MORALS AND DOGMA FOR THE 21ST CENTURY

A MODERN INTERPRETATION OF ALBERT PIKE'S GREATEST WORK

BRIAN A. CHAPUT
WILLIAM R. GOODELL
KEVIN K. MAIN
JAMES L. "JJ" MILLER IV

STONE GUILD PUBLISHING
PLANO, TEXAS
HTTP://WWW.STONEGUILDPUBLISHING.COM/

2009

Published By:

Stone Guild Publishing
P.O. Box 860475
Plano, TX 75086-0475
http://www.stoneguildpublishing.com/

First Paperback Edition Published 2009

ISBN-13 978-1-60532-013-7
ISBN- 1-60532-013-7

10 9 8 7 6 5 4 3 2

DEDICATION

This book is affectionately dedicated to:

❖   *Our families*, and especially our wives: Rachel Chaput, Lisa Main, and April Miller, who provided an unbelievable amount of emotional and personal support during this project. They endured with us everything that it took to get this work completed, while never once saying out loud, "You guys have completely lost your minds!" Without your help and support this would have never been possible. For this, we are eternally grateful.

❖   *The Craft*, we hope you enjoy this book and that it encourages you to pursue a more extensive and comprehensive Masonic education during your journey. We hope you take away from this book all that it has to offer and become a better father, son, husband, brother, citizen, and Mason for it.

❖   *The Brethren of Plano Lodge #768*, Plano, Texas, whose dedication and devotion to the principles of Freemasonry have made us better men, and for that, we offer this book to you. May the Young Masons Program continue to prosper and benefit you for generations.

It is our hope that this book invigorates the 21st Century Renaissance in Freemasonry and all that it has to offer humanity.

TABLE OF CONTENTS

ACKNOWLEDGEMENTS

First and foremost, we would like to disclose that we are all "black cap" 32° Masons, and none of us are past-anythings. We are everyday Masons: a Senior Warden, a Senior and Junior Steward, and a Master of Ceremonies all dedicated to making a difference. To this end, we want to tell everyone out there that you can make a difference in Masonry, because every step, great or small, moves the Fraternity forward.

Our families endured our taking on at least another full time job, in addition to our usual vocations and Lodge duties for the time it took to complete this work. Beware the famous last words, "This should take about 3-4 months." We have discovered the answer to the question: "I wonder why no one has ever done this before?" Brian kept going and going, picking up the slack along the way, all during his wife's pregnancy with their first child. Bill stuck it out, despite the oppressive workload at his day job, which kept building in magnitude and urgency. JJ bled red ink on every page at some point during the review process. Finally, Kevin pulled all of this together and made this idea a reality. Wow, I still cannot believe we did it.

All of that said, there is absolutely no way to accomplish such a task without the help of many others. These people have spent countless thousands of hours reading, reviewing, comparing, and making comments about each chapter, page, paragraph, and sentence.

We would like to sincerely thank Robert F. Pannell, James H. Abell, Jr., Ronald E. Lawrence, James L. "Jim" Miller III, Christopher Hayes, Brian Westmoreland, Harry F. Powell II, Mike Heidenreich, Lawrence H. Kester, and Charles E. McKay.

We also acknowledge the countless others who encouraged, inspired, and guided us along the way.

INTRODUCTION

Morals and Dogma is one of the most important books for Freemasonry, and every brother should utilize it as a tool to begin his Masonic education and development. Within its pages are lessons of honor, integrity, character, morality, and charity. These principles are timeless and in no way restricted to members of the Scottish Rite alone. The Blue Lodge and every other Masonic organization should actively teach and encourage the practice of these virtues. How the world might benefit if every lawyer, politician, businessperson, media figure, and civic leader in the civilized world took even one lesson from this book! How many of the current problems faced by Freemasonry and society as a whole might be resolved if more individuals practiced even one of the lessons contained within it? It is impossible to read even a small portion of this book and not be transformed through the contemplation of the ideas it contains.

Albert Pike created *Morals and Dogma* to communicate the intended lectures of the Ancient and Accepted Scottish Rite, which he expected the Brethren of the Rite to study in connection with the Rituals of the Degrees. In preparing the book, Pike was as much a compiler as author, extracting at least half of its content from those whom he felt represented the greatest writers, philosophers, and thinkers known in his time.

He incorporated the thoughts and words of others, continually changing and adding to the language of his source material and often mixing his own words with theirs. His motive for doing so was to yield the greatest value to his audience. Pike claimed only a small part of the credit of authorship, maintaining that the reader should regard every portion of the book as borrowed from "some old and better writer".

The reader should not interpret the lessons contained in the book as being sacramental, for they extend beyond the realm of Morality into the domains of Thought and Truth. The use of the word "Dogma" in its title is intended in the true and original sense of the word as "doctrine" or "teaching". It does not mean "dogmatic" as in the modern and offensive usage of the term. Every individual may freely accept or reject the words contained within the book as untrue or unsound. While the doctrines of the Rite do not specifically contain the ancient theosophical and philosophical speculations contained in the book, Albert Pike understood that it was in our interest to understand what the "Ancient Intellects" thought about such subjects. Our ability to understand and evaluate these speculations demonstrates the radical difference between our human and animal natures. To paraphrase the Canonist, Ludovicus Gomez: "Beliefs may grow old, vary with the times, and perish; otherwise, they may be reborn in opposition to the original and afterwards reach maturity."

As a Fraternity, we need to teach our Brethren what it means to be a Mason beyond paying dues and attending business meetings. We need to focus on the quality of our Masons and not the quantity. We need to reinforce our differences from other civic or charitable organizations and lift the fog that has obscured our path of progress and prosperity in recent years.

This book is far too important to the Scottish Rite to be lost forever. This "translation" of the work seeks to inspire a return to the basics and renew our belief in the importance of giving our new members a starting point for their Masonic journey and a foundation upon which to build. Volumes have been written about every aspect of the original edition of *Morals and Dogma*, but none of these efforts has made the beauty and lessons of the book any more accessible to the vast majority of our membership. Analysis and commentary is only useful when the source material is well understood. The neglect of the last several decades has rendered this work withered and fruitless, but it is as relevant today as it was in 1871. Its lessons need to be repeated again, and again, and again.

It is with an absolute reverence for Albert Pike and for the Ancient and Accepted Scottish Rite that the compilers of this work have endeavored to make *Morals and Dogma* more approachable and accessible to the modern reader. In no way do we intend to displace (or replace) his work from its exalted position, so rightly and fully deserved. Rather, through this effort, we hope to inspire our audience to read *Morals and Dogma* in its entirety and in the original language. Only in this way, can the Brethren of the Rite fully appreciate Albert Pike's sublime language and explore the book's deeper mysteries and speculations.

NOTES ABOUT THIS WORK

The layout of this book is designed to allow the reader to make a side-by-side comparison with the original edition of Morals and Dogma by Albert Pike. The numbers within the margins indicate the beginning of the corresponding page in the original version of the text. The order of the paragraphs on each page follows the order of those in the original version with only a few exceptions. In order to complete independent ideas within a single paragraph or to improve the flow of the dialogue within a page or chapter, we occasionally felt it necessary to move a sentence from one paragraph to another or a paragraph from one page to another. In every case, these changes improved the readability and flow of ideas without (in our opinion) changing the original author's intent.

We hope that this attention to detail provides everyone the opportunity to compare their own interpretation of the original text to the interpretation we have provided here.

In a few instances, we have also updated or modified historical and illustrative references and examples that have either changed or become obsolete since Albert Pike's time. While this will no doubt incite dissension among the purists, our chief aim is to help the reader better understand these lessons as they may be applied today. In each case, we have made every effort to provide a more contemporary reference that will bear the same significance for a 21st century reader that the original text would have inspired in its time. We believe that Albert Pike would approve of these slight changes. From his own words on page 29-30 of this new edition (page 37 of the original work):

> "...all truths are *Truths of that Period* and not truths for eternity. Whatever great fact had strength and vitality enough to make itself real, whether it be religion, morals, government, or whatever else, was a truth *for that era and only as good as the men who were capable of receiving it.*"

We encourage readers to submit any questions, concerns, or inconsistencies that you perceive in our interpretation to the following E-mail address: **feedback@morals-and-dogma.com**. We will diligently review and analyze any feedback we receive with the intention of improving subsequent editions of the work.

Morals and Dogma for the 21st Century

Lodge of Perfection

CHAPTER 1: APPRENTICE

THE TWENTY-FOUR-INCH RULE AND THE COMMON GAVEL

UNCONTROLLED or misdirected power is wasted like gasoline burned in the open air or unused electricity. It strikes out in the dark, finding no target, and recoils upon itself. It is the destruction and ruin of the volcano, the earthquake, the tsunami, and the tornado, which are devoid of growth and progress. Like the blind Polyphemus (Cyclops), unregulated force strikes at random and misses its target with enough momentum to fall headfirst onto the sharp rocks below.

The blind Power of the people must be regulated and managed by the Intellect of men, like the Power of electricity is managed by machines to lift the arms and turn the wheels which bore and rifle a canon or weave the most delicate lace. Intellect is the soul of the people. The Power of the people counsels and guides its leadership like the slender needle of the compass guides the ship while always pointing north. This Power must have a brain to think and laws to govern in order to attack the fortresses of superstition, despotism, and prejudice the human race has constructed. Only then, will its daring deeds produce permanent results, real progress, and glorious conquests. Thought is a power, and philosophy is the energy. They both take their aim at affecting the progress of mankind. When these Powers are reinforced with the two great motors of Truth and Love and guided by Intellect focused on using the RULE of Right and Justice, they generate the inspiration needed to begin the march of progress. The POWER of the Deity Himself is balanced by His WISDOM, and it only produces HARMONY.

Innovations and meaningful progress require focused POWER. Concerted actions organized upon the moral horizon in the mountain ranges of Justice, Wisdom, Reason, and Right can lose themselves in moral and ethical quagmires. They can lose their direction even when they originate from the purest ideals.

The history of the human race demonstrates that worthwhile progress

3

must be driven by noble deeds and lasting lessons of courage. Daring deeds create one class of guiding lights for man, and they are the shining examples inherent in the people. To strive, brave all risks, stumble, risk everything, persevere, be true to one's self, challenge destiny, face the possibility of a crushing defeat and the fear it inspires, to confront corrupt power, and to defy overreaching and excessive triumph are examples of the light that nations need to inspire them.

Throughout every society, there are always immense Powers in motion within the great caverns of evil found in the degradation, squalor, wretchedness, destitution, vices, and crime that are pervasive in the population. Ideas and progress are luxuries there because of the rampant greed and blind ambition born of two stepmothers – Ignorance and Misery. When public opinion is crystallized, the masses have the combined power of a large HAMMER, but their blows are only productive when used within the lines traced by the RULE of wisdom and discretion.

The momentum of the Power of the people is the Titanic power that allows for the formations of armies and fortifications. The dishonorable tyranny of the despots Claudius and Domitian is directly reflected by the offensive behavior of their subordinates. A dangerous and poisonous wind blows when the masses imitate the conscience of dishonorable leadership; the public authorities become corrupt, hearts become hardened, and character is abandoned. This was true under Caracalla, Commodus, Heliogabalus, and from the Roman senate under Caesar.

The power of the people, acting through armies and used to sustain despots, more often enslaves than liberates. In this example, despotism applies the RULE and power is the MACE of steel wielded by the soldier. The passive obedience of the people supports Kings and oligarchies. The might of an army wielded by tyranny is the manifestation of the cumulative weakness of a nation and leads to Humanity waging war against Humanity in the name of Humanity. So people willingly appease despotism, its workers submit to being despised and degraded, and its soldiers submit to being whipped.

Tyrants use the power of the people to enslave and subjugate them and then drive them as though they were workhorses or oxen teams. The spirit of liberty and innovation is replaced by the bayonet, and its principles are struck down by cannon fire. The monks mingle with the soldiers, while the militant zealots sing hymns for victory over the rebellion.

The HAMMER or MACE of POWER must be subordinate to the RULE because when military power is not subordinate to the civil power it will become a full blown and armed tyranny. It spawns a dynasty that begins to rot like the Third Reich or Russian Provisional Government until it deteriorates into the despotic Hitler or Stalin. This frequently *begins* where former dynasties *ended*.

The immense political and social power of the people is always exhausted by prolonging those institutions long since dead. These include governing mankind by embalming old dead tyrannies of Faith, restoring dilapidated dogmas, regilding faded and worm-eaten shrines, restoring ancient and barren superstitions, saving society by multiplying its parasites, perpetuating obsolete philosophies, enforcing the worship of symbols as the actual means of salvation, and tying the dead corpse of the Past, mouth to mouth, with the living present. This is why one fatality of Humanity is condemned to an eternal struggle with phantoms, superstitions, bigotries, hypocrisies, prejudices, formulas of error, and the pleas of tyranny. When viewed in a historical context, even wretched despots can appear respectable in the same way a mountain of rough volcanic rock, when viewed from a distance and in a haze, can appear smooth and beautiful. The sight of a single dungeon of tyranny is more effective than the most eloquent essay when it used to dispel the hated illusions of despotism. The French should preserve the Bastille, the Italians should preserve the dungeons of the Inquisition, the Germans should preserve the Concentration camps, and the Russians should preserve the Gulags as perpetual lessons of how the Power of the people maintained the Power, which imprisoned and destroyed the living.

Free governments become anarchy when the POWER of the people is unrestrained. Their Power must be channeled and redistributed into necessary activities such as establishing laws, institutions, and decisions for the Nation, just like the ancient Egyptian kings who channeled the flooding rivers of the Nile into sub-divided canals allowing it to fertilize the land rather than devastate it. There must be the *jus et norma*, the law and *Rule*, or *Gauge* of constitution and law governing the public power. To violate either, leads to the destruction of the other, rendering both dead and inert amid the ruin it has wrought.

The fundamental power of the people is derived from their popular will in motion, and it is symbolized by the GAVEL. THE GAVEL is regulated and guided within the limits of LAW and ORDER, which is symbolized by the TWENTY-FOUR-INCH GAUGE. These combine to produce the fruits of LIBERTY, EQUALITY, and FRATERNITY. Liberty regulated by law. Equality of rights in the eye of the law. Fraternity, or Brotherhood, with its duties, obligations, and benefits.

The *Rough* ASHLAR and the *Perfect* ASHLAR are jewels of the Lodge. The York Rite teaches that the rough Ashlar is "a quarry stone in its raw and natural state," and the perfect Ashlar is "a stone prepared by the hands of the workmen, to be adjusted by the working tools of the Fellow-Craft." They allude to the self-improvement of the individual craftsman, and you can read their explanations in the printed Monitors of the York Rite.

The Scottish Rite teaches the rough Ashlar is the PEOPLE as a mass, raw and unorganized. The perfect Ashlar is a cubical stone and the symbol of perfection representing the NATION whose rulers derive their powers from the consent of the governed. The people communicate their will through the laws and constitution which when properly combined form a harmonious government, symmetrical and balanced. Its powers should be properly distributed and duly adjusted.

When we draw a cube on a plane surface:

we have *three* visible faces and *nine* external lines drawn between *seven* points. The complete cube has *three* more faces totaling *six*; *three* more lines totaling *twelve*; and *one* more point, making *eight*. The cube became the symbol of perfection because the number of lines, *twelve*, include the sacred numbers 3, 5, 7, and 9 (3 times 3). Its own two figures 1 and 2 when added together total the sacred number 3.

6   Produced by POWER, acting by RULE, and prepared in accordance with the lines measured by the Gauge, the perfect Ashlar is an appropriate symbol of the Power of the people expressed as the constitution and laws of the Nation. The three visible faces represent the three branches of government. The Executive branch executes the laws. The Legislative branch makes the laws, and the Judicial branch interprets and enforces the laws. The three invisible faces are Liberty, Equality, and Fraternity, and they represent the three souls of a Nation – its vitality, spirit, and intellect.

●   ●   ●   ●   ●   ●

Although prayer is an essential part of our ceremonies, Masonry neither replaces nor seeks to imitate religion. The soul aspires toward the Absolute and Infinite Intelligence, the one Supreme Deity who is also characterized as an "Architect". Thought, meditation, and prayer are man's power of the mind used to navigate the ocean of the Unknown using his conscience as his compass. A spiritual magnetism connects the human soul with the Deity, and it creates the majestic illuminations of the soul that pierce the darkness with light.

Prayer is a logical and rational pursuit even though it cannot be used to persuade God to change His predestined plans. He produces predetermined effects through *His* forces of nature. Free will is our own part of these as we pursue our efforts to attain wealth, happiness, or a prolonged healthy life. Even if our effort is predestined, it is *our* effort made of *our free will*. So we pray. Free will is a power. Thought is a power. Prayer is a power. Man cannot be understood as a starting-point without the two great powers of Faith and Love. Prayers should be inspiring. Selfish prayers that beg, plead, and clamor are pitiful and should be avoided. To deny the effectiveness of prayer is to deny the power of Faith, Love, and Effort. When free will moves our hand to launch a pebble into the ocean, the effects never cease. Every word spoken is registered upon the airwaves for eternity.

Every Lodge is a symbolic Temple as a whole and in its details. The ⑦ Universe supplied man with the model used to raise the first temples to the Divinity. The arrangement of the Temple of Solomon, the symbolic ornaments which formed its chief decorations, and the dress of the High-Priest all had reference to the order of the Universe as it was then understood. The Temple contained many emblems of the seasons – the sun, the moon, the planets, the constellation Ursa Major and Minor, the zodiac, the elements, and other parts of the world. Hermes was the master of *this* Lodge of the Universe. He was also represented by Khūrūm (Hiram the architect), one of the other lights of the Lodge.

You will receive further instruction about the symbolism of the heavenly bodies, the sacred numbers, and the details of the Temple as you advance in Masonry. And while you are instructed to be patient, you are encouraged to study them on your own in the meantime. The sage and the philosopher seek to correctly interpret the symbols of the Universe and to penetrate God's thoughts by studying and deciphering his writings.

This understanding is asked and answered in the esoteric work of the Blue Lodge.

•   •   •   •   •   •

A "Lodge" is defined as "a certain number of Freemasons, duly assembled in a room or place, with the sacred writings, square and compasses, and a warrant or charter authorizing them to work." We will now examine the Lodge room or place where we meet, which represents some part of King Solomon's Temple.

The Lodge is supported by the three great columns, WISDOM, POWER (or STRENGTH), and BEAUTY. The Worshipful Master, Senior Warden, and Junior Warden represent these three columns. They are the perfections of everything, and nothing can endure without them. The York Rite teaches, "It is necessary for there to be Wisdom to conceive, Strength to support, and Beauty to adorn all great and laudable undertakings." The Apostle Paul states, "Do you not know that you are the temple of God and his spirit dwells in you? If any man desecrates the temple of God, he destroys God, for the temple of God is holy, and the temple is you."

The Wisdom and Power of the Deity are always in balance. The Deity's laws of nature and moral laws are not simply His Omnipotent mandates because 8 then they could also be changed by Him. Once changed, order would become disorder, good and right would become evil and wrong, honesty and loyalty would become vices, and fraud, ingratitude, and vice would become virtues. Unlimited Omnipotent power existing alone would not be constrained to consistency, and its decrees and laws would not be immutable. We are obligated by the laws of God because they communicate His infinite WISDOM and not because they are the expressions of His POWER or His WILL. They are His laws because they are right and not right because they are His laws. Perfect harmony in physics and the moral universe are the result of the balance between infinite wisdom and infinite power. Accordingly, Wisdom, Power, and Harmony constitute one Masonic triad.

The wisdom of a skilled Architect is displayed in the combination of strength, grace, beauty, symmetry, proportion, lightness, and ornamentation. God has done this in nature as evidenced by the tree, the human frame, the egg, and the cells of the honeycomb. The skill of the orator and poet is to combine power, strength, and energy with grace, style, musical cadences, the beauty of figures, and the entertainment of imagination. Likewise, in a Nation, the Titanic strength of the aggressive, industrial power of the people must be combined with the beauty of the arts, sciences, and intellect if a Nation is to succeed to the heights of excellence and its people be free. Harmony is achieved when Wisdom balances the beam of the scales between sympathy and conflicting actions. The great enigmas of the Sphinx are the reconciliation of the absolute power of God to the moral law, human responsibility, and free will and the congruity of His absolute wisdom, goodness, and mercy to the existence of evil.

You entered the Lodge between the representatives of the two columns, which stood on either side of the entrance porch at the eastern gateway to the Temple. According to the First and Second Book of Kings and confirmed in Jeremiah, these bronze pillars were four fingers thick, four cubits in diameter, eighteen cubits in height, and crowned with a capital of five cubits in height. (A cubit equals 1.707 feet.) Therefore, each shaft was 6 feet 10 inches in diameter, thirty feet eight inches in height, and the capitals added an additional eight feet six inches in height. The capitals were adorned by bronze pomegranates, covered by bronze network, and ornamented with bronze wreaths. The wreaths were similar to the shape of the seed vessel of the lotus flower, or Egyptian lily, which was a sacred symbol to both the Hindus and the Egyptians. The southern pillar (on the right) was named JACHIN, which is the Hebrew word for "*He shall establish.*" The northern pillar (on the left) was named BOAZ which is the Hebrew word for "*In it is strength.*"

Khūrūm (Hiram the Tyrian artisan) based the design of these columns upon the great columns consecrated to the Winds and Fire at the famous Temple of Malkarth in the city of Tyre. It is customary in York Rite Lodges to place a celestial globe on one column and a terrestrial globe on the other, but these are unnecessary if the objective is to imitate the original two columns of the Temple. The symbolic meaning of these columns will be explained later, but for now, it should be added that Entered Apprentices keep their working-tools in the JACHIN column.

The word *Jachin*, in Hebrew, is יכין. It was probably pronounced *Ya-kayan*, and as a verbal noun it means *He that strengthens* and *firm, stable, and upright. Jachin* also means *he will establish,* or *plant in an upright position* – from the verb בוך *Kūn* meaning *he stood erect. Jachin* probably meant *Active, Vivifying Energy and Power,* and *Boaz* meant *Stability or Performance* in the *passive* sense.

The word *Boaz* is בעז. The prefix ב means *"with"* or *"in"*. עז means *Strong, Strength, Power, Might, Refuge, Source of Strength, a Fort.*

The York Rite defines the Dimensions of the Lodge as "unlimited, and its coverings are the canopy of Heaven. The Mason should continually strive to ascend from the earth to Heaven with the aid of the three principle rungs of Jacob's ladder: Faith, Hope, and Charity. They admonish us to have Faith in God, Hope in Immortality, and Charity to all mankind." This ladder is also shown with nine rungs, its feet resting on the earth, and its top in the clouds with the stars shining above it. It represents the mystic ladder Jacob saw in his dream used by the angels of God who ascended and descended it. The addition of the three principal rungs to the symbolism is a modern and inconsistent adaptation.

The ancients knew of seven planets and arranged them in the following order: the Moon, Mercury, Venus, the Sun, Mars, Jupiter, and Saturn. There were seven heavens and seven spheres (planets) as evidenced by the monuments of Mithras which had seven alters or pyres. The seven lamps of the golden candelabrum were consecrated to the seven planets, and Clemens of Alexandria confirms in his Stromata that they represented the planets.

The ancients believed the human soul returned to Heaven by ascending through the seven spheres. The commentary on the Ennead of Plotinus by Marsilius Ficinus states, "The *Ladder* by which the human soul ascends to Heaven has seven degrees or steps." The Mysteries of Mithras carried to Rome under the Emperors had a seven rung ladder which was a symbol referring to this ascent through the spheres of the seven planets. Jacob saw the Spirits of God ascending and descending this ladder, and he saw the Deity Himself above it. The Mithraic Mysteries were celebrated in caves, where gates marked the four equinox and solstice points of the zodiac. The seven planetary spheres, which all souls must traverse when descending from the fixed stars of heaven to earth, were represented in the ceremonies by seven gates, one for each planet, through which they must pass when either ascending or descending.

Celsus confirms this through Origen who wrote in the Mithraic Mysteries that the symbolic image of this passage from the stars was a ladder reaching from Heaven to earth and divided into seven steps or stages, each affixed with a gate. At the summit, there was an eighth gate affixed to the stars. This symbol was similar to the seven-stage Pyramid of Borsippa near Babylon, where each stage was built of different colored vitrified brick. In the Mithraic ceremonies, the seven-rung ladder was the symbol of the seven stages of initiation through which a candidate passed, and many of those stages were very formidable trials.

The Lights of the Lodge allow you to see its details and ornaments, and you have been told of their York Rite explanations.

The *Holy Bible, Square, and Compasses* are the Great Lights in Masonry, but they also represent the *Furniture* of the Lodge because no Lodge exists without them. This requirement has at times been made a pretext for excluding Jews from our Lodges because they cannot regard the New Testament as a holy book. However, the Bible is only an indispensable part of the furniture of a *Christian* Lodge because it is the sacred book of the Christian religion, just as the Hebrew Pentateuch is in a Hebrew Lodge and the Vedas are in a Hindu Lodge. One of these sacred books, the Square, and the Compasses on an Altar are understood to be the Great Lights by which a Mason must walk and work.

The obligation of each candidate is always to be taken on the sacred book or books of his religion in order to make it more solemn and binding. This is the only reason you were asked about your religious creed.

The Square is two lines forming a right angle on a geometric plane. Using spherical trigonometry, the Compasses use circles to describe the science of spheres and the heavens. The square is an emblem of the body and the earth while the Compasses are an emblem of the soul and the heavens. The Compasses are also used in plane trigonometry to erect perpendiculars, and in this degree, it reminds you that, while both points of the Compasses are underneath the Square, you should only consider the moral and political meanings of these symbols and avoid the philosophical and spiritual explanations. The divine always mingles with the mortal, and the earthly mixes with the supernatural. It results in something almost spiritual in the most common day-to-day duties of life. Nations are not only political bodies but also political souls. Woe to the people who seek only material goals and forget the importance of a nation's soul, because a nation that worships at the altar of monetary reward can never lead a civilization. Worshipping money atrophies the mind, the muscles, and the will to move them. Religious or commercial domination by the state diminishes the cheerfulness of a nation and deprives them by limiting their perspective and their goals. A free nation that forgets that their souls need to be cared for will devote all its energy to material advancement. They make war only to serve their commercial interests. Citizens will begin to imitate the material leadership of the Nation and regard wealth, pomp, and luxury as the great goods of life. Such a nation creates wealth rapidly, distributes it badly, and degrades into the two extremes of grotesque opulence and misery. To a very few is the enjoyment of Privilege, Exception, Monopoly, and Feudality falsely and dangerously built upon the labor of the people, as though they were a blind Cyclops chained in the mines, factories, offices, workshops, and fields where their private misery props up the public power. The greatness of a nation is ill conceived when planted in the suffering of the people because there are no moral elements present to nurture and sustain its growth. Like an eclipsed star, the people have the right to return to light once the eclipse is complete and not sink further into darkness.

The York Rite teaches that the three lesser lights, or the Sublime Lights, are the Sun, Moon, and Worshipful Master. However, you are not told why they are lights because the Sun and Moon do not light the Lodge, unless they do it symbolically. Likewise you are not told what they are symbols of, because the *13* Moon does not govern the night with any regularity.

The Sun is the ancient symbol of the generative and life-giving power of the Deity, and it represents the male. Light was the source of life to the ancients, and God was the source of all light. God was the *essence* of Light, the *Invisible* Fire, developed as Flame and *manifested* as light and splendor. His manifestation and visible image was the Sun. Although the Sabeans seemed to worship the Sun, they really just observed it as the manifestation of the Deity.

The Moon is the symbol of the passive capacity of nature to produce, and it represents the female. It was also the symbol of Isis, Astarte, and Artemis (or Diana). The *"Master of Life"* was the Supreme Deity who ruled and was manifest in both the Sun and the Moon. Just as Zeus, the Son of Saturn, became King of the Gods; so did Horus (son of Osiris and Isis) become the Master of Life; and Dionysus (or Bacchus), like Mithras, become the author of Light, Life, and Truth.

●　　●　　●　　●　　●　　●

The Master of Light and Life, the Sun, and the Moon are symbolized in every Lodge by the Master and Wardens. It is the duty of the Master to dispense light to the Brethren, through the Wardens if necessary.

Isaiah said to Jerusalem, "the sun will go down no more, and the moon will not withdraw itself. The Lord will be your everlasting light, and the days of your mourning will be ended. Your people will be righteous, and they will inherit the land forever." Such is the existence of a free people.

Our northern ancestors worshiped a triad Deity: ODIN (the Almighty FATHER), FREA (his wife and emblem of universal matter), and THOR (his son the mediator). Above this triad ruled the Supreme God, "the author of everything that exists, the Eternal, the Ancient, the Living and Reverential Being, the Searcher into hidden things, the Being that never changes." In the Temple of Eleusis (a Greek sanctuary lit only by a single skylight in the roof and representing the Universe), the images of the Sun, Moon, and Mercury were represented.

The learned Bro∴ FRANCOIS DELAUNAY said, "The Sun and Moon represent the two grand principles for all generations, the active and passive, the male and the female. The Sun represents the actual light, and it shines upon the *14* Moon with its prolific rays. Both the Sun and the Moon shine their light upon the offspring HORUS (the Blazing Star), and together the three form the great

Equilateral Triangle. In the center of this triangle is the all-creating letter of Kabbalah, and it is where creation is said to have started."

The ORNAMENTS of the Lodge are said to be "the Mosaic Pavement, the Indented Tessel, and the Blazing Star." The Mosaic Pavement, or checkered pavement, is said to represent the ground floor of King Solomon's Temple, but there was no stone seen within the Temple because the walls were covered with cedar planks, and the floor was covered with fir planks. Because there was no stone floor visible, there was no "beautiful tessellated border surrounding it." However in England, anciently, the Tracing-Board was surrounded with an indented border, and it is only in America that such a border is put around the Mosaic pavement. The phrase tessellated pavement developed as a misuse of the word tassel. The indented or denticulated border and the four tassels representing Temperance, Fortitude, Prudence, and Justice are properly called a *tesserated* pavement. The Blazing Star in the center of the floor was "an emblem of Divine Providence commemorating the star which guided the wise men of the East to the place of Jesus' nativity."

The black and white checkered pavement symbolizes the Good and Evil Principles of the Egyptian and Persian creeds. It represents the warfare between Michael and Satan, the Gods and the Titans, Balder and Lok, light and darkness, Day and Night, Freedom and Despotism, and Religious Liberty and the Arbitrary Dogmas of religious zealots.

The edges of this pavement would be indented or denticulated like the teeth of a saw and have a finished edge to complete the bordering. The four corners of this bordering were then decorated by ornamental tassels.

It is unrealistic to depict the five pointed BLAZING STAR as an allusion to the Divine Providence or to make it commemorative of the Star that guided the Magi. Both explanations provide a modern interpretation that is inconsistent with the era when King Solomon's Temple was constructed. Originally, the BLAZING STAR represented SIRIUS, or the Dog Star, which foretold the flooding of the Nile. It also represented the God ANUBIS who was the companion of Isis during her search for the body of her brother and husband OSIRIS. It eventually became the image of HORUS, the son of OSIRIS. HORUS was the son of ISIS, and he was considered the author of the Seasons and the God of Time. ISIS was the universal nature, and Horus was the primitive matter, the inexhaustible source of Life, the spark of uncreated fire, and the universal seed of all beings. Then it became HERMES, the Master of Learning, whose Greek name means Mercury. The PENTALPHA became the sacred sign of the Magi and the prominent emblem of Liberty and Freedom because it blazes with a steady radiance by promising calm skies and fertile seasons to the nations after the storms and weltering elements of change, tumult, and good and bad Revolutions have passed.

Suspended over the Master's head in the East is an enclosed triangle with the Hebrew letter for YŌD [' or ＠]. In the English and American Lodges, the letter G∴ is substituted for YŌD because it is the first initial of the word GOD.

15

12

However, for a global fraternity this makes as little sense as if the letter D, the first initial of the word DIEU, were used in French Lodges. In Kabbalah, YōD is the symbol of Unity and the Supreme Deity, the first letter of the Holy Name, and the symbol of the Great Kabbalistic Triads. To understand its meanings, you need to study the Zohar, the Siphra de Zeniutha, and other Kabbalistic books. In summary, it is the Creative Energy of the Deity represented as a *point* in the *Circle* of immensity. In this Degree, it is the symbol of the unmanifested Deity, the absolute, who has no name.

Our French Brethren place the letter YōD in the centre of the Blazing Star. Our ancient English Brethren taught in the old Lectures, "The Blazing Star of Glory refers to the Sun, the grand luminary which enlightens the earth with its cheerful influence by dispensing blessings to mankind." In the lectures, it is an emblem of PRUDENCE, and the original definition of the word *Prudentia* means *Foresight*. Accordingly, the Blazing Star is regarded as an emblem of Omniscience, or the All-seeing Eye, which to the Egyptian Initiates was the emblem of Osiris the Creator. With the YōD in the center, it has the Kabbalistic meaning of the Divine Energy manifested as Light and creating the Universe.

There are six Jewels belonging to the Lodge. Three are *"Movable"* and three are *"Immovable"*. The Movable Jewels are the SQUARE, the LEVEL, and the PLUMB because they pass from one Brother to another. It is an improper modern innovation to label them immovable because they must always be present in the Lodge. The immovable jewels are the ROUGH ASHLAR, the PERFECT ASHLAR or CUBICAL STONE (and in some Rituals the DOUBLE CUBE), and the TRESTLE-BOARD or TRACING-BOARD.

The York Rite instructs, "The *Square* teaches Morality. The *Level* teaches Equality, and the *Plumb* teaches Uprightness of Conduct." These explanations may be read in the York Rite monitors.

•　　•　　•　　•　　•　　•

The York Rite also teaches that represented within every well-governed Lodge is a certain point within a circle. The point represents an individual brother, and the Circle is the boundary line of his conduct beyond which he is never to suffer his prejudices or allow his passions to betray him. However, this explanation does not *interpret* the symbols of Masonry.

More appropriately, the point within the circle represents God in the center of the Universe. It is also a common Egyptian sign for the Sun and Osiris and is still today used as the astronomical sign of the great luminary. In Kabbalah, the point is YōD irradiating the circular space with Light from God.

Our York Rite Brethren add, "This circle is embroidered by two perpendicular parallel lines, representing Saint John the Baptist and Saint John the Evangelist, and upon the top rest the Holy Scriptures (an open book). In going around this circle, the Mason touches upon these two lines and the Holy

Scriptures, and he keeps himself circumscribed by their guidance making it is impossible that he should materially err."

17   Some writers have speculated the parallel lines represent the Tropics of Cancer and Capricorn, which the Sun alternately touches upon at the Summer and Winter solstices. This idea is not practical because the tropics are not perpendicular lines. If these parallel lines were a part of the ancient symbol they probably had a more profound and *fruitful* meaning. Most likely, they had the same meaning as the twin columns Jachin and Boaz. The JUSTICE and MERCY of GOD are in equilibrium, and the result is HARMONY, because a Single and Perfect Wisdom presides over both. While the complete meaning is not for the Apprentice, the adept may find it in Kabbalah.

The Holy Scriptures are an entirely modern addition to the symbol, like the terrestrial and celestial globes on the columns of the portico. Consequently, this ancient symbol has been deprived of its original meaning with incompatible additions, like that of Isis weeping over the broken column containing the remains of Osiris at Byblos.

•   •   •   •   •   •

Masonry has a Decalogue for its Initiates.   These are its Ten Commandments:

I.   ⊕ ∴ God is the Eternal, Omnipotent, Immutable WISDOM and the Supreme INTELLIGENCE, the Never-ending LOVE.   You will adore, revere, and love Him. You will honor Him by practicing the virtues.

II.   ⊕ ∴ Your religion shall be to do good because it is a pleasure to you and not merely because it is a duty. You may become the friend of a wise man, but you shall follow his guidance. Your soul is immortal. Do nothing to degrade it.

III.   ⊕ ∴ You shall unceasingly battle vice. Do not do unto others that which you would not want them to do unto you. Be submissive to your fortunes and keep the light of wisdom burning.

IV.   ⊕ ∴ Honor your parents. Pay respect and homage to your elders. Instruct the young. Protect and defend infancy and innocence.

V.   ⊕ ∴ Cherish your wife and children. Love your country and obey its laws.

18 VI.   ⊕ ∴ Your friends should be a reflection of yourself. Misfortune should not estrange you from your friends. Do for their memory whatever you would do for them if they were living.

VII.   ⊕ ∴ Avoid and flee from insincere friendships. In all things, refrain from excess. Fear being the cause of a stain on your memory.

VIII.   ⊕ ∴ Allow no passions to become your master. Learn from observing the passions of others. Be tolerant of error.

IX.   ⊕∴. Listen often. Speak rarely. Act politely. Forget slights. Return good for evil. Do not misuse strength or superiority.

X.   ⊕∴. By studying others, you will learn to study yourself. Always pursue virtue. Be Just. Avoid idleness.

The greatest commandment of Masonry is this: "Love one another!" He who says he is in the light, but hates his brother, remains in the darkness.

These are the moral duties of a Mason. It is the duty of Masonry to assist in elevating the moral and intellectual level of society by bringing ideas into circulation and causing the minds of the youth to grow. Gradually teaching the axioms and promulgations of positive laws will place the human race in harmony with its destinies.

This is the duty and work apprenticed to every Initiate. Do not imagine you can affect nothing or in despair, you will do nothing. Many great deeds are accomplished during the small day-to-day struggles in a person's daily life, and over their lifetime, they become magnificent works. A determined and unseen bravery defends itself foot to foot in the darkness against the fatal invasion of necessity and corruption. There are many noble triumphs which no eye sees, which no renown rewards, and which no band of trumpets salutes. Life, misfortune, isolation, abandonment, and poverty are battlefields which have their *19* own heroes – sometimes obscure heroes who are greater than those who become famous. Every Mason should strive with this same bravery against those invasions of necessity and corruption, which infect nations as well as people. He should meet *them* foot to foot, even at midnight, to protect against the national wrongs and follies and to prevent the usurpation from that persistent problem of Tyranny. There is no more sovereign eloquence than the truth in indignation. The Protest of Truth is a necessity because it is more difficult for a people to keep their freedom than to gain it. This right continually protects against that event. There is Eternity in the Right, and the Mason should be the Priest and Soldier of that Right. If his country should be robbed of her liberties, he should not despair because the protest of the Right against the Event persists forever. The robbery of a people never becomes prescriptive, and the reclamation of its rights is barred by no length of time. A people may endure military usurpation, and subjugated Nations may kneel to conquering Nations while wearing a yoke under the stress of necessity. When this necessity disappears, if the people are fit to be free, the submerged country will reappear on the surface, and Tyranny will be judged by History to have murdered its victims.

Whatever occurs, we should have Faith in the Justice and Wisdom of God, Hope for the Future, and Loving-kindness for those who are in error. God makes His will visible to men during events and with obscure texts. Men make their translations of it forthwith, hasty, incorrect, full of faults, omissions, and misreadings. We see so short a distance along the arc of the great circle that few minds can comprehend the Divine. The most wise, calm, and profound decipher the hieroglyphs slowly. When they complete their text, the need may have long passed, and there already exist twenty translations in the public square – the most incorrect of these being the most popularly accepted interpretation. From each translation, a party is born, and from each misreading, a faction is spawned. Each party believes or pretends it has the only true text, and each faction believes or pretends it alone possesses the light. These factions consist of blind men who aim straight the arrows of their errors, striking skillfully with all the violence that springs from false reasoning. This is why we are often frustrated when combating misconceptions before the people. Antæus long resisted Hercules, and the heads of the Hydra (sea serpent) grew as fast as they were cut off. It is absurd to say that once wounded, *misconception writhes in pain and dies amid its worshippers* because truth conquers slowly. There is a bizarre vitality in Error. Truth shoots over the heads of the masses, and if a misconception is briefly overcome, it will with great certainty rise again and be as vigorous as ever. It will not die when its brains are beat out, and the most stupid and irrational misconception always seem to be the longest-lived.

20

Nevertheless, the Morality and Philosophy that is Masonry must not cease to do its duty. We never know at what moment success awaits our efforts – typically when we least expect it. Succeed or fail, Masonry must not bow to error or surrender to discouragement. There were a few Carthaginian soldiers taken prisoner at Rome who refused to bow to Flaminius and lost their lives, but their pride was intact. Masons should possess an equal level of determination in their souls. Masonry should be an energy finding its aim and effect in the betterment of mankind. The wisdom of Socrates combined with the humanity of Adam, produces a Marcus Aurelius, thus creating the man of wisdom from the man of enjoyments. Masonry should not be a watchtower for the curious to gaze with ease upon the misery of the world with no effect. The province of Masonic philosophy should be to hold the full cup of thought to the thirsty lips of men, to offer all the true ideas of Deity, and to harmonize conscience and science. Morality is Faith in full bloom. Contemplation should lead to action, the absolute be practical, and the ideal be made into air, food and drink for the human mind. Wisdom is a sacred communion, and when it ceases to be a sterile love of Science, it becomes the one and supreme method by which to unite Humanity and arouse it to concerted action. Then, Philosophy becomes Spiritual.

Like History and Philosophy, Masonry has eternal yet simple duties – to oppose self-serving, politically motivated clergy (Caiaphas), cruel and corrupt Judges (Draco or Jefferies), excessively opulent legislators (Trimalcion), Hitler as Emperor, or Stalin as Dictator. These are symbols of tyranny and corruption that infest, degrade, defile, and crush a nation. In the works published for use by the Craft, we are told that the three great tenets of a Mason's profession are Brotherly Love, Relief, and Truth. A Brotherly affection and kindness should govern us in all our interactions and relationships with our brethren, and a

21

general and liberal philanthropy should influence us in regards to all men. To relieve the distressed is a duty unique to Masons – a sacred duty, not to be omitted, neglected, or inefficiently complied with. Truth is a Divine attribute and the foundation of every virtue. Seeking and learning the Truth are the goals of every good Mason.

Masonry recognizes Temperance, Fortitude, Prudence, and Justice as the four cardinal virtues, as did the Ancients did. These are as necessary to nations as to individuals. A Free and Independent people must possess Wisdom, Forethought, Foresight, and Precaution, all of which are included in the meaning of the word Prudence. It must be temperate in asserting its rights and in its councils and be economical in its expenses. It must be bold, brave, courageous, patient under setbacks, undismayed by disasters, and hopeful amid calamities, like Rome when she sold the field where Hannibal had camped his army during his siege. No Cannæ, or Pharsalia, or Pavia, or Agincourt, or Waterloo can discourage her. Let her Senate sit in their seats until the Gauls pluck them by the beard. Above all things, she must be just, never surrendering to the strong or plundering the weak. She must act on the square with all nations, always keep her faith, be honest in her legislation, and upright in all her dealings. Whenever such a Republic exists, it will be immortal because rashness, injustice, intemperance, and luxury during prosperity, and despair and disorder during adversity are the causes of the decline and collapse of nations.

CHAPTER 2: THE FELLOWCRAFT

RELIGION in the Ancient Orient (East) consisted of parables inseparable 22 from philosophy. Originally, ancient theology combined many symbols and allegories such as the sun, moon, and the planets to represent reality. Eventually, this practice degenerated into a worship of heavenly bodies and imaginary stone, animal, and reptile Deities possessing human feelings, passions, appetites, and lusts. The Onion was sacred to the Egyptians because its many layers symbolized the concentric spheres of heaven. However, the popular religion could not satisfy the thoughts, longings, and greater aspirations of the Spirit, or the logic of reason. Initiates in the Mysteries were first taught with the use of symbols. A formal creed cannot communicate the many complex interpretations that symbols explain with illustrations. This makes the symbols a teaching tool for an abstract concept by inspiring a desirable *feeling* when a complete *idea* cannot be explained.

The knowledge now taught by books and letters was previously taught with symbols. Priests created or perpetuated rites and presentations whose meanings were more explicit, suggestive, and expressive to the eyes and mind than words.

Masonry still follows the ancient Mysteries method of teaching. Its ceremonies are like ancient mystic plays that use research and philosophy in the analysis of a problem. Its symbols are explained by the instruction given and the interpretations provided in the lectures. To become an accomplished Mason you must not be content to merely hear or reiterate the lectures, but you must use them to assist yourself in studying, interpreting, and developing your 23 own understanding and interpretation of the symbols.

•   •   •   •   •   •

Masonry is similar to the ancient Mysteries only in a qualified sense: it presents an imperfect image of their former brilliancy, the ruins of their grandeur, and a methodology that has weathered progressive alterations, social upheavals, political extremes, and the ambitious foolishness of its proponents. After leaving Egypt, the Mysteries were modified by the religious and cultural traditions in each country where they were transplanted. Every Initiate was obligated to uphold the established government, laws, and religion of their country. They were the forerunners to the priests who willingly shared philosophical truth with the masses.

Masonry is not the Coliseum in ruins. Rather, it is an Italian palace of the middle ages built on a massive stone substructure laid by the founders of Rome, the Etruscans. Many of the stones of the superstructure are taken from the dwellings and temples of the Hadrian and Antoninus eras, and then further modified with modern architectural improvements.

Masonry was the first advocate and champion of EQUALITY. It established for mankind the threefold heritage of FRATERNITY, EQUALITY, and LIBERTY. The Monastery had *fraternity* and *equality,* but no *liberty.* Christianity taught the doctrine of FRATERNITY but rejected political EQUALITY and LIBERTY by reinforcing the indoctrination of absolute obedience to the Pope and other sacred authorities.

An accidental byproduct of the original purpose of the Mysteries was teaching men how to recognize their duties to themselves and mankind by sharing the practical aspect of all philosophy and knowledge.

Truth is the river from which duty flows. It has only been a few hundred years since the new Truth emerged that MAN IS SUPREME OVER INSTITUTIONS AND NOT THEY OVER HIM. This Truth established that man has *natural* authority over *all* institutions, and he develops these institutions according to his needs rather than the institutions developing man according to their needs. While this may seem to be a very simple statement with which all people would agree, it was once a great new Truth that only appeared after governments had been in existence for at least five thousand years. This new Truth imposed new duties upon man. Man owed it to *himself* to be free. He owed it to his *country* to give *her* freedom or maintain her possession of it. It decreed Tyranny and Usurpation to be the enemies of the Human Race by making both temporal and spiritual Despots and Despotisms illegal. Man's sphere of Duty was significantly expanded, and Patriotism had a newer and more extensive definition that included Free Government, Free Thought, Free Conscience, and Free Speech! Those whose inalienable rights had been parted with, robbed of, or whose ancestors had lost them, had the *right* to promptly reclaim them. Truths frequently become perverted into misapplied falsehoods, and unfortunately *this* Truth was perverted into the Gospel of Anarchy shortly after it was preached.

Very early on Masonry recognized and understood how this Truth expanded our duties. As the original meanings of its symbols began to grow, it adopted the facade of Stonemasonry whose working tools supplied more appropriate symbols for these expanded duties. It aided in bringing about the French Revolution, but disappeared when the Girondists were guillotined. The Order was restored soon after, and it sustained Napoleon who, with saber, musket, and cannon, defended the great right of the People to choose even a Corsican General for their Emperor if it pleased them.

Masonry believes this Truth has the Omnipotence of God on its side which neither Pope nor Potentate can overcome. It is a truth deposited into the world's treasury, and it forms a part of the heritage that each generation receives, holds in trust, contributes to, and then bequeaths to the personal estate of mankind. Masonry recognizes that to develop any truth, human excellence of gift, or growth is to improve the spiritual glory of the human race. Anyone who helps a thought become a Truth writes on the same line with MOSES and JESUS OF NAZARETH, and he has an intellectual sympathy with the Deity Himself.

20

Manhood is the best gift Masonry can bestow upon man. Manhood, supported by science and philosophy is what Masonry was ordained by God to 25 bestow on its faithful followers. It does not promote sectarianism, religious dogma, or a rudimentary morality like that found in the writings of Confucius, Zoroaster, and Seneca or as learned on a grade school playground.

Philosophy and Science are not in opposition to Religion. Philosophy is the knowledge derived from observing the manifested interaction between God and the Soul, which is then developed into wise analogies. It is the intellectual guide needed by religious sentiment. True religious philosophy is an infinite search, or best estimate, as SOCRATES believed and not a system of indoctrination. Religious sentiment inspires and promotes the intellectual and moral progress of philosophy.

Science cannot advance if religion remains stationary. Science builds upon those matured hypotheses that other experiments have confirmed. Science combines what is truly valuable in both old modes of mediation. First is the *heroic,* or the system of action and effort. Second is the *mystical,* or the theory of spiritual and intellectual communion. GALEN said, "Listen to me for I am the leader of the Eleusinian Priests. The study of Nature is an important mystery that displays the wisdom and power of the Great Creator. *Their* lessons and demonstrations are obscure, but *ours* are clear and concise."

The best knowledge we can obtain of another man's Soul is furnished by his actions and lifelong conduct. More reliance and confidence should be given to these actions and conduct than the hearsay and rumors spoken by other men. God wrote the first Scriptures of the human race in science upon the Heavens and Earth. An understanding of the grass, trees, insects, and animals teaches us deeper lessons of love and faith than we could gain from reading FÉNELON and AUGUSTINE. Nature is the Bible of God opened before mankind.

Knowledge is convertible into power, but it is not Power itself. Theories are convertible into rules of utility and duty. Wisdom is Power, its Prime Minister is JUSTICE, and it is the perfected law of TRUTH. The purpose of Science and Education is to make a man wise, but if that fails, then that 26 knowledge has been wasted like wine poured onto the ground. To know the *formulas* of Masonry is of little value by itself, just like knowing how to speak an obscure African or Asian dialect. Even understanding the *meaning* of Masonic symbols is of little value unless it contributes to our wisdom, charity, and justice.

The true objective of your Masonic studies should be to build upon your estate of wisdom beyond merely adding to your knowledge. Masonry's goal is to teach its Initiates the great truths about their rights, interests, and duties. A man may spend an entire lifetime studying a single specialty of knowledge (for example: geology, botany, or microbiology) by memorizing names, words, and phrases derived from Greek and Latin, then classifying and reclassifying subsets of subsets. Unfortunately, at the end of his life, he is no wiser than when he began.

The wiser a man becomes, the less likely he will be to submit to chains or restraints on his conscience or his body. A wise man *knows* his rights and more highly *values* them because he is more conscious of his worth and dignity. His wisdom urges him to assert his independence, and he becomes more *able* to do it. He is also better able to assist others and his country when their very existence depends upon the same assertion. Knowledge by itself does not make someone independent or prepare them to be free. More often, it only makes them a more useful slave because Liberty is a curse to the ignorant.

Political science seeks to determine how institutions of political and personal freedom can be secured and perpetuated to protect freedom of thought and opinion from the despotism of monarchy, mob, and clergy. It also seeks to protect freedom of action within the limits of the law and to provide the Courts of Justice with impartial Judges and juries. In these courts, weakness and poverty should have equal influence with power and wealth. The military powers, *in war or peace,* should be in strict subordination to the civil power. It should be impossible to make arbitrary arrests for acts not defined by the law as crimes. Courts outside of common law such as Vatican Inquisitions, Star Chambers, and the Military Commissions of the nineteenth century should be non-existent. Education must be within the reach of all children. The right of Free Speech is absolute, and strict accountability of all public officers, civil and military, is necessary.

Masonry points to the sad history of the world as justification for imposing political and moral duties on its Initiates. Masonry does not need to turn back the pages of history to the chapter written by Tacitus, or to those chapters reciting the incredible horrors of despotism under Caligula, Domitian, Caracalla, Commodus, Vitellius, or Maximin. Masonry only needs to point to the genocide, destruction, and senseless killing wrought by Hitler, Stalin, and Pol Pot; to the centuries of calamity endured by the French nation under the selfish Bourbon kings during the long oppression of the feudal ages; to those times when the peasants were robbed and slaughtered like sheep by their lords and princes; to the lords who claimed the first fruits of the peasant's marriage bed; to the captured city that was given up to merciless rape and massacre; to the State prisons which groaned with innocent victims; and to the Church on the Eve of St. Bartholomew when it blessed the banners of pitiless murderers while singing hymns for the crowning mercy.

We could also turn to a later chapter detailing the reign of the Louis XV, when early adolescent girls were kidnapped to serve his lusts. The time when *lettres de cachet* (King's orders) filled the Bastille with persons accused of no crime, or with husbands whose crime was keeping the pleasures of their wife when she was also desired by those villains bearing royal orders of nobility. The people were ground between the upper and lower millstones of taxes, customs, and excises. All this happened while the Pope's diplomat and the Cardinal de la Roche-Ayman knelt devoutly on each side of the king's sequestered prostitute,

Madame du Barry, helping to put on her slippers before rising from her adulterous bed. To the French royalty, the people were merely beasts of burdens used for suffering and toiling.

Masonry cannot cause change by itself, but it can help as one of God's instruments. The true Mason labors strenuously to contribute to implementing his Order's great purposes. It is a Force and a Power that must exert itself. Masonry should always remember the noble allegory of the courageous Curtius who bravely sacrificed himself to save Rome from being eternally divided against herself. Masonry will TRY. It cannot ensure a refrain from combat between two religions who meet head to head like two rams protecting the darkness behind them on a bridge over the Infinite. When people no longer fear famine, plundering, prostitution, distress, misery, unemployment, and all the other cast of characters in the outlaw bands that patrol the forest of human events, then nations will gravitate around the Truth like the planets around the Sun, each in its own orbit without clashing or collision. Then freedom will reign supreme everywhere, encompassed by stars, crowned with the celestial splendors, and accompanied by wisdom and justice on either hand.

As a Fellowcraft, REASON, LOVE, and FAITH must guide you in your studies.

We will not discuss the differences in definition between Reason and Faith here, but it should be noted that even in the ordinary affairs of life we are governed far more by what we *believe* (FAITH and ANALOGY) than by what we *know* (REASON). The "Age of Reason", that was the French Revolution proved the folly of enthroning Reason supremely and exclusively. Reason has a fault when dealing with the Infinite because we must revere and believe it. Despite the calamities of the virtuous, the miseries of the deserving, the prosperity of tyrants, and the murder of martyrs, we *must* believe there is a wise, just, merciful, and loving God whose Intelligence and Providence is supreme over all. Faith is a necessity to mankind. Take pity on those who believe in nothing!

We believe another's soul is of a certain nature and possesses a certain quality. The soul is either generous and honest, or greedy and dishonest. It is either virtuous and amiable, or vicious and ill tempered. These qualities can be determined with a brief glimpse at the soul without a means of *knowing*. We venture our fortune on the signature of a complete stranger from the other side of the world with the belief they are honest and trustworthy. We believe events have occurred based upon the word of others. We believe one energy will act upon another in a multitude of other phenomena which Reason cannot explain.

We should *not* believe what Reason authoritatively denies or what is repulsed by the sense of decency, what is absurd or self-contradictory, what is at issue with experience or science, or what degrades the character of the Deity and makes Him vengeful, malignant, cruel, or unjust.

A person's Faith and Reason are uniquely their own. Their Freedom is in their faith of being free and in their will to be uncontrolled by power. The

28

29

Priests and Augurs of Rome or Greece did not have the right to require Cicero or Socrates to believe in the absurd mythology of the uncivilized. The Imams of Islam do not have the right to require a single Pagan to believe Gabriel dictated the Koran to their Prophet. Even if assembled in one conclave like the Cardinals, no Brahmin who ever lived could gain the right to compel a single human being to believe in the Hindu Cosmogony. No person or body of people *can* be authorized to decree what anyone shall believe about any tenet of faith. Except to those who first receive it, every religion and the truth of its inspired writings depend on *human* testimony, the internal affirmation judged by Reason, and the wise analogies of Faith. Each person must have the right to judge their truths for themselves, because no one else has a higher or better right to pass judgment than someone with equal intelligence and circumstance.

The Roman Emperor Domitian claimed to be the Lord God. He had gold and silver statues and images of himself placed throughout the known world. He claimed to be the God of all men and, according to Suetonius, began his letters: *"Our Lord and God commands...."* He also formally decreed that no one should address him in any other manner, either in writing or by word of mouth. The philosopher Palfurius Sura, who was Domitian's primary advocate and chief prosecutor, did not have the fundamental right to persecute those Christians in Rome and in the provinces who refused to recognize Domitian's divinity as *he* did.

Reason is not the only guide in morals or political science. Love or loving-kindness must accompany reason to prevent fanaticism, intolerance, and persecution, which lead to a morality that is too withdrawn and political principles that are too extreme. You must also have faith in yourself and in the people; otherwise your enthusiasm will be easily discouraged by setbacks and obstacles. Do not listen to Reason alone because Faith and Love can produce more Power to help someone scale to the loftiest heights of morality or become the Savior and Redeemer of a People. Reason must hold the helm, but Faith and Love supply the driving power since they are the engines of the soul. Without the impulsive tendency of Enthusiasm, Love, and Faith there would be no RIENZI, TELL, SYDNEY, WASHINGTON, or any of the other great immortal patriots.

• • • • • •

GENIUS rules with God-like Power, AND its principal lieutenants are FORCE and WISDOM. The most unmanageable men will follow a leader who has the knowledge to see and the will to do. Genius unveils to its counselors the hidden human mysteries whose words help rebuild the crumbled ruins and cast off the huge chains. Dishonesty and stupidity stand ashamed before it. Its glances bring down the senseless idols whose altars have been built on high places and in the sacred groves. Its single Yea or Nay repeals the wrongs of ages that are heard by the future generations. Its power is immense because its wisdom is immense. Genius is the Sun of the political sphere, and its ministers Force and Wisdom are the lighthouses that shine its light into the darkness and returns the reflecting Truth.

Progress is symbolized by the Mallet and Chisel. It alludes to the development of energies and the progress of intellect in the individual and the masses. Genius may place itself at the head of an unintelligent, uneducated, unmotivated nation, but the only mode of securing intellect and genius for rulers in a free country is to cultivate the intellect of those who elect them. The world is rarely governed by great spirits except at the birth or the dissolution of institutions. In periods of transition and upheaval, the Long Parliaments, the Robespierres and Marats, and the semi-respectabilities of intellect will too often hold the reins of power. The Cromwells and Napoleons come later. After Marius, Sulla, and Cicero comes the orator CÆSAR. Great intellect is typically too sharp for the granite of this lifestyle. Legislators tend to be very ordinary men because legislation is very ordinary work and the final compromise of a million minds. *31*

The power of money and the sword is poor and pitiful compared to the power of the intellect. One may have agrarian *lands* equally partitioned by agrarian laws, but intellect is man's own nontransferable estate given directly from God. Intellect is the most potent of weapons in the hands of a warrior. If people can comprehend Power in the physical sense first, then they will have much more reverence for intellect. Hildebrand, Luther, and Loyola fall powerless before intellect as if before an idol. The mastery of mind over mind is the only conquest worth having. The physical conquest injures both parties, and it dissolves in a breath. The great cable falls rudely down and snaps, and this barely resembles the dominion of the Creator. Intellect does not need a subject if it is bright as a flame and strong as a stream, because it will flow like a spring tide to the popular heart. In addition to the spoken word, intellectual action fascinates with the admiration of the Invisible. Knotted with Love, intellect is the golden chain that binds together mankind and retrieves water from the well of Truth.

The influence of man over man by intellect or wealth is a law of nature. Society is joined together with spirituality. A free country will endure where intellect and genius govern, but it will perish if they submit and let other influences govern. Every nation who has ever tried to govern by their smallest, most incapable, or barely respectable influences have perished. Without Genius and Intellect to govern, the Constitutions and Laws will slowly be ground into dust and then blown away by the winds.

Giving Intellect supreme authority in a nation is the only method of perpetuating freedom. It will compel a generous care for the people and the best efforts from its leaders. It will foster honorable and intelligent allegiance from those below. A public political life will protect men from self-corruption in sensual pursuits, improper acts, and ignoble greed by offering the noble ambition of a just and effective rule. Elevating the masses by teaching loving-kindness and wisdom develops the free State from the rough ashlar and fulfills the great labor Masonry desires to contribute.

We should all labor in building the great monument of a nation and the Holy House of the Temple. The cardinal virtues cannot be divided among men like land or professions. ALL are apprenticed to Duty and Honor.

Masonry is a challenging march toward Light for both the individual and the nation. Light is Virtue, Fortitude, Intelligence, and Liberty while Tyranny over the soul or body is darkness. The freest people are always in danger of relapsing into servitude. Wars can be fatal to Republics because out of necessity they create tyrants who consolidate their power and suffer from the hazards of evil counsel. When the petty and the dishonorable are entrusted with power, the administrators and legislators produce two parallel series of errors and blunders, ending in war and calamity and necessitating a tyrant to restore order. When a nation feels it is sliding backwards and down a hill, it is time for a supreme effort. People and nations will sell themselves into virtual slavery to gratify their passions and to exact revenge. The magnificent tyrants of the past are a glimpse of those to come in the future. The tyrant's plea of necessity is always available, and once in power, the tyrant's need of providing for his safety makes him brutally savage. Religion is a power he must control because its sanctuaries might rebel if left Independent. It then becomes unlawful for the people to worship God in their own way, and old spiritual despotisms are revived. People must then believe as the Power dictates or fear death, and if they do believe as they will, their land, house, body, and soul can be seized and branded with the royal crest. Stalin said to the Russian people, *"I am the State. The very shirts on your backs are mine, and I can take them if I so desire."*

Dynasties established in this manner endure like the Cæsars of Rome, the Emperors of Constantinople, the Caliphs, Stuarts, Spaniards, Goths, and the Valois until the people tire out and finish with lunatics and idiots, who *still* rule because there is no agreement between men to end the horrible bondage. The State crumbles internally and deteriorates further from the random blows of the external elements. The furious passions, sleepy disregard, indifference of human ignorance, and rivalry of social orders are as good for the kings as the swords of the armies. The executives and legislators will have all bowed down before the idol of the status quo for so long they are unable to go into the streets and choose another leader. So their impotent State floats down the muddied stream of Time until the tempest or tidal sea discovers the worm has consumed its strength and crumbles it into oblivion.

●   ●   ●   ●   ●   ●

Civil and religious Freedom must go hand in hand because Persecution matures them both. A people content to obey a priest's commands will also be content with Royalty by Divine Right because the Throne and the Church will conspire to sustain each other. They will produce disloyalty and contempt by smothering dissension while the battle for freedom rages on around them. They will chain passive citizens into servitude with a deep trance, only to be occasionally woken with furious fits of frenzy, which end with helpless exhaustion.

Despotism is easy to maintain in a land that has only known one master from its childhood. There is nothing harder than perfecting and perpetuating free government by the people because all citizens must think as leaders. It is easy for a mob to prop up a puppet who in a few days will fall lower than before. A free government grows slowly like individual human faculties or like the trees from the inner core outward. Liberty is not a birthright. It can be lost by the non-user as well as by the mis-user. Liberty depends far more on the universal effort than on any other human property. It does not have a single shrine or holy well of pilgrimage for the nation, but rather its waters should erupt freely from the soil everywhere.

The free popular will is trained to think for itself and act for itself. Its true strength only becomes known in its hour of adversity when its trials, sacrifices, and expectations are its own. It is neither cast down by catastrophe nor euphoric from success. While enslaved people surrender themselves at the first glimpse of adversity, free people stand tall with the strength of unity, self-reliance, mutual dependence, and assurance against all but the visible hand of God.

The vast power of endurance, forbearance, patience, and performance are only acquired by the continuous use of all these functions, like the physical exercise or the individual moral exercise.

The old maxim that eternal vigilance is the price of liberty is no less true 34 than it was 4,000 years ago. It is fascinating to observe the universal pretext that tyrants have used to take away national liberties. It was written in the laws of Edward II that the justices and sheriffs should no longer be elected by the people due to the riots and dissensions which had arisen because of it. The same reason was given long ago following the suppression of the popular election of the bishops. There is a witness to this untruth in still yet older eras when Rome lost her freedom. Her enraged citizens declared that tumultuous liberty is better than a disgraceful tranquility.

•   •   •   •   •   •

With the Compasses and Rule, we can trace the figures used in the mathematics of planes, or what is formally called GEOMETRY and TRIGONOMETRY. GEOMETRY, which the letter G. in most Lodges is *said* to signify, means the *measurement* of *land* or *earth*, or Surveying. TRIGONOMETRY is the measurement of triangles or angles and is the most appropriate word for the science intended to be expressed by the word "Geometry". Neither word has a sufficient definition for *what is above equaling what is below, immensity equaling immensity.* Pythagoras placed great importance in the Science of Numbers, which is found throughout the ancient religions, Kabbalah, and the Bible. The Science of Numbers is not sufficiently expressed by either the word *"Geometry"* or the word *"Trigonometry"*, because it also includes Arithmetic, Algebra, Logarithms, Calculus, and Differential Equations, which are used to resolve the great problems of Astronomy and Physics.

35

• • • • • •

Virtue is the heroic bravery to *do* the things believed to be true despite the enemies, temptations, and menaces of the flesh or the spirit. Man is accountable for the *up*rightness, not rightness, of his doctrine. Devout enthusiasm is far easier than good action, but the end product of thought is action. The sole purpose of Religion is to establish an Ethic, but the theory of political science is a worthless debate unless it is actually placed into practice.

The soul of man and every religious or political *credo* has two regions: the Logical and the Ethical. When these two regions are in harmony, a perfect discipline evolves. There are men who are logical Christians, just as there are men who are logical Masons. Yet ethically, they are non-believers in the strictest sense: intellectual believers but practical atheists. These men can write long essays of their logic in perfect faith, but they cannot carry out their Christian or Masonic doctrine because of the strength or weakness of the flesh. On the other hand, there are many logical skeptics, but ethical believers. There are many ethical Masons who have never undergone initiation, but as ethics are the purpose of religion so are ethical believers the most worthy. He who *does* right is better than he who *thinks* right.

Not all men are hypocrites whose conduct does not square with their sentiments. No vice is rarer or task more difficult than methodical hypocrisy. When the Advocate becomes a Power it does not logically follow that he was always a hypocrite. Only shallow, simple men judge others this way.

The truth is that creed has very little influence on a person's individual conduct in religion, or party conduct in politics. A Gospel of Love in the mouth is the embodiment of Persecution in the heart. Men who believe in the creed of eternal damnation and a literal sea of fire and brimstone ensure its penalty with the slightest temptation of appetite or passion. Predestination relies on the necessity of good works. Extraordinary pains are taken to show that Masonry is an abstraction that does not desire to wrongly interfere in worldly matters. Yet among Masons, as in life, the most minor infraction can cause one person to

36 speak ill of another behind his back. Then we find far from the "Brotherhood"

of Blue Masonry or the use of the word "Brother". The solemn pledges contained in it are ignored. Among Masons, as elsewhere, when there is a choice to be made, one might give his vote and influence, in politics and business, to the less qualified person in preference to the better qualified Mason simply out of spite. A brother takes an oath to oppose any unlawful usurpation of power, but then ambition permits him to become the ready and even eager instrument of a usurper. Another will call someone "Brother" then, with a lie whose authorship cannot be traced, betray him like Judas Iscariot, or strike him as Joab did Abner under the fifth rib. Masonry cannot change human nature, and it cannot make honest men out of scoundrels.

While you are engaged in studying these principles for future use, do not forget the words of the Apostle James: "For if anyone hears the word and does not take action, he is like a man looking at himself in the mirror, for he sees himself, walks away, and immediately forgets what kind of man he saw. Whoever looks into the perfect law of liberty and does this work without forgetting what he heard, this man shall be blessed in his work. Faith is dead and useless without works."

•   •   •   •   •   •

Political science uses simple and intelligible theories to erect free governments and frame free constitutions. No sound conclusion can be reached about these theories and constitutional questions except by implementing them both in debate and in practice. Do not timidly shrink from the responsibility of the true theory or veer from it for want of the logical license. Do not transgress against it with passion or a plea of necessity or expediency, because this results in a denial or invasion of rights, laws that offend against first principles, the appropriation of illegal powers, and the rejection and renunciation of legitimate authority.

The man of solid learning, large intellect, and religious sympathies will almost always be rejected over the showy, superficial, brazen, and self-conceited leader because the highest truths are not acceptable by the masses, even during the threat of danger and calamity to the State. The intellectual man is simply further away from the masses and legislative level.

When the Athenian statesman SOLON was asked if he had given his countrymen the *best* laws he replied, *"The best they are capable of receiving."* This comment is one of the most profound on record, and yet like all great truths, it is so simple as to be barely comprehended because it contains the whole philosophy of History. Its truth could have saved man a tremendous amount of vain and idle contention by leading them to clearer paths of knowledge about the Past. This comment says that all truths are *Truths of that Period* and not truths for eternity. Whatever great fact had strength and vitality enough to make itself real, whether it be religion, morals, government, or whatever else, was a truth *for that era and only as good as the men who were capable of receiving it.*

This is also true of great men. The intellect and capacity of a nation is strictly measured by the great men whom Providence gives to them and those they *receive.* There have always been men too great for their time or their people, and every nation only makes *such* men its leaders who it is capable of understanding.

Imposing ideal truth or law upon a simple or unqualified *real* man is vain and empty speculation. The laws of sympathy govern this, and they dictate which men are chosen to lead. We do not know what qualifications the sheep insist on in a shepherd, but the masses have little sympathy for men who are too highly intellectual. When the wisest statesman England ever had, EDMUND BURKE, rose to speak in the House of Commons, it emptied out as if Parliament was over for the day. There is very little sympathy between the masses and the highest TRUTHS. The highest truth and the most intelligent man are seen as a great unreality and falsehood to the masses. The most profound doctrines of Christianity and Philosophy are mere jargon and babble to the Indigenous Amazon Basin Indians, like the popular explanations of Masonic symbols provided to the multitudes who have filled the Temples to capacity. Catholicism was a vital truth in its earliest ages, but its later failings led to the birth of Protestantism. The doctrines of ZOROASTER were the best the ancient Persians were capable to receive, those of CONFUCIUS were the best for the ancient Chinese, and those of MOHAMMED were the best for the Arabs of his age. Each was a Truth for that time, and each was a GOSPEL preached by a REFORMER. People so unfortunate as to remain content with stagnate understandings, while others have attained a higher Truth, should be pitied for their ignorance and misfortune, not persecuted.

People are not easily convinced of the truth or capable of comprehending it. The subtle human intellect can weave its webs over even the clearest vision. It is wishful to ask unanimity from a jury, but it is virtually impossible to ask it from a large number of people on a single point of political faith. Rarely do two people in any Congress or Convention agree because politicians can barely agree with *themselves.* If the political church seeks supremacy but has an indefinite number of tongues, then how can we expect men to agree about matters beyond the comprehension of the senses? How can we accomplish the Infinite and Invisible without a chain of evidence? Ask the small sea waves what they murmur among the pebbles! How many of those words that come from the invisible shore are lost, like the birds, during the long passage? How vainly do we strain the eyes across the long Infinite! We must be content with the pebbles that have washed onto the beach since we are unable to explore the hidden depths.

The Fellowcraft is taught not to become arrogant in his knowledge because pride in unsound theories is worse than ignorance. Humility becomes a Mason. Take some of the quiet, sober moments of life and add together the two ideas of Pride and Man. Then view him as a creature in a span of time walking through infinite space in all the grandeur of his littleness! Perched on a speck in the Universe with every wind of Heaven blowing into his blood as his soul floats away from his body, the coldness of his death sounds like the melody from a string. Like dust on the wheel, day and night he is rolled along the heavens through a labyrinth of worlds with all the creations of God flaming on every side even further than his imagination can reach. Does this person make for himself a crown of glory, deny his own flesh, and mock his friend who is made from the same dust to which both will soon return? Does the proud man not err? Does he not suffer? Does he not die? Is his reason ever stopped short by difficulties? Do his acts ever succumb to the temptations of pleasure? Is he free from pain when he lives? Does disease not also claim him as their prey? Can he escape the common grave when he dies? Pride is not the heritage of man. Humility should dwell with frailty and atone for ignorance, error, and imperfection.

A Mason should not be over-anxious for office and honor no matter how certain he may feel he has the capacity to serve the State. He should neither pursue nor refuse honors, because it is better to enjoy the blessings of fortune and submit without regret to their loss. The greatest deeds are not done in the bright lights of the media or before the eyes of the people. He whom God has gifted with a love of solitude possesses an additional sense of the vast and noble scenes of nature. Here is where we find the healing ointment for the wounds received from the pitiful shifts of policy, and this reverence of solitude is the surest wellness against the ills of life.

Fortitude is nobler than solitude because it is less passive. Solitude is a dismal selfishness that prohibits the exertion for others, and it is only dignified or noble when it is the temporary getaway from where oracles issue guidance to mankind. Solitude of this nature is the sole seclusion, which a good and wise man will covet or appreciate. The very philosophy that makes a man covet the *quiet* will make him avoid the *uselessness* of the hermit's lifestyle. LORD BOLINGBROKE would have received very little praise from his haymakers and ploughmen if he had looked with an indifferent eye upon an extravagant Prime Minister and a crooked Parliament. Very little interest would have been given to his vegetable garden if they had caused him to forget he was happier on a farm than he could be in a Senate and had made him forego all concern for re-entering the political arena as a legislator.

Some education stimulates the Intellect but leaves the heart more barren or hardened than before. There are ethical lessons in the laws of the heavenly bodies, earthly elements, geography, chemistry, geology, and all the material sciences. Objects and properties are symbols of Truths. Science that does not teach moral and spiritual truths is dead and decaying with little more real value than committing to memory a long list of unconnected dates, or the Latin names of plants, bugs, and animals.

Christianity began with the burning of the false gods by the people. Education begins with the burning of our intellectual and moral idols of prejudices, notions, vanity, worthless, and cowardly purposes. It is especially necessary to shake off the love of material gain because with Freedom comes a longing for material advancement. In the race for wealth men are ever falling, rising, running, and falling again while the absolute fear of poverty deepens the lines on many a noble's forehead. The gambler grows old as he counts the cards, and life's worries drive Youth away before its time. People live like high performance engines; a hundred years in a hundred months. Meanwhile the atlas becomes the Bible, and the diary becomes the Book of the Morning Prayer.

This greed becomes the misleading and dishonest practice in which the capitalist earns unscrupulous profits at the expense of the lives of the laborers. His speculations coin a nation's agonies into personal wealth with all the devilish machinery of Mammon, the God of Money. Greed for money and greed for office are the two twin columns at the entrance to the Temple of Moloch. It is doubtful whether the latter, blossoming into falsehood, trickery, and fraud is not even more deplorable than the former. These malevolent twins work to gain control of unfortunate subjects and render their souls to wither, decay, and at last die. The souls of half the human race leave them in this manner long before they die.

•   •   •   •   •   •

Alexander the Great coined a saying which survived his conquests: *"Nothing is more noble than work."* Only work can keep even kings respectable. When a king acts like a king, it is an honorable office that gives tone to the manners and morals of a nation. It sets the example of virtuous conduct and restores the spirit of chivalry enabling young men to be nurtured to real greatness. We must always strive for the idea of real work, since work and wages *will* go together in men's minds even in the most royal institutions. The sleep that follows work is always sweeter than the sleep that follows rest.

Let no Fellowcraft imagine the work of the least influential person is not worth doing because there is no limit to the possible effect a good deed, a wise word, or a generous effort may have. Nothing is really small, and whoever is open to the deep penetration of nature knows this. Although no absolute satisfaction may be given to philosophy, by circumscribing the cause or limiting the effect, the man of thought and contemplation experiences great pleasure in viewing the disbanding of forces that results in unity. These work to unify. Destruction is not annihilation, but rather the first step in regeneration.

Algebra can be applied to the movement of the clouds, and the shining star helps the rose to grow. But no thinker would conjecture to say the perfume of the hawthorn has no impact on the constellations. Who can calculate the path and position of the atom? How do we know the creation of

41

worlds is not determined by the falling effect of a single grain of sand? Who knows where the butterfly effect ends? Who understands the reciprocation between the infinitely great and the infinitely small? Who sees how the ripple effect echoing from the abysses becomes the tsunami or the avalanche of creation? It is all in equilibrium through necessity. There are intricate relationships between beings and things, and from the sun to the earthworm, there is no waste because they all need each other. Light does not carry terrestrial perfumes into the deep blue without first knowing what to do with them. The night distributes its stellar fragrance to the sleeping plants, and every bird has the thread of the Infinite in its claw. Germination includes the impact of a meteor, the tap of a swallow's bill, and the breaking of an egg. It all leads forward to the birth of an earthworm or the arrival of a Socrates. Between the telescope and the microscope, which has the better view? A bit of mold is like a bouquet of flowers, and a nebula appears like an ant-hill of stars.

There is another and more wonderful construction of intellect and matter. The elements and the principles are mingled, combined, married, and multiplied by each other to the point where the material world and the moral world are brought into the same light. Phenomena are perpetually folding back upon themselves, while time keeps marching forward. The vast astronomical changes in the universe come and go in completely random patterns shrouding all in the invisible mystery of their beginnings. The universe remembers all dreams from every sleep, creating an amoeba here, imploding a star there, oscillating and propelling itself to make the force of Light, and the development of Thought. When disseminated it is indivisible. It dissolves everything except that unified or one-dimensional point without length, breadth, or width. The MYSELF reduces everything to the Soul-atom level and makes everything develop towards God while unifying all activities from the highest to the lowest in the obscurity of a dizzying process. The flight path of an insect within the movement of the earth is only subordinate to the knowledge of the law of motion for the comet in the heavens, the knowledge of fluid dynamics, and the course of a drop in a body of water. The whole process of understanding must be developed in the mind where we might see the first gear as an atom and the last wheel as the zodiac.

Consider the consequences of a single act upon destiny and fate. A peasant-boy guides Blücher's artillery to the correct road fork and enables him to reach Waterloo in time to save Wellington from an embarrassing defeat. This enabled the kings to imprison Napoleon on an island prison. The careless machining of a tank or plane by an untrustworthy mechanic causes its breakdown on the field of battle, the battle is lost, and the destinies of empires are changed. A generous officer permits an imprisoned monarch to end his game of chess before leading him to the executioner's block. Meanwhile the revolutionary leader dies, and the imprisoned monarch re-ascends to the throne. An unskilled craftsman repairs the compass but by malice or stupidity misarranges it, the ship mistakes her course, and the ocean swallows an oracle preparing to write a new chapter in the history of the world. What we call accident is but the unbreakable chain of the intricate network between all created things. The locust hatched in the Arabian sands, the small worm that destroys the cotton-boll, the drought making famine in the Orient, the closing mills and starving workmen and their children in the Occident with riots and massacres are as much God's will as the earthquake. The fate of nations depends more on these accidents than on the intellect of its kings and legislators. Both World Wars ended by shaking the world to its very foundation. These wars were caused by the acts of ambitious generals, crazed fanatics, ambitious legislative zealots, and fools from obscure country parishes, among others. The energy of universal causation between action and reaction penetrates everything from the planets to the particles in a sunbeam. FAUST with his typeset and LUTHER with his sermons created greater results than Alexander or Hannibal. A single thought sometimes suffices to overturn a dynasty, and a silly song did more to unseat James II than the acquittal of the Bishops. Voltaire, Condorcet, and Rousseau uttered words that will ring throughout the ages for change and revolutions.

Although life is short, the influences of what we say or do are immortal. No calculus equation has yet pretended to identify the law of proportion between cause and effect. The hammer of an English blacksmith striking a contemptuous government official led to a rebellion that almost became a revolution. Even done by the feeblest or humblest of persons, the word well spoken or the deed fitly done cannot change their effect since it became inevitable and eternal. The echoes of the greatest deeds may fade away, and to human judgment, it seems to have been done without result. Yet the unconsidered act of the poorest of men may fuel the fire that ignites the powder kegs that tear apart an empire with a massive explosion.

The terrible and truthful power of a free people is often at the disposal of a single and seemingly unimportant individual. Free people feel with one heart and can lift up their innumerable arms for a consolidated blow. There is no graduated scale for the measurement of the influences of different intellects upon the masses. Peter the Hermit held no office, yet what an event he provoked!

•   •   •   •   •   •

The political point of view has but a single principle: LIBERTY is the sovereignty of mankind over itself. Where two or more of these sovereignties intersect the State begins, but there is no relinquishment in this association. Each sovereignty contributes equally to the whole common law to create an identity of concession called EQUALITY. The common law is the protection of everyone by everyone, which is called FRATERNITY.

Liberty is the summit, and Equality is the base. Equality is civility by *44*
every citizen having equal opportunity politically and equal opportunity
religiously.

The catalyst of Equality is free and mandatory education beginning with
the right to learn reading, writing, and arithmetic. Then we must *obligate* high
school upon all and *offer* trade school or college to all. Education is Light!
Everything comes from Light, and everything returns to it. The same
opportunity for everyone brings forth an equal society.

We must be in touch with the thoughts and feelings of the masses to be
wise and do any good work. A person must be evaluated by how they have put
to use the gifts Nature has given them and not for any wealth Fortune has given
them with her blind old eyes. We profess equality in the Church and in the
Lodge, but we will all be equal in the eyes of God when He judges the earth. We
should cheerfully sit together in friendship and fellowship for the brief moments
that constitute life.

A Democratic Government definitely has its defects because it is made
and administered by men and not by the Wise God. It cannot be concise and
swift like the despot, but when its fury is aroused, it develops its latent strength
and the sturdiest opponent trembles. Its domestic rule is tolerant, patient, and
indecisive. People are brought together first to differ and then to agree.
Affirmation, negation, discussion, and solution are the means of attaining truth.
The enemy will usually be at the gates before their babble is drowned out by the
chorus of consent. In the Legislative office, deliberation often defeats decision,
and Liberty and Tyrants can only play the fool.

Refined society requires more detail to its regulation. The advances of
successful States will be imitated by the old and the new, but the difficulty of
success lies in discovering the right path through the chaos and confusion. The
reconciliation of mutual rights and wrongs is also more difficult in democracies.
We cannot clearly see or easily estimate the relative importance of national issues
from our first level view because each of us looks at them through our own set
of personal experiences. These issues must be viewed and assessed in the
context of all national issues.

Shameless dependence on constituents or politicians, or being in debt to *45*
the favor of a Tyrant is a miserable condition. It is rare to find a man who can
speak honestly and frankly about the plain truth without fear, favor, or affection
from either the Emperor or the People.

Assemblies of men almost always lack faith in each other, and they stand
divided unless the terrible pressure of calamity or external danger produces
cohesion. The constructive power of these assemblies is generally insufficient.
The current triumphs in Europe have been in tearing down and destroying
institutions and not in building them up. But Repeal is not Reform, and time will
bring with it the Restorer and Rebuilder.

Speech is grossly abused in Republics. If the use of speech is glorious, then its abuse is the most villainous of vices. Plato said, "Rhetoric is the art of ruling the minds of men." However, in democracies it is very common to *hide* thought in words, to *overlay* it, and to speak nonsense. The glitter of these intellectual bubbles is mistaken for the glorious rainbow of genius, as the worthless iron pyrite is continuously mistaken for gold. Even intellect is reduced to jugglery, used to entertain the masses by keeping many thoughts in motion but only handling them briefly. In all Congresses, there is an inexhaustible flow of babble, and a Faction's clamorous deceit in discussion is no better than the screech of parrots or the crying of monkeys. No matter how fluent, the mere talker is barren of deeds on judgment day.

Some people are well skilled in fencing with their tongue, being marvelous at speech, but misers in deeds. Too much talking or over thinking destroys the power of action. In human nature, the thought can only be made perfect by the deed. Silence is the mother of thought and deed. The loud trumpeter is not the bravest of the brave because steel, not brass, wins the day. The doer of great deeds is usually slow and inarticulate in speech. Some people are born and bred to betray. Patriotism is their trade, and speech is their capital. No noble spirit can plead like Paul and be as false to itself as Judas.

Too often, deception rules in republics even though it always seems to be in the minority. Its guardians are self-appointed, and the unjust prosper more than the just. Like the roar of the night-lion, the Despot drowns out the birthright of free speech and the clamor of free voices becomes a novelty for the enslaved.

It is a rare accident when republics select their wisest, or even the least incompetent from the pool of completely incompetent, to govern and legislate for them. The people revere learned and knowledgeable genius when it takes charge, but if genius only moderately offers itself for office, then the people will firmly reject it even when it is a necessity to the salvation of the State. When genius battles the showy, superficial, arrogant, ignorant, brazen, and the imposter, the result will always be the same. Yet like the verdicts of juries, the Legislatures and the People sometimes make the right choice by accident.

Political offices rain down from the Heavens upon the just and the unjust. The Roman politicians laughed in each other's faces at both their own audacity and the simplicity of the masses. Politicians are not needed to lead the people astray because they readily deceive themselves. No matter how a Republic begins, it will still be in its infancy when idiocy has been promoted to high places, and treachery and dishonesty has infected all of its sanctuaries. The most unscrupulous partisanship will prevail even in respect to judicial appointments. Every improper promotion confers an undeserved favor that causes a hundred honest people to suffer from its injustice.

The country is stabbed in the chest when those who are brought into the esteemed positions of authority should have instead slithered into the dimly lit gallery. Every ill-gained token of Honor is stolen from the Treasury of Merit.

The entry and promotion within public service affects both the rights of individuals and those of the nation. The injustice of bestowing or withholding office from those pursuing it must be so intolerable in democratic countries that the least trace of it should be treated like the scent of Treason. All citizens of equal character do not have an equal claim to knock at the door of every public office and demand admittance. When any man presents himself for public service, he has a right to aspire to the highest office immediately, but only if he can demonstrate that he is more competent than everyone else who offers *47* themselves for the same post. The paved avenues to honor and offices should be available to anyone worthy of them, but the entry into that post can only be made through the door of merit. Whenever anyone unfairly and disreputably attains such a high post and is later found to be an absolute failure, they should at once be removed and convicted, for they are the worst kind of public enemy.

When people sufficiently proclaim themselves, others should be proud to give them the benefit of the doubt. When the power of promotion is abused by the People, the Legislature, or the Executive, rectification of the unjust decision falls to the Judicial Branch because it is a gross shortsightedness to be incapable of finding someone deserving. The eyes and mouth of both the Press and the Public should denounce and condemn injustice wherever it rears its terrible head. If someone looks long, hard, and honestly, they will identify the necessary merit, genius, and qualification.

"The tools to the workmen!" is the only principle that will save a Republic from the destruction of civil war or dry rot. No Republic has ever survived an attempt to govern by the minority.

However glaring and gross the inherent defects of democratic governments are, we only need to glance at the reigns of Hitler, Stalin, Mao, Pol Pot, Tiberius, Nero, and Caligula, to see their obvious advantages. The incredible cruelty, wickedness, and insanity of these Tyrants demonstrate the difference between freedom and despotism is as wide as the difference between Heaven and Hell. Let those who complain of the fickle humors and impulsiveness of a free people read Pliny's character of Domitian. If a great person in a Republic cannot win office without descending to the low arts, whining beggary, and the judicious use of sneaking lies, let them remain in the private sector and use the pen. Tacitus and Juvenal held no office, so let History and Satire punish the pretenders and crucify the despots. The revenge of intellect is terrible and just.

Let Masonry use the pen and the printing press against the Demagogue in the free State and against the Tyrant in the Despotism. Five thousand years of history offers many examples of violated rights and the sufferings of people who *48* instigated such protests, as possible, with each period of history. Under the

Cæsars there was no insurrection, but there was Juvenal who aroused the indignation that replaced Gracchi. Under the Cæsars there was the exile of Syene, but there was also the author of the Annals. The dark reign of the Neros should be reflected by the work of the engraver preparing the text to be poured with a concentrated and biting prose.

Despots may be an aid to intellectuals, but restricted speech is terrible speech. The writer must double and triple his style when silence is imposed by a Tyrant. There springs from this silence a certain mysterious fullness in the filtered and solid thoughts. Compression in the events of history produces conciseness in the historian. The durability of some celebrated prose is only a concise byproduct of the Tyrant's ways. Tyranny constrains the writer to a shortened diameter that results in an increased strength of words. Hardly sufficient upon Verres, the Ciceronian period would lose its edge upon Caligula.

The Demagogue is the forefather to the Despot. Anyone who will falsely ingratiate those who have offices to appoint will betray like Iscariot and prove to be a miserable and pitiful failure. The new Junius will give such people their deserved lashings, and History will make them immortal in infamy, since their influences culminate in ruin. The Republic that employs and honors those "who willingly crawl into the sewage of a promised office," will weep tears of blood for its fatal error because such supreme folly is the fruit of damnation. Let the complete justice and truth of every noble heart strike such persons like a thunderbolt! The very least each citizen should do is condemn it with their vote and ostracize it by denunciation.

The Czars were absolute and had it in their power to select the best qualified for public service. The forefather of a dynasty or a monarchy in its prime does not allow deceit and shallowness to thrive, prosper, or ascend to power as it does in Republics. Not all speak in the Parliament of a Dictator, as they do in the Congress of a Democracy, because the incompetent do not go undetected there *all* their lives.

Dynasties rapidly decay and lose steam as they dwindle into idiocy. Even the dull or brazen Members of Congress are at least the intellectual peers of the vast majority of kings and dictators. The great men, Julius Cæsar, Charlemagne, Cromwell, Napoleon, and Churchill were reigns of right because they were the wisest and the strongest. The incapables and imbeciles followed and encroached, and their fear made them cruel. For example, after Julius came Caracalla and Galba; after Charlemagne, the lunatic Charles VI. Similarly, the Saracenic dynasty dwindled out; the Capets, the Stuarts, the Bourbons, and the last of these produced Bomba, the ape of Domitian.

●　　●　　●　　●　　●　　●

Mankind is cruel by nature. The barbarian, the tyrant, and the civilized fanatic enjoy the sufferings of others like children enjoy the contortions of puppet shows. Absolute Power cannot be anything except cruel because it fears for the safety of its own tenure.

Dynasties invariably cease to have competent rulers after a few generations, and they become shams, governed by ministers, favorites, or courtesans. They may also become like those old Etruscan kings, lounging in their royal golden robes for days and months while doing nothing. Those who complain of the short-comings of democracy should ask themselves if they would prefer being governing by; the mistress Du Barry or Pompadour in the name of a Louis the XV; Caligula who made his horse a consul; or Domitian, "that most savage monster," who sometimes drank the blood of his relatives or entertained himself by slaughtering the most distinguished citizens at the city gates where fear and terror kept watch. After all, the Laws and the Constitution of a free government are above the Incompetents because the Courts correct their legislation, and the future will be the final Grand Jury who passes judgment on their decisions. What is the value of civil office that is void of intellect and knowledge when compared to the trials before Jeffries, the tortures in the dark caverns of the Inquisition, the Alvabutcheries in the Netherlands, the Eve of Saint Bartholomew, the Sicilian Vespers, the Great Purges, or the Final Solution?

●   ●   ●   ●   ●   ●

The Abbé Barruel, in his *Memoirs for the History of Jacobinism,* declared that Masonry in France gave as its secret the words Equality and Liberty and then left them for every honest and religious Mason to explain as would best suit his principles. However, French Masonry unveiled in the higher Degrees the "true" meaning of those words as interpreted by the French Revolution. He also excused English Masons from his denunciation because he said, "in England, Masons are peaceful subjects of the civil authorities, and no matter where he resides he does not engage in plots or conspiracies against even the worst governments. He goes on to state that England was disgusted with an Equality and a Liberty whose consequences had been felt in the struggles with her Lollards, Anabaptists, and Presbyterians. It had "purged English Masonry" from all explanations tending to overturn empires, although there still remained adepts whose disorganizing principles were bound to the Ancient Mysteries."

Effective Masonry flew the banners of Freedom and Equal Rights while it was in rebellion against temporal and spiritual tyranny. Masonry was outlawed in 1735 by an edict of the States of Holland. In 1737, Louis XV forbade it in France, and in 1738, Pope Clement XII issued his famous Bull of Excommunication against it, which was renewed by Benedict XIV. In 1743, the Council of Berne also outlawed it, and the title of the Clement XII's Bull is, "The Condemnation of the Society of Conventicles *de Liberi Muratori,* or of the Freemasons, under the penalty of *ipso facto* excommunication, the absolution from which is reserved to the Pope alone, except at the point of death." This

50

Bull empowered all bishops, laymen, and inquisitors to punish Freemasons, "as severely suspected of heresy" and to use the civil authority to put them to death, if necessary.

●   ●   ●   ●   ●   ●

False and degrading political theories meet their death after brutalizing the State. For example, assume that government offices and their employment are to be awarded for services rendered to political parties, and soon they become the prey and spoils of faction. The Republic becomes a mass of corruption and gangrene begins to rot the flesh of the State. In the end, all unsound theories morph themselves into one foul and loathsome disease of the political body. Like man, the State must make a constant effort to *stay* on the paths of virtue, honesty, and integrity. The habit of electioneering for office culminates in bribery *with* office, and begging for office leads to corruption *in* office.

An elected man has established a visible trust from God as plain to see as if the commission were notarized. A nation cannot renounce these Divine decrees any more than Masonry can, and it must labor to do its duty knowingly and wisely. We must remember that in free States as well as in despotisms, Injustice is the spouse of Oppression, and they are the fruitful parents of Deceit, Distrust, Hatred, Conspiracy, Treason, and Unfaithfulness. When assailing Tyranny we must use Truth and Reason as our chief weapons. Like the old Puritans, we must march into battle against the abuses that spring from within a free government with the flaming sword in one hand and the Oracles of God in the other.

The citizen, who cannot conduct the smaller purposes of public life, certainly cannot achieve the larger ones. The vast powers of endurance, forbearance, patience, and performance of a free people are only acquired by the continuous exercise of these functions, like physical exercise is required for physical health. If the individual citizens do not have them, the State will also be without them. The essence of a free government is the people should be as concerned in making the laws as they are with administering them. No person should be more ready to administer and obey these laws than the people who helped to make them. The business of government is carried out for the benefit of all, and every participant should give counsel and cooperation.

Another rocky reef on which the fates of free States are wrecked is the tendency to segregate the citizens by creating castes, or the perpetuation of the *jus divinum* (divine law) to perpetuate family dynasties in public office. The more democratic the State, the more certain this result because of the natural course of events and the apathy of human nature. Although free States have a strong tendency to advance towards centralized power, it does not originate from deliberate evil intention. Executive powers swell and grow to excessive dimensions because the Executive is always aggressive with respect to the nation. Government offices are created to reward partisans with public appointments. The strongest of the dregs and lower strata of the mob obtains large representation first in the lower offices and lastly rise to the Senates. Then Bureaucracy raises its bald head, bristling with pens, girded with spectacles, and adorned with ribbon. The art of Government evolves like a Craft, and its guilds 52 tend to become very exclusive like those of the Middle Ages.

Political science may be improved as a subject of speculation, but it should never be divorced from the real world of national necessity. The science of governing men must always be practical rather than philosophical. Political science does not have the same amount of positive or universal truth as the hard sciences, because what is true in one country may be very false in another. What is false today may become true in another generation, or the truth today may be overturned by the judgment of tomorrow. The goal of political policy is to distinguish the temporary from the enduring, to separate the suitable from the unsuitable, and to make forward progress possible. The theories of the political doctors are no better than the divinity doctors both lacking in the actual knowledge, experience, and communion of labor. The reign of such a caste with its mysteries, its zealots, and its corrupting influence may be as fatal as that of despots because thirty tyrants are thirty times worse than one.

There is a strong temptation for those in power to become as slothful and impotent as the weakest of absolute kings. They will relapse into apathy and indifference if given the power to rid themselves of great and wise men and will replace them with idiots when fancy prompts them. Organized and cunning if not enlightened, the central power is the law making body created by the people to remedy wrongs with the rule of justice. It soon supplies itself with all the required machinery to become ready and apt for all kinds of interference. The central power may not be able to suggest the best scientific solution to a problem, but it has the easiest means of placing an idea into action. If the goal to be attained is a large one, it will require a large comprehension, which is a proper action of the central power, but if it is a small goal, it may be thwarted by debate and disagreement. The central power must be an arbitrator when the people are too averse to change, too slothful in their own business, unjust to a minority, or even oppressive to the majority. The central power must take the reins when the people drop them.

France became a centralized government more from the apathy and ignorance of its people than the tyranny of its kings. When the private sector is given over to the direct guardianship of the State and completed government 53 forms are required for the simple repair to the belfry of a country church, a people are in their twilight. The dawn of social life nurtures men in idiocy. When the central government feeds part of the people, it is preparing for all to be slaves. When it begins to direct city and county affairs, the people are already enslaved. The next step is to regulate labor with quotas and wages by function.

Whatever follies the free people may commit, even putting legislative powers into the hands of the incompetent and dishonest, they do not despair. EXPERIENCE, that powerful teacher, will make them wiser with time by writing its lessons on the hearts of those who have been desolated by calamity and wrung with agony. Deception, distortion, and shameful begging for votes will some day cease to suffice. Have FAITH against evil influences and discouragements, and struggle on! FAITH is the Savior and Redeemer of nations. During the twilight of the Crusades when Christianity had grown weak, profitless, and powerless, the Arabs came like a cleansing hurricane. At dawn when the battle of Damascus was about to be fought, the Christian bishop went to the gates of the city and opened the Testament of Christ before the army. The Christian general THOMAS laid his hand on the book and said, *"Oh God! IF our faith be true, aid us, and deliver us from the hands of our enemies!"* But KHALED, the Arab, *"the Sword of God"* who had marched from victory to victory exclaimed to his wearied soldiers, *"Let no man sleep! There will be rest enough in the house of Paradise. Sweet will be the rest never to be followed by labor."* The Arab faith had become stronger than the Christian faith, and it won the battle.

The Sword is also an emblem of SPEECH in the Bible. The vision of the apocalypse during John's exile on Patmos was really an essay in the name of the ideal world to come. A tremendous satire was spoken in the name of Religion and Liberty with a fiery barrage smiting the throne of the Cæsars with a sharp, two-edged sword coming out of the mouth of the Image of the Son of Man who was encircled by the seven golden candlesticks and holding in his right hand seven stars. Isaiah said, "the Lord has made my mouth like a sharp sword." Hosea replied, "I have slain them by the words of my mouth." The author of the apostolic letter to the Hebrews said, "The word of God is quick, powerful, and sharper than any two edged sword capable of piercing, even dividing the soul and spirit." "The sword of the Spirit is the Word of God," says Paul, writing to the Christians at Ephesus. "I will fight against them with the sword of my mouth," it says in the Apocalypse to the angel of the church at Pergamos.

· · · · · ·

The spoken debate may roll on strongly like the great tidal wave, but it dies on the beach and does not make vast inroads. It is heard by few, remembered by still fewer, and it fades away like an echo into the mountains leaving no token of power. It is nothing to the living and coming generations of men. It is the *written* human speech that gives power and longevity to human thought. This longevity makes all human history part of one individual life.

A rock is a solid writing surface, but it requires a journey to read it. There is only one copy, and Time wears on it. Writing on skins or papyrus was another method, but only the rich could afford it. The Chinese stereotyped the wisdom of old sages and the passing events as unchangeable. The process tended to suffocate thought and hinder progress, for there is a continual wandering in the wisest minds. Unfortunately, Truth writes her last words on the pages that Error has made and often mended.

Printing made the written word prolific. Thenceforth the orator spoke in front of listening nations, while the author wrote decrees, *urbi et orbi,* and posted them throughout the market places remaining invisible to human sight if he chose. The printed word sealed the doom of tyrannies, because satire and sarcasm became as influential as armies. The unseen hands of the Juniuses and other anonymous authors could launch the thunderbolts that made ministers tremble. One whisper from the printed word fills the earth as easily as the magnificent speeches of Demosthenes filled the Agora, and it can be heard at the opposite end of the earth as easily as in the next street. It travels at the speed of light under the oceans. It makes the masses as one person and speaks to it in the same common language that elicits a sure and single response. Thus, printed speech passes into thought and then promptly into action, and a nation truly becomes one throbbing pulse with one large heart. Men become invisibly present as if spiritual beings. The unknown or forgotten thinker who sits in an Alpine solitude among the hills and silent herds may flash their words to all the cities and over all the seas with the printed word.

Choose thinkers to be Legislators and avoid liars. Wisdom is rarely grandiose. Weight and depth of thought are not synonyms with fluency, although the shallow and superficial are generally more expressive and frequently pass for eloquent. The general rule of politics is the more words used, the less thought given. The man who endeavors to say something worth remembering becomes meticulous and concise in every sentence like Tacitus. The masses love a steady, general stream, but the trinkets of babble that decorate it do not cover its real shortcomings.

Logical subtleties are not as valuable to public men. The Christian faith has it, but not as much as it once did. It is a subtlety that might have entangled Plato, and it has competed in its complexities with the mystic lore of Jewish Rabbis and Indian Sages. This subtlety does not convert the heathen. It is a vain task to balance the great thoughts of the earth on the fingertips of debate. It is not this kind of warfare that makes a belief triumphant in the hearts of the non-believers. What works is the actual power that lives in Faith.

The political philosophy of subtle logic is useless. Its cleverness rarely stirs or convinces the hearts of the people. The true apostle of Liberty, Equality, and Fraternity makes it a matter of life and death. A true apostolic fire flashes conviction into the soul like lightning. The true word is a two edged sword. Matters of government and political science can be fairly dealt with only by sound reason and the commonsense logic of the wise. The intuitive thinkers rarely succeed in becoming leaders of men. A buzzword, sound bite, or a catchphrase is more persuasive with the people than logic, especially if it is the least bit spiritual. When a political prophet stirs the dreaming stagnant nation to throw out the false idols from their places, his words will be from God's own mouth and thundered into the conscience. He will reason, teach, warn, and rule. The real "Sword of the Spirit" is more brilliant than the brightest blade of Damascus. Such men rule a nation with the strength of justice, wisdom, and power. The men of logical subtlety often rule well, because in practice they forget their finely spun theories and use the effective logic of common sense. When great hearts and large intellects are left to rust in private life, the country is in her deterioration even if its beard has not yet grown or grayed because then only the small attorneys, political hacks, the unskilled and unethical, or the practitioners in disreputable courts are made into national Legislators.

A free country must have the freedom of speech, and the State *must* listen to the meanderings of folly, the screechings of its geese, the brayings of its asses, and the golden oracles of its wise and great men. Even the despotic old kings allowed their wise fools to say what they liked. The true alchemist can extract lessons of wisdom from the babblings of folly. He will hear what a man has to say, even if he only seeks to prove himself the prince of fools, because even a fool will sometimes have something to say. There is some truth in all men unless they are forced to speak the words of other men. Even the idiot may occasionally point his finger in the right direction.

A nation must learn to forget. An ill fate awaits those who cannot learn the new because they cannot forget the old. To unlearn is to learn, and it is sometimes necessary to learn the forgotten again. The antics of fools make the current follies more tolerable, and the fashions are made absurd by the caricatures which lead to their demise. The clown and the jester serve a useful purpose. Like Solomon, the brilliant artificer and craftsman searches the earth for his materials, then he transforms the misshapen matter into glorious workmanship. The world is conquered more by the brain than the brawn, but an assembly cannot talk forever. Once it has listened long enough, it quietly puts the silly, the shallow, and the superficial aside, and it sets to work.

Groupthink runs in the most crooked channels. It is harder to trace or follow than the blind currents of the ocean, because no notion is too absurd that it may not find acceptance there. The master workman must mold these notions and impulses with his two handed hammer. They twist out of the way of the hammer swings and are invulnerable against logic. The mace, the battleaxe, the great double-edged two-handed sword must deal with follies, but the rapier is no better against them than a wand unless it be the forged from ridicule.

The SWORD is also the symbol of *war* and the *soldier*. Like thunderstorms, wars are often necessary to purify the stagnant atmosphere. War is not a demon without remorse or reward as it restores the brotherhood in letters of fire. War is the baptism of blood and fire by which men can be reformed when they are seated on the couch of ease and indolence, possessed by Pretence and Incapacity while littleness seeps into all the high places of State. War is the hurricane that brings the essential equilibrium of Power and Wisdom.

The appeal of nations to God is the acknowledgment of His might. It lights the beacons of Faith and Freedom, and it stokes the fire through which the earnest and loyal pass to immortal glory. There is in war the quenchless sense of Duty, the stirring sense of Honor, the doom of defeat, the incense of success, and the measureless solemn sacrifice of devotedness. Even in the heat and smoke of battle, the Mason can find his brother and fulfill the sacred obligations of Fraternity.

TWO, or the Duad, is the symbol of Antagonism; of Good and Evil, Light and Darkness, Cain and Abel, Eve and Lilith, Jachin and Boaz, Ormuzd and Ahriman, Osiris and Typhon.

THREE, or the Triad, is most significantly expressed by the equilateral and the right-angled triangles. There are *three* primary colors or rays in the rainbow: *blue, yellow,* and *red.* They combine to make the *seven* colors. The Trinity of the Deity has been a cornerstone in all creeds, in one form or another. He creates, preserves, and destroys. He is the generative *power,* the productive *capacity,* and the *result.* According to Kabbalah, the immaterial man is composed of *vitality,* (the breath of *life), soul* (or *mind),* and *spirit.* Salt, sulfur, and mercury are the great symbols of the alchemists, and to them man was body, soul, and spirit.

FOUR is expressed by the square, or four sided right-angled figure. A 58 river flowed from the symbolic Garden of Eden that was divided into *four* streams; PISON, which flowed around the land of gold, or light; GIHON, which flowed around the land of Ethiopia or Darkness; HIDDEKEL, which flowed eastward to Assyria; and the EUPHRATES. Zechariah saw *four* chariots coming from between two mountains of bronze. The first chariot was pulled by *red* horses, the second by *black,* the third by *white,* and the fourth by *grizzled,* "and these were the four winds of the heavens that will go forth on the Earth from before the Lord." Ezekiel saw *four* living creatures each with *four* faces and *four* wings. Their faces were of a *man,* a *lion,* an *ox,* and an *eagle,* and *four* wheels were mounted upon their *four* sides. Saint John beheld the *four* beasts: the LION, the young OX, the MAN, and the flying EAGLE. *Four* was the signature of the Earth. This is why, in the 148th Psalm, those who must praise the Lord on the land were *four* times *four* and *four* particular living creatures. Visible nature is described as the *four* quarters of the world and the *four* corners of the earth. The old Jewish saying is "there are *four* which take the first place in this world; *man,* among the creatures; the *eagle* among birds; the *ox* among cattle; and the *lion* among wild beasts." Daniel also saw *four* great beasts rise from the sea.

FIVE is the Duad added to the Triad. It is expressed by the five pointed or blazing star, the mysterious Pentalpha of Pythagoras, and it is permanently connected to the number *seven.* Christ fed His disciples and the multitude with *five* loaves and *two* fishes, and there remained *twelve* fragments, which is *five* and *seven* baskets full. He again fed them with *seven* loaves and a few little fishes, and there remained *seven* baskets full. The *five* small planets Mercury, Venus, Mars,

Jupiter, and Saturn, plus the two great planets the Sun and Moon, constituted the *seven* ancient celestial spheres.

SEVEN was the peculiarly sacred number. There were *seven* planets and spheres presided over by *seven* archangels. There were *seven* colors in the rainbow. The Phœnician Deity was called the HEPTAKIS or God of the *seven* rays. There are *Seven* days of the week, and *seven* and *five* make twelve, the number of tribes and apostles. Zechariah saw a golden candlestick with *seven* lamps, *seven* pipes to the lamps, and an olive tree on each side. He said, "the *seven* eyes of the Lord shall rejoice, and he shall see the plum line in the hand of Zerubbabel." John, in the Apocalypse writes *seven* epistles to the *seven* churches regarding *twelve* promises. What is said to the churches in praise or blame is completed in the number *three*. The refrain, *"who has ears to hear."* etc., has *ten* words, or *three* plus *seven,* and the *seven* is *three* plus *four.* The *seven* epistles are also *three* plus *four.* In the seals, trumpets, and vials of this symbolic vision, the *seven* are *four* plus *three.* He who sends his message to Ephesus, "holds the *seven* stars in his right hand and walks amid the *seven* golden lamps."

In *six* days or periods, God created the Universe and rested on the *seventh* day. Of clean beasts, Noah was directed to take by *sevens* into the ark and of fowls by *sevens,* because in *seven* days the rain was to begin. On the *seven*teenth day of the month, the rain began, and on the *seven*teenth day of the *seventh* month, the ark rested on Ararat. When the dove returned, Noah waited *seven* days before he sent her forth again, and again *seven* days after she returned with the olive leaf. Enoch was the *seventh* patriarch including Adam. Lamech lived 777 years.

There were *seven* lamps in the great candlestick of the Tabernacle and the Temple representing the *seven* planets. *Seven* times Moses sprinkled the anointing oil upon the altar, and there were *seven* days of consecration for Aaron and his sons. A woman was unclean *seven* days after childbirth. A person infected with leprosy was isolated *seven* days, *seven* times the leper was sprinkled with the blood of a slain bird, and *seven* days afterwards, he must remain out of his tent. *Seven* times while purifying the leper the priest was to sprinkle the consecrated oil, and *seven* times, he was to purify the house by sprinkling the blood of a sacrificed bird. *Seven* times the blood of the slain young bull was sprinkled on the mercy seat and *seven* times on the altar. The *seventh* year was a Sabbath of rest, and at the end of *seven* times *seven* years, came the great year of jubilee. *Seven* days the people ate unleavened bread in the month of Abib. *Seven* weeks were counted from the time of first putting the sickle to the wheat, and the Feast of the Tabernacles lasted *seven* days.

Israel was in the land of Midian *seven* years before Gideon delivered them. The young bull sacrificed by him was *seven* years old. Samson told Delilah to bind him with *seven* green willow branches, and she wove the *seven* locks of his head and afterwards cut them off. Balaam told Barak to build for him *seven* altars. Jacob served *seven* years for Leah and *seven* for Rachel. Job had *seven* sons and *three* daughters, making the perfect number *ten*. He had *seven* thousand sheep and *three* thousand camels. His friends sat down with him *seven* days and *seven* nights. His friends were ordered to sacrifice *seven* young bulls and *seven* rams. Again at the end, he had *seven* sons and *three* daughters, and two times *seven* thousand sheep, and lived an hundred and forty or two time *seven* times *ten* years. Pharaoh saw in his dream *seven* fat and *seven* lean cows, *seven* good ears and *seven* wilted ears of wheat; and there were *seven* years of feast and *seven* of famine. Jericho fell when *seven* priests with *seven* trumpets made the circuit of the city on *seven* successive days; once each day for six days and *seven* times on the seventh. "The *seven* eyes of the Lord," says Zechariah, "run across the whole earth." Solomon took *seven* years to build the Temple. *Seven* angels in the Apocalypse pour out *seven* plagues from the *seven* vials of wrath. The scarlet colored beast on which the woman sits in the wilderness has *seven* heads and *ten* horns, and so does the beast that rises from the sea. *Seven* thunders uttered their voices. *Seven* angels sounded *seven* trumpets. *Seven* lamps of fire for the *seven* spirits of God burned before the throne, and the Lamb that was slain had *seven* horns and *seven* eyes.

EIGHT is the first cube composed of *two.*

NINE is the square of *three* and represents the triple triangle.

TEN includes all the other numbers. It is especially *seven* plus *three,* and it is called the number of perfection. Pythagoras represented it by the TETRACTYS, which had many mystic meanings. This symbol is sometimes composed of dots, points, commas, or yōds, and in Kabbalah it is the letters of the name of Deity and is thus arranged:

$$\text{י}$$
$$\text{י} \quad \text{י}$$
$$\text{י} \quad \text{י} \quad \text{י}$$
$$\text{י} \quad \text{י} \quad \text{י} \quad \text{י}$$

The Patriarchs from Adam to Noah are *ten* in number, and there are *ten* Commandments.

TWELVE is the number of lines of equal length that form a cube. It is the number of the months, the tribes, and the apostles. It is the number of the oxen under the Brazen Sea, and of the stones on the breastplate of the high priest.

$$\bullet \quad \bullet \quad \bullet \quad \bullet \quad \bullet \quad \bullet$$

$$\bullet \quad \bullet \quad \bullet \quad \bullet \quad \bullet \quad \bullet$$

CHAPTER 3: THE MASTER

All religious expression IS symbolism, because we can only *describe* what we can *see*. The true forms of religion are THE SEEN. The earliest educational tools used were symbols, which differ in meaning according to external circumstances, imagery, and the level of a person's knowledge or education. Language is symbolic as it relates to mental and spiritual action. All *words* first have a *material* sense, but they may become spiritual *non*-sense to the uneducated. The word "retract" means to *draw back* and is used symbolically when we "retract" a *statement*. A picture of an arm drawn back could also express this idea. Another example is the word "*spirit*" which is derived form the Latin verb *spiro* (*breathe*) and means "*breath*".

Simply showing a symbol to someone does not mean they will associate the same meaning to it that you do. Philosophers attach explanations and stories to their symbols so the intended meaning can be more easily understood than just using the symbol alone. Gradually, the meaning of these stories and explanations is lost as contradictions and inconsistencies are introduced during their communication to others. Finally, these stories are abandoned for definitions and formulas, and the language will no longer express the complete meaning intended by the original stories. Reducing a symbol to spoken words cannot communicate to *you* the *exact* meaning it has for *me*, so religion and philosophy are further reduced to an argument about the meaning of words. The most abstract expression that language can supply for DEITY is a *sign* or *symbol* for an object beyond our comprehension. The signs and symbols of OSIRIS and VISHNU are not more accurate than their images or names, but they are less sensuous and explicit. We can avoid sensuousness with simple negation. Spirit is not matter, but spirit is - spirit.

An example of the symbolism of *words* is the York Rite phrase: "I will always *hail*, forever conceal, and never reveal." The word "*hail*", was altered from the phrase, "From whence do you *hail?*"

The word *hail* is really "*hele*", from the Anglo-Saxon verb *helan,* which means to *cover, hide,* or *conceal. Helan* is derived from the Latin verb *tegere,* which means to *cover* or *roof over.* "That ye fro me no thynge woll hele," says Gower. "They *hele* fro me no priuyte," says the Roman de la Rose. "To *heal* a house," is a common phrase in the western England area of Sussex where a person who roofs a house with slate tiles is called a *Healer.* Therefore, to "*heal*" means the same as to "*tile*", which is itself symbolic and primarily means to *cover* a house with *tiles* but also means to *cover, hide,* or *conceal.* Thus, language can also be symbolism whose words are as misunderstood and misused as the more important symbols.

Symbolism continually becomes more complicated. All the powers of Heaven were reproduced on earth until the art and ignorance of error wove a web of fiction and allegory that the wit of man, with his limited means of explanation, will never unravel. Even the Hebrew Theism became involved in symbolism and image-worship, probably adapted from an older creed in the remote regions of Asia. The worship of the Great Semitic Nature God (AL or ELS, and its symbolic representations of JEHOVAH Himself) was not confined to poetical or illustrative language. The priests were monotheists, but the people were idolaters.

64 The dangers of symbolism afford an impressive lesson in regards to the similar risks associated with the use of language. Imagination takes the place of reason or leaves it helplessly entangled in its web. Proper names are complicated by it, and the means are mistaken for the ends. The interpretation is taken for the object, and the symbols seize an independent character as truths and persons. PLUTARCH warns of a necessary but also dangerous path to approach the Deity by saying, "mistaking the symbol for the object can lead to a ridiculous superstition, but trying to avoid the extreme can also plunge the meaning into the hideous gulf of irreverence towards religion."

CICERO said the Mysteries teach us the first principles of life. The term "initiation" is used for good reason because the Mysteries teach us to live more happily and agreeably, and they soften the pains of death with the hope of a better afterlife.

The Mysteries were a Sacred Drama that demonstrated the legends significant to both nature's changes and the visible Universe where the Divinity was revealed to both the Pagan and Christian. Nature is the great Teacher of mankind because it is the Revelation of God. Nature does not attempt to force or indoctrinate a particular creed or specific interpretation. It simply displays its symbols without any explanations. It is the text without commentary. Error, heresy, and persecution have their origins in the glossy commentary of mankind. The earliest instructors adopted and adhered to the lessons of Nature using the methods She imparted. Beyond the current traditions or the sacred and enigmatic recitals of the Temples, the Mysteries provided the spectators few explanations. Initiates were to form their own opinions, like in the school of nature. No other method could have been more appropriate to every degree of cultivation and capacity. Instead of using the technicalities of language, nature's universal symbolism discloses its secrets to every one in proportion to his education and intellect. This ensured their moral and political meanings were within the reach of everyone, even if their philosophical meanings were only understood by a few.

These mystic shows and performances were not the reading of a lecture, but the beginning of a problem intended to arouse the initiate's dormant intellect 65 by requiring research. They had no hostility towards Philosophy, the great expounder of symbolism, although its ancient interpretations were often incorrect and ill founded. The migration from symbolism to dogma is fatal to the beauty of expression, and it leads to intolerance from this flawed perfection.

•   •   •   •   •   •

The ancients struggled to express the *nature* of the soul by comparing it to FIRE and LIGHT. Does any of our accumulated knowledge provide us a better or clearer idea of its nature today? By teaching the great doctrine of the divine nature of the Soul, explaining its longings for immortality, and proving its superiority over the souls of the animals (who have no Heavenly aspirations), we have hopelessly taken refuge in having no better explanation of the soul than the ancients did. Although they erred with respect to the soul's place of origin, they literally understood the mode and path of its descent. However, the Initiates probably perceived these explanations as allegories designed to make the ideas more meaningful and impressive to the mind.

We should no more laugh in self-conceit at these stories than we would at the *bosom* of Abraham being a home for the recently deceased *spirits*, or the New Jerusalem with its walls of jasper, and edifices of pure gold and precious stones. PAUL said, "I knew a man who made it to the third Heaven. While he was in Paradise, he heard divine words too sacred for a person to utter." The antagonism and conflict between the spirit and the body is greater than he portrays in his writings, and nowhere is the Divine nature of the soul more strongly asserted. PAUL said, "With the mind I serve the law of God, but with the flesh I serve the law of sin. The Spirit of God leads the sons of God, and the sincere expectation of the people awaits the manifestation of these sons of God. The people shall be delivered from the bondage of corruption and old age, and into the glorious liberty of the children of God."

•   •   •   •   •   •

Despotism and Democracy may both lead to the existence of falsehood and deceit. Despotism makes people false, treacherous, and deceitful out of fear, while Democracy makes people false, treacherous, and deceitful as a means of attaining celebrity, power in office, and wealth. Experience proves these vile and detestable vices will grow and spread rapidly in a Republic. When office, celebrity, and wealth become the gods of a people, the most unworthy and unfit will aspire to office and fraud will become the highway to wealth. The land will reek with falsehood, and hard work will lie and deceive. When the offices are open to all, those with the merit, integrity, and dignity of unsullied honor will rarely attain it, and only then by accident. To serve the country well will cease to be a reason why the great, wise, and learned should be selected to render service. Other, less honorable qualifications will become more prevalent such as adapting one's political opinions to the prevailing winds: defending, apologizing for, and

66

justifying the popular follies; advocating the expedient and the plausible; caressing, ingratiating, and flattering the elector; begging like a trained seal for their vote; professing friendship for a competitor then backstabbing them with innuendo; spreading rumors, or being present when they are uttered and not speaking out against them. Everyone has seen these dirty deeds put into practice to the point where success cannot be had with certainty by more honorable means. The result is a State ruled and ruined by ignorant and shallow mediocrity, brazen self-conceit, and the vanity of immature intellect.

The faithless and the false in public and political life will also be faithless and false in private. The jockey in politics, like the jockey on the racecourse, wants to win at all costs. He will always attend to his own interests first, and whoever leans on him will be horsewhipped. His ambition is disgraceful, and he will seek to attain office or any other coveted object by equally disgraceful means.

At length, office and honor are divorced. Any office where the small and shallow, the villain, and the trickster are deemed competent and fit to serve, ceases to be worth the ambition of great and capable men, because the weapons used are unfit for a gentleman to handle. The habits of unprincipled lawyers are made into law in the legislatures. They squabble over the fraudulent details while the fate of the nation and millions of lives are at stake. Even States are produced by treachery and brought forth by fraud, and insidious acts are justified by legislators claiming to be honorable. Contested elections become decided by perjured votes or party considerations, and the worst practices of corruption are revived and exaggerated in Republics.

It is very strange how reverence for truth, chivalry, loyalty, scorn of littleness, scorn of unfair advantage, faith, godliness, and generosity diminish among citizens and statesmen as civilizations advance. During the Victorian era, the statesman, the businessman, the taxpayer, and the soldier were all heroic figures who only feared God. However within one hundred years, the same people under the same Republic find nothing is *less* heroic than the statesman, the businessman, the shrewd speculator, the taxpaying middle class, each fearing only man and not God at all. Admiration for greatness dies out and it is dishonorably replaced by an envy in which everyone is in the way of many others on the road to celebrity or wealth. There is an unjust feeling of satisfaction when a great statesman is toppled from his high estate, and this makes it a misfortune, if not a crime, to be above the common level.

We would assume that a nation in distress would receive counsel from its wisest citizens. Quite the contrary. Great people seem unusually scarce when they are most needed, and small people seem unusually bold. These trying times are when the marginally sufficient, visually impotent, sophomorically immature, and flashy incompetent are most dangerous. When France was at the height of revolutionary agony and in desperate need of great leadership, she was instead being governed by an assembly of petty, provincial quibblers, and Robespierre,

Marat, and Couthon ruled in the place of Mirabeau, Vergniaud, and Carnot. England suffered similarly from weak leadership when she was governed by the Rump Parliament after having beheaded her king. Napoleon extinguished one body and Cromwell the other.

Fraud, perjury, trickery, and deceit in national affairs are the signs of decadence in States. They always precede upheavals or paralysis. Bullying the weak and cowering to the strong is the policy of a nation governed by the barely adequate. The electoral tricks for office are then re-enacted in the Senates, and the Executive dispenses patronage, instead of money bribes, primarily to the most unworthy men at the ruin of the Republic. The Divine nature of man disappears, and it is replaced with greed and selfishness. Sad but true, this story characterizes the constituents of many leaders whose greed has turned them into Swine like the allurement of the Greek goddess Circe. ₆₈

• • • • • •

The Great Teacher Jesus said, "You cannot serve the God of Man and the God of Money." When the thirst for wealth becomes too great, it will be sought honestly and dishonestly by frauds and encroachment, by the scoundrels of trade, the heartless greedy speculators, and by gambling in stocks and commodities. All of these soon demoralize an entire community. Some people will speculate upon the needs of their neighbors and the distresses of their country. Cunning scams aided by mindless gullibility will burst market bubbles impoverishing the masses with ground shaking bankruptcies more fatal than giant earthquakes. Fraudulent contracts, a collapse of the currency, the crash of banks, the inflation of Government securities, and the liquidated savings of the poor all ravage the very young and the very old, filling the graveyards and insane asylums with residents. In contrast, the professional opportunist or the speculator thrives during the misery. If their country is fighting for her very existence, they aid her by depreciating her money so they may accumulate great amounts of it with very little outlay. If their neighbor is distressed, they buy his property for pennies. If they administer an estate, it will be found to be insolvent and the orphans become paupers. If their bank collapses, they will be found to have withdrawn their money in time. Society worships and fawns over its money-and-credit kings like the old Hindus and Egyptians worshipped and fawned over their worthless idols. No wonder people believe there is another world in which these injustices will be atoned for with fire and brimstone when they see their friends of these ruined families begging the wealthy speculators for charity to prevent the orphaned victims from starving. ₆₉

• • • • • •

Nations are particularly greedy for commerce and territory. Commerce leads to the violation of treaties, encroachments upon feeble neighbors, and the plundering of their coveted lands. Republics are as greedy and unprincipled as Despots, never learning from history that unrestrained expansion by plundering and fraud has its inevitable consequences in its own destruction or enslavement. When a nation begins to plunder its neighbors, the words of its doom are already written on the walls. God has already decreed a judgment upon unrighteous conduct in national affairs. When a war slashes the vitals of a nation, let it reflect upon whether it has been guilty of these injustices, and if so, let it humble itself in the dust!

When a nation exceeds the just and fair limits of a reasonable prosperity it has become consumed by the spirit of commercial greed and possessed by the demons of commercial gluttony. Greed is a corrupt and demoralizing passion more unscrupulous than raw ambition and more hateful than vengeance. The infected nation is to be regarded as the enemy of the human race. To grasp at the lion's share of commerce has always proven to be the ruin of Nations, because it requires consistent and detestable injustices. They forge a selfish and crooked policy that forbids a Nation that only cares for itself to make allies with other nations.

Commercial greed in Asia and Africa during the 1800 has caused more atrocities, greater plundering, and a higher cost in human lives than the more noble ambition of the expanded empire of Consular Rome. A nation that only pursues global commerce becomes selfish, calculating, and dead to the noblest impulses and sympathies that should inspire other nations. It will submit to insults that diminish its honor rather than risk threatening its commercial interests with war. It will also be caused to wage unjust war under false and frivolous excuses, while its free people cheerfully associate with despots so they can crush a commercial rival.

The corrupt and calculating self-interest of a nation's commercial greed will ultimately displace the Honor and Generosity, which elevated it to greatness. Greed made both Elizabeth and Cromwell the protectors of Protestants against the prevalent, crowned Tyranny and Persecution beyond the four seas of England. The greedy nation's soul petrifies like the soul of the person who makes gold and money his gods. The Despot will occasionally act nobly and generously to help the weak against the strong or the right against the wrong. But commercial greed is egotistic, grasping, faithless, overreaching, crafty, cold, stingy, selfish, calculating, and solely controlled by considerations of self-interest. Because it is heartless and merciless, it has no sentiments of pity, sympathy, or honor to make it pause during its remorseless career. It simply crushes all that impedes its progress under the heel of commerce.

War fought for a great principle makes a nation noble. War fought for commercial supremacy based upon a false pretext is shameful, and it shows to what dishonorable depths men and nations can descend. The slave trade in East Africa, the Middle East, and Southeast Asia is no different to the people operating it than the trade in steel, oil, or diamonds because they are consumed by greed. Commercial greed places no value on people's lives, as it quiets its own conscience by steadily attempting to justify itself to God.

Justice is a process of administering that exact measure of reward which a person's merit decrees, or punishment which their error (or crime) deserves. The justice of a father is not inconsistent with the forgiveness he grants for the errors and offenses of his child. The Infinite Justice of God does not consist in doling out exact judgments of punishment for human frailties and sins. People are inclined to define very narrow notions of what is right and wrong into the laws of justice, and then insist that God adopt them as His law. People continually try *71* to dignify their own shameful love of revenge and retaliation by labeling it justice. They measure behavior with their own little tape measure and call it God's law of justice.

Justice does not involve strictly governing our conduct with rigid legal rules. If a community were to enforce the strictness of this rule, then written over its gates should be the warning, which DANTE says, is written over the great gate of Hell: "LET THOSE WHO ENTER HERE LEAVE HOPE BEHIND!" It is unethical and immoral to pay the lowest market wage to the laborers in the fields, factories, or offices for their labor as long as they are physically able to work. Otherwise, when sickness or old age overtakes them, their family will starve. God will curse with calamity those who allow the children of its unemployed or infirm laborers to eat the boiled grass of the fields to fight starvation, or mothers who strangle their children so they may buy food for themselves with the charitable pittance given for burial expenses. The rules of what is normally termed *"Justice"*, may be formally observed among the fallen spirits that make up the aristocracy of Hell.

●　　●　　●　　●　　●　　●

Justice divorced from sympathy is selfish indifference. The sympathy that acknowledges the mutual struggle and cooperation needed to survive can even be observed among the freshwater algae found in the tiniest bit of scum from a stagnant pond. Throughout nature, there are an unlimited number of animals who provide each other with a level of sympathy and assistance beyond what humans are inclined to regard as the strict law of justice.

We only need to reflect briefly to be convinced that the individual man is just a small fraction of the whole unit of society, inseparably connected to the rest of mankind. His actions, interconnected with the will and thoughts of others, make or break his fortunes, control his destinies, render honor or *72* dishonor, and are his life or death. The infectious and contagious physical and moral epidemics, the popular delusion of public opinion, enthusiasms, and the other great moral and intellectual phenomena, test and confirm the universal sympathy. The vote of a single man, the utterance of self-will, ignorance, conceit, or spite can decide an election and place Absurdity, Incompetence, or Corruption into the legislature. This action will ultimately lead the country into war, destroys fortunes, slaughters our sons, renders our life's work worthless, and pushes us helplessly into the grave.

These considerations should teach us that justice to ourselves and others is the same thing. We cannot define our duties with mathematical lines ruled by the square. Instead, good deeds must fill the great circle of humanity traced by the compasses, which place us at the point in its center like a drop of water in the great Pacific. The particles of an atom are bound by a mysterious law of attraction to every other atom in the mass. We term this attraction sympathy. The physical and moral welfare of others cannot be indifferent to us because we have a direct and personal interest in the public morality, prevailing intelligence, the well-being, and the physical comfort of the people at large. The ignorance, destitution, consequential degradation, brutalization, and demoralization of the people are noxious plagues that must be dealt with because they cannot be ignored, escaped, or avoided.

Justice is uniquely essential to nations. History and the Eternal Wisdom both teach that the unjust Nation is doomed to calamity and ruin. "Righteousness dignifies a nation, but immorality disgraces it. Righteousness establishes the Throne. Let the lips of the Ruler pronounce the Divine sentence, and his mouth will make no wrong judgment!" A nation is predestined for destruction if it uses fraud and violence to increase its territories, to encroach on the weak and plunder their possessions, to violate its treaties and obligations, and to substitute the urgency of greed for the law of honor and fairness. The nation and the individual are both bound to the inevitable and eternal consequences of these wrongs.

No wrong is ever really successful. Written by the Infinite God against all that is unjust, this sentence is inherent to the nature of mankind and the Universe. The gain of injustice is a loss, and its pleasure is suffering. Wickedness often seems to prosper, but its success is also its defeat and shame. If its consequences miss the offender, then they will certainly fall upon and crush his children. It is a philosophical, moral, and physical truth that God threatens the descendants to the third and fourth generations with the evils of their parents, who violated His laws. Deceit proves to be a failure and the day of reckoning always comes to the nation and to the individual.

Hypocrisy is the tribute paid to virtue and justice by vice and corruption. It is Satan trying to dress himself in the angelic clothing of light. Hypocrisy by man and nation are both equally detestable in morals, politics, and religion. The following are as common as they are infamous and disgraceful: to perform injustice under the pretense of equity and fairness; to criticize vice in public but commit it in private; to pretend to possess a charitable opinion while objectionably condemning it; to profess the principles of Masonic beneficence but close an ear to the crying of distress and suffering; to praise the intelligence of the people but plot to deceive and betray them with their own ignorance and simplicity; to preach of purity but embezzle; to honor , then abandon a sinking cause; to act uninfluenced by selfish motives but sell one's vote for position and power; to wear the uniform of the Court of God while loyally serving the Devil; to pretend to believe in a God of mercy and a Redeemer of love but persecute those of a different faith; to underbid a widow's house after making a long prayer for the deceased; to preach fidelity but wallow in lust; to advise humility but be more proud than Satan; to pay tithe but refuse more important matters of the law, judgment, mercy, and faith; and to appear outwardly righteous but be full of hypocrisy and savagery. Indeed, all of these are like the white marble graves, which appear beautiful on the surface, but inside they are full of the foulness and putrification of the bodies of the dead.

Under the pretense of duty, the State cloaks its ambition under the banner of "extending the sphere of freedom" to annex other States or Provinces through violence or other obsolete, hollow, and fraudulent means. An Empire 74 founded by a successful soldier will claim its ancient or natural boundaries and then make necessity and safety its tagline for open robbery. Both the Nazis and the Soviets gained footholds in Europe by establishing a continual need for extending their territory by force. Without a plea, the great Despotisms divided between themselves a Kingdom, dismembered Poland, and prepared to wage war over the Eastern European states. A plea to maintain the balance of power only yielded destruction for those States.

The thirst for power is insatiable for people and nations. When Rome was the mistress of the world, the Emperors caused themselves to be worshipped as gods. The Church of Rome laid claim to everyone's soul, and despotically ruled everyone's life from the cradle to the grave. It sold and bartered pardons for past and future sins, while it claimed to be infallible in matters of faith. It decimated Europe to purge it of heretics, and it decimated the Americas to convert the Mexicans and Peruvians. It awarded and deposed thrones and wielded excommunication and banishment to close the gates of Paradise against whole Nations. Conceited with his defeat of the Aztecs and the Incas, the King of Spain (Philip the Second, who was married to the Queen of England) strived to conquer Protestantism in the Netherlands with his "invincible" Armada and force that kingdom back into allegiance with the Papal throne. Napoleon crowned his relatives and generals on thrones and divided amongst them half of Europe. The Czars ruled over an empire larger than Rome, but history always repeats itself - acquisition, dismemberment, ruin. God makes judgments of all that is unjust.

The highest goal of human ambition seems to be to subjugate the *will* of others and imprison the *soul,* because it is the exercise of the highest power. It is the root of all indoctrination and propaganda, from Mesmer, to the Church of Rome, to the Soviet Republic. It is also the religious doctrine of Joshua and Mohammed. Masonry alone preaches Toleration for the right of man to abide

75 by his own faith and the right of all States to govern themselves. It opposes the monarch and the despot seeking to extend their boundaries by conquest, and the Church claiming the right to suppress heresy with fire and steel.

When wronged, it is a natural reaction to desire revenge. Revenge has always been "a kind of wild justice" for discouraging wrongs by making them fruitless and their punishment certain. We convince ourselves that our desire for revenge is more to prevent the repeat of the wrong than for our own satisfaction. We also believe our vengeance should be rewarded with immunity and profit, because to submit to being cheated is to encourage the cheater to continue. We are quick to regard ourselves as instruments of God for inflicting His vengeance. But revenge is always taken in anger, and is therefore unworthy of a great soul whose serenity should not be disturbed by ingratitude or villainy. The misery perpetrated by scoundrels is as unworthy of our anger as that done by the insects and beasts. When we crush the snake or slay the wolf, we should do it with no more anger or feeling of revenge than we have in pulling weeds in the yard.

If it must be in human nature to take revenge by way of punishment, let the Mason consider that by doing so he is God's agent. His revenge should be measured by justice and tempered by mercy. The law of God states the consequences of wrong. Cruelty and crime shall be punished. The injured, wronged, and indignant are as much His instruments to enforce that law as are the diseases, public humiliation, the verdict of history, and the damnation of the future. No one will disagree that the following should not be punished: the Inquisitor who has racked and burned the innocent; the Spaniard who chopped the Indians into pieces and fed the mangled limbs to his bloodhounds; the military tyrant who shot men without trial; the corrupt who has robbed or betrayed his State; the fraudulent banker who has bankrupt widows and orphans; the public officer who has violated his oath; the judge who has sold injustice; or the legislator who has enabled Incompetence to ruin the State. Let the injured and the sympathizing be the instruments of God's just vengeance, but always out of a higher feeling for justice than mere personal revenge.

76 Every moral characteristic of mankind finds its start among the animals of the wild. The cruel foulness of the hyena, the savage piracy of the wolf, the merciless rage of the tiger, and the cunning treachery of the panther are all found in mankind. These characteristics should excite no other emotion when found in people, than when found in beasts. Why should the honorable person be angry with the geese that hiss, the peacocks that strut, the asses that bray, and the apes that chatter even when they wear the human form? It is more noble to forgive than to take revenge, and we should neither obsessively despise those who wrong us, nor feel the anger to take revenge.

You are in the region of LIGHT at the sphere of the Sun, * * * * the great source of light for the Earth. ZAHAB is the Hebrew word for *gold* or *Light*. In the great Eastern allegory of the Hebrews, the River PISON encompasses the land of *Gold* or *Light*, and the River GIHON encompasses the land of *Ethiopia* or *Darkness*.

We do not know any more about light than the ancients did. Even among modern physicists, light may behave as a particle and at other times as a wave. They resolve that paradox by deciding that it is either both or neither. To the ancients, light was an outflowing from the Deity, and we still view it today as the proper symbol for truth and knowledge. We also believe the upward journey of the soul through the Spheres is symbolic, but we are equally uninformed about the soul's origination at birth and its destination after death. The ancients strived to have *some* belief and faith, *some* creed about those points. But today, people are satisfied to believe that the soul is *something* separate from the body without concern whether it existed before or after. No one asks whether it originated from the Deity, is created from nothing, or generated like the tissue of the body from the father and the mother? We can safely accept the symbols of the ancients until we have a better belief than the soul is of a Divine nature, originating in a sphere nearer the Deity, and returning to It when freed from the body to be purified of all the impurities and sin which the body has 77 contaminated it with.

Humanity worships Longevity. It is no coincidence that thousands of years ago, men worshipped the Sun. The Parsees continue that worship today. Originally, they looked beyond the orb to the invisible God whose manifestation generated life with the Sun's outflowing light. Long before the Chaldæan shepherds watched it from their plains, the Sun regularly arose in the morning like a god, set again in the west like a king retiring for the evening, and returned again the next morning in the same array of majesty. It was this steadfast, immutable character of the Sun that the men of Baalbec worshipped. His light-giving and life-giving powers were secondary qualities. The characteristic of God that compelled their worship was the reflected light they saw and its enduring and consistent quality of Deity. Beyond Olympus, beyond the Pillars of Hercules, He went home every evening and returned every morning to behold the temples they built to his worship. The Nations that personified him as BRAHMA, AMUN, OSIRIS, BEL, ADONIS, MALKARTH, MITHRAS, and APOLLO, grew old and died. Moss grew on the capitals of the great columns of his temples, and he still shined on that moss. Grain by grain his temples crumbled into dust and were carried away by the winds, and still he shined on the crumbling columns and doorsills. The roofs crashed to the pavement, and he shined in on the Holy of Holies with unchanging rays. It is no wonder that people worshipped the consistency of the Sun.

There is a water plant whose broad leaves prevent the rolling drops of water from uniting, just like arguments on points of faith, politics, or religion never unite while rolling over the surface of the mind. An argument that convinces one mind has no effect on another, because few intellects or souls have any logical power or capacity. There is an angle in the human mind that makes false logic more effective than the truth with nine-tenths of those who are regarded as people of intellect. Even among the judges, not one in ten can argue 78 logically. Each mind sees the truth distorted through its own set of experiences. Truth is like matter in the spherical state to most people, like a drop of cold water on the surface of a red-hot metal plate as it dances, trembles, spins, but never comes into contact with it. The mind may be plunged into truth yet not even be warmed by the immersion, like a hand plunged into boiling water, not noticing a thing.

• • • • • •

Khairūm or *Khūrūm* is a compound word. The German scholar Gesenius renders *Khūrūm* by the word *noble* or *free-born*: *Khūr* meaning *white, noble*. It also means the opening of a window or eye socket. *Khri* also means *white*, or an *opening;* and *Khris*, the orb of the Sun as in *Judges* 8:13 and *Job* 9:7. *Krishna* is the Hindu Sun-God. The Parsi word *Khur* is the literal name of the Sun.

From *Kur* or *Khur*, the Sun, comes Khora which is also a name of Lower Egypt. Bryant said in his Mythology that the Sun was called *Kur;* and Plutarch said the Persians called the Sun *Kūros*. *Kurios*, meaning *Lord* in Greek, like *Adonaï* meaning *Lord* in Phœnician and Hebrew, and was also applied to the Sun. There were many places sacred to the Sun, and called *Kura, Kuria, Kuropolis, Kurene, Kureschata, Kuresta,* and *Corusia* in Scythia.

The Egyptian Deity called by the Greeks *"Horus"* was *Her-Ra*, or *Har-ocris*. *Hor* or *Har*, the Sun. *Hari* is a Hindu name for the Sun. *Ari-al, Ar-es, Ar, Aryaman, Areimonios*, the AR meaning *Fire* or *Flame*, are of the same kindred. *Hermes* or *Har-mës, (Aram, Remus, Haram, Harameias)*, was Kadmos, the Divine Light or Wisdom. *Mar-kuri*, says Movers, is *Mar*, the Sun.

In the Hebrew, AOOR, אור, is *Light, Fire,* or the *Sun*. The Greek historian Ctesias said, *Cyrus* was so named from *Kuros*, the Sun. Hesychius says *Kuris* was Adonis. Apollo, the Sun-god, was called *Kurraios*, from *Kurra*, a city in Phocis. The people of *Kurene*, originally Ethiopians or Cuthites, worshipped the Sun under the title of *Achoor* and *Achōr*.

The ancient annals of Tsūr document the principal festivity of *Mal-karth* (the incarnation of the Sun) was celebrated at the Winter Solstice. The festival held at Tsūr represented his *re-birth* or his *awakening,* and it was celebrated with a pyre on which the god was supposed to regain a new life through the aid of fire. This festival was celebrated in the month of *Peritius (Barith),* the second day of which corresponded to the 25th of December. *Movers* said, KHUR-UM, 79 King of Tyre, was the first to perform this ceremony. We learn these facts from *Josephus, Servius* on the Æneid, and the *Dionysiacs* of *Nonnus*. It cannot be a random coincidence that in Rome the *Dies Natalis Solis Invicti,* the festal day of the invincible Sun was celebrated on the same day. HAR-*acles* was worshipped at Tsūr under the title HERCULES. Accordingly, while the temple was being built and during the winter solstice at Tsūr, the death and resurrection of a Sun-God was annually represented by Solomon's ally using the pyre of MAL-KARTH, the Tsūrian Haracles.

AROERIS or HAR-*oeris,* is the elder HORUS. The word is from the old Hebrew root that has the form *Aūr,* or with the definite article prefixed, *Haūr* is Light. It also means *the* Light, splendor, flame, the Sun, and its rays. The hieroglyphic of the younger HORUS is the point in a circle. The hieroglyphic of the Elder was a pair of eyes. The festival held on the thirtieth day of the month *Epiphi* represented when the sun and moon were supposed to be in the same right line with the earth and was called *"The birth-day of the eyes of Horus".*

In a papyrus published by Champollion, this god was styled *"Haroeri,* Lord of the Solar Spirits, the beneficent eye of the Sun." Plutarch calls him *"Har-pocrates"* but there is no trace of Plutarch's reference in the hieroglyphic legends. He is the son of OSIRIS and ISIS, and he is shown sitting on a throne supported by *lions.* The same word means *Lion* and *Sun* in Egyptian. Accordingly, Solomon made a great ivory throne, plated with gold, upon a pedestal of six steps. A lion was paced at each riser and upon the top stair, making seven lions on each side, for a total of fourteen.

Again, the Hebrew word חי, *Khi,* means *"living;"* and ראם *râm* means *"was, or shall be, raised or lifted up."* The latter is the same as רום, ארום, חרם, *rōōm, arōōm, harūm,* whence *Aram,* for Syria or *Aramæa* meaning *High*-land. *Khairūm,* therefore, would mean *"was raised up to life, or living."*

So, in Arabic, *hrm,* an unused root, meant *"was high", "made great", "exalted",* and *Hîrm* means an *ox,* which is also the symbol of the Sun in Taurus at the Vernal Equinox.

KHURUM, therefore, improperly called *Hiram,* is KHUR-OM. It is the same as *Her-ra, Her-mes,* and *Her-acles,* the *"Heracles Tyrius Invictus",* the personification of Light and the Son, the Mediator, Redeemer, and Savior. From the Egyptian word *Ra* came the Coptic word *Oūro,* and the Hebrew word *Aūr,* all meaning Light. *Har-oeri,* is *Hor* or *Har,* the chief or *master.* *Hor* is also heat, while *hora* is season or hour. The royal name rendered *Pharaoh,* was PHRA, which is pronounced *Pai-ra* and means Sun.

The legend of the contest between *Hor-ra* and *Set,* (or *Set-nu-bi,* the same as *Bar* or *Bal)* is older than the strife between *Ostris* and *Typhon.* It goes back to at least the nineteenth Egyptian dynasty. In the Book of the Dead, it is called "The day of the battle between Horus and Set." The later myth connects itself with Phœnicia and Syria. The body of OSIRIS went ashore at *Gebal* or *Byblos,* sixty miles above Tsūr. Take notice that the names of each of Khūrūm's murderers contain the name of the Evil God Bal.

•   •   •   •   •   •

Har-oeri was the god of TIME and Life. The Egyptian legend involves the King of Byblos who cut down the tamarisk tree containing the body of

80

61

OSIRIS to make a column for his palace. While employed in the palace, Isis took possession of the column, removed the body from it, and carried it away. Apuleius describes Isis as "a beautiful female whose long thick hair hung in graceful ringlets over her divine neck." She was often shown in procession with female attendants, holding ivory combs, while dressing and ornamenting the royal hair of the goddess. The palm-tree and the lamp in the shape of a boat also appeared in the procession. If our Masonic allegory is not a mere modern invention, it does allude to these legends.

This relationship is also confirmed by this hieroglyphic picture copied from an ancient Egyptian monument, and it also enlightens you about the Lion's grip and the Master's gavel.

81   אב, in the ancient Phœnician characters ⊿ℵ, and in the Samaritan 𐤀𐤁, AB, (the two letters representing the numbers 1 and 2) or Unity and Duality, means *Father,* and is a primitive noun common to all the Semitic languages. It also means an Ancestor, Originator, Inventor, Head, Chief or Ruler, Manager, Overseer, Master, Priest, Prophet.

אבי is simply Father. When it precedes another word, the preposition "of" is implied, for example אבי-אל, Abi-Al, is the Father of Al.

The final Yōd means "my". So אבי by itself means "My father". דויד אבי means David my father, II *Chronicles* 2:3.

ו (Vav), ending is the possessive pronoun "his". אביו, *Abiu* (which we read *"Abif"*) means "of my father's". Its full meaning, as related to the name of Khūrūm, is "formerly one of my father's servants (or slaves)."

The name of the Phœnician artificer in Samuel and Kings is חירם and חירום [II *Samuel* 5:11; I *Kings* 5:15; I *Kings* 7:40]. In Chronicles it is חורם, with the addition of אבי [II *Chronicles* 2:12] and of אביו [II *Chronicles* 4:16].

It is unnecessary to add the word *"Abif"*, or *"Abiff"*, to the name of the artificer. It is almost as absurd to add the word *"Abi"*, which was a *title* and not part of the *name.* Joseph says [*Genesis* 45:8], "God has made me *'Ab l'Paraah,* as Father to Paraah (Vizier or Prime Minister)." Haman was called the Second

Father of Artaxerxes, and when King Khūrūm used the phrase "Khūrūm Abi" he meant the artificer he sent Schlomoh was the principal or foreman in his line at Tsūr.

A medal copied by Montfaucon exhibits a female nursing a child, holding ears of wheat in her hand, with the inscription Iao. She is seated on clouds with a star at her head and three ears of wheat rising from an altar before her.

HORUS was the *mediator* who was buried for three days, regenerated, and triumphed over evil.

In Sanscrit, the word HERI means *Shepherd* and *Savior,* and CRISHNA is called *Heri,* or as JESUS called Himself the *Good Shepherd.*

חור, *Khūr,* means an opening of a window, cave, or eye, and it also means white.

חר also means an opening, and noble, free-born, or high-born.

חרם KHURM means consecrated or devoted. In Ethiopic, it is the name *82* of a city, [*Joshua,* 19:38]; and of a man, [*Ezra* 2:32, 10:31; *Nehemiah* 3:11].

חירה, *Khirah,* means nobility or of noble race.

Buddha is said to have personally understood the essence of the Hindu Trinity. Hence, the three meaning one monosyllable (*Om or Aum*) applies to him the same as Brahma-Vishnu-Siva. He is the same as Hermes, Thoth, Taut, and Teutates. One of his names is Heri-maya or Hermaya, which are the same name as Hermes and Khirm or Khūrm. In Sanscrit, Heri, means *Lord.*

A learned Brother places over the two symbolic pillars from right to left, the two words ⳢᎩ⳩ and ᒿ∇Ꮖ, יהו and בעל. IHU and BAL are followed by the hieroglyphic equivalent, of the Sun-God Amun-Ra. Is it a coincidence that in the name of each murderer are the two names of the Hebrew Good and Evil Deities: for *Yu-bel* is *Yehu-Bal* or *Yeho-Bal?* The three final syllables of the names, *a, o,* and *um* make A∴U∴M∴ the sacred word of the Hindus representing the Trinity-God who was Life-giving, Life-preserving, and Life-destroying. He was represented by the mystic character **Y**.

The real *Acacia* is a thorny evergreen, which grew around the body of Osiris. It was a sacred tree among the Arabs who made it the idol Al-Uzza, which Mohammed destroyed. It is an abundant bush in the Desert of Thur, and the "crown of thorns" placed on the forehead of Jesus of Nazareth was made of it. It is a proper symbol of immortality because of its tenacity for life. When used as a doorpost, it has been frequently known to take root again and sprout new branches above the threshold.

•   •   •   •   •   •

Every nation must have periods of trial and transition, especially if it engages in war. At some point it is certain to be governed by demagogues appealing to every corrupt element of the prevailing times; influential corporations; currency traders; petty attorneys; confidence men; speculators;

adventurers; or a dishonorable oligarchy enriched by the distresses of the nation and fattened on the miseries of the people. The deceitful visions of equality and the rights of man end, and the plundered State can only regain real liberty by being purified with fire and blood.

In a Republic, political parties will position themselves around the positive and negative poles of an issue or opinion, but the intolerant spirit of a triumphant majority will prevent any deviation from the standard it has established for itself. Freedom of opinion will be declared and feigned. People will exercise it at the peril of being banished from the political circles of those in power who prescribed the policy to be followed. Obedience to the party line and its current whims go hand in hand. Political independence only occurs in an elderly state where a person's opinions grow from the acts that they have been constrained or sanctioned to perform. Flattery of the individual (or the people) corrupts both the recipient and the flatterer. It benefits no one. A Cæsar securely seated in power cares less for his office than he would in a free democracy. His appetite for his office will not become excessive, as that of a free people will, until it becomes insatiable. The effect of liberty is to allow individuals to do what they please, when they please. Do not risk congratulations, which may soon be turned into complaints. Flattery is justly called a crime, because it tends to mislead those in power, who are prone to misuse that power.

The first principle in a Republic should be, "wages or privileges from the community are only to be given for public services rendered, and the offices of magistrate, legislature, and judge are not birthrights." This is a single sentence lesson of Truth and Wisdom for all nations, which every person can understand. If a tidal wave of despotism overthrew the world and destroyed all the institutions protecting freedom so they could no longer be remembered among men, this sentence would be sufficient to rekindle the fires of liberty and revive the race of free men.

However, to *preserve* liberty it must be added that: "a free nation never confers office as a reward, especially for questionable services, unless she seeks her own ruin. All officers are *employed* by her only in consideration of their will and ability to render service in the future, ensuring only the best and most competent are always preferred."

Hereditary succession is the only rule which can be compromised and still make it possible to preserve the liberties of the State. No other rule entrusts the power of making laws to those who have an instinctive sense of injustice, which enables them to detect evil, and corruption in their most secret hiding places. It gives them the moral courage and brave independence to drag the perpetrators into the light of day and call down upon them the scorn and indignation of the world. These people are never the flatterers of the masses. The time always comes to a Republic when its most prominent leaders are people devoid of any reputation, statesmanship, tolerance, ability, or information.

They are mere political bigots who owe their places to trickery and *want* of qualifications. These Republics die and the world is none the wiser for what they have said or done. Their names sink to the bottomless pit of oblivion, and their acts of folly or deceit cursed the political body and proved its ruin.

Politicians in a free nation are generally hollow, heartless, and selfish. Their own glorified prestige is the purpose of their patriotism. With secret satisfaction, they watch the fall or removal of one whose loftier genius or superior talents overshadow their own self-importance, or whose integrity and incorruptible honor are in the way of their own selfish ends. The influence of the petty antagonists is always against the great man, because *His* rise to power may last a lifetime. One of their own kind will be more easily displaced with each of them hoping to succeed him. So it comes to pass that people who are 85 unfit to be the lowest clerks shamelessly aspire and actually win the highest offices. It seems that incompetence and marginal adequacy are the surest passports to high office.

The consequence is that those who are competent and qualified to serve the people refuse to enter into the struggle for office. The wicked and crafty political doctrine that "anything goes" is an incentive for every species of scoundrel to seek even the highest offices of the nation. Reliance upon the power of a magnanimous spirit is gone. The sympathizing impulses of a great soul are gone. Stirring and moving the people to generous, noble, heroic, wise and strong action are gone. Like the trained dog standing on its hind legs and begging with its front paws, politicians fawn, flatter, and beg for votes. Rather than descend to this, the competent and qualified persons stay scornfully distant, refusing to court the people, while acting on the maxim that "mankind has no claim to demand that we shall serve them in spite of themselves."

• • • • • •

It is unfortunate to see a nation split into factions, each following its own great or brazen leader with a blind, unreasoning, unquestioning hero-worship. It is contemptible to see a nation divided into political parties whose leaders are petty and corrupt, whose sole end is the spoils of victory. Such a nation is in the last stages of decay and near its end no matter how prosperous it may seem. It may argue over the weather and the earthquake, but it is certain that no government can be conducted by the people and for the people without a rigid adherence to those principles that our reason supports as certain and sound. These principles must be the tests of political parties, people, and measures. Once established, these principles must be uncompromisingly applied requiring everything to either rise to the standard or be declared against it. People may betray, but principles never can. Oppression is the inevitable consequence of misplaced confidence in a treacherous person. It is not the result of the working or application of a sound, just, and well-tried principle. Compromising fundamental principles in order to unite political parties of incompatible creeds is a fraud that will end in ruin due to the just and natural consequence of fraud. Once your theory and creed are established, accept no departure from it on any grounds, especially expediency. This is the Master's word. Do not yield it to flattery or force, and let no defeat or persecution rob you of it! A person who blundered once with statesmanship will blunder again because political near-sightedness does not improve with age. These blunders can be as fatal as crimes. There will always be more impostors than genuine leaders among public men, more false prophets than true ones, more prophets of Baal than of Jehovah, and Jerusalem will always be in danger of the Assyrians.

Sallust wrote, "a State once corrupted by luxury and idleness may, by its mere greatness collapse under the burden of its vices." While he was writing, Rome had already played out her masquerade of freedom. Causes other than luxury and sloth destroy Republics. If small, their larger neighbors absorb them. If large, the cohesive force is too weak to hold it together, and they break apart under their own weight. The raw ambition of petty people cannot prevent a nation's collapse from distressing issues because they lack wisdom in their councils. Usurpation of power plays its part, and incompetence seconds corruption. The storm rises and the fragments of the fragile raft are scattered across the sandy shores, providing another lesson for mankind to disregard.

•   •   •   •   •   •

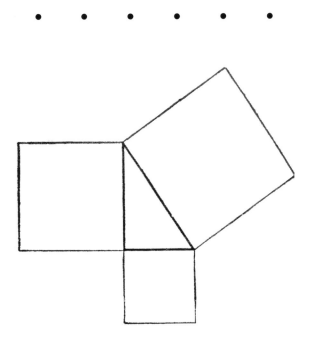

The Forty-Seventh Proposition is older than Pythagoras. "In every right angled triangle, the sum of the squares of its two perpendicular sides is equal to the square of its hypotenuse ($a^2 + b^2 = c^2$)."

The square of a number is that number multiplied by itself. Thus, 2 *87* squared is 4, and 3 squared is 9.

The first ten numbers are: 1, 2, 3, 4, 5, 6, 7, 8, 9, 10; their squares are.....................................1, 4, 9, 16, 25, 36, 49, 64, 81, 100; and.. 3, 5, 7, 9, 11, 13, 15, 17, 19 are the differences between each square and the one preceding it, which give us the sacred numbers 3, 5, 7, and 9.

The squares of 3 and 4, added together, equal the square of 5, and the squares of 6 and 8 equal the square of 10. Therefore, if a right angle triangle is formed from a base measuring 3 or 6 parts, and the perpendicular measures 4 or 8 parts, the hypotenuse will equal 5 or 10 parts. And if a square is drawn on each side of the triangle, these squares can be subdivided into single squares equal in number to the square of the hypotenuse.

The Egyptians arranged their deities in Triads: the FATHER (the Spirit, Active Principle, or *Generative* Power), the MOTHER (Matter, the Passive Principle, or *Conceptive* Power), and the SON (*Issue* or *Product,* the Universe, or produced from the two principles). In ancient Egypt, these were OSIRIS, ISIS, and HORUS. In the same manner, PLATO described *Thought* (the *Father),* Primitive *Matter* (the *Mother),* and *Kosmos* the *World* (the *Son),* and the Universe was animated by a soul. Triads of this kind are found in Kabbalah.

PLUTARCH said in his book *De Iside et Osiride,* "the better and more divine nature consists of three things: Intellect, or that existing within; Matter; and *Kosmos,* or that produced from these two. Plato wants to call the Intelligible the 'Idea, Exemplar, and Father;' Matter is the 'Mother, Nurse, and the place and vessel of generation; and the issue of these two is 'the Offspring and Genesis,' but the KOSMOS is the word signifying equal *Beauty* and *Order,* or the Universe itself." (Beauty is symbolized by the Junior Warden in the South.) Plutarch adds that both the Egyptians and Plato compared the universal nature to what they called the most beautiful and perfect triangle in that nuptial diagram. The triangle is right angled, its sides are respectively 3, 4, and 5, and "we must suppose the perpendicular is designed to represent the masculine *88* nature, the base the feminine, and the hypotenuse is the offspring of both. Accordingly, the perpendicular represents OSIRIS, or the prime cause. The base represents ISIS, or the receptive capacity. And the hypotenuse represents HORUS, or the offspring of the two. The first number which is composed of even and odd integers is 3; and 4 is a square whose side is equal to the even number 2; but 5 is generated by the preceding numbers 2 and 3, and it is said to have an equal relation to both of them as its common parents."

● ● ● ● ● ●

The *clasped hands* are another symbol that was used by PYTHAGORAS. It represented the sacred number 10, which contained all the preceding numbers and the number expressed by the mysterious TETRACTYS. Both he and the Hebrew priests borrowed this figure from the Egyptian sacred science, and it should be included again among the symbols of the Master's Degree. The Hebrews designed it with the letters of the Divine name:

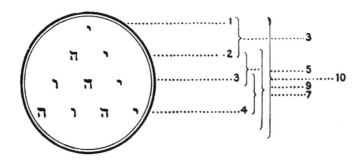

Thus, the *Tetractys* leads you to both the study of the Pythagorean philosophy of numbers and to Kabbalah, which will aid you in discovering the True Word and understanding, what was meant by "The Music of the Spheres". Long before his time, nature had designed her own cube roots and squares, and modern science continues to confirm the ideas of Pythagoras with regard to the properties of numbers and how they govern in the Universe.

●　　●　　●　　●　　●　　●

89　　All of the POWERS at man's disposal, under his control, or subject to his influence are his *working tools*. The friendship and sympathy that bond heart to heart are like the force of cohesion which make the sandy particles into the solid rock. This law of cohesion prevents the planets and suns from chaotically dissolving into the most basic atomic particles. Without the ties of friendship, affection, and love, mankind would be a raging hoard of wild and savage beasts of prey. The sand hardens into rock under the immense pressure of the ocean, occasionally aided by the irresistible energy of fire. When the pressure of calamity and danger is upon an order or a country, the members or the citizens will be more closely united by the cohesion of sympathy and inter-dependence.

Morality is a power. It is the magnetic attraction of the heart to Truth and Virtue. The compass needle points unerringly to the north carrying the mariner safely over the trackless ocean through storm and darkness until his glad eyes behold the beneficent beacons that welcome him to a safe and hospitable harbor. The hearts of those who love him are made happy by the subtle, inconspicuous, and unerring monitor that guided him through the stormy waters. A feeling of helplessness and fear rushes upon a sailor who finds the needle of his compass has drifted too far eastward or westward and no longer points true. The same would be said if the great axioms of morality were to fail, leaving the human soul helplessly adrift and at the mercy of the uncertain, faithless currents of the deep.

Honor and Duty are the North and South stars of a Mason. The Mason who loses sight of these is no longer governed by their compassionate and potential power. He becomes lost, shipwrecked, sinks out of sight, and disappears unnoticed and unmissed.

The power of electricity, like that of sympathy, instantaneously flashes over the nerves of nations with great thoughts, worthless suggestions, noble acts, and dishonorable natures. The powers of growth and immortality, *90* expansion and contraction, give birth to the wonderful achievements of electricity, which have parallelisms in the individuals, nations, and the moral world. Growth is a necessity for people and nations, and its termination is the beginning of decay. Man has long prepared for the earthquakes that crush nations into pieces, overturn thrones, and swallow States. Revolutions have deep roots in the past, and the power exerted is in direct proportion to the previous restraint and compression. The true statesman should see the progression of causes that in due time produces Revolutions, and he who does not is but a blind leader of the blind.

The great changes in nations are slowly and continuously made, like the geological changes of the earth. They are the water falling from Heaven as rain and dew, slowly disintegrating the granite mountains. The water erodes the plains, leaving hills and ridges as monuments to itself. It carves out the valleys, fills the seas, widens the rivers, and after the lapse of thousands and thousands of silent centuries, the great alluvial plains are prepared for the growth of that plant whose seeds employ the looms of the world. The abundance or destitution of these crops will determine whether the weavers and spinners of other countries have work or starve.

Public Opinion is an immense power, but its currents are inconsistent and incomprehensible. Nevertheless, in free governments, it reigns supreme, and the statesman is tasked with finding the means to shape, control, and direct it. Once this is done, it is either conservative and beneficial, or liberal and destructive. The Public Opinion of the civilized world is International Law, and it is a power so great that it can even force the victorious despot to be generous or aid an oppressed people in their struggle for independence.

Habit is a great power. Even in trees, it is second nature, and it is as strong in nations as in men. So are the Prejudices, which (like the passions) are given to men and nations. They are valuable powers if properly and skillfully applied, but very destructive if improperly handled.

The strongest and most immense powers are the Love of Country, *91* National Pride, and the Love of Home. Encourage them all. Insist upon them in your elected leaders. A permanent home is necessary for patriotism. National pride is but theory and illusion to people who move from country to country to country. A migratory race will have little love of country.

Eloquence is a mighty power. If you have it, use it to teach, advise, and advance the people. Do not mislead and corrupt them. Corrupt and unethical orators are the assassins of public liberties and public morals.

Free Will is a power whose limits are still unknown. It is the power of free will that allows us to see the spiritual and divine in mankind. There is a correlation between man's will and the Creative Will whose action seems so incomprehensible. It is the people of *will* and *action* that govern the world, not the people of intellect only.

Finally, the three greatest moral powers are FAITH, HOPE, and CHARITY. Faith is the only true WISDOM, and it is the very foundation of all government. HOPE is STRENGTH, and it insures success. CHARITY is BEAUTY, and it alone makes the animated, united effort possible. These powers are within the reach of all men. Moved by these powers, Masonry could bring tremendous good to the world, unless she has ceased to possess them.

Wisdom in the man, statesman, king, or priest consists of an appreciation of these powers. However, the fate of nations often depends upon the disregard of some of them. How many lives have hung upon the incomplete or incompetent evaluation of the power of an idea: the reverence for a flag, the blind loyalty to a form or constitution of government, or the concept of a Fatherland!

What errors in political economy and statesmanship have been committed as a result of the over or under-estimation of particular values, or even the non-estimation of some of them! It is asserted that everything is the product of human labor, but the gold or diamond accidentally found is not. What is the value of the labor bestowed by the farmer upon his crops when compared to the value of the 92 sunshine and rain without which his labor produces nothing? Labor creates commerce by adding to the value of the goods produced in the fields, the mines, the factories, the offices, and then by transporting them to different markets.

Who can estimate the value of morality, strength, moral worth, and intellectual knowledge in a nation? These are the sunshine and rain of the State. The wind with its changing currents is a suitable symbol for the erratic persona of the masses, its passions, its heroic impulses, and its enthusiasms. Woe to the statesman who does not estimate these values!

Music and song are also sometimes found to have an indeterminable value. Every nation has some song of a proven value, more easily counted in lives than dollars. The Star Spangled Banner to America, the Marseillaise to revolutionary France, or Hail to the Queen in the U.K.

Peace is an inestimable element of prosperity and wealth. Social interaction and the association of men in beneficent Orders have an indeterminable value. The illustrious examples of a nation's Past, the memories and immortal thoughts of her great and wise thinkers, statesmen, and heroes are the invaluable legacy of the Past bequeathed to the Present and the future. All of these not only have the higher, more luxurious, and priceless values, but also an actual *monetary* value since it is only when they are functioning together that human labor can create and accumulate wealth. They are the chief elements of material wealth in addition to the national fortitude, heroism, glory, prosperity, and immortal honor.

●   ●   ●   ●   ●   ●

Providence has appointed the three great disciplines of *War, Monarchy* and *Priesthood,* to use what the CAMP, PALACE, and TEMPLE symbolize to train the people intelligently for all the great purposes of society. When virtue and intelligence become standard qualities of the masses, the lasting result will be free governments. Such governments are impossible without them. Man advances in increments. Solving one pressing calamity gives him the courage to attempt the solution of the remaining evils. It renders people more sensitive to the problems or perhaps sensitive for the first time. Serfs that agonize under the whip are not distressed about their political rights. Once freed from slavery, they become sensitive to political oppression. Liberated from arbitrary power, they begin to   93 scrutinize the law and desire to be governed by what they deem the best law. When the civil or temporal despotism has been set aside and the municipal law has been molded to the principles of an enlightened legislation, they may realize they are living under a priestly or ecclesiastical despotism and also desire reform there.

The advance of humanity is slow. It often pauses and sometimes moves backwards. Despotisms do not retire or yield ground to self-governing communities. Churches and priesthoods do not relinquish their old task of governing men with imaginary terrors. Nowhere do we see a populace that could be easily freed from such a government. We do not see the great religious teachers seeking to discover truth for themselves or for others. Rather, they continue to rule contentedly by whatever dogma is already established. They are as much bound by their necessity to govern as the populace is by their need of government. Poverty in its most hideous forms still exists in the great cities, and the cancer of pauperism has its roots in the hearts of great kingdoms. People there take no measure of their wants or of their own power to supply them, but live and multiply like the beasts of the field. Providence apparently has ceased to care for them. Intelligence never visits them, or it appears as some new development of villainy. War has not ceased, and there are still battles and sieges. Homes are in chaos, tears, anger, and spite make hells where there should be heavens. Thus, Masonry is even more necessary! So wide is the field of its labors! So great is the need for it to be true to itself, awaken from its apathy, and repent of its dereliction to its true creed!

Work, death, taxes, and sexual passion are essential and permanent conditions of the human existence, but they render perfection, and a thousand year life on earth, impossible. The decree of Fate is that the vast majority of men must work to live, and they cannot find the time to cultivate intelligence. Knowing they are to die, most people will not sacrifice their present pleasures for greater ones in the future. The love of woman never ceases, but it can have a terrible and uncontrollable fate if obsessive and untempered. Society can be improved. Free government *is* possible for States, and freedom of thought and conscience is not *wholly* utopian. We already see that Emperors prefer to be elected by universal suffrage. States are transferred to Empires by vote, and the Empires are administered with the spirit of a Republic. They are little more than democracies with a single head, ruling through one man, one representative, instead of an assembly of representatives. Priesthoods that still govern must now come before the laity to argue that they *should* govern, and they are obliged to invoke the very reason that they are bent on undermining.

Everyday, people become freer because the freedom of mankind lies in its reason. A person can reflect upon their own future and conduct, analyze its consequences, and lay down rules for constant guidance. They are relieved from the tyranny of sense and passion and at any time enabled to live according to the light of the knowledge that is within them. Herein lies the freedom of man in regard to the necessity imposed by the omnipotent God. So much light equals so much liberty. When the emperor and the church make appeals to reason, there is naturally universal suffrage.

No one needs to lose courage or believe that labor for the cause of Progress will be labor wasted. There is no waste in nature of Matter, Power, Act, or Thought. A Thought is as much the end of life as an Action. A single Thought sometimes works better results than a Revolution, even Revolutions themselves. Still, there should not be separation between Thought and Action. The true Thought culminates in life, and all wise and true Thought produces Action. It is generative like the light. Knowledge acquired perseveringly induces habits of sound Thought. The multitude of workers cannot acquire it, and most people achieve a very low standard of it. Knowledge is incompatible with the ordinary and indispensable activities of life. A whole world of error and work produce one reflective man. The most advanced nations have more ignorant citizens than wise. They have more poor than rich and more habitual laborers than reasoning, reflective men. The proportion is at least a thousand to one. Unanimity of opinion is the same. It only exists among the masses who do not think, and the political or spiritual priesthoods prevent it by trying to guide and govern them. When men begin to reflect, they begin to differ, and the greatest problem is finding counsel who will not attempt to be tyrants. This is very important in respect to the heart more than the head. Every man earns his share of the product of human labor, by hard work, trickery, or deceit. Honorably acquired, useful knowledge is too often used to pursue an activity that is not honest or reasonable, thus making the studies of youth far nobler than the practices of adulthood. The farmer's interaction with the earth, the skies, and the plants tends to make him earnest, provident, and grateful, while the lawyer's interaction in the courts makes them quarrelsome, crafty, envious, and intolerable.

Masonry seeks to be a generous, content, compassionate guide. In all great structures the sound of the hammer and the clink of the trowel should always be heard somewhere. With faith in man, hope in the future of humanity, and loving-kindness in mankind, Masonry and the Mason must always work and teach. Let each do his part for which he is best fitted. The teacher is also a workman, like the navigator and the lighthouse keeper, who work together to share the treasures of the world with the people of their port.

Masonry has helped to cast down idols and grind to dust the links of the chains that held men's souls in bondage. This progress is evident by people openly discussing and debating politics and religion without fear of prison or death. No doctrines can be apprehended as truths if they contradict the truths given to us by God. Long before the Protestant Reformation began, a monk who was afraid to speak aloud a word of his anti-papal and personal beliefs 96 instead wrote them on parchment, sealed the perilous record, and hid them in the massive walls of his monastery. He had no one he could trust to share his secret or pour out his soul. His only consolation was to imagine that in a future age someone might find the parchment. He hoped the seed would sprout and not have been planted in vain. What if every truth had to lie dormant for hundreds of years, like the parchment inside the monastery? Speak it again and again, and let fate take its chance!

The rose of Jericho grows almost six inches high in the sandy deserts of Arabia. After the flowering season, it loses its leaves and dries up into a withered ball. It is uprooted by the winds, carried, blown, and tossed across the desert. Finally, it falls into the sea. Feeling contact with the water, it unfolds itself, expands its branches, and drops its seeds from their seedpods. Once saturated with water, these pods are carried back to the shore by the tide. Many are lost, just as many individual lives of men are lost or useless. Many find their way back from the seashore into the desert where they grow and flower like their ancestors, waiting to be blown into the sea again. God will not be less careful to provide for the germination of the truths you may bring forth. He said, *"Cast your bread upon the waters, and after many days it shall return to thee again."*

Initiation does not change. Through all the ages we find it in its same form again and again. The last disciples of Martinez Pasquale are still the children of Orpheus, and they adore the advocate of the antique philosophy, the Incarnate Word of the Christians.

Pythagoras, the great philosopher of numbers, visited all the sanctuaries of the world. He went into Judæa, where he was circumcised so that he might be admitted to the secrets of Kabbalah, which the prophets Ezekiel and Daniel communicated to him, but not without some reservations. Then he was admitted to the Egyptian initiation with the recommendation of King Amasis, but not without some difficulty. The power of his genius overcame the language barriers, and he himself became a Master.

97 Pythagoras defined God as a Living and Absolute Truth clothed with Light.

He said the Word was Number manifested by Form.

He made all descend from the *Tetractys,* that is to say, from the Quaternary.

He said God is the Supreme Music, whose nature is Harmony.

Pythagoras gave the magistrates of Crotona this great religious, political, and social precept:

"Any evil is preferred over anarchy."

Pythagoras said, "As there are three divine notions and three intelligible regions, there is also a triple word, because the Hierarchical Order always manifests itself in threes. There are the simple word, the hieroglyphical word, and the symbolic word. They are the word that expresses, the word that conceals, and the word that signifies. The whole sacred intelligence is in the perfect knowledge of these three words."

Pythagoras covered his doctrine with symbols, but carefully avoided personifications and images, which he thought could produce idolatry.

The Holy Kabbalah, or the tradition of the children of Seth, was carried from Chaldæa by Abraham. Joseph taught it to the Egyptian priesthood, and Moses recovered and purified it. It was concealed under symbols in the Bible and revealed by the Savior to Saint John. It is contained in that Apostle's Apocalypse entirely under sacred figures similar to those of all antiquity.

The Kabbalists consider God the Intelligent, Animating, Living Infinite. For them, He is not the aggregate of existences, nor the existence in the abstract, nor a Being philosophically definable. He is *in* all, *distinct* from all, and *greater* than all. His name is beyond words, and His name is only capable of expressing the human ideal of His divinity. Man is not capable of comprehending what God is in Himself.

God is the absolute of Faith, and the absolute of *Reason* is BEING, יהוה. *"I am what I am,"* is an accepted translation of this.

98 Reason and science demonstrate that the modes of Existence and Being balance each other in equilibrium according to harmonious and hierarchical laws. But a hierarchy is produced in ascending order, and it tends to become monarchical. Reason cannot pause at a single chief without being alarmed by the abysses, which seem to exist above this Supreme Monarch. Therefore, it silently gives order to the Faith it adores.

Science and reason support the notion that God is the most grand, most holy, and most useful of all man's aspirations. Upon this belief, morality rests with its eternal authorization. The belief in humanity is the most real phenomena of being. If this were false, nature would confirm it, because nothingness would give form to life, and God would be and not be at the same time.

This philosophic and indisputable reality was termed "The Idea of God" by the Kabbalists. This name contains all others, its ciphers contain all the numbers, and the hieroglyphics of its letters express all the laws and things of nature.

BEING IS BEING. The reason of Being is in Being. The Beginning is the Word, and the Word in logic formulated Speech is the spoken Reason. The Word is in God, and it is God Himself manifested in the Intelligence. This is what is beyond all the philosophies. We must believe this under the penalty of never truly knowing or fear relapsing into the absurd skepticism of Pyrrho. The custodian of Faith represented by the Priesthood rests entirely upon this basis of knowledge, and in its teachings, we must recognize the Divine Principle of the Eternal Word.

Light is not the Spirit, as the sacred Indian priests believed. Rather, Light is the instrument of the Spirit. It is not the body of the Protoplasts as the Theurgists of the school of Alexandria taught, but it is the first physical manifestation of the Divine inspiration. God eternally creates it, and man modifies and multiplies it.

The high magic is styled "The Sacerdotal Art" and "The Royal Art". In Egypt, Greece, and Rome it shared the greatness and decadence of the Priesthood and Royalty. Every philosophy hostile to nationalist worship and to its mysteries was also hostile to the great political powers that would lose their grandeur if they ceased to be the images of the Divine Power in the eyes of the masses. Every Crown is shattered when it clashes with the Tiara.

While writing to Dionysius the Younger about the nature of the First Principle, Plato said, "I must write to you in riddles so if my letter is intercepted whoever shall read it may not comprehend it. All things surround their King, and they exist because of Him. He alone is the cause of good things. Second for the Seconds, and Third for the Thirds."

A complete summary of the Theology of the Sephiroth is contained in those few words. "The *King*" is AIN SOPH, the Being Supreme and Absolute. From this center, *which is everywhere,* all things come forth, but we understand it in three manners and three different spheres. In the *Divine* world (ATZILUTH), or the First Cause, the whole Eternity of Things in the beginning existed as Unity. While Eternity moved forward, clothed with form, the attributes that constitute matter and the First Principle are One Primary, yet not the VERY Illimitable Deity, incomprehensible and indefinable. Matter is manifested by the Creative Thought. It is littleness compared with infinity. All we can know of the Very God *is* compared to His Wholeness only as an infinitesimally small fraction of a unit, compared with an infinitely large number of Units.

The World of Creation is that of Second Causes (the Kabbalistic World BRIAH). The Autocracy of the First Principle is complete, but we only conceive the Cause of the Second Causes. Here it is manifested by the Binary, and it is the Creative Principle passive. Finally, in the third world YETZIRAH (Formation), it is revealed in the perfect Form, the Form of Forms, the World, the Supreme Beauty and Excellence, the Created Perfection. The Principle is at once the First, the Second, and the Third, since it is All in All, the Centre and Cause of all. We are not admiring *the genius of Plato* here. We only recognize *the exact knowledge of the Initiate.*

100 The Apostle Saint John did not borrow the philosophy of Plato for the opening of his Gospel. Rather, Plato drank from the same springs with Saint John and Philo. In the opening verses of John's paraphrase, he ponders the first principles of a dogma, which are common to many schools of thought. He uses language very similar to Philo, whom he had evidently read. The philosophy of Plato could *yearn toward* the Word made by man, and the Gospel could give Him to the world.

The most foolish and dangerous of superstitions are doubt and skepticism: doubt in the presence of Being and its harmonies, and skepticism in the face of the eternal mathematics and the immutable laws of Life, which make the Divinity present and visible everywhere. Thought is not a consequence, the result of the organization of matter, or the chemical action or reaction of its particles. To the contrary, because Thought is manifested and realized in human and divine action, it proves the existence of an Entity, or Unity, that thinks. The Universe is the Infinite Statement of an infinite number of Infinite Thoughts that emanate from an Infinite and Thinking Source. The cause is always at least equal to the effect. Matter cannot think or cause itself, or exist without cause, nor could nothing *produce* either powers or things. In a void, no Powers can exist. Recognize a self-existent Power, its Intelligence, or an Intelligent cause of it, and at once GOD IS.

The Hebrew allegory of the Fall of Man is a variation of the universal legend symbolizing one of the most universal allegories of science.

Moral Evil is Falsehood in actions, and Falsehood is Crime in words.

Injustice is the essence of Falsehood, and every false word is an injustice.

Injustice is the death of the Moral Being, just as Falsehood is the poison of the Intelligence.

The perception of Light is the dawn of the Eternal Life in Being. The Word of God creates the Light, and it seems to be spoken by every Intelligence that can recognize Forms. The Light exists in its splendor for those eyes that 101 gaze at it. Amorous of the beautiful spectacle of the Universe, the Soul focuses on the luminous writing of the Infinite Book called "The Visible", and as God did on the dawn of the first day, utters the sublime and creative word, "LET THERE BE! LIGHT!"

Seek the mysteries of death during life, not once you are beyond the grave. Salvation or damnation begins here in the terrestrial world where it has its own Heaven and Hell. Even here on Earth, virtue is rewarded and vice is punished. Occasionally, it seems evil-doers are exempted from the instruments of good and evil, wealth and riches, and good fortune seems to be showered upon them. Woe to the unjust person who possess the golden key, because for *them* it only opens the gates of Hell.

The true Initiates recognize the benefit of hard work and sorrow. A German poet wrote, "sorrow is the unknown shepherd's dog who guides the flock of men." To learn to suffer and die are the disciplines of Eternity.

The allegorical picture of Plato's Cebes, which Dante depicted in his Divine Comedy, is the description that many painters of the middle age used in their depictions of this philosophical and magical monument. It is both a complete moral synthesis and the most audacious demonstration ever given of the Grand Arcanum, whose secret revelation would overturn Earth and Heaven. No one should expect to be given its explanation! Anyone who passes behind the veil that cloaks this mystery understands its indescribable nature. It is death to those who win it by surprise, as well as to him who reveals it.

This secret is the Royalty of the Sages. It is the Crown of the Initiate whom we see re-descend victorious from the summit of Trials, in the fine allegory of Cebes. The Grand Arcanum makes him master of gold and the light, which are the same thing. He has solved the problem of squaring the circle. He directs the perpetual movement, and he possesses the Philosopher's Stone. Here the Adepts will understand us. There is neither interruption in the work of nature, nor gaps in her work. The Harmonies of Heaven correspond to those of Earth, and the Eternal Life accomplishes its evolutions in accordance with the same laws of nature. "God has arranged all things by weight, number, and measure," says the Bible. This luminous doctrine was also practiced by Plato.

102

Humanity has only had one religion and one worship. This universal light has had its uncertain mirages, its deceitful reflections, and its shadows. But once the nights of Error are over, we see it reappear again, one and pure like the Sun.

The grandeurs of worship are the life of religion, and although Christ may wish for poor ministers, the Sovereign Divinity does not wish for meager altars. Some Protestants have not learned that worship is a style of teaching, and we must avoid creating the image of a mean or miserable God to the people. The sanctuaries that resemble poorly furnished offices or inns, and ministers who dress like paupers, cause religion to be perceived as a strict formality with God as a Justice of the Peace.

We scoff at the Augurs. While it is easy to scoff, it is very difficult to comprehend. Did the Deity leave the whole world without Light for 4,000 years only to illuminate a little corner for the brutal, ignorant, and ungrateful people of Palestine? Why always slander God and the Sanctuary? Were there never any priests who were not rogues or villains? Could no honest and sincere men be found among the sacred priests of Ceres, Diana, Dionysus, Apollo, Hermes, or Mithras? Were they all deceived like the rest? Who deceived them for centuries without betraying themselves? Cheats are not immortal! Arago said outside of the pure mathematics, anyone who utters the word "impossible" is lacking in prudence and good sense.

The Kabbalists say the true name of Satan is Yahveh reversed. Satan is not a black god but the negation of God, the absence of God. The Devil is the personification of Atheism or Idolatry.

This is not a *Person,* but a *Power* created for good, but easily made to serve evil. *This Power is Liberty or Free Will,* and the Greek God PAN presides over its physical generations. Then came the goat of the Sabbat, brother of the Ancient Serpent and the Light-bearer or *Phosphor,* of which the parts have been perverted to create the legend of Lucifer.

103   Gold is condensed Light. The sacred numbers of Kabbalah are styled the "golden numbers" and the moral teachings of Pythagoras are the "golden verses." For the same reason, a mysterious book of Apuleius, in which an ass is prominent, was called "The Golden Ass".

The Pagans accused the Christians of worshipping an ass. This criticism originated with the Samaritan Jews, who calculated the data of Kabbalah in regard to the Divinity by Egyptian symbols. They also represented the Intelligence with the figure of the Magical Star adored under the name of *Remphan.* Science was symbolized by Anubis, whose name they changed to *Nibbas.* The common faith or trust was represented by *Thartac,* a god depicted with a book, a cloak, and the head of an ass. According to the Samaritan Doctors, Christianity was the reign of *Thartac* when blind Faith and common trust were constructed into a universal oracle and preferred to Intelligence and Science.

Synesius, the Bishop of Ptolemaïs, was a great Kabbalist but of doubtful orthodoxy. He wrote, "the people will always mock those things that are easy to understand. They need to have illusions. A Spirit that loves wisdom and contemplates the Truth at hand is forced to simplify it to encourage the people to accept it. Parables are necessary to the people. The Truth becomes deadly to those who are not strong enough to contemplate it in all its brilliance. If the priestly laws permitted alternate conclusions about the allegory of words, I would accept their proposed dignity on the condition that I might be a philosopher at home and a narrator of parables in public. What is there in common between the ignorant masses and the exalted wisdom? The truth should be protected, and the masses provided with a teaching tool that accommodates their imperfect reason."

Moral disorder produces physical ugliness, which can lead to those frightful faces which tradition assigns to the demons.

The first Druids were the true children of the Magi. Their initiation came from Egypt and Chaldæa, the pure sources of the original Kabbalah. They adored the Trinity under the names of *Isis* or *Hesus* the Supreme Harmony; of *Belen* or *Bel* which means Lord in Assyrian and corresponds to the name of ADONAÏ; and of

Camul or *Camaël* which in Kabbalah personifies the Divine Justice. Below this triangle of Light they portrayed a divine reflection composed of three personified rays: first the *Teutates* or *Teuth* which was the Word or the formulated Intelligence which was also the same as the *Thoth* of the Egyptians; second was Power and Beauty whose names varied like their emblems; and thirdly, the sacred number 7, a mysterious image which represented the progress of the dogma and its future realizations. This symbol was a young veiled girl holding a child in her arms, and they dedicated this image as "The Virgin who will become a mother or the *Virgini pariturœ.*" 104

Hertha or Wertha, was the young Isis of Gaul, the Queen of Heaven, and the Virgin who was to bear a child. She held the spindle of the Fates which were half filled with white wool and half filled with black. She presided over all forms and symbols, weaving the garment of the Ideas.

One of the most mysterious figures of Kabbalah is contained in the Enchiridion of Leo III and represents a reversed equilateral triangle inscribed in a double circle. On the triangle are written the prophetic Tau, the two Hebrew words of the Ineffable Name אלהם and צבאות, ALOHAYIM or the Powers, and TSABAOTH or the Starry Armies and their guiding spirits. These words also symbolize the Equilibrium of the Powers of Nature and the Harmony of Numbers. To the three sides of the triangle belong the three great Names יהוה, אדני, and אגלא, IAHAVEH, ADONAÏ, and AGLA. Above the first is written in Latin, *Formatio,* above the second *Reformatio,* and above the third, *Transformatio.* Creation is assigned to the FATHER. Redemption or Reformation is assigned to the SON. Sanctification or Transformation is assigned to the HOLY SPIRIT. This provides for the mathematical laws of Action, Reaction, and Equilibrium. IAHAVEH is also the Genesis or Formation of dogma by the signification of the four letters of the Sacred Tetragram. ADONAÏ is the realization of this dogma in the Human Form and in the Visible LORD who is the Son of God or the perfect Man. AGLA (formed from the initials of the four words *Ath Gebur Laulaïm Adonaï*) expresses the synthesis of the entire dogma and the totality of the Kabbalistic science indicated by the hieroglyphics, from which this admirable name is formed the Triple Secret of the Great Work.

Masonry, like all Religions, Mysteries, Hermeticism, and Alchemy, *conceals* its secrets from all except the Adepts, Scholars, or the Elect. It uses partial explanations and misinterpretations of its symbols to mislead those who deserve to be misled, to conceal the Truth from them, and to draw the Light away from them. Truth is not for those who are unworthy, unable to receive it, or those who would pervert it. God Himself incapacitates many people, leading the masses away from the highest Truth, but giving them the power to attain as much of it as is appropriate for them to know. Every age has had a religion suited to its capacity. 105

The Teachers, even of Christianity, tend to be the most ignorant of the true meaning they teach. There is no book of which so little is known as the Bible. To most who read it, it is as incomprehensible as the Zohar.

Therefore, Masonry jealously conceals its secrets and intentionally leads the conceited interpreters astray. There is no sight under the sun more pitiful and ludicrous than the spectacle of the Prestons and the Webbs, trying to "explain" the old symbols of Masonry by adding to and "improving" them, or by inventing new ones. The Point within the Circle, traced between two parallel lines is a purely Kabbalistic figure. Preston and Webb then superimposed the Bible, placed upon it a ladder with three or nine rungs, and provided an uninspiring interpretation of the whole symbol so profoundly absurd that it actually excited admiration.

CHAPTER 4: SECRET MASTER

MASONRY is a series of allegories used as teaching tools for the important 106 lessons in morality and philosophy. As you advance, you will find them to be a dignified, comprehensive, and harmonious system.

The lessons of morality, the scientific instruction, and the symbols explained during the first three degrees are the product of the increasing accommodations the ceremonies and lessons have made through the ages. They serve the needs and intellect of the Pupil and the New Initiate to begin their Masonic journey. Originally, the symbols were used to *conceal*, not *reveal*, the principles of morality when learning was confined to a select few. These ancient yet simple Degrees are viewed like the broken columns of a roofless Greek temple, in their humbled and disfigured greatness, their broken pieces worn by time and altered by modern additions and modified interpretations. In spite of all of this, the first three degrees are still the three respected columns on the portico to the gateway of the great Masonic Temple.

You have now taken the first steps toward the inner sanctuary of the Temple. You are on a path that leads to the slope of the mountain of Truth, and your success depends upon your discretion, dedication, and reliability. 107

You do not become a Mason by simply learning what is commonly called the "work" or even by becoming familiar with its traditions, although this is a good start. There is much more to Masonry than what you learned from the allegories and traditions. Masonry has a history, a literature, and a philosophy. You must follow the rivers of knowledge to their sources at the springs located in the distant past. There you will find the origin and meaning of Masonry.

A few basic lessons in architecture, a few universally accepted maxims of morality, and a few trivial traditions, whose real meanings are unknown or misunderstood, no longer satisfy the devoted student of Masonic truth. Those desiring to really understand the beautiful and harmonious lessons of Freemasonry must read, study, reflect, and critically analyze. The true Mason is enthusiastic about acquiring knowledge. He appreciates that the books and antique symbols of Masonry are a complete system handed down to us with the intellectual riches of the Past. The details of this system shed much of the light on the history of Masonry and prove its claim to be acknowledged as the benefactor of mankind.

Knowledge is the most real and genuine of human treasures. Knowledge is Light. Ignorance is Darkness. Knowledge is the *development* of the human soul, and its acquisition is the *growth*. Knowledge has within it the *power* to grow, acquire, and develop, just as the acorn develops from the shoot, into the plant, and finally into the oak tree. We must regard the dignity and advantage of knowledge, learning, and immortality which human nature most aspires to. The raising of families and houses starts generation. Buildings, foundations, and monuments start the desire of memory, fame, and celebrity."

108 The human soul aspires to have both our influences and our names survive us as living forces once we are in the grave. It aspires that our works be read, our actions spoken of, and our names recollected and mentioned kindly as evidence that our lives positively influenced some portion of mankind. "The monuments of genius and learning are much more durable than the monuments of power. Without the loss of its message or meaning, the verses of Homer have continued twenty-five hundred years or more during which time an infinite number of palaces, temples, castles, and cities have been built, prospered, decayed, and destroyed. The true pictures and statues made for Cyrus, Alexander, Cæsar, or even the recent Kings are lost with time, and their imperfect copies lose the truth of the life. Man's real genius and knowledge remains preserved in books, exempted from the wrong of time, and capable of perpetual renovation. They cast the seeds of knowledge into the minds of generations, provoking and causing infinite actions and opinions across the ages. No matter how many ships, trains, planes, cars, telephones, or computer networks can transport wealth, commodities, and information from place to remote place, the knowledge and messages contained in these books is a hundred times more effective across the ages, making that distant history participate in our wisdom, illumination, and inventions today."

It is a necessity for truly noble souls to learn, attain knowledge, and be wise. Accordingly, teaching, communicating that knowledge, and sharing that wisdom with others is very noble work.

The son of David said, "There was a little city with only a few men. A great King came, besieged it, and built large bulwarks against it. A poor wise man delivered the city, yet no one honored him because he was poor. But I say wisdom is better than strength, even though the poor man's wisdom was despised, and his words were not honored." Whenever you have the chance to

109 perform a good deed for mankind, just do it, even if your reward will only be indifference and forgetfulness. The son of David added, "In the morning sow the seed. In the evening do not withhold your hand, for you do not know which seed will prosper or whether both will be equally good." Sow the seeds of good deeds, no matter who will reap them. You have leaned that you are enabled to do good, so do *it*, because *it* is right. You will find your reward in each act.

The noblest destiny of man is attaining truth to better serve our brethren, our country, and mankind. As a Secret Master, this is your goal, your destiny in life from this point forward.

To achieve this goal, you must arm yourself for the long and difficult struggle! Pleasure will beckon you on one hand, and Indolence will invite you upon the other. You can resist the allurements of both with discretion, dedication, and fidelity.

Discretion is indispensable to the Mason. It is the most important lesson taught to the Entered Apprentice. Our obligations require us to perform serious and burdensome duties for Masons personally unknown to us when they request our aid. By failing to fulfill these obligations, we would be branded as false Masons and faithless men. These consequences demonstrate how profound a mistake it would be to communicate our secrets to those who are not Masons. These secrets then give a non-Mason the opportunity to demand the help or favor from a brother they themselves are not obligated to return.

The secrets of our brethren, when communicated to us as such, must be kept sacred provided they do not violate the law. We have a stronger duty to obey the law, because it is the will of the People. Edicts handed down by the arbitrary will of a despotic power are contrary to the law of God or the Great Laws of Nature. They are destructive of the inherent rights of man, hostile to *110* the right of free speech, free thought, or free conscience. It is lawful to rebel against this type of tyranny and strive for its abolishment.

Obedience to the Law does not mean submission to tyranny. We are not required to sacrifice every dignified principle or offer despotism the admiration of applause. As every new victim of despotism yields to tyranny, he *could* lift his voice in still louder flattery. He *could* fall at their feet and graciously beg for the honor of kissing that bloody hand which has been lifted against the helpless, or he *could* do more. He *could* implore God not to ascend to Heaven too soon because he has the sad remembrance of what these people and souls have done. He *could* constrain his tongue to be false, contort his features to the likeness of that passionate adoration which he wishes to express, or bow down on his knee, but he cannot constrain his heart. The virtue of the helpless must have a voice that is not drowned out by contemptible hymns and acclamations of crimes being shrouded as virtues in the name of God. If the Mason does nothing to prevent this, he is even more contemptible.

Laws that are the fair expression of the will and judgment of the people are the enactment of every individual as a whole. These laws must be consistent with the law of God, the great law of nature, the pure and abstract right as tempered by necessity, and the general interest free from the private interests of individuals. If these conditions are met, everyone is obligated to uphold these laws because they are the collective will and solemn judgment of all, from which there is no appeal.

This Degree teaches you the duty of obedience to the law. The one true and original law conforms to reason and nature. It applies to everyone, invariably, and eternally calls for the fulfillment of duty and the abstinence from injustice. It calls with that irresistible voice whose authority is acknowledged wherever heard. This law cannot be abolished, diminished, or sanctioned by any law of man. A whole senate or a whole people cannot avoid its paramount obligation. It does not require a commentator to make it intelligible, nor is it one thing in Rome, another in Athens, or one thing now and another in the future. But forever and in all nations it is, has been, and will always be the law of the One TRUE and everlasting God, the great Author and Promulgator, the Common Sovereign of all mankind, who is Himself One.

It is our duty to obey the laws of our country. Be careful that prejudice, passion, extravagance, affection, error, and illusion are not mistaken for conscience. Nothing is more common than to fake a conscience in public actions because the truth cannot be concealed. The disobedient refuse to submit to the laws by pretense to conscience. Disobedience and rebellion then become conscience, neither of which have any knowledge, revelation, truth, charity, reason, or religion. Conscience is bound to the laws. Right or sure conscience is consistent reasoning reduced to the practice of conducting moral actions. Perverse conscience is founded in extravagance or affections, and it is the deformity of conscience or the malice of affections. Conscience must be taught by nature and God, conducted by reason, made dynamic by debate, assisted by choice, instructed by sober principles, and then it *is* right. The general measures of justice are the laws of God. They constitute the general rules of government for the conscience. Necessity also has a large voice in the order of human affairs, the development of human relationships, and the administration of human laws. Like a great river that is divided into streams, then channels, then particles, these general rules are derived by the laws, customs, punishments, and contracts dictated by the despotism of necessity that does not allow perfect justice, abstract reasonableness, or equity to be the sole rule of civil government in this imperfect world. This paradox requires every law to be created to provide the greatest good to the greatest number of people.

When you make a vow to God, do not procrastinate in fulfilling it. It is better that you do not take a vow than to take one and not honor it. Do not let your tongue be vulgar with your language, or your heart be impulsive before God. Carefully assess any decision that involves a promise, but once the promise or pledge is made, remember that anyone who fails to fulfill their obligation will also be disloyal to their family, friends, country, and God.

Fides servanda est: Faith pledged must always be kept. This was a maxim and an axiom even among the pagans. The virtuous Roman said, "Either do not allow what seems expedient to be corrupt, or if it *is* corrupt, do not let it seem to be expedient." Nothing is so valuable or urgent that you should risk depriving yourself of a good name or robbing yourself of integrity and honor. He who violates his promised word is unspeakably corrupt. Once given, the word of a Mason must be defended, like the word of a knight in the times of chivalry. The judgment by the brethren upon anyone who violates his pledge should be as stern as the judgments of the Roman Censors. Good faith is as revered among Masons as it was among the Romans. Like them, we believe that chaos is better than corruption, and like the knights of lore, death is better than dishonor.

Accordingly, be faithful to the promises you make, to the pledges you give, and to the vows that you take, since to break any of them is unethical and dishonorable.

Be faithful to your family. Proudly perform all the duties of a good father, a good son, a good husband, and a good brother.

Be faithful to your friends. True friendship should survive all the changes, conflicting opinions, challenges, and upheavals of life.

Be faithful to your country. Prefer its dignity and honor to any degree of celebrity and honor for yourself. Act in its interest rather than your own. The pleasure and gratification of the masses is often at odds with their welfare.

Be faithful to Masonry. This means being faithful to the best interests of mankind. Work to improve the standard of Masonic character and enlarge its sphere of influence by precept and example. Publicize its teachings of Liberty, Equality, and Fraternity to everyone because it is the Great Apostle of Peace, 113 Harmony, and Good will amongst men.

Masonry is useful to all people. To the educated, it offers them the opportunity of exercising their intellect with topics that will complement and improve their own knowledge and morality. To the uneducated, it offers them exceptional guidance they can use to better themselves both personally and professionally. To the young, it provides them the beneficial principles, good examples, and conventional customs necessary to begin a successful life. To the journeymen, it furnishes them with noble and useful methods to find friends and brothers in countries where they would otherwise be isolated and lonely. To the worthy man in misfortune, it gives assistance. To the afflicted man, it lavishes consolation. To the charitable man, it enables him to do more good by uniting him with those who are also charitable. And to those capable of appreciating its importance, they will enjoy friendships founded on the same principles of religion, morality, and charity.

A Freemason should be a man of honor, conscience, and committed to duty. He should be independent in his opinions, of good morals, submissive to the law, and very devoted to his family, his country, and to humanity. He should be kind and charitable to his brethren, a friend to all virtuous men, and be ready to assist his brethren by all means in his power.

By doing these things, you will be faithful to yourself, your brethren, and to God. This will earn you the honor, name, and rank of SECRET MASTER.

CHAPTER 5: PERFECT MASTER

THE Master Hiram Abif (Khūrūm) was an industrious and honest man.   *114*
What he was employed to do he did diligently, well, and faithfully. He received
no wages he did not earn. Industry and honesty in a man are the virtues taught
in this Degree. They are common and unadorned virtues, but should not be
beneath our notice. Those who do not work add no value to society and
therefore do not earn love or respect. Masonry neither loves nor respects the
idle, or those who live only by the opportunities afforded by the surrounding
society. Least of all are those parasites that exclusively live from society's
handouts. Those who are lazy feel unrestrained in conduct and are likely to
become immoral in behavior. True honesty, which ought to be a common
qualification in all humanity, is a rare trait to be found. To do anything earnestly,
steadily, faithfully, and honestly appears to ask little of our moral character. Yet,
even in the most common and homely application of these virtues one can attain
the character of a Perfect Master.

Idleness is the death of a living man. An idle person is so useless towards
any of the purposes of God (or of man) that his net contribution is like one who
is dead. He is unconcerned in the changes and necessities of the world around.
The idle person only lives to spend their time selfishly. They enjoy the fruits of
the earth provided to them. Like vermin, when their time comes, they die and
perish, and the time between has seen nothing accomplished. They neither
plough nor reap. They have added no value to society, or worse, have been
mischievous in its final contribution.

If man is not idle with their time, then it is considered a worthy effort in
life. Man is great and virtuous if he is not swayed by criminal or bad habits. He
who continues to read good books will have great knowledge, if he has the   *115*
facilities about him for its use.

St. Ambrose and St. Augustine divided every day into equal blocks of
time for the employment of knowledge, service, and meditation. They spent
eight hours for rest and recreation. Another eight hours they spent for charity,
assisting others, conducting their personal business, reconciling their dislikes,
improving their own vices, correcting their errors, instructing their ignorance,

and conducting the duties of their usual vocation. The other eight hours they spent in study and prayer towards God.

One thinks, at the age of twenty, that life is too long a span of time for all that we have to learn and do. There seems an incredible distance between our age and that of our grandparents. However, when one is at the age of sixty, one halts and reflects at life's journey. One finds himself attempting to note, tally, and balance the achievements and endeavors of life against time and provided opportunity. One finds that we have made life much too short by wasting too much time. One then continues to deduct from our total years those days and hours that we slept beyond our needs. We deduct those working hours in the days when we did not muster a single constructive thought. We deduct the days we idly and willfully waited to pass in order to attain some real or fancied object that lay in the future. These idle hours are worse than those wasted in follies and personal amusement, or misspent towards useless or unprofitable enterprises. One regrets to acknowledge that we could have done more with ten years well spent than we have accomplished with forty years in our adulthood.

The soul's work is to learn and to do! The soul grows as truly as an oak grows. The tree takes the carbon dioxide from the air with the dew, rain, light, and nutrients from the ground. By a mysterious chemistry, it transmutes these into sap, fiber, wood, leaf, flower, fruit, color, and perfume. Similarly, the soul absorbs knowledge and with a divine alchemy changes that into its own substance where it grows larger from within using its own force and power.

The soul, like the body, has senses that should be nurtured, cultivated, 116 grown, and refined so the soul itself can grow in stature and proportion. One who cannot recognize a fine painting, a statue, a noble poem, a sweet harmony, a heroic thought, a noble deed, the wisdom of philosophy, the elevation of mind and spirit, or the knowledge of the loftiest truths as more important than the value of the stock markets merely lives on the level of the commonplace. These characters pride themselves on the inferiority of their soul's senses. These dull senses develop the inferior and imperfect soul.

The duties of every Mason who desires to imitate the Master Hiram Abif (Khūrūm) should be to sleep little and study much; to say little, but hear and think much; to learn what we may be able to do and then earnestly and vigorously do it. These duties may be required of us for the good of our brothers, our country, and mankind.

A Mason's duty as an honest man is straightforward and basic. It requires us to be honest in contracts, sincere in assertions, simple in bargaining, and faithful in performance. Speak the truth. Do not lie, either in a little matter or in a great one, not in substance or in circumstance, not in word or deed. Do not pretend something is true, if it is false. Do not cover the truth. Let the other party understand your agreement or denial with your work. One who deceives another by speaking in a manner so as to mislead or not be understood by the other party, is still a liar and, in practice, a thief. A Perfect Master must equally avoid deception and that which is false.

Let your prices be in accordance with that measure of good and evil which is established in the accounts of the wisest and most merciful men skilled in that practice or commodity. The profits of your business should be earned without scandal and achievable by all persons of similar capability.

In your business with others, do not try to take all that is strictly allowed by law. Keep something within your powers. There is a latitude in the gain received from buying and selling. Do not take every penny that is lawful, or which you think is legally obtainable. For, although it be lawful, it is not always prudent or safe. He who gets all he legally can, this time, will possibly be tempted to gain a little more the next time, and that might be unlawful.

Fear of poverty should not excuse a man to be oppressive or cruel in negotiating. A man should modestly, diligently, and patiently entrust his final 117 estate in God. Allow the interest to be earned naturally, and leave the ultimate success of your estate to Him.

Do not withhold the wages of the worker. Every selfish reason used to detain wages beyond the proper time is unjust and uncharitable. This uncharitable act squeezes the worker causing tears to flow and blood to run. One should pay according to the agreement or according to the worker's needs, whichever is more appropriate.

Religiously keep all promises and covenants. Keep them even if they were made to your disadvantage. Do not let any established promise of yours be broken, even if by accident. Let nothing make you break your promise, contradict your statement or ignore agreements you established with others. The only exceptions are those acts that are unlawful, impossible, out of your power, or intolerably inconvenient and of no advantage to the other.

Let no man take wages or fees for work that he cannot do, or cannot complete. One should be careful not to arrange a contract if the work cannot be performed profitably, with ease, or find a positive advantage in it. Let no man set aside for his own use what God or the government has intended for society. That is against the ideals of both Justice and Charity.

Taking advantage of others, making their condition worse, or their possession smaller while we benefit and profit is against the rules of equity, justice, and charity. We will not do unto others what we would not have done unto ourselves as we grow richer upon the ruins of their fortune.

It is not honest to receive anything from another without equitable payment. The trickster who cheats the money out of others is dishonest. No Mason should take that which belongs to another man. No honest man should receive money for what he has not earned. Similarly, the merchant who sells an inferior product at a high price, or the speculator who takes advantage of the distresses of others for his profit are neither fair nor honest. They are the lowest of people and unfit for future immortality.

Every Perfect Master should desire to live, deal, and act so that on his deathbed he can honestly claim that no man is poorer for his wealth. Everything he received he earned honestly. No witness should stand before God, and claim that by His Divine rules of equity, the house, land, and money bequeathed to his survivors should be another's entitlement and not his estate's proper legacy. It is certain that God is just, and He will sternly enforce every trust. He will decree a full and adequate compensation to all we impoverish, defraud, or take from, without fair consideration and equivalent payment at the time of transaction.

Therefore, be careful not to receive wages you have not earned! You will have wronged another if you do because you have taken what belongs to someone else. Whether you take wealth, rank, influence, reputation, or affection, you will eventually be held to balance your actions and settle your accounts from this life.

CHAPTER 6: INTIMATE SECRETARY (CONFIDENTIAL SECRETARY)

THIS Degree teaches you to be zealous, faithful, impartial, good, and a 119 peacemaker, if dissention or dispute arises among the brethren.

Duty is the magnetism that controls the moral compass that guides the Mason's course through the rough seas of life. The stars may not always shine, but the compass always points true as an aide to navigate life safely. The mariner follows the compass's silent bidding when he is beyond sight of land, and the ocean is without a landmark. He never doubts that it points true to the north. Similarly, if the moral ideals of honor and integrity do not clearly define the path in the face of trouble and adversity, then the unerring force of duty will still show the true course to avoid dishonor. To recognize and perform his duty is a Mason's sole concern, with or without reward. It does not matter to the Mason if his devotion to duty bears no witness, or that humanity will not know his actions and faithfulness.

Reflection will teach that Fame is most limiting. A person who seeks happiness in fame and the repetition of his name by others, might spend his life in self-promotion. He will never expand his horizons beyond the little, constructed world of his.

If he imagines the world to be filled with the knowledge of his actions and attempts to count the people who will sing of his fame, he will never count 120 everyone. He will need to subtract all those who do not observe the fame of others, all those who imagine themselves too important to take notice of another's activities, all who are too selfish to acknowledge anything beyond themselves, all who are attracted by constancy of ideas, all who are too busy with personal pursuits, and all who ignore the matters of life. Then, he will find his fame much less than at first thought or hoped. He would notice that few men are that inspiring beyond a small circle of peers. Therefore, we should not waste our time in the pursuit of fame. It is necessary that we focus on higher prospects for our legacy, as the Roman general Scipio Africanus focused on his work rather than seek fame and title among the Romans. When we contemplate our future and eternal state, we find that the hope of hearing our praises or achieving the rewards that mankind can bestow upon us are inconsequential.

We are born not only to benefit ourselves. Our country will claim her share and our friends will claim their share. Everything the earth produces is for man. So too are man's accomplishments meant to benefit mankind. We are obliged to do good to one another. We should use nature as our guide and contribute to society where needs arise. It may be by a reciprocation of duties, by receiving, or by giving. Sometimes we need to help cement human society with the arts, industry, or our personal resources.

Allow others to be praised in your presence. Entertain their glory with delight. Do not disparage them, lessen their report, or make an objection towards their praise. Do not think the advancement of someone else is a lessening of your own worth. Do not discredit a man by showing his weakness to him and causing his discomfit. Do not report these weaknesses to disgrace him, lessen him, or to set yourself above him. Do not praise yourself or dispraise another, unless there is some worthy end for it.

Remember that we usually disparage others for little real reason. When a man is highly commended, we are quick to judge him unworthy, if we can find one sin or inferior account of him. We should judge ourselves more severely than another. We should remember that whatever good praise anyone could say of us, we know of many unworthy, foolish, and perhaps worse actions ourselves. Moreover, any of those deeds, when done by another person, would be enough to ruin their reputation, with *us*.

If we are to think of people as wise, of keen perception, just, and appreciative when they praise and make idols of *us*, we should not then call them unlearned, dull-witted, ill, and poor judges when our neighbor is pronounced for public fame.

Every man has enough sins, trouble, evil, and failings to suggest that an interest in the affairs of others could be motivated by envy and an ill intent. The charitable man will be attentive and inquisitive into the motivation and order of a well-run group, or towards the virtues of a great person. However, he will not take notice of any piece of knowledge that others would keep hidden under lock and key. He will ignore the items that blush to see the light of day or are shameful and private in nature.

It should be sufficient to exclude any man from the society of Masons who is not impartial and generous with his actions, his opinions, and his testimony. Someone who is selfish, needy, censorious, or ungenerous will not remain within the strict boundaries of honesty and truth very long, and will commit an injustice eventually. He who loves himself too much will love others too little. He who regularly levels harsh judgment on others will soon give unjust judgment.

The generous and charitable man freely gives more to others than he receives. On the final day, he would prefer to know that he has given more than he received in life. In order for his life to balance the favors received and given, he would have much to receive and would have great wealth attributed to the soul. Those who return favors with forgetfulness and ingratitude merely add to the wealth due to others instead of diminishing their portion. Similarly, he who expects favors in return for all he gives is not charitable and spends all of his wealth with nothing left for his soul. One who cannot return a favor is also bankrupt, whether this inability arises from poverty of spirit, vileness of soul, or financial hardship. He who gives, not because he expects a return, but because it is a good and right thing to do is the generous man.

Even the wealthy man with a large portfolio of investments is still poorer than the man whom many owe large returns of kindnesses and favors. The wealth of any man, beyond a moderate amount, that is only *invested* with, and he *never* truly used represents capital that is reserved for selfish benefit and not for bettering humanity. This is the same as favors unreturned and kindness unreciprocated.

122

An abundant and generous spirit makes men humane, gracious, open-hearted, frank, sincere, intending to do good, mild-mannered, contented, and an advocate for humanity. They protect the feeble against the strong. They protect the defenseless against those who prey on them. They aid and comfort the poor. They are the guardians, under God, of his innocent and helpless constituents. They value friends more than riches or fame, and gratitude more than money or power. They are noble by God's decree, and their names and flags are found in heaven's great book of heraldry. A man cannot be a gentleman or a Mason unless he is generous, charitable, and impartial. Masonry strives to be liberal with that which is ours, to be just and generous, and to give even when giving deprives us of luxury or comfort.

He who is worldly, greedy, or carnal must change before he can become a good Mason. If we are governed by natural inclination instead of by the call of duty, we are a great distance from the true Masonic light. Similarly, if we are unkind, severe, censorious, or abusive in our relationships through life, we are misguided. If we are unfaithful parents, bad children, harsh bosses, faithless employees, treacherous friends, bad neighbors, bitter competitors, corrupt or unprincipled politicians, or oppressing business people, we are unworthy of being a true Mason.

Masons must be kind and affectionate to each other. Frequenting the same temples and kneeling at the same altars. They should feel respect and kindness for each other, which their common approach to one God should inspire. We need more of this spirit of ancient fellowship and brotherly love among us. There should be more sympathy, forgiveness, and care for each other's faults, improvement, and good fortune. There should be no shame to use the word "*brother*".

Nothing should be allowed to interfere with the kindness and affection of a Mason. Not in the spirit of business which can be absorbing, eager, unscrupulous, and ungenerous in its dealings, intense and bitter in its competition, or low and wretched in its purposes. Nor should being ambitious,

123 selfish, greedy, restless, underhanded, proud, envious, vain, unjust, unscrupulous, or slanderous interfere.

Someone who does me a favor has bound me to make a thankful return. The obligation does not come by covenant, contract, or express intention. It is the nature of the favor that is the obligation of duty, which springs up within the spirit of the person. This person finds it is more natural to love a friend and to do good for the act of doing good, than to return evil when evil is done. A man may forgive an injury, but he must never forget a good deed. One that refuses to do good to those he is bound to love, or to love one who was good to him, is unnatural and untrue to his affection. He must think the entire world was born to serve him and this shows the greediness in his character. His greed is worse than a black hole, which envelopes all within its grasp. Yet the black hole furnishes the energy for new stars and galaxies and contributes back to its environment. Our duty is to those who help us. We are to hold high-regard and esteem for them and to love them for their goodness. According to their kindness, we should obligate ourselves to return to them proportionate services, duty, or profit, as we can, as they need, or as the opportunity presents itself.

Forgiveness does not imply forgetting, approval, or acceptance of misdeeds or unkindness done to us. It does mean the recognition that one cannot continue to live with bitterness, anger, and the desire for revenge against the perpetrator of the wrong. It represents a laying down of the hurt and anger in order to get on with one's life. Forgiveness may not help the person being forgiven, but the benefits to the person doing the forgiving are immense. He has laid down his burden, cleansed his soul, cleared his head, and moved on to a brighter future.

The generous man does not want to see dissention and dispute among his brethren. Only low and selfish people delight in discord. It is the poorest occupation of humanity to work at making men think worse of each other. One sees the press and the pulpit as the new court of public opinion. One of the duties of the Mason is to make man think better of his neighbor and to mediate, not aggravate difficulties. A Mason should bring together those who are estranged, keep friends from becoming foes, and persuade foes to become friends. To do so, one needs to control of his own passions. He should not act rashly or hastily. He must not be easily offended or angered.

Anger is the professed enemy to guarded thought and intention. It is a storm, which no man can be heard while standing in. If you counsel it gently, you will be disregarded. If you urge it and be vehement, you only provoke it more. Anger is neither righteous nor honorable. It makes unavoidable trouble in a marriage. It makes friendships, societies, and communities intolerable. It worsens the evils of drunkenness. It makes the happiness of wine run to madness. It makes innocent humor into the beginning of argument. It turns

124 friendships towards hatred. It makes a man lose his wits, his reasoning, and his rhetoric when in engaged in a dispute. It turns the desire for knowledge into an

itch for argument and bickering. It makes the powerful overbearing. It turns justice into cruelty, and judgment into oppression. It changes discipline into boring routine, and it encourages hatred of generous institutions. Anger encourages malicious thoughts on a prosperous man and unsympathetic feelings towards an unfortunate person.

Therefore, you must first control your temper and govern your passions. Then you have equipped yourself to keep peace and harmony among other men, more especially the brethren. Above all else, remember that Masonry is a realm of peace, and that *"among Masons there should be no contention but that noble contention, or rather emulation, of who can best work and best agree."* There is no Masonry where strife and hatred exist among the brethren. Masonry is Peace, Brotherly Love, and Harmony.

Masonry is the great Peace Society of the world. Wherever it exists, it works to prevent international troubles and disputes. It strives to bind Republics, Kingdoms, and Empires together into one great treaty of peace and friendship. If Masons knew their strength and put value in their oaths, it would not struggle in vain so often.

If we cannot agree, humanity is doomed to conflict. Who can count the horrors and woes accumulated in just one war? Masonry is not dazzled with all of war's pomp and circumstance, nor its glitter and glory. War comes with its bloody reach into our homes. It takes from thousands of homes those who once lived there in peace and comfort among the tender ties of family and kindred. War drags them away, to die of fever or exposure due to improper attention or in infectious climates. They are hacked, torn, and maimed in the battles. They fall on bloody fields and rise no more. They are pulled away in awful agony to noisy and horrid hospitals. The groans of the battlefield are echoed in sad sighs of bereavement from thousands of affected homes. There resides a skeleton in every house and a vacant chair at every table. The returning soldier brings back to his home even worse sorrow, battle fatigue, loss of friends, and the memories of the horrors of war. The country is demoralized by this activity. The national mind is brought low from the high and noble interchange of kind purpose and intent with other peoples, to wrath, revenge, lowly pride, and a habit of measuring brute strength in battle. Government treasuries are spent wastefully. This money could build ten thousand houses of worship, hospitals, universities, or build a grand transportation infrastructure across the continents. If that treasure were lost to the sea, it would be calamity enough. But, in war it is put to *125* worse use as it is expended in cutting the veins and arteries of human life and it ceases not until the earth is flooded with a sea of mankind's blood.

Such are the lessons of this Degree. You have vowed to make them the rule, the law, and the guide of your life and conduct. If you do so, you will be equipped and entitled to advance in Masonry. If you do not, you have already gone too far.

CHAPTER 7: PROVOST AND JUDGE

THE lesson this Degree teaches is JUSTICE. It is to be employed in our 126 decisions, judgments, and interaction with other men.

In a country that practices trial-by-jury, every person can be called to act as a judge. One can be asked to judge based on fact or law as presented. The consequences of judging poorly are heavy burdens, which that person must carry.

Those who are tasked with the responsibility of judgment should judge all persons uprightly, morally, justly, and impartially. Judgment should be blind and not swayed by power, wealth, popularity, or even needs of the poor. No one will dispute that this is the cardinal rule of justice, though many fail to follow it. Those who fail in this must do more. They must divest themselves of prejudice and bias. They must listen patiently, remember accurately, and weigh carefully the facts and arguments presented to them. They must not jump to conclusions or form opinions before they have heard every argument. They must not presume guilt in crime or fraud. Their judgment must not be ruled by the stubborn pride of their own opinion. They must not be too easily swayed by the views and arguments of others either. In deriving a motive for the act, one should not presume the best (nor the worst) motivations. They should reason that a just and fair motive might exist, as they would want, if the rest of the world sat as their judge. They must not allow a multitude of minor circumstances to be pieced together as sound evidence in an attempt to prove some greatness of perception or wisdom like Sherlock Holmes. Do not assume, but rely on proof. These are sound rules for every juror to follow.

In mankind's dealings with others, there are two kinds of injustice. The 127 first is direct injury. Those who have the power to stop an injury from occurring but do nothing perform the second injustice. *Active* injustice may be done in two ways: by force or by fraud. Fraud is the more detestable. Force is lion-like and fraud is fox-like, yet both are opposed to social duty.

Every wrong done by one man to another's person, property, happiness, or reputation is an offense against the law of justice. The scope of this Degree's teachings is vast. Masonry strives to establish and enforce the laws of justice within its system, and it seeks the most effective means of preventing wrong and injustice.

To this end, Masonry teaches this great and momentous truth: once done, wrong and injustice cannot be undone. Once committed, the consequences of the act are eternal and part of an irrevocable past. There is no eraser, rewrite, or do-over for life's actions. Once performed, the wrong will foster its own rebalancing justice as certainly as the acorn leads to the oak. The consequences of a deed are punishment. It needs nothing further. Those involved in its doing cannot be separated from it, and this burden will weigh their conscience as a punishment. A wrong done to another is also an injury to our own nature. It is an offense against our own souls and a disfigurement of the image of the "Beautiful and Good". True punishment is the consequence of a deed's effect, and not the execution of a sentence. Punishment is ordained to follow the guilt by the laws He enacted as the Creator and Legislator of the Universe, and not by the decree of God as a judge. Punishment is not an appendant deed, but is the ordinary and logical consequence of an action. Therefore, its burden must be carried by the wrongdoer, and through him, it may continue to pass onto others. It is the decision of the infinite justice of God, in the form of law.

There can be no deflection, buy-out, or protection from the natural effects of wrongful acts. God will not prevent the act or its consequence. In that strict sense, there can be no forgiveness of sins. One may repent of an act and the soul corrected, but the injury is done. A wrong might be redeemed by subsequent efforts, and the stain it left may be removed through the struggle, suffering, and persistence of correcting the wrong. Yet all the effort, endurance, and fortitude of that soul are exhausted by merely regaining what was lost, rather than raising itself to loftier heights. We must always see a vast difference between someone who has ceased to do evil and someone who has never done evil.

Someone who believes that wrong deeds lead to inevitable consequences, despite attempts to rectify them, will be more principled and conscientious in their conduct than someone who believes that penitence and pardon will correct any unfavorable chain of events. We would do less wrong and injustice if we believed that everything done is permanent. If we believe the Omnipotence of God cannot *uncommit* a deed, cannot make that *undone* which has *been done*, then every act of ours must play out its part in the world according to the everlasting law. It must remain forever permanently inscribed in the archives of Universal Nature.

If you have wronged another, you may grieve, repent, and resolve against any such weakness in the future. As far as it is possible, you may make reparations and amends. The injured party may forgive you. However, the deed is *done* and not all the powers of Nature can make it *undone*. The consequences to the body and soul, though unperceivable, *are there* and inscribed in the records of the past to propagate throughout time.

Repentance for a wrong done purifies the heart and makes amends for the future, but it cannot erase the past. The committing of a wrong is an irrevocable act. However, it does not stop the soul from doing right in the future. Its consequence cannot be cancelled, but the soul can be corrected. Though permanent and wrong, evil done does not call for hopelessness. It calls for efforts more energetic than before. Repentance is valid because it can better the future even if it cannot erase the past.

The sound waves in the air, once set into motion by the human voice, do not cease to exist as its source becomes silent. The attenuating sound waves quickly become inaudible to human ears. Despite the lack of human perception, these waves continue to travel and interact until every atom over Earth has been affected somehow due to that portion of energy that has been conveyed to it. These will continue to influence atoms throughout the future. The atmosphere is one vast library recording all that man has ever said or whispered. In its constantly changing, but unending vibrations are forever encoded and recorded all those vows and promises from the earliest to the latest. This repository of man's statements perpetually affects the movements of all particles for all eternity. God can read what is stored in this library He created, even though we cannot.

Earth, air, and ocean are the eternal witnesses to the acts we have done. No motion from natural causes or human agency is ever complete. The wake from every boat that has ever sailed the surface of the ocean continually registers its effect on the future movements of all the surrounding particles. The laws of the Almighty forever connect every criminal to the affects of his crime. Every atom of his body will retain some movement derived from that very muscular effort by which the crime was perpetrated.

What if our senses could be enhanced in a future time so as to enable us to perceive and trace the consequences of our poor words and evil deeds, rendering our remorse and grief as eternal as those consequences themselves? A moral creature can conceive no more fearful punishment than to see a wrong deed's effects it performed, knowing that it will continue forever.

By its teachings, Masonry works to restrain men from committing unjust, wrong, and outrageous acts. Though it does not endeavor to occupy the place of religion in life, its code of morals are based upon principles beyond municipal laws. It condemns and punishes offenses that neither civil law punishes nor public opinion condemns. In the Masonic law, to defraud in business, cheat in sport, deceive in law, or defame in politics is considered equal with theft. Just as a deliberate lie is the same as perjury, slander to robbery, and seduction with murder.

It especially condemns those wrongs in which one persuades and encourages another to participate. *He* may repent for the deed. *He* may, after

129

130 agonizing struggles, regain the path of virtue. *His* spirit may reclaim its purity through anguish and strife, but the weaker fellow whom he led astray, whom he made an accessory in guilt, whose downward course, the first step of which he taught, he is now unable to stop and must witness. What forgiveness of sins can help him there? He may share in the guilt, but he cannot share in the repentance and amendment. *There* is his perpetual and inevitable punishment, which no repentance can rectify, and no mercy can pardon.

Let us be just when judging other men's motives. We know little of the real merits, or demerits, of any fellow human. We can rarely say with certainty that this man is guilty of more than what is before us. We can rarely certify that a man is very good or very wicked. Often, the lowest or simplest men leave behind excellent reputations. Rarely is there one among us who has not been on the verge of committing a crime or wrongful act at some point in his life. Every one of us can look back with fear and see the time when our feet stood upon the slippery cliff that overhung the abyss of guilt. If temptation had lingered longer, had been a little more urgent, if poverty and destitution had pressed us a little harder, or if a little more wine had further reduced our intellect, dethroned our judgment, and aroused our passions, our feet would have slipped from moral certainty. We would have fallen, never to rise again.

We might be able to say, "*This* man has lied, pilfered, forged, embezzled money entrusted to him while *that* man has gone through life with clean hands." But we cannot say the former had not struggled against temptation, though unsuccessfully, under which the second would have succumbed much more quickly. We can say which has the cleanest *hands* before *man*, but we cannot confirm who has the cleanest *soul* before *God*. We may be able to say *this* man has committed adultery and *that* man has ever been chaste. Yet, we cannot tell if this innocence is due to the coldness of his heart, the absence of motive, the presence of fear, or the degree of the temptation. Nor can we tell if the fall of the other was preceded by the most vehement self-contest, caused by the most over-powering frenzy, and atoned for by the most reverential repentance. Generosity as well as stinginess may be a natural predisposition. In the eye of Heaven, a long life of charity in one man may have cost less effort, indicate less

131 virtue, and caused less sacrifice of interest, than a few rare unknown acts of kindness delivered by duty from the reluctant and unsympathetic nature of another man. There may be more merit, self-sacrifice, and moral greatness in a life of outward failure, sin, and shame than in what appears to be a career of stainless integrity.

When we condemn the fallen soul, how do we know that we would not have fallen just like him, when tempted like him, and perhaps with less resistance? How can we know what we would do if we were unemployed, gaunt, hungry, desperate for food, and our children cried from famine? *We do not fall, because we are not tempted enough!* This fallen man may be as honest as the next at heart. How do we know that our daughter, sister, or wife could resist the abandonment, desolation, distress, and temptation that sacrificed the virtue of their poor sister of shame? Perhaps they have not fallen only because they have not been so tempted! We wisely pray that we may not be exposed to this level of temptation.

Human justice must always listen to the circumstances. How many judicial executions have been committed through ignorance of insanity! How many men were hung for murder but were wrongly convicted? Their hearts were as clean of the deed as the jury and judge that sentenced them! It could be conjectured that the administration of laws, in every country, is but one gigantic mass of injustice and wrong. God bears witness better than man. The most abandoned criminal may continue to keep a little light burning in a corner of his soul. While those who walk proudly in the light of glory and fame may have extinguished this light in their soul if they had only been tried and tempted like that poor outcast.

We do not even know the *outside* life of men. We are not competent to rule on their *deeds*. We do not know half the wicked or virtuous acts of our closest companions. We cannot say with certainty that our closest friend has not committed a particular sin or broken a particular commandment. Let each man ask his own heart! How many of our best and worst acts and qualities are unknown to our closest confidants?! How many virtues does the world give us credit for which we do not truly possess? How many vices do they condemn us for which we are not bound?! There are only a small portion of our evil deeds and thoughts that ever come to light, and it is out of redeeming grace that the 132 largest portion is known only to God.

It is only when we are generous that we can be just in judging other men. We should assume the power of judging others only when the duty is forced upon us, because we are certain to err and the consequence so serious. No one should wish for the office of judge, because the title assumed is a grave and burdensome responsibility. Yet we all assume it. Man is always ready to judge and condemn his neighbor although he would acquit himself of his judgment's consequences. Therefore, exercise this responsibility with caution, charity, and generosity. Otherwise, when passing judgment, you may commit a greater wrong than what you condemn, and the consequences will be eternally upon your soul.

The faults, crimes, and follies of other men are important to us. They form a part of our moral discipline. Similarly, the war and bloodshed abroad and the financial scandals also concern our moral welfare, because they affect our thoughtful hearts. The public may attempt to ignore the miserable victim of his own vice, or that shattered wreck of a man may move the masses to laughter or scorn. To the Mason, this man before him is the form of sacred humanity, an erring human bearing a desolate, forlorn, and forsaken soul. The Mason's thoughts about this poor wretch will be far deeper than indifference, ridicule, or contempt. All human offenses will be looked upon by the Mason, not as a scene of mere mean toils and strife, but as a whole system of dishonesty, evasion, circumventing, forbidden indulgence, intrigue, and ambition in which men are struggling against each other in solemn conflicts for the benefit of their own mortal being instead of the immortal mind. It is a sad and unworthy struggle among humanity that is taken with displeasure. This displeasure must change to sympathy, because the stakes by which these games are played are not as envisioned or imagined by man. For example, a person strives for a title or office and finally gains it, but he may have risked his soul for it through the devotion to self-service, uncharitableness, defamation, and deceit.

Good men are proud of their goodness. They are respectable. Dishonor does not come near them, and their approval carries weight and influence. Their robes are unstained, and the poisonous breath of a defamatory mouth has never spoken their name. It would be easy for them to look down with scorn upon the poor and degraded offender. It would be easy to side step him and pull close his coat so that he may not be soiled by his touch! Yet a man of virtue would not do this. He would come to the aid of the hated, the sinners, the prostitutes, the outcasts, and the pariahs of the ancient world.

Many people think better of themselves in relationships if they can identify the sin of others! When they review the list of their neighbor's fits of bad temper or poor conduct, they often feel a secret exuberance. This contradicts their own claims to wisdom, moderation, and virtue. Many even take pleasure in knowing the sins of others. This is the case when someone has had happy thoughts while comparing his own virtues to his neighbors' faults.

The power of compassion is too infrequent in the world. The controlling influences of love and kindness, calm over passion, grave displeasure with grief, and pity for the offender demonstrate the commanding majesty of perfect character. A Mason should treat his brethren who go astray in this manner. Do not treat them with bitterness, good-natured easiness, worldly indifference, philosophic coldness, or a looseness of conscience that accounts everything well and will pass under the seal of public opinion. Treat them with charity and pitying loving-kindness.

The human heart will not willingly submit to what it finds wrong in other people's human nature. It must yield to what is divine and pure within us. The wickedness of my neighbor cannot be brought to submission when he is in the light of my wickedness. He will not fully repent of his sins while I have anger for these vices. My faults cannot be ignored when trying to level reasoning to stop his faults. This is why impatient reformers, denouncing preachers, hasty rebukers, angry parents, and irritable relatives generally fail in their several attempts to reclaim an erring soul.

A moral offense is sickness, pain, loss, and dishonor to the immortal soul of man. It is guilt and misery on top of that. It is disaster that brings God's disapproval, the loathing of virtuous men, and the soul's own displeasure. Deal faithfully, patiently, and tenderly with this evil! It is not a matter to deal with for petty provocations, for personal conflicts, or for selfish matters.

Speak kindly to your erring brother! God pities him. Providence waits for him. Heaven's mercy yearns toward him, and Heaven's spirits are ready to welcome him back with joy. Let your voice be in unison with all those powers that God uses for a soul's recovery!

If someone defrauds you and rejoices in it, they are to be pitied most among all human beings. They have more deeply injured themselves than you. God regards them with mingled displeasure and compassion and His judgment should be your rule and law. Among the benedictions from the Holy Mount, there is not one for this kind of person, but for the merciful, the peacemakers, and the persecuted they are free and voluminous.

We are all people of like passions, tendencies, and influences. There are portions in all of us that might have been manipulated to the worst of crimes through a process of successive negative influences and moral deterioration. The wretch whom the mob follows to the scaffold with curses may be no worse than any one in that crowd. Anyone of them might have become that same wretch under similar circumstances. He should be condemned for the crime, but also deeply pitied for the sake of his soul and ours.

It is not appropriate for the weak and sinful to be vindictive to even the worst criminals. We owe much to the good Providence of God as He compels us to be more virtuous. However, we all have within us the capacity to be pushed to sinful excess. Perhaps we could have fallen just as others did but with even less temptation. Perhaps we have already performed acts that would be less excusable than their great crime if we were to view it proportionately to the temptation or provocation received. Compassion and sorrow for the victim should balance our detestation of the crime. Take as an example the terrorist who murders in cold blood. He is the man you or I might have become with similar backgrounds. Orphaned or abandoned in childhood, immoral parents, perverted beliefs, no friends in youth, evil mentors, ignorance, lacking moral cultivation, temptations of sinful pleasure, grinding poverty, hopelessness, vices, addictions, outcast from society, forgotten love, or crushed affections all could have led any one of us to act the same. We might have been raised with the belief of bloody and universal defiance. We could easily be the one to wage war with our fellow man, live the reckless life, and die the death of the remorseless killer. Humanity pleads with us to pity the murderer. His head once rested on a mother's bosom. He was once the object of sisterly love and endearment. Perhaps his hand once clasped another loving hand at the altar, but it is now red with blood. Pity him for his blighted hopes and his crushed heart! It is conceivable that weak-willed and erring creatures may stray from the true and moral path of life as we might. We should view the crime as tempted souls might. It may be that when God weighs men's crimes, He will take into consideration their temptations and adverse circumstances. His law may consider the opportunities for moral correctness or reconciliation with the

135

offender. It may be that in proportion, our own offenses will weigh heavier than the murderer's, though man's laws and judgments may state otherwise.

Therefore, let the true Mason never forget the solemn command necessary to be observed at every moment of a busy life: "JUDGE NOT, OR YOU WILL BE JUDGED: FOR WHAT EVER JUDGMENT YOU MEASURE ON OTHERS, THE SAME WILL ALSO BE MEASURED ON YOU." This is the lesson taught to the Provost and Judge.

CHAPTER 8: INTENDANT OF THE BUILDING

136 THIS Degree teaches the important lesson that no one is entitled to advance in the Ancient and Accepted Scottish Rite who have not studied and applied themselves in Masonic learning and laws. The Degrees of this Rite are not for those content with the work and ceremonies, and those who do not seek the mines of wisdom that are buried beneath its surface. You still advance toward the Light, toward that blazing star in the distance which is a symbol of the Divine Truth given by God to man. It has been preserved for man despite all the changes from all ages within the traditions and teachings of Masonry. How far you advance will depend entirely on yourself. Everywhere in the world, Darkness struggles with Light, and its shadows come between you and Truth.

For some time you will be exclusively occupied by living in the morality of Masonry. First, you must learn to practice all the virtues that it teaches. As they become familiar and you breathe its morality unconsciously, then you will be prepared to receive its lofty philosophical instruction. You will be ready to climb the heights to the summit where Light and Truth rule. Systematically, men must advance towards Perfection, and each Masonic Degree is meant guide you there. Each teaches us to develop a particular duty. Presently, you are taught charity and benevolence. You are to be an example of virtue to your brethren. You are 137 taught to correct your own faults and strive to correct those of your brethren.

As in all Degrees, you see the emblems and names of Deity. Masonry primarily seeks to perpetuate the true knowledge of Deity's character and attributes. The first of the Masonic duties is to appreciate His infinite greatness and goodness, to rely implicitly upon His Providence, and to revere Him as the Supreme Architect, Creator, and Legislator of the universe.

The Battery of this Degree and the five circuits (circumambulation) you made around the Lodge allude to the five points of fellowship so that you will always remember them. The duties are written in God's great code of law. Go upon a brother's errand or to his relief, even if barefoot and at midnight. Remember him in your prayers to Deity. Keep his secrets in your heart, and protect him against malice and evil speaking. Guide him when he is about to stumble and fall and aid him in his efforts at reformation. Give him timely, honest, and good counsel. These are the first duties of Masonry.

The first sign of this Degree expresses our uncertainty and humility when we inquire into the nature and attributes of the Deity. The second sign is our profound awe and reverence when we contemplate His glories. The third sign is our sorrow when we reflect upon our insufficient practice of duties and imperfect compliance with His laws.

The unique characteristic of man is his search for, and following of, the truth. When our normal cares and concerns are quiet, we find ourselves desiring to see, hear, and learn. The knowledge of obscure and wonderful things is essential on the path to living happily. Human nature finds Truth, Simplicity, and Candor most favorable. By applying sound judgment and seeking Truth, we can find virtue among anything. Virtue preserves Human Society by giving to every man his due and observing faithfulness in our contracts. Virtue is in the greatness of a spiritual and free mind. Virtue is attainable through Moderation by keeping order and regularity in all our words and through Temperance in all our actions.

138 Masonry rigorously preserves that enlightened faith which produces the sublime Devotedness, the opinion of Charity, the spirit of tolerance, peace, hope, and happiness, and a devotion to duty. Masonry has always spread faith with passion and grace. It works today more zealously than ever. A Masonic conversation rarely is spoken that does not show the advantage and need for faith. Recall the two fundamental principles of all religions; love of God and love of neighbor. Masons carry these principles in their hearts to spread to their families, friends, and neighbors. While the narrow-minded Sectarians weaken the religious spirit, Masonry preserves and strengthens it. Masons form one great Society over the world and carry the banner of Charity and Benevolence. They extend that spirit in purity and simplicity because it has always existed in the depths of the human heart. It has existed in the most ancient forms of worship even where superstitions forbade its recognition.

A Masonic Lodge should resemble a beehive with all members fervently working together for the common good. Masonry is not for dispassionate souls and narrow-mindedness that cannot comprehend its lofty and sublime mission. Uninspired souls are disliked. The labor that sparks zeal and enthusiasm in Masons is comforting the unfortunate, promoting knowledge, teaching truth and purity in religion and philosophy, familiarizing men with respect for order and justice, and showing the path to real happiness. It prepares for that glorious time when all the peoples of Humanity will unite as one family by the bonds of Toleration and Fraternity.

We will not expand or elaborate upon these ideas. We mention them to you as ideas that you may reflect upon at your leisure. If you continue to advance in the Degrees these ideas will be unfolded, explained, and developed further.

Masonry does not practice impractical or extravagant rules of conduct because these are of no regard to reputable, practical teachings. It does not ask the impossible or difficult of its initiates. Every just, upright, and honest man can obey its statutes, no matter what his faith or creed. Its goal is to get the greatest good from man without demanding that he be perfect. It does not interfere with religions or question their practices. It teaches the truths written *139* by God upon the heart of man. It teaches the most excellent ideals of duty. These were developed through meditation and reflection by wise and educated persons, confirmed though loyalty to their meaning by the good, and certified accurate by every pure mind's response to them. Masonry cannot authoritatively establish moral practice in men nor does it arrogantly imagine that moral certainty is attainable.

This world with its splendid beauty, thrilling interests, glorious works, and noble and holy affections cannot be disparaged by Masonry. We are not to detach our hearts from this earthly life and fix our interests upon Heaven alone. This life is not defined as empty, fleeting, or unworthy with only Heaven deserves love and meditation. Masonry teaches that man has special duties to perform and a destiny to fulfill on Earth. This world is more than a mere portal to the next. This life is important and worthy of concern today. The Present is our stage while the Future is for speculation and trust. Man was created upon Earth to live, enjoy, study, love, improve, and make the most of it. He should lavish his affections and his efforts on it where his influence can operate. It is his house and not a tent. It is his home and not merely a school. Man was not sent into *this* world to be constantly longing, dreaming, and preparing for *another*. He is to do his duty and fulfill his destiny on this earth, now. Man must do all that lies in his power to improve it and make it a place of increased happiness for himself, those around him, and those who are yet to be born. His current life is part of the immortal self, and *this* world is among the stars and heavens.

Though Masonry helps us, can mankind prepare for that Future it longs for? The Unseen cannot hold a higher place in our affections than the Seen, Familiar, and Present. The law is a Love of Life, its interests, and its adornments. It is by a love of this world that we find ourselves engrossed in the interests and concerns of Earth. It is not a sensual love, nor the love of wealth, fame, ease, power, or splendor. It is a love of Earth as the garden which the Creator lavished with miracles of beauty as the habitat of humanity, though the arena of its conflicts, it is the scene of unlimited progress and the dwelling of the wise, good, active, loving, and dear. It is the place of opportunity to develop the noblest passions, loftiest virtues, and most tender sympathies even if by means of *140* sin, suffering, and sorrow.

Those who endeavor to persuade men to despise this world and all its beauty make pointless strides. They live here but benefit no one. God did not take all that time and effort in forming, framing, furnishing, and adorning the world so that those who He created to live in it would despise it. It should be enough to simply not love it as much as others, but it is pointless to try to stop all affections and passions in human nature. As long as honor, virtue, and industry exist in this world there will be ambition, emulation, and drive among the best and most accomplished men. If these were not prominent among men, we would find more violence, vice, and wickedness in every nation of the world.

Those who have a real interest and affection for this world will work to improve it. Those who under-value this life become full of complaint and discontent and have no interest in the welfare of others. Masons must feel that to serve here and now is worth our efforts. We must be content with the earthly world that God has given us until He moves us to a spiritual one. He could not deem this an unworthy world because He is here with us.

Do not defame the whole world by speaking of it as a home for a poor, toiling, drudging, ignorant, and dishonorable humanity. Do not discredit your family, friends, town, city, or country this way. The world is a wonderful and exciting place, and you should be thankful to live in it. If this life is worthless, immortality would be also.

Mankind has a heavy hand in the technology and machinery that connects our lives across the whole world. Yet, there is refinement within society that exists due to these interactions. Machines rush around the earth expanding our reach, tasks, responsibilities, needs, and businesses. The machines *141* often work with difficulty. They are cumbersome, loud, and collide frequently. However, the concepts and ideas that fuel our enterprise are usually motivated by the comforts, affections, and hopes of society. These motives become mixed with greed and often obstruct the noble actions. Alas, he who looks cynically on all this technology is not so wise because he has lost the sense of good that created it. If you can be, or have, just one friend, it is a wondrous good fortune that we could use to offset all the other problems of our social nature. If you have a place to call home, a sanctuary of walled and shielded joy, we could offset all the other ruins around life. If you can be a social man and speak real thoughts despite any controversy or opinion that will always outweigh any external arguments.

In the visible repulsive and annoying aspect of society, we are likely to lose the real sense of its invisible blessings. As in Nature, it is not the obvious that is so beautiful. It is not the soils, rains, fields, nor even the flowers. The beauty lies in that which is invisible, yet perceptible. Though unobserved, the most beautiful is the spirit of wisdom, and it is found throughout the world and society.

What makes man struggle? If man were only responsible for himself, he would throw down his working tools and live freely. He might wander through the world in its wild and untamed form, barren of anything noble. His home is the invisible bond to the world. It is the good, strong, and noble faith people have in each other which gives the highest character to business, trade, and commerce. Honesty is the rule. Fraud occurs in business, but it is the exception to the rule. No fraud in the world can break the great bond of human confidence. If it could, trade and business would halt, and all the cities of the world would crumble into ruin. You hold good, through his bond, the character of a man on the other side of the world, who you never have seen and who you never will. The most striking feature of any political state is the universal will of the people to be governed for the benefit and wealth of its citizens; not its government, constitution, laws, statutes, judicial power, nor its police. If we take that restraint away from the people, no government on earth could stand.

The most valuable teaching of Masonry is that we do not minimize this life. We should not cry when we reflect on the destiny of a newborn child on earth. Like the Hebrews, we should celebrate the birth of a child with joy. Their birthdays should be festivals. 142

Those who claim to have experienced life and found little merit in it are not for Masonry. Similarly, those who have concluded that life is more misery than happiness because their work is hard, their plans are frustrated, and their friendships have ceased are not Masons. Unfortunately, these people do not find pleasure, honor, or merit in life's path. They only see it as boring, dull, and worn.

Masonry finds no reverence for God among the people who belittle or despise the existence that He has established for us. Masonry does not preach of one spiritual or future world that is in competition with our current state. Rather it compares these worlds and views both as one system. This world must strive to emulate that world. It holds that a man may make the best of both worlds at the same time. By improving this world for others, he prepares himself for the next world. Masonry instructs its initiates that this world's meaningful duties are the works of God meant to be performed by man. It does not look upon this life as lost time. It does not regard efforts here as trivial or unworthy to the immortal soul within. Masonry encourages its practitioners to look cheerfully upon the world as a theatre worthy of action, exalted usefulness, and rational, innocent enjoyment.

Life is a blessing even with all its evils and to deny that is to destroy the foundation of all religion. Religion's foundation is the universal belief that God is good. If we ridicule humanity and our very existence with contempt and scorn, we destroy the basis of religion. If we considered the Earth a prison with no blessing, except our eventual escape from it, we would extinguish the fundamental light of faith, hope, and happiness. We would destroy Truth's foundation in God's goodness. All of man's highest actions would remain constrained by distrust, depression, and despair.

Our perseverance through sorrow and suffering is evidence of love of life. Our attachment to familiar places (e.g. our home or birthplace) throughout life proves how dear the ties to family and society are. We remember misery more than happiness because it is not our usual state of mind. Misery is strange for us and we are aware of its presence. Happiness lives with us and sometimes 143 we forget it because it rarely disturbs our order of thoughts, but agony remains an epic in our life. We remember our miseries because they are uncommon. They are like a natural disaster that is recorded for history because it is an extraordinary event to humanity, yet surrounding this event are significant unrecorded periods of peace and happiness in society. We mark the times of calamity but do not mark the many happy days of regular enjoyment in our memory or speak of them when we give thanks. Human nature is less able to recall the peaceful moments, easy sensations, bright thoughts, quiet dreams, or the multitude of affections life provides. These support us almost unconsciously because it carries us calmly and gently.

Life is good. It is a glorious experience for billions. Human virtue clothes life with the splendors of devotedness, charity, and heroism. The crown of sacrifice is upon its head. The soul shines brightly through this worldly and sometimes darkened life. The humblest life can feel its connection with its Infinite Source. There is something immortal in these bodies of ours. The mind stretches to infinity and its thoughts flash to the boundless, immeasurable, and infinite. It senses far into the future and desires to be a powerful influence upon future generations. It wants to know its wonderful Author, gain wisdom from the Eternal Stars, and provide reverence, gratitude, and love to the Ruler of all realms. It strives to be immortal, far into the Future through its influence. It makes life worthy and glorious.

144   Life is the wonderful creation of God. It is light from darkness, and it is power in motion. Life was created from a void and that contrast sparks wonder and delight. Life is a spring from within the infinite and overflowing Goodness. From the moment it gushes up to light to the time it flows into the ocean of Eternity, that Goodness attends to this glorious gift. There is joy in its infant voice, happiness in the steps of its youth, satisfaction in its strong maturity, and peace in its old age. There is good for the charitable, virtue for the faithful, and victory for the valiant. Even in this simple life there is an infinity to accommodate those good, boundless desires. There are blessings upon its birth; there is hope in its death, and eternity in its potential. Thus, to the Mason this Earth is both the origin and goal of immortality. Life buries many under the rubbish of its vanities, but to the Mason, life is the height of meditation where Heaven, Infinity, and Eternity are spread before and around him. To the wise, pure, and virtuous this life is the beginning of Heaven and an important part of that immortality.

God has designated that a contented spirit is a remedy for all the evils in the world. We may have to accept poverty or lack of fortune if we are proportionately to allow ourselves to experience contentedness and composure. No man is poor who finds himself content. In contrast, one has chosen his own inadequate condition if he is full of fortune but desires more. The virtue of contentedness is the conclusion of all the old moral philosophy, and it is to be used universally in the course of our lives. Contentedness is the only tool that eases the burdens of the world and the bitterness from poor luck. It is reasonable for us to comply with this Divine Providence. It governs the entire world and orders us to the service of His great family. God dispenses His gifts as He pleases. We do not want to complain about the conditions He has divined for us.

Good or bad, we make our fortunes. When we react with fear, impatience, pride, or envy because God lets loose a sickness, scorn, poor luck, or a Tyrant upon our lives, then that calamity will strongly affect us. If we know how to manage the noble principles, are fearless in the face of dishonesty, despise impatience, perceive foolish pride as disgraceful, and prefer poverty to *145* greed, then may we control a focused mind and continue to smile if our fortunes reverse and Fate becomes ill-natured towards us.

If you lose your land, do not also lose your even temper. If you must die sooner than expected, do not die irritably. When a man is content, there is no chance for evil within him. To a man, nothing should cause misery except the unreasonable. No man can be forced to abandon his freedom. Only when he first bows to serve only life and death, pleasure and pain, or hope and fear is he enslaved. Command your passions, and you are freer than the ancient Parthian Kings.

When someone corrects us, we should accept it as constructive criticism because they will be more truthful than our best friends would. While we can forgive the anger found in the conveyance, we can make use of the accusation for personal improvement. Just as the OX walks straightest when weary, we walk the straightest moral path after surviving wearying accusations from our enemies. These criticisms can be better for our character building than flattering comments that lead to pride and carelessness.

If you become unemployed, take refuge in honest retirement and be indifferent to further gain. When the storms blow hard and the rain dampens everything, we must not sit down and cry in it. We must rise up to defend ourselves against the elements with a warm garment, a good fire, and a dry roof. Similarly, when a sad moment beats our spirits, we can turn it into positive action if we are resolved to do so. With calmness and patience, we shelter ourselves from self-pitying. If our patience is tested, and we respond with heroic endurance, all the temporary suffering has rewarded us enough. A wise man will control his environment and thereby influence his own contentedness more than all the outside influences could.

Do not compare your condition to the people above you. Secure your content by comparing your life against the thousands with whom you would not change places. There are great soldiers without the victories of Alexander the Great or Genghis Khan. He should rejoice that he is not defeated like the many generals who battled Napoleon or Rommel. One is not poor for not possessing the wealth of a Rothschild, Rockefeller, or Walton. One should rejoice that he *146* does not need to beg for charity. There may be many who have more wealth or who may be more fortunate, but many are more miserable when compared to your possession and fortune.

Though unfortunate, there will always be something left for us. It may be a merry appearance, cheerful spirit, good conscience, the Providence of God, the hopes of Heaven, charity, a loving wife, friendships, light, air, or any of the beauties of Nature. It may be that we can read, discuss, and meditate with quiet understanding. With these blessings, we should be happy despite our moments of sorrow, and we should become upset only if we were to lose them all. Be content in life to withstand our little handful of thorns.

Enjoy the blessings God sends you everyday. If instead there are evils, bear them patiently and calmly for this is still our experience on this day. Yesterday is gone and can do nothing more for us. Tomorrow is unavailable for our improvement. Today is all we have to count on. When our fortunes change, our spirits could remain unchanged if we always expect a reversal of fortune and reserve an expectation of sorrow. The blessings of immunity, security, liberty, and integrity deserve gratitude through our whole life. We are constantly rescued from unseen calamity, which could render our present sorrow to obscurity from which we would gladly trade back to our current condition.

Separate your desires from your fortune and condition. Do not measure your fortune by what you desire. Do not let your whims, bad habits, or ambitious principles rule your actions, but let your needs and nature govern. It is bad to be vicious and impatient, but not to be poor. What is the measure of our possession or wealth when comparing our real needs? Is the large bear that grazes over an entire mountain wealthier than the little bee that feeds on just the dew or manna that falls from those storehouses of Heaven, clouds, and Providence every morning? Both have possession suitable to their needs.

There are some fortunes that cannot coexist with a fair condition. If you desire one thing, you will give-up another. Unless you are content with one you will lose the comfort of both. If you desire learning, you must have the time and money to pursue it. If you desire honors of State or political distinctions you must, "be ever in the public, gather experience, do all men's business, keep all company, and have no leisure at all." If you desire to be rich, you must be frugal. If you desire to be popular, you must be generous with yourself. If you want to be a philosopher, you must despise the riches of establishment. If you would be famous as the general Epaminondas in his time, you must also accept the poverty he endured, because it added luster to his character and envy to his fortune. His virtue would not have been so excellent otherwise. If you want to have the reputation of a martyr, you must accept the persecution necessary. If you desire to be a benefactor against the world's injustice, then you must expect to see the general populace embrace lesser men who promote what is easy and popular over yourself who promotes what is right for society.

147

God can bring good out of evil. It is one of His glories. Therefore, we should trust in Him to govern His world as He pleases. We should be patient while we wait for enlightenment or improvement in our fortunes.

A Mason's must not be content from selfishness, because he should care for the condition of others equally. This world will always have wrongs to forgive, suffering to alleviate, sorrow asking for sympathy, necessities and poverty to relieve, and ample occasion for charity and good deeds. Someone who enjoys his own comforts and luxuries more after comparing them with the hungry, ragged, destitute, and shivering misery of others is not content, but selfish and unfeeling.

The saddest sights on earth are those of men who are wealthy and lazy in life as well as those who are workaholics and are miserly towards others. Those people who turn a deaf ear to cries of appeal and a blind-eye to suffering are far worse than the man whose hasty anger carried him to violence or crime. Faithless servants are those who hoard or embezzle what God has intended for the impoverished and destitute. The true Mason earns the right to be content when he lives and works for himself *and* for others. He is sympathetic to those who deserve and need his assistance.

"Charity is the great channel through which God passes all His mercy upon mankind. We receive absolution of our sins in proportion to the forgiving of our brother. This is the rule of our hopes and the measure of our desire, and on the judgment day, the great sentence upon mankind shall be proportionate with our charity. God himself is love, and every act of charity in us is part of the Divine nature."

Masonry reduces these principles to practice. Hereafter, it expects you to *148* be guided and governed by them. It especially teaches these principles to those who are employers. It forbids him to fire an employee if they will starve without income. It forbids him to contract with anyone for too low of a price that they must sacrifice their time and effort to fulfill their obligation, effectively selling their life with the labor they provide.

These Degrees are intended to teach more than morals. The symbols and ceremonies of Masonry have many meanings. They conceal more Truth than they disclose. They merely hint at it. Their various meanings are only to be discovered through great reflection and study. Light symbolizes Truth. Just as light is separable into a rainbow of colors, truth is separable into various components. It is the responsibility of Masonry to teach all these truths and not just the moral truths. We must teach the great and essential principles of political, philosophical, and religious truths. Symbolic meanings require great teachers, dedication to learning, and significant contemplation. The sphinx was merely a symbol, and to whom has it disclosed its inner most meaning? Who knows all the symbolic meanings of the pyramids?

Next, you will learn of the primary enemies of human liberty as symbolized by the assassins of the Master Hiram Abif (Khūrūm). In their fate you will see foreshadowed what we hope will overtake those enemies of humanity, against whom Masonry has struggled for so long.

CHAPTER 9: ELECT (ELU) OF THE NINE

ORIGINALLY created to reward fidelity, loyalty, obedience, and devotion, this Degree is dedicated to bravery, devotedness, and patriotism. Your obligation alerts you to the duties you have assumed. They are summarized in the simple mandate; "Protect the oppressed against the oppressor, and devote yourself to the honor and interests of your Country."

Masonry is experimental and practical. It is not sentimental, "speculative", or theoretical. It requires self-sacrifice and self-control. It frowns upon vices, and it interferes with many of our superficial pursuits and pleasures. It penetrates beyond sentiment without action. It has substance beyond moralizers and philosophers fine theories and beautiful expressions. It goes to the very depths of our hearts, reprimanding our selfishness and meanness, accusing our prejudice and passion, and fighting the armies of our vices.

Masonry wages war against the acts of passion among the world of nice thoughts. The reality is that this world has admirable sayings but foul practices, and good laws but bad deeds. In our world, dark passions are restrained by custom while ceremony remains hidden from itself by beautiful sentiments. This terrible irony has existed in all ages. Catholic sentiments have often masked infidelity and vice. Protestant ideas often praise spirituality and faith, but neglect basic truth, openness, and generosity. Liberal Rationalism has refinement that soars to heaven in its dreams, but on earth it wallows in the mire of incomplete deeds.

There may be volumes of Masonic opinion but a world with little or no Masonry. There is a vague and general idea of Masonic charity, generosity, and impartiality among many people. However, most people do not actively perform virtuous deeds, practice habitual kindness, implement self-sacrifice, or exhibit generosity. Masonry dances around them like the brilliant Northern lights. There are occasional flashes of generosity, moments of just and noble thought, and transient brilliance of imagination, but there is nothing pure and Masonic in their heart, which remains cold and inhospitable. These people do nothing and achieve no victories over themselves. They make no progress and they stand motionless in the Northeast corner of the Lodge as when they first stood there as Entered Apprentices. They have not made an effort to build their morality or improve the world by their actions and example. They are not determined, resolute, or regular in their cultivation of Masonry. Their Masonry takes its place in unfocused words and deeds that are shamefully barren of real results.

Most men have concepts but no principles. Concepts are temporary, general, and reactionary sensations that do not rise to virtuousness. Everyone feels them because they rise spontaneously in every heart. Principles are permanent rules of action and controlling influences of goodness and virtue that shape our conduct. Masonry insists upon principles.

The story of human nature is that while we agree with the right, we still pursue the wrong. No one promotes injustice, fraud, oppression, desire, revenge, envy, or slander. How many are guilty of them despite our condemnation of these? It is common for us to be inflamed, unjust, oppressive, or slanderous of an accused person when told of wicked injustice, cruel oppression, slander, or misery inflicted by the accused on the innocent. How angry a man can become at the greed and pride he sees in others!

151   A great Preacher said, "You are inexcusable when you judge, for when you judge another, you condemn yourself. You that judge, do the same wrongs." It is amazing to listen to some men talk of virtue and honor when their life denies both. It is interesting to hear the marvelous skill by which many bad men can quote Scripture. The use of good words and holy texts comfort their evil consciences when twisted to support their actions and marginalize their bad deeds. Be aware that the more a man talks about Charity and Toleration, the less he usually has of either. The more he talks about Virtue, the less he has of it. He speaks of the abundances of the heart, but he does not often practice it. Meanwhile, the vicious and lewd often express disgust at vice and sexuality. These forms of hypocrisy are not as rare as we would think.

In the Lodge, virtue and vice are only matters of reflection. We have little opportunity for the practice of either. Masons yield to virtue with ease and readiness, because there is nothing to it, and it is easy and safe to reflect upon these matters in the lodge. But tomorrow when they wake-up surrounded by competition and worldly gain, their passions will be stirred at the opportunities available, and all their concern for virtue and all their disdain for selfishness, greed, and sensuality vanish like smoke in the wind.

During the time at the Lodge, their emotions and sentiments are sincere and real. Men may be sincerely interested in Masonry, but still lack virtue. It is not always hypocrisy. Men often pray religiously, but they are constantly guilty of bad, base, ungenerous, and unrighteous acts, making the crimes in our courts barely worse.

A man may be good in general but very bad in particular. He might be good in the Lodge, but bad in the outer-world. He could be good in public, but bad toward his family. Maybe he is good at home, but bad among strangers. Many men truly desire to be good Masons and sincerely say so. However, at a particular instance, he will not wish to be a good Mason if he is required to resist a certain passion, sacrifice a certain indulgence, control his appetite at a feast, or keep his temper in a dispute. Even if he wants to do so, he might not be able to resist his worse impulses.

The duties in life are still more than this. The law expects all citizens to *152* serve and potentially sacrifice for country before considering the safety of their own lives. This is no different than it was in Roman times when the phrase was coined, "Necesse est ut eam, non ut vivam." (If I must go, it is not necessary that I should live.)

How ungrateful it is to slink away, die, and have done nothing to reflect the glory of Heaven! How barren is the tree that lives, spreads, and burdens the ground, but leaves not one seed, not one good work for a generation after him! Not everyone can leave the same legacy, but everyone can leave something in proportion to his or her capability. Your life is meaningless if you leave nothing for the future. The path to Heaven is long and difficult when you try to go alone.

Industry is fruitful. It may not bring joy with profit, but it will prevent mischief with preoccupation. An angel always waits to reward Diligence. The man who did nothing for the world, but live and die is unworthy of life! The liberty to do anything is a gift from Heaven and the power to use it well is a great fortune from Deity.

Masonry is action. Its Initiates are required to WORK actively and earnestly for the benefit of their brothers, their country, and all humanity. It is the protector of the oppressed. It comforts the unfortunate. In Masonry, it is a nobler honor to enable progress and reform, than to enjoy rank or office with lofty titles. It is the advocate for the people in the interest of mankind. It hates bold power and forceful seizures. It pities the poor, the mournful, and the dejected while it strives to improve the ignorant, sunken, and degraded.

Masonry's efforts to improve the people's condition and the resources it gathers to do so are the proof of its loyalty and fidelity to that purpose. It is the *153* aid to the education of children. An intelligent population, knowledgeable of its rights, will know its power, and it will not be oppressed for long. Without a stable and virtuous populace, the top of society's pyramid will be worthless because of the need of stability in its base. It is never safe for a nation to rest on the lap of ignorance. If ever there was a time when tranquility was ensured through ignorance that time is long past. Ignorance and stupidity constantly live in fear and terror. The improvement of the population is the security of liberty for all, but if neglected, the politeness, refinement, and knowledge accumulated in our societies will one day perish like dry grass in the blaze of popular uproar.

It is not the mission of Masonry to engage in conspiracies against the civil government. It does not spread the propaganda of a creed or theory. It does not proclaim itself the enemy of kings or judge of republics, but it is the advocate of liberty, equality, and fraternity. It has no alliances with any sect of theorists, dreamers, or philosophers nor does it control or prevent its Initiates independent thoughts. It exists apart from all other sects and creeds. It has its own calm and simple dignity under every government. Masonry is still what it was before humans walked on the soils of Mesopotamia or Egypt or colonized Southern India, Media, or Europe.

Masonry gives no favor to anarchy or immorality. It does not provide illusions of glory and extravagant emulation of the ancients. It does promote a thirst for liberty. It teaches moral virtue is the only sure guarantee for the protection of political freedoms. It is the soldier for the sanctity of laws and the rights of conscience.

154   Needs, rights, and justice must govern the making, administration, and regulation of laws in society. It sees the necessity of rules and laws in the affairs of man. It knows that when man focuses on personal ambition he neglects the peace and safety of the community and country. To ensure civility, man may require rule and government by those of abstract thought, free intellect, and broad wisdom over the majority without unanimity. Society trusts that God will work His great and wise purpose eventually though man may struggle and err in our interpretation and implementation. We must wait to ensure our actions are forward steps on the path to Truth and good.

It hopes and longs for the day when all men will be elevated and enjoy the freedom from the evils that afflict the earth. It does not preach revolution to those who are fond of kings. It does not preach rebellion when it will end in disaster, defeat, trade one tyrant for another, or exchange multiple despots for one.

Masonry sympathizes wherever free people govern themselves and vigorously strive to maintain their nation. It detests the tyrants, oppression, coup d'etats, and the misuse of lawful powers. It frowns upon cruelty and the disregard for civil and human rights. It loathes the greedy employer, and it lightens the burdens of hunger, shelter, want, and dependence shackled to the worker. It fosters kindness towards others, even to the poorest and most unfortunate.

Masonry cannot be used anywhere to teach toleration for the cruel, reduce the moral hatred for the guilty, or corrupt and brutalize the human mind. The fear of punishment will never make a Mason an accomplice to corruption or to the barbarity of his countrymen. A Mason would never buckle to the pressure of the powerful should they desire to condemn a satirist as a libeler or treasonous in a court of justice.

155   The Mason must keep his duty and perspective even if all law and liberty were trampled under the feet of demagogues, partisans, fanatics, or armed gangs. Even if great crimes were perpetrated by the highest powers in the land and their power was strong, a Mason must do what is right by duty. If a mob overthrew law and legal procedure and publicly demanded blood for a crime performed out of passion, insanity, or absentmindedness, the Mason would continue to guard their rights from the masses. For true words boldly spoken or unpopular acts

bravely done, the Masonic juror must take the proper perspective and be uninfluenced by powers-that-be. Duty alone will make him stand with a noble firmness between the human predators and their prey.

The Mason would prefer to pass his life in privacy and obscurity to feed freely his soul with good deeds and noble actions. The most splendid throne of the universe is a tormented place, cursed with the tendency to make good situations into bad actions. He has lived life well if he has produced any great and laudable works. He serves society well if he provides material or spiritual peace and relieves the burdens of poverty, dependence, and oppression on others. He serves his country well if he aides in securing peace beyond its borders and helped reconcile differences between people and government within its borders. He serves well if his countrymen elect him to protect and preserve their laws and goodwill. If he does these things, then he provides his part to society with the best intent and action. Then, he may close the book of life, even if he wants to read a page or two more, for his life has been good by every measure.

Masonry teaches that power is delegated for the good of the People. If this power is perverted from its purpose, the trust becomes broken, and the right path must be resumed. Resistance to illegitimate use of power is a duty which man owes to himself, his neighbor, and God. He should strive to assert the duty God gave him at Creation. Neither ignorance nor incivility can stop this principle. It is wrong for man to suffer under oppression when he should act. It preserves within him the original ideals of Providence. It opposes the arrogant assumptions of Tyrants and vindicates the independence of humanity. 156

The wise and well-informed Mason will always be a devoted follower of Liberty and Justice. He vigorously supports and defends them whenever needed. Liberty's struggle is not just for a country. It is the cause of humanity. His country is where the people understand the value of political justice, and they are prepared to assert it. His country is where he contributes, teaches, and spreads these principles making the real happiness of mankind. He desires the benefit of justice in every country.

The true Mason associates the honor of his country with his own. Nothing contributes more to the beauty and glory of a country than the preservation of its civil and religious liberties. World history remembers the names of patriots who honorably defended their countries from its enemies.

Masonry supports justice that is equitable in its administration and not denied, sold, or delayed to anyone. A country should care for its poor. No one should starve, be homeless, or search in vain for work. The children should not be overworked, and the employee should not be shorted pay, overworked, or mercilessly punished. God's great laws of mercy, humanity, and compassion should be enforced by civil law and public opinion. Working to enable the fortunate time when divine law is universally understood and obeyed is as patriotic as a soldier fighting on the front lines for his country. A Mason struggles against censure, discredit, immorality, and evil conduct.

Fortitude and toughness are not reserved for war, but one can practice them at great difficulties and against vicious assailants. People who battle cruelty, oppression, and abuse fight for a country's honor. Honor is as important as existence. The fight against disgraceful abuses within one's country is as hazardous as, but more discouraging than, the fight against enemies on a battlefield. It deserves equal, if not greater, reward.

The ancient Greeks and Romans used the virtuous love of liberty in defeating their tyrants. This virtue prompted them to seize the sword, and it provided them the strength to use it. With skill, they accomplished their task amid the public cries of praise and joy. They did not attempt an action of such danger with doubtful purpose. As evidence of their dedication to this glorious virtue, they were rewarded with laurel wreaths and their memories were engraved for timeless fame by their countrymen.

Those who fight the abuses of old laws may not receive such laurels. Denouncing acts of ancient, superstitious cruelty on humanity may not promote one to fame among the populace. Rigorous work against all perpetrators of all wrongs could be received with suspicion rather than glory. Reward will be scarce when one assails the abuses and violations of the established order. The Mason will overcome and emerge victorious even when contending with long-held opinions, superstitions, prejudices, and fears among men. If a Mason tries, but fails, against the mighty body of prejudice and passion, his elevated virtue will still merit fame just as in battle, the front-line may fall despite eventual victory by the army.

If his country turns to ruin, he has lived too long. There is no joy in life after such an event, and man does not need to live. Similarly, the purpose of life is lost if one can be content amid the abuse, disgrace, cruelty, dishonor, misery, destitution, brutalization, meanness, or revenge that make his country a pariah among generous nations. Life is worthless if one does strive to prevent or remedy these problems.

It is not often that a country is at war, and not everyone can have the privilege of offering his life in the country's defense. However, in the patriotic labors of preventing, remedying, and reforming evils, oppressions, wrongs, cruelties, and outrages every Mason can unite against them. Everyone can affect something, and share in the honor and glory of its result.

The famous names throughout history are few and easily counted. But there are nameless millions who spend their time planning and preparing for humanity's final destiny. They gather and amass the kindling that will light and warm us when the spark from heaven descends. Numberless are the settlers, pioneers, engineers, and artisans who attend the march of intellect and humanity. Many of them advance to pave the way for those who follow. They clear the obstacles to progress and earn their reward. When they diligently and faithfully pursue their calling, they will enjoy the calm happiness resulting from hard work. The sweat of their brows will improve humanity, and it will ease the path for those that follow. When human victory is finally achieved, they will deserve a share of the glory, just as the bravest soldiers who fought at Marathon, Tours, Gettysburg, Ain Jaloot, Waterloo, Catalaunian, Stalingrad, Normandy, and Midway. If he falls in life but not in spirit, he will be counted as a representative of all the brother-heroes. Within his family, he will be honored, and that is the closest affirmation of an approving conscience from someone else we can earn. If he fell in the fight, and his place at the dinner table is vacant, that place will become sacred. He will be often spoken of at home during those long winter evenings, and his family will be considered fortunate to have produced such a hero.

Life's greatness is not measured by hours and days, but by what we have done for our country and countrymen. A useless life is short, even if it lasts a century. The life of Alexander was as long as that of the oak tree, though he died at thirty-two. You can do a lot in a few years, or you can do nothing over a *159* lifetime. If you only exist to gain wealth, offices, or titles, you have not lived at all. You would have no right to expect immortality. You must participate in work towards progress all around you.

Therefore, remember what this Degree charges you to do. Defend the weak against the strong, the unpopular against the mob, and the oppressed against the oppressor! Always be vigilant and mindful of the interests and honor of your country! May the Grand Architect of the Universe give you strength and wisdom to enable you to perform these duties well and faithfully!

CHAPTER 10: ILLUSTRIOUS ELECT (ELU) OF THE FIFTEEN

THIS Degree is devoted to the same causes as the Elu of Nine. 160
Additionally, it is dedicated to the causes of Toleration and Generosity against
political and religious Fanaticism and Persecution. It is also dedicated to the
causes of Education and Enlightenment over Incivility and Ignorance. You have
forever devoted your hand, heart, and intellect to these ideas.

Toleration is the understanding that everyone has an equal right to their
opinion and faith. Generosity lies in knowing that no single human can be
certain of truth or be *surely* in possession of truth. In the conflict of opposing
faiths, everyone should feel that the opposing opinion, being equally honest and
sincere, could also contain truth. Whatever one firmly and conscientiously
believes is truth to *him*. Toleration and generosity teach understanding that is the
mortal enemy of fanaticism. Fanaticism persecutes and crusades against
opinions it imagines to be contrary to the law of God or deems contrary to its
own principles and dogma. Education and enlightenment are the most powerful
means to render fanaticism and intolerance powerless.

A true Mason does not belittle the honest convictions and ardent zeal
toward what someone else believes to be truth and justice. A Mason will deny 161
the right of any man to condemn another's faith or opinion as heretical and
punishable. Only Deity can exercise that privilege. A Mason does not support
actions that endanger the peace of great nations. He does not approve of those
who serve their own selfish interest by sponsoring philanthropy in order to avoid
contact with others or labor while proclaiming themselves holier than others for
their actions.

A Mason knows that such follies can be more disastrous than the
ambitions of kings. Intolerance and bigotry are infinitely greater curses to
mankind than ignorance and error. Error is better than persecution! Any
opinion is better than torture! It is absurd for a person surrounded by vast
mysteries to torture and kill others simply because they do not hold the same
opinions regarding the most profound of those mysteries. Persecution is absurd
when it quarrels over the interpretations of what is really beyond the
comprehension of anyone, persecutor or persecuted.

Masonry is not a religion. Anyone who makes it a religion falsifies and deprives it of its proper nature. The Hindu, Jew, Muslim, Catholic, and Protestant each profess their particular religion. Over time and through the law, they work to promote and retain their beliefs despite other religions. The social and religious laws adapted to the practices, manners, and prejudices of particular countries are the work of men.

Masonry teaches in its preserved purity the primary doctrine of the old primitive faith, which is the foundation of all religions. All that ever existed have a foundation of truth and are overlaid with human errors. The primary truths were quickly corrupted and combined with fictional stories and these were taught to the first followers. Masonry is the universal morality. It is suitable to all inhabitants of the earth and to men of all creeds. It has taught nothing less than the truths that safeguard the well-being of humanity. Those who attempt to label it for their vengeance, political ends, and missionary pursuits, only pervert its goodness for their own selfish purposes.

Humanity passed the era of sacrifices and mythology, which became identified with its early years on this world. Still, we find that it is easy for humans to retain these superstitions than to pass further in development. If we view human nature like the unadventurous Nomadic Tartar who wants to keep his flock on the same close-cropped land through life, we see Masons as the progressive men who roam onward "to fresh fields and new pastures."

The progressive man is the true Mason. The best Mason does the work of life with the power of business. The life of the upright worker, professional, merchant, or farmer working with the powers of thought, justice, and love is a great performance of Masonic duty. The regular use of strength by a strong man or wisdom by a wise man is the *work* of the strong or the wise. The regular work of Masonry is living a practical life, using all power in its proper arena and for its proper function. The divine attributes of Truth, Justice, and Generosity will manifest in a life defined by these qualities. This is the effective rule of Masonry. A declaration of one's beliefs, joining the Order, assuming the obligations, and assisting in the ceremonies are all of value in Masonry. However, the natural form of Masonry is goodness and morality living a true, just, affectionate, and faithful life motivated as a good man. It is loyal obedience to God's law.

The good Mason always does the right thing from a love of duty and not simply because a law commands him to do it. By being true to his mind, conscience, heart, and soul, he will feel little temptation to do to others what he would not want done to him. He will deny himself for the benefit of his brother. His *desire* to do right as part of his duty attracts those who are needy to him, with both ultimately benefiting. The poor or oppressed do not look to him in vain. You find such men in all the great religions of the civilized world. Among the Buddhists, Protestants, Hindus, Catholics, Muslims, Jews, and many others are kind fathers and generous citizens, unimpeachable in their business and wondrous in their daily lives. You see their Masonry in their work and in their recreation. It appears in all the forms of their individual, domestic, social, religious, or political activities. True Masonry internally is morality externally. The action follows the thought. *Eminent*, lofty morality becomes philanthropy. The true Mason not only loves his family and country, but all humanity. He counts the good and the evil among his brothers. He has more goodness than his daily life can hold. Goodness from him nourishes thousands around him. When he is not busy with the duties that lie along his path, he will seek them out. He is not only *willing*, he has a *longing* to do good, to spread truth, justice, generosity, and Masonry over all the world. His daily life is an expression of his Masonry, given as perpetual goodwill to all men.

    The true Mason lives this outward life as naturally as the beaver builds or the mockingbird sings. From the perennial spring, the stream swells, nourishing the meadow for new greenery, and bursting perfect beauty into bloom. Masonry does the work it was meant to do. The Mason does not sigh, weep, or grimace. He lives right on. When he finds his life marked with error and sin, he plows the barren spot with remorse, sows it with new seed, and the old dirt springs forth new life. Established forms of thought, action, or feeling do not confine him. He accepts what his mind regards as true, what his conscience decides is right, and what his heart deems generous and noble. He disregards all else. Even if the ancient and honorable of the Earth request he bow to them, he stubbornly bends only at the bidding of his dignified soul. Masonry is not a bondage to men but a freedom before God. His mind acts on the universal law of intellect, his conscience reacts to the moral law, and his affections and soul act upon their respective laws. God strengthens him and communicates with him through mind, conscience, affection, and soul.

    The old philosophies of religion from ancient times do not suffice now. The duties of life are to be done, and we are to do them with a conscious obedience to the law of God and not our own loving, selfish gain. Sins of trade need correction. Morality and philanthropy are needed everywhere. Errors need eradication so we can replace them with new truths, radiant with the glories of Heaven. The great wrongs and evils in Church, State, domestic, social, and public life need to be corrected and outgrown. Masonry cannot forsake public dialogue throughout life. It must journey in the open, appear before crowds, and teach men by deeds, for life by example is more eloquent than statements.

    This Degree is primarily devoted to TOLERATION. It emphatically promotes the leading ideas of this Ancient Art. A belief in one True God and a moral and virtuous life constitute the only religious requisite needed to enable a man to be a Mason.

    Masonry remembers the terrible tortures used to subdue new religions and extinguish old ones. It remembers the wars against people of all sexes and ages by the troops of Moses and Joshua, because they did not fear the God of the Hebrews. It remembers those persecuted, tortured, and killed for worshiping a God with the wrong name. It remembers how the thumbscrew, rack, whip, gallows, and the stake were used on the Covenanters, Non-Conformists, Cathars, Quakers, Jews, and a vast array of others. There were many victims of the ruthless persecutors from Roman Emperor Diocletian, General Alva, the Inquisitors, Crusaders, and Fundamentalists. It remembers Archbishop Cranmer of Canterbury holding his arm in the fire until his hand dropped off in the fire as a sign that he no longer was in error. It sees the persecution of Peter and Paul, the martyrdom of Stephen, and the trials of Ignatius, Polycarp, Justin, and Irenaeus. It remembers the suffering of the Pagans under the Catholic Emperors. It remembers the suffering of the Catholics of Ireland under English rulers Elizabeth and Henry. It remembers the Roman Virgins placed naked before the hungry lions. It remembers the ordeal of young Margaret Graham who was tied to a stake at low-water mark and left to drown, who sang hymns to God until the waters swallowed her head. Masonry remembers everyone from all ages who suffered from hunger, nakedness, peril, prison, the rack, the stake, and the sword. It remembers all of them, and it shudders at the list of human atrocities throughout history. Oppression is still practiced in the name of religion. Men are murdered because of religious intolerance. In almost every religious State, there are laws that forbid freedom of speech on matters regarding religion. Too often, the gallows reach from the pulpit.

There are many examples that warn man of the evils that originate from religion. There were the sacrificial fires to Moloch in Canaan and Syria. There were the wars in the name of Astarte, Cybele, and Jehovah through Asia Minor. There were the cruelties of the Imperial Pagan Torturers. There were the unspeakable torments from the Inquisitions from Italy to Spain. There were the atrocities upon the victims of the Crusades and the Arab Conquest. These were the atrocities instigated by religious groups. There are many horrors committed against religion from secular entities as with the Holocaust. There were fiendish cruelties to which Switzerland, France, the Netherlands, England, Scotland, Ireland, Germany, America, and all nations have been witnesses or participants. Never have these nations been powerful enough to learn and deter these mistakes and errors from future generations. The evidence rests with how man continues to remember and describe God as having cruel and vindictive actions toward the erring humans. These descriptions bestowed on Deity by man demonstrate man's tendency to revert to violence and oppression.

Man does not have the right to claim the unexercised power of God. Man cannot condemn and punish others for his own beliefs. If born in a Protestant land, we are of that faith. If we had been born in the shadows of St. Peter's Cathedral in Rome, we would have been Catholic. If we were born in Jerusalem, we would simply believe in God and humanity. If our first breaths were in Istanbul, we would state, "*Allah il Allah*, God is great and Mohammed is his prophet!" Birthplace and education determine our faith. Few people practice a religion because they have studied its convictions, verified its authenticity, and made an educated and informed judgment after weighing other faiths first. Only one person in ten thousand will know anything about the *proofs* of their faith. People believe what they are taught. The most fanatical also know the least about the evidences on which their creed is founded. With rare exception, facts and testimony are not the groundwork of faith. It is an unavoidable principle of mankind that men will accept the beliefs of those among whom he is born and reared without question. His faith resists all evidences to the contrary. He will disbelieve even his own senses when they provide contrary input rather than yield the religious beliefs he grew up knowing.

What is truth to *me* is not truth to *another*. The same arguments and evidences that convince one mind make no impression on another. The differences in men start at birth. No man is entitled to assert that he is right when other men of equal intelligence hold the opposite opinion. Each person will think it impossible for the other to be sincere in his or her conviction. Ironically, each is equally in error. *"What is truth?"* is a profound question. It is the most suggestive one ever asked. Many beliefs from ancient and present times seem incomprehensible. They startle us with a new glimpse into the human soul. It is a mysterious thing that becomes more mysterious as we witness its workings. Take for example a man who is superior in intellect and learning, but he believes something so absurd that there would be no merit in a scientific proof to invalidate his statements. One cannot conceive and sincerely believe he is both sane and honest. *And yet he is both.* His reasoning is as perfect and honest as any other.

The imaginations of a lunatic are realities *to him.* Our dreams are realities *while they last*, and the memories are equivalent with those from our time awake. No man can say that *he* has as clear possession of the truth as surely as an object. When men hear multiple opinions that are diametrically opposed to each other, who decides which is the Truth? How can either side say with certainty that they have it? We do not know what the truth is. The fact that we believe and feel certain in our own belief is not proof of the truth. Even what seems to be fact to us is still capable of doubt. Man cannot be accountable for the rightness of his faith, only for the *up*rightness of it.

This is why man does not have the right to persecute another for his belief. If one man can persecute another because he is certain that the other's belief is erroneous, the other man has similar, equal rights to persecute the first.

The truth is tainted with our prejudices and preconceptions. Truth comes to us bent and distorted like the image of a rod through water. An argument convinces the mind of one man, but rebounds like a ping-pong ball from another's mind. It is of no benefit to have a particular excellent, sound, and philosophic faith, if one cannot separate it from prejudice and passion.

Masonry wisely requires no more than a belief in One Great All-Powerful Deity, the Father and Preserver of the Universe. It teaches adherents that toleration is one of the prime duties of every good Mason. It is a component of charity, without which we are mere hollow images of true Masons.

166

No evil has afflicted the world as much as the intolerance of religious opinion. If all the people slain by persecution were brought to life they would make a great nation. If they were not murdered their offspring could have provided great advancement in civilization and enlightenment to the world. But it is primarily among these civilized nations these religious wars have been waged. The money and the human labor lost to these wars could have made the earth a beautiful garden. If man could put away his evil passions, we can still grow this garden of humanity, and all would be as happy as in Eden.

No man truly obeys Masonic law by merely tolerating those whose religious opinions are opposed to his own. Every man's opinions are his own private possession. All men are equally entitled to keep their opinions. *Merely tolerating* an opposing opinion is assuming it is wrong. This attitude claims the *right* to persecute silently and holds our *toleration* as a virtue. The Mason's creed maintains that no man has any right (in any way) to interfere with the religious beliefs of another. It holds that each man is independent and rules his own belief. It implies that one person's belief is a matter separate from everyone who does not entertain the same belief. If there were a right to persecution at all, it would be a mutual right in all cases. One party would have the same right as the other to sit as judge over each other's case. Truly, God is the only judge who can rightfully decide between them. Masonry defers the matter to that great Judge. It opens its doors wide and invites all to enter and live in peace and harmony. Any man from every religion is invited if he will lead a virtuous and moral life, love his brother, help the sick and distressed, and believe in the ONE, *All-Powerful, All-Wise, everywhere-Present* GOD, *Architect, Creator, and Preserver of all things.* True Masons pay a most profound homage to the belief in His universal law of Harmony, the vast, infinite circle of Life and Death, and the INEFFABLE NAME! For His thousands of blessings pour on us, let us feel the sincerest gratitude now and forever!

We should be tolerant of each other's creed, because in every faith there are excellent moral principles. In the South of Asia, Zoroaster taught the following lessons; "On beginning a journey, the Faithful should turn his thoughts toward Ormuzd (the supreme deity) and profess with purity of heart, that He is the King of the World; he should love Him, pay homage to Him, and serve Him. He must be upright and charitable, despise the pleasures of the body, avoid pride, arrogance, vice, and falsehood as the worst sins of which man can be guilty. He must forget injustice and not avenge himself. He must honor the memory of his parents and relatives. At night, before going to sleep, he should examine his conscience, and repent of the faults which weakness or ill-fortune had caused him to commit." A man was required to pray for strength to maintain the Good and obtain forgiveness for his errors. It was his duty to confess his faults to a Magus (wise priest), a virtuous layman, or the Sun. Fasting and starvation were prohibited and it was his duty to nourish the body and to maintain its vigor so that his soul would have strength to resist the Genius of

Darkness. He needed to be strong that he might attentively read the Divine Word and have the courage to perform noble deeds.

In Northern Europe, the Druids taught devotion to friends, tolerance for wrongs, love of deserved praise, prudence, discretion, humanity, hospitality, respect elders, disregard for the unseen future, temperance, contempt of death, and a chivalrous devotion to women. Listen to the following principles from the Hava Maal (Sublime Book of Odin).

"If you have a friend, visit him often. The path will grow over with grass, and the trees will soon cover it if you do not constantly walk upon it. He is a faithful friend who, having but two loaves, gives one to his friend. Never be the first to end a friendship as sorrow devastates the heart of those who have no one but himself to talk with. A virtuous man will have some vice, and a bad man will have some virtue. Happy is the person who obtains the praise and goodwill of men, because what depends on the will of others is hazardous and uncertain. Riches disappear in the blink of an eye, and they are the most inconstant of friends. Flocks and herds perish, parents die, friends are mortal, you yourself will die but the one thing that cannot die is the judgment passed on the dead. Be humane toward those you meet on the road. If the guest that comes to your house is cold, give him warmth. If a man needs food and dry clothes, provide them to him. Do not mock the elderly, for sensible words often come from the wrinkles of age. Be moderately wise but not overly judicious. Let no one desire to know his fate if he could sleep tranquilly without it. There is no crueler disease than for one to be upset with our lot in life. The glutton eats himself to death. The wise man laughs at the fool's greediness. Nothing is more harmful to the young than excessive drinking. The more one drinks the more they lose their *169* reason. The bird of forgetfulness sings to those who intoxicate and waste away their souls. Devoid of sense, man believes he will live forever if he avoids confrontation and danger. Nevertheless, if the swords and arrows spare him, old age will provide no sanctuary. It is better to live well than to live long. When a man sparks the fire in his house, death will come before it goes out."

The Hindu books provide many similar principles. "Honor your father and mother. Never forget the benefits you receive. Learn while you are young. Submit to the laws of your country. Seek the company of virtuous men. Only speak of God with respect. Live on good terms with your neighbors. Remain in your proper place. Speak ill of no one. Do not mock anyone's bodily infirmities. Relent when you pursue a conquered enemy. Strive to acquire a good reputation. Take counsel with wise men. The more one learns, the more he acquires the ability to learn. Knowledge is the most permanent wealth. Do not favor ignorance. The true use of knowledge is to distinguish good from evil. Do not shame your parents. What one learns in youth, endures like an engraving in rock. He that is wise knows himself. Let books be your best friends. When you turn one hundred years-old, you can finally cease with your duty to learn. Deceive no one, not even your enemy. Wisdom is a treasure that maintains its value everywhere. Speak pleasantly, even to the poor. It is better to forgive than to take vengeance. Gaming and fighting lead to misery. There is no true worth without the practice of virtue. To honor our mother is the most fitting homage we can pay the Divinity. There is no peaceful sleep without a clear conscience. He who breaks his own word poorly understands his own interest."

Twenty-five centuries ago, the following Chinese Ethics were shared:

"Confucius said, 'SAN! My doctrine is simple, and easy to be understood.' THSENG-TSEU replied, 'That is certain.' Confucius left and the disciples asked what their master meant. THSENG-TSEU responded, 'The doctrine of our Master consists solely in being upright of heart, and loving our neighbor as we love ourselves.'"

A century later the Hebrew law said, "If any man hates his neighbor . . . then shall you do to him, as he had thought to do to his neighbor . . . Better is a neighbor that is near, than a brother far off . . . You shall love your neighbor as yourself."

At the same time, SOCRATES said, "You shall love your neighbor as yourself."

Three generations earlier, ZOROASTER had said to the Persians: "Offer up your grateful prayers to the Lord, the most just and pure Ormuzd, the supreme and adorable God who declared to his Prophet Zardusht: 'Do not do to others what you would not desire done to yourself. Do to the people what is agreeable to be done to you.'"

The same doctrine was taught in the schools of Babylon, Alexandria, and Jerusalem. A Pagan declared to Rabbi HILLEL that he was ready to embrace the Jewish religion if he could summarize back to him the whole law of Moses while standing on one foot. Hillel replied, "That which is hateful to you, don't do to your neighbor. This is the whole of the law. The rest is commentary – go and learn it."

CONFUCIUS said, "Nothing is more natural, simpler than the principles of morality which I endeavor, using helpful maxims, to teach to you . . . It is humanity, which is that universal charity among all humans without distinction. It is uprightness, which is correctness of spirit and heart, that makes one search for truth in everything and desire it without deceiving oneself or others. Finally, it is sincerity or good faith which is that frankness and openness of heart, tempered by self-reliance that excludes all deception and disguising in speech and in action."

The mission of Masonry is to be the forerunner of moral improvement, spreading useful information and furthering intellectual refinement. Education will hasten the day when knowledge will chase away ignorance and error, even from the base of the great social pyramid. This is a high calling of splendid talents and perfect virtues. Masonry should send forth those whose genius, and not their ancestry, elevate them. They will open the temple of science to all. Their own example makes the humblest men eager to climb steps that are no longer inaccessible, so that they too can enter the open gates of knowledge burning in the sun.

The highest intellectual pursuits are perfectly compatible with the daily *171* chores of the workingmen. A keen enjoyment for the high truths of science belongs equally to every portion of mankind. As philosophy was taught under the Portico, in the sacred groves of Athens, and in the old Temples of Egypt and India, so should Knowledge be dispensed and the Sciences taught in our Lodges. Its Lectures become like the teachings of Socrates, Plato, Agassiz, and Cousin.

Real knowledge does not permit trouble or disbelief. Its progress is the forbearer of generosity and enlightened toleration. Anyone who fears these ideals may be assured that they come to dispel the evils of tyranny and persecution that haunted the dark but are now gone from the sky. Hopefully, the time will soon come when men will not be ignorant and yield to the vile principles of judging and mistreating their fellow-creatures based on subjective opinions and prejudice, instead of the merit of their actions.

When we respect those who conscientiously differ from ourselves, we can effectively enlighten ignorance from our side and the other. With education and debate, we affect the only kind of unanimity that may be desirably produced among rational thinkers, that coming from earnest conviction after the free discussion.

Therefore, the Elu of the Fifteen should lead his fellow-citizens. He should not lead in frivolous amusements or in degrading pursuits. He should lead the noble task of enlightening his countrymen. He should leave his name highlighted by the honors most worthy of our rational nature and not with crude fame or splendid objects of uselessness. His name should be associated with the spread of knowledge, wisdom, and acts of kindness. He should be gratefully remembered by at least a few whom his actions have rescued from ignorance and vice.

In the words of the great Roman we say, "Men closely approach the Deity when they confer benefits on men. To serve and do good to as many people as possible is the greatest fortune of all, and there is nothing finer in your *172* nature than the desire to do this." This is the goal for every man and Mason who prizes the enjoyment of happiness or sets a value upon a spotless reputation. If mankind shall enjoy the privilege of viewing the legacy and effects of its mortal efforts, charities, toils, and sufferings after its time, it will be the moral benefactors who will enjoy this reflection. The benefactors of humanity will be in a state of exalted purity and wisdom. They will enjoy and delight in triumph by tracing the remote effects of their enlightened benevolence through the improved condition of humanity. On reflection, they will be happy with the changes they see, even if they contributed in a small degree. Knowledge becomes Power. Virtue shares the Empire. Superstition is dethroned. Tyranny exiled. Real Humanity is achieved.

Looking back, the ungratified will be the founders of dynasties, the conquerors of empires, the Caesars, Alexanders, and Tamerlanes, the Kings, Councilors, Presidents, and Senators. They will have nothing to revere, because they primarily lived for their party and for their country incidentally by frequently sacrificing the good of the citizens for their own aggrandizement. These people will only be left with the monuments to their inglorious fame.

Masonry requires nothing impossible of its initiates and adherents. It does not demand them to climb to lofty and sublime peaks of a theoretical and unpractical virtue. These ideals are as high, cold, remote, and inaccessible as the eternal snows that blanket the shoulders of the Himalayan Mountains. It asks only what is easy. It overtasks no one's strength. It asks no one to go beyond his means and capacity. It does not expect one whose profession provides little more than the necessities for himself and his family, or whose time is occupied with his usual vocation, to neglect the business by which he and his family live. It does not request that he devote himself and his means to the diffusion of knowledge among men. It does not require him to publish books for the people. It does not request that he lecture, found academies and colleges, or build libraries to the ruin of his private affairs.

Masonry does require and expect every man to do something within and according to his means. There is no Mason who *cannot* do *some*thing at the very least work in association with others.

If a Lodge cannot aid in the founding of a school or an academy, it can still do something. It can educate one boy or girl, or at the very least the child of some poor or departed brother. It should never be forgotten that the poorest forgotten child that seems abandoned to ignorance and vice may hold the untapped wisdom and virtue of a Socrates, the intellect of a Bacon or Einstein, the genius of a Shakespeare, or the capacity to benefit mankind of a Washington. By rescuing this child from the darkness in which he exists and giving him the means to education and development, the Lodge may confer upon the world as great a gift as that given by Johann Fust and Johannes Gutenberg with the printing press. It may perpetuate the liberties of a country, change the destinies of nations, or write a new chapter in the history of the world.

We never know the total importance of the acts we perform. The daughter of the Pharaoh thought little of what she was doing for the human race, or the unimaginable consequences that depended on her charitable act, when she drew the little child of a Hebrew woman from among the reeds that grew along the bank of the Nile and determined to rear it as if it were her own.

How often has an act of charity, costing the doer little, given the world a great painter, musician, or inventor?! How often has such an act developed the ragged boy into the benefactor of his race?! What small and apparently unimportant circumstances have hinged on the fates of the world's great conquerors? There is no law that limits the reward obtained from a single good deed. The widow's penny may be as acceptable to God and produce as great

173

results as a rich man's expensive offering. The poorest boy, helped by charity, may come to lead armies, control senates, decide peace and war, or dictate to cabinets. His magnificent thoughts and noble words may become law many years hereafter to millions of people yet unborn. 174

The opportunity to provide significant good does not occur often. It is foolish for someone to be idle and expect grace to influence his legacy for future generations. However, he may hope for a legacy through his many actions in life. He can expect to benefit the world as men attain any result: through continuance, persistence, steadiness, and uniform habit of work. He must labor for the enlightenment of the world.

It is always through steady labor, dedication to work, time management, and constant diligence that we secure the strength of real excellence and not by any process of trickery. Demosthenes built his immortal speeches clause by clause and sentence by sentence. Newton pioneered his methods using the steps of an ascending geometry to define the Heavens. It was also how Le Verrier added a planet to our Solar System.

It is wrong to believe that those who left behind the most incredible monuments of intellect were different only because of their talent. Their hard work is hardly remembered or noted. They were no different from the rest of humanity. In truth, they owe their glory to the tireless application of these everyday talents that are infused among us all. We now highlight and remember the names of these glories.

Do not belittle genius. It is lit by a direct inspiration from Heaven. We should not overlook the steadfastness of purpose, the devotion to a single object or the labor given. It is not from a great leap of thought, but built bit by bit as the strength of the mind may bear it. The accumulation of many small efforts (instead of a few large ones), combined with inspired movements, create the marvelous. From this combination, great results are achieved that write the enduring records in history, on the face of the earth, and on man.

We must not overlook the elements which genius owes to her 175 achievements. We must acknowledge qualities such as patience, effort, resolve, and industry that have a share in supporting a distinct and illustrious benefactor among humanity.

We must not forget that great results are usually produced by a combination of many contributions. The invisible molecules of water vapor, each separate and distinct from the other, rise from the oceans, bays, gulfs, lakes, rivers, swamps, and flooded plains to become the clouds. These fall as dew, showers, rain, and snow upon the Earth's broad plains and jagged mountains to make the great waterways that serve as the life-blood of a country.

Masonry can do great things if each Mason is content to do his share and unites his efforts through wise counsel towards a common purpose. "It is for God, as the Omnipotent, to do mighty things in a moment, but growth to greatness by degrees is the course that He has left for man."

If Masonry will be true to its mission and Masons are true to their obligations, then great results will be attained. Together, Masons and Masonry should earnestly and without fail pursue a career of charity. Remember that our contributions to the cause of charity and education earn the greatest credit when it costs something. Great work will be accomplished when charity requires us to give up a comfort or forego a luxury. If we steadily and regularly give aid to Masonry's great ideas for human improvement always, then we may be sure that great Masonic results will be attained and a great Masonic work will be done. Then, Masonry will not be seen as degenerate, unable, or in decay.

CHAPTER 11: SUBLIME ELECT (ELU) OF THE TWELVE OR PRINCE AMETH

THE duties of a Prince Ameth are to be earnest, true, reliable, and 176 sincere. He is to protect the people against illegal demands and extortion. He is to struggle for their political rights. He is to see that those who receive the benefits of Government bear the burdens of it.

You are to be true to all men.

You are to be frank and sincere in all things.

You are to be purposeful in doing your duty.

No one should regret that he or she relied on your commitment, your promise, or your work.

The greatest distinguishing characteristic of a Mason is sympathy for others. He understands that the human race is one great family. This surrounding family connects with him by unseen links through a network of circumstance, woven by God.

Feeling this sympathy, his first Masonic duty is to serve others. During his first entrance into the Order, he ceases to be isolated and becomes one member of a great brotherhood. He assumes new duties toward every Mason that lives, and all Masons at the same moment assume duties toward him.

These duties are not confined to Masons. He assumes many duties toward his country and the suffering masses. They are all his brothers, and God hears them no matter how muffled their misery may be. By all proper means of persuasion, influence, and effort he is bound to defend them against oppression, 177 extortion, and tyranny when occasion requires.

He labors equally to defend and improve people. He does not flatter to mislead them, placate to rule them, lie to humor them, declare they can never err, or declare that their voice is the voice of God. He knows the safety, continuance, and longevity of every free government depends upon the virtue and intelligence of the people. Weapons and force cannot take liberty away when people have acquired it through institution, courage, justice, temperance, and virtue, and when it has taken root in the hearts and mind of the people. Those who would take it from them by treachery will face impossible odds.

A Mason knows that if people neglect the art of peace, once released from the toils of war, they will find their interests are steered by the military industrial complex. If the peace and liberty of a nation are defended by a perpetual state of war, and it sees virtue and praise in war, it will find peace adverse to its interest. The state of war will become more distressing, and their imagined liberty will be the worst of slaveries. Unless people use genuine knowledge and sincere morality to clear their mind from error, ignorance, passion, and vice, there will always be those who submit to the chains of war. Despite all of man's triumphs, wartime and its aftermath will be opportunities for the extortion of wealth and power from the people by playing to their ignorance, prejudices, and passions.

The nation that does not limit the inclination of its wealthy to wallow in greed, ambition, and pleasure will deny any luxuries for the people of future generations. The nation that does not work to reduce poverty, teach the poor, help the weakest avoid sin and vice, or ensure the industrious workers don't starve will find that it has encouraged more uncontrolled tyranny domestically than it ever could encounter abroad. The children of these tyrants of greed will continue to corrupt the county if left to their own devices. Those with power acquired through greed, ambition, sensuality, selfishness, and luxury of their class or position will always promote the degradation, misery, drunkenness, ignorance, and brutalization of the masses for the continuation of their own of security and benefit.

These are the first enemies to be subdued. This constitutes the campaign of Peace. These bloodless triumphs, though difficult, are more honorable than the trophies earned by slaughter and plunder. If a nation is not successful with this at home, it achieves nothing to be victorious over the enemies in the field.

A nation will only hasten its own ruin if it believes that it is better to raise taxes, to increase revenues, and drain the life-blood of its people in order to increase its stature and prowess internationally. When the priority of a nation's power and mighty forces are focused on rivaling foreign nations, swallowing foreign territory, making deceitful treaties and alliances, ruling weaker states, and policing hopeless provinces with fear and force, it has appropriated its goodwill and surpluses to the wrong endeavors. It should seek to administer true and unbiased justice for its own people. If a nation does not strive to relieve and raise the condition of its workforce, tend to the injured, aid the distressed, settle the unsatisfied, and restore to everyone their own, then that nation and those people are not serving their own basic needs, and the nation is out of equilibrium. The people will realize too late that neglecting these basic functions of government has only precipitated despair and ruin. Grand designs and mighty benefits cannot come before basic services for the people. These mighty sounding benefits will distract attention from the simple and necessary considerations.

Every age presents its own special, difficult, and near impossible problem to solve. This age presents for consideration to all thinking men its own question. How can a populous and wealthy country, blessed with free institutions and a constitutional government, enable the masses to have steady work at fair wages, eliminate starvation, protect its children, access and learn real *knowledge*, equip them to keep their moral duties, exercise the privileges of freemen, and entrust them with the important and yet dangerous right to vote?

Even in richest and most civilized countries, the citizens are fortunate if they have been able to feed, clothe, and shelter themselves and their families throughout their lives. We cannot fully explain why this is. God, being infinitely merciful and wise, has ordered it among all nations, and therefore it seems to be His unquestionable law.

He seems to have enacted His law, and no community has found a   *179* means to abolish it yet. When a country becomes populous, wealth will concentrate in the hands of the few, and all others are more and more at their mercy. Eventually, the work of laborers and artisans ceases to be worth much, if anything. The masses crawl about in rags, starving and begging for work.

While every ox and horse that has worth and can work is fed, man is not always treated as well. The pursuit of employment and fair wages becomes the great focus of a man's life. The employer can survive without the employee and discharge him whenever that labor ceases to be profitable. The moment that the weather is most stormy, food scarcest, and rent highest, the employer will turn him out to starve. When the laborer is sick, his wages stop. He will have no pension provided for his retirement when old. His children cannot be sent to school. They must work, or else they too will starve. The strong and able-bodied man works for pennies a day. The mother shivers over a small fire when the temperatures freeze. Her hungry children cry themselves to sleep, and afterwards, she sews by the dim light. For mere living expenses, she exchanges her life for the work of her needle.

Among the poor and destitute nations, fathers and mothers slay their children to receive the death benefits so that, with the price of one child's life, they may continue the life of those that survive. Little girls with bare feet sweep the street-crossings when the winter wind forces them to beg piteously for pennies from those who wear warm furs. Children grow up in squalid misery and brutal ignorance. Want compels virgin and wife to prostitute their bodies. Women starve, freeze, and lack proper shelter night after night. Hundreds of families are crowded into tenements, shanties, and projects that are numerous with horrors and teeming with polluted air and disease. Men, women, and   *180* children huddle together in their filth. All ages sleep indiscriminately together. Even in a great and free Republic in its full vigor of youth and strength, too many people live below the poverty line and require charity.

How does a nation deal with this apparently inevitable, evil, and mortal disease? By far, poverty is the most important of all social problems. What can be done with too many laborers? How can any country last when brutality coerces, ignorance votes, and politicians only represent themselves and not the people? How can a nation survive if trouble and vice are elected to hold senate seats? Those villains reek with the odors of hell, the track, the brothel, and the gambling halls where vices are laudable. How can the country endure if wisdom and authority are not available?

Masonry will do all in its power, by direct labor or cooperation, to improve, instruct, inform, and protect the people. It will attempt to improve their physical condition, relieve their miseries, supply their wants, and minister to their necessities. Every Mason must do all that is in his power for this good work.

It always was, is, and will be true that to be free is the same as to be devoted, wise, just, restrained, frugal, un-indulgent, noble, and brave. To be the opposite of these is to be a slave. As usually happens, through appointment and retributive justice of the Deity, people who cannot moderate their passions, and are slaves to their lusts and vices, find themselves under the rule of those they hate and are made to submit in servitude. This is unjust.

Above all things, let us not forget that mankind is one great brotherhood. All are born to encounter suffering and sorrow and, therefore, bound to sympathize with each other.

No tower of Pride has ever been high enough to lift its owner above the trials, fears, and frailties of humanity. No human hand has nor ever will build the wall that will keep out affliction, pain, and infirmity. Sickness, sorrow, trouble, and death are rules that level everything. They do not discriminate between rich and poor. The primary desires of life and the great necessities of the soul give immunity to no one. They make all poor and weak. They put prayers in the mouth of every human being as truly as a beggar begs.

The principle of misery is not evil. To err is human, and the consequences provide us wisdom. All elements and all laws of things around us lead to this end. Though paths may be painful and full of error and mistakes, this is the design of Providence. It leads us to truth and happiness. If erring only taught us to err, if mistakes affirmed our rashness, if misery by indulgence made us hopeless slaves to vice, then suffering would be truly evil. On the contrary, all of these are designed to encourage improvement in ourselves. Suffering is how virtue disciplines. Virtue is infinitely better than happiness, because it embraces all essential happiness. It nourishes, invigorates, and perfects happiness. Virtue is the prize of mankind's contested race and hard-fought battle. It is worth all the fatigue and wounds endured. Man should battle calamity with a brave and strong heart. He must master it and not let it become *his* master. He is not to abandon his post when trial and peril come, but stand firm until the great word of Providence instructs him to fly or sink. With resolution and courage, the Mason is to do the work that is appointed to him. He is to work towards that goal, which rises high and bright before him, even when facing a darkening cloud of human calamity. The portion of life assigned to sorrow is noble and high in purpose. None suffer forever and without purpose. It is the object of God's wisdom and His Infinite Love for us to obtain infinite happiness and glory.

True liberty lies in virtue. He who yields to passion is not free. He who is in bondage is not free, even with a noble master. Examples are the best and most lasting lectures, and virtue is the best example. He who has done good deeds and set good precedents with sincerity is happy. His worth shall outlive time. He whose good deeds are pillars of remembrance truly lives after death and adds to His glory. Good works are like seeds that return a continuing harvest to us. The memory of noble action is more enduring than monuments of marble.

Life is a school. The world is a place of instruction and discipline. It is *182* not a prison, penitentiary, palace, arena, or playground. Life provides us moral and spiritual training. The entire course of this great school of life is an education in virtue, happiness, and future existence. The moments of Life are its exams, and the human conditions are its grades. All our efforts are its lessons. Families are the main departments for moral education. The various circles of society are its secondary grades, while the Kingdoms and Republics are its universities.

Riches, Poverty, Laughter, Sorrow, Marriages, Funerals, the kept and broken promises of life, fitness, fortune, misfortune, and pain are all lessons. Events are not carelessly flung together. Providence does not school one man and protect another from lessons learned through trial-by-fire. It does not have rich favorites and poor victims. One event happens to all. One end and one design concern and drive all men.

The prosperous man is still at school. Perhaps he thought he was special and greatly important, but he has been a pupil all along. He perhaps thought he was a Master and had nothing more to do than direct and command. However, there is a Master above him, the Master of Life. *He* does not look at our appearance, claims, aids, or tools of learning, but at our learning itself. He puts the poor and the rich at the same level and measures only progress in learning as their differences.

In prosperity, if we learn moderation, restraint, impartiality, modesty, humbleness to God, and generosity to man, then we are entitled to be honored and rewarded. However, if we learn selfishness, self-indulgence, wrongdoing, vice, forgetting our less fortunate brothers and scoff at the Providence of God, then we are unworthy and dishonorable. The eyes of Heaven and all wise men see everyone equally, though some were reared in affluence and schooled as their noble ancestors were. They see us as though we had nothing before them. The simplest of human justice does not look at the school, but at the scholar. The law of Heaven will not look beneath that mark.

The poor man is at school too. Let him be sure that he learns, rather *183* than complaining. Let him hold onto his integrity, impartiality, and his kindness of heart. Let him be wary of envy and bondage to keep his self-respect. The body's labors are nothing. Let him beware of the mind's erosion and degradation. While he works to better his condition, let him be more eager to better his soul. While poor, let him always be willing to learn poverty's great lessons of emotional strength, cheerfulness, contentment, and unquestioned confidence in God's Providence. With these, as well as patience, calmness, self-control, equity in judgment, and affectionate kindness, the humble dwelling may be sacred and more dear than the grandest palace. Above all things, let him ensure that he does not lose his independence. If he is poorer than poor, let him not push himself as a lazy, helpless, despised beggar that preys upon the kindness of others. Every man should choose to have God as his Master rather than man. He should not attempt to escape from his school. Through dishonesty, he may fall into that condition, which is worse than disgrace, where he can have no respect for himself.

The ties of Society teach us to love one another. It is a miserable society when the absence of this affectionate kindness is replaced by formalities, decorum, graceful civility, politeness, and a polished insincerity. It is a miserable society indeed, when ambition, jealousy, and distrust rule in the place of simplicity, confidence, and kindness.

The good social state also teaches modesty and gentleness. We learn to be patient quiet, and better than society's opinion of us, but not cynical or bitter. We learn to be gentle, candid, and affectionate. These we learn from the neglect of the world, injustice, and the popularity of those who are immoral or unfit.

Death is the great Teacher. It is stern, cold, unyielding, and certain. The collected might of the world cannot overcome it. Life cannot be bought by King or acquired by beggar. It cannot be brought back for a moment, even with the wealth of all the Empires. This is a lesson for us. It teaches us that our frailty, our feebleness, and the Infinite Power are beyond us! It is a fearful lesson that never becomes accepted. It walks upon the earth in dreaded mystery and lays its cold hand upon all. It is a universal lesson that applies everywhere to all people. Its message comes every year and every day. The years past are crowded with its sad and solemn mementoes. Death's finger traces its handwriting on the walls of every home.

184   Death teaches us of the Duty to act our part well. It teaches us to fulfill the work we are assigned to us. When one is dying, and once dead, there is only one question: *Has he lived well?* In death, the only evil is what was made in life.

There are hard lessons in the school of God's Providence, yet the school of life has its lesson plan carefully arranged to man's powers and passions. There is no extravagance in its teachings. Nothing is done for the sake of today's effect. The whole course of human life is a conflict between troubles and difficulties, and when rightly conducted, its effect is progress and improvement. It is never too late for man to learn. All of life, not just a small part, is the school. Even when entering old age, there should not be a time when one should lay aside their eagerness to master the effort, or cheerfully apply oneself to it. Throughout life man walks in patience, strife, and sometimes in darkness. Patience brings perfection. Strife brings triumph. The storm clouds of darkness bring flashes of lightning that make visible the path to eternity.

Let the Mason be faithful in the school of life and all its lessons! Let him not fail to learn. Let him take care in ensuring what lessons are learned. Let him not age, and only show indifference and sloth. Do not let him be zealous in acquiring everything but virtue. Do not let him labor only for himself. Let him not forget that the humblest man that lives is his brother, and has a claim for his sympathies and kind duties. For beneath his rough garments may beat a heart as noble as the best of princes.

> God, who counts by souls, not stations,
>   Loves and pities you and me;
> For to Him all vain distinctions
>   Are as pebbles on the sea.

The other duties taught in this degree are no less important. A Mason is told that Truth is a Divine attribute and the foundation of every virtue. Frankness, reliability, sincerity, straightforwardness, and plain dealing are but different modes in which Truth manifests itself. No Mason will willingly deceive anyone, even if dead, absent, innocent, or entrusted to him. He owes noble justice to all, for they are the most certain tests of human equity. Cicero claimed that only the most forgotten of men would deceive him, and he would have been uninjured if he had not been trusting. All the noble deeds through all the ages have come from men of truth and courage. The always-truthful man is also virtuous and wise. He possesses the greatest guards of safety, because the law does not have power to hurt the virtuous, nor does bad luck ruin the wise.

The basis of Masonry is morality and virtue. It is by studying one and practicing the other that the conduct of a Mason becomes irreproachable. The good of Humanity is its principal goal. Disinterestedness (selflessness) is one of the first virtues that it requires of its members because that is the source of justice and charity.

He will be passionate for the duties that virtue and society impose upon him. To be good he will pity the misfortunes of others. He will be humble without meanness. He will be proud without arrogance. He will renounce hatred and revenge, and he will be the enemy of vice. He will prove himself to be forgiving and tolerant without extravagance. He will revere wisdom and virtue. He will respect innocence. He will be persistent and patient in adversity and modest in prosperity. He will avoid every irregularity that stains the soul and infects the body. By following these actions, a Mason will become a good citizen, a faithful husband, a tender father, an obedient son, an honorable friend, and a true brother.

Masonry imposes these duties upon us, because it is proper and significant *work*. Anyone who imagines that he is a Mason by merely taking the first three Degrees is strangely deceived. He may wrongly believe that having leisurely stepped upon that small elevation without labor, exertion, self-denial, and sacrifice, that there is nothing more to be *done* in Masonry.

Is it true that nothing remains to be done in Masonry?

Do we no longer see one Brother sue another from his Lodge regarding matters that could be easily settled within the Masonic family circle?

Has hatred, banned between Brethren, disappeared from our sights? Do Masons of high rank refrain from it, or do they bow low, submit to it, and violate their obligation?

Do Masons still form uncharitable opinions of their Brethren, establish harsh judgments, and judge their own actions by a different rule than their Brethren?

Does Masonry do everything it can for charity? Has it done all it should for the cause of education?

Are political disputes conducted without violence and bitterness?

Do Masons not defame or denounce their Brethren who differ with them in religious or political opinions?

What grand social problems or useful projects do we engage in our discussions? Where in Lodge are lectures regularly delivered for the real instruction of the Brethren? Don't our meetings transpire with the discussion of minor matters of business, settlement of points of order, questions of mere administration, and the admission and advancement of Candidates, whom we then fail to instruct afterwards?

In what Lodge are our ceremonies explained and clarified? They have been corrupted by time until their true features can hardly be deciphered. Where do we teach those great primitive truths of revelation that Masonry has preserved for the world?

We have dignified-sounding titles. Are those who possess them qualified to enlighten the world with respect to the goals and objects of Masonry? To the descendants of those Initiates who governed empires: does your influence enter into practical life, and does that influence efficiently operate on behalf of well-regulated and constitutional liberty?

Your debates should be friendly conversations. You need agreement, union, and peace. Why then do you use words that excite rivalries and jealousies? Why permit controversy and ambitious claims? Do your own words and acts agree with each other? If you do not practice Masonry, how can you encourage it on others?

You continually praise each other and elaborately commend the Order. In every way, you assume that you are what you should be. Nowhere do you look upon yourselves as you really are. Is it true that all our actions are in the pursuit of virtue? Explore the recesses of your own heart. Let us examine ourselves with an impartial eye and answer our own questions! Can we testify to the rigid performance of all our duties, or even *half* of them?

Let us do away with offensive self-flattery! Let us be men if we cannot be sages! The good laws of Masonry cannot wholly change man's nature. It enlightens him. It points out the true way, but it cannot lead only by repressing the fire of their passions and conquering selfishness. Regrettably, these tend to conquer, and Masonry is forgotten!

After praising each other all our lives, there are always excellent Brethren who shower unlimited eulogies over our coffins. Every one of us who dies is a model for all the virtues. We are the children of the celestial light even if we are void of the accolades in this life. In Egypt, among our old Masters, where Masonry was practiced more than displayed, no one could gain admission to the sacred asylum of the tomb until he had passed under the most solemn judgment. A grave tribunal sat in judgment upon all, even the kings. They said to the dead; "Whoever you are, give account to your country of your actions! What have you done with your time and life? The law interrogates you, your country hears you, and Truth sits in judgment of you!" Princes came there to be judged, escorted only by their virtues and their vices. A public accuser recounted the history of a dead man's life and threw the light from the torch of truth on all his actions. If it were judged that he had led an evil life, his memory was condemned in the presence of the nation, and his body was denied the honors of burial in the tomb. What a lesson old Masonry taught to the sons of the people!

Is it true that Masonry is decaying? Is it true that acacia, once withered, provides no shade? Is Masonry no longer marching on the frontline of Truth? No! Is freedom universal? Have ignorance and prejudice disappeared from the earth? Are there no longer hostilities among men? Do desire and lies no longer exist? Do toleration and harmony prevail among religious and political sects? Masonry has much work to accomplish. Though this is greater than the twelve labors of Hercules, Masonry must advance steadily and with determination. It *188* must seek to enlighten the minds of the people, reconstruct society, reform laws, and improve all society's morals. The eternity in front of us seems as infinite as the one behind us. Masonry cannot cease to labor for social progress without ceasing to be true to itself and ceasing to *be* Masonry.

Chapter 12: Grand Master Architect

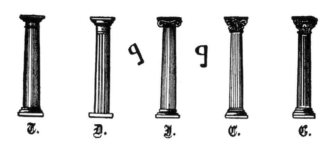

T.   D.   I.   C.   C.

THE great duties taught by the lessons and the working-tools of the *189* Grand Master Architect demand much from us, and take for granted the capacity to perform them faithfully and fully. They bring us to reflect upon human nature and the vast power and capacity of the human soul. It is this idea that we invite to your attention in this Degree. Let us begin to rise from earth toward the stars.

The human soul always struggles toward light, God, and the Infinite. It struggles especially in its suffering. Words can barely scrape the surface of the depths of sorrow. The thoughts that writhe in silence have no emblem or symbol. They go into the stillness of Infinity and Eternity. Enough thoughts enter there that cannot be properly worded. These thoughts do not want human sympathy as much as higher help. There is loneliness in deep sorrow that only Deity can comfort. The mind struggles alone with calamity, and it seeks a solution from the Infinite Providence of Heaven, which leads directly to God.

We are not conscious of many parts of human nature yet. One desire is to wake that sleeping consciousness into action and lead the soul up to Light. This can be done through the pen, pencil, or dialogue. We are unconscious to the intensity and wonderful awe of that life within us. Health and sickness, joy and sorrow, success and disappointment, life and death, and love and loss are *190* familiar words upon our lips yet we do not know to what depths they go within us.

We never seem to appreciate what *any*thing means or is worth, until we have lost it. Within us are many organs, nerves, and tissue that perform silently and without thought for years. We are unconscious of their value. When injured we discover their value, and find out how instrumental they were to our happiness and comfort. We never realize the full significance of the words "property", "ease", and "health". Nor do we comprehend the wealth in the meaning of, "parent", "child", "beloved", and "friend" until the thing or the person is taken away. When the bright, visible object is replaced by the awful, lonely shadow, we stretch out our hands and hearts in vain into *nothingness*. We strain our eyes in the dark and dismal void. Yet, in that absence, we do not *lose* the object that we loved. It only becomes more identifiable to us. Our blessings not only brighten with departure, but they are solidified into continuing reality. Love and friendship receive their everlasting seal under the cold stamp of death.

Beneath all the commonplace of life lies a dim consciousness of its infinite mystery and grandeur. There is an inspiring majesty around us, even among the mundane. As the simple peasant from the Italian Apennines Mountains is asleep at the foot of a pillar within a majestic Roman church, he does not truly hear or see what is around. He dreams only of the herd he feeds, or the ground he tills in the mountains. Yet, the choir's symphonies fall softly upon his ears, and the glorious arches are dimly noticed through his half-slumbering eyelids.

Similarly, the soul cannot quite lose the sense of where it is and what is above and below it, however preoccupied by the necessities of daily life. The area tread in life may be small. The paths of its steps may be well defined and well worn. The objects it handles, easily grasped, and worn out with daily uses. It may be that among such things we all live. We live our simple life, but Heaven is above us, around us, and near to us. Eternity is before us and behind us. The suns and stars are our silent witnesses and watchers. We are enveloped by Infinity. Infinite Powers and Infinite spaces encircle us. The reverent arch of Mystery spreads above us, and no voice ever violates its space. Eternity is enthroned within Heaven's endless starry heights. No utterance or word ever came from those far-off and silent spaces. Above, below, and around is the majesty that stretches to infinity. Beneath it is this little struggle and conflict of life on this busy anthill of Time.

From this anthill, many sounds emerge into the silent and all-surrounding Infinity. There is the babble from the streets, the sounds of music and reveling, the stir of the multitude, the shouts of joy, and the shrieks of agony. Outside the audible, from the innermost depths of man goes up a prayer, an imploring request for revelation. A cry in silent agony praying for the arch of mystery to break and the stars, that is ever above the turbulence of mortal troubles, to speak. It implores them to find a voice, and to have the mysterious heavens come nearer to mankind. It wants them all to tell us what they alone know: information about the loved and lost, answer what we are, and tell us where we are going.

A dome of incomprehensible wonders encloses man. What is within and without man should fill his life with majesty and sacredness. Something from heaven that is sanctified and sublime has been downloaded into the heart of everyone that lives. No one is so low and abandoned that they do not have some traits of that sacredness left within them still. This something may be so opposite his general reputation that he chooses to hide it from everyone. There is some sanctuary in his soul, where no one may enter. There one stores the memory of a child, image of a revered parent, adoration of a pure love, or echo of a kind word once spoken to him, as echoes that reverberate forever.

Life is more than negativity, superficiality, or worldliness. Our existence is haunted with thoughts, far beyond its own comprehension, which some regard as the memory of a pre-existent state. So it is with all of us, in this worn track of our worldly pilgrimage. There is more here, than the world we observe. Life is not simply to live. An unseen and infinite presence is here. It is the sense of something greater than what we possess. It is a seeking for a good beyond all the void wastes of life. It is a crying out of the heart for understanding. It is a memory of the dead still touching some thread in this great curtain of mystery that hangs over us.

We all have clues that we are capable of better things than we realize. A *192* great crisis could pressure us to develop these powers within us, beyond the conscientious bias of our spirits. From time to time Heaven calls forth those better talents within us. There are few families in the world selfish enough that, if one in it had to die and was to be selected by the others, it would be utterly possible for the parents and children to choose the victim. Each member would say, "I will die, but I cannot choose." If that dire circumstance were upon families, it would be remarkably vast how many would step forth freed from ordinary selfishness and say, "Let the blow fall on me!" There are greater things within all of us than the world or even *we* notice. If only we could and would seek them out. It is one part of our Masonic culture to *find* these traits of power and sublime devotion. We are to revive the faded nobleness of generosity and self-sacrifice for it has been a gift of God's love and kindness almost forgotten to our souls. It tries to induce us to yield ourselves to their guidance and control.

One impartial law presses upon all conditions of men. In all situations and fortunes, the *mind* gives them character. Character is defined by what is inside the person, not what surrounds that person. A king might be a mean, degrading despot yet a slave of ambition, fear, voluptuousness, and every vile passion. The peasant might be the real monarch, the moral master of his fate as a free and sublime being. He is more than a prince in happiness and more than a king in honor.

Man is not driftwood upon the sea of his fortunes, helpless and irresponsible upon the tide of events. Out of similar circumstances, different men can bring very different results. The same hardships, difficulties, distress, poverty, or misfortunes that wear down one man will build-up another and makes him strong. This is the very attribute and glory of man that chiefly distinguishes him from the animal. He can alter his circumstances to the intellectual and moral purposes of his nature. This is the power and mastery of his will.

The power of moral will as developed in the child is a new aspect of his nature. It is a power brought and delegated from Heaven. A human has never sunk so low that he could not find the power, God's gift, to rise. Because God commands him to rise, we know he *can* rise if he obeys. Every man should use *193* this power to make all situations, trials, and temptations tools to promote his virtue and happiness. He is not the creature of circumstance. *He* creates and controls *them* for his moral being by making them to be all that they are: evil or good.

Life is what we make it. The world is what we make of it. The eyes of the cheerful and of the sad are fixed upon the same creation even though they perceive it differently. To some, it is all beauty and gladness. They see the waves of the ocean roll in light and the mountains covered with day. To them life shines upon every flower and every tree that moves with the breeze. Everywhere there is more than the eye beholds. There is a presence of joy within the hills, valleys, and waters. Others mournfully gaze at the same scenes. Everything has a dull, dim, and sickly appearance. The grumbling noise from the brook is inharmonious to them. The great roar of the sea has an angry and threatening tone. The solemn music of the forest sings the requiem of their lost and departed happiness. The light shines glaringly on their eyes and bothers them. The passing of the seasons is like a funeral procession. They sigh and turn impatiently away. The eye recreates what it sees, but the mind interprets it. The ear can hear, but the mind is able to make its own songs and noise. The world outside is reflected by the inner world.

Let the Mason never forget that life and the world are what we make them. It is through our social character that we want to adapt to society, relationships, and pursuits for the world. To the selfish, cold, insensible, haughty, presuming, proud, demanding, jealous, sensitive, violators, offenders, rude, violent, dishonest, and sensual their social condition will present annoyances, disappointments, and pains according to their character. Kind affections will not be attracted to selfishness. The cold-hearted must expect to meet coldness, the proud will meet arrogance, the passionate will meet anger, and the violent will meet rudeness. Those who forget the rights of others, must not be surprised if their own are forgotten. Those who stoop low to embrace their worldly senses must not wonder why others do not seem concerned to bend and lift them back up to the respect of the world.

To the gentle, many will be gentle. To the kind, many will be kind. A good man will find goodness in the world. An honest man will find honesty among mankind. A man of principle will find principle and integrity in the minds of others.

There are no blessings given which the mind cannot convert into evil. The mind can build any trial into a noble blessing. Virtue may gain strength from temptation instead of being vanquished and subdued by it. It is true that temptations have great power and virtue often falls. The temptations are not as mighty as our virtue is feeble, and hearts weak. We rely too much on the strength of our defenses, and allow these temptations to make approaches at leisure. The offer of dishonest gain and guilty pleasure make the honest man more honest, and the pure man purer. They raise his virtue to the height of a towering displeasure. The occasion and opportunity of a tempting chance will

194

148

become the defeat and disgrace of the tempter. The honest and upright man does not wait for temptation to be at his doorstep.

To the impure, dishonest, false-hearted, corrupt, and sensual occasions come every day from everywhere in every thought and imagination. He is prepared to give-in before the temptation approaches. He *makes* occasions, opportunities, and evil *thoughts* come. He throws wide open his heart and welcomes vice and entertains them with a lavish hospitality.

The business of the world corrupts and degrades one's mind. To another mind, the world feeds and nurses nobleness, independence, integrity, and generosity. Pleasure is a poison to some while it is nourishment to others. To one, the world is a great harmony, sweet with the music of infinite melodies. To another, it is noisy, like a huge factory with the clang of machinery that deafens the ears and is pure madness. Life is substantially the same thing to all who live. 195 Some rise to virtue and glory. Others sink to shame and damnation as they undergo trials and yet enjoy the same privileges.

Being thorough, faithful, and giving your best effort to improve is the path to success and the highest happiness. To sigh with human misfortune is only for the mind's undeveloped state. A mind is miserable due to its own fault. Under the Providence of God it is appointed as both punisher and corrector of its faults. In the long run, the mind will be happy in proportion to its loyalty and wisdom. When miserable, the mind creates its problems, holds them, and complains. That complaint is really the *confession* that *it* created its own problems.

A certain degree of spirituality enters into a large part of every life. You cannot carry out business without some faith in man. You cannot even dig in the ground without an expectation of the unseen result. You cannot think, reason, or step without faith in your inward, spiritual principle. All the central affections, bonds, hopes, and interests of life involve the spiritual. You know that if that central bond were broken, the world would soon evolve into chaos.

Believe in God. He is our Father. He has a paternal interest in our welfare and improvement. He has given us powers by which we may escape from sin. He has predestined a life of endless progress toward perfection and knowledge of Himself. As every Mason, you should believe this so you can live calmly, endure patiently, labor with determination, sacrifice cheerfully, hope unwaveringly, and be the victor in the great struggle of life. Take away any one of these principles and what remains for us? Say that there is no God and no way for hope, reformation, triumph, or heaven to come, what are we to do? If there is no rest for the weary after this life, if there is no place with God for the suffering and inconsolable soul, what is our hope? What if God was simply blind *Chance*? What if He was *some*what our expectation of Him? What if He was *nothing* that we expect? What if he was emotionless, passionless, and the Supreme *Apathy* by which all things are indifferent? What if he was the jealous God who vengefully visits the sins of the fathers on the children? What if He 196 was really an arbitrary supreme *Will* who has made it *right* to be virtuous and wrong to lie and steal, because IT was His *pleasure* at the time, and He retained the power to reverse that law? What if He was an inconstant, cruel, bloodthirsty, savage Deity, and we were but the sport of chance and the victims of despair? What if we were surrounded by darkness, struggling with obstacles, toiling for barren results and empty purposes, distracted with doubts, and misled by false rays of light? What if we were wanderers with no path, no hope, and no home as doomed and deserted mariners on a dark and stormy sea, without compass or stars, tossed helmless upon the angry waves with no blessed port in the distance whose guiding-light invites us to its welcome rest?

The faith taught by Masonry dispenses the theory that there is no God. That faith is indispensable to the attainment of the great achievements of life. It must have been designed to be a part of life. We are made for faith, and there must be something for us to believe in. We cannot grow healthily or live happily without faith. Therefore, it is *true*. A soul would sink into sin, misery, darkness, and ruin if one cut the principles of Masonry from it. The faith in God, in immortality, in virtue, and in correctness of conduct is essential to man. If we could cut off all sense of these truths, the man would sink to the level of an animal.

No man can suffer and be patient, struggle and conquer, learn and be happy without conscience, hope, justice, wisdom, and a forgiving God. We must embrace the great truths taught by Masonry, and follow them to live happily. *"I put my trust in God,"* is the declaration of Masonry. It advocates against the belief of a cruel, angry, and vengeful God to be feared and not revered by His creatures.

Society, with its relationships, is as much a creation of heaven as are the systems of the universe. If gravity, which bonds all worlds and systems to each other, was suddenly absent, the universe would fly into chaos. Similarly, if we were to sever all moral bonds that hold society together, Truth and Integrity from an unseen authority above and a conscience within, would immediately descend into anarchy and ruin. We teach, as a principle of things, that religion is as certain and true as gravity.

Man needs faith in moral principles, in virtue, and in God. Faith is as necessary to the guide of man as instinct guides an animal. Therefore, faith within man has a mission as true in God's Providence as instinct. The pleasures of the soul must depend on certain principles. They must recognize a soul's responsibilities, conscience, and the sense of a higher authority. These are the principles of faith. Everything in the universe has fixed laws and principles for its action such as the star in its orbit, the animal in its activity, the man in his functions. Likewise, man has certain laws and principles as a spiritual being. His soul does not die from lack of sustenance or guidance. To the reasonable soul, there is ample provision available. It would be strange if there were no answer to the cry of the soul, tortured by want, sorrow, and agony. The total rejection of all moral and religious belief would strike a principle from human nature. Faith is as essential to humanity as gravitation is to the stars, instinct to animals, and oxygen to the body.

God has declared that life shall be a social state. We are members of a civil community. The life of that community depends upon its morality. Public spirit, intelligence, uprightness, self-restraint, kindness, and domestic purity will make it a happy, prosperous, and enduring community. Widespread selfishness, dishonesty, indulgence, libertinism, corruption, and crime will make it miserable, immoral, and ruinous. Society lives one life together, with one heart, and one pulse for its existence. One stream of life flows, with millions of intermingled branches and channels, through all the homes of human love. One sound as an ecstatic jubilee or a mournful sigh, comes from the combined dwellings of the *198* whole nation.

The Public is not an abstraction. What is done to the Public, against its interest, law, or virtue does not press lightly on its conscience. It is a vast expanse of individual lives: an ocean of tears, an atmosphere of sighs, or a universe of joy and gladness. The public suffers as million suffer and it rejoices as millions rejoice. What a vast crime is committed by the one who dares to strike the Public Welfare! He is a criminal, whether a private man, lobbyist, agent, contractor, legislator, magistrate, secretary, or president, who encourages corruption in the shameful sale of position or office, or contributes anything to that which sows dissension and weakens the bonds that bind a nation together! He who dares to pierce that mighty heart is wicked for he strikes at the heart from which our existence is flowing!

Do we have equal interest in the virtue of those whom we love!? In this virtue alone is gathered an unequalled treasure. Do we care for a brother or a friend if we do not first care for his honor, fidelity, reputation, and kindness? How respectful is the conduct of a parent! How sacred this reputation! No blight that falls on a child compares with a parent's dishonor. Every parent wishes to have their child do well and pours upon them all their parental love, in the desire that they *may* do well. Parents hope that the child may be worthy of their cares and pains and that they might walk with honor and happiness. Thus, they cannot walk one-step without virtue. Such is life and its relationships. A thousand ties embrace it, like a web of lace, the nervous system, the transistors of a microchip, or the strings of an instrument capable of sweet melodies, but easily put out of tune or broken, by rudeness, anger, and selfishness.

If life was made insensible to pain or pleasure and the human heart were hard, then greed, ambition, and sensuality might cut paths through it and no one would care to protest. If we could be patient under the load of a superficial life, we could bear burdens as the beasts bear them. Then, *like* beasts, we might turn all of our thoughts to the earth. No call from the great Heavens above would *199* change us from our plodding and earthly course.

However, we art *not* insensible brutes. We cannot refuse the call of reason and conscience. Our soul is capable of remorse. When the great irregularities of life press down upon us we weep, suffer, and are full of sorrow. Sorrow and agony desire other companions than the secular and worldly. We are not willing to bear those burdens of fear, anxiety, disappointment, and trouble on our heart without any object or use. We are not willing to suffer, sick and afflicted, to have our days filled with calamity and grief instead of comfort and joy without advantage or compensation. We will not barter away the dear treasures of the suffering heart, sell the life-blood from a failing body, or shed our tears of bitterness and anguish for nothing. Human nature though frail, feeling, sensitive, and sorrowing cannot stand to suffer for nothing.

Everywhere, human life is a great and solemn order of affairs. Man suffers, enjoys, loves, hates, hopes, and fears while chained to the earth. Yet he also explores the expanses of the universe and has the power to commune with God and His angels. Around these actions of our existence, the curtains of Time are drawn. There are openings that give us glimpses of eternity. God looks down upon this scene of our human trials. The wise and good through all ages have come together with their teachings and blood. Everything that exists around us, every movement in nature, every counsel of Providence, every act of God, centers upon one point: His trust in man. Even if the ghosts of the departed could come through the doors of our homes at night, and the dead could glide through the aisles and sit in our Masonic Temples, those teachings would be no more eloquent and impressive than the realities of life. Already, these memories of years misspent, these ghosts of opportunities missed, point to our conscience and cry continually in our ears, "*Work while the day lasts! for the night of death comes, in which no man can work.*"

There is no public mourning for the troubles of the soul. Men weep when the body dies. When it is carried to its final resting place, they follow it with sad and mournful procession. Yet for a dying soul, there is no open grief and for the lost soul, there are no rites.

The mind and soul of man have a value that nothing else has. They are worth a care, which nothing else is worth. The individual should be more interested than anything else. The stored treasures of the heart, the unknown depth of its reserve to be mined, boundless realms of Thought, that armada of man's hopes and best affections are brighter than gold and dearer than treasure.

Little is really known of the mind. It is *all* which man permanently *is*, his inward being, his divine energy, his immortal thought, his boundless capacity, and his infinite ambition. Nevertheless, few value it for what it is truly worth. Few see the mind in another light. For through the rags which poverty clothes it, shrouded by the burdens of life, amidst the worldly troubles, wants, and sorrows, it is elusive in thought. Few acknowledge and cheer it among that humble lot. Few feel the nobilities of earth, or the glory of Heaven is found there.

Men do not sense the worth of their own souls. They have pride in their mental capacities, but they do not perceive the intrinsic, inner, and infinite *worth* of their own mind. A poor man will feel like a mere ordinary creature when admitted to a palace, amid the splendors, though he is still a moral and immortal being. He sees wealth in others around him, has a degrading envy, and feels himself as a humbler creature because others, by measure, are rich above him. He forgets his own mind's intrinsic and eternal dignity. Men tend to respect each other according to wealth, higher rank, higher office, loftier opinions, commanding more votes as the favorite of people and power.

The difference among men is in the faculty of communication. It is not so much in their nature and intrinsic power. Some have the capacity to utter and translate their thoughts into words. All men, more or less, *feel* those thoughts. The glory of genius and the joy of virtue, when rightly revealed, are shared among many minds. When eloquence and poetry speak, many rejoice. When glorious arts, statues, paintings, and music become audible and visible people are moved. When patriotism, charity, and virtue speak with an exciting power, the 201 hearts of millions glow with joy and ecstasy. If it did not move, there would be no eloquence. For eloquence beseeches other hearts and provides the capacity and power to *make* other hearts respond. No one is so low, as to not be occasionally touched with the beauty of goodness. No heart is made of material so common as to not respond with every fiber to the call of honor, patriotism, generosity, and virtue. The poor will die in defense of family and children just the same. The poor, lost, scorned, abandoned, and outcast woman will call-on and nurse those who are dying with her very hands. The pickpocket will scale burning walls to rescue a stranger from the dangerous flames.

This capacity in man is the most glorious! It is a power to commune with God and His Angels. Communication concentrates the moral splendors of the universe as the reflection of the Uncreated Light. The soul gives value to the things of this world. It is only by raising the soul to its rightful elevation above all other things that we can comprehend the purposes of this earth. No scepter, throne, building, monument, or empire can compare with the wonder and grandeur of a single thought. That thought alone can comprehend the Maker of all. Thought is the key that unlocks all the treasures of the universe. It is the power that reigns over space, time, and eternity. Under God, it is the Sovereign Dispenser of all blessings and glories that lie within the compass of possession and the range of possibility. Virtue, Heaven, and Immortality exist alone in the perception, feeling, and thought of the glorious mind.

My Brother, I hope that you have listened to and understood the Instruction and Lecture of this Degree and that you feel the dignity of your own nature. I hope that you feel the vast capacities of your own soul for good or evil, and I will proceed briefly to communicate to you the remaining instruction of this Degree.

The Hebrew word, in its old Hebrew and Samaritan character, suspended in the East over the five columns, is ADONAI, one of the names of God. It is usually translated as Lord. It is this name, which the Hebrews always substitute 202 for the True Name, which was ineffable for them.

The five columns of the five different orders of architecture are emblematical to us of the five principal divisions of the Ancient and Accepted Scottish Rite:

1.--The *Tuscan*, to the three blue Degrees, or the primitive Masonry.
2.--The *Doric,* to the ineffable Degrees, from the fourth to the fourteenth, inclusive.
3.--The *Ionic*, to the fifteenth and sixteenth, or second temple Degrees.
4.--The *Corinthian*, to the seventeenth and eighteenth Degrees, or those of the new law.
5.--The *Composite*, to the philosophical and chivalric Degrees intermingled, from the nineteenth to the thirty-second, inclusive.

The North Star, always fixed and unchangeable for us, represents the point in the centre of the circle. It represents Deity in the centre of the Universe. It is the special symbol of duty and of faith. To it, and the seven ancient planets that continually revolve around it, mystical meanings are attached. If you should be permitted to advance, you will learn these when you are made acquainted with the philosophical doctrines of the Hebrews.

The Morning Star rising in the East, Jupiter, or as called by the Hebrews Tsydoch, *Just*, is an emblem to us of the ever-approaching dawn of perfection and Masonic Light.

The three great lights of the Lodge are symbols of the Power, Wisdom, and Beneficence (charity) of the Deity. These three are also symbols of the first three *Sephiroth*, or Emanations of the Deity, according to Kabbalah. These are called: *Kether*, the omnipotent divine *will*; *Chokmah*, the divine intellectual *power* to *generate* thought; and *Binah*, the divine intellectual *capacity* to *produce* it. The latter two are usually translated *Wisdom* and *Understanding*, and reflect the *active* and the *passive*, or *positive* and *negative*. We will not elaborate on these right now. They are represented by the columns Jachin and Boaz, which stand at the entrance to Masonic Temples.

In another aspect of this Degree, the Chief of the Architects [רב בנים, Rab Banaim,] symbolizes the constitutional executive of a free government. The Degree teaches us that no free government can long endure, when the people cease to select the best and the wisest for their magistrates and statesmen. When, the people fail to participate, they permit factions and special interests to select for them the shallow, weak, ignoble, and obscure. Into these hands are trusted the country's destinies. There is a "divine right" to govern, but it is meant to be invested with the ablest, wisest, and best of every nation. "Counsel is mine, and sound wisdom: I am understanding; I am power; by me kings do reign and princes decree justice; by me princes rule, and nobles, even all the magistrates of the earth."

203

My Brother, for the present let this be enough. We welcome you among us to this peaceful retreat of virtue, to participate in our privileges, and to a share in our joys and sorrows.

CHAPTER 13: ROYAL ARCH OF SOLOMON

WE will not debate whether the legend of this Degree is historic or 204 merely an allegory containing a deeper truth and a more profound meaning. If it is a myth, then you must find out for yourself what it means. It is certain that the word, which the Hebrews were never permitted to pronounce, was commonly used by Abraham, Lot, Isaac, Jacob, Laban, Rebecca, and among foreign tribes before the time of Moses. It recurs a hundred times in the lyrical outpourings of David and other Hebrew poets.

We know that for centuries the Hebrews were expressly forbidden to pronounce the Sacred Name. Wherever it did occur in life, they replaced it with the word *Adonai*. When *Adonai* was written, the vowels (Masoretic points) were not included under the consonants of the word. The knowledge and true pronunciation of the Word was thought to hold extraordinary and supernatural powers. The Word itself, when worn as a talisman protected against personal danger, sickness, and evil spirits. We know that all this was superstition. It was natural to the people then and disappeared as they became enlightened. It is not useful for a Mason today.

Note that this sanctity for the Divine Name or Creative Word was common to all ancient nations. The Sacred Word HOM was thought by the ancient Persians, who were among the earliest emigrants from Northern India, to hold a mysterious power. They taught that the world was created by its use. In 205 India, it was forbidden to pronounce the word AUM or OM, as it was the Sacred Name of the One Deity represented by Brahma, Vishnu, and Shiva.

The superstitious notions regarding the power of the Word (and hence the prohibition against pronouncing it) could not be part of the pure, primitive religion. It could not have been part of the secret teachings of Moses. The full knowledge of it was confined to Initiates. Maybe the idea was an ingenious invention for the concealment of some Name or truth whose meaning was made known only to a *select few*. If so, the notions regarding the Word grew in the minds of the people among ancient nations in error. These original truths, symbols, and allegories became misunderstood through time. Allegories have always been vehicles of truth for the sages. When taken literally by the ignorant, they spread nothing but error.

The Masoretic points were added to Hebrew writing long after the beginning of the Christian era. Prior to this, the pronunciation of a Hebrew word could not be known only from the characters in which it was written. It is *possible* that the true pronunciation of the name of Deity was forgotten and lost. It is certain that the true pronunciation is not represented by the word Jehovah. Therefore, *that* is not the true name of Deity, and it is not the Ineffable Word.

The ancient symbols and allegories had more than one interpretation. They would have a *double* meaning, and sometimes *more*, with one serving as the envelope of another. Thus, the *pronunciation* of the word was really a symbol. The pronunciation and the word were lost once the knowledge of the true nature and attributes of God faded from the minds of the Jewish tribes. This is *one* interpretation. Although *true*, it is not *the inner and most profound interpretation.*

Figuratively, men forgot the *name* of God when they lost the inner *knowledge*. They began worshipping heathen deities, burning incense on the high places, and performing rituals like the passing of their children through the fire for Moloch.

The attempts of the ancient Israelites and the Initiates to determine the True Name of the Deity and rediscover its pronunciation, like the loss of the True Word, are an allegory. It represents the general ignorance of the true nature and attributes of God. It also represents the proneness of the people of Judah and Israel to worship other deities, and their lower, erroneous, and dishonorable notions of the Grand Architect of the Universe. Everyone shared these views except a few favored, select persons. Even Solomon built altars and sacrificed to Astarte (the goddess of the love) and Molech (the Ammonite god). He built high places for Chemosh (the Moabite deity) and Molech. The true nature of God, like His name, was unknown to them. They worshiped the calves of Jeroboam as they did in those made for them by Aaron in the desert.

Most of the ancient Hebrews did not believe in the existence of only one God until a later period in their history. Their popular ideas of Deity were simple. Even while Moses was receiving the law upon Mount Sinai, the people forced Aaron to make an image of the Egyptian god Apis, and they fell down and adored it. They were always ready to return to the worship of the gods of Egypt (Mitzraim). Soon after the death of Joshua, they became worshippers of the false gods of the surrounding nations. Amos the prophet said to them, while speaking of the time since the Exodus, "You have brought the tabernacle of Maloch and Cain your idols, the star of your god, which you made to yourselves."

Among them, as among other nations, the varied concepts of God were formed according to their intellectual and spiritual capability. The poor and ignorant invested God with the common attributes of humanity. The virtuous and gifted invested pure and moral attributes. These concepts gradually improved, purified, and ennobled as the nation advanced in civilization. They are viewed by God having the lowest attributes in the historical accounts, later being amended with prophetic writings, and reaching the highest elevation among the poets of the nations.

Among *all* the ancient nations, there was one faith and one idea of Deity for the enlightened, intelligent, and educated, and there was another for the masses. The Hebrews were no exception to this rule. To the masses, Jehovah was like the gods of the nations around them, except that He was *their* God. He was the God of the family of Abraham, Isaac, and Jacob. Eventually, He became the *National* God. He was *more powerful* than the other gods worshipped by their neighbors. This idea is expressed with the statement, "Who among the gods is like you, O Jehovah?" 207

The Deity of the early Hebrews talked to Adam and Eve in the garden of Eden as He walked in it during the cool of the day. He conversed with Cain. He sat and ate with Abraham in his tent. He permitted Abraham to bargain with Him and to persuade Him to change His first determination regarding Sodom's punishment. He wrestled with Jacob. He showed Moses His goodness, though not His face. He dictated the minutest regulations and gave the exact dimensions of the tabernacle and its furniture to Moses. He insisted on and delighted in sacrifices and burnt offerings. He was angry, jealous, vengeful, wavering, and irresolute. He allowed Moses to reason with His resolve to destroy His people. He commanded the performance of acts of barbarity against others. He hardened the heart of Pharaoh. He repented for the destruction that He had said He would do to the people of Nineveh, which caused disgust and anger in Jonah.

These were the popular notions of Deity. Either the priests did not have a better notion, or they did not bother to correct these notions. Perhaps, the popular intellect was not free enough to allow them to conceive a better Almighty.

These were not the ideas of the intellectual and enlightened among the Hebrews. It is certain that *they* possessed a knowledge of the true nature and attributes of God. Among other nations, similar knowledge was known among men such as Zoroaster, Menu, Confucius, Socrates, and Plato. The difference was that these doctrines were esoteric and only for a limited audience. Therefore, they did not have to communicate them to the people at large. They were communicated in Egypt, India, Persia, Phœnicia, Greece, and Samothrace as greater mysteries to the Initiates.

The communication of this knowledge and its secrets (some perhaps lost) constituted what we now call *Masonry, Free-* or *Franc- Masonry*. That knowledge was *the Lost Word*, which was made known to the Grand Elect, Perfect, and Sublime Masons. It would be wrong to pretend that the *forms* and ceremonies in those ages were the same as those of Masonry today. The present name of the Order, its titles, and the modern names of the Degrees were not used then. Even the Blue Lodge cannot trace its *authentic* history *with its present three Degrees* 208 further back than the 18th century. By whatever *name* it became known in any country, Masonry existed as it now exists, in spirit and at heart. It existed before Solomon built the temple and before the first humans immigrated into Southern India, Persia, and Egypt.

The Supreme, Self-existent, Eternal, All-wise, All-powerful, Infinitely Good, Pitying, and Merciful Creator and Preserver of the Universe was one and the same, by any name, to the intellectual and enlightened men of all nations. The name was nothing but a symbol and a representation of His nature and attributes. The name AL, or EL, represented his remoteness above men and His *inaccessibility.* BAL and BALA represented *might.* ELOHIM represented various *potencies.* IHUH represented *existence* and the *generation* of things. Among the Eastern names, none was a symbol of a divinely infinite love, tenderness, or all-embracing mercy. As MOLOCH or MALEC, He was an omnipotent *monarch* with a tremendous and irresponsible *Will.* As ADONAI, He was a LORD and *Master.* As EL *Shaddai,* He was a *potent* DESTROYER.

The primary object of the mysteries was to communicate true ideas of Deity. In the Mysteries, Hiram (Khūrūm) King of Tyre and Hiram (Khūrūm) Abif the Master obtained their knowledge of Him and His attributes. That knowledge was the same as taught to Moses and Pythagoras.

Nothing prevents you from considering the whole legend of this Degree (like the Master's Degree) an allegory representing the perpetuation of the knowledge of the True God in the temples of initiation. Through the subterranean vaults, you might understand the places of initiation, which were generally underground in the ancient ceremonies. The Temple of Solomon presented a symbolic image of the Universe. In its arrangements and furniture, it resembled all the temples of the ancient nations that practiced the Mysteries. The system of numbers was closely connected to religion and worship. Though unknown to the vast majority of those who use them, they are full of esoteric meaning. These meanings have been passed down to us in Masonry. Numbers had a reference to Deity, represented his attributes, and figured in the framework of the world, time, and space. They formed the basis of that framework. Universally, these were regarded as sacred and expressing the order, intelligence, and words of the Divinity Himself.

The Holy of Holies of the Temple formed a cube. When drawn on a two-dimensional surface, a solid cube has nine visible *lines,* and there are three visible sides or faces. This was in harmony with the number *four,* which the ancients used to represent *Nature.* Four was the number of substances, physical forms, elements, cardinal points, seasons, and *secondary* colors. The number *three* always represented the Supreme Being. Therefore, to the ancient Mason the name of the Deity engraved upon the *triangular* plate was sunk into the *cube* of agate. It teaches us that the true knowledge of God, His nature, and His attributes was written by Him upon the pages of the Book of Universal Nature. Those who apply the required amount of intellect may read it. *The Master Mason's*

Word is the knowledge of God written there. Masonry has always been the interpreter.

Inside the Temple, all the decorations were connected mystically and symbolically with the same system. The ceiling was starred like the heavens. It was supported by twelve columns, which represented the twelve months of the year. The border that ran around the columns represented the zodiac. One of the twelve celestial signs was appropriated to each column. The brazen sea was supported by twelve oxen with three looking to each cardinal point of the compass.

Today every Masonic Lodge represents the Universe. We are told that each extends from the rising to the setting sun, from the South to the North, from the surface of the Earth to the Heavens, and from the center to the circumference of the globe. In it are represented the sun, moon, and stars. Three great torches in the East, West, and South form a triangle and give it light. The Delta, or Triangle, suspended in the East encloses the Ineffable Name. The mathematical equality of its angles and sides indicates the beautiful and harmonious proportions that govern the sum and details of the Universe. Those sides and angles also represent, by the number three, the Trinity of Power, Wisdom, and Harmony that presided at the building of this marvelous work. These three great lights also represent the great mystery of the three principles of *210* creation, destruction, and regeneration regarded as sacred by all beliefs in their own Trinities.

The luminous pedestal, lighted by the perpetual flame within, is a symbol of that light of *Reason* given by God to man. By reasoning, man is able to understand the Book of Nature, the chronicles of thought, and the revelation of the attributes of the Deity.

The three Masters Adoniram, Joabert, and Stolkin, represent the True Masons who seek knowledge for pure motives so they may be better enabled to serve and benefit their fellow man. The discontented and presumptuous Masters are buried in the ruins of the arches representing those who strove to acquire it for the unholy purposes of gaining power over others or gratifying their pride, vanity, or ambition.

The Lion that guards the Ark represents Solomon and holds the key to open it in his mouth. He is the Lion of the Tribe of Judah. He preserves and communicates the key to the true knowledge of God, His laws, and the profound mysteries of the moral and physical Universe.

We are told that ENOCH [חנוך, Khanoc] walked with God three hundred years after reaching the age of sixty-five. He, "walked with God, then he was no more, for God had taken him." His name signified in Hebrew is INITIATE or INITIATOR. The legend of the columns of granite, brass, and bronze erected by him is probably symbolic. That of bronze, which survived the flood, is supposed to symbolize the mysteries to which Masonry is the legitimate successor. Therefore, from the earliest times, Masonry was the custodian of the great philosophical and religious truths generally unknown to the world and handed down in an unbroken tradition veiled by symbols, emblems, and allegories.

The legend of this Degree is partially interpreted. It is of little importance whether it is historical. Its value consists in the lessons that it teaches and the duties that it bestows upon those who receive it. The tales and allegories of the Scriptures are not less valuable than real history. Rather, they are more valuable, because ancient history is not very instructive. The legend and myth conceal and symbolically reveal truths.

There are more profound meanings concealed in the symbols of this Degree. They are connected with the philosophical system of the Hebrew 211 Kabbalists, which you will learn if you advance. They are revealed in the higher Degrees. The *lion* [ארי, אריה, *Arai, Araiah*] which also signifies *altar*, still holds in his mouth the key to the riddle of the sphinx.

There is one application of this Degree that you are now entitled to know. Remembering that Hiram the Master is the symbol of human freedom, you would probably discover these for yourself.

It is not enough for a nation to *gain* liberty. They must *secure* it. They must not entrust it to be kept or held by any one man. The keystone of the Royal Arch of the great Temple of Liberty is a fundamental law, charter, or constitution. It is the form and written expression of the fixed thought of the people. It may also be the result of the slow growth and consolidation of centuries of thought and action. It should be the same in war as in peace. Liberty cannot be hastily changed or violated without punishment or effect. It is sacred like the Ark of the Covenant, which none could touch and live.

A permanent constitution is rooted in the affections and expressions of the will and judgment of the people. It is built on the instincts and habits of the established thought of the people. It has an independent judiciary, an elected legislature of two branches, an executive responsible to the people, and the right of trial by jury to guarantee the liberties of a nation. If it is virtuous, restrained, without luxury, without lust of conquest, and without the follies of visions of impossible perfection, it can protect these liberties.

Masonry teaches its Initiates that the pursuits and occupations of this life, its activity, care, ingenuity, and the development of this nature given us by God, tend to promote His great design for making the world. We are not at war with the great purpose of life. It teaches that everything is beautiful in its time, place, and appointed office. It asserts that everything which man does assists salvation if rightly and faithfully done. If he obeys the principles of his calling, he will be a good man. It is only by neglect of the task set for him by Heaven, idleness, or violation of its charitable and lofty spirit that he becomes a lesser man. The appointed action of life is the great training of Providence. If man commits 212 himself to it, he will need neither churches nor ordinances except to *express* his religious respect and gratitude.

There is a religion of work. It is not merely the stretching of limbs and the straining of ligaments to complete tasks. It has meaning and intent. A living heart pumps blood into the working, toiling arm. Kind affections inspire and mingle with man's labors. They are the *home* affections. Labor toils elsewhere. It applies itself in cities or in the vessels of commerce across the world. Home is the center. Labor always goes home with its earnings to support and comfort others. These are sacred offerings to the thought of every true man, like a sacrifice at a golden shrine. Many problems are found amid the toils of life. Many harsh and hasty words are spoken, yet the work goes on despite being wearisome, hard, and exasperating. The home needs to be a place where age, sickness, helpless infancy, gentle childhood, and feebleness must not go unattended. If man had no impulse other than selfishness, the society and life we see around us would not exist.

The lawyer who fairly and honestly presents his case with a feeling of true self-respect, honor, and conscience to help the jury arrive at the right conclusion is acting with a religious part. He has a conviction that God's justice reigns there. He leads a religious life that day or else he feels that right and justice are not part of his religion. If he has appealed to his conscience once, if he has spoken of religion and God once, or if he has an inward purpose, conscious intent, and desire that justice should triumph, he must lead a good and *religious* life. He made a most essential contribution to that religion of life and society. It is the cause of equality between men, truth, and correct action within the world.

Books do not need to be sermons, pious exercises, or prayers to be of a religious nature in the Masonic sense. Whatever teaches pure, noble, and patriotic sentiments is religious to Masonry. The religion of Masonry values all that touches the heart with the beauty of virtue and the excellence of an upright life. These are the Gospels of literature and art. These Gospels are preached from many books, paintings, poems, fiction, reviews, and newspapers. It is painful, erroneous, and shortsighted to fail to view these organizations of Heaven's allowance as always good and great. We must understand that God does not only speak from the pulpit.

There is also a religion of society. In business, there is a sacred faith of man in man, which goes beyond the normal sale, exchange, price, and payment. It is great when we show confidence in the integrity of another. It is great when we feel the other will not swerve from the correct, honest, straightforward, and conscientious course for any temptation. His personal integrity and conscientiousness are the image of God to us. When we believe in *it*, it is a great and generous act, just as when we believe in the moral virtue of Deity.

In lively gatherings for amusement, good thoughts and affections of life flow and mingle. If *they* did not, these gatherings would be as dreary as a den of outlaws. When friends meet, hands are warmly pressed and the eyes light up and with the rich feeling of gladness. There is a religion between their hearts. Each

213

appreciates the True and Good in the other. It is not policy, self-interest, or selfishness that induces charm around a meeting, but it is the halo of bright and honest affection.

The brilliance of friendship and affection shines like the soft sky over the entire world. It shines in all places where men meet, walk, and work together. It is not restricted to lovers' retreats, marriage-altars, or homes of purity and tenderness alone. It is over all tended fields, workshops, highways, and city streets. No sidewalk has escaped the scene of such offerings of mutual kindness. There is no doorpost or fence that the beating heart of friendship has not pressed against. How many elements are in the stream of life flowing around us? Surely, everywhere is *that* honest, heartfelt, unbiased, and inexpressible affection.

Every Masonic Lodge is a temple of religion. Its teachings are instruction in these religions. It teaches neutrality, affection, toleration, devotedness, patriotism, truth, sympathy for those who suffer and mourn, pity for the fallen, mercy for the erring, relief for those in need, Faith, Hope, and Charity. We meet there as brothers to learn, know, and love each other. We greet each other gladly. We overlook each other's faults and are respectful of each other's feelings. We are ready to aid each other's needs. This is the true religion revealed to the ancient patriarchs. Masonry has taught this for centuries and will continue to teach it as long as time endures. If unworthy passions, selfishness, bitterness, vengeful feelings, contempt, dislike, or hatred enters there, they are intruders and unwelcome strangers who have come uninvited.

There are many evils, bad feelings, hate, contempt, and unkindness throughout the world. We cannot be blind to the evil present in life. *All* is not evil. We still see God in the world. There is good within evil. Mercy provides wealth to those in poverty and sorrow. Truth and simplicity live amid many traps and false arguments. There are good hearts among the rich as well as the poor.

Love clasps firmly, amid all the superficial and polished distractions. Fidelity, pity, and sympathy hold the long, night watch by the bedside of the suffering neighbor, even amid poverty and misery. Devoted men go from city to city to assist those afflicted by terrible ailments. Women, though well born and refined, nursed wounded soldiers in hospitals before it became fashionable to do so. Even poor, lost, and pitiless women tended the ill with a patient and generous heroism. Masonry and its similar Orders teach men to love each other, feed the hungry, cloth the naked, comfort the sick, and bury the friendless dead. God finds and blesses these kind works.

There is some good in all lawful pursuits. There is a divine spirit breathing in all affections. The ground on which we walk is holy ground. There is a natural religion of life that answers to the religion of nature. There is a beauty and glory in Humanity, in answering to the loveliness of beauty, soft landscapes, rolling hills, and the wonder of the starry heavens.

Men can be virtuous, self-improving, and religious *in* their careers. Those positions were made precisely for that purpose. All the social relations, friendship, love, and ties of family were made to be holy. These ties are religious when they conform to their true spirit, but not when we resist the simple tasks they require. These careers do not *exclude* religion. They *demand* it for their own perfection. We may be religious laborers, physicians, lawyers, artisans, engineers, painters, or musicians. We may be religious in all the work and fun of life. Our life may be a religion with the earth as its altar, its incense in the breath of life, and its fires kindled by the brightness of Heaven. *215*

The thought that rejects the limits of our visible existence is tied to our frail life. The soul reaches outward and asks for freedom. It looks through the frosted window of our senses towards immeasurable creation. It knows that beyond it stretches the infinite and everlasting paths.

Everything within and without us should cause our minds to have a sense of admiration and wonder. We are a mystery encompassed with mysteries. The connection between the mind and matter is a mystery. The communication between the brain and every part of the body and the power and action of our will remind us of this. Every memory is more than a story in a land of make-believe. The power of movement is as precious as the power of thought. Memory and the dreams that are the echoes of forgotten memories are both inexplicable. Universal harmony and cohesion dictate infinite complications. Every step we take in our homes affects the order of the Universe. We are all connected by thought, just as we are connected with the matter and forces of the Universe and the past and future generations of man.

The simplest object before our eyes completely defies our understanding, as do the workings of the most distant stars. Every leaf and every blade of grass holds within the secrets that no human will ever fathom. No man can identify the principle of life. It is an unsolvable mystery. Wherever we place our hand, we lay it on a mystery. Wherever we walk, we tread upon wonders. The sands of the sea, clods of the field, water-worn pebbles on a hill, and the masses of rock are repositories of a text that is much older, more significant, and more sublime than all the ancient ruins of man. They offer more information than all the defeated and buried cities that past generations have left upon the earth. *216* They are the library of the Almighty.

A Mason's great business in life is to read these books of teaching. It is to discover that life is not simply working but the hearing and learning of wisdom. The old mythology is just a page in these books. It gave the world a spiritual nature. The book of Science, with its many pages, spreads the same tale of wonder before mankind.

We shall be just as happy in the afterlife as we are pure and upright here, but no more than that. We shall be just as happy as our character prepares us to be, but no more. Like our mental character, our moral character is not formed in a moment. It is the habit of our mind. It is the result of a lifetime of many thoughts, feelings, and efforts all bound together by many ties. The great *law of Retribution* states that all of our coming experiences are affected by our present actions. Our future must answer for our present. If one moment is sacrificed to vice, then it is sacrificed *forever* and lost. An hour's delay on the right path will put us behind in the pursuit of happiness. Every sin will be equally answered for, even by the best of men. It will be answered according to the full measure of its ill-gotten gains and according to the rule of unwavering impartiality.

The *law of Retribution* weighs on every man, whether he thinks of it or not. It follows him throughout his life. Its steps never falter nor tire. Its eyes never blink or close for sleep. If it were otherwise, God's laws would not be impartial. There would be no moral dominion and no light shed upon the mysteries of Providence.

Whatever a man sows, he shall reap. There is nothing else to harvest. What we are doing today and tomorrow is done for good or evil, whether it is serious or light-hearted. Each thought, feeling, action, and event of every hour contributes to the creation of our character. All these things will judge us. Every bit of influence that contributes to our joys, woes, and character will be sorted and scrutinized. Particle by particle, every word and action will have to answer during judgment.

Therefore, let us take care of what we sow. An evil temptation comes during the opportunity for unrighteous gain, sinful indulgence, pleasure, or socializing. If we yield, we plant a seed of bitterness and sorrow. Tomorrow we may be threatened with discovery where, agitated and alarmed, we cover the sin and bury it deep in falsehood and hypocrisy. It lies concealed in the fertile soil of similar vices. Sin does not die. It thrives and grows. More and more germs of evil gather around this cursed root. Finally, from that single seed of corruption, a horrible and habitual lying and vice springs up in the soul. We take each downward step with aversion, but a frightful power urges us onward. The hell of debt, disease, dishonor, and remorse gather as a shadow on our steps. These are the beginning of our sorrows. The deed may be done in a single moment, but the conscience never dies, memory never sleeps, guilt never evolves to innocence, and remorse never ushers peace.

Beware if you are tempted to evil! Beware what you hope for in the future! Beware what you write in the archives of eternity! Do not wrong your neighbor, or the remorse will never cease in its bitterness! Do not break into the house of innocence and steal its treasure, or when many years have passed over you, the moan of its distress will still be heard in your ears! Do not build a throne of ambition in your heart. Do not be busy with circumventing devices or selfish schemes, or else desolation and loneliness will find you. A long future stretches forth! Do not live a useless, impious, or injurious life! That life is bound with the never-ending principle of retribution and the elements of God's creation, which will never cease. They continue forever to unfold with the ages to eternity. Do not be deceived! God has formed your nature and you must live according to his designs. His law can never be repealed, nor His justice eluded. *"A man reaps that what he has sown,"* forever and ever.

CHAPTER 14: GRAND ELECT, PERFECT, AND SUBLIME MASON (PERFECT ELU)

IT is for each individual Mason to discover the secrets of Masonry 218 through reflection and meditation of its symbols as well as wise consideration and analysis of the sayings and work. Masonry does not implant her truths through repetition. She states them briefly once, hints at them darkly, or interposes a cloud between them and the eyes that would be dazzled by them. "Seek, and you shall find," knowledge and truth.

The practical object of Masonry is the physical, moral, intellectual, and spiritual improvement of an individual and then society. Only through promoting and spreading truth can either be affected. The miseries of men and misfortunes of nations owe their condition to falsehoods in their doctrines and principles. Public opinion is rarely correct on any point. From its collective opinions, there are truths that should be substituted for the many errors and prejudices. There are few truths that public opinion has not hated or persecuted as heresy at some point in its history. Many of these errors were perceived as truths radiating from the presence of God at different times. These moral maladies of man and society need to be treated with boldness, prudence, and discretion because they are the fruit of false doctrines, morals, politics, and religious inclinations.

Much of the Masonic secret manifests itself without speech. It reveals 219 itself to those who partially comprehend the Degrees and their relation, as they are exposed to them. It is revealed easily to those who have advanced to the highest Degrees of the Ancient and Accepted Scottish Rite. From the first Degree of Entered Apprentice the Rite raises a corner of the mysterious veil when it declares that Masonry is a respectful method of *worship*.

Masonry strives to improve the social order by enlightening men's minds, warming their hearts, promoting love and goodness, and inspiring them with the great principle of fraternity. It requires the language and actions of its disciples to conform to the principles that they shall enlighten each other, control their passions, detest vice, and pity the vicious as if they were afflicted with a wretched malady.

Masonry is the universal, eternal, and unchanging religion God planted in the heart of humanity. No creed has ever survived that was not built upon its foundation. It is the base to their superstructure. "Pure and undefiled religion before God is this: visit the fatherless and widows and keep himself unsoiled from the world." "Is not *this* the path I have chosen? To loose the ties of wickedness, remove heavy burdens, free the oppressed, and break every yoke?" The ministers of this religion are all Masons who comprehend and are devoted to it. Its sacrifices to God are its good works. It sacrifices disorderly passions and self-interest upon the altar of humanity. It perpetuates efforts to attain all the moral perfection for which man is capable.

The duties of a Mason are to make honor and moral duty the steady beacons that guide lives through troubled and stormy times. Its duty is to do what is right because it is right and not because it will ensure reward, gain admiration, be "best policy", be more prudent, or be more advisable. It acts because it *is* right, and therefore *ought* to be done. It battles error, intolerance, ignorance, and vice. It is to take pity on those who err, show tolerance even towards intolerance, teach the uneducated, and labor to make the selfish generous. These are some of the duties of a Mason.

A good Mason is one that can look at death without fear and understand its duty. He can endure all the labors of life with just the support of his soul. He 220 can be generous with or without riches. He is not saddened by another's riches or happy when fortune finds him. He does not change with wealth or poverty. He can view another man's possessions as calmly as if it were his own. He spends his own resources as if another entrusted them to him. He does not spend wastefully, foolishly, nor miserly. He does not measure favors by weight or number but by the circumstances of the other party. He never counts his charity too expensive if the receiver is worthy. He acts out of conscience and not for opinion's sake. He is as careful with his thoughts and actions in public. He thinks as much of himself as society. He is free and cheerful with his friends while being charitable and forgiving of his enemies. He loves his country, thinks of its honor, and obeys its laws. He desires nothing more than to do his duty and honor God. Such a Mason acknowledges that his life is the life of a good man. He may calculate his impact not by days, but against the zodiac and the circle of his virtues.

The whole world is but one republic, with each nation as a family and the individuals as the children. Masonry does not detract from the duties to these nations but it creates a new family of men. It is composed of the men of many nations and languages that are bound together by science, morality, and virtue.

Essentially philanthropic, philosophical, and progressive, it holds a firm belief in the existence of God, His providence, and the immortality of the soul as the basis of its dogma. Its objective is to practice and spread the virtues of moral, political, philosophical, and religious truth. Through all the ages, its purpose has been "Liberty, Equality, and Fraternity" within a constitutional government, and it supports *law, order, discipline,* and *subordination* to legitimate authority. Its plan is organized *government*, not *anarchy*.

It is not a political party or a religious sect. It embraces all parties and all sects to form a vast fraternal association. It recognizes the dignity of human nature and man's right to freedom. It does not place one man below another, except when speaking of ignorance, sin, crime, and insubordination to lawful *221* authority.

It is philanthropic. It recognizes the truth that all men have the same origin, common interests, and should cooperate for the same end.

It teaches its members to love, assist, support, and share each other's pains, sorrows, joys, and pleasures. It teaches us to guard reputations, respect opinions, and tolerate errors in each other as it applies to faith and belief.

It is philosophical because it teaches the great Truths concerning the nature and existence of one Supreme Deity and the immortality of the soul. It revives the Academy of Plato and the wise teachings of Socrates. It reiterates the maxims of Pythagoras, Confucius, Zoroaster, and Jesus.

The ancients thought humanity acted under the influence of the opposing Principles of Good and Evil. The Good urged men toward Truth, Independence, and Devotedness. The Evil urged them toward Falsehood, Servility, and Selfishness. Masonry represents the Good Principle and constantly struggles against the Evil one. It is the Hercules, Osiris, Apollo, Mithras, and Ormuzd at the everlasting battle with the demons of ignorance, brutality, corruption, falsehood, dishonor, intolerance, superstition, tyranny, meanness, rudeness, arrogance, racism, and bigotry.

When tyranny and superstition, the twin-powers of evil and darkness, reigned over all the lands, subjugated all nations, and seemed invincible, immortal mysteries of truth were invented to avoid its persecution. The allegory, symbol, and emblem were created in these mysteries to transmit its doctrines by a secret initiation. Today, we have retained the ancient symbols and portions of its ancient ceremonies. It displays its great principles in every civilized country. It smiles past the efforts kings and religious leaders took to crush it out of existence.

Man's views of God contain only as much truth as the human mind is capable of receiving by reason or revelation. The truth must be limited to bring *222* it within the capabilities of finite human intelligence. By being finite, we cannot completely form a correct or adequate idea of the Infinite. Because we are material beings, we cannot form a clear concept of the Spiritual. We understand the infinity *of* Space and Time, and we know of the spirituality *of* the Soul. However, the *idea* of infinity and spirituality eludes us. Even Omnipotence cannot infuse infinite concepts into a finite mind. Not without entirely changing the fabric of our being could God pour the complete knowledge of His own nature and attributes within the narrow confines of our human capacities.

Human intelligence cannot truly grasp it and nor could human language fully express it. Out of necessity, the visible defines how we measure the invisible.

The consciousness of the individual can only reveal *itself*. His knowledge cannot pass beyond the limits of his own material being. His concepts of things *are only his concepts*. They are not those things *itself*. The INFINITE is the principle of the Universe while *our* ideas and concepts are *finite* and can only apply to finite beings.

Deity is not an object of *knowledge*, but of *faith*. It is not approached by *understanding*, but by *moral sense*. It is not *conceptualized*, but *felt*. All attempts to define the Infinite by Finite explanations are only concessions to man's frailties. Shrouded in obscurity, separated from human comprehension by our limited imagination, we know our thoughts are restrained and they must retreat in weakness. The Divine Nature is a concept on which man is barely entitled to assert his opinion due to his lack of authority on the subject. The philosophic intellect is painfully aware of its own insufficiency.

Yet it is here that man most definitively asserts, classifies, and describes God's attributes. Here man draws a map of God's nature and lists an inventory of God's qualities, feelings, impulses, and passions. Man then attacks his neighbor who simply has made a different map and inventory. There is no common understanding and toleration as *Man's* God is an *incarnate* Divinity and exhibits human characteristics. The imperfections in man force their limitations on the Infinite. It clothes the Inconceivable Spirit of the Universe in forms that are understandable and relate to our senses and intellect. These are derived from our imperfect nature, which is part of God's creation.

223   We are all mistaken to some degree. The cherished dogmas within each of us are not the pure truth of God, as we fondly believe. They are simply our own special form of error, our own guesses at truth, and our mind's interpretation of the refracted and obscured rays of light that fall upon us. Our belief systems have their day and then cease to be. They are but scattered lights from God. He is more. Perfect truth is not attainable. We call this a Degree of Perfection, yet what it teaches is imperfect and defective. Still, we are not to drop our pursuit of truth. We are not content and accepting of our errors. It is our duty to press forward with the search for a *more perfect* truth. Though absolute truth may be unattainable, we can continually diminish the amount of error in our views. Thus, Masonry is a continual movement towards light.

Not all errors are harmless. Those that are most dangerous entertain concepts of the nature and attributes of God that are unworthy. This is why Masonry symbolizes the True Word as lost. The true word of a Mason is not the entire, perfect, and absolute truth regarding God. The word is simply the highest and noblest concept of Him that our minds are capable of forming. This *word* is really Ineffable because one man cannot properly communicate his own concept of Deity to another man. Every man's concept of God must be individually proportioned to the learning, intellect, and morals of that man. God *is* what man conceives of Him. He is the reflected image of man himself.

Every person's idea of God changes with teaching, retention, and intellectual formulation. If anyone is content with a *lower* image of Him than his intellect is capable of grasping, then he defines that which is false *to him*, as well as false *in fact*. If his concept is anything but the highest he can reach, he must *feel* it to be false. If we adopt older concepts as our own, then *our* concepts of God are those of more ignorant and narrow-minded peoples, and we are thinking worse of God. We are claiming a more limited view of His nature. Humanity's knowledge grows year by year, and we should develop a better sense of Him as we move towards perfection. The clearest description we can form is the closest to the truth. If we acquiesce to any lower or older understanding, we have an untruth. We should feel it is an indignity to Him to promote the concept of Him as a cruel, shortsighted, erratic, unjust, jealous, angry, and vindictive Being. When we examine our thoughts of His character and we can conceive of a loftier, nobler, higher, more charitable, more glorious, and more magnificent character, then these thoughts within us are closer to the true concept of Deity. *We cannot imagine anything greater than Him.* 224

In order for religion to connect with and influence the populace, it must be simplified and relayed with an amount of error as previously discussed. It is described by the lowest common denominator and is far below the standard attainable by higher capacities. If religion were as pure as the most educated human intellect could fathom, it would not be understood by anyone less educated. He would be ineffective. Truth as comprehended by the philosopher would not similarly be understood by another. The capability of a person to understand would likewise be subject to the teacher and their capacity for learning. Therefore, popular religion is like elementary education whereby it must necessarily be simplified, and hence incorrect as described. It has good intention and attempts to steer us to the right path with the goal of ensuring that most of the people can quickly comprehend most of its aspects. Popular religion does not change its essence and spiritual ideas from True religion as much as it changes the forms, symbols, and dogmas to embody it. Only those who pursue it deeper develop a more refined and more correct view by constantly refining their views and understanding of the subject matter. They proceed, just as one might evolve a view from elementary school through high school, college, and a doctoral program on a subject. One must have the learning and background in religion to correctly understand and interpret a deeper and truer meaning in True religion. Across many points, the truest religion cannot be correctly understood by the uneducated, or even those highly educated in different matters. The truest religion would not be consoling, guiding, or supporting to the majority of humans. The doctrines of the Bible are not clothed in the language of strict truth. They are fitted to relay the practical essentials of a doctrine to those uncultured and uninformed people of that era. A perfectly pure faith, free from outside influences, of noble theism, and of lofty morality, would find too little in common with the daily toils of man for prompt reception by his mind and heart. Hence, Truth might not have reached each of us today if it had not borrowed the wings of Simplicity, with Error to carry its message across the ages.

The Mason regards God as a Moral Governor as well as the Original Creator. He is close-by and not merely found far away in the infinite space and time of Eternity. We conceive Him taking a watchful and presiding interest in the affairs of the world. He continues to influence the hearts and actions of men.

To a Mason, God is the great Source of the World, Life, and Matter. Man, with his physical and mental frame is His direct work. He believes that God has made men with differing intellectual and physical capacities. Some are enabled by intelligence to comprehend and decipher the truths that are unknown and hidden from the masses. He believes that when God wills for mankind to make a great leap forward or achieve a new discovery, He selects and raises 225 someone with an extraordinary and powerful intellect. These minds give birth to new ideas and provide better interpretations of the Truths that are vital to Humanity.

We hold that God has structured all things in this beautiful, harmonious, and mysterious Universe so that mankind continuously builds one great mind after another from its collective learning. From time to time, great minds reveal to men the truths that further our collective understanding. We find our advancement towards Truth limited only by the speed of what can be digested and used by man. He arranges nature and events to develop people within the world who are endowed with a higher mental and moral organization. From these, grand truths and sublime spiritual light will inevitably arise.

Whatever Hiram really was to us, at least he is the imagined apex of humanity in its highest phase. He is an example of what man should become in the course of time as he progresses toward the realization of his destiny as an individual. He was gifted with a glorious intellect, noble soul, fine composition, and perfectly balanced moral being. He is an example of what humanity may be and what we believe it will be in God's good time. He was *the possibility of humanity made real.*

The Mason believes that God has organized this gloriously perplexing world with a purpose and a plan. He holds that every man born to the earth has a duty to perform, a mission to fulfill, and a baptism, trial, or initiation to undergo. Every great and good man possesses some portion of God's truth. He must proclaim this truth to the world and it must have meaning within him. He believes all the strong, wise, and intellectual people of the world are endowed to provide instruction, advancement, and elevation for mankind. That kind of endowment and inspiration is pervasive throughout all of mankind and is not limited to a few writers of Jewish, Christian, or Muslim backgrounds. It is the consequence of the faithful use of our skills. God is its source, each man is its subject, and Truth is its only test. Inspiration differs only in refinement and degrees of learning, intellect, wisdom, and morality of the soul. It is not limited to one religion, sect, age, or nation. It is as vast as the world and as common as the one God. It was not given to a few men, in the infancy of mankind to hold monopoly over truth and bar God from man's soul. We are not born in the twilight and decay of our world. The stars are as beautiful now as then. The oldest Heavens are still fresh and strong. God is still everywhere throughout 226 nature. He is everywhere that a heart beats with love or Faith and Reason speak their truths, as He is in the hearts of mystics and prophets. No soil on earth is more holy than a good man's heart, for nothing is more full of God. Inspiration is not provided only to the learned, great, or wise. Inspiration is endowed to every faithful child of God. As the open eye takes in light, the pure in heart witness God. He who lives true to himself feels God as a presence within his soul. His conscience is the voice of Deity.

Christians, Jews, Muslims, Hindus, Buddhists, Confucians, and Zoroastrians can assemble around the altar of Masonry as brothers and unite in prayer to the one God who is above *all* the false gods (the Baalim). Masonry leaves the Initiate to seek the foundation of his faith and the hope within its written scriptures. Masons find truths written by God upon the heart of man and throughout nature. The principles of religion and duty which are determined through meditation, confirmed by good and wise men's allegiance, and proved by their acceptance among every free mind are charged to Masons. Everyone accepts these fundamental principles.

The Mason does not pretend certainty nor imagine that a certainty is attainable. He has confidence that, if there were no written revelation for man to debate, he could safely have hope and trust in the principles that move and guide him, because his reason, instinct, and consciousness prove to him that they would still exist. He can find a solid foundation for his religious belief with these deductions of the intellect and convictions of the heart. His reasoning provides proof of the existence and attributes of God. He feels that those spiritual instincts are the voice of God in his soul. They fill his mind with a sense of his relationship to God. They provide a conviction in the charity of the Creator and Preserver. They secure a hope of a future existence. His reason and conscience point to virtue as the highest good and lay a path of purpose in man's life.

He studies the wonders of the Heavens, the laws and revolutions of the Earth, the mysterious beauties and adaptations of the animal kingdom, and the moral and material constitution of humans. He is filled with fear and wonder. He is satisfied that God IS. He knows that a Wise and Good Being is the creator 227 of the starry Heavens above him and the moral realms within him. His mind finds a foundation for its hopes, worship, and principles to act in the Universe. It provides a place to grow a deep, full soul bursting with thoughts that cannot be articulated.

There are sublime commandments that need no miracle or voice from above to force our allegiance and assure us of their divine origin. These truths are understood by every reflective mind. If obeyed, they are intended to make Earth a Paradise and raise man to just below the angels. They include understanding the worthlessness of ceremonies and the need for active virtue in its place. They confirm that a pure heart is security for a pure life. They declare that government of thought is the originator and forerunner to action. They promote the ideas of universal philanthropy and love for all men. They encourage us to do unto others as we would have done to ourselves and to be right, just, and generous. These truths also include the forgiveness of injuries and self-sacrifice for duty, humility, sincerity, and *being* that which we *seem* to be. They command obedience by their correctness and beauty. They are the law in all ages, in every country around the world. God revealed them to man from his beginning.

To the Mason, God is our Father in Heaven. To be His children is sufficient reward for peacemakers. To see His face is the highest hope of the pure in heart. He is always there to strengthen His true worshippers. We owe Him our deepest love and our most humble and patient submission. His worship is seen in a pure, charitable, and generous heart. We must live and act as if He were constantly present. In death, we are at His merciful disposal. We hope and believe that death is but the initiation to a better life. His wise decrees forbid a man to regard his death with lazy contentment.

Masonry's teachings about conduct toward man and reverence to God are universal among all religious men and offer little room for debate among mankind. He is our *Father*, and we are all *brothers*. These truths are apparent to both the unlearned and wise, the busy and the leisurely. No priest is needed to teach or endorse these. If every man conformed to them we could end barbarity, cruelty, intolerance, uncharitableness, faithlessness, treachery, vengeance, selfishness, and all the vices and evil passions of humanity.

The true Mason holds that a Supreme God created and governs this world. He believes that He governs it by wise, just, charitable, steady, unwavering, and unalterable laws. He believes agony and sorrow are for *his* correction, *his* strengthening, and *his* development. These laws are the best that could be made for our happiness and purification. They provide the opportunity for everyone, from the common to the most noble, to work on their virtues. They are best adapted for us to work out the vast, reverent, glorious, and eternal designs of the Great Spirit of the Universe. Though a man may be in misery, he believes that nature has showered equal blessings and sunshine upon others from the very same unchanging equation of life. Time is pressing onward to fulfill its mighty purpose. It is an honor and a reward to have contributed to humanity's course through time, even as a victim. A Mason takes this steady view of Time, Nature, and God. He bears his lot in life without objection because it is his part of a system ordained by God. He believes God does not lose sight of *him* while

228

176

overseeing the operation of the Universe. He understands that if he should suffer pain or calamity that it was established when the Universe was created and the chain of events ordained through time. He believes that God considers his own good deeds equal with the notable achievements of humanity through time.

With these beliefs, he attains a degree of virtue that is the highest humanity can reach amid *passive* excellence. He finds his reward in the reflection that he is an eager and cooperative aid to the Creator of the Universe and in the noble understanding that he is worthy and capable of this sublime concept despite his sad destiny. He is entitled to be called a Grand Elect, Perfect, and 229 Sublime Mason. He is content to fall early in the battle if his body would form a stepping-stone for the future advancement of humanity.

If God is perfectly good, then He could not have us suffer pain without reason. Either we receive an antidote to evil within us, or such pain is necessary to the grand scheme of the Universe, which is good in its whole. The Mason submits to it in either case. He would not suffer unless it was the order of things. If a man believes that God cares for His creations, then (no matter his creed) he cannot doubt that it would only happen if it were better for himself or for the greater good of humanity. To complain and grieve is to challenge God's will, and it is worse than unbelief.

The Mason's mind is nobler upon enlightenment and reflection. He ascends toward a more divine life. He loves truth more than rest. He prefers the peace of Heaven to the peace of earthly paradise. His loftier mind is heavy with worries. He knows man does not live by pleasure and materialism alone, but by God's power. He knows that the only true rest and peace comes with the final rest and reward from a life filled with good works. He accepts that trouble is found everywhere on the path to Heaven. He must prepare himself for the necessary work of life that requires constant attention. If one does not find comfort in the furnished temples and churches of tradition, then he must labor to build his own house for his own system of faith and thought.

The power in the hope of success, not reward, should stimulate and sustain us. Our objective, not our self-interest, should be our inspiration. Selfishness is a sin. When we consider eternity, selfish desires are simply not important. We should not work through life to achieve Heaven or Bliss but out of Duty.

Usually, we have to combine our efforts with thousands of others, contributing and carrying forward a great cause. Our specific sacrifices cannot be accurately measured. If we are to assist and prepare the way for the future arrival of some great achievement among humanity, our portion of contribution 230 may not be realistically measured. Few of those who have labored with patience, secrecy, and silence to bring about political or social change for humanity have lived to see that change implemented, and fewer have witnessed appreciable returns from their labor. Still fewer were able to define what weight their efforts contributed to the achievement of that change. Many will doubt if these exertions will make a difference. Thus discouraged, they cease all effort.

Undiscouraged, the Mason strives to elevate and purify his *motives* just as he works diligently with the conviction that there is truly no such thing as wasted effort. In all labor, there is something to be gained. All sincere exertion in a righteous and unselfish cause is *necessarily* followed by an appropriate and proportionate success. *No* bread cast on the waters can be wholly lost. *No* seed planted in the ground can fail to sprout in due time and measure. In moments of despair, we may doubt if our cause will triumph and, if it does, whether we have contributed to its triumph. We take comfort in the knowledge that God knows our immeasurable contribution. He sees every exertion we make and can assign the exact degree each assisted to gain victory over social evil. No good work is done in vain.

The Grand Elect, Perfect, and Sublime Mason will not deserve that honorable title if he does not have strength, will, and energy. He must have a Faith that feeds upon the desire and thought of humanity's victory. It must be content with its own portion, fighting when it should, and finding joy in the battle, even in defeat.

The accumulated filth and misery from mankind's centuries, the Augean Stables of the World, require a mighty river to cleanse them thoroughly. Our labors are drops we add to the river to swell and bolster its force to accomplish the deed. God notices this even if man does not. He whose zeal is deep and serious, will not care foremost that his drops should be distinguishable from the 231 mighty torrent of cleansing waters. To make them distinct, he would have to keep his portion separate to flow by itself, where it would have far less of the desired effect for mankind.

The true Mason will not take care to ensure that his name is labeled on the coins he casts into God's treasury. He is satisfied knowing he has worked with a purity of purpose towards a good cause, and he *must* have contributed to its success. The *degree* in which he has contributed is a matter of little concern for him to measure. The unselfish is satisfied knowing that having contributed to a success, however obscure or unnoticed is sufficient reward. Let every Grand Elect, Perfect, and Sublime Mason cherish this faith. It is his duty. It is the brilliant and never-fading light that shines from within the symbolic pedestal of alabaster on which rests the perfect cube of agate, the symbol of duty that is inscribed with the divine name of God. He who is industrious is a good laborer and a worthy employee. He who selflessly sows seeds that others will reap is a noble person and worthy of reward.

The Mason does not promote an undervaluing of this life among others. He does not view this life as an insignificant and unworthy portion of existence, because that would require unnatural, morbid, or insincere feelings. Masonry teaches us that the future will correct the social evils we see about us today. This life is but a step on the path to achieving that correction. Without action today, it will be unattainable, but we may not see the cure in this lifetime. Denial of progress does injury to virtue and society. Life is real, serious, and full of duties to perform. It is our initiation to immortality. Those who have affection and deep interest for this world's state will work for its improvement. Those whose affections are deflected to Heaven easily submit to the miseries of earth. They deem these problems as hopeless, fitting, or pre-ordained. They comfort themselves with the idea of their future compensation. It is a sad hypocrisy that those completely given to religious contemplation and to making religion and virtue rule their hearts are often most apathetic toward improving this world's problems. In many cases, they conserve the imperfect state by being hostile to political and social reform, as it might divert men's energies from thoughts of eternity.

The Mason does not fight instincts, emaciate his body, belittle what he sees to be beautiful, demean the wonderful, and distance himself from what is 232 dear and precious. He does not deny his nature, which God has given him, to struggle to achieve what He has *not* bestowed. He knows that man was created as a mixed being of body and mind. He is not only a spiritual being. The body is fit and needs the material world with its full, rightful, and allotted share. His life is guided by a recognition of this fact. He does not deny his body boldly and then suffer to admit its weakness and inevitable failings. He believes that his spirituality will continue to exist in the next stage of his being, the spiritual body. His body will be left behind at death, but until then God meant for it to be commanded and controlled and not painfully neglected, despised, or ignored for the soul.

The Mason is concerned about the fate of the soul, its continued and eternal being, and the events in which it will become fully developed. These are topics of profound interest and refining contemplation. These thoughts occupy much of his leisure time. He returns to them as he becomes familiar with the sorrows and troubles of this life, as his hopes are dashed, and as his visions of happiness fade away. When life has wearied him, when he is worn, and when the burden of his years weigh heavy on him, the balance of his thoughts slowly shift to the next life. He clings to his beliefs with a feverish tenacity and will not listen to the forbidding decree of others. These are the privileges earned by the worn, weary, and bereaved.

His contemplations of the Future shine light on the Present for him. It develops the higher aspects of his nature. He strives to accommodate the respective claims of Heaven and earth upon his time and thoughts. He works to give proper proportion to performing the duties and interests of this world while preparing for the next. He weighs his actions between the cultivation of his own character and public service.

The Mason does not indoctrinate. He entertains and speaks his own convictions and leaves others free to do the same. He only hopes for the time,

233 even if it takes ages, when all men shall form one great family of brothers. At that time just one law, the law of love, shall govern God's whole Universe.

My brother, believe as you want. If you feel there is a God in the Universe and man is unlike other living creatures due to his immortal soul, then we welcome you among us. You may carry the title of Grand Elect, Perfect, and Sublime Mason with humility and consciousness of your faults, as we all do.

There are secret meanings behind the *twelve* Apostles of Christ and *seventy-two* of his Disciples. There is hidden meaning when John addressed his criticisms and warnings to the *Seven* churches, which is the number of Archangels and of the then known Planets. Near Babylon, the Tower of Babel at Borsippa had Seven Stages and was a pyramid of Seven stories. At Ecbatana, the capital of the Medianites, there were Seven concentric walls each of a different color. Thebes had Seven gates, and Seven is repeated throughout the story of the flood. There are ten Sephiroth (Emanations of God). Three Sephirah are in one class, and seven in another, repeating the mystic numbers of Pythagoras. Seven Amshaspandan (archangels) are invoked with Ormuzd. Seven inferior Rishis of Hindustan were saved with the head of their family in an ark. Seven ancient personages alone returned with the British Druid Hu from the valley of grievous waters. There were Seven Heliadae (sons) whose father Helios, the Sun, crossed the sky in a golden chariot. There are Seven Titans, children of Kronos, or Saturn. There were Seven Korybantes. There were Seven Cabeiri being the sons of Sydyk. There were Seven primeval Celestial spirits of the Japanese. There were Seven "seeds" that escaped the flood and began anew from the summit of Mount Albordi. Seven Cyclopes were said to have built the walls of Tiryns and Mycenae.

Origen quotes Celsus who tells us that the Persians symbolized the two-fold motion of the fixed stars and moving planets and how the Soul passes through their successive spheres. For the mystic Mithraic Rites of initiation practiced in holy caves they erected a "high *ladder*". On the Seven steps of this ladder were Seven gates or portals, according to the number of the Seven principal heavenly bodies. Initiates passed through these gates until they reached the summit of the whole. This passage was styled a transmigration through the spheres.

234 Jacob saw in his dream a *ladder* set on the earth. Its top reached to Heaven, and the Angels (Malaki Alohim) ascended and descended on it. Above it stood IHUH, declaring Himself to be Ihuh-Alhi Abraham. The word translated as *ladder* is סלם *Salam* (from סלל, *Salal*) and means raised, elevated, reared up, exalted, or piled heap, *Aggeravit.* סללה Salalah, means a heap, rampart, or other unnatural accumulation of earth and stone. סלע, *Salaa* or *Salo*, is a rock, cliff, or boulder and is a name of the City of Petra. We find no ancient Hebrew word to designate a pyramid.

The symbolic mountain Meru was ascended by Seven steps, or stages. All the pyramids and artificial tumuli and hillocks thrown up in flat countries were imitations of this fabulous and mystic mountain for the purpose of worship. These were the "High Places" where heathen idolaters sacrificed to foreign gods.

The pyramids were sometimes square, and sometimes round. The sacred Babylonian tower (מגדל, Magdol), dedicated to the great Father Baal, was an artificial hill of pyramidal shape and built of Seven stages of brick. Each stage was of a different color representing the Seven planetary spheres according to the respective color of each planet. Meru was said to be a single mountain with three peaks and thus a symbol of the Trimurti. The great Pagoda at Tanjore was six stories surmounted by a temple, making a total of seven, and on this were three spires or towers. An ancient pagoda at Deogur was surmounted by a tower, providing for the mystic egg and trident. Herodotus tells us that the Temple of Baal at Babylon was a tower composed of Seven towers resting on an eighth that served as its base. It diminished in size from the bottom to the top, and Strabo tells us it was a pyramid.

Faber thinks that the Mithraic *ladder* was really a pyramid with Seven stages, and each provided a narrow door through which the aspirant passed to reach the summit. Then he descended through similar doors on the opposite side of the pyramid. The ascent and descent of the Soul was thus represented.

All Mithraic caves and all the ancient temples were intended to symbolize the Universe. A Temple was regularly called the habitation of Deity. Every temple was the world in miniature. The entire world was one grand temple. Most ancient temples were roofless. Hence, the Persians, Celts, and Scythians strong dislike of artificially covered buildings. Cicero says that Xerxes burned the Grecian temples on the express ground that the whole world was the Magnificent Temple and Habitat of the Supreme Deity. Macrobius says that the entire Universe was determined by many to be the Temple of God. Plato pronounced that the real Temple of the Deity was the world. Heraclitus declared that the Universe, diverse with animals, plants, and stars was the only genuine Temple of the Divinity.

The Temple of Solomon was symbolic as seen with its sacred numbers and astrological symbols in its historical descriptions. The details of the reconstructed building as seen in Ezekiel's vision bears witness to this. The Apocalypse completes the demonstration and shows the Kabbalistic meanings of its entirety. The *Symbola Architectonica* is found on the most ancient edifices. These mathematical figures and instruments, adopted by the Templars, are identical with those on the gnostic seals. They connect their dogma with the Chaldæan, Syrian, and Egyptian philosophies. The secret Pythagorean doctrine of numbers was preserved by the monks of Tibet, Hierophants of Egypt, Eleusis at Jerusalem, and circular Chapters of the Druids. They are consecrated in the mysterious writing, the Apocalypse of Saint John.

All temples were surrounded by pillars, which recorded the number of the constellations, signs of the zodiac, or cycles of the planets. Each one was a microcosm, or symbol, of the Universe that had the starred vault of Heaven for its roof or ceiling.

All temples were originally open at the top, having the sky for a roof. Twelve pillars described the belt of the zodiac. Whatever the number of the pillars, they were mystical. At the Temple of Abury, the Druids reproduced all the celestial orbits by its columns. Around the temples of Chilminar in Persia, Baalbec in Lebanon, and Takht-e Soleiman in West Azerbaijan stood *forty* pillars. On each side of the temple at Paestum in Italy were fourteen pillars recording the Egyptian cycles of the dark and light sides of the moon as described by Plutarch, and the whole thirty-eight that surrounded them recorded the two meteoric cycles often found in the Druidic temples.

Three hundred and sixty columns surrounded the theater built by M. Aemilius Scaurus in Rome. Three hundred and sixty stones surround the Kaaba at Mecca and the Temple on Iona in Scotland.

Morals and Dogma for the 21st Century

Chapter of Rose Croix

CHAPTER 15: KNIGHT OF THE EAST OR OF THE SWORD OR OF THE EAGLE

THIS Degree is symbolic, like all of the Degrees in Masonry. Although 237 based upon historical truth and authentic tradition, it is still an allegory. The two primary lessons of this Degree are Fidelity to obligation and Constancy and Perseverance when facing difficult and discouraging situations.

Masonry is engaged in a crusade against ignorance, intolerance, fanaticism, superstition, greed, and error. It does not sail the smooth seas with a steady breeze from the prevailing winds bound for a welcoming harbor, but it meets and must overcome many opposing currents, treacherous winds, and dead calms.

The largest obstacles to its success are the apathy and faithlessness of its own selfish members and their moral and intellectual indifference to the world. The enduring voice of Masonry is ignored in the daily stress, pressure, and turmoil of life, business, and politics. The first lesson learned when engaged in any great work of reform or beneficence is that men are fundamentally careless, uncommitted, apathetic, and indifferent to anything that does not benefit their own immediate personal welfare. As man struggles towards perfection, the great 238 works of mankind are indebted to the efforts of a few individual men and not to the united efforts of many. The enthusiast who that imagines he can inspire the multitudes with his own enthusiasm is grievously mistaken. The realization of this mistake is typically followed by discouragement and disgust. The curse of the benefactor of man is to successfully work, pay, and suffer through the obstacles and hindrances necessary to accomplish a great work, only to have those who opposed or denied him assistance receive the praise and reward.

The man who endeavors to serve, benefit, and improve the world is like a swimmer struggling against a river's rapid current. Many waves surge over his head, beat him back, and frustrate him. Most people will yield to the stress of the current and float downstream to the shore or be swept over the rapids. Only the stout, strong heart and vigorous arms will struggle on toward ultimate success.

Stationary and motionless people impede and disturb the current of progress, like the solid rock or dead tree resting firmly on the river bottom around which the water must whirl and eddy. Our progress is impeded by Masons who doubt, hesitate, are discouraged, or do not believe in man's ability to improve. Those who do not work for the interest and general well-being of humanity and who expect others to do everything while they idly sit applauding (or perhaps predicting failure), frustrate progress as certainly as the rock.

There were many such people at the rebuilding of the Temple: prophets of evil and misfortune; the uncommitted, indifferent, and apathetic; those who stood by and sneered; and those who thought they did enough service to God if they occasionally applauded. The ravens croaked ill omens and whisperers preached about the idiocy and futility of the effort. The world is full of these kinds of people, and they are as abundant today as they were then.

However, despite the gloomy and discouraging prospect of indifference within and bitter opposition without, our ancient brethren persevered. 239 Whenever success is uncertain, remote, and contingent, the only question we should ask ourselves as real men and Masons is, "What does our duty require?" Do not consider what will be the result or reward if we perform our duty. Move forward with the Sword in one hand and the Trowel in the other!

Masonry teaches that God is a Paternal Being. He has an interest in His children as conveyed by the title *Father*. This interest is absent in all the systems of Paganism and is not taught in any of the theories of philosophy. It is an interest in the glorious beings of other spheres, the Sons of Light, the dwellers in Heavenly worlds, and also in us (the poor, ignorant, and unworthy). He has pity for the dishonest, pardon for the guilty, love for the pure, knowledge for the humble, and promises of immortal life for those who trust and obey Him.

Life is miserable without a belief in Him. The world is dark, and the Universe is disrobed of its splendors. The intellectual bond to nature is broken, and the charm of existence is dissolved. Hope is lost, and the mind wanders through the infinite desert of its perception without attraction, instinct, destiny, or purpose.

Masonry teaches that God foresees all the events and actions that take place in the universe and the eternal succession of ages. Because He comprehends all, man's free will should be His instrument like all the forces of nature.

Masonry teaches that He forms the soul for a purpose. Built in its proportions and fashioned by infinite skill, its nature, necessity, and design are virtues emanating from His spirit. It is formed, molded, fashioned, balanced, and proportioned so perfectly and exquisitely in every part, that sin introduced into it is a misery. Vicious thoughts fall upon it like drops of poison, and guilty desires breathing on its delicate fibers form deadly plague-spots. The soul is made for virtue and not vice. Purity, rest, and happiness are its end. Trying to change the laws of human nature is as vain as attempting to sink a mountain to be level with its valley, turn back the waves of the angry sea from the shores, cease the thunder upon the beach, or halt the stars in their swift orbits. Be upright and virtuous is one of the laws uttered by God's voice that speaks through every nerve, fiber, force, and element of the moral constitution He has *240* given us. If tempted, we must resist. We must govern our unruly passions and hold reign on our sensual appetites. This is part of the great law of harmony that binds the Universe together. It is not the mere command of arbitrary will, but the edict of Infinite Wisdom.

God is good, and we know what He does is right. The works of creation, changes of life, and destinies of eternity are all spread before us as the gifts and advice of infinite love. The love of God is always working on good and glorious tasks beyond our thought and comprehension. We cannot understand God's love because it is *too* glorious for us to understand. God's love takes care of everything and neglects nothing. It watches over all. It provides for all. It makes wise decisions for all ages; for infancy, childhood, maturity, and in every scene of this world; for want, weakness, joy, sorrow, and even sin. All is good, well, and right and it shall be so forever. Through all ages, the light of God's beneficence will disclose all, consummate all, and reward all who deserve to be rewarded. Then we will see what we now can only believe. The cloud will be lifted, the gate of mystery will be passed, and the full light will shine forever as the symbolic light of the Lodge. Then our trial will yield us triumph, and our heartache will be filled with gladness. We will then feel that the only true happiness is to learn, advance, and improve, which cannot happen unless we begin with error, ignorance, and imperfection. We must pass through the darkness, to reach the light.

CHAPTER 16: PRINCE OF JERUSALEM

WE no longer expect to rebuild the Temple at Jerusalem. It is only a 241 symbol to us, because the world and every upright heart are God's Temple. Establishing the New Law and Reign of Love, Peace, Charity, and Toleration builds that Temple which is most acceptable to God. Masonry is now engaged in this effort. We no longer need to travel to Jerusalem to worship, offer sacrifices, or shed blood to appease the Deity. The woods and mountains are our Churches and Temples for worshiping God with a devout gratitude. Wherever the humble and remorseful heart silently offers up its adoration is God's house and the New Jerusalem.

The Princes of Jerusalem are no longer magistrates judging between the people, nor is their number limited to five. Their duties remain substantially the same, and their insignia and symbols retain their old significance of Justice and Equity. Their duties are to settle and heal dissensions, restore peace and harmony, soothe dislikes, and soften prejudices. They know that peacemakers are blessed.

Their emblems have been explained. They are part of the language of Masonry that is the same now as it was when Moses learned it from the Egyptian Priests.

We continue to observe the spirit of the Divine law as explained to our ancient brethren when the Temple was rebuilt. The book of the law was once again opened:

"Execute true judgment. Show mercy and compassion to every person. Do not oppress the widow, the fatherless, the stranger, or the poor. Do not imagine evil against your brother in your heart. Speak the truth to your neighbor, 242 execute the judgment of Truth and Peace, and make no false oath, for I hate all of these said the Lord."

"Let those who have power rule in righteousness. The Princes of Jerusalem rule in judgment. A judge should be a hiding place from the wind, a shelter from the storm, a river of water in a desert, and the shadow of a great rock in a weary land. The work of justice will be peace, and its result is tranquility and security. Wisdom and knowledge will stabilize the times. Walk righteously, speak uprightly, and despise the gains of oppression and the corruption of bribery. Do not cover your ears to the cries of the oppressed or close your eyes to the crimes of the powerful. Then you will dwell on high ground, and your place of defense will be armed with heavy munitions."

Do not forget these precepts of the old Law. Remember that every Mason is your brother, however humble, and the working man is your peer! Remember that all Masonry is work and that the trowel is an emblem of the Degrees of this Council. Labor is both noble and dignifying, and it is intended to develop a man's moral and spiritual nature. It should not be deemed a disgrace or misfortune.

Everything around us is moral in its behavior and influences. When we awaken, the serene and bright morning calls us to a new life and gives us existence again. His mercies visit us in every bright ray and glad thought, and they call for gratitude and contentment. The hushed silence of the early dawn; the holy twilight with its cooling breeze and lengthening shadows; the sweltering noontide; the stern and solemn midnight; the Spring, Autumn, and Summer that bring forth the ever-renewed wonders of the world; and Winter that gathers us around the evening fire. All these touch the spiritual life within us and direct our lives to either good or evil. The idle hand of the wristwatch and the shadow from the shaft on the sundial often fall upon the conscience.

243 A life of labor is not a state of inferiority or degradation. The Almighty has not cast humanity's lot beneath the quiet shovels or amid pleasant groves and lovely hills with no tasks except to rise, eat, lie down, and rest. He has ordained that *Work* will be done in all the dwellings of life, every productive field, every busy city, and on every wave of every ocean. He did this because it pleases Him to give man a nature destined to higher ends than simply a lazy calm or irresponsible, profitless existence. Work is the necessary and proper element for harnessing the energies of this nature.

Masonry teaches this as a great Truth and a moral landmark that should guide the course of all humanity. It teaches its followers that the work of their daily life is spiritual and their tools, services, and products are designed for spiritual ends. By embracing this, their daily lot may become a sphere for the noblest improvement. The activities of our leisure time should be designed to prepare our minds for the *action* of Life. We should hear, read, and meditate so we may *act* well because the *action* of life is the great arena for spiritual improvement. There is no task of industry or business, in the field or the forest, on the wharf or the ship's deck, in the office or exchange that does not have spiritual ends. Every aspect of our daily labors was especially ordained to teach us patience, calmness, resolution, perseverance, gentleness, impartiality, and kindness. There are not any working tools or implements that are not a part of the great spiritual instrumentality.

All the relations of life, like those of a parent, child, brother, sister, friend, associate, lover, beloved, husband, and wife, are moral. Every living tie and thrilling nerve bind them together. They cannot subsist a day or even an hour without putting the mind to a trial of its truth, fidelity, patience, and integrity.

A city is an extended form of moral action. Every act or event that 244 occurs in it has a purpose, ultimately good or bad, and is, therefore, moral. Every action performed has a motive, and motives are the special jurisdiction of morality. Equipment, houses, and furniture are symbols of what is moral, and in a thousand ways, they provoke right or wrong feelings. Everything we own administers to our comfort, luxury, pride, gratitude, selfishness, vanity, thoughts of self-indulgence, or the merciful remembrances of the needy and destitute.

Everything acts upon and influences us. God's great law of sympathy and harmony is as effective and inflexible as His law of gravity. A sentence embodying a noble thought may stir our blood. A noise made by a child may worry or aggravate us, but both influence our actions.

We all vaguely appraise the world of spiritual objects, influences, and relationships that surrounds us. Anyone who communicates with the spiritual scene around them hears the voice of the spirit in every sound, sees its signs in every passing form, and feels its impulse in all action, passion, and being lives a charmed life. All around us lie the mines of wisdom. There is a secret in the simplest, a wonder in the plainest, and a charm in the dullest of things.

People are naturally inclined to seek wonder. They travel far and wide to see the majesty of old ruins, the imposing forms of the remote mountains, great waterfalls, and galleries of art. Yet a world of wonder is all around us. We can find it in the setting sun, the evening stars, the magic of springtime, the blossoming of the trees, the strange transformations of the butterfly, the Infinite Divinity, and His boundless revelation. There is no better splendor than that which sets its morning throne in the golden East and no dome as sublime as that of Heaven. There is no beauty as fair as that of the blossoming earth and no place like that home which is hushed and embraced by the humblest walls and roof.

These are the symbols of things far greater and far higher. They are the timeless clothing of the spirit wrapping the immortal nature. In this show of circumstance and form, the stupendous reality stands revealed. Let man be as he is, a living soul in harmony with himself and with God. His vision becomes *245* eternity; his sanctuary becomes infinity, and his home becomes the bosom of all embracing love.

The great problem of Humanity is played out in the humblest homes, but not more than in the highest. A human heart throbs beneath the beggar's cloak, and that alone stirs the Prince's mantle with its beating. The beauty of Love, the charm of Friendship, the sacredness of Sorrow, the heroism of Patience, and noble Self-sacrifice are the beauty and power that make life what it is. They are the priceless treasures and glory of humanity and not things of condition. All places and all landscapes are clothed with the majesty and charm of virtues such as these.

A million moments will come to each of us during the normal course of our life. Varying every hour, they will require us to restrain our passions, subdue our hearts to gentleness and patience, resign our own interest to another's advantage, speak words of kindness and wisdom, raise the fallen, cheer the fainting and sick in spirit, and soothe and relieve the weariness and bitterness of their mortal lot. Every Mason will have plenty of opportunity for this. They cannot be written on his tomb, but they will be written deep in the hearts of friends, family, and the acquaintances all around him. They will be credited in the great book of accounts, and their eternal influences will be on the great pages of the Universe.

Brethren, let us all aspire to such a destiny! Let us all strive to obey these laws of Masonry! May He encourage our zeal, sustain our hopes, and assure us of success. Then will our hearts become true temples of the Living God!

CHAPTER 17: KNIGHT OF THE EAST AND WEST

246

THIS is the first of the Philosophical Degrees of the Ancient and Accepted Scottish Rite. It is the beginning of a course of instruction that will reveal the heart and inner mysteries of Masonry. Do not worry if you have often thought you were about to gain light but found disappointment. Truth has always hidden beneath symbols and allegories. Veil after veil has to be penetrated before the true Light is obtained and the ultimate truth revealed. Human Light is only an imperfect reflection of the Infinite and Divine.

We are about to begin the study of the ancient Religions which once ruled the minds of men. Their ruins are scattered on the plains of the great Past 247 like the broken columns of Palmyra and Tadmor washing away in the sands of the desert. Those old, strange, and mysterious creeds are shrouded in the mists of antiquity. They mysteriously walk along the line that divides Time from Eternity. Forms of strange, wild, and startling beauty mingle with shapes that are monstrous, grotesque, and hideous.

The religion taught by Moses emphasized the principle of exclusion and borrowed from all the creeds it interacted with. The learned and wise enriched it with the best principles of the religions of Egypt and Asia. During the wanderings of the Jews, it was influenced by everything that was impure or seductive in the pagan manners and superstitions. It was different during the time of Moses and Aaron than it was during the time of David and Solomon, and different still at the time of Daniel and Philo.

When John the Baptist made his appearance in the desert, all the old philosophical and religious systems were moving toward each other. The conquests of Alexander and the establishment of the Greek colonies and dynasties unified the existing doctrines. The mixing of the different nations that resulted from the wars of Alexander brought together the doctrines of Greece, Egypt, Persia, and India. All the barriers that had previously kept the nations apart were torn down. The People of the West readily combined their beliefs with those of the East, while the Eastern peoples hurried to learn the traditions of Rome and the legends of Athens. The Philosophers of Greece eagerly adopted the beliefs and doctrines of the East. The Jews and Egyptians (until then the most exclusive of peoples) adopted Greek and Roman eclecticism.

248 Christians also mixed the old and new teachings of Christianity and Philosophy. An intelligent man who is devoted to one system of thought rarely displaces it with another in all its purity. People will take any creed that is offered to them. The distinction between esoteric and exoteric doctrine easily gained a foothold among many of the Christians. Philosophers believed that the writings of the Apostles were incomplete and only contained the seeds of another doctrine. They believed that Philosophy must provide the systematic organization and development that Christianity was lacking and that the writings of the Apostles only addressed the articles of the vulgar faith for the general public. The mysteries of knowledge were transmitted to the superior minds of the Elect. These mysteries were handed down from generation to generation in esoteric traditions. They named this science of the mysteries "Gnosis".

The Gnostics derived their leading doctrines and ideas from Plato, Philo, the Zend-Avesta, Kabbalah, and the sacred books of India and Egypt. They provided Christianity the cosmological and religious speculations of the ancient Eastern religions and merged them with the Egyptian, Greek, and Jewish doctrines previously adopted by the Neo-Platonists.

The Gnostics taught that all beings came from God, progressively degenerated, will be redeemed, and will return to the purity of the Creator. The Eastern culture of contemplation, mysticism, and intuition dictated its doctrines. Its language corresponded to its origin. It had all the magnificence, imagery, inconsistencies, and mobility of the figurative style.

249 Behold the light that originates from an immense center of Light. It spreads its benevolent rays everywhere. Spirits of Light originate from the Divine Light. All the springs that nourish, embellish, fertilize, and purify the Earth originate from the same ocean. All Numbers begin with and resemble one primitive number. They are composed of its essence, but they vary infinitely. Words are divisible into many syllables and elements contained in the primitive Word, but they are infinitely various. All Intelligences originated from a Primary Intelligence, and they resemble it though displaying an infinite variety of existences.

Gnosticism revived and combined the old doctrines of the East and West and found justification for doing so in many passages of the Gospels and the Pastoral letters. Christ spoke in parables and allegories, John borrowed the enigmatical language of the Platonists, and Paul often indulged in difficult rhetoric that was only clear to the Initiates.

The birthplace of Gnosticism was probably in Syria or Palestine. Most of its teachers wrote in a corrupted form of Greek used by the Hellenistic Jews, in the Septuagint, and the New Testament. There was a striking similarity between their doctrines and those of Philo of Alexandria. Three philosophic and religious schools (Greek, Egyptian, and Jewish) were located in the city.

Pythagoras and Plato, who were the most mystical of the Greek Philosophers, taught the esoteric doctrines and the distinction between the initiated and profane. Between them, they had traveled to Egypt, Phœnicia, India, and Persia. The chief doctrines of Platonism were found in Gnosticism. Among these were the beliefs that Intelligence came from God, that man would stray in error, and his spirit would suffer. They saw the search for Truth and reunion with God as a hopeless and continuous effort. They viewed Man's soul as a mixture of the pure and divine with the irrational. Lacking knowledge of the creation, they believed that angels or demons governed the planets and dwelled within them. All beings would be reincarnated by returning to the Cosmos, whose ruler was the Supreme Being. In these two systems, we discover some of *250* the ideas that form a part of Masonry. In the present debased condition of the symbolic Degrees, they are disguised with fiction and absurdity. The ideas are casually hinted at but often completely overlooked.

The distinction between the esoteric and exoteric doctrines, which was strictly Masonic, has always been preserved among the Greeks. The mysteries of Theosophy were found in all the Greek traditions and myths. After the time of Alexander, the Greeks turned to the schools of Egypt, Asia, Ancient Thrace, Sicily, Etruria, and Attica for instruction, dogmas, and mysteries.

Everything we know of the Jewish-Greek School of Alexandria comes through two of its leaders. Aristobulus and Philo were Jews of Alexandria in Egypt. The school originated in Asia and owed its language and studies to Greece. It tried to show that all the philosophical truths of other countries originated in Palestine. Aristobulus declared that all the facts and details of the Jewish Scriptures were allegories that concealed the most profound meanings and that Plato had borrowed his best ideas from them. A century later, he influenced Philo, who tried to show that the Hebrew writings, with their system of allegories, were the true source of all religious and philosophical doctrines. According to Philo, the literal meaning of the writings was for the uneducated alone. Anyone who has meditated on philosophy, been purified by virtue, and improved himself by contemplation of God and the intellectual world discovers a different order of things. He becomes an initiate of the mysteries and understands that the simple or literal meaning is an imperfect image. A historical fact, figure, word, rite, custom, parable, or vision of a prophet hides the most profound truths. Whoever has the key of science will interpret everything according to the light he possesses.

Once again, we see the symbolism of Masonry and the Candidate's search for light. "Let men of narrow minds withdraw with closed ears," Philo says. "We teach the divine mysteries to those who have received the sacred *251* initiation, practiced true piety, and who have not been enslaved by empty words or preconceived opinions."

Philo believed the Supreme Being was the Primitive, the Archetype of Light, and the source of the rays that illuminate Souls. God was also the Soul of the Universe, acting everywhere. He fills and limits His whole Being. His Powers and Virtues fill and penetrate all. These Powers are Spirits separate from God. They are the "Ideas" that Plato personified. He is without beginning and lives in the prototype of Time.

His image is THE WORD, a form more brilliant than fire, but not the *pure* light. This LOGOS dwells in God. Within His intelligence, the Supreme Being makes the types or ideas of everything that is to become reality in this World. The LOGOS is the vehicle by which God acts on the Universe, like the speech of man.

The LOGOS is the World of Ideas that God has used to create visible things. He is the most ancient God, more ancient than the World. He is the representative of the LOGOS. The highest *Intelligence* is called *Archangel* and is the *symbol* and *representative* of all spirits, even those of mortals. He is also Adam, the model of primitive man.

God alone is Wise. The wisdom of man is only a reflection and image of the Wisdom of God. He is the Father and His WISDOM is the mother of creation. He united Himself with WISDOM and provided the germ of creation. In turn, Wisdom brought forth the material world. He created only the ideal world and modeled the material world after it. The Intellectual City was the *Thought* of the Architect who created it according to the plan of the Material City.

The Word is not only the Creator, but it occupies the place of the Supreme Being. All the Powers and Attributes of God act through Him. He represents the Human Family and is their Protector and Shepherd.

252 God gave man the Soul or Intelligence, which existed before the body, and united it with the body. Reason comes from God through the Word. In man, there are irrational impulses and passions that produce disorder. The body is taken from the Earth, and God hates the rational Principle that animates it. The rational soul that God has provided is captive in the body that encompasses it. Man's present condition is not like his original condition, in which he was the image of the Logos. He has fallen from his first place, but he may free himself from the bonds of the body again by following the guidance of WISDOM and the Angels whom God has charged to aid him. God has permitted the existence of evil *to furnish mankind the means to exercise our liberty* in fighting against it. The souls, purified by light, rise to Heaven to enjoy perfect happiness. Bodies are centers for passion and evil desire, and evil souls go from body to body. The familiar arguments of these doctrines will be recognized by all those who have read the Epistles of St. Paul.

Masons are familiar with the doctrines of Philo. To him, the Supreme Being was a center of Light whose rays penetrate the Universe. All Masonic journeys are a search for that Light. The sun and moon in our Lodges are symbols of that Light, and Darkness is its main enemy. They fight with each other for the rule of the world. The Candidate symbolizes that struggle as he wanders in darkness and is brought to light. The world was not created by the Supreme Being but by a secondary agent, His WORD, assisted by an INTELLIGENCE or WISDOM. Here is the hidden meaning of the need to recover "the Word" and the symbolism of our two columns of STRENGTH and WISDOM, the two parallel lines that bound the circle which represents the Universe. The visible world is the image of the invisible world, and the essence of the Human Soul is the image of God. Its goal is to free itself of its body, so it may ascend to *253* Heaven when it is purified. This is the meaning (almost forgotten in our Lodges) of the method for preparing the candidate for apprenticeship and the tests and purifications he faces in the first Degree of the Ancient and Accepted Scottish Rite.

Philo did not incorporate Egyptian or Eastern elements into his eclecticism. However, there were other Jewish teachers in Alexandria who did. The Jews of Egypt were slightly jealous and hostile toward the Jews of Palestine, especially after the erection of the sanctuary at Leontopolis. Therefore, they admired and magnified those scholars who had resided in Egypt like Jeremiah. "The wisdom of Solomon" was written in Alexandria in the time of St. Jerome and attributed to Philo. However, it contains principles that contradict his. It personifies Wisdom and separates its believers from the Profane with the same argument that Egypt had long before taught to the Jews. That distinction existed from the beginning of the Mosaic creed. As the adopted son of Pharaoh's daughter, Moses was required to be an Initiate in the mysteries of Egypt. *Thouoris* was the daughter of *Sesostris-Ramses* and was the Regent of Lower Egypt at the time of Moses' birth. She was also a Priestess of HATHOR and NEITH. As her adopted son, Moses would have lived in her Palace and presence for forty years. During that period, he was barely acquainted with his fellow Jews. In many of his laws, we find the intention of preserving the separation between the common people and the Initiates, which he learned in Egypt. Moses, Aaron, the High Priests, the Council of 70 Elders, Solomon, and all the Prophets were in possession of a higher science. At the least, Masonry is the lineal descendant of this higher science, known as THE KNOWLEDGE OF THE WORD.

AMUN was the Supreme God. He was called "*the Celestial Lord, who sheds Light on hidden things.*" He was the source of divine life and power symbolized by the *crux ansata*. He contained all the attributes that the Ancient Eastern Theology *254* assigned to the Supreme Being. He was the Pleroma or "*Fullness of things*". He was the Sun-God and contained everything, including the LIGHT, in Himself. He was unchanging in the midst of his changing worlds. He *created* nothing, but everything *originated* from Him. All the other Gods were just manifestations of Him.

The Ram was His living symbol, which you see reproduced in this Degree, lying on the book with seven seals on the tracing-board. He caused the creation of the world by the Primitive Thought or *Spirit* using his *Voice* or the

WORD. The *Thought* or *Spirit* was personified as the Goddess NEITH. She was a deity of *Light* and the mother of the Sun. The Creative *Power*, another manifestation of God with its Divine *Intelligence*, produced the Universe. This was symbolized by the egg issuing from the mouth of KNEPH. PHTHA came from that egg and was the image of the Supreme Intelligence and the principal agent of Nature. PHRE or RE was the Sun, whose symbol was a point within a circle. He was the son of PHTHA. His wife TIPHE, the celestial firmament, was represented on many monuments and was clothed in blue or yellow. Her garments were sprinkled with stars and accompanied by the sun, moon, and five planets. She was the symbol of Wisdom and represented the Seven Planetary Spirits of the Gnostics presiding over the earthly world.

Though unknown for a hundred years to those who have practiced it, the symbols of this Degree refer to these old doctrines. The lamb, the yellow hangings covered with stars, the seven columns, candlesticks, and seals all recall them.

The Lion was the symbol of ATHOM-RE, the Great God of Upper Egypt. The symbols for RA, MENDES, and APIS were the Hawk, Eagle, and Bull respectively, which are seen under the platform on which our altar stands.

The first HERMES was the INTELLIGENCE or WORD of God. Having 255 compassion for a mankind without law and wishing to direct them on the right path, God sent OSIRIS and ISIS. They were accompanied by THOTH, the incarnation of the first HERMES who had taught mankind the arts, sciences, and the ceremonies of religion. OSIRIS was the Principle of Good. TYPHON, like AHRIMAN, was the source of all that is evil in the moral and physical order. Like the Satan of Gnosticism, he was associated with Matter.

From Egypt or Persia, the Neo-Platonists and Gnostics borrowed the idea that man is under the influence of the Moon, Mercury, Venus, the Sun, Mars, Jupiter, and Saturn.

The Jews of Syria and Judea were the direct precursors of Gnosticism, and their doctrines contained eastern elements. They had contact with the East during two different periods that familiarized them with the doctrines of Asia, especially of Chaldæa and Persia. While living in Mesopotamia with the Chaldæans, Assyrians, Medes, and Persians, they adopted many of the doctrines of their conquerors. Their descendants did not want to leave Persia, even when they were allowed to do so. They had their own areas with governors and judges from among their own people. Many of them held high office, and their children were educated with those of the highest nobles. Daniel was the friend and minister of the King and Chief of the College of the Magi at Babylon. Mordecai 256 was the Prime Minister, and his cousin Esther was the Monarch's wife.

The Magi of Babylon were teachers of figurative writings, interpreters of nature and dreams, astronomers, and priests. After their captivity, the Jews developed a number of sects derived from their teachings. The *Aions* of the

Gnostics, *Ideas* of Plato, *Angels* of the Jews, and *Demons* of the Greeks corresponded to the *Ferouers* of Zoroaster.

A great number of Jewish families remained permanently in their new country. One of the most celebrated of their schools was at Babylon, and they quickly became familiar with the doctrine of Zoroaster. From the Zend-Avesta, they borrowed everything that could be reconciled with their own faith, and these additions spread into Syria and Palestine.

In the Zend-Avesta, God is Illimitable Time, and no origin can be assigned to Him. His nature and attributes are so inaccessible to the human mind that He can only be the object of silent Veneration. Creation took place through emanation from Him. The first emanation was the primitive *Light* and from that descended ORMUZD, the King of Light. By the "WORD", *Ormuzd* created the world. He is its preserver and judge, Holy and Heavenly. He is Intelligence, Knowledge, and the First-born of Time invested with all the Powers of the Supreme Being.

He is, strictly speaking, the *Fourth* Being. He had a *Ferouer* (a pre-existing Soul) that Plato called a *type* or *ideal*. He is said to have existed from the beginning in the primitive *Light*. That *Light* was just a small part of the whole, and His *Ferouer* was an ideal. Likewise, ORMUZD can be considered *the First-born* of ZEROUANE-AKHERENE. "THE WORD" of Masonry is the LIGHT toward which all Masons travel.

He created six Genii called *Amshaspands*, who surround his Throne. They communicate with inferior spirits and man, transmitting their prayers to Him. They serve as models of purity and perfection. Thus we have the *Demiourgos* of Gnosticism and the six *Genii* that assist him. These are the Hebrew Archangels of the planets.

The names of these *Amshaspands* are Bahman, Ardibehest, Schariver, Sapandomad, Khordad, and Amerdad.

The fourth, SAPANDOMAD, created the first man and woman.

ORMUZD also created 28 *Izeds*, of whom MITHRAS is the chief. With *Ormuzd* and the *Amshaspands*, they watch over the happiness, purity, and preservation of the world. They are models for humanity and the interpreters of prayers. With *Mithras* and *Ormuzd*, they make a *pleroma* (or complete number) of 30, corresponding to the thirty Aions of the Gnostics and the *ogdoade, dodecade*, and *decade* of the Egyptians. *Mithras* was the Sun-God called upon and soon confused with OMUZD. Eventually, MITHRAS eclipsed *Ormuzd* himself.

The third order of pure spirits is more numerous. They are the *Ferouers*, which were the THOUGHTS or IDEAS of Ormuzd. They are superior to man, protecting him during his life on earth and from evil after his resurrection.

AHRIMAN was the second emanation, pure like ORMUZD. His pride and ambition made him jealous of Ormuzd. The Eternal condemned him to dwell in darkness for 12,000 years. During that period, the struggle between *Light* and *Darkness, Good* and *Evil* would cease.

257

AHRIMAN refused to submit and fought against ORMUZD. For each of the good spirits created by his Brother, he created an equal number of Evil Ones. The seven *Amshaspands* were opposed by seven *Archdevs*. The *Izeds* and *Ferouers* were opposed by an equal number of *Devs* who brought *Poverty, Maladies, Impurity, Envy, Chagrin, Drunkenness,* and *Falsehood* into the world.

258   Ahriman's symbol was the Dragon, which was confused by the Jews with Satan and the Serpent-Tempter. After a reign of 3000 years, Ormuzd created the Material World in six periods, calling into existence Light, Water, Earth, plants, animals, and Man. Ahriman shared in the creation of earth and water. Ormuzd could not exclude the Master of Darkness, so they also jointly produced Man. With his Will and Word, Ormuzd produced a Being that was the symbol and source of universal life for everything that exists under Heaven. He placed in man, the pure Life that comes from the Supreme Being, but Ahriman destroyed that pure principle and its body. From its recovered and purified essence, Ormuzd made the first man and woman. Ahriman then seduced and tempted them with wine and fruit.

At times during the next 9000 years, Ahriman and Darkness will be triumphant. Assisted by the Good Spirits, the Triumph of Good is decreed by the Supreme Being, and the period of that triumph will certainly arrive. When the world is most afflicted by evil, three Prophets will come to bring relief to mortals. SOSIOSCH, the leader of the Three, will regenerate the earth and restore it to its primitive beauty, strength, and purity. He will judge the good and the wicked. After the resurrection of the good, he will lead them to a home of everlasting happiness. Ahriman, his evil demons, and all wicked men will be purified in a torrent of melted metal. The law of Ormuzd will reign everywhere. All humanity will be happy and join with Sosiosch in singing the praises of the Supreme Being.

These doctrines were borrowed by the Pharisaic Jews and more fully adopted by the Gnostics. They taught of the restoration of all things to their original, pure condition. They hoped for the happiness of their admission to the feast of Heavenly Wisdom.

The doctrines of Zoroaster originated in Bactria, an Indian Province of Persia. They included both Hindu and Buddhist elements. The main idea of Buddhism is that matter subjugates the intelligence, and intelligence will free

259   itself from slavery. Lao-Tsu said, "Before the chaos that preceded the birth of Heaven and Earth, a single Being existed. I know not its name, but I call it *Reason.* Earth is the *symbol* and *model* for Man; Earth for Heaven; Heaven for Reason; and Reason for Itself." This mirrors the *Ferouers, Ideas,* and *Aions* or the REASON, INTELLIGENCE, SILENCE, WORD, and WISDOM of the Gnostics.

The main belief system among the Jews after their captivity was that of the Pharisees, who borrowed much of their doctrine from the Persians. Like them, the Pharisees claimed to have exclusive and mysterious knowledge unknown to the masses. They taught that a constant war was waged between the

Empire of Good and that of Evil. They attributed sin and the fall of man to demons. They believed in the special protection of the righteous by beings who were agents of Jehovah, and their beliefs reflected those in the Holy Books. It is likely that these ideas originated in the East.

They called themselves *Interpreters* and claimed exclusive possession of the true meaning of the Holy Writings. Successive generations of Initiates claimed that these ideas had been transmitted from Moses to them. Their clothing, their belief in the influences of the stars and the immortality and transmigration of souls, and their system of angels and astronomy were foreign.

Jewish opposition to these foreign teachings led to the rise of Sadduceeism.

This Degree is especially concerned with the *Essenes* and *Therapeuts*. The intermingling of Eastern and Western rites is unmistakable in the creeds of these two sects.

Their beliefs were distinguished by simple meditations and moral practices. Their morality shared the Zoroastrian principle that it was necessary to 260 free the soul from material concerns. This led to a system of abstinence opposed to the ancient Hebraic ideas.

The life and actions of these mystical groups, particularly their prayers at sunrise, appear to match the requirements of the Zend-Avesta for the faithful adorer of Ormuzd.

The Therapeuts lived around Alexandria in Egypt, and the Essenes lived in Palestine near the Dead Sea. Nevertheless, there was a striking similarity in their ideas. The Jews of Egypt tried to harmonize their doctrines with the traditions of Greece. The doctrines of the Therapeuts developed many similarities to the Pythagorean and Orphic ideas on one side and those of Judaism on the other. The Jews of Palestine adopted the Eastern doctrines of Persia. This influence was particularly strong in Kabbalah, which was more extensive in Palestine than Egypt. Kabbalah furnished the Gnostics with some of their most striking theories.

Christ often spoke of the Pharisees and Sadducees. He never mentioned the Essenes, but His doctrines greatly resembled those of the Essenes.

John the Baptist was the son of a Temple Priest, and his mother was of the family of Aaron. He drank neither wine nor strong drink. He wore haircloth with a girdle of leather and ate the food of the desert where he dwelled. He preached in the country around the Jordan, emphasizing a baptism of repentance and the need to prove repentance by *reformation*. He taught the people charity and Liberality, the merchants justice, equity, and fair dealing, and the soldiers 261 peace, truth, and contentment. He taught the need for a virtuous life and the folly of relying on their descent from Abraham.

He denounced both the Pharisees and Sadducees as a generation of vipers who were threatened with the anger of God. He baptized those who confessed their sins. He preached in the desert where the Essenes lived. He was imprisoned before Christ began to preach. Matthew mentions him without explanation, as though his history was too well known to need one. "In those days," he says, "came John the Baptist, preaching in the wilderness of Judea." John's disciples frequently fasted. They and the Pharisees came to Jesus asking why *His* Disciples did not fast as often as they did. Jesus did not denounce *them*, as was His habit was with the Pharisees.

From prison, John sent two disciples to ask of Christ: "Are you he that is to come, or do we look for another?" Christ referred them to His miracles as an answer and declared to the people that John was a prophet. He said that no greater man had ever been born, but the humblest Christian was his superior. He declared John to be Elias, who was to come.

John had denounced Herod's marriage to his brother's wife as unlawful. For this, he was imprisoned and finally executed to gratify her. After his disciples buried him, Herod and others thought he had risen from the dead and appeared again in the person of Christ. The people all regarded John as a prophet. Christ silenced the Priests and Elders by asking them whether John was inspired. They were afraid to arouse the anger of the people by saying that he was not. Christ declared that he came, "in the way of righteousness." Ordinary people believed him, though the Priests and Pharisees did not.

John was often consulted by Herod, who showed him great deference. His doctrine taught *some* creed older than Christianity, which prevailed among the people and merchants. The Jews that adopted his doctrines were neither Pharisees nor Sadducees, but the common people. They must, therefore, have been Essenes. Christ argued for baptism as a sacred rite, which was well known and long practiced.

In the 18th chapter of Acts, we read, "And a certain Jew named Apollos, mighty in the Scriptures, came to Ephesus. This man *was taught in the way of the Lord*, and, being fervent in spirit, *he spoke and taught diligently the things of the Lord, knowing only the baptism of John.* He began to speak boldly in the synagogue, and when Aquilla and Priscilla heard, they took him and taught him *the way of God* more perfectly."

Translating into common language, it might read, "And a certain Jew named Apollos came to Ephesus. He had learned in the mysteries the true doctrine regarding God, having received no other baptism than that of John." He knew nothing regarding Christianity, having lived in Alexandria.

St. Augustine said, "the Christian religion is called that not because of the thing itself, but because it later received this name. The thing itself, which is now called the Christian religion, *was really known to the Ancients."* The disciples were first called "Christians" at Antioch when Barnabas and Paul began to preach there.

The Wandering Jews or Exorcists, who used the Sacred Name in exorcising evil spirits, were no doubt the Therapeutae or Essenes. We read in the 19th chapter of Acts, verses 1 to 4, "that while Apollos was at Corinth, Paul, having passed through the upper parts of Asia Minor, came to Ephesus. Finding certain *disciples*, he said to them, 'Have you received the Holy Ghost since you became Believers?' They said to him, 'We have not so much as heard that there *is* any Holy Ghost.' He said to them, 'In what, then, were you baptized?' They said, 'In John's baptism.' Paul said, 'John indeed baptized with the baptism of repentance, saying to the people that they should believe in Him who was to come. When they heard this, they were baptized in the name of the Lord, Jesus."

The nearly Christian faith taught by John was probably the doctrine of the Essenes, and John probably belonged to that sect. The place where he preached, his frugal diet, and the doctrines he taught all prove it conclusively. There was no other sect that he *could* have belonged to *except* the Essenes.

Paul wrote to the brethren at Corinth about their disagreements. Rival sects had developed that supported Paul, Apollos, and Cephas. Some of them denied the resurrection. Paul urged them to follow his doctrines and sent Timothy to gain their adherence.

According to Paul, Christ was to come again. He was to put an end to all other Kingdoms and Death itself. He would then be merged once more with God.

The forms and ceremonies of the Essenes were symbolic. According to Philo, they had four Degrees. The members were divided into two Orders, the *Practici* and *Therapeutici*. The latter were contemplative and medical Brethren, and the former were active, practical businessmen. They were Jews by birth and had a greater affection for each other than the members of any other sect. Their brotherly love was intense. They fulfilled the Christian law: "Love one another." They despised riches, and no one had more than any other. The possessions of one were combined with those of the others. Their piety toward God was extraordinary. Before sunrise, they never spoke a word about profane matters, but used the same prayers they had received from their ancestors. Before light, their prayers and hymns had ascended to Heaven. They were faithful, true, and Ministers of Peace. They had mysterious ceremonies and initiations into their mysteries. The Candidate promised that he would practice fidelity to all men, especially those in authority.

Their word was their bond. They avoided swearing and considered it worse than perjury. They were simple in their diet and way of life, and they despised death. They cultivated the science of medicine and were very skillful. They considered it a good omen to dress in white robes. They had their own courts and passed righteous judgments. They kept the Sabbath more rigorously than other Jewish sects did.

Their chief towns were Engaddi and Hebron. Engaddi was about 30 miles southeast of Jerusalem, and Hebron was about 20 miles further south. Josephus and Eusebius speak of them as an ancient sect, and they were no doubt the first among the Jews to embrace Christianity. Their faith and doctrine had many points of resemblance to Christianity and were very much the same. Pliny regarded them as a very ancient people.

During their prayers, they turned toward the rising sun. They observed the Law of Moses with scrupulous fidelity and were never idolaters. They held all things in common and despised riches. Everything they needed was supplied by the administration of Curators or Stewards. A Tetractys of round dots was revered among them. This was a Pythagorean symbol, but their beliefs more nearly resemble those of Confucius and Zoroaster. These may have been adopted while they were prisoners in Persia.

265 Their demeanor was sober and chaste. They submitted to the superintendence of governors appointed by themselves. Their time was spent in labor, meditation, and prayer, and they were most attentive to every call for justice, humanity, and moral duty. They believed in the unity of God and thought that the souls of men had fallen from the regions of purity and light into the bodies they occupied. They did not believe in the resurrection of the body, but in the resurrection of the soul. They believed in future rewards and punishments and disregarded the ceremonies or external forms required by the Law of Moses in the worship of God. They believed the words of Moses were meant to be understood in a mysterious sense and not according to their literal meaning. They offered no sacrifices, except at home. They worked to isolate the soul from the body and carry it back to God.

Eusebius says, "The ancient Therapeutea were Christians, and their ancient writings are our Gospels and Epistles."

The ESSENES were one of the Eclectic Sects of Philosophers and held PLATO in the highest esteem. They believed that true philosophy, the greatest and most salutary gift of God to man, was scattered through all the different Sects. Consequently, it was the duty of every wise man to collect it from where it lay dispersed and use it to destroy impiety and vice.

The Essenes observed the Solstice festivals in a distinguished manner. They revered the Sun, not as a god, but as a symbol of light and fire. They lived in restraint and had established places similar to the monasteries of the early Christians.

The writings of the Essenes were full of mysticism, parables, enigmas, and allegories. They believed in the esoteric and exoteric meanings of the Scriptures and found a basis for that in the Scriptures themselves. They found it in the Old Testament, as the Gnostics found it in the New. The Christian
266 writers (even Christ himself) recognized that all Scripture had an inner and an outer meaning.

One of the Gospels says, "To you, it is given to know the mystery of the Kingdom of God. To men *that are without*, all these things are done in parables. Seeing, they may see but not perceive, and hearing, they may hear but not understand. The disciples came and said to him, 'Why do you speak the truth in parables?' He answered and said, 'Because it is given to *you* to know the mysteries of the Kingdom of Heaven, but to *them* it is not given.'"

The fourth chapter of Paul's Epistle to the Galatians says that the facts of the Old Testament are *an allegory*. In the third chapter of the second letter to the Corinthians, he says he is a minister of the New Testament appointed by God, "not of the letter, but of the spirit; for the letter kills." Origen and St. Gregory believed the Gospels were not to be taken literally. Athanasius teaches that, "If we understand sacred writing according to the letter, we would fall into the most enormous blasphemies."

Eusebius said, "Those who interpret the Holy Scriptures philosophize over them and teach their literal sense by allegory."

Our knowledge of the Kabbalistic doctrines is the Sepher Yehzirah (written in the second century) and Zohar (written sometime later). Both contain material that is much older. Characteristically, they go back to the time of the exile. They teach that everything flows from a source of infinite LIGHT. THE ANCIENT OF DAYS and the KING OF LIGHT existed before everything else. THE KING OF LIGHT, THE ANCIENT, is ALL THAT IS. He is not only the real cause of all Existences, but He is Infinite (AIN SOPH). He is HIMSELF.

In Indian doctrine, the Supreme Being is the cause of everything and the only real Existence. Everything else is illusion. In Kabbalah, He is the Supreme Being who is unknown to all. The world is His revelation and exists only in Him. His attributes are reproduced there in various aspects and in different degrees. The Universe is His Holy Splendor, but it must be revered in silence. All beings sprang from the Supreme Being, and the closer a being is to Him, the more perfect that being is.

A ray of Light from the Deity is the cause and principle of all that exists. It is at once Father and Mother of All. It penetrates everything, and without it, nothing can exist. The FIRST-BORN of God, the Universal FORM that contains all beings, came from this double FORCE represented by the two parts of the word I∴H∴U∴H∴.

This First-Born is the Creative Agent, Conservator, and animating Principle of the Universe. It is THE LIGHT OF LIGHT. It possesses the three Primitive Forces of the Divinity: LIGHT, SPIRIT, and LIFE. It gives Light and Life and is considered the generative and conceptive Principle (the Primitive Man or ADAM KADMON). It has revealed itself in ten emanations or *Sephiroth*, which are not ten different beings or even beings at all. They are sources of life and the archetypes of Creation. They are *Will, Wisdom, Understanding, Mercy, Severity, Beauty, Victory, Glory, Stability,* and *Kingdom*. These are the attributes of God, by which He reveals Himself. It is a profound truth that the human mind cannot perceive God in his works. We know only what the Visible reveals about the Invisible.

Wisdom was called NOUS, LOGOS, and INTELLECT or the WORD. *Understanding* corresponds to the Holy Ghost of the Christian Faith.

Beauty is represented by green and yellow. *Victory* is YAHOVAH-TSABAOTH, the column of Jachin on the right hand. *Glory* is the column of *Boaz* on the left hand. Our symbols appear repeatedly in Kabbalah. LIGHT, the object of our labors, appears as the creative power of Deity. The circle was the special symbol of the first Sephirah, Kether (the Crown).

268   We will not yet consider the four Kabbalistic Worlds of *Aziluth, Briah, Yetzirah,* and *Assiah,* which correspond to *emanation, creation, formation,* and *fabrication.* One is inferior to the other, and the superior always encircles the inferior. Nothing that exists is purely material. Everything comes from God and exists by the Divine ray that penetrates creation. Everything is united by the Spirit of God

The WORD was also found in the Phœnician creed. A WORD of God created the world. It was written in starry characters and communicated to the adepts of the human race. The faith of the Phœnicians came from the ancient worship of the Stars, and Light and Fire are its most important agents. They adored the Heavens with its Lights, calling it the Supreme God.

Everything comes from a Single Principle that is the Moving Power of All and governs all. The union of Light with Spirit is the Life of everything and penetrates everything. It should be respected and honored everywhere.

The Chaldæan and Jerusalem Paraphrasts tried to make the phrase DEBAR-YAHOVAH (the Word of God) a personality. In the Jerusalem Targum, the phrase "And God created man," is, "And the Word of IHUH created man."

269   In Genesis 28: 20-21, Jacob says, "If God IHIH ALHIM will be with me...then shall IHUH be my ALHIM, and this stone shall be God's House IHIH BITH ALHIM." Onkelos paraphrases it, "If the word of IHUH will be my help...then the word of IHUH shall be my God".

In Genesis 3: 8, "The Voice of the Lord God" (IHUH ALHIM) becomes "The Voice of the Word of IHUH".

Wisdom 9: 1 says, "O God of my Fathers and Lord of Mercy! who has made all things with Your word."

In Wisdom 18: 15 we have, "Your Almighty Word leapt down from Heaven."

Philo speaks of the Word as being the same as God. In several places, he calls it the Second Divinity, the Image of God, and the Divine Word that made all things.

When John began to preach, the great questions concerning eternity and the creation of matter had long been argued.

Jewish doctrine attributed creation to the direct action of the Supreme Being. The Theosophists of the other Eastern Peoples placed at least two intermediaries between God and the world. They felt that placing only a single Being between them decreased the Supreme Majesty. The distance between God, who is perfect Purity, and matter, which is base and foul, was too great for them to clear with a single step. Neither Plato nor Philo could so impoverish the Intellectual World.

Cerinthus of Ephesus thought this distance was too great for the Supreme Being to have created the material world. Below the Ancient of Days, one, two, or more Existences were imagined to play a direct role in the creation of the material and mental universe. 270

We have already considered many of the speculations on this idea. To some, the world was created by the LOGOS or WORD. To others, the beginning of creation was the emanation of a ray of LIGHT that created the principle of *Light* and *Life*. That creation resulted from the Primitive THOUGHT and created the inferior Deities, a succession of INTELLIGENCES, and the DIVINE REASON. No restraints were put on the Imagination. Abstractions became Existences and Realities. The attributes of God personified became Powers, Spirits, and Intelligences.

God was the *Light of Light, Divine Fire, Abstract Intelligence,* and the *Root* or *Seed* of the Universe. *Simon Magus,* founder of the Gnostic faith, believed that the manifestations of the Supreme Being, as FATHER, SON, CHRIST, or HOLY SPIRIT were just different *forms* of the same God. To others, they were real and distinct beings.

Eastern imaginations reveled in the creation of these Inferior Intelligences, the Powers of Good and Evil, and the Angels. We have spoken of those imagined by the Persians and the Kabbalists. In the Talmud, every star, nation, and town has a Prince of Heaven as its Protector. JEHUEL is the guardian of fire, assisted by *Seraphiel, Gabriel, Nitriel, Tammael, Tchimschiel, Hadarniel,* and *Sarniel.* These seven are represented by the square columns of this Degree. The columns of JACHIN and BOAZ represent the angels of fire and water. Basilides 271 believed that God was nameless and contained and concealed in Himself, the Plenitude of His Perfections. To the Essenes and Gnostics, the Ideas, Conceptions, or Manifestations of the Deity were all God. They were nothing without Him, but they were more than what we now understand by the word *ideas.* They had a middle existence between our modern ideas and the intelligences or ideas elevated to the rank of genii by Eastern mythology.

Basilides theorized that these personified attributes of Deity were the *First-born* or *Mind.* From this comes *Logos* or THE WORD, which provides *Intellect. Wisdom* follows, leading to *Power,* and *Righteousness* comes from Power. The whole number of successive emanations was 365. The Gnostics represented this with the mystic word *Abraxas.* It identified God as he was manifested, but not the Supreme and Secret God Himself. These three hundred and sixty-five Intelligences compose the totality or *Plenitude* of the Divine Emanations.

The Ophites believed there were seven inferior spirits: *Michael, Suriel, Raphael, Gabriel, Thauthabaoth, Erataoth,* and *Athaniel,* who were the genii of the stars called the Bull, Dog, Lion, Bear, Serpent, Eagle, and Ass respectively.

Ialdabaoth, Iao, Adonai, Eloi, Orai, and *Astaphai* were the genii of Saturn, the Moon, the Sun, Jupiter, Venus, and Mercury.

The WORD appears in all these creeds. It is the *Ormuzd* of Zoroaster, the *Ain Soph* of Kabbalah, the *Nous* of Platonism and Philonism, and the *Sophia* or *Demiourgos* of the Gnostics.

272   All these creeds recognized the different manifestations of the Supreme Being, but they recognized that His identity was immutable and permanent. That was Plato's distinction between the unchanging Being and the perpetual flow of things, which incessantly changes.

The belief in some form of dualism was universal. Those who believed that everything came from God also believed that there were two adverse Principles of Light and Darkness, of Good and Evil. In Central Asian doctrines, there was a second Intellectual Principle opposed to the Empire of Light. In Egypt, the second Principle was Matter and was related to Emptiness, Darkness, and Death. According to this idea, matter could only be animated indirectly by a principle of divine life. Through Satan, matter resists any influences that would spiritualize it.

Many believed that there were two governing Principles. The first was the Unknown Father (the Supreme and Eternal God), living in the center of the Light and content with the perfect purity of His being. The other was the eternal Matter, which they considered the source of all evils, the mother and dwelling-place of Satan.

Philo and the Platonists believed there was a Soul of the world that created visible things and acted as the agent of the Supreme Intelligence.

The Apocalypse or Revelation comes from the East and is very old. The story it relates is older still. It tells of the great struggle of Light, Truth, and Good against Darkness, Error, and Evil. It is the ancient myth of Ormuzd and his Genii against Ahriman and his Devs, and it celebrates the final triumph of Truth against the combined powers of men and demons. The ideas and imagery are borrowed from every quarter, and allusions are made to doctrines of all ages.

273   We are continually reminded of the Zend-Avesta, the Jewish Codes, Philo, and the Gnosis. The Seven Spirits surrounding the Throne of the Eternal at the beginning are the Seven Amshaspands of Parsism. The Twenty-four Ancients remind us of the Mysterious Chiefs of Judaism and foreshadow the Eons of Gnosticism and the twenty-four Good Spirits that Ormuzd created and enclosed in an egg.

The Christ of the Apocalypse, First-born of Creation and the Resurrection, is invested with the characteristics of Ormuzd and Sosiosch from the Zend-Avesta, the Ain Soph of Kabbalah, and the Carpistes of the Gnostics. The idea that the true Initiates and the Faithful become Kings and Priests is common to the Persian, Jewish, Christian, and Gnostic doctrines. The identification of the Supreme Being as the Alpha and Omega is Zoroaster's definition of Zerouane-Akherene.

The immeasurable depths of Satan, his temporary triumph by fraud and violence, his names of the Serpent and Dragon, and the conflict of Good and Evil are found in the Zend-Avesta, Kabbalah, and the Gnosis.

In the Apocalypse, we even find the Persian idea that regards some of the lower animals as Devs or vehicles of Devs.

Every philosophy of the East sought victory in the guardianship of the earth by a good angel, the reward of the earth in heaven, and the final triumph of good and holy men.

The gold and white clothing of the twenty-four Elders is a sign of lofty perfection and divine purity.

The Human mind labored, struggled, and tortured itself for ages to explain what it felt. Numerous abstractions of the imagination were the result. *274*

One grand idea always emerged, prominent and unchangeable, out of this confusion. God is great, good, and wise. Evil, pain, and sorrow are temporary and serve a wise and beneficent purpose. They *must* be consistent with God's goodness, purity, and infinite perfection, and there *must* be a method of explaining them, if we could only find it. Ultimately, Good will prevail, and Evil will be defeated. God alone *can* do this, and He *will* do it through His Redeemer.

The objective of all doctrines is the annihilation of evil and the restoration of Man to his original state by a Redeemer.

This Redeemer is the Word or Logos, the Ormuzd of Zoroaster, the Ain Soph of Kabbalah, and the Nous of Platonism and Philonism. The Redeemer was sought by all the People of the East, as shown in the Gospel of John and the Letters of Paul. All the energies of the writers are devoted to showing that Jesus is the Christ that all these nations were expecting.

This Degree symbolizes the great contest between good and evil in anticipation of the appearance and the advent of the Word or Redeemer. The doctrines of the Essenes, as taught by John the Baptist, greatly resembled those taught by Jesus. Palestine was full of John's disciples, and the Priests and Pharisees did not dare deny John's inspiration. His doctrine had also extended to Asia Minor and made converts in luxurious Ephesus as well as Alexandria in Egypt. They readily embraced the Christian faith that they had not heard before.

These old controversies have died away, and the old faiths have faded *275* into oblivion. Masonry still survives, as vigorous and strong as when philosophy was taught in the schools of Alexandria and under the Portico. It teaches the same truths that the Essenes taught by the shores of the Dead Sea and John the Baptist preached in the Desert. These truths were gathered by the Essenes from the doctrines of the East and the West, from the Zend-Avesta and the Vedas, Plato and Pythagoras, India, Persia, Phœnicia, Syria, Greece, and Egypt. We are called Knights of the East and West because these doctrines came from both. Masonry has garnered up these purified doctrines in her heart of hearts and delivered them to us. God is One, immutable, unchangeable, infinitely just, and good. Light will finally overcome Darkness, Good will conquer Evil, and Truth will be victorious over Error. These truths are the religion and Philosophy of Masonry.

It is useful to study the speculations and ideas of the older doctrines. Knowing what is worthless, you may value and appreciate more the plain, simple, sublime, and universal truths. They are the Light by which Masons have been guided on their way. Wisdom and Strength, like imperishable columns, have sustained and will continue to sustain its glorious and magnificent Temple.

CHAPTER 18: KNIGHT ROSE CROIX (PRINCE ROSE CROIX)

EACH of us applies the symbols and ceremonies of this Degree to our 276 faith as seems proper. Some see the legend of the Master Hiram foretelling the condemnation and sufferings of Christ or the unfortunate Grand Master of the Templars. Likewise, the ceremonies of this Degree receive different explanations, and everyone should interpret them for himself without being offended at other interpretations.

The universal character of Masonry enabled two Kings, worshippers of different Deities, to sit together as Masters while the first temple was built and to sit with others in the same Lodge as brethren.

Early worshippers didn't meet in Temples made with human hands. 277 Stephen, the first Martyr, said, "God doesn't dwell in Temples made with hands." They met in the open air for prayer and thanksgiving. They adored the God of Light who represented Good as darkness represented Evil.

Our ancestors resolved the existence of Evil by imagining the existence of a Principle of Evil that, having first fallen, then tempted man to his fall. They believed there would be a future life gained by purification and trial and a Redeemer who would overcome the Evil Principle. The Redeemer would be born to a Virgin and suffer a painful death.

Krishna was raised and educated among Shepherds. At the time of his birth, a Tyrant ordered all male children to be slain. It is said that He performed miracles, even raising the dead. He washed the feet of the Brahmins and was meek and lowly of spirit. He descended to Hell, rose again, and ascended to Heaven. He charged his disciples with teaching his doctrines and gave them the gift of miracles.

The first Masonic Legislator preserved by history was Buddha. A thousand years before the Christian era, He reformed the religion of Manous. He called all men to the Priesthood, regardless of caste, who felt inspired by God to instruct men. They formed a Society of Prophets under the name of Samaneans and recognized the existence of a single uncreated God. The 278 worship of this God required the obedience of all the beings He created. The doctrines of Buddha spread throughout India, China, and Japan. The Priests of Brahma united together against Buddhism, exterminating its followers. Their sacrifices enabled the doctrine that produced a new Society called the Gymnosophists. A large number fled to Ireland with their doctrines, and there they erected the round towers still visible.

The Phœnician Cosmogony was the Word of God, written in astral characters and communicated by the Demi-gods to Humanity. Their doctrines resembled the Ancient Sabeism that was followed by King Hiram and Hiram Abif. In these doctrines, the First Principle was half material and half spiritual. From this came the WORD, creation, and generation. A race of men arose who adored Heaven and its Stars as the Supreme Being and whose different gods were incarnations of the Sun, Moon, Stars, and Ether. *Chrysor* was the great fiery power of Nature. *Baal* and *Malakarth* were representations of the Sun and Moon.

Man had fallen, but not because of the serpent's temptation. The Phœnicians believed the serpent shared the Divine Nature and was sacred. He was thought to be immortal, unless slain by violence. In his old age, he consumed himself and became young again. The Serpent in a circle, holding his tail in his mouth, was a symbol of eternity. With the head of a hawk, he had a Divine Nature and was a symbol of the sun. One Gnostic sect saw him as a benevolent symbol of wisdom. He was also symbolized by the brazen serpent erected by Moses in the desert.

"Before the chaos that preceded the birth of Heaven and Earth," said Lao-Tzu, "a single Being existed, immense and silent, immutable and always acting. I don't know the name of the Being, but I call it Reason. Man is modeled on the earth, the earth on Heaven, Heaven on Reason, and Reason on itself."

Isis said, "I am Nature. I am the parent of all things, the sovereign of the Elements, and Queen of the Shades, venerated by the whole world in many forms with various rites and many names. The Egyptians worship me with proper ceremonies and call me by my true name, Isis the Queen."

The Hindu Vedas define the Deity as:

"He who surpasses speech, and through whose power speech is expressed. He is Brahma.

"He whom Intelligence cannot comprehend and through whose Power the nature of Intelligence can be understood. He is Brahma.

"He who cannot be seen and through whose power the organ of seeing sees. He is Brahma.

"He who cannot be heard and through whose power the organ of hearing hears. He is Brahma.

"He who cannot be perceived by scent and through whose power the organ of smelling smells. He is Brahma."

"When God decided to create the human race," said *Arius*, "He made a Being that He called The WORD or The Son so that this Being might give existence to men." This WORD is the *Ormuzd* of Zoroaster, the *Ain Soph* of Kabbalah, and the *Wisdom* or *Demiourgos* of the Gnostics.

That is the True Word that our ancient brethren sought as the priceless reward for their labors on the Holy Temple. The Word of this Degree reminds us of the Infinite Reason that is the Soul of Nature. It is the Duty of every Mason to believe in and revere it. **280**

John begins his Gospel with, "In the beginning was the Word and the Word was with God and the Word was God. All things were made by Him, and without Him, nothing was made. In Him was Life, and the life was the Light of man. The Light shines in darkness, and the darkness cannot contain it."

It is an old tradition that this passage was from an older work. Philostorgius and Nicephorus state that when Emperor Julian began to rebuild the Temple, a stone was removed that covered the mouth of a deep square cave. One of the laborers was lowered by a rope and found a cubical pillar in the centre of the floor. On the pillar lay a roll or book, wrapped in a fine linen cloth, in which (in capital letters) was the preceding passage.

It is clear that John's Gospel is a refutation of the Gnostic teaching. At the outset, he states the current doctrine regarding the creation by the Word. He then demonstrates that this Word was Jesus Christ.

The first sentence, in our language, would read, "When the process of creation or evolution of beings inferior to God began, the Word came into existence and was. This word was the immediate or first emanation from God. It was God Himself. By that Word everything that is was created." Tertullian says that God made the World out of nothing by means of His Word, Wisdom, or Power.

Philo believed the Supreme Being was the *Primitive Light* or *Archetype of Light*, whose rays illuminate Souls. He is the Soul of the World and acts everywhere. He Himself fills and defines His whole existence, and His forces fill and penetrate everything. His Image is the WORD [LOGOS] which is more brilliant than fire, but not pure light. This WORD dwells in God. Within His Intelligence, the Supreme Being frames the Types of Ideas for all that He creates. **281** The WORD is the Vehicle by which God acts on the Universe. God has created visible things through the World of Ideas. These concepts are borrowed from Plato. This WORD is not only the Creator ("*by Him was everything made that was made*"), but acts in the *place* of God. All the Powers and Attributes of God act through him. As the first representative of the human race, he is the protector of Men and their Shepherd, the Son of Man.

Man was created in the image of the WORD, but that is not his actual condition. He has fallen from that exalted position because of his unruly passions. He may rise again by following the teachings of Heavenly Wisdom, by the aid of Angels (commissioned by God to aid him in escaping the entanglements of the body), and by fighting Evil. God allowed Evil to exist solely to provide Man a means of exercising his free will.

The Supreme Being of the Egyptians was *Amun*. He was a secret and concealed God, the Unknown Father of the Gnostics, the Source of Divine Life, and the original Light. He *creates* nothing, but everything *comes* from Him. All the other Gods are his manifestations. His utterance of a Word created *Neith*, the Divine Mother of all things and the Primitive THOUGHT and FORCE that puts everything in movement.

Osiris was the image of this Supreme Being and the Source of all Good in the moral and physical world. He was the constant foe of Typhon, the Genius of Evil, and the Satan of Gnosticism. Har-Oeri, the Redeemer and Son of Isis and Osiris, will finally defeat him.

In the Zend-Avesta of the Persians, the Supreme Being is *Time without limit* (ZERUANE AKHERENE). He had no origin, and was enveloped in His own

282 Glory. His Nature and Attributes were so inaccessible to human Intelligence, that He was the object of silent veneration. His first emanation was the Primitive Light, and from this Light emerged *Ormuzd*, the *King of Light*. By the WORD, Ormuzd created the World in its purity. He is its Preserver and Judge and a Holy and Sacred Being. He is Time without limit and wields all the powers of the Supreme Being.

According to the Persian Zend-Avesta, man contained a pure Principle that came from the Will and Word of Ormuzd. It was joined with an impure principle coming from Ahriman, the Dragon, or the principle of Evil. The first man and woman were tempted by Ahriman and had fallen. The war between *Ormuzd* with his Good Spirits and *Ahriman* with his Evil ones was to last twelve thousand years.

Good Spirits assist pure souls, and the Triumph of the Good Principle will infallibly arrive. At the moment when the earth will be most afflicted with evils, three Prophets will appear to bring assistance to mortals. Sosiosch, Chief of the Three, will regenerate the world and restore it to its primitive Beauty, Strength, and Purity. He will judge the good and the wicked. After the universal resurrection of the Good, the pure Spirits will conduct them to an abode of eternal happiness. Ahriman, his evil Demons, and the entire world will be purified by a torrent of burning, liquid metal. The Law of Ormuzd will rule everywhere, and all men will be happy. They will join with Sosiosch to sing the praises of the Supreme Being.

The Kabbalists and Gnostics adopted these doctrines, with some modifications.

Apollonius of Tyana said, "We shall render the most appropriate worship to God. We will present no offerings and kindle no fire, for He needs nothing.

283 The earth produces no plant, animal, or anything else that would not be impure in His sight. Addressing Him, we must use only the higher word which is the silent inner word of the spirit. From the most Glorious of all Beings, we must ask for blessings."

Strabo said, "This one Supreme Essence embraces us all, the water, land, Heavens, and Nature. This Highest Being should be worshipped in sacred groves without images. There the devout should lay themselves down to sleep and expect signs from God in dreams."

Aristotle said, "It has been handed down in a mythical form that there are Gods and that The Divine encompasses all nature. This has been added for the purpose of persuading the masses and for the interest and advantage of the State. Men have given the Gods human forms and have represented them with other forms. If we separate the original principle that the first Essences are Gods, we will find that this has been divinely said. It is probable that philosophy and the arts have been found and lost many times, and such doctrines may have been preserved as the remains of ancient wisdom."

Porphyry said, "The ancients represented God and his powers with images. They used visible images to represent the invisible. The ignorant consider the images to be nothing more than wood or stone. Those who are ignorant of writing see nothing in monuments but stone, nothing in tablets but wood, and in books but a tissue of paper."

Apollonius of Tyana believed that birth and death are only in appearance. Matter that separates itself from the one substance (the one Divine essence) seems to be born. When released from the bonds of matter, it seems to die. There is a transformation between becoming visible and becoming invisible. There is one essence which alone acts and suffers, becoming all things to all men.

284

The Neo-Platonists replaced the Supreme Essence with the idea of the Absolute. This Supreme Entity is the first, most simple principle and is outside of existence itself. We cannot assign attributes to it. Even crediting the Absolute with consciousness or self-contemplation would imply a quality (which is contradictory to its nature). The Supreme Entity can only be known by an intellectual intuition of the Spirit, transcending itself, and freeing itself from its own limitations.

The concept of finding such an absolute through the Spirit was united with a certain mysticism. This combination resulted in a transcendent state of feeling that communicated the abstraction of the nature of the Absolute in a manner the mind would receive as reality. The highest end the spiritual life could reach was the absorption of the Spirit into the super-existence or the revelation of that super-existence to the transcended Spirit.

The New Platonists' idea of God was that of One Simple Original Essence exalted above all. He is the only true Being and that from whom all Existence, in its several gradations, has emanated. He is first and the head of all other Gods. In these Gods His perfection is expanded and becomes knowable. They serve to exhibit, in different forms, the image of the Supreme Essence. They are the mediators between man and the Supreme Unity.

Philo said, "He who doesn't believe the miraculous, simply as the miraculous, neither knows God nor has ever sought Him. Otherwise, he would

285 have understood, by simply observing the miracle of the Universe, that these miracles are God's Providence and are merely child's play for the Divine Power. The truly miraculous has become despised through familiarity. The universal, although insignificant, overwhelms us with amazement through our love of novelty."

The Alexandrian Jews tried to purge any trace of the human form from idea of God. By the exclusion of every human passion, it was reduced to something devoid of all attributes and wholly transcendental. The mere Being (the Good or the Absolute of Platonism) was substituted for the personal Deity of the Old Testament. Soaring upward, the mind achieves the intellectual intuition of this Absolute Being. It can affirm nothing but existence and sets aside all other determinations as beneath the exalted nature of the Supreme Essence.

Philo makes a distinction between those who are in the proper sense Sons of God, having raised themselves to the highest Being, and those who know God only in His mundane form. The latter consider the LOGOS to be the Supreme God and are the sons of the Logos, rather than of the True Being.

Pythagoras said, "God is not the object of sense or subject to passion. He is invisible, intelligible, and supremely intelligent. In His body, He is like the *light,* and in His soul He resembles truth. He is the universal *spirit* that spreads itself over all nature. All beings receive their *life* from Him. There is but one God, and He is not seated above the world. Being Himself all in all, He sees all the beings that fill His immensity. He *produces everything.* He orders and disposes everything. He is the REASON, LIFE, and MOTION of all being."

"I am the LIGHT of the world. He that follows Me shall not walk in DARKNESS but shall have the LIGHT OF LIFE.", said Jesus.

286 God appeared to Moses in a FLAMING bush that was not consumed. He descended upon Mount Sinai like the smoke of a *furnace.* He went before the children of Israel, as a pillar of cloud by day and as a pillar of *fire* by night. "Call on the name of *your* Gods," said Elijah to the Priests of Baal, "and I will call upon the name of ADONAI. The God that answers *by fire,* let him be God."

According to Kabbalah and the doctrines of Zoroaster, everything that exists has emanated from a source of infinite light. *The Primitive Being,* THE ANCIENT OF DAYS, existed before all things. This title is frequently given to the Creator in the Zend-Avesta, the Code of the Sabeans, and the Jewish Scriptures.

The world was His Revelation and only existed in Him. His attributes were reproduced there with various modifications and in different degrees. The Universe was His Holy Splendor, His Mantle. He was to be adored in silence, and perfection was gained with a nearer approach to Him.

The PRIMITIVE LIGHT filled all space before the worlds were created. When the Supreme Being decided to display His perfections, He withdrew within Himself, formed a void, and brought forth His first emanation as a ray of light.

It was the cause and principle of everything that exists and united both the generative and conceptive power.

Man was seduced by the Evil Spirits most remote from the Great King of Light. They were from the fourth world of spirits, Assiah, and their chief was Belial. They wage constant war against the pure Intelligences of the other worlds who are the guardians of man. In the beginning, all was unison and harmony, full of divine light and perfect purity. The Seven Kings of Evil fell, and the Universe was troubled. The Creator took from the Seven Kings the principles of Good and Light and divided them among the four worlds of Spirits. He gave the first three worlds the Pure Intelligences. Those Spirits of the fourth were *287* only given feeble glimmerings of light.

After the conflict between these and the good angels has continued its appointed time, the Eternal Himself will come to correct the Evil ones. He will deliver them from the bodies that hold them captive, re-animate and strengthen the ray of light they have preserved, and re-establish that primitive Harmony.

The Gnostic Marcion said, "The Soul of the True Christian, adopted as a child by the Supreme Being, receives from Him the Spirit and Divine Life. It is led and confirmed in a pure and holy life. If it completes its earthly career in charity, chastity, and sanctity, it will one day be released from its body as the young bird escapes its egg. It will share in the bliss of the Good and Perfect Father, re-clothed in an aerial body, and made like the Angels in Heaven."

You see, my brother, the meaning of Masonic "Light". You see why the EAST of the Lodge, where the initial letter of the Name of the Deity is suspended over the Master, is the place of Light. Light is Good, and darkness is Evil. In all ages, Masons have sought that Light, the true knowledge of Deity. Masonry marches steadily onward toward the Light that shines in the great distance. It is the Light of the day when Evil, overcome and vanquished, shall fade away and disappear forever. Life and Light will be the one law of the Universe and its eternal Harmony.

The Degree of Rose Croix teaches three things. It discusses the unity, immutability, and goodness of God. It illustrates the immortality of the Soul and teaches of a Redeemer's ultimate victory and annihilation of evil and wrong.

It replaces the three pillars of the old Temple with three that have already been explained to you. They are Faith (in God, mankind, and the individual), Hope (in the victory over evil, the advancement of Humanity, and a hereafter), *288* and Charity (relieving the wants and tolerating the errors and faults of others). Being trustful, hopeful, and indulgent in an age of selfishness and harsh and bitter judgment are the most important Masonic Virtues. They are the old pillars of the Temple under different names. He is wise who judges others charitably. He is strong who is hopeful. There is no beauty like a firm faith in God, our fellows, and ourselves.

The second apartment (which is hung in mourning), the shattered columns of the Temple, and the brethren bowed down in the deepest despair represent the world under the tyranny of the Principle of Evil. In this world, virtue is persecuted and vice rewarded. The righteous starve for bread, and the wicked live richly. Insolent ignorance rules, and learning and genius are subordinate. It is a world where Kings and Priests trample on liberty and the rights of conscience. Freedom hides in caves and mountains, and servility and flattery fawn and thrive. The cry of the widow and orphan, starving for lack of food and shivering with cold, rises to Heaven. Men willing to labor are starving, and they and their families beg plaintively for work when the owner closes his business. Here one who grows rich by cheating and abusing the poor is treated with honor in life and death. Here war has never ceased. One may recall the sorrow of the Craft for the death of Hiram, the grief of the Jews for the fall of Jerusalem, the misery of the Templars at the ruin of their order and the death of De Molay, or the world's agony and pangs of woe at the death of the Redeemer. Any of these may serve to illustrate the sorrow we feel in this present condition.

289   The third apartment represents the consequences of sin and vice and the hell made of the human heart by its passions. We may see here a parallel to the Hades of the Greeks, the Gehenna of the Hebrews, the Tartarus of the Romans, or the Hell of the Christians.

The fourth apartment represents the Universe freed from the insolent dominion and tyranny of the Principle of Evil. It is brilliant with the true Light that flows from the Supreme Deity. When sin and wrong are abolished and the great plans of Infinite Eternal Wisdom are realized, all God's creatures shall know that God's goodness and beneficence are as infinite as His power. One may see in this the unique mysteries of a faith or creed or an allusion to any past occurrences. Let each of us apply its symbols as he pleases. To all of us they symbolize the universal rule of Masonry and its three chief virtues, Faith, Hope, and Charity. We labor here to no other end. These symbols need no other interpretation.

The obligations of our Ancient Brethren of the Rose ✝ were to fulfill all the duties of friendship, cheerfulness, charity, peace, liberality, temperance, and chastity. They were to avoid impurity, haughtiness, hatred, anger, and every other vice. They took their philosophy from the old Theology of the Egyptians, as Moses and Solomon had, and borrowed its hieroglyphics and the ciphers of the Hebrews. Their principal rules were to practice the profession of medicine charitably and without fee, advance the cause of virtue, enlarge the sciences, and convince men to live simply.

It is not important to know the origin of this Degree or which rites have practiced it throughout history. It is very old. Its ceremonies are different in different countries, and it receives various interpretations. If we were to examine all the different ceremonies, their emblems, and their formulas, we would see that it all belongs to the primitive and essential elements of the order. All
290   practice virtue. All labor, like us, for the elimination of vice, the purification of man, the development of the arts and sciences, and the relief of humanity.

None will admit an adept until he has been purified at the altar of the symbolic Degrees. Differences of opinion about the age and genealogy of the Degree and the variations in the practice (ceremonial and liturgical) are not important if all revere the Holy Arch of the symbolic Degrees. It is the first and unalterable source of Freemasonry.

If brethren of a particular religious belief have been excluded from this Degree, it shows how gravely the purposes and plan of Masonry may be misunderstood. Whenever the door of any Degree is closed against anyone who believes in one God and the soul's immortality because of the other tenets of his faith, that Degree is no longer Masonry. No Mason has the right to interpret the symbols of this Degree for another or to refuse him its mysteries.

Listen to *our* explanation of the symbols of the Degree and then give them whatever further interpretation you think fit.

The *Cross* has been a sacred symbol from the earliest Antiquity. It is found upon all the enduring monuments of the world. Buddha was said to have died upon it. The Druids cut an oak into its shape. They considered it sacred and built their temples in that form. It points to the four corners of the world and was the symbol of universal nature. Krishna is said to have died upon a cruciform tree that was marked with a cross. The cross was also revered in Mexico.

Its particular meaning in this Degree is that given by the Ancient Egyptians. *Thoth* or *Phtha* is represented on the oldest monuments carrying the *Crux Ansata*, or *Ankh* (a Tau cross, with a ring or circle over it). He is seen with it on the double tablet of Shufu and Noh Shufu (builders of the greatest of the Pyramids) at Wadi Meghara. The Ankh was the hieroglyph for *life* and with a triangle preceding it meant *life-giving*. To us, it is the symbol of the *Life* that emanated from God and of the Eternal Life that everyone hopes for.

The ROSE was sacred to Aurora and the Sun. It is the symbol of *Dawn*. As a representation of the resurrection of Light and the renewal of life, it is the dawn of the first day and the resurrection. The Cross and Rose together hieroglyphically represent the Dawn of Eternal Life that all Nations have hoped to obtain with the arrival of a Redeemer.

The *Pelican* feeding her young is an emblem of the large and bountiful beneficence of Nature, the Redeemer of fallen man, and of the humanity and charity that ought to distinguish a Knight of this Degree.

The *Eagle* was the living Symbol of the Egyptian God *Mendes* or *Menthra* who was one with *Amun-Re*, the God of Thebes and Upper Egypt.

The *Compass* surmounted by a *crown* signifies that, regardless of the high Masonic rank achieved by a Knight of the Rose Croix, equality and impartiality must govern his behavior.

Many meanings have been assigned to the word INRI, inscribed on the Crux Ansata over the Master's Seat. The Christian Initiate sees it as the initials of the inscription upon the cross of Christ (*Iesus Nazarenus Rex Iudaeorum*).

291

Anciently, wise men connected it with one of the greatest secrets of Nature, universal regeneration. They saw it as *Igne Natura renovatur integra* (the whole of nature is renovated by fire). The Alchemical or Hermetic Masons used this aphorism, *Igne nitrum roris invenitur*. The four letters are the initials of the Hebrew words that represent the four elements: *Iammim* (the seas or water), *Nour* (fire), *Rouach* (air), and *Iebeschah* (dry earth). Its meaning to us does not need to be repeated.

The CROSS ✕ was the Sign of the Creative Wisdom or Logos, the Son of God. Plato said, "God expressed him with the figure of the letter X, a cross laid upon the universe." Mithras marked his soldiers' foreheads with a Cross.

292

We constantly see the Tau and the Resh joined. In old Samaritan, these two letters stand for 400 and 200 (the sum of which is 600). It is the Staff of Osiris and his monogram. The Christians later adopted it as a Sign. A medal of Constantius bears the inscription, *"In hoc signo victor cris."* An inscription in the Duomo at Milan reads, *"X et P Christi-Nomina-Sancta-Tenei."*

The sign of the Egyptian God Canobus was a **T** or a ✝. The Vaishnavas of India have the same Sacred Tau, to which they add crosses and triangles (✿). The garments of the priests of Horus and the dress of the Lama of Tibet were covered with these Crosses (✠). The Sectarian marks of the Jains and the badge of the Sect of Xac Japonicos resembled a Swastika. Though reviled today for its connection to Adolf Hitler's Nazi party, it was widely used for centuries as a solar symbol or cross.

On the ruins of Mandore, in India, are the mystic triangle and interlaced triangle (✿). It is also found on ancient coins and medals excavated from the ruins of Oojein and other ancient cities in India.

Lament, with us, the sad condition of the Human race in this vale of tears! Grieve for the darkness of the bewildered soul, oppressed by doubt and worry.

Every human soul is sad at times and every thoughtful soul at times despairs. There are very few who are not sometimes startled and terrified by the awful questions that they ask in their innermost depths. Some Demon seems to torture it with doubts and crush it with despair, asking if its convictions are true and its faith well founded. It questions whether the Universe is ruled by a God of Infinite Love and Beneficence or by some great remorseless Fate and iron

293 Necessity. "What are we," the Tempter asks, "except puppets on a stage. O Omnipotent destiny, pull our strings gently! Dance us mercifully off our miserable little stage!"

The Demon whispers, "Is it not the vanity of man that causes him to pretend to himself that he is like God in intellect, sympathies, and passions? Is not his God just his own shadow, projected in gigantic outlines upon the clouds? Does he not create for himself a God in his own image by adding indefinite extension to his own faculties, powers, and passions?"

"Who," the Voice that will not be silent whispers, "has ever thoroughly satisfied himself with his own arguments regarding his own nature? Who ever demonstrated to himself with certainty that he was an immortal spirit living temporarily in the body? Who has demonstrated that the intellect of Man is different from that of the wiser animals? Who has done more than utter nonsense and incoherencies regarding the difference between the instincts of the dog and the reason of Man? The horse, dog, and elephant are as conscious of their identity as we are. They think, dream, remember, argue with themselves, plan, and *reason*. What is the intellect and intelligence of man but the intellect of the animal in a higher degree or larger quantity?"

The Voice asks, "In what Respect have the masses of men proven themselves either wiser or better than the animals in whose eyes a higher intelligence shines than in *their* dull, unintellectual ones. How have they proven themselves worthy of, or suited for, an immortal life? Would that be a prize of any value to the vast majority? Do they show any capacity for improvement or fitness for a state of existence in which they would not bow to power? What would be the value of a Heaven where they could not lie, libel, and practice deceit for profitable returns?"

Sadly, we look around us and read the gloomy and dreary records of the old, dead, and rotten ages. More than twenty centuries have past since Christ was crucified, and His Doctrines are not yet even nominally accepted as true by a fourth of mankind. Since His death, uncounted numbers of human beings have lived and died in total unbelief of all that is essential to Salvation! How many souls have flocked up toward the eternal Throne of God to receive His judgment?

The Religion of Love has often proven to be the Religion of Hate. Heresies grew up before the Apostles died. Sects fought and each persecuted the other as they gained power until the soil of the Christian world was watered with the blood of martyrs.

"By what right", whispers the Voice, "does this savage, merciless, and persecuting animal try to convince itself that it is *not* an animal like the wolf, hyena, and tiger and that it is a noble creature, destined to be immortal? What other immortality could this selfish creature enjoy? Of what is it capable? Doesn't immortality begin *here,* and isn't *life* a part of it? How will death change the base nature of the base soul? Don't those other animals have the same right as man to expect a resurrection, an Eternity of existence, or a Heaven of Love?"

The world improves. Man will stop persecuting when the victims become too numerous and strong to submit to it. When that source of pleasure is closed, men will turn their cruelty on animals and other living things below them. Depriving other creatures of the life that God gave them out of mere savagery is the amusement of man who prides himself on being the Lord of Creation and a little lower than the Angels. If he can no longer torture his fellow man, he can hate, slander, and find delight in the thought that he will bask in the luxuries of

294

295

Heaven while watching the writhing agony of those who were justly damned for daring to hold opinions contrary to his own.

After the armies of the despots cease to slay and ravage, the armies of "Freedom" take their place and slaughter, burn, and ravage. Each age re-enacts the crimes, as well as the follies, of its predecessors. War still turns fruitful lands into deserts, and God is thanked in the Churches for bloody butcheries. The remorseless devastators are crowned with laurels and receive ovations.

Not one in ten thousand men has any aspirations beyond his daily needs. In this and all other ages, most men are born to be beasts of burden like the horse and ox. Profoundly ignorant, they think and reason like the animals they work with. For them, God, Soul, Spirit, and Immortality are just words without any meaning. The God of most of the Christian world is Bel, Moloch, Zeus, or at best Osiris, Mithras, and Adonaï under another name. The Statue of Olympian Jove (worshipped as the Father) is found in a Christian Church that was once a Pagan Temple. The statue of Venus is revered as the Virgin Mary. Men do not believe in their hearts that God is either just or merciful. They fear and shrink from His lightning and dread His wrath. They only think they believe that there is an afterlife, judgment, and punishment for sin. Yet they will persecute those who do not believe what they themselves imagine they believe, calling them Infidels and Atheists. To the majority of mankind, God is just the reflected image of an earthly Tyrant on his Throne, but more powerful, inscrutable, and implacable.

In the cities, the lower classes are equally without faith and hope. The others have a blind faith imposed by education and circumstances. The worlds of science and philosophy grow ever more distant from the world of belief. Faith and Reason are not opposites in equilibrium, but antagonistic and hostile to each other. The result is the darkness and despair of skepticism seen as rationalism.

In large areas of the world, humanity still kneels, like camels, to take up and carry burdens for its tyrants. If a Republic occasionally rises, it soon falls in blood. Kings don't need to make war upon it to crush it. They only need to leave it alone, and it soon destroys itself. When an enslaved people shake off their chains, it may be asked,

> Shall the braggart shout
> For some blind glimpse of Freedom, link itself,
> Through madness, hated by the wise, to law,
> System and Empire?

Everywhere in the world, labor is the slave of profit. A man is fed only so long as he works well for the owner. There are famines, pestilence, brutality, misery, squalor, ignorance, and hatred in the human cesspools and sewers everywhere.

Even so, the Voice says, this race is not satisfied to see its multitudes destroyed by mysterious epidemics. It must always wage war. There has not been a time when the world was at peace. Men have always been murdering each other somewhere. Armies have always lived by the toil of the farmer. War has exhausted the resources, wasted the energies, and ended the prosperity of Nations. Now it burdens future generations with crushing debt, borrows against the future, and brings upon nations the shame and infamy of dishonest repudiation.

Sometimes, the fires of war light up half a Continent at once. The flames will flicker and die away, and the fire will smolder in its ashes only to break out again with a renewed and more concentrated fury. Sometimes, the storm of war howls over small areas only. At other times, its lights cover the whole globe. War is experienced everywhere, and nowhere is safe. No people fail to perform the horrible blasphemy of thanking the God of Love for victories and carnage. Chants of praise are still heard after acts of terrorism committed by religious fanatics. Man's ingenuity and inventive powers are commissioned to develop infernal instruments of war to more quickly and effectively maim and kill. *298*

When we dream of Utopia and believe that man is not, after all, a half tamed tiger, we are startled to find that the thin mask of civilization is ripped away. We lie down to sleep on the slopes of Mount Vesuvius. The volcano has been inert for so long that we believe its fires have been extinguished. The clustering grapes and green leaves of the olive tree tremble in the soft night air. Above us shines the peaceful, patient stars. The crash of a new eruption wakes us. We see the volcano hurling its fires to the stars and the lava pouring down its sides. The roar and screams of Civil War are all around us. The great armies roll along and leave behind them smoking and depopulated deserts. The pillager is in every house, taking the morsel of bread from the lips of the starving child. Laws, Courts, Constitutions, Christianity, Mercy, and Pity disappear. God seems to have abdicated, and Moloch reigns in His place. The Press and Pulpit rejoice in universal murder and urge the extermination of the Conquered. Human predators win the gratitude of Christian Senates with plunder and murder.

Commercial greed deadens the sympathy of Nations. It makes them deaf to the demands of honor, generosity, and the appeals of those who suffer under injustice. The universal pursuit of wealth dethrones God and pays divine honors *299* to Mammon and Beelzebub. Selfishness rules supreme, and achieving wealth becomes the goal of life. The villainies of legalized gambling becomes epidemic, and treachery is just evidence of shrewdness. Political office falls prey to vocal minorities, and the Country is torn by its own hounds. The villains it has carefully educated plunder it when it is helpless.

By what right, the Voice demands, does a creature engaged in robbery and slaughter claim to be superior to the savage beasts?

The shadow of horrible doubt falls upon the soul that would love, trust, and believe. The darkness that surrounded you was a symbol. It doubts the truth of Revelation and the existence of a beneficent God. It asks itself, "Is it useless to hope that Humanity will move any closer to perfection?" When it advances in one respect, it seems to regress in another as if in compensation. It asks itself whether man is the plaything of a blind, merciless Fate. It wonders whether all philosophies are delusions and all religions are fantastic creations of human vanity and self-conceit. When Reason is abandoned as a guide, don't all faiths have the same claims to sovereignty and implicit credence?

He wonders whether Man's belief in an afterlife is based on the calamities, oppressions, and miseries of the Good. Doubting man's capacity for unbounded progress here, he doubts the possibility of it anywhere. If he does not doubt God's existence, he cannot silence the incessant whisper that the miseries and calamities of men are of no more significance or importance in the *300* eyes of God than those occurring to other material beings. This is not a picture painted by the imagination. Many thoughtful minds have doubted and despaired. How many of us can say that our own faith is so well grounded and complete that we never hear those painful whisperings within the soul? Blessed are those who never doubt and whose souls never know that Awful Shadow, the absence of the Divine Light.

To explain the existence of Evil and Suffering, the Ancient Persians believed there were two Principles or Deities in the Universe, one Good and the other Evil. They were constantly in conflict with each other for control, alternately overcoming and being overcome. The SAGES believed the One Supreme was superior to both and for *them*, Light would prevail over Darkness in the end. Good would prevail over Evil, and Ahriman and his Demons would abandon their wicked and vicious natures and share the universal Salvation. It did not occur to them that the existence of the Evil Principle did not explain suffering or the existence of Evil. Man is often content with simple answers that ignore the hard questions. He cannot believe that the world rests on nothing but is content when taught that it is carried on the back of an elephant who stands on a tortoise. Many have found great happiness in the belief in a Devil who relieved God of the infamy of being the Author of Sin.

Faith isn't sufficient for everyone to overcome this great difficulty. They, like the concerned father of *Mark 9:14-29*, say, "*Lord! I believe!*" but then they add, "*Help me overcome my unbelief!*" Without coinciding reason and Faith, they remain in the darkness of doubt.

301 Only those focused solely on the material life are uninterested in these great Problems. Animals do not consider them. It is characteristic of an immortal Soul that it would try to satisfy itself about its immortality and understand this great enigma. Anyone who is not troubled or tortured by these doubts and speculations shouldn't be regarded as wise or fortunate.

However we see Faith, it begins where Reason ends and must have a foundation in Reason, Analogy, Consciousness, or human testimony. The worshipper of Brahma has implicit Faith in what seems to us false and absurd.

His faith isn't supported by Reason, Analogy, or the Consciousness, but by the testimony of his Spiritual teachers and Holy Books. The Muslim also believes based on the positive testimony of the Prophet. No faith, however absurd or degrading, has ever lacked foundations of testimony and Holy books. Miracles supported by unimpeachable testimony have always been used as a foundation for Faith, and modern miracles are better authenticated than ancient ones.

Faith must flow from some source within us when the evidence for our belief is not presented to our senses, or it won't be the assurance of the truth.

For a limited class of truths, the Consciousness or the instinct for the truth of things is the highest possible evidence of certainty.

Reason will eventually lead us *away* from the Truth regarding things of the Infinite if we only believe our senses or what can be logically proven. To Human reason, an Infinite Justice and an Infinite Mercy (or Love) in the same Being are inconsistent and impossible. It can be *demonstrated* that one excludes the other. Reason can demonstrate that, since the Creation had a beginning, an Eternity must have elapsed before the Deity began to create. 302

When we look at the Heavens, glittering with stars, we feel our own insignificance in the scale of Creation. If the Ancients had our modern understanding of the stars, Sun, Moon, and Planets, much of what has been religious faith would never have developed.

To them, all the lights of the sky were created only to give light to the earth. The earth was assumed to be the only inhabited part of the Universe. The world and the Universe were synonymous terms. Men had no idea of the immense size and distance of the heavenly bodies. In Chaldæa, Egypt, India, China, and Persia, the Sages knew what the heavens were and always had an esoteric creed that was only taught in the mysteries. No Sage believed the popular creed. To them, the Gods and Idols were symbols of great and mysterious truths.

The majority thought that the attention of the Gods was always centered upon the earth and man. The Grecian Divinities inhabited Olympus, an insignificant mountain of the Earth. Neptune, Pluto, and Persephone came to the Court of Zeus from their respective dwellings. God came down to Sinai from Heaven and dictated the Hebrew law to His servant Moses. The Stars were the guardians of mortals, whose fates and fortunes were read in their movements, conjunctions, and oppositions. The Moon was the Bride and Sister of the Sun and, like the Sun, was made for the service of mankind.

If we examine the vast nebula of Hercules, Orion, and Andromeda, we will find that they resolve into Stars more numerous than the sands on the seashore. If we realize that each of these Stars is a Sun, our world seems to shrink into an incredible insignificance. 303

The Universe, which is the uttered Word of God, is infinite in extent. There is no empty space beyond creation on any side. The Universe, which is the Thought of God pronounced, has always existed. The forms of creation

225

change, but the Universe itself is infinite and eternal, because God Is, Was, and always Will Be.

Reason has to admit that a Supreme Intelligence, infinitely powerful and wise, must have created this boundless Universe. Reason also tells us that we are as unimportant in it as the microscopic organisms that float upon the air or swim in a drop of water.

The foundations of our faith, resting upon the imagined focus of God on our race, are rudely shaken when the Universe broadens and expands. The darkness of doubt and distrust rests heavy on the Soul.

The methods we use to satisfy our doubts only increase them. *Demonstrating* the necessity for a cause of the creation merely indicates the necessity of a cause for that cause. The argument for a plan and design only moves the difficulty a step further off. We rest the world on the elephant, the elephant on the tortoise, and the tortoise on nothing.

The radical distinction between men and beasts cannot be attributed to the difference between Reason (belonging only to Man) and animal instinct. If 304 the mental processes exhibited by animals that think, dream, remember, plan, and communicate their thoughts to each other are similar to those in man, the theory that an immaterial Soul explains these processes in the *human* being is absurd. The true unsolvable mystery is that organized matter can think or even feel at all. "Instinct" is a word without a meaning or else it means inspiration. It is either the animal itself or God *in* the animal that thinks, remembers, and reasons. Instinct, as we understand it, would be the most wonderful of mysteries. It would be the direct, immediate, and constant promptings of the Deity, because animals are not merely machines to be controlled.

Must we *always* remain in this darkness of uncertainty and doubt? Is there no method of escaping from this labyrinth except by a blind faith that explains nothing?

In Chronicles, King Solomon placed two huge columns of bronze in front of the entrance to the Temple. One was called Jachin and the other Boaz. The Masonry of the Blue Lodges doesn't give an explanation for these symbolic columns. If they were not intended to be symbols, they were subsequently understood to be such.

We are certain that everything *within* the Temple was symbolic, and the whole structure was intended to represent the Universe. We may conclude that the columns of the portico also had a symbolic significance.

The key to their true meaning may be discovered. Two opposing 305 principles are necessary for creation so that harmony may result from their balance. This is the second principle of *Kabbalah*. It is indicated by all the sacred hieroglyphs of the Ancient Sanctuaries and the rites, so little understood by Initiates of Ancient and Modern Freemasonry.

The Zohar declares that everything in the Universe is governed by the mystery of "the Balance" or Equilibrium. In the Sephiroth, Wisdom and Understanding, Severity and Benignity, and Victory and Glory constitute pairs.

Wisdom and Understanding are represented symbolically in Kabbalah as male and female. So are Justice and Mercy. Strength is intellectual Energy or Activity, and Establishment or Stability is the intellectual Capacity to produce. They are the POWER of *generation* and the CAPACITY of *production*. God creates by WISDOM and establishes by UNDERSTANDING. These are the two Columns of the Temple. They are opposites like Man and Woman, Reason and Faith, Omnipotence and Liberty, and Infinite Justice and Infinite Mercy. They were the columns of the intellectual and moral world and a symbol of the balance that was necessary to the grand law of creation.

Every Force must have a Resistance to support it, and every light must have a shadow. For every positive, there must be a negative.

For the Kabbalist, Light represents the Active Principle, and Darkness represents the Passive Principle. They made the Sun and Moon symbols of the two Divine Sexes and the two creative forces. They credited woman with Temptation and the first sin, but also with the first labor (the maternal labor of redemption). From darkness, light is reborn. The Void attracts Fullness. The emptiness of poverty and misery attracts charity, pity, and love. Christ 306 completed the Atonement on the Cross by descending into Hell.

Justice and Mercy are opposites. Their co-existence seems impossible, and being equal, one cannot annihilate the other and reign alone. The mysteries of the Divine Nature are beyond our comprehension. In all nature, harmony and movement are the result of the equilibrium of opposing or contrary forces.

The analogy of opposites provides the solution to the most interesting and difficult problem of modern philosophy, the balancing of Reason and Faith, Authority and Liberty, Science and Belief, and the Perfection of God and Imperfection of Man. If science or knowledge is the Sun, Belief is the Moon. Faith is the Supplement of Reason. It comes from Reason, but can never be confused with it. The encroachments of Reason on Faith or Faith on Reason are eclipses of the Sun and Moon. They simultaneously render both the Source of Light and its reflection useless.

Science is destroyed by systems that are nothing but beliefs. Faith succumbs to reasoning. For the two Columns of the Temple to support the edifice, they must remain separate and parallel to each other. As soon as they are brought together, they are overturned and the whole structure falls.

Harmony is the result of a balance of forces. When this is lacking in government, it will be a failure, because it is either Despotism or Anarchy. All theoretical governments end in one or the other. Enduring Governments are not made in the mind of the philosopher or in a Congress or Convention. In a Republic, forces that seem opposites give movement and life. The Spheres are held in their orbits and caused to revolve harmoniously by two opposing forces.

307 If the centripetal force overcame the centrifugal, the rush of the Spheres to the Central Sun would annihilate the system. Instead of consolidation, they would be shattered into fragments.

Man is a free agent though Omnipotence is all around him. To be free to do good, he must be free to do evil. The Light requires the Shadow. A State is as free as an individual in any just government. The freedom of the State is limited only by the freedom allowed it by the Nation, just as an individual has only the liberty that God has given him. These are opposites, but not antagonistic. In a union of States, the freedom of the States is consistent with the Supremacy of the Nation. When either obtains permanent mastery over the other, they cease to be in *equilibrium.* The weaker will be annihilated, and without resistance, the stronger rushes into ruin.

When the balance of Reason and Faith is destroyed, the result is Atheism or Superstition (disbelief or blind credulity). The leaders of the Faithful and the Faithless both rule as tyrants.

"*Whoever God loves, he chastises,*" is an expression that formulates a whole dogma. The trials of life are the blessings of life if one has a Soul that is worthy of salvation. "*Light and darkness,*" said ZOROASTER, "*are the world's eternal ways.*" The Light and Shadow are everywhere and are always in proportion. It is only by trial that men and Nations gain initiation. The agonies of the garden of Gethsemane and the Cross on Calvary preceded the Resurrection and were the means of Redemption. It is with prosperity that God afflicts Humanity.

The Degree of Rose Croix is devoted to and symbolizes the final triumph of truth over falsehood, liberty over slavery, light over darkness, life over death, and good over evil. It teaches the great truth that, in spite of the existence of Evil, God is infinitely wise, just, and good. The affairs of the world follow no rule of right and wrong that we can comprehend, but all *is* right because it is the *308* work of God. All evils, miseries, and misfortunes are like drops in the vast current that is sweeping onward (with His guidance) to a great and magnificent result. At the appointed time, He will redeem and regenerate the world, and the Principle, Power, and existence of Evil will end. God will choose the method and instruments of this end. He may employ a Redeemer that has already appeared or one who has yet to come. It is not for us as Masons to decide. Everyone must judge and decide for himself.

Meanwhile, we labor to hasten the coming of that day. The morals of antiquity are ours. We recognize every teacher of Morality and every Reformer as a brother in this great work. The Eagle is the symbol of Liberty and the Compasses of Equality. The Pelican represents Humanity and our order of Fraternity. Laboring for these principles with Faith, Hope, and Charity, we wait with patience for the final triumph of Good.

No one Mason has the right to decide the degree of veneration that another shall feel for any Reformer or Founder of Religion. We neither reject nor endorse any particular creed. Whatever higher attributes the Founder of the

Christian Faith had, none can deny that He taught and practiced a pure and elevated morality, even at the risk and ultimate loss of His life. He was not only the benefactor of a disinherited people, but a model for mankind. He loved the children of Israel. He came to them. To them alone He preached that Gospel which His disciples later carried to foreigners. He would have freed the chosen People from their spiritual bondage of ignorance and degradation. As a lover of all mankind, He laid down His life for the emancipation of His Brethren. He should be an object of gratitude and veneration to all.

The Roman world felt the pangs of its approaching fall. Paganism, its Temples shattered by Socrates and Cicero, was in decline. The God of the Hebrews was unknown beyond the limits of Palestine. The old religions had failed to give happiness and peace to the world. The babbling and wrangling philosophers had confused men's ideas, until they doubted everything and had *309* faith in nothing. Mankind was divided into two great classes, the master and the slave.

Then, a voice in the small Roman Province of Judea proclaimed a new Gospel for a crushed, suffering, and bleeding humanity. Liberty of Thought, Equality of all men in the eye of God, and universal Fraternity became the new doctrine. It was the old Primitive Truth uttered once again!

Man is once more taught to look upward to his God rather than seek an infinitely remote God, hidden in impenetrable mystery. He is a good, kind, beneficent, and merciful God. He loves the creatures He has made with a love that is immeasurable and inexhaustible.

Jesus of Nazareth, the "Son of man", is the teacher of the new Law of Love. He calls to Him the humble, poor, and outcasts of the world. The first sentence that He pronounced blesses the world and announces the new gospel, "Blessed are they that mourn for they shall be comforted." He pours the oil of consolation and peace upon every crushed and bleeding heart. Everyone who suffers is His follower. He shares their sorrows and sympathizes with all their afflictions.

He raises up the sinner and the Samaritan woman and teaches them to hope for forgiveness. He pardons the woman caught in adultery. He doesn't select His disciples from the Pharisees or Philosophers, but from the low and humble. He heals the sick and feeds the poor. He lives among the destitute and the friendless. He said, "Suffer the little children to come unto me, for of such is the kingdom of Heaven! Blessed are the humble-minded, for theirs is the kingdom of Heaven. Blessed are the meek, for they shall inherit the Earth. Blessed are the merciful, for they shall obtain mercy; and the pure in heart, for they shall see God. Blessed are the peacemakers, for they will be called the *310* children of God! First be reconciled to your brother, and then come and offer your gift at the altar. Give to him that asks of you. If someone asks to borrow from you, do not turn him away! Love your enemies. Bless those that curse you. Do good to those that hate you and pray for those that despitefully use you and persecute you! Do to others as you would want done to you, for this is the law and the Prophets! He that does not take his cross and follow Me is not worthy of Me. I give this new commandment to you: that you love one another as I have loved you. By this, all will know that you are My disciples. Greater love has no man than this that a man lay down his life for his friend."

He sealed the Gospel of Love with His life. The cruelty of the Jewish Priesthood, the ferocity of the mob, and Roman indifference to barbarian life nailed Him to the cross, yet He died uttering blessings upon humanity.

He bequeathed His teachings to man as an inestimable inheritance. Perverted and corrupted, they have served as a basis for many creeds and have been the warrant for intolerance and persecution. We teach them in their purity. They are our Masonry and good men of all creeds can subscribe to them.

God is good and merciful. He loves and sympathizes with the creatures He has made. His finger is visible in all the movements of the moral, intellectual, and material universe. We are His children and objects of His paternal care and regard. All men are our brothers. We are to supply their needs, pardon their errors, tolerate their opinions, and forgive their injustice. Man has an immortal soul, a free will, and a right to freedom of thought and action. All men are equal in God's sight, and we best serve God by humility, meekness, gentleness, kindness, and the other virtues. These are "the new Law", the "WORD", which the world has waited for. Every true Knight of the Rose will revere the memory of He who taught it and be tolerant of those who view Him as something more.

311 Philo said, "The contemplative soul, unequally guided, sometimes towards abundance and sometimes towards barrenness, is illuminated by the primitive ideas that emanate from the Divine Intelligence when it ascends toward the Sublime Treasures. When it descends, it falls within the domain of those Intelligences that are called Angels. When the soul is deprived of the light of God, it no longer enjoys more than a feeble and secondary light and the understanding of words only."

"Let the narrow-souled withdraw, having their ears sealed up! We communicate the divine mysteries only to those who have received the sacred initiation, practice true piety, and are not enslaved by empty words or the doctrines of pagans."

"You Initiates whose ears are purified, receive this in your souls never to be lost! Reveal it to no Profane! Keep and contain it within yourselves, as an incorruptible treasure more precious than everything. It is the knowledge of the Great Cause, Nature, and that which is born of both. If you meet an Initiate, besiege him with your prayers, that he will teach you new mysteries that he may know and don't rest until you have obtained them! Moses, the Friend of God, initiated me in the Great Mysteries, but having seen Jeremiah, I recognized him as an Initiate and a Hierophant. I follow his school."

We, like him, recognize all Initiates as our Brothers. We belong to no one creed or school. In all religions, there is a basis of Truth and pure Morality.

We respect all creeds that teach the cardinal tenets of Masonry. We admire and revere all teachers and reformers of mankind.

Masonry also has her mission to perform. Her traditions reach back to the earliest times, and her symbols date back beyond the monumental history of Egypt. She invites all men of all religions to enlist under her banners and to war against evil, ignorance, and wrong. You are now her knight and to her service your sword is consecrated. May you prove a worthy soldier in a worthy cause!

MORALS AND DOGMA FOR THE 21ST CENTURY

COUNCIL OF KADOSH

CHAPTER 19: GRAND PONTIFF

THE true Mason works for the benefit of future generations and for the advancement and improvement of his country. Poor ambition limits these efforts to a single life. Everyone wants to survive their funerals, to live afterwards in the permanent good they have done for mankind, rather than fade with the fragile pages of fleeting memory. Most people desire to leave behind something that will live beyond their final day. That instinctive impulse is given by God and found in the rudest human heart. It is the surest proof of the soul's immortality. To plant the trees that will shelter our children after we are dead, is as natural as to love the shade of those our fathers planted. The most uneducated laborer painfully conscious of their own inferiority and the poorest widowed mother giving her life-blood to those who pay only for the work of her needle will work and save to educate their children so they may take a higher station in the world. They are the world's greatest benefactors.

Through the influences that survive him, man becomes immortal before the general resurrection. Consider the Spartan mother who gave her son his shield and said, "WITH IT, OR UPON IT!" She too made a law that survived her and inspired the Spartan soldiery who later demolished the walls of Athens and aided Alexander in his conquest of the East. The widow who gave Marion the fiery arrows used to burn her own house so it could no longer shelter the enemies of her country legislated more effectively for England than Locke, Shaftesbury, or many a Legislature has done since that State won its freedom.

It was of little importance to the Kings of Egypt and the Monarchs of Assyria and Phœnicia that the orphan of a Jewish woman was adopted by the daughter of Sesostris Ramses, slew an Egyptian who oppressed a Hebrew slave, and then fled into the desert to remain there forty years. Moses might have otherwise become the Regent of Lower Egypt. Known to us only because of a tablet on a tomb, he became the deliverer of the Jews. He led them from Egypt to the frontiers of Palestine and made a law for them, out of which grew the Christian faith and ultimately shaped the destinies of the world. Moses, the old Roman lawyers, Alfred of England, the Saxon Thanes and Norman Barons, the old judges, chancellors, and the makers of the canons lost in the mists, and shadows of the Past are our legislators, and even today we obey the laws that they enacted.

Napoleon died upon the barren rock of his exile. His bones were carried to France by the son of a King and they rest in the Hopital des Invalides in Paris. His Thoughts still govern France. He, and not the People, dethroned the Bourbon and drove the last King of the House of Orleans into exile. In his coffin, he, and not the People, voted the crown to the Third Napoleon. He, and not the Generals of France and England, led the united forces against the grim Northern Despotism.

Mohammad announced to the Arabian idolaters his new creed, *"There is but one God, and Mohammad, like Moses and Christ, is His Apostle."* For many years, he taught and preached the Koran unaided, then with the help of his family and a few friends, then with many disciples, and finally with an army. The religion of the wild Arabian enthusiast spread over Asia converting the fiery Tribes of the Great Desert. It built up the Saracen dynasties and conquered Persia, India, the Greek Empire, Northern Africa, and Spain. It dashed the surges of its fierce soldiery against the fortifications of Northern Christendom. The Law of Mohammad still governs a fifth of the human race as the Turk, Arab, Persian, and Indonesian still obey Him and pray with their faces turned toward Mecca. He rules and reigns in the smallest corners of the East.

Confucius thought still influences the laws of China. The thoughts and ideas of Lenin and Stalin still exert influence Russia. Plato and the other great Sages of Antiquity still reign as the Kings of Philosophy and have dominion over the human intellect. The great Statesmen of the Past still preside at the United 314 Nations. Burke still lingers in the House of Commons and Berryer's sonorous tones will long ring in the Legislative Chambers of France. Sam Rayburn's precedents still govern many of the functions of the U.S. House of Representatives.

Tamerlane built his pyramid of fifty thousand human skulls, and when he wheeled away his vast armies from the gates of Damascus to find new conquests and build other pyramids, a young John Faust, the son of a poor artisan, was playing in the streets of Mentz. His apparent importance in the scale of beings was compared to that of Tamerlane, a grain of sand on the earth. Tamerlane and all his shaggy legions have passed away and become shadows. But printing, the wonderful invention that John Faust commercialized, has exerted a greater influence on mankind's destinies and overturned more thrones and dynasties than all the bloodstained victories from Nimrod to Napoleon.

Long ago, the Temple built by Solomon and our Ancient Brethren sank into ruin when the Assyrian Armies sacked Jerusalem. The Holy Land remains a place of turmoil. The Kings of Egypt and Assyria, who were peers of Solomon, are forgotten and their histories are now only fables. The Ancient Orient is a shattered wreck bleaching on the shores of Time. The Wolf and the Jackal howl among the ruins of Thebes and Tyre and the sculptured images of the Temples and Palaces of Babylon and Nineveh are excavated from their ruins and carried away to foreign lands. But the Son of a poor Phœnician Widow who served as Grand Master with the Kings of Israel and the King of Tyre in a quiet and peaceful Order increased in stature and influence while defying the angry waves of time and the storms of persecution. Age has not weakened its foundations, shattered its columns, nor marred the beauty of its harmonious proportions. In the time of Solomon, primitive barbarians peopled the inhospitable, howling wildernesses in France, Britain, and the New World, unknown to Jew or Gentile 315 until the glories of the Orient had faded. Now the Order has built new Temples and taught its millions of Initiates those lessons of peace, good-will, and toleration. It learned reliance on God and confidence in man when the Hebrew and the Giblemite worked side by side on the slopes of Lebanon and the Servant of Jehovah and the Phœnician servant of Bel sat together with the humble artisan in Council at Jerusalem.

The Dead govern and the Living obey. After death, if the Soul sees what occurs upon this earth as it watches over the welfare of those it loves, then its greatest happiness must be to see the current of its beneficent influences widening out, like streams widening into rivers, and shaping the destinies of individuals, families, States, and the World. Its most bitter punishment is seeing its evil influences causing the mischief and misery that curse and afflict humanity long after both name and memory are forgotten.

We do not know among the Dead who control our destinies. The human race is intertwined by those influences and sympathies, which in their truest sense do make human fates. Humanity is the unit of which one man is but a fraction. What other people in the Past have done, said, and thought forged the great iron network of circumstance that surrounds and controls us all. We take our faith on trust. We think and believe as the Old Lords of Thought command us, and Reason is powerless before Authority.

The Thoughts of the dead Judges of England, Rome, and Greece live on, even though their ashes have been cold for centuries. We could settle our estate in a particular way, but the prohibition of the English Parliament from the reign of the first or second Edward comes echoing down the long avenues of time and tells us we shall not exercise the power of disposition as we wish. We would gain advantage over another except for the thought of the old Roman lawyer who died before Justinian, or that of Rome's great orator Cicero, nullifies the act and makes the intention ineffectual. Moses forbids this act, and Alfred forbids that one. We could sell our land but certain marks on perishable paper tell us that our father or remote ancestor ordered otherwise, and the arm of the dead emerges from the grave and prohibits the transaction. When about to sin or err, *316* the thought and wish of our dead mother, spoken when we were children in words that fell upon deaf ears and were long forgotten, flash in our memory and hold us back with a resistless power.

The living shall obey the dead, and once we are dead, for better or worse, the living will obey us. The Thoughts of the Past are the Laws of the Present and the roadmap to the Future. What we say and do that has no effect beyond our lives is unimportant. What lives on as part of the great body of law enacted by the dead is the only act worth doing and the only Thought worth speaking. The desire to do something that will benefit the world, when neither praise nor malice can reach us in the grave, is the noblest ambition considered by man.

This is the ambition of a true and genuine Mason. Knowing the slow processes by which the Deity brings about great results, the Mason does not expect to sow and reap in the same lifetime.

With rare exceptions, it is the steadfast fate and noblest destiny of great and good people to work and let others reap the harvest of their labors. Someone who does good only to be repaid in kind, thanks, gratitude, reputation, or the world's praise is like the Shylock who loans money so that after a few months he receives it back with interest. Distinguished service is typically repaid with slander, criticism, ridicule, disregard, or ingratitude. This is not a misfortune. However, those who lack the wit to see, the sense to appreciate the service, or the nobility of soul to thank or reward the benefactor of this kind are a pitiful lot. His influences will live on and the great Future will obey whether it recognizes or disowns the leader.

Miltiades was fortunate that he was exiled and Aristides that he was ostracized. The Redeemer, Jesus Christ, was not unfortunate, but those who repaid Him by nailing Him upon the cross as though He had been a slave or criminal for the inestimable gift He offered them and for a life passed in working for their good were very unfortunate. The persecutor dies and rots, and the Future utters his name with hatred, but his victim's memory he has unintentionally immortalized and made glorious.

317 If not for slander and persecution, the Mason who would benefit mankind must look for apathy and indifference in those whose good he seeks and those who should seek the good of others. When a great Reformer appears and a new Faith springs up and grows with supernatural energy, the progress of Truth is slower than the growth of oaks. He who plants need not expect to gather. The Redeemer, at His death, had twelve disciples. One betrayed him and one deserted and denied Him. It is gratifying enough for us to know that the fruit will mature in its due season. Who will gather it does not concern us in the least. It is our responsibility to plant the seed. It is God's right to give the fruit to whom He pleases, and if not to us, then our action is that much more noble.

The true office of a Mason and the proudest destiny of a man to sow that others may reap; to work and plant for those who will reside on earth when we are dead; to project our influences far into the future and live beyond our time; to rule as the Kings of Thought over those who are yet unborn; and to bless those with the glorious gifts of Truth, Light, and Liberty who will not know the name of the humanitarian nor care in what grave his unregarded ashes are deposited.

The great and beneficial developments of Nature are produced by slow and often imperceptible degrees. Only the work of destruction and devastation is rapid. The Volcano, Earthquake, Tsunami, Tornado, and Avalanche leap suddenly to life with a fearful energy and strike with an unexpected blow. Mount Vesuvius buried Pompeii and Herculaneum in a night. Lisbon fell flat in a breath when the earth rocked and shuddered. The Alpine village is erased in one bound of the avalanche and the ancient forests fall like grass before the mower when the tornado leaps upon them. Pestilence slays its thousands in a day, and the stormy oceans strew the sandy beaches with shattered navies.

Many years before the Norman Conqueror stamped his mailed foot on the neck of a defeated Saxon England, some wandering barbarian on a continent then unknown to the world planted an acorn. He died and was forgotten but the *318* acorn laid there while the mighty force within it continued working in the darkness. A tender shoot gently rose and, fed by the light, air, and dews, put forth its leaves and lived because the elk or buffalo did not trample and crush it. The years marched by and the shoot became a sapling and its green leaves came and went with the Spring and Fall. The years came and went, William the Norman Bastard parceled out England among his Barons, and still the sapling grew. The dews fed its leaves, and the birds built their nests among its small limbs for many generations. The years still came and went, and the Indian hunter slept in the shade of the sapling, Richard the Lionheart fought at Acre and Ascalon, and King John's bold Barons wrestled from him the Magna Carta. The sapling had become a tree, and it still grew, thrust out its great arms, and lifted its head still higher toward the Heavens in defiance of the storms that roared through its branches. When Columbus sailed his tiny ships to the unknown Western Atlantic and Cortez and Pizarro bathed the cross in blood and the Puritan, Huguenot, Cavalier, and Quakers sought refuge beyond the ocean, the Great Oak still stood firmly rooted, vigorously, stately, and proudly domineering over all the forest without concern for all the centuries that had hurried past since the Indian had first planted the little acorn. Yet, if someone had sat and watched every instant from the moment when the feeble shoot first pushed its way into the light until the eagles built their nest among its branches, they would have never seen the tree or sapling grow because it happens so slowly.

Many centuries long ago, before the Chaldæan Shepherds watched the Stars or Khufu built the Pyramids, one could steer an aircraft carrier where there are now a thousand islands breaking the surface of the Indian Ocean, and the deep sea fishermen would never have found any bottom. But below these waves are countless billions of tiny living creatures made by the Almighty Creator and fashioned by Him for the work they had to do. There they worked beneath the waters, each doing its allotted share and entirely ignorant of the result which God *319* intended. They lived and died, incalculable in numbers and almost infinite in the succession of their generations, each adding his molecule to the gigantic work that went on there under God's direction. He has chosen to create great Continents and Islands and still the coral-insects live and work, as when they made the rocks that lie beneath the Ohio valley.

God has chosen to create. Where firm land now exists once chafed and thundered the great prehistoric ocean. For ages upon ages, the minute shields of infinite myriads of coral and the stony stems of their fossils sank into its depths, and under the vast pressure of the waters, they hardened into limestone. Raised slowly from the ocean floor by His hand, these quarries now lie beneath the soil of every continent hundreds of feet thick. From these remains of the countless dead, we build palaces and tombs just as the Egyptians built their pyramids.

The Great Sun looks earnestly and lovingly upon all the broad lakes and oceans and the invisible vapors rise to meet him. In the upper atmosphere, they are condensed to mist, gather into clouds, and float around in the ambient air. They sail with its currents and hover over the oceans, rolling huge masses around the stony shoulders of great mountains. Condensed still more by changes in temperature, they fall upon the thirsty earth in gentle showers, pour upon it in heavy rains or storm against it during the Equinox. The showers, rains, and storms pass away, the clouds vanish, and the bright stars shine clearly upon the happy earth once more. The raindrops sink into the ground, gather in subterranean reservoirs, flow in subterranean channels, and bubble up to the surface in springs and fountains. From the mountainsides to the valleys, the silver threads of water begin their long journey to the ocean. Slowly uniting, they widen into brooks, then streams, rivers, and finally become a Mississippi, Amazon, Nile, Yangtze, or Danube rolling between its banks mighty, majestic, and effortlessly creating vast alluvial valleys to be the granaries of the world. They are navigated by the millions of ships of commerce, serve as great highways, and become the impassable boundaries of rival nations. These rivers are always returning to the ocean the drops of vapor that had descended from it as rain, snow, and hail upon level plains and mountains that caused them to recoil for many miles before the headlong surge of their great tide.

320 So it is with the combined Human effort. The invisible particles of vapor combine and connect to form the mists and clouds that fall as rain on the thirsty continents and bless the great green forests, wide grassy prairies, waving meadows, and fields by which we live. The infinite number of drops that the glad earth drinks are gathered into springs, streams, and rivers to level the mountains, elevate the plains, and feed the large lakes and unquenchable oceans. All human Thought, Speech, and Action done, said, thought, and suffered upon the Earth combine and flow into one broad, irresistible current toward those great results, which are determined by the will of God.

We build slowly but destroy quickly. Our Ancient Brethren built the Temples at Jerusalem with an untold number of hammer blows that hewed and squared the cedars, quarried the stones, and carved the intricate ornaments, which became the Temples. Stone after stone, by the combined effort and industry of the Apprentices, Fellowcrafts, and Masters, the walls steadily rose. Slowly the roof was framed and fashioned. Many years elapsed until the Houses stood finished and ready for the Worship of God, a gorgeous splendor in the sunny atmosphere of Palestine. But the action of an ignorant, barbarous Assyrian Spearman, a drunken Roman, or a Gothic Legionary of Titus, motivated by a senseless impulse, brutality stoked a blazing fire that within a few short hours consumed and melted each Temple to a smoking mass of black unsightly ruin.

Therefore, be patient my Brother and wait!

The issues belong to God: but to do right, belongs to us.

Do not become weak or weary in doing good! Do not be discouraged at man's apathy, disgusted by their follies or tired of their disregard! Do not care for results and returns, but only keep sight of what needs to be done and do it. Leave the results to God! Soldier of the Cross! Sworn Knight of Justice, Truth, and Toleration! True and Good Knight! Be patient and work!

The Apocalypse, that sublime Kabbalistic and prophetic Summary of all 321 the figures, divides its images into three groups of seven, and after each group there is to be silence in Heaven. There are Seven Seals to be opened, Seven mysteries to know, Seven difficulties to overcome, Seven trumpets to sound, and Seven cups to empty.

To those who receive the nineteenth Degree, the Apocalypse is the representation of a Sublime Faith, aspiring only to God and despising the Evil identified as Lucifer. The name Lucifer (the Morning Star, the Son of the Morning) was derived from the ancient Latin word for *Light-bearer* first used in the fifth century Vulgate translation (Latin) of the Holy Bible. What a strange and curious name to give to the Symbol of Darkness! Centuries later, the work of poets like Dante and Milton equated the name Lucifer with Satan. Does Lucifer bear the brilliant *Light* that blinds the feeble, sensual, and selfish Souls? Absolutely! Traditions are full of Divine Revelation and Inspiration, and genuine Inspiration is not restricted to one Age or one Creed. Plato and Philo were similarly inspired.

The Apocalypse is as obscure as the Zohar.

It is written hieroglyphically with numbers and images, and the Apostle John often appeals to the intelligence of the Initiated. "Let he who has knowledge understand this." "Let he who understands this calculate it," he often says after an allegory or the mention of a number. Saint John was the favorite Apostle and the Depository of the Secrets of the Savior and, therefore, did not write to be understood by the masses.

The Sepher Yetzirah, the Zohar, and the Apocalypse are the most complete embodiments of Occultism. They contain more meanings than words. Their expressions are as figurative as poetry and exact as numbers. The Apocalypse sums up, completes, and surpasses all the Science of Abraham and of Solomon. The visions of Ezekiel by the river Chebar and of the new Symbolic Temple, are equally mysterious expressions veiled by figures of the puzzling dogmas of Kabbalah, and their symbols are as misunderstood by the Commentators as those of Freemasonry.

Seven is the Crown of the Numbers, because it unites the Triangle of the Idea to the Square of the Form.

The more effort the great Priests made to conceal their absolute Science, the more grandeur they added to the explanations and multiplied the number of symbols. The huge pyramids, with their triangular sides of elevation and square bases, represented their Metaphysics founded upon the knowledge of Nature. The knowledge of Nature had for its symbolic key the gigantic form of the huge Sphinx, which has hollowed its deep bed into the sands while keeping watch at the feet of the Pyramids. The Seven monuments called the Wonders of the World were the magnificent Commentaries on the Seven lines that composed the Pyramids and on the Seven mystic gates of Thebes.

The Septenary (Number 7) philosophy of Initiation among the Ancients may be summed up as follows:

Three Absolute Principles are but One Principle. Four elementary forms are but one. Both form a Single Whole, composed of the Idea and the Form.

The three Principles were:

1°. BEING IS BEING.

In Philosophy, it is the identity of the Idea, of Being, or Reality. In Religion, the first Principle is THE FATHER.

2°. BEING IS REAL.

In Philosophy, it is the identity of Knowing, and of Being, or Reality. In Religion, the LOGOS of Plato, the *Demiourgos* is the WORD.

3°. BEING IS LOGIC.

In Philosophy, it is the identity of the Reason and Reality. In Religion, Providence is the Divine Action that makes real the Good, and in Christianity, we call it THE HOLY SPIRIT.

The *union* of all the Seven colors is *White*, which is the symbol of GOOD. The *absence* of all is *Black* and is the analogous symbol of EVIL. There are three primary colors, *Red*, *Yellow*, and *Blue*, and four secondary colors, *Orange*, *Green*, *Indigo*, and *Violet*. God displays all of these to mankind in the rainbow. They also have their analogies in the moral and intellectual world. The number *Seven*, continually appears in the Apocalypse. Composed of *three* and *four*, these numbers relate to the last Seven of the Sephiroth. Three answer to BENIGNITY or MERCY, SEVERITY or JUSTICE, and BEAUTY or HARMONY; and four to *Netzach*, *Hod*, *Yesod*, and *Malkuth* or VICTORY, GLORY, STABILITY, and DOMINION. The same numbers also represent the *first* three Sephiroth: KETHER, CHOKMAH, and BINAH, or *Will*, *Wisdom*, and *Understanding*, which including DAATH (*Intellection* or

Thought), are also four. DAATH is not regarded as a Sephirah, but as the Divine Action.

The Sephiroth are commonly figured in Kabbalah as constituting a human form, the ADAM KADMON or MACROCOSM. The universal law of Equilibrium is demonstrated three times; the Divine Intellectual, Active and Masculine ENERGY; the Passive CAPACITY to produce Thought; and the action of THINKING. From MERCY and SEVERITY flows HARMONY. From VICTORY (an Infinite overcoming) and GLORY flows STABILITY or PERMANENCE, and it is the perfect DOMINION of the Infinite WILL.

The last nine Sephiroth are included, because they have flowed forth from KETHER, or the CROWN. Each flowed in succession from and remains included in the one preceding it. The Will of God *includes* His Wisdom, and His Wisdom is His Will specifically developed and acting. This Wisdom is the LOGOS that creates. By uttering the letter YOD, it creates the worlds first in the Divine Intellect as an Idea, then invested with form it became the fabricated World or the Universe of material reality. YOD and HE are two letters of the Ineffable Name of the Manifested Deity. They represent the Male and the Female, the Active and the Passive in Equilibrium. The VAV completes the Trinity and the Triliteral Name, and this Divine Triangle is the repetition of the *He* that becomes the Tetragrammaton.

The ten Sephiroth contain all the Sacred Numbers, *three, five, seven, nine,* and the perfect Number *Ten.* These correspond with the Tetractys of Pythagoras.

BEING IS BEING, *Ahayah Asar Ahayah.* This Principle is the "BEGINNING".

In the Beginning IS, WAS, and WILL BE, the WORD or the REASON that *Speaks.*

The Word is the reason of belief, and it includes the expression of Faith that makes Science a living thing. The Word is the Source of Logic, and Jesus is the Word Incarnate. The balance between Reason and Faith, Knowledge and Belief, Authority and Liberty, has become the defining paradox of our times.

Wisdom is the Creative Agent of God in the Kabbalistic Books of the Proverbs and Ecclesiastes. In other parts of the Hebrew writings, *Debar Iahavah* is the Word of God. It is by His uttered Word that God reveals Himself to us in the visible, invisible, and intellectual creation, as well as our convictions, consciousness, and instincts. This is how certain beliefs are universal. The conviction of mankind that God is good led to the belief in a Devil, the fallen *Lucifer* or *Light-bearer,* Shaitan the Adversary, Ahriman, and Typhon. This belief helped to explain the existence of Evil and make it consistent with the Infinite Power, Wisdom, and Benevolence of God.

Nothing surpasses and nothing equals is a Summary of all the doctrines of the Old World. Those brief words engraved by HERMES on "The Emerald Tablets" are the Unity of Being and the Unity of the Harmonies. They are the progressive and proportional scale of the Word, the ascending and descending, the immutable law of the Equilibrium and the proportioned progress of the universal analogies. The relation of the Idea to the Word gives the measure of the relation between the Creator and the Created. The necessary mathematics of the Infinite are proved by the measures of a single corner of the Finite and are expressed by a single proposition of the Great Egyptian Priest:

"What is Superior is as that which is Inferior, and what is Below is like that which is Above, to form the Marvels of the Unity."

CHAPTER 20: GRAND MASTER OF ALL SYMBOLIC LODGES

325 THE true Mason is a practical Philosopher who using the plans traced by nature and reason builds upon the moral edifice of knowledge. He should find in the relation of all the parts of this edifice the principle and rule of all his duties and the source of his pleasures. He improves his moral nature, becoming a better man and finds the means of multiplying his acts of beneficence. Masonry and Philosophy have the same object and same end, the worship of the Grand Architect of the Universe, acquaintance and familiarity with the wonders of nature, and the happiness of humanity.

As Grand Master of all Symbolic Lodges, it is your special duty to aid in restoring Masonry to its primitive purity. You have become an instructor, but Masonry has long wandered in error. It degenerated from its primitive simplicity to a system distorted by error and ignorance. Less than three hundred years ago, its organization was simple and altogether moral. Its emblems, allegories, and ceremonies were easy to understand and their purpose and object easily seen. It was limited to a very small number of Degrees, and its constitutions were like those of a Society of Essenes written in the first century of the modern era. The Essenes organized early Christianity like Masonry or the school of Pythagoras, without deviations or absurdities. It was Masonry; simple, significant, religious, philosophical, and worthy of a good citizen and philanthropist.

326 Innovators and inventors overturned that primitive simplicity and displaced the Masonic Truth. The drama of a horrid vengeance, the dagger, and the bloody head appeared in the peaceful Temple of Masonry without sufficient explanation of their symbolic meaning. Excessive oaths shocked the candidate and became entirely inappropriate or they were wholly disregarded. Initiates were subjected to tests and compelled to perform acts, which, if real, would have been despicable. More than 800 Degrees of one kind or another were simply invented. Infidelity and even Jesuitry were taught under the guise of Masonry. The rituals were copied and mutilated by ignorant men who rendered them illogical and irrelevant. The degrees became so corrupted, that it has become impossible to restore their original meanings.

The largest portion of the Degrees recognized by the Ancient and Accepted Scottish Rite and the Rite of Perfection were discontinued or merely communicated. These Rites resembled those old palaces and castles that were built during different eras and according to different needs, but they collectively formed an adverse and conflicting whole. Judaism, chivalry, superstition, and philosophy were strangely combined and found standing hand in hand within the Temples of Peace and Concord. The whole system became a distorted patchwork of ideas overlaid and disfigured by absurdities resulting from ignorance, fanaticism, and an imaginary mysticism.

The world laughed at the pretensions, overblown explanations, and meaningless, grandiose titles. The Initiate could only feel embarrassed by the world's ridicule. Although we have retained some of these titles, their meanings are consistent with the Spirit of Equality, which is the foundation and law of Masonry. The Masonic *Knight* devotes his hands, heart, and intelligence to the Science of and professes himself the Sworn Soldier of Truth. The *Prince* aims to be a *Leader* in virtue and good deeds. The *Sovereign* is Supreme only because of the law and constitutions he administers and by which he is also governed. The titles, *Puissant, Potent, Wise,* and *Venerable* indicate the power of Virtue, Intelligence, and Wisdom sought by those placed in high office with the vote of their brethren. The remaining titles and designations have an esoteric meaning consistent with modesty and equality that needs to be understood by those who receive them. As Master of a Lodge, it is your duty to instruct your Brethren in the qualifications that are required of those who claim office. They are not pompoms or ribbons to be worn in sophomoric imitation of the times when the Nobles and Priests were masters and the people were slaves. In all true Masonry, the Knight, Pontiff, Prince, and Sovereign are only the first among equals and the cordon, clothing, and jewel are symbols and emblems of the virtues required of all good Masons.

The Mason no longer has to kneel to present his petition or receive the answer to it. He only has to kneel to his God, to whom he appeals to for honor, integrity, perseverance, and guidance. No one is degraded by kneeling to God at the altar, or when receiving the honor of Knighthood. Kneeling is not required for other purposes in Masonry. God gave man a head to stand erect with an upright posture. We gather in our Temples to learn and cherish the just and upright conduct which a man is required to maintain and we never require our Initiates to bow the head. We respect people because we respect ourselves. If modesty is a virtue, false humility and pandering are dishonorable. Noble pride is the most real and solid basis of virtue. People should humble themselves before the Infinite God, but not before his erring and imperfect brother.

Be diligent that no Candidate, in any Degree, is ever required to submit to any degradation. Make it an absolute rule that real Masonry requires nothing which a Knight or Gentleman cannot honorably submit to and accept.

During the 19th century, the Supreme Council for the Southern Jurisdiction of the United States undertook the overdue task of revising and reforming the work and rituals of the thirty Degrees under its jurisdiction. Retaining the essential and prominent ideas of the Degrees and rejecting their absurdities, it made them into a logical system of moral, religious, and philosophical instruction. Favoring no creed, it uses the old allegories detailed in the Hebrew and Christian books and the Ancient Mysteries of Egypt, Persia, Greece, India, the Druids, and the Essenes to teach the Great Masonic Truths.

The Ancient and Accepted Scottish Rite no longer incorporates a spirit of vengeance. It has not allowed Masonry to play the assassin to avenge the death of Hiram, Charles the 1st, or Jacques De Molay. It has now become what Masonry was meant to be, a Teacher of Great Truths inspired by an honorable and intelligent reason.

It is no longer ruled by chance, lack of thought, ignorance, or perhaps less worthy motives. Now it is a system suited to our habits, manners, ideas, and toleration. It is no longer a conglomeration of Degrees with chronological errors and contradictions, powerless to spread light, information, and moral and philosophical ideas. *329*

The decorations of many of the Degrees shall be left out whenever the expense would interfere with the duties of charity, relief, and good will. They should only be used by wealthy Valleys who can contribute to those entitled to their assistance. The regalia of all the Degrees may be acquired at minimal expense, but it is the option of each Brother to procure or not procure the dress, decorations, and jewels of any Degrees other than the 14th, 18th, 30th, and 32d.

We do not teach that the legends of our rituals are the literal truth. They are parables and allegories of Masonic instruction and full of useful and interesting information. They represent the different phases of the human mind and its efforts and struggles to comprehend nature, God, and the existence of sorrow and evil. We learn wisdom by studying the speculations of the Philosophers, Kabbalists, Mystics, and Gnostics and we learn folly by trying to explain what we are not capable of understanding. Everyone is free to interpret our symbols and emblems in a manner most consistent with their beliefs and whenever we provide an explanation, it is because it is generally accepted by all. The Degrees may be conferred in any country or city upon the subject of an absolute government or the citizen of a Free State. Honoring God, regarding all men as our Brethren, and making himself useful to society by his labor are the Masonic lessons taught to all Initiates in all the Degrees.

Masonry teaches Liberty, Fraternity, and Equality by making men fit to receive them with the moral power of an intelligent and enlightened People. It does not plot and conspire revolution or encourage people to revolt against the constituted authorities. It recognizes the great truth that freedom follows fitness for freedom and it strives to prepare men to govern themselves. *330*

Masonry teaches the master to show humanity and charity to the apprentice and it teaches the employers to have consideration and humanity for those who depend upon labor for their living.

As Master of a Lodge, you are to impress these duties on your brethren. Teach the worker to be honest, punctual, faithful, and obedient to all proper orders. Teach the employer that every man or woman who desires to work has the right to do so. Those who cannot work because of sickness, loss of limb, poor health, or old age have a right to be fed, clothed, and sheltered. A Mason ignores Masonry and God if he closes his offices, workshops, or factories when they do not earn a sufficient profit and then downsizes workmen into destitution. He also ignores Masonry when he reduces the wages of a man or woman so low that their families cannot be clothed, fed, and housed, or by overwork, they must give their life and blood in exchange for their wages. His duty as a Mason requires him to continue to employ workers who would otherwise suffer from hunger and cold or to theft and vice. He should pay them fair wages even though it may reduce his profits or decrease his capital. God has only loaned him that wealth and he is agent to invest it.

The symbols of the moral virtues and intellectual qualities of Masonry are the tools and implements that belong exclusively to the first three Degrees. They serve to remind the Mason who has advanced that his new rank is based upon the humble labors of the symbolic Degrees.

331 The Initiates should be inspired by the idea that Masonry is essentially WORK that teaches and practices LABOR, and it is also emblematic. Three kinds of work are necessary for the preservation and protection of mankind and society; manual labor symbolized in the three blue Degrees; labor in arms symbolized by the Knightly or chivalric Degrees; and intellectual labor symbolized by the Philosophical Degrees.

We have preserved and multiplied the symbols that have a true and profound meaning. We have also rejected many of the obsolete and trivial explanations without reducing Masonry to a cold metaphysics that rejects everything which comes from the imagination. The ignorant and conceited may challenge our symbols with sarcasms, but they are brilliant veils that protect the Truth. They are respected by those who know the ways to reaching a man's heart. The Great Teachers frequently used allegories for instruction and to avoid offending their students. We have been careful to prevent our emblems from becoming so obscure that they require preposterous and contrived interpretations. We should not burden ourselves with strange and impenetrable teachings that prevent or interfere with instruction. We should also not create the impression that there are concealed meanings that are only communicated to the most reliable Brothers, because this is contrary to good order and the well-being of society.

The Duties of the *Instructors* (the 4th to 8th Degrees) are to reinforce to the younger Masons the words, signs, tokens, and other work of the Degrees they have received. They also explain the meaning of the different emblems and teach the moral instruction they communicate.

The Directors of the Work (the 9th, 10th, and 11th Degrees) report to the Chapters the regularity, activity, and the direction needed to make the work in the lower Degrees practical and profitable. In the Symbolic Lodges, they should 332 encourage the zeal of the workmen and advocate new projects and endeavors for the good of Masonry, the country, and mankind. They should give fraternal advice when they fall short on their duty and, when necessary, bring against them the severity of Masonic law.

The Architects (the 12th, 13th, and 14th Degrees) should be selected from Brothers knowledgeable in the preceding Degrees and capable of discussing

Masonry and questions of moral philosophy. They should always be prepared with a lecture that communicates to the Brethren useful knowledge or good advice.

The Knights (the 15th and 16th Degrees) wear the swords. They are bound to prevent and rectify the injustice in the world and Masonry to the best of their abilities. They must protect the weak and bring oppressors to justice and their works and lectures must be based upon this spirit. They should investigate whether Masonry fulfills its principal purpose of aiding the unfortunate. In the Blue Lodges, they should offer propositions that end any abuses and prevent or correct negligence. Those who have attained the rank of Knights are the most suitable to being appointed and charged with determining those who need and are entitled to charity from the Order.

Only those with enough reading and knowledge to reasonably discuss the great questions of philosophy should be admitted into the higher Degrees. The Orators of the Lodges, Councils, and Chapters should be selected from these Brethren. They are compelled to suggest the measures necessary to keep Masonry faithful to the spirit of its institution. They must be loyal to Masonry's charitable purposes and shed the light and knowledge needed to correct any abuses that have crept in. All of this will make it the great Teacher of Mankind.

It will be your duty as Master of a Lodge, Council, or Chapter, to teach your Brethren the details of the general plan and separate parts of the Ancient and Accepted Scottish Rite. This includes teaching its spirit, design, harmony, regularity, duties of the officers and members, and the particular lessons taught by each Degree.

When presiding over any assembly, do not close it without first reminding the Brethren of the Masonic virtues and duties that are displayed upon the Trestleboard of this degree. It is imperative. Do not forget that more than three thousand years ago, ZOROASTER said, *"Be good, be kind, be humane, and be charitable; love your neighbors; give comfort to the sick; forgive those who have done you wrong."* More than twenty-four hundred years ago, CONFUCIUS also quoted those who had lived before, *"Love your neighbor as yourself: Do not do to others what you would not wish be done to yourself: Forgive wrong doings. Forgive your enemy, be reconciled to him, give him assistance, and invoke God on his behalf."* 333

Do not let the morality of your Lodge be inferior to the Persian or Chinese Philosopher.

Promote to your Brethren the teaching and everyday practice of the morality of the Lodge, without regard to time, place, religion, or people.

Urge them to love one another, be devoted to one another, and be faithful to their country, the government, and its laws. Serving their country is the payment of a dear and sacred debt.

Respect all forms of worship and tolerate all political and religious opinions. Do not blame or condemn the religion of others and do not seek to make converts. Be content if, like the religion of Socrates, they have veneration for the Creator, good deeds, and a grateful acknowledgment of God's blessings.

Socialize with all men, assist those who are unfortunate, and cheerfully postpone your interests to that of the Order.

Make it the constant rule of your life to think, speak, and act well.

Place the sage above the soldier, noble, or prince and use the wise and good as your model.

Make certain that your professions, practices, teachings, and conduct always agree.

Make this your motto: Do that which you *should* do, regardless of the result.

My Brother, these are some of the duties of the office of this Degree. Perform them well and by doing this you will gain honor for yourself and advance the great cause of Masonry, Humanity, and Progress.

CHAPTER 21: NOACHITE OR PRUSSIAN KNIGHT

YOU are charged in this Degree to be modest, humble, and free from vanity and conceit. Do not be wiser in your own opinion than the Deity or find fault with His works. Don't try to improve upon what He has done. Be modest in your interactions with other people, slow to think evil of them, and reluctant to accuse them of evil intentions. A thousand printing presses are busily engaged in maligning the motives and conduct of people and making one person think the worst of another. Seldom is anyone found, even accidentally, trying to make a person think better of someone else.

Slander and libel were never as widespread as they are today. The most private and inconspicuous personality is not protected against their poisoned arrows. Distinguished public service only makes their hatefulness and invective more eager and unscrupulous.

The evil is widespread and universal. No man, woman, or household is safe from this new Inquisition. No act is so pure or praiseworthy that the unscrupulous spreader of lies will not brand it a crime. No motive is so innocent or praiseworthy that he will not claim it is criminal. Journalism pries into private lives, gloats over domestic tragedies, and deliberately invents and circulates unfounded lies to make money for themselves or create political advantage.

We do not need to expand upon these evils. They are apparent to, and regretted by, everyone. Therefore, it is the duty of every Mason to do everything in his power to lessen or remove them. We should have nothing to do with the errors and sins of other people who do not personally affect us. The journalist has no mandate that makes him the Judge of Morality. There is no obligation for us to announce our disapproval of every wrongful, inconsiderate, or improper act that every other person commits.

We should do for others as we would want done for us. We should not defame, reproach, or belittle anyone for their faults or shortcomings. We have enough work to do in improving ourselves rather than lowering the perception of those around us. Masons and everyone of good will should strive to improve society as a whole instead of merely improving our own self-image. Negative attacks directed at others destructively drag down the standard for everyone. This caustic negativity has degraded journalism, politics, and the civility of general discourse between people. We must approach every situation with the intention of bettering humanity.

Usually, the scorn placed on people's actions by those who have appointed themselves Keepers of the Public Morals is undeserved. Often it is not only undeserved, but praise is deserved instead of blame. When the blame is deserved, it is almost always exaggerated and therefore unjust.

A Mason will wonder how anyone can libel a person who has fallen. If he has any nobility of soul, he would sympathize with their disasters and spare some pity for their folly and wretchedness. Nature cursed them with souls that

would cruelly add to an intolerable wretchedness. When a Mason hears of any person who has fallen into public disgrace, he should have compassion with their mishap and not make them more miserable. Libeling a name that is already
336 damaged is like beating a whipped man with an iron rod and will seem inhuman and cowardly.

The man who does wrong and commits errors often has a quiet home, a loving wife, and innocent children who do not know of his past errors and lapses. If they do, they may love him better because he has erred and repented. Every attack directed at this husband and father strikes at the wife and children but that does not stop the brutal journalist and politician. They continue to strike the innocent family as they hold their heads high and call on the people to praise and admire them.

Dishonorable people frequently have arrogant and boastful postures. Arrogance is the weed that grows on the public landfill. It is from the rankness of the garbage that it gets its growth. Being modest and unaffected by our superiors is a duty, a courtesy to our equals, and a nobleness to our inferiors. There is no greater arrogance than denouncing another person's errors and faults by someone who understands nothing but makes it their business to smear deserving people.

The occupation of the spy has always been seen as dishonorable. With rare exceptions, editors and partisans have become perpetual spies upon the actions of other people. Their malice makes them cunningly attentive and quick to find fault. They will even distort those things that had honest intent. They hinder others in order to make them fail. They expose the vices of other people for the world to gaze upon and bury their virtues underground so that none may recognize them. If they cannot hurt with the truth, they will do it with
337 speculation, and if all else fails, they will fabricate lies out of nothing. They know the public will believe them, because it easier to believe than disprove a statement. It is against the morality of journalism to allow a lie to be disputed where it began. Even if it is contradicted, a slander raised will never die because it will find many people to preserve it.

This is the age of falsehood. In the past, if a person was suspected of lying, it was enough to ruin their reputation. It has become unusual for a partisan or politician to always and scrupulously tell the truth. Lies are now a regular part of all campaigns and controversies. They are stockpiled and valued at a market price according to their profitability and effectiveness.

If people spent any time considering the imperfections of humanity, then they would spend less time publicizing condemnations. Ignorance gives disparagement a louder voice than knowledge. Wise men would rather know, than tell. Relentless criticism is the fault of unforgiving wit. The heaviest criticism will come where there is no judgment, because self-examination would make all judgments charitable. If we know of vices in other people, it would be an act of charity to conceal them provided that did not encourage them to keep doing it. The most despicable action a person can perform is to defame the worthy person.

There is only one rule for the Mason in this matter. If any person has virtue and the Mason is called to speak of them, let him speak impartially. If there are vices as well, the Mason should let the world hear of them from someone else. Although an evil man deserves no pity, his wife, parents, children, or other innocent people who love him may. The thug's trade is no more respectable today than it was two hundred and thirty years ago in Venice. Where we lack experience, Charity requires us to think the best and leave what we do not know to the Searcher of Hearts. Mistakes, suspicions, and envy often injure *338* a good name and there is less harm in giving them the benefit of the doubt.

Finally, the Mason should be humble and modest towards the Grand Architect of the Universe. Do not question His Wisdom or set a personal and imperfect sense of Right against His Providence and dispensations. Do not attempt to explore the Mysteries of God's Infinite Essence, mysterious plans, and Great Nature, which we are not capable of understanding.

Avoid those vain philosophies that try to account for everything without admitting that there is a God, separate and apart from the Universe, and which transforms Universal Nature into a God and worships It alone. Avoid those Philosophies that annihilate the Spirit and believe no testimony except that of the bodily senses and makes the actual, living, guiding, and protecting God fade into a mere abstraction and unreality.

The Mason should not associate with theorists who criticize the delays of Providence, try to hasten the slow speed it has imposed on events or who neglect the practical for impossibilities. Nor should he associate with those who think they are wiser than God, know His aims and purposes, or can see a shorter and more direct way of attaining them than it pleases Him to use. He should not theorize with the anarchist or those who would have equal distribution of property with no discord in the harmony of the Universe, no compulsory labor, and no starvation or destitution.

The Mason should not spend his life building a new Tower of Babel or attempting to change that which is fixed by God's inflexible law. He should yield to the Superior Wisdom of Providence and believe that events are ordered by an Infinite Wisdom that leads to a great and perfect result. He should be satisfied to follow the path pointed out by that Providence and to labor for the good of the human race. He should not build another Tower of Babel under the belief that by ascending it he will be so high that God will disappear or be superseded by material forces. Standing humbly and reverently upon the earth while looking *339* with awe and confidence toward Heaven, he should be satisfied that there is a real God, a person not a formula, a Father, and a protector who loves and sympathizes. The eternal ways by which He rules the world are infinitely wise, no matter how far they may be above the feeble comprehension and limited vision of man.

CHAPTER 22: KNIGHT OF THE ROYAL AXE OR PRINCE OF LIBANUS

340 THE lessons of this Degree are purely Masonic and include SYMPATHY with the working class, respect for labor itself, and resolve to do good *work* for our generation. Masonry has made the working-man a Hero through its principal legend and a companion of Kings. The idea is simple, true, and sublime. From first to last and beginning to end, Masonry is *work*. It reveres the Grand *Architect* of the Universe. It commemorates the *building* of the Temple. Its principal emblems are *the working tools* of Masons and Artisans. It preserves the name of the first *worker* in *brass* and *iron* as one of its passwords. When Brethren meet together, they are at *labor*. The Master is the *overseer* or foreman who sets the craft to labor with good and wholesome instructions. Masonry is the epitome of WORK.

Masonry is found in the hands of brave, forgotten men that made this a great, populous, and cultivated world for *us*. It is the sum of *all* work including what is *forgotten*. Each *real* and heroic soul in some part helped fell the forest, shape the land, drain the marsh, build the harbor wall, develop wise processes, cultivate crops, establish industry, or perform a true and valiant deed. These are the real conquerors, creators, and caretakers of all great and civilized nations. When faithfully performed, genuine work has eternal benefits. It is as eternal as the Almighty Founder and World-builder Himself. All work is noble. God does not rest forever. Similarly, there is no life of ease for the real man. The Almighty Maker did not create the Universe long-ago only to sit back and watch it *go* ever since. That belief leads to Atheism. Faith in an Invisible, Unnamable, and Directing Deity who is everywhere in all we see, all our work, and all we suffer through is the essence of all faith.

The existence of all Gods coincides with a Sublime Work. It is the Infinite battle against Infinite labor. Our highest rite is termed the Worship of 341 Sorrow because the son's inheritance is a crown of pain and not a noble crown. Man is not destined to be happy simply by finding and loving pleasant things. His destiny is to work and be fulfilled by that labor, and he is only *un*happy when he cannot truly work. The days, months, and years pass quickly. The night comes when no man can work, and our happiness or unhappiness vanish and no longer matter. Yet our work cannot be undone, and it will not vanish, because the product of our labors is Eternal.

The STRENGTH a person has within is composed of morality, intelligence, patience, perseverance, faithfulness, logic, insight, ingenuity, and energy. It is recorded by the WORK they perform. To work is to test oneself against Nature and Her unerring, everlasting laws. She will return a true verdict of their efforts. The noblest Epic tells of a mighty Empire, slowly built by a series of heroic deeds. It illustrates the mighty conquest over chaos. Deeds are greater than words. Though silent, they have a life and grow. Deeds fill the approaching void in Time and prepare a bright future for all humanity.

Labor is the truest representation of God, the Architect and Eternal Maker. Noble Labor is the King of this Earth, and it sits on the highest Throne. Men without labor or duty are like trees planted on rocky cliffs where the roots have only crumbled the earth beneath them. It is natural for a man to suffer in life. Nature scorns the man who sits isolated from all work, want, danger, and hardship. Work is the road to victory over hardship. There are those who pride themselves that they do not need to work or challenge their minds. They are like the swine who also accomplish nothing constructive.

The leader of mankind stands at the forefront of humanity and faces the danger that frightens all the followers. Hercules was worshipped for his twelve labors. The Czar of Russia became a carpenter in the shipyards of Saardam, where he developed the leadership skills that made him Peter the Great. Cromwell worked, as did Napoleon, through the ranks of the military, and it caused his efforts to have positive effects upon humanity, in spite of the methods they used against their enemies.

There is a constant nobleness and sacredness in work. Man should always be enlightened and remember this high calling. A person who actually and earnestly works always has hope. Idleness fuels perpetual Despair, because individuals perfect themselves by working. Useless lands are redeveloped into farms, ranches, and stately cities. Man ceases to be useless through these efforts. Even with the worst labors, the soul of man is peaceful and harmonious from the moment he begins to work. Doubt, Desire, Sorrow, Remorse, Indignation, and Despair shrink from the man who resolutely commits himself to his task. Labor is life. From the heart of the worker rises his God-given Power. Almighty God gives him his Sacred, Celestial Life-essence and it fully awakens to all its nobleness when work duly begins. Through work, man learns Patience, Courage, Perseverance, Tolerance, Responsibility, and the aspiration to improve and do better. Only through labor will man continually learn and improve his virtues. There is no Rite of stagnation and inaction, only for activity and exertion. The deepest truth is embodied in that saying of the old monks: "*laborare est orare* (labor is prayer)." "He prays best who loves best all things great and small." Can man love except by working earnestly to benefit those whom he loves?

"Work and receive well-being," is the oldest of Gospels. Though unspoken and inarticulate, it is permanent and enduring. Work makes Disorder its constant enemy, and it attacks, subdues, and reorders it. Our Masonic duty, as commanded by the Highest God, is to challenge Chaos with Intelligence, Divinity, and ourselves. We are to attack tirelessly and strike ignorance, stupidity, and brute force with wisdom. In the name of God, we are not to rest until we succeed. Through work, He speaks with more inspiration than heard in the thunders of Sinai. The Unborn Generations, old Graves, Kingdoms of Heaven and Hell, boundless Space, and endless Time all speak to us with gentleness and silence telling us to work hard while we still have today. All Labor rises to its summit in Heaven. To labor with muscle, sweat, brain, and heart is to worship, and it is the greatest thing found under the canopy of Heaven. Labor is not a curse from the Deity upon the tired and weary. Without labor there could be no true advancement in human civilization and human nature. Without work, pain, *343* and sorrow how would human virtues develop? How would Patience, Perseverance, Submission, Energy, Endurance, Fortitude, Bravery, Justice, and Self-Sacrifice develop as the noblest aspects of the Soul?

Do not let those who work complain or be humiliated! Let them look up and see their fellow-workmen in God's Eternity. They *alone* survive there. Even with the weak human memory, they *alone* will survive Time as Saints and as Heroes.

Good fortune descended on primitive man directly from God. A Supreme God prescribed whatever duty lay before for him. To the primitive man, the Universe was a Temple, and living his life was his form of Worship.

Duty always forbids us to be idle. It is most honorable to work upon that which lies before us, and to do with our hands and minds as needed and as we are able. Farmers, ranchers, professionals, builders, inventors, scientists, poets, advocates, writers, and all workers stand upon one common level to form one host, marching onward from the beginning of human existence. Each worker is entitled to our sympathy and respect as a brother.

It was well conceived to give the Earth in its darkness to mankind for him to labor and improve. It was appropriate to provide raw materials in the mountains, forests, and oceans for man to transform into splendor and beauty. We transform and improve because the act of creating splendor and beauty is better than those goals alone. Exertion is more noble than enjoyment. The laborer is better and more honorable than the lounger. Masonry stands up for the nobility of labor because it is Heaven's intent that we work for human improvement. This concept has been broken over time, but Masonry seeks to rebuild it again. It is broken because most people work only as a necessity, submitting to it as a degrading obligation. People desire nothing more on earth than to escape from its requirements and although they fulfill the great law of labor, they completely miss the true spirit of it. They fulfill it with their muscles, but they break it with their will.

Masonry teaches that the road to improvement is through manual or mental labor. However, man is not compelled to work under the imperfect teachings in today's civilizations. To the contrary, he is allowed to sit down, fold *344* his hands, and glorify idleness. We live in a time that views work as disgraceful or demeaning, and we need to do away with it. It is wrong to be ashamed of the labor, workshop, muddy field, calloused hand, or dirtied and weathered clothes. To be ashamed of work and envious of the robes of idleness and vanity is treason to Nature, impiety to Heaven, and a breach of Heaven's great Ordinance.

WORK is the only true and genuine nobility, whether it is the work of the brain, heart, or hand.

Labor is a more charitable service than man admits or comprehends. Work has measurable benefits to an individual even if its great spiritual gains remain hidden. Work teaches an individual discipline, develops the energies, nurses the virtues, and provides the classroom for improvement. Every worker, from the child who gathers wood for the family fire to the strong man who pours molten steel, is following a Wisdom from far above and fulfilling the grand design, even if it is unknown to them.

The great law of human industry is that all human improvement comes from applying the power of our hands and minds to a task in an attempt to achieve a desired result. We are not like animals in this world, eating the spontaneous vegetation in the fields with rest as our reward. Mankind is sent to dig the soil, troll the seas, and work in cities for business and factories for manufacturing. The world is the great school of industry. An artificial aspect of society divides mankind into the leisure and labor classes, but this is not the intention of Providence.

Labor is man's great function and unique distinction. It is his privilege to be separated from the animals that only eat, drink, and sleep. He becomes a worker and with the hands of ingenuity, he builds his own thoughts into Nature. He fashions these into forms of grace and fabrics of convenience converting them for mankind's improvement and happiness. This is the greatest distinction that man has over other animals.

The Earth and the Atmosphere are man's laboratory and not his trash can. With spade, plough, mineshafts, furnaces, forges, steam, electricity, and amid the noise of new machinery, man should always be working, experimenting, and developing. Man must improve what limits his best qualities. Man must always be a worker. While his cares and toils develop, the splendors of Heaven surround him. His thoughts of the infinite are contemplated, and a deep philosophy and admirable intellect are refined. Man can become or achieve nothing without work. Without work, he cannot truly improve or experience happiness. The idle must hunt down the hours as their prey. To them, Time is an enemy clothed with armor, and they must kill it or die themselves. It has never been right for anyone to do nothing. A person cannot experience life if they are exempt from all care and effort, allowed to lounge, walk, ride, and feast without duty. God made a law against it. No human power can nullify it, and no human ingenuity can evade it.

The idea that wealth should be acquired over the course of thirty years and that it should suffice for the remainder of one's life is a misconception about the purpose of work. The notion that all of life's contributions are accomplished in a seemingly brief portion of it and that afterwards one is relieved from the cares of work and self-denial, is a mistake. It is a misconception about the true nature and design of our efforts and our responsibility to improve the condition

345

of humanity. The common perception of accumulating wealth for the sake of securing a life of ease, gratification, escape, and self-service in our golden years is entirely wrong.

The Mason should live his entire life to its fullest and enjoy it daily as it passes. He will live richer and die poorer. It is better for him to forget the hollow dream of a future selfishness and indulgence. He should address the business of life as the classroom of his worldly education. He should accept that if he earns an exemption from the necessity of work, it does not give him an exemption from social employment. It is wise to know that a body at work is a happy body, whether it is working physically or mentally. He should feel that the reasonable exertion of his physical and mental powers should be regarded as good discipline, a wise rule, and a training for the soul in its nobler endeavors in the spheres of higher activity.

There are lawful and earnest reasons why a Mason may desire fortune. 346 He may desire to fill some palace, itself a work of art, with the product of lofty genius. He may desire to be the volunteer, friend, and helper of humble worth. He may desire to seek out where failing health or adverse fortune press hard upon men and alleviate the bitterest hours with his attendance and attention. He may desire to stand up for the oppressed and press for their rights and equality. He may desire to build and provide institutions of learning and the arts for the masses and run it for maximum social benefit. He may desire to develop better methods for the survival of the poor by devising a plan for their elevation in knowledge and virtue. If a man has sufficient heart and mind to do good things with wealth and use it for leveraging further good work, better thoughts, more enlightened motives, and enhancing the success of actions, then he may lawfully desire fortune. If desire for fortune does nothing more for humanity than for the individual, then there is no reason why someone should desire it.

What is glorious in the world that is not the product of physical or mental labor? What is history without its record? What are the treasures of genius and art without their work? What are cultivated fields without toil? The bustling markets, the glass and steel cities, and the revered empires of the world are really just great storehouses of labor. The pyramids of Egypt, the castles and cathedrals of Europe, the lost cities of Peru and Mexico, and the vast temple complexes of Asia are the tracks left by the mighty footsteps of labor. Without work, antiquity would not exist, and there would be no memory of the past and no hope for the future.

Even complete laziness rests on the treasures that work has gathered through its gains. He who does nothing, but does not starve, is the physical testimony to work *somebody* did at *sometime*. Masonry does not honor this inaction. It honors the Worker. It honors the person who produces and contributes to the treasury of human efforts. It does not revere those who only consume and take from the treasury of good deeds done. It honors those who fight their battles and do not shrink with cowardice from the fierce elements to

347 the comforts of luxury. It honors strong muscle, nerves of steel, brave hearts, sweating brows, and contemplative brains. It honors the great and beautiful offices of humanity being man's toil, paternity, and industry with woman's tasks of maternity, nurture, and organization. It esteems wise teachings and patient learning. It respects the caretakers that preside over the State and the laborer that toils in the workshop, field, and office.

God has made a world of poor men, not rich men. They must toil for subsistence. This is the best endeavor for man, and it is his arena for self-improvement. If the whole world could acquire enough wealth (and one man is as much entitled to it as another when he is born) or have one generation store up enough provision to last for the next generation to stop working, the whole human society would be destroyed. Mankind cannot lay down their tools together, though some may rest today and some tomorrow, or some establish an estate of luxury for their children. All industry would cease without the necessity for sustenance. All improvement would stop with no demand for exertion. Fortune would dissipate and mischief would reign supreme without a healthful, industrious society to prevent it. The world would sink and rot in the grave of its own vices.

Poor men as scholars, professionals, artisans, artists, philosophers, poets, and geniuses have advanced most of the noble achievements across time. It is good for a person to possess seriousness, sobriety, moderation, restraint, and pressure to perform. His body was not made for excess luxuries, and it will sicken and die with them. His mind was not made for triviality and indulgence, and it will grow weak and small with them. Anyone who pampers their body with luxury and their mind with indulgence leaves the adverse consequences of these actions to their children and descendants. Inheritance without a proper work ethic will lack the energy to *keep* and sustain its wealth. Wealth through generations decreases rapidly, and the third generation usually finds itself *without* the benefit of that inheritance. This generation then needs to learn to rise again 348 through work and suffering. Despite this repetition in history, we are all anxious to put our children on the road to inherited wealth. Unfortunately, this inherited indulgence and luxury lead to vice, degradation, and ruin.

If accumulated wealth were used to develop culture at home and works of philanthropy abroad, encourage the studies of art, building academies, and schools, or raising the intellect of the world, then there would never be too much of it. However, if the aim of wealth is to have rich furniture, expensive entertainment, build enormous houses, and aid vanity, then there should be less of it. Wealth allows for elegance, luxury, hospitality, and enjoyment in proportion to its reward and service of higher aims. When it serves only for personal benefit, then it serves peril and evil.

The evils of wealth do not infect just individuals and families. It also spreads through the Cities, Republics, and Empires. Throughout history, wealth has always encouraged corruption and downfall. A civilization never survived the trials and temptations of wealth. Great wealth does not spread the virtues of personal energy, self-denial, and moral virtue. You do not find patriotism, faith, virtue, fortitude, and strength among those of wealth, ease, and indulgence in a country.

The great civilizations have always toiled and labored to build the nation while opulence and luxury betray its greatness. This law is universal among all great empires. From the Phœnicians of Sidon and Tyre to the great nations of Babylon, Palmyra, Persia, Egypt, Judea, Greece, Ottoman Empire, China, Rome, and many more good examples. All prove the destructive tendencies of immense wealth. These nations were weakened by their own vices before being overwhelmed by enemies. When wealth finds us, we must become more generous and charitable, rather than more selfish and indulgent. The alternative is written in the history of the fallen empires.

Most people desire something distinct and ennobling in life. The people 349 who have the most honorable goals are usually the happiest and most satisfied in their pursuits. Artists, mechanics, engineers, inventors, and everyone who seeks to develop beauty with their work seem to enjoy it most. This enjoyment is one of the fundamental rewards that employment gives to our demands in life. Gathering and fattening one's wealth does not provide the same physical happiness and satisfaction as bringing a piece of machinery to perfection and order with your hands. Wealth is subjective, while the physical item is now better than it was. The ability to show improvement to yourself, others, and the item is most satisfying. Building something physical has its rewards. Wealth building is not the same. It is an artifact of what might be, of potential, but it is nothing itself. This is evident when wealth is used for display, pomp, ease, vanity, selfish pleasure, or mere luxuries for these disappear when the money disappears. When wealth is used towards philanthropy, relief, sustenance, or for another noble object, it carries a more permanent reward and a different significance.

There is a painful worry among the masses that their pursuits do not supply anything useful to society and that they will never be recognized for their honest efforts. Why should one work if the world will not know of your existence? Why work if no one will be able to perpetuate their name on canvas, marble, books, oratory, or leadership?

The answer is that every person has to work for himself. This is a greater work than that of genius, and its work is nobler than that performed in fine materials. This work is done in his own soul and intellect. There is nothing more noble or grand in the universe. Therefore, even the simplest worker can achieve the same results from their work as any artist, author, statesman, or general could hope to achieve in their lifetime.

The great author or artist only portrays what every person should be. They *conceive* or *conjecture* what we should *do*. They conceive and represent moral beauty, fortitude, love, devotion, forgiveness, and the soul's greatness. They portray virtues that are admirable. To become these ideals through our daily lives is the practical realization of those great ideals of art. It is the true art in life. The best aspect of written Heroes, faith of Truth's martyrs, beauty of love captured on canvas, and words of Truth and Right from the Eloquent are what any person may feel or practice in daily life. The life and work of virtue are more noble than any work of genius. It is nobler to *be* a hero than to *describe* one. It is better to *endure* martyrdom than to *paint* it. It is better to *do* right than to *plead* for it. Action is far greater than writing. A good person is a nobler object than any great author's object. There are only two things worth living for: to do what is worth writing about; and writing what is worth reading. The greater of these is in *doing*.

Every person simply has to *do* the noblest thing that any other person can do or *describe*. There is no obstacle preventing someone from performing those duties with courage, cheerfulness, energy, and dignity. Therefore, let no Mason deem his life to be mediocre, difficult, vain, unprofitable, toilsome, or anything less than immortal. No one knows if the great prizes in life are for other people. The reality is that no matter how noble an act described by the author or illustrated by the artist is portrayed, it is not action. It is always more noble to go and *perform* the deed instead of describing it, or even *serving* as the model that inspires others to act.

The loftiest action ever described is not more noble than the actions we do in our daily lives. Our lives are filled with temptation, distress, bereavement, and death, and the noble action is greater in light of our other influences. Through the Providence of God, one of the laws of humanity is there is an opportunity for every person to perform the noblest action. People will not perform their highest virtues in extraordinary situations. There are few opportunities in life when all eyes are upon us, our energy is flowing, and our vigilance is alert, that virtue is demanded of us. Usually we find our tests in silence and seclusion, with only our own honesty as witness. Virtue does not seek praise or reward, and it levels its advantage selflessly.

Masonry seeks the noble in everyday life. It works to highlight, support, and admonish the more extraordinary virtue of ordinary life and not the ordinary virtue of an extraordinary life. The actions and good effects done during the private, daily struggles of life are the highest glory. What is done through suffering and from the inner spirit and depths of the heart while maintaining a cheerful exterior shall inherit a brighter crown.

In the biography of a Masonic life, one bright word is written, and from every angle there is a blazing, ineffable splendor surrounding it. That word is DUTY.

Masonry seeks to secure all labor with permanent employment for appropriate compensation. It seeks to quicken the arrival of a time when no one shall suffer from hunger or poverty due to lack of effort if they are willing and able to work. It seeks a time when no one should be forgotten because they have been overtaken by sickness in the midst of their labor. These are part of your duties as a Knight of the Royal Axe. If we can succeed in making a portion of God's creation a little better, more productive, more cheerful, and more worthy of Him, we shall succeed. If we can make one or two hearts a little more wise, courageous, hopeful, and happy, then we shall have done the worthy *work* of Masonry, that work which is acceptable to our Father in Heaven.

CHAPTER 23: CHIEF OF THE TABERNACLE

AMONG the Ancient Nations, there were both public and private worship, the latter was known as the Mysteries. The ceremonies of initiation prepared those for admission into these Mysteries.

The most widespread of the ancient Mysteries were about Isis, Orpheus, Dionysus, Ceres, and Mithras. Many nations received the knowledge of these Mysteries from the Egyptians before they spread into Greece. Even the British Isle Druids learned the celebrations of Dionysus from the Egyptians.

The Athenian celebration of the Mysteries of Eleusis honored the God Ceres, and they absorbed all the other Mysteries. Other nations began to neglect their own Mysteries in favor of celebrating the Eleusinian Mysteries and soon all of Greece and Asia Minor were filled with its Initiates. They spread throughout the Roman Empire and far beyond. The Roman Cicero verified this when he stated, "Those are the holy and dignified Eleusinian Mysteries whose initiates include the people of remote lands." The Byzantine historian Zosimus proclaimed that they included the whole of the human race, while the Athenian Aristides called them the common temple of the whole world.

There were the little and the great Mysteries in the Eleusinian feasts. The little was only a preparation for the great. Everybody was admitted to the little and there was an ordinary novice introductory period of three to four years.

Clement of Alexandria stated the great Mysteries taught of the Universe. It was the completion and perfection of all instruction. It viewed things as they were seen, and nature's works were made known.

The ancients claimed that the Initiates would be happier after death than other mortals. After leaving their bodies, the souls of the common masses would become entangled and remain buried in the darkness of Earth. However, the souls of the Initiates would fly to the Fortunate Isles, the abode of the Gods.

Plato said the purpose of the Mysteries was to reestablish the soul's primitive purity and state of perfection, which had been lost. Epictetus said, "Whatever is done therein has been developed by our Masters for man's instruction and to correct his morals."

The Neo-Platonist philosopher Proclus alleged that initiation elevated the soul from a material, sensual, and purely mundane life to a celestial communication with the Gods. A variety of objects, forms, and species were shown to Initiates to represent the first generation of the Gods.

Purity of morals and an elevation of the soul were required of the Initiates. Candidates were required to have a spotless reputation and irreproachable virtue. As examples, Nero did not dare to present himself at the Mysteries after murdering his mother. On the other hand, Antony presented himself for initiation as testimony and proof of his innocence in the death of Avidius Cassius.

265

Initiates were regarded as the only fortunate men on earth. Aristophanes stated, "the beneficent daystar shines upon us alone. We alone receive pleasure from the influence of its rays. As initiates we practice towards citizens and strangers every possible act of justice and piety." It is not surprising that initiation became considered as necessary to them as the Christians later deemed baptism. It was regarded as a dishonor to be denied initiation into the Mysteries.

The great orator, philosopher, and moralist Cicero said, "It seems to me that Athens has produced nothing as great as the Mysteries. It has replaced a wild and ferocious life with humanity and civility of manners. The appropriately use the term *initiation* because through them we learn the first principles of life to live in a manner more consoling and agreeable, and they soften the pains of death with the hope of a better afterlife."

Where the Mysteries originated is not recorded. It is thought that they came from India through Chaldæa (Mesopotamia) into Egypt and then were carried to Greece. Whatever lands they passed through, they were practiced among all in that nation. The Thracians, Cretans, and Athenians each claimed 354 the honor of its Invention and insisted they had borrowed nothing from any other nation.

Throughout Egypt and the East, all religion was a mystery. In Greece, the primary reason a distinction was made with the Mysteries was due to the superficial popular theology that left many unsatisfied. Although religion in a broader context could supply that need, the Mysteries were an acknowledgment of the insufficiency of popular religion to satisfy the deeper thoughts and aspirations of the mind. The vagueness in symbolism communicated what the more tangible and conventional creed could not. The Mysteries acknowledged the secrecy of its subject by their indefiniteness. It treated a mysterious subject mystically, and it endeavored to illustrate what it could not explain by creating the feeling. It made learning tools from images of the concept that never became too obvious or familiar.

The instruction now taught in books was once learned by these symbols. As we already learned, the priests invented and perpetuated a display of rites and exhibitions that were more attractive and suggestive to the eye and the mind.

After time, the institution became less religious and more moral and political. In Egypt, the civil magistrates had influenced the ceremonies for political ends. The sages who carried them to Asia, Greece, and Northern Europe were all kings or legislators. The chief magistrate presided over those of Eleusis and was represented by an officer titled *King* while the Priest played a subordinate part.

The Powers revered in the Mysteries were of Nature Gods. They could not be addressed as mere heroes because their nature was super heroic. The Mysteries taught the doctrine of the Divine Oneness (Theocracia). It was considered a more solemn expression of religion because they did not entirely conceal the truths. They strived for a more solemn explanation of the symbols of the popular religion in a more impressive form. The essence of all the Mysteries was the concept of a single, unapproachable Being, eternal, and unchanging with Nature whose various powers were separately symbolized. These powers were revealed to the senses in the never-ending cycle of movement, life, and death. Eventually, these powers became distinct pieces in their treatment and were expressed Polytheistically as separate deities. The Mysteries offered a perpetual problem to excite the curiosity that contributed to the pervasive need for religion. If nothing useful from the simple and intelligible religion could be used, it found excitement in a reverential contemplation of the obscure.

355

Nature's truths are free from the opinions asserted about it. The earliest instructors of mankind adopted her lessons and adhered to her method of disclosing them. They attempted to teach an understanding with visual aids and the majority of it was conveyed through this ancient and impressive "exhibition". The Mysteries were a sacred drama of the visible Universe in which divinity was revealed by exhibiting significant keys to Nature. These teachings were important to and harmonious with most religions. Beyond the traditions and sacred recitals at the temples, the spectators were provided with few explanations. They were left to make inferences for themselves, just like with nature.

The method of indirect suggestion by using allegory or symbols is a more effective form of instruction than the plain lecture. By habit, mankind is indifferent to what is acquired without effort. "The initiated are few though many bear the thyrsus (a symbol in Dionysus' Mystery)." It would have been impossible to provide a lesson capable of being learned by every degree of cultivation and capacity in humanity. Therefore, it was explained with a representation of Nature using her symbolism instead of language. It invited endless research, but it also rewarded the simplest inquirer. It disclosed its secrets to everyone in proportion to their intellect and comprehension.

Lacking in any formal or official statement of those important truths, the plays of the Mysteries certainly contained suggestions and lessons. Many believed the Mysteries were adapted to elevate the character of the spectators. Even in well-cultivated and learned ages it was discouraged to teach these lessons except under a veil of allegory because these lessons lost their value in proportion to any part mechanically learned as a rigid truth. The Mysteries enabled them to speculate about the purposes of existence and the means to improve it by allowing them to live better and to die happier.

356

These mystic shows and performances revealed a contemplative problem. Unlike the traditional religion that uses books, creeds, or lectures, these problems and presentations did not exclude itself from further research. They were not hostile to philosophy but viewed it as the great initiator, Mystagogue, or Arch-Expounder of the symbolism. Although Greek interpretations of Philosophy, old myths, and symbols were in many instances flawed, in many ways they were also correct.

These impressive exhibitions were the best method available to inspire the dormant intellect. They required the use of imagination to seek, compare, and judge for itself rather than simply following prescribed routines of creed. The eventual change from reliance on symbolism to unchallenged dogma is fatal to this inspiriting form of expression. Similarly, the change from a fundamental faith to the adherence to dogma is also fatal to the search for truth and purity in our thoughts.

Philosophy, like the Mysteries, often reverts to the natural method of teaching with expressions and interpretation. Socrates is said to have avoided using lectures or dogma in his teachings. Instead, he preferred to awaken the minds of his students and develop the ideas of their interpretations. Both philosophy and the Mysteries sought to avoid filling minds with preprogrammed and subjective opinions.

Masonry continues to use this ancient method of teaching. The instruction is provided through interpretation of the symbols provided, and the lectures are partial and incomplete interpretations of those symbols. To become an accomplished Mason you must not be content to only hear and understand the lectures, but you must study, interpret, and develop the symbol's meaning for yourself with the lecture's aid.

The earliest interpretations had expressed far more than could be clearly comprehended. The mind received these vague impressions left by mysterious analogies. These were the most appropriate and energetic representations of the phenomena seen around them. The Mysteries and the symbols of Masonry are images of the analogies of Nature. Neither of these reveals new secrets to those who are unprepared or incapable of interpreting their significance.

In the old Mysteries, the symbolism and ceremonies of the instructor (Hierophant) were found within a similar mythical entity who united Human Attributes with the Divine. Like Hermes, Zoroaster, Buddha, or Jesus, he becomes the God whose worship he started. He teaches men about civilization, song, and Nature. Through death, he comes to symbolize that Nature due to his body's permanent connection to it. This earthly comfort is an essential interpretation of religion.

The Mysteries embraced, represented, and described the three great doctrines of Ancient Theosophy: God, Man, and Nature. Dionysus Mysteries described him as the God of Nature or the essence of the life of Nature. He prepared in darkness for the return of life, or for who was the Light, and its expected Change. He was theologically the same as Hermes, Prometheus, or Poseidon. In the Aegean Islands, he was similar to Butes, Dardanus, Himerus, or Imbros while in Crete he appeared as Iasius or Zeus. In Crete, his worship was revealed and the symbols became misunderstood by the indevote among them. In Thracia, he is the robed Bassareus, who is the same as Sabazios of the

Phrygian Korybantes. He was also associated with the mystic Iacchus, son of Ceres, and with the dismembered Zagreus, son of Persephone.

The symbolic form of the Mysteries told of THE ONE and THE MANIFOLD as its infinite illustration. It contained moral lessons designed to guide the soul through life and to have happiness in death. The story of Dionysus was profound and significant. He was the creator of the world and the guardian, liberator, and Savior of souls. As God of the multicolored mantle, he was the personification across the ages of life in its innumerable forms.

The spiritual regeneration of man was performed in the Mysteries with the second birth of Dionysus as the offspring of the Highest. The symbols of this regeneration were the elements that affected Nature's periodic purification. The mystic fan symbolized air. The torch signified fire. Water symbolized itself as the cleanser of all things and the source of all life.

The ritual portrayed the soul's reformation and training for a moral purity, which was proclaimed at Eleusis. Only those, "of clean hands and ingenuous speech, free from all impurities, and with a clear conscience," were invited. The initiated Euripides and Aristophanes said, "Happy is the man who purifies his life and reverently consecrates his soul in the group worship of the God. He does not utter a profane word. Let him be just and kind to the stranger and neighbor. He should not let himself become excessive in anything unless his spirit becomes dull and heavy. Keep the impure, the lying, treacherous, and selfish far from the mystic dance of our worship. Keep all those whose practices are more like the riot of Titans than to the regulated life of the Orphic, or the Curetan, Priests of Idaean Zeus." ₃₅₈

Elevated beyond his worldly senses and unable to account entirely for what he had been exposed to, the devotee seemed to become proportionately more divine as they lessened the worldly ties. He seemed to elevate and become a demigod. In their imagination, the initiated alone were considered beatified, blissful, enjoying the true life, and seeing the Sun's true luster. They sang praises to their God beneath their mystic groves that mimicked the paradise of Elysium, and they were regenerated by the pleasant influence of their dances.

It was said, "Those who Persephone (goddess of the underworld) guides in her mysteries and who take her instruction and spiritual nourishment, rest from their labors and know strife no longer. Happy are those who witness and comprehend these sacred ceremonies! They are made to know the answers to the riddle of existence by observing life's aim and death as determined by Zeus. They gain a benefit more valuable and enduring than the grain bestowed by Ceres. They are exalted for their scale of intellectual existence and obtain sweet hopes to console them at their death."

The original ceremonies of initiation were few and simple. As the great truth of the original revelation faded from memory and wickedness flourished on the earth, it became more necessary to discriminate between the initiates. The mysteries lowered a veil of secrecy by requiring longer times, more tests, and schools of instruction for the candidates. Using pomp and ceremony, they heightened the opinion of the degree's value and importance.

We agree that the Mysteries and their rites eventually lost much of their meaning and reasoning by the steady corruption of time and interpretation. Despite this, for ages the Mysteries must have remained pure with the doctrines of natural religion and morals taught with the highest reverence despite later interpretations of them. The proof is provided by the highest regards the most virtuous, learned, and philosophic of the ancients speak of the Mysteries.

The rites of initiation became successively more complicated. Signs and tokens were created so the Children of Light (the initiated) could easily recognize each other. Different Degrees were added as the Initiated numbers grew to provide a method for protecting the greater secrets. Those within the inner chambers of the Temple could wield the influence and power of the Order.

Anciently, the Mysteries were created to begin a new life of reason and virtue. The initiates were taught the concept of the One Supreme God. They were taught the theories of death, eternity, immortality, the mysteries in Nature, the restoration of the soul to that state of perfection, and the concepts of reward and punishment after death. The uninitiated were labeled "Profane" and unworthy of public employment or secret knowledge. They were eventually termed Atheists and were to receive an everlasting punishment beyond the grave.

Everyone could be initiated into the lesser Mysteries, but few were permitted into the more secret doctrines hidden in the greater Mysteries. These inner secrets of the Mysteries were impenetrable to the outsiders. They were secured by oaths and penalties considered appalling in their severity. Knowledge of the Hieroglyphics could only be obtained through initiation. This allowed the knowledge to be passed through the writings that decorated the walls, columns, and ceilings of the Temples. These inscriptions were believed to have been communicated to the Priests by a revelation from the celestial deities.

The ceremonies were performed at night and were typically located underground or within a pyramid. They used many means to excite the candidate's worldly senses. Over time, numerous ceremonies were added to the degrees. These included the wild, romantic, dreadful, and appalling to enhance the few expressive symbols of the original primitive observance. Pyramids, caverns, pagodas, or labyrinths were used for initiation, because the ceremonies required many rooms, cells, passages, and wells. In Egypt, a primary site for the Mysteries was the island of Philae in the Southern Nile where the magnificent Temple of Osiris stood and its relics were preserved.

In Egypt, India, Phœnicia, Israel, Greece, Britain, Rome, and wherever else the Mysteries were known, the Priesthood protected their exclusivity by making the ceremonies higher and wider to preserve their own power. The purity of all religions does not continue for long. Rank and title overtake the early simplicity, and unprincipled and corrupt men put on God's robes only to serve the Devil. Luxury, vice, intolerance, and pride dominate frugality, virtue, gentleness, and humility among the theocracy. It changes the altar from a place of service to God to a throne from which to reign over men.

The Kings, Philosophers, and Statesmen who learned the wise, great, and good lessons from the Mysteries were able to postpone the self-destructive tendencies of their Priesthood. It is important to note that St. Zosimus (later a Pope) suggested that the neglect of the Mysteries after Emperor Diocletian abdicated his position was the primary reason for the decline of the Roman Empire. In the year 364 AD, the Proconsul (administrator) of Greece refused to discontinue the Mysteries, despite a law from Emperor Valentinian. He decided that if he prevented the people from performing them for the welfare of mankind, then those people would be driven to desperate actions. The Mysteries continued to be practiced in all of Greece and Rome for several centuries after Christ, in Athens until the 8th century AD, and in Wales and Scotland until the 12th century AD.

Indians originally practiced the Patriarchal religion. Even the worship of Vishnu was cheerful and social with song, dance, music as well as food, drink, and aromatic perfumes.

The Mysteries most likely began in India, and their allegories taught the original truths. We do not detail the ceremonies of initiation in their Mysteries within these pages, but we will use general language below, except where something from those old Mysteries remains in Masonry.

The Initiate was given a cord with three threads (*zennar*) braided as to   *361* make three times three. This represents our cable-tow, and it was an emblem of their triune (three-in-one) Deity. We remember this by the three senior officers of our Lodge, presiding in the three quarters of that Universe which our Lodge represents. The symbol has also been carried forward with our three greater and three lesser lights, our three movable and immovable jewels, and the three pillars that support the Lodge.

The Indian Mysteries were conducted in underground caverns or grottos hewn from solid rock. The Initiates worshiped the Deity who was symbolized by the solar fire. The candidate truly wanted light after wandering in darkness. The worship of God as the Source of Light was taught. The vast Temple caves of Elephanta in India were hewn out of the rock, and 60,000 square feet was used for initiations. Similarly, the caverns of Salsette with over 300 apartments were also used for initiations.

The periods of initiation were regulated by the waxing and waning moon cycles. The Mysteries were divided into four steps or Degrees. The candidate might receive the first at eight years of age, when he was given the cord of three threads (zennar). Each Degree taught something about perfection. As described in the Hitopadesha fables, "Let man practice virtue, whenever he enjoys one of the three or four religious Degrees. Let him be even-minded with all created things, and that disposition will be the source of virtue."

After various ceremonies primarily related to the unity and trinity of God, the candidate was clothed in a seamless linen garment, and he remained under the care of a Brahmin until he was twenty years of age. He continued to study and practice virtues while he underwent the probationary period for the second Degree. There he was consecrated by the sign of the cross that pointed to the four quarters of the compass. The cross was honored as a striking symbol of the Universe and was used in many nations throughout antiquity. The Indians integrated it into the shape of their temples, too.

Next, he was taken to the Holy Cavern blazing with light. Inside sat the three chief priests (Hierophants) gloriously robed in the East, West, and South who represented the Trimurti, or the triune Indian Deity of Brahma, Vishnu, and Shiva. The ceremonies began with a song to the Great God of Nature. It was followed with this address, "O mighty Being! Greater than Brahma! We bow down before You as the primal Creator! Eternal God of Gods! The World's Mansion! You are the Incorruptible Being, distinct from all things transient! You are before all Gods, the Ancient Absolute Existence, and the Supreme Supporter of the Universe! You are the Supreme Mansion, and by You, O Infinite Form, the Universe was created."

After being taught the first primitive truth, the candidate was to make a formal declaration. He would be obedient to his superiors. He would keep his body pure. He would think before speaking. He committed to observe obediently when receiving the doctrines and traditions of the Order. He was to maintain the strictest secrecy with the hidden and esoteric mysteries. After this declaration, he was sprinkled with water (hence *baptism*), and the Passwords of that Indian Degree were whispered in his ear. He removed his shoes and walked three times around the cavern. From this, we see its influence on our three circuits and the origin of why we were neither barefoot nor shod.

The Gymnosophist Priests (ancient Hindu sect) brought their science and doctrines from the banks of the Euphrates to Ethiopia. Their principal College was at the city of Meroe where the Mysteries were celebrated in the Temple of Amun, renowned for its oracle. Ethiopia became a powerful theocratic State and preceded Egypt in civilization. Above the King was the Priest who had authority in the name of the Deity even over the King's life. At the time, Egypt was only composed of the Thebaid, which was Middle Egypt and the Delta. The Ethiopian kingdom was strong and ruled the Nile Delta for a period of time. This ruling Sacerdotal Caste was later replaced by a dynasty of warriors. The magnificent Kingdom of Axum has portions of its obelisks, hieroglyphics, temples, tombs, and pyramids near the ancient City of Meroe that date back to 5000 BC and are older than the pyramids of Giza.

Taught by Hermes, the Priests wrote of the hermetic sciences, the occult, and added their own discoveries with the revelations of the Sibyls (prophetess). They studied the abstract sciences, discovered geometrical theorems (which Pythagoras afterward learned from them), calculated eclipses, and composed an

362

equivalent to the Julian calendar nineteen centuries before Julius Caesar. They made practical investigations for the necessities of life, and they communicated their discoveries to the people. They cultivated fine arts and inspired people with enthusiasm. Ultimately, this affected the layout of the city of Thebes, the Crocodilopolis Labyrinth, the Temples at Karnak, Denderah, Edfu, and Philae, the monolithic obelisks, and Lake Moeris that was made into the reservoir of the country.

Egyptian Initiates exhibited a high level of science, lofty morality, and immense knowledge. Many men of rank and fortune desired this wisdom and sought admission to the Mysteries of Osiris and Isis despite the complicated and terrible trials.

The Mysteries traveled from Egypt to Phœnicia where they were celebrated at Tyre. The names were changed, as from Osiris to Adonai or Dionysus, but they still revered the Sun. Later, the Mysteries were passed to Assyria, Babylon, Persia, Greece, Sicily, and Italy. In Greece and Sicily, the name Osiris changed to Bacchus. The name Isis changed to Ceres, Cybele, Rhea, and Venus.

Bishop Bar Hebraeus stated, "Enoch was the first to invent books and different sorts of writing. The ancient Greeks declared that Enoch was the same as Mercury [Hermes] Trismegistus, and that he taught the sons of man the art of building cities, and enacted admirable laws. He discovered the knowledge of the Zodiac, and the course of the Planets. He showed man the worship of God, the fast, prayer, charity, offerings, and tithes. He forbids certain foods and drunkenness, and he appointed festivals with the assent of each of the Zodiacal Signs."

The historian Manetho found his sources on certain pillars he discovered in Egypt. Thoth, regarded as the predecessor to Mercury [Hermes], is purported to have made inscriptions upon them in sacred letters and in a sacred dialect. After the flood, they were translated from that sacred dialect into Greek and placed in the private recesses of those Egyptian Temples. These pillars were in subterranean tombs, outside of Thebes and beyond the Nile not far from the Colossi of Memnon, which are described as winding underground corridors. It is believed they were made by people skilled in the ancient rites. They were built in several places amid fear of the Deluge that the memory of their ceremonies would be obliterated.

From Egypt sprang a man of consummate wisdom. He was initiated with the secret knowledge of India, Persia, and Ethiopia. His Egyptian compatriots named him Thoth or Ptah, the Phœnicians named him Taautus, the Greeks named him Hermes Trismegistus, the Muslims named him Idris, and the Rabbis named him Enoch. Nature chose him as her favorite son and lavished on him all the skills necessary to study and know her thoroughly. The Deity had instilled in him the arts and sciences so he might instruct the whole world.

He invented things necessary for life and named them. He taught men how to write their thoughts and arrange their speech. He instituted the ceremonies of observance for the worship of the Gods. He observed the course of the stars, invented music, exercise, arithmetic, medicine, metallurgy, and the lyre with its three strings. He regulated the three Greek tones of the voice, the *sharp* was taken from autumn, the *grave* (or flat) from winter, and the *middle* (or circumflex) from spring (there were only three Greek seasons). He taught the Greeks how to interpret terms and things and hence, they gave him the name of *Hermes* [Ἑρμῆς], which meant *Interpreter*.

In Egypt, he provided hieroglyphics and selected certain people whom he judged fit to receive his secrets. They were to be capable of attaining the throne and the first offices in the Mysteries. He organized them and created *Priests of the Living God*. He instructed them in science and art while explaining the symbols that veiled them. In the Mysteries 1500 years before Moses, Egypt revered ONE SUPREME GOD called the ONLY UNCREATED. Under Him, they revered seven principal deities. Hermes is attributed with the concealment, *veiling*, of the original Indian worship. It was Moses who later *revealed* these laws of Hermes, but he only changed away from the plurality of the mystic Gods.

The Egyptian Priests stated that on his deathbed Hermes said, "Here I have lived an exile from my true country, now I will return there. Do not weep for me because I return to that celestial country where each goes in his turn. There is God. This life is but a death." This is the same creed as that of the Buddhists. They believed that God occasionally sent a Buddha to earth to reform men, to wean them from vice, and lead them back onto the path of virtue.

Hermes communicated secrets by teaching the sciences to the Initiates. These secrets were imparted with a terrible oath of allegiance under the condition that they should never divulge them, except to those who, after long trial, should be found worthy to succeed them. Even the Kings were prohibited from revealing them as punishable by the pain of death. This secret was styled the Sacerdotal Art and it included alchemy, astrology, magic, the science of spirits, etc. He gave them the key to the Hieroglyphics of all these secret sciences. They were considered sacred and kept hidden in the most secret places of the Temple.

Egyptians honored and respected the initiated Priests for their great secrecy and the sciences they taught. They were regarded by other nations as the college, repository, and sanctuary of the arts and sciences, and these mysteries excited the curiosity of others. Orpheus is said to have transformed himself into an Egyptian. There he was initiated into Theology and Physics. He made these ideas and the reasoning of his teachers so completely his own that his Hymns reflect an Egyptian Priest more than a Greek Poet. He was the first to carry the Egyptian stories into Greece.

Pythagoras, in his thirst for learning, agreed to circumcision in order to be allowed as one of the Initiates. There the sciences were revealed to him in the innermost part of the sanctuary.

The Initiates of a particular science wrote mysteriously whenever their works touched on the subject of the Mysteries. They continued to conceal their science under a veil of fiction just as they were instructed by stories, enigmas, allegories, and hieroglyphics.

With the destruction of the Egyptian cities and almost the entire Kingdom by the Persian King Cambyses II in the year 525 BC, most of the Priests dispersed around the Mediterranean, to Greece, and elsewhere. They took their sciences with them and continued to teach through the obscurities of their stories and hieroglyphics. They did this to ensure that if a commoner overheard or oversaw it, they would continue to know and comprehend nothing substantial. All of the later writers drew from these sources eventually. *366* Unfortunately, the Mysteries had been concealed under so many unexplained layers that many absurdities occurred in its interpretation. These misinterpretations then spread from Greece across the earth.

In the Greek Mysteries established by Pythagoras, there were three Degrees. A preparation period required five years of abstinence and silence. A candidate was rejected if he was found to be rash, quarrelsome, or materialistic.

In the lectures, Pythagoras taught mathematics as a method to prove the existence of God from observation and reason. Grammar, rhetoric, and logic were taught to improve one's reasoning. Arithmetic was taught because he believed it was the foundation of man's improvement. Geometry, music, and astronomy instilled knowledge of what was truly good and useful to man.

He taught the method to obtain knowledge of the Divine laws through the imitation of the perfection of God. This was done by purifying the soul from imperfections, searching for truth, and practicing virtue. If his system did not help to expel vice and instill virtue then it was in vain. He taught the two best things were to speak the truth and to help one another. He was careful to teach the virtues of Silence, Temperance, Fortitude, Prudence, and Justice. He taught of the immortality of the soul, the Omnipotence of God, and the need of personal holiness to qualify for admission into the Society of the Gods.

We owe the instructions of the Fellowcraft Degree to Pythagoras although this Degree is still an imperfect reproduction of his lectures. We also find many of the explanations of the symbols. He arranged his assemblies due East and West, because he held that Motion began in the East and proceeded to the West. The Lodges are also due East and West. We state that because the Master represents the rising Sun, he must be in the East. Similarly, the pyramids were built precisely aligned to the four cardinal points. The expression that our Lodges extend upward to the Heavens is derived from the Persian and Druidic custom of having no roof on their Temples except the sky.

367 Plato developed and spiritualized the philosophy of Pythagoras. Even the Christian bishop Eusebius of Caesarea admitted that Plato had touched the threshold of Truth.

The Druidical ceremonies came from India with the migration of the Celtic people. The Druids were originally Buddhist. The word *Druid*, like the word *Magi*, signifies wise or learned men and, appropriately, they were philosophers, magistrates, and divine priests.

There were surprising similarities between the Temples, Priests, doctrines, and worship of both the Persian Magi and British Druids. The Gods of Britain were the same as the Cabeiri Deities of Samothrace. Osiris and Isis also appeared in their Mysteries but with the names of Hu (Sun) and Ceridwen (Moon). Like the early Persians, their Temples were enclosed with huge unfinished stones. The temples were either circular or oval, and some were shaped as a circle with a huge serpent attached. To this day, some remain and are feared, venerated, and awed by the people. The circle was an Eastern symbol of the Universe that an Omnipotent Deity governed. This Deity's center was everywhere yet his circumference was nowhere. From this, the egg became a universal symbol of the world. Some of the Temples had wings, and referred to Kneph, the winged Deity of Egypt that represented the soul of man. At *Navestock*, England there has survived a site where one of the temples stood. Some other temples were shaped like a cross and were found as far away as Ireland and Scotland.

The periods for initiation into the Druidical Mysteries were at the equinoxes or solstices. During the times when they originated, this corresponded with February 13th, May 1st, August 19th, and November 1st. The annual celebration was May-Eve and the preparations started at midnight on April 29th. At midnight, the initiations were performed, and they consisted of three Degrees. On May-Eve when the initiations were over, fires were started at all megalithic monuments on the island. These burned all night to introduce the Mayday celebration in honor of the Sun.

Alternately, Odin carried the Gothic Mysteries Northward from the East. He was a great warrior and adapted them to suit his purposes and the capacities of his people. He placed twelve Hierophants (priests) over these celebrations. They also served as Priests, Counselors of State, and supreme Judges of the people.

368 He held the numbers three and nine in veneration. He, himself, was probably an Indian Buddha. Every thrice-three (nine) months, thrice-three nine victims were sacrificed to their triune God.

The Goths had three great festivals. The most magnificent began with the winter solstice and was in honor of Thor, the Prince of the Thunder. It was the longest night in the year, and it marked the point from which the Sun begins its Northward ascent and commemorated Creation. The Norse termed it mother-night to signify creation, when light from primitive darkness came forth into the world. This was the *Yule, Juul,* or *Yeol* feast that later was merged into the Christmas celebration. Thor was the Sun, the equivalent of the Egyptian Osiris, while Kneph was the Phœnician Baal. At this feast, initiations were celebrated, and they took place in large, intricate caverns like the Mithraic caverns. This complex terminated in a spacious vault where the candidate *was brought to light.*

Joseph was an initiate. After he interpreted Pharaoh's dream, he was placed in charge of the land of Egypt and made the Prime Minister. Pharaoh had him ride around in the second-in-command chariot, while having ABRECH (bow down)! announced before him. Additionally, the King gave him the new name Tsapanat-Paanakh and married him to Asanat, the daughter of Potai Parang, the Priest of On (Heliopolis) at the Temple of Athom-Re and thus completely naturalized opposition to the Pharaoh. Joseph could not have that marriage and received that high dignity without being an initiate in the Egyptian Mysteries. When his Brethren came to Egypt, the Egyptians in his court could not eat with them because that would have been abomination even though they ate with Joseph. He was special and not regarded as a foreigner. When he brought his brethren back and charged them to take his cup, he said, "Don't you know that a man like me practices divination?" This statement was made with the understanding that Egyptians of high rank were initiated in the Mysteries and familiar with the occult sciences.

Moses must have also been initiated. He was reared in the court of the Pharaoh as an adopted son of the King's daughter until he was forty years old. He was instructed in all the learning of the Egyptians. He later married the daughter of Jethro, another Priest of On. Historians Strabo and Diodorus Siculus both assert that he was a Priest of Heliopolis. There was known relationships between Moses and the Priesthood before he sought refuge in the Desert. Josephus describes Moses' successful command of an army sent by the King against the Ethiopians. Simplicius of Cilicia asserts that the doctrines Moses taught to the Hebrews were the same ones he had received in the Egyptian Mysteries. Clement and Philo, both of Alexandria, claim Moses was a Theologian, Prophet, and interpreter of the Sacred Laws. Manetho, cited by Josephus, says he was a Priest of Heliopolis and his original Egyptian name was Osarsiph.

The Hebrew Priesthood's powers, privileges, immunities, and sanctity of ritual closely imitated the Egyptian rites. Moses made *public* the worship of the Deity whom the Egyptian Initiates worshipped in private. He continuously tried to prevent the people from relapsing into their former mixture of Chaldæan and Egyptian superstitions and idolatry. Even Aaron, upon the first discontent restored the worship of the Egyptian God Apis (bull-deity) when he made the golden calf.

The Egyptian Mysteries where the Priests taught to believe there was one God, Supreme and Unapproachable. He *conceived* the Universe by His

369

Intelligence before He *created* it with His Will and Power. They were not Materialists who believed that only matter exists, nor were they Pantheists who believed that God is everything, or everything is God. They taught Matter was not eternal and not coexistent with the great First Cause, but it was created by Him.

The early Christians also received the Mysteries as taught by the founder of their Religion. Those primitive truths passed to them from the Egyptians, through the Jews, and were preserved by the Essenes. They adopted the building of the symbolic Temple as their objective, and they preserved the old Scriptures of the Jews as their sacred book and fundamental law. These additions furnished many of our Degrees with new initiation words and formulas, but these have also been corrupted by time and misinterpretation.

370   My Brother, this is the doctrine of the first Degree of the Mysteries, or Chief of the Tabernacle to which you have been admitted. The moral lessons are devotion to the service of God, unbiased zeal, and constant work for the welfare of humanity. You have received hints of the true objects and purposes of these Mysteries. Be content and patient. As you advance, you will receive a more complete understanding of them and the sublime doctrines they teach.

CHAPTER 24: PRINCE OF THE TABERNACLE

THE ancient theology utilized symbols for instruction almost exclusively, 371 because visual learning was an easy method for conveying understanding. Ancient expressions for communication of religious knowledge were signified through visual clues. The first teachers used this method of instruction to produce an endless amount of significant symbols and hieroglyphics. These lessons were like the quaint riddles of the Sphinx as they tempted the curious, but were risky to the adventurous interpreter. The Oracle of Delphi did not *declare* or *conceal*, but only "*implied* or *signified*". It was said, "The Gods disclose their intentions to the wise, but their teaching is incomprehensible to fools."

The Ancient Greek Sages, and those of other lands, concealed true meanings by teaching with indirections and puzzles. Their lessons were learned with visual symbols or with audible "parables and legends". The Israelites considered it their sacred duty to keep oral traditions and teachings unchanged through all their generations. Objects, actions, symbols, and ceremonies were used to explain the intentions of the Gods, and they were treated like mystic signs and omens from dreams because both required thought and skillful interpretation to be understood. Fortune-tellers, Diviners, Interpreters, and Sages could interpret and learn of Wisdom and the Will of Heaven by contemplating, appreciating, and comprehending nature's similarities with man's trials.

The Mysteries were a series of symbols, and anything spoken consisted of sacred explanations only slightly altered by the current traditions of physical or moral speculation when combined with the original ancient events. Nature 372 essentially became her own teacher represented by an arbitrary symbol for instruction. The ancient views of the relationship between the human and divine were dramatic in their forms.

The symbolic and philosophic systems have always been closely related to the stories of the important qualities in all ages, the writings of the religious leaders of all nations, and the rituals of the secret and mysterious societies. A harmonious and uniform set of principles has been compiled in this manner.

Symbolic instruction is the preferred and ancient method used throughout all ages as a system of communicating the complex. The Deity used material images to reveal and enforce His sublime truths to mankind. Jesus taught with symbols and parables, and the Druids embodied their knowledge in mysterious signs and symbols. The Welsh poet Taliesin described initiation by saying, "The secrets were imparted to me by the old Giantess (*Ceridwen*, or *Isis*), without the use of audible language. . . I am a *silent* proficient."

Initiation was the place to teach the truths of early revelation, the existence and attributes of one God, the immortality of the Soul, rewards and punishments of the afterlife, the phenomena of Nature, the arts and sciences, morality, legislation, philosophy, philanthropy, psychology, and the other occult sciences.

The Egyptian Priests were aware of the ideas collected from the Priests of India, Persia, Syria, Arabia, Chaldæa, and Phœnicia. The rational Indian philosophy migrated into Persia and Chaldæa and then gave birth to the Egyptian Mysteries. The development of Hieroglyphics in Egypt can be traced to the early symbols and figures of the mineral, animal, and plant kingdoms used by the Indians, Persians, and Chaldæans. Their primitive philosophies were the origination of the newer philosophies of Pythagoras and Plato.

373 The illustrious philosophers and legislators of Antiquity were pupils of the initiation who made moral changes to the ancient religions due to their incorporation and extension of these Mysteries. The Mysteries prevented man from the primitive barbarism and chaos of early and popular superstitions. Zoroaster and Confucius drew their doctrines from the Mysteries. Clement of Alexandria spoke of the Great Mysteries, "Here ends all instruction. Nature and everything is seen and known." Philosophy, God, Truth, and all the sciences were taught, and these oral and written traditions reached back to the first age of the world. Had only moral truths been taught to Initiates, the Mysteries would never have received the magnificent praises from the most enlightened men of Antiquity such as Pindar, Plutarch, Isocrates, Diodorus Siculus, Plato, Euripides, Socrates, Aristophanes, Cicero, Epictetus, and Marcus Aurelius among others.

According to Plato's *Phaedo* dialogue, Socrates stated, "It is obvious that the Mysteries were established by men of great genius. They strove to teach us using enigmas that those who are not purified of thought and action will not understand. Those who have purged their sins to be virtuous will be admitted to the abode of the Deity. . . . The initiated are certain to attain the company of the Gods."

Vettius Agorius Praetextatus was a respected and virtuous man and was Proconsul of Achaea in the 4th century, among other titles. He petitioned the Roman Emperor to preserve the Eleusinian Mysteries in Greece because depriving the Greeks of them would make life dreary and comfortless.

Initiation was a descent into a mystical death and the infernal regions where every sin, imperfection, corruption, and evil was purged from life by fire and water. The perfect and fully initiated (*Epopt*) was *regenerated, new-born*, restored in *life, renovated* in existence, and brought to *light* and *purity* under Divine Protection.

Language and hieroglyphics were adapted to the celebrations and their highest meanings were preserved for those who received the highest Degree. This highest knowledge was restricted to a few who controlled the learning, 374 morality, and politics of the nations where the Mysteries were practiced. They were so efficient at restricting knowledge of the meanings of their hieroglyphics to the highest Degree that over time their meaning and interpretations were lost to everyone. Where these hieroglyphics were used in both higher and lower

Degrees, additional and different meanings were assigned in the higher Degrees. People eventually pretended these sacred hieroglyphics and language was that used by the Celestial Deities. Anything that increased the mystery of initiation was added to the ritual, and the name of the ceremonies possessed both a charm and wild fears. The greatest ecstasy and joy was expressed by the word that signified the pass into the Mysteries.

The Priesthood composed one third of the Egyptian population. Their influence increased through the Mysteries, and they spared nothing to impress the people of their importance. They represented it as the beginning of a new life of reason and virtue. The initiated expected the best in death and eternity, comprehended the hidden mysteries of Nature, had their souls restored to perfection, and upon death was to enter the celestial mansions of the Gods. The concepts of future reward or punishment were prominent features in the Mysteries. They believed in happiness and good-fortune during this time and would be protected against danger. Those who refused to be initiated were scorned, considered unworthy of public employment or private confidence, and doomed to eternal punishment as unholy and irreligious. Betraying, discrediting, or deriding the Mysteries was a death sentence at the hands of public vengeance.

Through the time of Cicero in the first century BC, the Mysteries had retained much of their original sanctity and purity. In the first century AD, Nero did not dare to celebrate the Mysteries after committing a horrible crime. Even in the early 4th century AD, Constantine the Great was not permitted to celebrate the Mysteries because he had murdered his relatives.

Everywhere, the Mysteries were like a funeral celebrating the mystical 375 death and restoration to life of a divine or heroic entity. The details of the legend and mode of death were varied between the different Countries that practiced them. The explanations covered astronomy to mythology.

The Legend of the Master's Degree is but another rendition of the Mysteries that reaches to antiquity. Whether this legend originated in Egypt or if it evolved from India or Chaldæa will never be known. We do know the Hebrews received their Mysteries from the Egyptians, and we *are* familiar with *their legend*. Joseph and Moses were Egyptian Initiates who knew of the fable of OSIRIS as the Sun, the Source of Light, and the Principle of Good, and of TYPHON as the Principle of Darkness and Evil. It is the truth about an abstract and spiritual meaning that is hidden in material forms and figures. The myths of Gods and Heroes concealed the astronomical details and the operations of Nature that were other symbols of higher and more profound truths. Only uncultivated intellects have persisted to view the Sun, Stars, and Nature as Divine and fit for Human Worship, but they will continue to do so while this world lasts and forever remain ignorant of the great Spiritual Truths that are hieroglyphically expressed.

A brief summary of the Egyptian legend will demonstrate the main idea upon which the Hebrew Mysteries were based.

Osiris was an ancient King of Egypt, and became the Sun. Isis was his wife, the Moon. His history poetically and figuratively tells of the annual journey of the Great Luminary of Heaven through the different Signs of the Zodiac.

Typhon was his brother who was filled with envy and malice towards Osiris. He sought to seize his throne while Osiris was absent, but Isis frustrated his plans. He resolved to kill Osiris instead. He persuaded Osiris to enter a coffin that he then flung into the Nile. Isis eventually recovered the body and hid it in a forest. Typhon found its hiding spot, cut the body into fourteen pieces, and scattered the pieces. After tedious searching, Isis found only thirteen pieces as the fish had eaten the last (the privates). She replaced the fourteenth part with wood and buried the body at the Island of Philae in the Nile where a magnificent temple was erected in honor of Osiris.

376

Isis and her son Horus fought and killed Typhon. She gloriously reigned until after her death, she was reunited with her husband in the same tomb.

Born of the earth, Typhon was depicted with a feathered upper body, scaled arms and legs, serpents coming from every side of him, and a fire-breathing mouth. Horus became the God of the Sun. These depictions were similar to the Greek Apollo who slew the great serpent Python.

The serpent symbolized Typhon (צפעני, Tsapanai . . life), and meant *life* like Eve. The form of the serpent symbolized life among all of nature. Astronomically toward the end of autumn, the constellation Virgo seems (according to the Chaldæan astronomical sphere) to crush the head of the serpent with her heel to foretell the coming of winter when life seems to retire from all beings and nature. This is why Typhon, the serpent, as a symbol of winter is depicted around the Terrestrial Globe surmounting the heavenly cross in the Catholic Temples. If the word Typhon is derived from *Tupoul*, it describes an apple tree (*mala*, evils), and it is the Hebrew origin of the fall of man. Typhon means usurper and signifies the human passions that expel wisdom from our hearts. In the Egyptian Fable, Isis wrote the sacred word to help humanity while Typhon tried to erase the word as fast as she wrote it. In terms of morals, this name signifies *Pride*, *Ignorance*, and *Falsehood*.

Isis first found the body where it had floated ashore near Byblos, and a shrub of *erica* (heather), or tamarisk, had grown into a tree around the casket that protected the body of Osiris. This is the source of our sprig of acacia. Anubis, the jackal-headed God, aided Isis in her search for the body. He was Sirius, the Dog-Star, and was the friend and counselor to Osiris, the inventor of language, grammar, astronomy, surveying, arithmetic, music, medical science, legislator, teacher of the worship of the Gods, and engineer in the building of Temples.

377

The shutting of Osiris's body in the chest was termed the *aphanism* (concealment) in the Mysteries just as the Sun is concealed below the Tropic of Capricorn at the Winter Solstice. The recovery of the body parts of Osiris by Isis was termed the *Euresis* (discovery). As in all the Mysteries, the candidates experience a representative ceremony of this event. This fable's main facts were similar in all countries where the prominent Deities were a male and female pair.

In Egypt, the pair was Osiris and Isis, in India it was Mahadeva (Shiva) and Bhavani, and in Phœnicia they were Tammuz (or Adonis) and Astarte. In Phrygia, the pair was Attis and Cybele, in Persia – Mithras and Asha, in Samothrace and Greece – Dionysus and Rhea, in Britain – Hu and Ceridwen, and in Scandinavia – Odin and Frigg. In all instances, the Deities represented the Sun and the Moon.

The Mysteries of Osiris, Isis, and Horus seem to be the model used in subsequent ceremonies among the other nations of the world. Those of Attis and Cybele in Phrygia, Ceres and Proserpina in Rome, Demeter and Persephone at Eleusis and around Greece were just copies of the Egyptian Mystery. Plutarch, Diodorus Siculus, Lactantius, and other writers refer to this, but in the absence of other proof this is supported by the similarity of the story of these Deities. The ancients held Ceres as the same as Isis while Dionysus was the equivalent to Bacchus and Osiris.

In Plutarch's legend of Osiris and Isis there are many details beyond those we have mentioned. Osiris married his sister Isis and worked with her to improve mankind. He taught agriculture, built temples to Gods, established worship, patronized the arts and sciences, and introduced iron and gold to metallurgy. Isis invented laws and assisted Osiris in his works. Osiris went forth with his army to civilize man and teach the people agriculture.

His brother Typhon killed him when the sun was in the sign of the Scorpion, or the Autumnal Equinox. Synesius claims they were rival claimants to the throne of Egypt just as Light and Darkness contend over the world. Plutarch adds that the birth of Horus occurred when the moon was full and in the sign Taurus, the sign of the Vernal Equinox and opposite the Scorpion.

378

Plutarch asserts that Isis established the Mysteries to represent these events. Images, symbols, and religious ceremonies reproduced it. Consolations for the misfortunes of man and lessons of piety were included. Those who began these Mysteries were trying to strengthen religion and give man lofty hopes of faith. These principles were taught to them in extravagant ceremonies but with a sacred veil of allegory.

The Greek historian Diodorus Siculus speaks of the famous columns erected near Nysa, Turkey in memory of Osiris and Isis. On one wall was the inscription, "I am Isis, Queen of this country. I was instructed by Hermes. No one can destroy the laws that I have established. I am the eldest daughter of Saturn, most ancient of the Gods. I am the wife and sister of Osiris the King. I first made known to mortals the use of wheat. I am the mother of Horus the King. In my honor, the city of Bubaste was built. Rejoice, O Egypt, rejoice, land that gave me birth!" . . . and on the other was written, "I am Osiris the King, who led my armies into all parts of the world from India, North into Asia, around Europe, and to the Ocean. I am the eldest son of Saturn. There is no place in the world I have not reached, bestowed my benefits, and made known my discoveries." The rest was illegible.

In her search for the body of Osiris, Isis sought out Anubis, son of Osiris and his sister Nephte. He was Sirius, the brightest star in the Heavens. With Anubis, she had learned that the sacred chest had stopped with the body of Osiris near Byblos. She seated herself near a fountain sad and silent, shedding a torrent of tears. Courtly women of Queen Astarte came and spoke to her, 379 dressed their hair, and poured perfumed ambrosia over it. Isis became employed as nurse for the Queen's child in her palace. There, she discovered one of the columns made of the *erica* (tamarisk) that had grown over the chest containing Osiris. Due to its uniqueness, it had been cut down by the King to be fitted as a column in his palace. He was not aware that it still contained the coffin. When Isis learned of this situation, she seized the column, extracted the coffin and Osiris' body, and fled with it wrapped in thin drapery and perfume.

Ignorant of its significance, Blue Masonry still has the emblem of a woman weeping over a broken column, holding in her hand a branch of acacia (or tamarisk), while Time standing at her back combs out the ringlets of her hair. This represents *Isis* at Byblos weeping near the broken column of the King's palace that had contained the body of Osiris, while Horus as the God of Time pours ambrosia over her hair.

Nothing of this legend was historical. It was all allegory or sacred fable, and it contains a meaning known only to the initiates of the Mysteries. All the incidents had astronomical associations with a deeper meaning than *that* explanation and twice veiled. These Mysteries were like those of Eleusis. The Greek traveler Pausanias (who was initiated) said the Greeks regarded the Mysteries as the best way to lead men to religion. Aristotle said the mysteries were the most valuable religious institution par excellence. The Temple of Eleusis was regarded as the common sanctuary of the entire earth, and there the noblest and best aspects of religion were brought for man.

The Mysteries' object was to inspire men and comfort them in life's miseries with the hope of a happier future for mankind, and an eternal bliss after death.

Cicero said the Initiates received lessons for a more agreeable life and hope for their life after death. Socrates stated that those admitted to the 380 Mysteries possessed glorious hopes for eternity. Aristides said they brought comfort to the Initiates for this life, an ability to persist with the existing evil, and the ability to pass to a happier state after death.

Isis was the Goddess of Sais in Egypt where the Feast of Lights was celebrated in her honor, and the secret "Mysteries of Night" were celebrated to represent Osiris's sufferings, death, and restoration to life.

The King of Egypt frequently co-existed with the Priesthood because they were both initiated when he attained the throne. Likewise, the First Magistrate (Archon-King) at Athens supervised the Mysteries indicating the powerful union between the Priesthood and Royalty that was a political tool between legislators and kings in the early nations.

Herodotus tried to explain the reasons why Egyptians deified animals: "If I were to explain the reasons, I would disclose those holy matters which I wish to avoid, which I am only to discuss out of necessity. The Egyptians have at Sais the tomb of someone whom I am not permitted to state, but it is behind the Temple of Minerva." To the Greeks, Minerva was the embodiment of Isis who frequently had this inscription quoted, "I am all that was, that is, and will be. No mortal has yet unveiled me." Herodotus continued, "At night we enact at the lake the accidents which happened to he who is unnamed. These are the Egyptian Mysteries and while I am versed in them, I compel myself to silence. Regarding the ceremonies for Ceres, I cannot speak beyond what the obligations allow me."

The great object of initiation into the Mysteries was simple: to civilize mankind, ease their ferocity, and introduce society to the betterment of their life. Cicero was convinced the Eleusinian Mysteries were the greatest gift provided by Athens to other nations because its effects civilized men, improved their *381* manners, taught morality, and *initiated* them to the type of life they were worthy of. He added that mankind owes these Goddesses, Ceres and Proserpina, the first elements of moral life, the first means of sustenance, knowledge of laws, regulation of morals, and examples for improved manners among civilized man.

In Euripides' story, Bacchus said to King Pentheus that his new rites (the Dionysus Mysteries) deserved to be learned because all impurities were forbidden. These Mysteries of Wisdom created a greater wisdom among the initiated Barbarians than even the uninitiated Greeks possessed.

The political and religious objectives taught by the Mysteries were duty to man, respect for the Gods, and obedience to their laws. The Roman poet Virgil writes about this in verse borrowed from the initiation ceremonies, "Teach me to respect Justice and the Gods." The Greek priests (Hierophants) impressed that great lesson upon the Initiates after they witnessed the representation of the Infernal regions. Virgil describes the different punishments suffered by the wicked in Tartarus (Hades) and specifically of King Sisyphus within its confines.

The Greek geographer Pausanias stated his point after seeing the representation of the punishments of Sisyphus and the daughters of Danaus at the Temple in Delphi that the crime meriting punishment was their contempt for the Mysteries of Eleusis. The Priests of Eleusis taught the dogma of punishment in Tartarus for crimes that included contempt for and disregard of the Holy Mysteries. Respect for justice and laws were the object of this institution with the needs and interest of religion being subordinate to it. Religion was a means to instill respect for these laws more surely. The religious opinions were in the *382* hands of the legislators and properly administered were sure to be closely obeyed and support civilization.

The Mysteries were more than simple observations about the formulas of nature with ceremonies to teach them, and it went beyond reminding men of the ancient conditions of man prior to civilization. The chief portion of the ceremonies led men to piety by teaching morals and the knowledge of a future life.

Agricultural symbols were used in the ceremonies, such as the ear of wheat where one of the words and has been preserved in Masonry. However, the main references were to astronomical phenomena. Much was taught regarding the brutality and degradation of man before the Mysteries spread. However, most of these allusions were metaphysical and highlighted the ignorance of the uninitiated rather than talk of the wild life of early man.

The Mysteries of Isis and most of the Mysteries had an underlying political objective. They meant to improve society, perfect its manners and morals, and bind society with stronger bonds than what civil laws can impose alone. The ancients invented the Mysteries from their exhaustive resources, science, and wisdom to make its legislation perfect. Their philosophy was to secure the happiness of man by purifying his soul from mortal and troubling passions that cause social disorder. The Mysteries use of all the sciences was evidence of the genius and profound knowledge that created it and helped subdue the human heart's desires.

It is a great mistake to believe they were invented to deceive and fool mankind. Over time, they may have degenerated into deception and misinterpretation, but they were pure in the beginning. If they were incorrect at their conception, then the wisest and noblest men of antiquity were complicit in their efforts. Eventually the allegories of the Mysteries, including Tartarus with its punishments, Minos, and the judges of the dead, were misinterpreted by the unlearned. They came to be misunderstood and were wrong in their interpretations, but originally they were true and recognized as merely arbitrary forms in which truths were enveloped.

383 The objective of the Mysteries was to create peace on earth through virtue, and for man's efforts he was taught that his soul was immortal. Error, sin, and vice must have their consequences from the immortal and inflexible laws. The crude representation of physical torture in Tartarus was just the allegory for the certain, unavoidable, and eternal consequences that are God's law. The poets and priests promoted and popularized the doctrines of the soul's immortality and punishment for sin and vice in this life to ensure the people accepted them. The versions relayed to the masses were decorated and accessorized with charm and spectacles of magic and illusion.

They depicted the virtuous man's happy life after death and the horrors destined to punish the immoral. The delights and horrors of these religious dramas were named the *initiation* and *mysteries*, and they were enacted within the darkened sanctuaries. Its secrecy, exclusivity, and tests excited man's curiosity. The scenery, decorations, pomp, props, and drama attracted their attention while respect, fear, hope, sadness, and delight were instilled in the Initiate through the dignity and majesty of the ceremony and its actors.

The Priests (Hierophants) were intelligent men who understood how to control man's attention, and they used all their means to impress the importance of their ceremonies. They preferred to perform their ceremonies at Night to achieve the desired veil of Secrecy, which assisted the ceremony's impressiveness and illusion upon the Initiate. To fill the mind with religious awe, the Temples were surrounded by thick groves and the ceremony's cavern was dimly lit to focus the mind.

Demetrius Phalereus wrote that the word *mystery* was a metaphor to denote the secrecy and awe the darkness and gloom was to inspire. Almost all the celebrations were at nighttime and referred to as nocturnal ceremonies. Initiations for the Mysteries of Samothrace, Isis, and Bacchus all took place at night. Euripides stated there is something noble and imposing at night.   384

The genius of Mystery is that it conceals a secret knowledge that man is by nature curious and desirous to know. Adding obstacles that slow or prevent fulfillment of that desire only increases man's curiosity. The ancient Legislators and Priests used this fundamental human characteristic to attract people to their sanctuaries. By this man sought the Mysteries' lessons, which otherwise might have been received with indifference if enacted as civil and public law. The Mysteries claimed they were duplicating the Deity and its method of interaction with man by hiding from man's earthly senses the laws that govern the Universe. They proclaimed that secrecy and allegories were used to conceal the highest truths to excite man's curious nature and cause him to personally investigate these truths within the Mystery's framework. Those who were told the highest truths were bound under oath never to reveal them except to the initiated. If someone uninitiated was within the Temple or if the secrets were revealed to the uninitiated, the Mysteries outlined the severest penalties against them including death and excommunication from the group.

Eurymedon, the Priest of Ceres (Hierophant) in Athens, accused Aristotle of impiety against the Gods for having performed ritual rites for his wife Pythias similar to those used in the worship of Ceres. From Athens, he fled to his mother's estate of Chalcis in Euboea. To clear his name of this accusation, he called for the erection of a Statue to Ceres in his will. After drinking a cup of hemlock, Socrates talked of sacrificing to Aesculapius, the God of Medicine to free his legacy from the suspicion of Atheism. A price was set to kill Diagoras of Melos (the Atheist) for revealing and demystifying the Secret of the Mysteries. Andocides the orator and Alcibiades Scambonides were also accused of similar crimes against the Mysteries. Both had to answer for their actions before the inquisition at Athens where the People sat in judgment. Aeschylus, the founder of the Greek Tragedy, was accused of disclosing the Mysteries in some of his plays, and he was acquitted only after proving that he had never been initiated.

While comparing Philosophy to initiation, Seneca stated only the adepts could know the most sacred ceremonies but even the masses knew many of its laws. This is illustrated by the concepts of the reward and punishment for this world's actions in the afterlife. The ancients revealed and impressed these truths with the aid of enlivened senses and imagination by the use of pomp of mystery, ceremony, mystic words, and magic.

Using the same techniques, they taught of the soul's origin, its fall to the earth, the spheres and elements, and its eventual return to its source. Its union with earthly matter weighed the soul and slowed its return although its essence was as pure and bright as ever. These metaphysical ideas were difficult to comprehend, so they were taught to the Initiates with representations of figures, symbols, and allegories. There is no idea so abstract that man cannot express it with images the senses can recognize.

The difficulty of obtaining admission enhanced the attraction of Secrecy. Obstacles and suspense furthered man's curiosity. Those who wanted to gain initiation into the Mysteries of the Sun and of Mithras underwent many trials. They started with easy challenges and worked through degrees towards the most cruel and dangerous tests. Saint Gregory of Nazianzus termed these as *tortures* and mystic *punishments*. According to the Byzantine Suda, no one could be initiated until he had passed unharmed through the trial which proved that his soul was virtuous and was unmotivated by passions. It was reported that there were twelve primary tests and maybe more.

The Eleusinian initiation trials were severe, though not as terrible as those of Mithras. The suspense of a several year waiting period between admission into the *inferior* and initiation into the *great* Mysteries was a type of torture to the curiosity and desire it encouraged. Masonry keeps this memory alive with the *ages* of those of its different Degrees. Pythagoras was tried like this before the Egyptian Priests admitted him to the secrets of their sacred science. By use of his patience and ability to defeat all obstacles, he succeeded in obtaining admission and receiving the lessons of their society. Within the Jewish community, the Essenes required all candidates to pass several tests (or Degrees) before they were admitted as one among them.

A *fellow-citizen* before initiation became a *brother* afterwards. The religious fraternity united him through a stronger and tighter bond with other initiates. Even the weak and poor could more easily appeal for assistance from the powerful or wealthy through the fellowship of religious association.

The Initiate was regarded as the favorite of the Gods. Heaven opened its treasures to him. Fortunate during life, the Initiate could promise himself eternal bliss after death through his favor within the Heavens.

The Priests on the Island of Samothrace, promised their initiates favorable winds, prosperous voyages, and the CABEIRI and the DIOSCURI (Castor and Pollux are the Twins, Gemini) would appear for them in raging storms and provide calm and smooth seas. Aristophanes wrote that those initiated in the

Mysteries on Samothrace were simple men who were lucky enough to escape the storms of the Aegean Sea.

The Mysteries of Orpheus considered its Initiates purified, released from evil, and provided the happiest of hopes in life. He was prompted to say, "I have emerged from evil and attained good." The initiates of the Mysteries of Eleusis believed the pure splendor of the blazing Sun was only for them. They thought Demeter and Persephone (or the Romans Ceres and Proserpina) inspired them, gave them wisdom, and counsel as Pericles perceived.

Initiation erased errors, banished misfortune, filled the heart of man with joy in life, and gave him blissful hope at death. Socrates said the Goddesses Demeter and Persephone lead man away from his early, barbaric life by providing hope for blissful eternity after death. Aristides stated the benefits received from the ceremonies were joy, deliverance, liberation from ills, and the hope in death of passing to a more fortunate state. Theon claimed initiation to the Mysteries was the source of the greatest blessings. The happiness promised was not limited to mortal life but extended beyond the grave. The afterlife of the *387* Initiate began a period of pure and limitless bliss. The Mysteries of Cybele and Attis and its Korybantes promised eternal life to Initiates.

Apuleius wrote that while Lucius was still in the form of an ass, he addressed his multitude of prayers to Isis. He speaks of her the same as the one God worshipped by different names across the world as the Queen of Heaven, Ceres, Venus, Diana, and Proserpina. She appeared to Lucius as a beautiful female, "over whose divine neck her long thick hair hung in graceful ringlets." Isis addressed him saying, "The mother of Universal nature attends your prayers. The mistress of the Elements, earliest of the generations, Supreme of Deities, Queen of the dead, chief of those in Heaven, and combined form of all the Gods and Goddesses is with you. With my approval, I govern the heights of the luminous Universe, the winds of the ocean, and the depths of the underworld. My Sole Divinity is worshipped by all nations over the Earth in many forms, titles, and rites."

Isis directs Lucius on how to proceed at her festival to obtain his human shape again. She said, "Throughout the remainder of your life, until the last breath has gone from your lips, you are devoted to serve me.... Under my protection, your life will be happy and glorious and when your days are done you will descend to the underworld and inhabit the paradise of the Elysian fields. Even there you will worship me as your patron. If through diligent obedience, religious devotion, and incorruptible chastity you prove yourself worthy of divine favor then you shall feel my powerful influence. Your life will be prolonged beyond its Ordinary length."

Lucius saw the image of Isis in the festival procession. On either side of her were female attendants who, "made believe with motion and gesture to comb and ornament Isis' royal hair with ivory combs." The initiated followed clad in linen robes. "The women's hair was perfumed and wrapped in a transparent *388* covering. The men were thoroughly shaven and represented the terrestrial stars of the religion. Their bald heads exceedingly shined."

Finally, there was the procession of the Priests dressed in white linen robes. The first held a lamp in the shape of a boat with a flame emitting from a hole in its middle. The second priest held a small altar, the third a golden palm tree, and the fourth displayed the form of a left hand with the palm open and expanded to, "represent equity and fair-dealing. The left hand is an appropriate emblem for this because it is slower and less dexterous than the right hand."

After Lucius had recovered his human form with the help of Isis, the Priest said to him, "Misfortune has no grasp on those who our Goddess has chosen for her service and vindicated with her majesty." The people declared he was fortunate to be "born again and at the service of the Holy Ministry."

When Lucius pleaded with the High Priest to initiate him, he was told that only the initiated who received special command from Isis could enter the ministry because otherwise one might be depraved, destructive, rash, sacrilegious, or commit an act deserving injury. He continued, "For the gates of the underworld and our life here, we are in the hands of the Goddess. *The ceremony of initiation into the Mysteries is to suffer death* with a dangerous chance for resuscitation. The Goddess, in her Divine wisdom, selected people who the secrets of her religion could be entrusted. They must stand on the threshold of this life and *through her Providence be born again* to start a new career with a new existence."

After a waiting period, Lucius was to be initiated. He was escorted to the baths to bathe, and after the Priest asked forgiveness of the Gods, he was sprinkled with the clearest and purest water and escorted back to the Temple. Apuleius stated, "After giving me instructions that I cannot reveal, he requested that I restrain my appetite for the next ten days by not eating meat or drinking wine."

389 The ten days elapsed and the Priest led him to the inner recesses of the Sanctuary. He wrote, "Studious reader, perhaps you are anxious to know what was said and done therein. I would tell you if it was lawful to divulge and you were allowed to hear and know it. Despite the fact that an indiscrete disclosure would assign a penalty to you and me, I will tell the truth for fear that you would be tormented too long by this religious longing and suspense. Listen to what I relate. *I approached the abode of death and I pressed the threshold of Proserpine's Palace. I was transported through the elements and led back again. At midnight, I saw the bright light of the sun shining, and I stood in the presence of the Gods, the Gods of Heaven, and the Underworld below. I stood near them and worshipped.* I have told you things that you cannot necessarily understand, and these are beyond the comprehension of the masses, which I can explain without committing a crime."

The usual ceremonies were completed by the dawn. He was then consecrated by being clothed in twelve gowns, crowned with white palm leaves, and displayed to the people. The rest of that day was a celebration and festival of his rebirth. After the third day, the religious ceremonies were repeated with a fast-breaking, "*followed by a final consummation of ceremonies.*"

A year later, he was told to prepare for initiation into the Mysteries of "the Great God, Supreme Parent of all the other Gods, the invincible OSIRIS." Apuleius stated, "although the ceremonies of both Deities are different, there is a connection between them BECAUSE THE ESSENCE OF BOTH DIVINITIES IS IDENTICAL."

We can guess what was taught in the Mysteries regarding the Deity by the following hints in the language of Lucius's prayer to Isis: "Holy and Perpetual Preserver of the Human Race! You are always generous, cherishing, and offering Your maternal affection to the unfortunate humans. Your generosity never rests. You stretch forth Your healing right hand over land and sea to protect mankind, disperse the storms of life, untangle the web of fate, temper fortune, and restrain the evil influence of the stars. *You are adored by the Gods in Heaven, revered by the Gods of the underworld, obeyed by the stars, rejoiced by Divinities, served by the elements and the seasons!* At Your command the winds blow, clouds gather, seeds grow, buds germinate, *the Earth revolves*, AND THE SUN PROVIDES LIGHT. IT IS YOU WHO GOVERNS THE UNIVERSE AND RULES TARTARUS." 390

Then, he was initiated to the nighttime Mysteries of Osiris and Serapis. Later, he was initiated to Ceres at Rome, however Apuleius had nothing to say of these ceremonies and initiations.

The ruler (Archonship) of Euclid excluded all bastards, slaves, and Epicureans (materialists) from initiation. The Epicureans denied Providence and could not be initiated. These restrictions were progressively interpreted until it was established that the gates of Elysium would only open for Initiates whose souls were purified and regenerated in the sanctuaries. Initiation alone was never considered sufficient. Plato teaches us the soul had to be purified of every stain and sin against it, and this provided the soul with virtue, truth, wisdom, strength, justice, and self-restraint.

Isocrates and Theon stated those who committed homicide were forbidden to enter the Temples as were magicians, frauds, imposters, and charlatans. The impious or criminal were also rejected. The *Augustan History* documents that before the Mysteries were celebrated, public notice was given so that no one should apply except those who were faultless in their consciences and certain of their innocence.

The Initiate was required to be free of any stain on his heart or hands. Porphyry of Tyre said at death, man's soul should be free of all hate, envy, and other passions. He should *be as pure as the Mysteries require him to be*. Murderers, perjurers, and other criminals against God and man could not be admitted. 391

The subject of Justice was repeatedly lectured to the Initiate in the Mysteries of Mithras. Virgil expressed the great moral lesson of all the ceremonies of the Mysteries in a single line, *to practice Justice and revere the Deity*. This told men to be just like the Gods who require it or punish infractions against it. The Initiate could gain the favor of the Gods only if he respected the rights of society and humanity. Aristophanes' chorus of Initiates said, "The sun burns with a pure light only for those admitted to the Mysteries, you must observe its laws among strangers and citizens." Initiates' rewards were attached to their social virtues and not to initiation alone. They needed to be faithful to these laws and duties. Bacchus allowed no one to participate in his Mysteries except those who were pious and just. Compassion for another's misfortune was a precious virtue taught by initiation. The Roman poet Juvenal said, "Nature has made us compassionate by providing us with tears. Our feelings are our most admired senses. What man is truly worthy of the Mysteries if he has no compassion for the misfortunes of others?"

The Mysteries of Eleusis forbid from Initiation anyone who had conspired against the state, were complacent with knowledge of conspiracy, committed treason, surrendered advantage to the enemy, provided benefit to enemies, or failed to fulfill their duty as good and honest citizens. To be admitted, one had to have lived equitably and well enough to prove the Gods did not hate him.

The Initiates became a society of virtuous men who worked to free their souls from the oppression of their passions and to develop strong social virtues. The Elysian Initiates were required to be virtuous upon acceptance and entrance to the sanctuaries, which caused it to be misunderstood that the Elysian fields were created only for the virtuous souls.

The nature and details of the afterlife's doctrines and their rewards and punishments, as developed in the Mysteries, are uncertain. There are few sources of information available to us. We know the ceremony represented scenes of Tartarus and the judgment of the dead, but we do not know how these allegories were explained. We do not need to repeat the descriptions of Elysium and Tartarus. We simply need to know the Mysteries taught of the soul's immortality, and the consequence of sin leads to suffering, pain, remorse, and agony.

Ceremonies are imperfect symbols as our purifications are in constant need of renewal as soon as we purify our past. New moments of life bring new error. Purification is like a bottomless pit that can be forever fed, but never full.

All initiation prepares us for the great change of death. Baptism, anointing, embalming, and funerals are symbols of preparation similar to Hercules' initiation before descending to the Underworld. These highlight the mental change that should precede our renewal and continued existence. Death is the true initiation and sleep is the minor mystery. To the Egyptian, this final rite united him with his God. It has the same promise for all who are duly and truly prepared.

The body was a temporary prison for the soul. The Father of the World allowed these chains to be broken and He provided a means of escape in Nature. Egyptians, Pythagoreans, Orphics, Silenoi, and others from antiquity shared the idea that death is far better than life. Real death resides with those who are oblivious to the control their earthly passions and fascinations have over their life. True life begins when the soul is freed for its return.

Therefore, Dionysus was in a sense *the* LIBERATOR by presiding over life 393 and death, like Osiris. He freed the soul, guided its migration beyond the grave, and protected it from falling under the domain of matter through reincarnation. He worked to exalt and perfect the soul's nature by purification and his Mysteries. Quoting from traditional and mystic sources Socrates said, "The great subject of philosophy is *Death*. He who pursues philosophy correctly *is studying how to die*."

All souls are part of the Universal Soul who is Dionysus (δαιμονιος), and he leads them back to their home through real and symbolic purification for their earthly journeys. He is the Priest, *Mystes*, Hierophant, or Spiritual Mediator of Greek religion.

The soul is a God *within* the mind. Its power is capable of becoming immortal by practicing the good and contemplating the beautiful and true. The transportation to the Elysian fields was mythically understood because everything earthly must die. Like Oedipus, man is imperfect at birth and his Elysium can exist only beyond the grave. Dionysus died and descended to the underworld, and his epic became the great Secret of the Mysteries, just as Death is the Grand Mystery of existence. His death, like Nature's periodical decay and restoration, was one of the symbols of the rebirth (*palingenesis*) of man.

Man was descended from the elemental Forces, Titans, and Gods. He learned of the Pantheistic Deity who created the Universe and commemorated this with his sacramental observance of this mysterious epic. Universal life invigorates him with the promise of regeneration, because death is an inseparable precedent to receiving life, just as a seed must die to produce a plant. The Earth itself dies for the birth of Dionysus. The *phallus*, or obelisk, is a significant symbol at a tomb or place of resurrection for the Deity at Lerna in Greece or Sais in Egypt.

Dionysus descended to the Underworld to recover his second mother 394 Semele (Virgo) and bring her back to the Gods as Thyone. Dionysus was also the son of Persephone and linked with her return to the Underworld every year. Dionysus had his retreat in the Underworld and this helped mark the winter season. The seasons were represented by alternating symbols of the bull and the serpent as Dionysus. These alternating symbols marked the change of seasons and the continuity of Time. The stern and dark always gave way to the beautiful and bright.

Being both somber and bright with anticipation was an aspect contemplated by the Mysteries. Human suffering is to be consoled by the knowledge of the terrible trials of the Gods and the persistent changes between life and death. It was appropriately symbolized with the sacrifice of the Bull and the extinguishing and relighting of a torch. This heightened the emotions in the candidate by alternating grief and joy in a similar method to the passions of Nature in all her changes.

The greater Eleusinian Mysteries were celebrated over several days in the month of Boedromion (late summer) in the Greek calendar. With crops planted and the year waning toward winter, the mind was allowed serious reflection. The first days passed in sorrow, anxious silence, fasting, atoning, and purification. Sorrow and lamentation then changed and Iacchus (Dionysus), represented with a crown of myrtle and holding a lighted torch, started the joyful procession to Eleusis. During the following night, the initiation was performed complete with its imposing revelation. The first scene was performed in the outer court (πϛοναος) of the sacred Temple amid utter darkness. The meditating God illuminated this Nocturnal Mystery as a single star and torch. The candidates were awed with sounds and noises while they made their way through the gloom of their soul's nighttime migration. This is comparable to the passage through the Valley of the Shadow of Death. Just like Psyche's trials to retrieve Cupid, every man must pass through the Underworld before reaching Heaven. After some time, the doors to the inner sanctuary (*adytum*) were opened and a supernatural light streamed from an illuminated statue of the Goddess. Enchanting sights, sounds, songs, and dances heightened the initiate's sense of supreme joy and the symbolic reunion with the Gods.

Due to the lack of direct sources or evidence detailing these ceremonies and their meanings, we must deduce the deities' characteristics from their symbols and myths, or direct testimony regarding the value of the Mysteries.

Nature's cycle is exhibited in the death of a seed to give birth to a plant. Nature connected divine concepts with ordinary events to become the simple and beautiful mystery in most religions from the Zend-Avesta to the Gospel. Like Persephone, this divine power is the decaying seed soon destroyed. The principle of destruction is associated with Artemis. Still, Artemis-Persephone is also the young Kore as Savior (Soteria) who leads the Spirits of Hercules and Hyacinthus to Heaven.

The Mysteries used many other symbols. The dove, the myrtle wreath, and others were symbols of life rising from death. Man's condition is also decaying and dying yet immortal.

Socrates' *Phaedo* and Virgil's *Aeneid* describe the events of Tartarus with its ceremonies of the judgments of the dead by Minos, Aeacus, and Rhadamanthys. These plays helped teach the lessons of the Mysteries. They taught the Initiates to always be prepared to answer to the Supreme Judge with a pure and spotless heart. As Socrates discussed in Plato's *Gorgias*, a soul stained with crimes descends into the Underworld and is very troubled. Plato stated that adhering to Justice and Wisdom is our duty. If we utilize these in our life, someday we may ascend the road towards heaven and avoid the evils of the subterranean Underworld as the soul travels its thousand-year journey. In

Phaedo, Socrates taught we should free our soul of its passions to be ready when Destiny summons us to the Underworld.

The Mysteries taught moral truth, veiled in a fable and made into an impressive spectacle using art and natural magic to add to its impression. They were determined to prepare men for the horrors of death and alleviate the fear of complete annihilation. The dialogue *Axiochus* stated death is a passage to a happier state. Still, one must have lived well to attain fortune in death. The idea of the immortality of the soul consoled the virtuous and religious man. To all others, it came with menaces, despair, terrors, and alarms that disturbed their rest for all their life.

The allegorical horrors of the Greek Tartarus within the Underworld became materially real to the interpretation of the uninitiated masses. As time progressed, even the Initiates may have even incorrectly understood the allegory. According to myth, the condemned and sinning souls were placed within a triple-walled prison in Tartarus surrounded by the fiery waves of the River Phlegethon in Hades. The great gate to the prison had columns of solid adamantine, which no one could cut except the Gods. Tisiphone, one of the Erinyes (Furies), was the warden clothed in bloody robes atop the prison tower lashing her whip upon the inmates. The crack of the whip across the bodies of the condemned, their cries, groans, screams, and clash of the chains mingled in a horrific harmony. The Erinyes tortured the guilty according to their various sins. The abyss within the prison was guarded by the fifty devouring heads of Hydra. Among the inmates was Tityos, who was restrained in a prone position so the vultures could feed on his entrails. Sisyphus was condemned to forever roll his rock up the hill. Ixion was bound to a spinning, fiery wheel with only occasional quiet. Tantalus was tortured by eternal thirst and hunger always just beyond his grasp despite wading in a pool of water and just below the low hanging fruit of a tree above his head. The daughters of Danaus had their pointless eternal tasks. In Tartarus, the beasts and venomous animals bit and stung while the flames continually consumed bodies to add fuel to the endless agony. All these images were vividly presented to the Initiates as the terrible price for sin and vice. Honesty and virtue were held as urgent pursuits to avoid this scene for eternity.

The ceremonies of the Mysteries and its horrors were explained to the Initiates as only symbols of the torture, remorse, and agony the soul and immortal spirit would receive. However, the symbols were weak and insufficient to the reality because all material images and symbols are incomplete versions of what is just beyond our senses and comprehension. The Priest (Hierophant), imagery, paintings, drama, horrors, sacrifices, mysteries, and solemn silence of the sanctuaries were still very symbolically impressive. These plays and images made the imagination of the Initiate the teacher of his own intellect.

It was also taught there were opportunities for the atonement of sins except in the most deplorable cases. The tests of *water*, *air*, and *fire* represented the way the soul could be purified over many years and again rise toward the ethereal regions. If the soul was heavy with sins and vice, the path and ascent would be more tedious. The Initiates were taught that pain, sorrow, misfortune, and remorse were the inevitable *consequences* of sin and vice. Effect flows from cause. Each sin and every act of vice slows the soul causing more time for it to cover the ground during its advance toward perfection. It was also taught that the ground lost could never be fully recovered as if the sin had never happened, and each soul would be conscious of every act of vice or baseness it did while on earth throughout all of eternity. These acts make the distance to ultimate perfection and peace far greater.

The truth and doctrine taught in the Mysteries was although slight and ordinary offences could be atoned for through penance, repentance, charity, and prayer, grave crimes were mortal sins and beyond any remedy. The Mysteries of Eleusis refused Nero. The Pagan Priests let Constantine know there was no remedy for his soul after murdering his wife, perjury, and other assassinations.

The ancient initiation's objective was to improve man and perfect his intellect. The nature of the human soul, its origin, destination, and relation to the body and to Nature formed this mystic science. These were the lessons directed to the Initiate. It was believed that initiation helped him work towards perfection by preventing the divine part within him from being plunged into the gloom of the earthly and material that would impede its return to the Deity. To them the soul was not an abstract concept, but the essence of life and thought. It was in material form, but not the same brute, inert, inactive, lifeless, motionless, formless, and lightless matter of this world. It was thought to be active, reasoning, and thinking. Its homeland was in the heavens of the Universe, and it descended only to illuminate, animate, enliven, and fill the form of matter. The soul continuously tries to connect with its natural home by freeing itself from the material anchor that holds it down. The souls of men are formed from this divine substance, infinitely delicate, active, and luminous. Man *lives* when the soul unites with the body.

Pythagoras taught these lessons. He learned them from the Egyptian Mysteries in his initiation and purification of his soul. Virgil wrote that the spirit of Anchises taught them to Aeneas. All the ceremonial atonement in the Mysteries were symbols of the intelligent soul purging vice and sin to free it from its material and earthly prison. Then it might return unimpeded to the eternal source from which it came.

These concepts developed into the theory on transmigration of the souls, which stemmed from an allegorical teaching by Pythagoras. Those who reviewed these thoughts after his death interpreted them literally. Likewise, Plato developed his teachings from the lessons of the Mysteries and Eastern thought, and he applied the symbolic language of these sources to Philosophy. He attempted to prove the immortality of the soul through debate and deduction whereas the Mysteries taught with symbols that could be *felt* by the conscious. The Roman Cicero also followed the Mysteries in teaching the Gods originated from mortal men but the difference was that their great virtues allowed their souls to be raised to immortality after death.

Transmigration of the soul is the belief that a soul is reincarnated into a form that best fit the virtuousness or viciousness of this life's actions. A vicious person would be passed into the body of an animal whose nature was like their actions as a human. The virtuous could avoid these transmigrations and free themselves to return to the eternal source in heaven. These concepts were developed from direct teaching, or from an untaught meaning in an allegory represented within the rituals of the Mysteries. The Neoplatonic philosopher Proclus Lycaeus said the Initiates prayed for the good fortune of being delivered *399* from this material Evil so they could be restored to their true life and final place of peace. This idea would exhibit the animals and monsters before the Initiate prior to seeing the light of hope and virtue that he would desire.

Plato said the soul could not free itself from its ills until they were restored to their primitive condition within the world. The sins and vices contracted within the realm of fire, earth, and air had to be overcome. He held that the way to Heaven was to practice distinguishing virtue in one of three ways. Pindar and the Jews held the same number of paths to righteousness. The Manichaeans said there were five ways to distinguish the virtuous soul.

Cicero said ancient wisdom and interpretations of the will of the Gods taught us this life was a period of atonement for the crimes of a previous life. The religious ceremonies and initiations of the Mysteries taught the soul passed through several states on its path to Heaven. The pains and sorrows of this life were atonement for prior faults.

Porphyry of Tyre informed us the idea of transmigration of souls originated among the Persians and Magi. The East and the West have held these views from ancient times. Herodotus found the concept among the Egyptians. They claimed the period of transmigration in the cycle from one human body, to animals, fish, birds, and back to another human body took three thousand years. Empedocles held that souls might even become plants. Within the plant kingdom, the laurel was the noblest while in the animal kingdom the lion was supreme. Both the laurel and lion were consecrated to the Sun, which the soul would return to in Eastern belief. The Kurds, Chinese, and Kabbalists held similar doctrines. The Gnostics, Origen Adamantius, and the initiated Greek Bishop Synesius also believed this. The Bishop prayed, "O Father, grant that my soul may not be plunged again into the vices of earth but let it be reunited with the light!" Even the Disciples of Christ asked if a blind man was being punished for a sin committed before his birth.

Virgil taught of the preexistence of the soul in his celebrated allegory developed from the doctrines of the ancient philosophers taught in the Mysteries. The souls emanated from the eternal fire which also fired the Stars *400* and was in all of Nature. Virgil wrote about the three modes of purification of the soul within the Mysteries of Bacchus by fire, water, and air. These were symbols of the passage of the soul into different material bodies through transmigration.

The human soul's relation to the rest of nature was part of the science of the Mysteries. Man was brought face to face with all of nature. The mystic egg symbolized the world and its surrounding envelope and was shown at the side of the Sun-God. The Orphic egg was holy to Bacchus in his Mysteries. Plutarch stated that it was an image of the Universe and contained everything in its bosom. The Neoplatonist philosopher Ambrosius Macrobius said, "Consult the Initiates of the Mysteries of Bacchus, who honor the sacred egg with special veneration." The rounded form of its shell that surrounds and confines within it the principles of life is symbolic of the world as the universal principle of all things.

The egg symbol was borrowed from the Egyptians who held it as Osiris, the source of Light, whom Diodorus Siculus said was born from that famous egg. In Thebes and Upper Egypt, he was shown emitting it from his mouth, the first principles of heat and light as the Fire-God, Vulcan, or Ptah. Even in Japan, we see the egg being used as a symbol. The famous Mithraic Bull whose attributes Osiris, Apis, and Bacchus all borrowed might have carried the egg between their horns. Orpheus styled Bacchus "the two-horned God" in his hymn.

Orpheus was the author of the Greek Mysteries, and he carried the use of this symbol from Egypt to Greece. He taught that uncreated and chaotic matter existed from eternity and contained the Principles of all Existences although they were unordered and intermingled as light with darkness, dry with humid, and heat with cold. From this eternal chaos issued the shape of the immense egg containing the pure matter of the first substance. This was divided into the four elements, and from this, heaven and earth and everything else was created. He taught this grand idea of the Cosmos in his Mysteries. Therein, the Hierophant explained the meaning of the mystic egg that was seen by the Initiates within the Sanctuary.

401 The early and primitive organization of Nature was presented to the initiates who wanted to learn its secrets. Clement of Alexandria might have said that initiation taught the physiology of nature.

In the Mysteries of the new Orphic, the Light-God Phanes emerged from the egg of chaos. The Persians believed in the great egg of Ahura Mazda (Ormuzd). Sanchuniathon informs us Phœnician theology taught chaos was in the form of an egg. He added, "The lessons of the Son of Thabion, first Pries of the Phœnicians, were made into allegories combining physics and astronomy. He taught the other Priests who presided at initiations and sought to astonish others with their faithful transmission of these lessons to their successors and the Initiates."

The Mysteries also taught the Universal Cause was divided into the Active and Passive causes. Osiris and Isis as heaven and earth symbolized these two causes. These two First Causes from the great Universal Cause were the two great Divinities. Varro related the worship of the two was taught to the Initiates at Samothrace and wrote, "As taught in the initiation into the Mysteries at Samothrace, Heaven and Earth are regarded as the two first Divinities. They are the Gods worshipped on that Island. Their names are consecrated in the books of our Augurs (Roman priests). One of them is male and the other is female. They have the same relation to each other as the soul does to the body, or humidity does with dryness." In Crete, the Korybantes built an altar to Heaven and Earth in a cypress cove at Knossos for the celebration of their Mysteries.

The two Divinities, as Active and Passive Principles of the Universe, frequently were symbolized as the reproductive parts of man and woman. This was not considered indecent in those days. The *Phallus* and *Vagina* were emblems of generation and production. They appeared in the Mysteries. The Indian Lingam stone, boat and mast, and point within a circle represented the philosophical union of the two great Causes of Nature. These work together actively and passively to generate all beings. Gemini symbolized this at the period when the Sun was in their Sign at the Vernal Equinox (spring) and when they were Male and Female. The Phallus was taken as a sign from Taurus the Bull, when at about 600 BC he opened the spring equinox and was thereafter used in the Ancient World as the symbol of the creative and generative Power. *402*

Proclus Lycaeus said the Initiation of Eleusis started by invoking the two great causes of nature, the Heavens and Earth. They successively addressed each a prayer. They viewed themselves as the Father and Mother of all generations and determined it was their duty to perform the prayer. The union of these two aspects of the Universe was theologically called a *marriage*. The early Christian Tertullian accused the Gnostic Valentinians of borrowing these symbols from the Mysteries of Eleusis although he admitted those Mysteries were explained in a decent manner by representing the powers of nature. He was not a philosopher able to comprehend the sublime esoteric (hidden) meaning of these symbols. These will be taught to you in more advanced Degrees.

The Christian Fathers were happy to ridicule the use of these symbols. In the early times, their meaning was not reviled by the Roman Church but was worn by the innocent and virtuous alike. It is wiser for us to search for the meaning of these symbols. Diodorus Siculus said the Egyptians and other societies consecrated the symbolic Phallus and honored the Active Force of universal generation in all things. We learn from the geographer Ptolemy it was revered among the Assyrians and Persians for the same reasons. Proclus reflected of the twelve great Divinities of the Zodiac, six signs were male and six were female.

The other division in nature noted by all men and civilizations and remembered in the Mysteries was Light and Darkness, Day and Night, and Good and Evil. The Great Symbolic Egg reminded the Initiates of this division of the world. Plutarch wrote of the dogma of Providence and cited the famous Mystic

Egg of Zoroastrianism and the Mysteries of Mithras. These two principles of Light and Darkness were regarded as the foundation of the Ancient Theology, Festivals, Mysteries, Greeks, and Barbarians, but it was lost in the darkness of time.

403

Scenes successively showed these two principles of Darkness and Light to the Initiates in the Mysteries of Eleusis. First, darkness was displayed with its illusions and ghosts followed by brilliant lights blazing around the statue of the Goddess. Dio Chrysostom said the candidate passed into a mysterious and beautiful temple where mystic scenes were exhibited to him. His ears were stunned by many voices. Darkness and Light passed before him. Themistius from Constantinople similarly described the Initiate as full of fear and religious awe when he was about to enter into that part of the sanctuary inhabited by the Goddess. He wavered, as he was uncertain in what direction to advance through the profound darkness that enveloped him. Then the Priest opened the entrance to the innermost sanctuary and removed the robe that hid the Goddess resplendent with divine light. The dark and gloomy atmosphere vanished and glowing enthusiasm took over. His soul was lifted out of the depression it had plunged into, and the purest light succeeded the thickest darkness.

Stobaeus preserved a fragment of Themistius's writing where we learn the Initiate was kept in an unknown state of emotion until his initiation was completed. Every sight was an alarm to his senses, his soul was kept in a state of astonishment and terror, and fear gripped his body until he was shown the Light. This astounding Light was the scene of Elysium with its quaint meadows and clear skies. Here he sees the dancing and festival while hearing harmonious voices and majestic chants from the Priests while the sacred spectacle is displayed before him. When free from his sins and vice he mingles with the other Initiates all crowned in flowers. The holy festival with dancing, singing, and drinking are celebrated in the ethereal realm of Ahura Mazda (Ormuzd).

404

The Mysteries of Isis had the candidate pass through the valley of the shadow of death to a place between worlds where the two principles clash and contend on the way to a brilliant region dominated by the sun where all darkness is lost. He would then dress himself as the Sun-God (Visible Source of Ethereal Light) of the Mysteries and pass from the empire of darkness to light. After arriving at the threshold of the Underworld (Pluto or Hades), he ascended to highest heaven (Empyrean Heaven) where the Eternal Principle of Light of the Universe resides and souls emanate.

Plutarch stated the two Principles were the basis of all Mysteries. They were venerated within the religious ceremonies and Mysteries of Greece. Osiris and Typhon, Ahura Mazda (Ormuzd) and Angra Mainyu (Ahriman), and Bacchus and the Titans represented these dueling principles. Phanes, the primeval God of Light, emerged from the Sacred World Egg and passed the scepter of kingship to his daughter Night (Nyx) in the Mysteries of Bacchus. Night and Day were two of the eight Gods in the Mysteries of Osiris. The tale of Persephone's and Adonis's six month stay in the upper world, or place of light, and six months in the lower world or place of darkness, was an allegory of the division of the Universe.

The initiation's association with the Equinoxes demonstrates the Mysteries referred to the persistent contest between these two principles of light and darkness. The Equinoxes refer to the perpetual separation and alternating domination between the two throughout time. The purpose of the celebrations proved the relationship between the two principles and the soul. The Emperor Julian said, "We celebrate the august Mysteries of Ceres and Proserpine at the Autumnal Equinox so the Gods will not permit the malignant Power of Darkness to rule over us as it is about to rule over Nature." The Roman Historian Sallust made the same remark about the relation of the soul to the periodical march of light and darkness during the year. He explained the mysterious festivals of Greece related the same purpose. In all the explanations given by Macrobius of the Sacred Fables regarding the Sun worshipped under the names of Osiris, Horus, Adonis, Attis, Bacchus, etc., we know they referred 405 to the two great Principles of Light and Darkness and their eternal contest. The triumph of the light of day over the length of night was celebrated in April and a converse ceremony was held in Autumn. Macrobius asserted that the ceremonies of mourning and rejoicing alternating referred to the administration of the world perennially by these principles.

This brings us to the tragic portion of these religious scenes and the allegory of the victory and vanquishing of the Principle of Light against Darkness each year. The most mysterious part of the ancient initiations was the part that still exists in Masonry and is found in the death of our Grand Master Hiram (Khir-Om). Herodotus only adds a veil of mystery and silence. He speaks of the Temple of Minerva (or Isis) whose Goddess is the Mother of the Sun-God. At Sais, Egypt these Mysteries were termed *Isiac*. He spoke of a Tomb within the Temple near the rear of the Chapel and against the wall, "It is the tomb of a man, whose name I conceal. Within the Temple were great obelisks [*phalli*] and a circular lake paved with stones that had a defensive wall as an embankment. It seemed as large as the one at Delos (Delos is where the Mysteries of Apollo were celebrated). In this lake, the Egyptians celebrated their Mysteries at night and represented the trials of the God I spoke about above." This God was Osiris, who was killed by Typhon, descended to the Underworld, and was restored to life.

Masons remember this with the Tomb of Hiram (Khir-Om), his death, and his rising from the grave. The Mystery ceremony was a symbol like Hiram's restoration to life. The brazen Sea in the Temple at Jerusalem was the lake. Herodotus added, "I practice a silence regarding these Mysteries and most of which I am acquainted. I will speak little of the initiations of Ceres, which was known as the Thesmophoria festival among the Greeks. What I shall say does not violate my oath to the religion."

The Christian Apologist Athenagoras quoted this passage to show the Statue and Tomb of Osiris displayed in Egypt to represent his tragic sufferings. He remarked the Egyptians had mourning ceremonies to honor, lament, and sacrifice for the death of their Gods who passed into a state of immortality.

406   We can combine these different ancient rays of light from the various Mysteries' sanctuaries that still shine upon us today. We can compile them through their hints to learn about the object and genius of these secret ceremonies, even if exact details are absent.

The Egyptians worshipped the Sun through Osiris. The tragic death of Osiris was an allegorical story of the Sun in which Typhon represented Darkness. The ordeal and death of Osiris in the Mysteries of the Night was an image of the mystical phenomena of Nature. The conflict between the two great Principles who share the empire of Nature influences our souls. While the Sun was not born, killed, or raised back to life, these events are an allegory of events that veil a higher truth.

Horus (Apollo or Sun) as the son of Isis also died and was restored to life by his mother. The priests of Isis celebrated these great events with a mourning festival followed by a joyous celebration.

The Mysteries of Phœnicia were established to honor Tammuz and Adonis (Sun), and the spectacle of his death and restoration was shown to the Initiates. We know from Johannes Meursius and Plutarch a corpse of a young man was depicted to the Initiates. Flowers covered his body, women mourned for him, and a tomb was established for him. The feasts for Tammuz and Adonis passed to Greece, which we learn from Plutarch and the Roman poet Ovid.

The Mysteries of Mithras (Sun-God) in Asia Minor, Armenia, and Persia lamented and celebrated the respective death and resurrection of the God. According to Julius Firmicus, a corpse representing Mithras was displayed to the Initiates. Later, his restoration was announced, and they rejoiced in the God's restoration to life. Three months earlier, a festival was celebrated to honor his infant birth on December 25th (the eighth day before the New Moon [Calends] of January).

The Greek Mysteries of Bacchus (Dionysus) included the scene of the God's death by the Titans, his descent into hell, subsequent resurrection, and the return to his Principle from where he had descended to unite himself with
407   matter. On the islands of Chios and Tenedos in the Aegean, they sacrificed a man by fire to commemorate his death.

According to Diodorus Siculus, in Phrygia of the Western Anatolia, the mutilation and suffering of the Sun-God Attis was the tragic scene of the Mysteries of Cybele, the mother Goddess. The scene of the corpse of a young man who had funeral honors and tears shed over him was established here.

On the island of Samothrace, the Mysteries of the Cabeiri (the great Gods) were practiced. This included the death scene of one of the Cabeiri Gods by the others, and the dead God was resurrected with the aid of Hermes. Ancient Astronomers named the Gemini Constellation's Twins with the names of the two other Cabeiri, who were Castor and Pollux. In some stories and star charts, the twins were depicted as Apollo and Hercules, and these are two names for the Sun. The writer Athenion said that the young slain Cabeirus was the same as the Dionysus (Bacchus) of the Greeks who was reborn with the aid of Hermes and found on the island Naxos. The Pelasgians (ancient inhabitants of Greece) who settled Samothrace celebrated these Mysteries and worshipped the Cabeiri Castor and Pollux as patrons of navigation.

The oracle and tomb of Apollo was at Delphi where his body laid while Dionysus (Python), the Polar Serpent, took over the Oracle and signified the three months of winter, cold, and darkness. Apollo returned and Dionysus leaves for Hades on March 25th, the Vernal Equinox.

On Crete, Jupiter Ammon (Amun or Zeus) was the Sun in Aries and was painted with the sign of the equinox, the Ram. Martianus Capella claimed Jupiter Ammon was the same as Osiris, Adonai, Adonis, Attis, and the other Sun-Gods, and he had a tomb with a religious initiation around it. One of the principal ceremonies consisted of clothing the Initiate with a lambskin. From this ceremony, we see an ancient practice that led to the white lambskin apron used in Masonry today.

These ceremonies, festivals, funerals, resurrections, anniversaries, tombs, and monuments to the Sun-God (in whatever name) had one objective: to tell the allegorical story of events that happened to the Light of Nature and its battle with the dark Principle of Matter. The Supreme Deity wills the same struggle within our material bodies and our spiritual soul. Clement of Alexandria said the Mysteries' murders, tombs, and religious tragedies had a common foundation but *408* different elaborations that made the fictitious death and resurrection of the Sun, Soul of the World, principle of life, great cause, principle in the Sublunary World, the Eternal Light, and source of our intelligence their primary purpose.

It was said that Souls were purified by going to the Sun. Porphyry of Tyre said the Sun was one of the gates through which the soul ascended towards its home of Light and the Good. The Dadoukos (the first officer, after the Priest) was the Demiurge or Maker of the Universe in the Mysteries of Eleusis. He was placed within the Temple to receive the candidates and represented the Sun receiving souls.

It was believed that a change in fortune of the Father of Light had an influence on the destiny of all souls because they were both from the same substance. We learn this from the Emperor Julian and Sallust the Roman historian. Souls are afflicted when he suffers and rejoice when he triumphs. The Mysteries received the benefit from God's suffering and death by the Principle of the Power of Darkness along with His restoration to life. The High Priest of Mithras said, "His death is your Salvation," and this was the great secret of the religious tragedy. The restored God of Light reestablished His rule over

Darkness, and virtuous Souls share in His triumph and glory because their purity did not work against Him or His power while He conquered.

The agents of the Universal Cause, and its orderly arrangement were shown to the Initiates. The Universe was man's first model for a Temple reared to the Divinity. The arrangement of the Temple of Solomon, its symbolic ornaments and decoration, and the High Priest's regalia all referenced the order of the world, as confirmed by Clement of Alexandria, Josephus, and Philo. Clement wrote the Temple contained many symbols of the Seasons, Sun, Moon, planets, Ursa Major and Minor, the constellations, the zodiac, elements, and other parts of the world.

409

Josephus protested the Hebrews' charges of other nation's impiety by citing that the High Priest's Robes, the construction of the Tabernacle, the Sacrificer's robes, and the Sacred vessels represented the whole World. The Temple was divided into three parts of which two represented the Earth and Sea and were open to all men. The third represented Heaven and God's dwelling place, but it was reserved for Him alone. The twelve loaves of Showbread represented the twelve months of the year. The Candlestick represented the twelve signs of the zodiac through which the Seven Planets ran their courses. The seven lights were the planets. The four colors of the veils represented the four elements. The tunic of the High Priest was the earth and the nearly blue Hyacinth was the Heavens. The ephod was four colors to represent all of nature, his gold was Light, the breastplate was earth, the two clasps of Sardonyxes were the Sun and Moon, and the twelve precious stones arranged in groups of threes around the breastplate were the Seasons, the twelve months, and the twelve signs of the zodiac. The loaves of showbread were in two groups of six also like the signs of the zodiac, above and below the Equator, and male or female. Clement the Bishop of Alexandria and Philo both adopt all these explanations as true.

Hermes used the name Tabernacle (Great Tent) to refer to the Zodiac. In the Royal Arch Degree in America, the Tabernacle has four veils of different colors and an associated banner for each. The colors are White, Blue, Crimson, and Purple while the banners show the images of the Bull, Lion, Man, and Eagle from the Constellations. These represented the constellations associated with the Equinox and Solstice dates and were known from about 3000 BC as the Royal Stars in Persia. The four stars and constellations were Aldebaran from Taurus, Regulus from Leo, Fomalhaut from Aquarius, and Antares from Scorpio. Each of the veils had three words and three signs upon the banner, which were associated with its division of the Zodiac headed by the four Stars. The four signs of Taurus, Leo, Scorpio, and Aquarius were termed the *fixed* signs and each was assigned a veil.

According to Clement and Philo, the Cherubim represented the two hemispheres of the heavens. Their wings were the vault of heaven and time was established by the revolution of the Zodiac in the heavens. The Cherubim were described as having four faces comprised of the Lion, Bull, Eagle, and Man.

Philo spoke of the winged Cherubim, "For the Heavens Fly". Images of these 410 winged creatures have been connected with those excavated at Nimrud. These creatures may have been adopted as beneficial symbols too. The Sun was known to enter Taurus at Spring (Vernal Equinox), Leo at the Summer Solstice, Scorpio was substituted for Aquila the Eagle due to its malignant influence at the Autumnal Equinox, and Aquarius at the Winter Solstice.

Clement said the candlestick with its seven branches symbolized the seven planets each arranged and well regulated to preserve their proportion and harmony with the sun at the center. Philo described the lamps as arranged in two sets of three with three above and three below the sun, for a total of seven branches. The middle branch represented the Sun, the mediator of celestial harmony. He is also represented as the fourth, and middle, note in the musical scale as Philo and Martianus Capella remarked.

Near the candlestick were other symbols for the heavens, earth, and plant kingdoms. The whole temple was a microcosm of the world. The candlesticks with four branches were symbols of the elements and seasons. Those with twelve branches were symbols of the zodiac signs. The candlestick with three hundred and sixty lamps symbolized the number of days in the year (as known at the time). The architect placed two columns of bronze at the entrance porch. The circular brazen sea was supported by four groups of three bulls each, facing the four cardinal directions and alluding to the Vernal Equinox. Hiram built two earlier temples at Tyre for the God's Melqart and Astarte, Josephus stated. At the Temple of Astarte in Tyre, there were two large columns at the entrance porch. The Tyrian Temple's great columns were consecrated to the winds and to fire. Astarte was given reign over the world by her husband Melqart, and she wore a helmet with the image of a bull on her head to symbolize her dominion. The throne of Solomon, the throne of Horus in Egypt, and the throne of the Sun in Tyre were all built alike with bulls on its arms and resting upon lions that referred to the Vernal Equinox and Summer Solstice, respectively.

Sabazios was the Father God of the Sky in ancient Thrace. Macrobius said the Greek Bacchus cults adopted his worship and built him a temple in Thrace with its round architecture representing the world and the sun. A circular hole in the roof admitted sunlight into the sanctuary. There it seemed to blaze 411 from the heights of Heaven removing all darkness from within the temple that symbolized the world. Within this temple the trial, death, and resurrection of Bacchus was represented.

Similarly, the Temple of Eleusis had a hole in the roof for light. Dio said this sanctuary differed only in size with the Universe. Within the sanctuary, the great lights of nature were mystically represented, and played a part in its rites. The images of the Sun, Moon, and Mercury were represented (Mercury was like Anubis with Isis). These three lights are the three lights in a Masonic Lodge where Mercury is substituted for the Master of the Lodge.

Eusebius named the main officers of the Mysteries of Eleusis. First and greatest was the *Hierophant* who was robed and symbolized the Demiurge, or Grand Architect of the Universe. Second was the *Dadoukos* who represented the Sun as the torch-bearer and incense-burner. Next, the alter-bearer represented the Moon and was called Epibomos. The last main officer was the *Hieroceryx* bearing the caduceus and represented Mercury. The different symbols and ceremonies were not allowed to be shared with the masses, so we do not know the attributes, emblems, and ornaments of these and other officers of Eleusis.

We read the ceremonies were considered marvelous and astonishing to the Initiates whose senses were filled in the rites of Initiation. The Hierophant had noble features, long hair, great age, dignity, deep voice, long trailing robes, and sat upon a throne as the Motive-God of Nature. He was portrayed as busy in His work and was hidden under a veil that no mortal could hope to raise. His name was concealed from all, just as the name of the Demiurge was ineffable.

The Dadoukos wore a long robe and was longhaired with a headband and he was charged to lead the Initiates in their procession and Purification. When Callias II held the office, he fought at Marathon in his priestly robes and the Persians mistook him as a King.

We do not know the function of the *Epibomos* at the altar who symbolized the moon. The moon was considered one of the two great gates and natural homes for the soul. Through it, they could ascend and descend between heaven and Earth. Mercury was charged with conducting souls through the two great gates, and when they went between the sun to the moon they passed by him. He admitted and rejected Initiates according to their purity and was called the Sacred Herald (Hieroceryx). Mercury was charged to exclude the masses from the Mysteries.

The same officers are in the Mysteries of Isis as described by Apuleius. All officers were dressed in white linen robes closed tightly across the chest and tailor fit to their feet. They were processed in order to start the ceremony. The first held a lamp in the shape of a boat. The second carried an altar while the third carried a golden palm tree and the caduceus. These three are the same as the top officers of Eleusis after the Hierophant. After these, one carried an open hand and poured milk on the ground from a golden vessel shaped as a woman's breast. The hand represented justice while the milk alluded to the Milky Way along which souls descended and ascended. Two others followed, one carried a fan and the other carried a water vase. These two symbols represented the purification of souls by air and water. Earth was the third symbol of purification represented by an ox led by the next officer.

A magnificently decorated ark followed bearing the image of the reproductive organ of Osiris (or maybe both sex organs, the generating and producing Powers). According to the Egyptian fable, when Typhon dismembered the body of Osiris into fourteen pieces he cast the genitals into the Nile where the fish devoured them. Attis is said to have mutilated himself as his

412

Priests did in imitation. Adonis was wounded in his genitals by the boar. All of these stories represent the loss of the Sun's generative power when it reached the Autumnal Equinox and began its descent to the region of darkness and winter. In older monuments, the Scorpion is depicted biting that part of the Vernal Bull.

Apuleius described the joyful sight of the, "one who carried at his chest an impressive likeness of the Supreme Deity that was not like man, cattle, bird, beast, or any living creature. It was an exquisite, novel, and impressive invention of originality. It was an ineffable symbol of the religious mysteries to be *413* contemplated in profound silence. Its figure was like a small urn of polished gold, hollowed out, rounded at the bottom, and covered with Egyptian hieroglyphics. The spout was not raised. Rather it extended laterally. The opposite side had a handle with a similar lateral extension. On the top was an asp (cobra), curling its body into folds and stretching upward with its head flared."

The serpent in its folds with its head raised and flared is seen on many monuments because it was the royal sign of the Pharaohs. The cobra was the Phoenix of all the serpents. The vase or urn was the vessel with its spout from which the priests are shown pouring the *cruz ansata* (Tau Cross) and *scepters* over the kings in the many monuments of Egypt.

In the Mysteries of Mithras, a sacred cave was established to receive the Initiates. It was selected and decorated to represent the world. The Greek Eubulus said Zoroaster first introduced the custom of establishing caves for ceremonies. Later, caves were used on Crete for Jupiter's ceremonies, in Arcadia for Pan, and on the Island of Naxos for Bacchus. The Persians Mysteries of Mithras were celebrated in a cave and fixed the seat of that God, the Father of Generation (Demiurge) at the Vernal Equinox with the world's North to his right and South to his left.

Porphyry said Mithras presided over the Equinoxes bearing a sword and seated on the Bull as the symbolic animal of the Demiurge. The equinoxes were the gates the souls passed through when traversing between the hemisphere of light and darkness. In old theology, the Milky Way passed near these gates and was the pathway of souls. According to Pythagoras, the numerous souls comprised that luminous belt in the sky.

According to Porphyry, the souls followed a progressive route through this world among the fixed stars and the planets. The Mithraic cave displayed the zodiac, constellations, seven planetary spheres that the soul must traverse, and the four gates marked by the equinoxes and solstices through which souls were able to enter or exit the worlds of light and darkness around the earth. *414*

Through Origen, we learn from Celsus the Mithraic Mysteries used the symbolic imagery of a ladder in the soul's passage among the Stars when between Earth and Heaven. This ladder reached between Heaven and Earth and was divided into seven steps on each of which was a gate. At the top was an eighth gate for the fixed stars. The first gate was Saturn whose slow path in the sky was symbolically represented by lead. The second gate was Venus whose soft splendor and easy flexibility was represented by tin. The third gate was Jupiter who being solid and dry by nature was given the symbol of brass. The fourth gate of Mercury was tireless, wise, and was represented by iron. The fifth gate of Mars was marked by an unequal and variable nature and was symbolized by copper. The sixth gate of the Moon was represented by silver. The seventh gate was the Sun and was symbolized by gold. This order was not the natural order for these bodies and is mysterious to us as if we were to count the days of the Week *backwards* Saturday through Sunday. This was ordered by the harmonic relation of the fourth (the Sun), claimed Celsus.

There was a close connection between the Sacred Science of the Mysteries and ancient astronomy and physics. The grand spectacle in the Sanctuary was the order of the Known Universe (Nature) surrounding the soul of the Initiate just as it was when it first descended through the planetary gates, across the gates of the equinoxes and solstices, along the Milky Way, and was enclosed within matter. The Mysteries also presented the candidate sensible symbols of the invisible forces that govern the visible Universe. Virtues, qualities, and powers with matter that maintain its order were shared as Porphyry informs us.

According to ancient philosophers, the world was not purely material and mechanical. A great Soul was found everywhere and it enlivened the entire Universe and its parts. A great Intelligence directed its movements and harmony. Thus the Universe, as the symbolic egg, was composed of two parts being the Soul and the Intelligence. To the Universe, these were like each man's intellect and soul.

Orpheus taught this concept of the Unity of God. His hymn is proof in its fragments quoted by many of the early Church Fathers such as Justin, Tatian, Clement of Alexandria, Cyril, and Theodoret while Eusebius of Caesarea quoted it whole through Aristobulus. The Mysteries objective was to teach of the LOGOS (word), NOUS (intellect), man's incarnation, death, resurrection, transfiguration, union with matter, division of the visible world, return to Unity, the origin of the soul, and the soul's destiny.

The Emperor Julian explains the Mysteries of Attis and Cybele by the same principles of the demiurge, Intelligence, descent into matter, and return to Unity. These are extended by the Emperor to explain the Mysteries of Ceres. Sallust the Philosopher does the same and affirms a secondary intelligent Force in God that descends into matter to organize it. These mystical concepts formed part of the doctrines and ceremonies of initiation that meant to unite man with the World and the Deity. According to Clement, the final stage of perfection was the contemplation of nature, real beings, and causes. Sallust defines this correctly. The Mysteries were a method to perfect the soul, give it dignity, and remind it of its nobility, origin, immortality, and relation with the Universe and the Deity.

Real beings mean *invisible* beings, as *genii* or the *faculties* or *powers* of nature (Aeons). It can also include things that are not part of the *visible* world, or the *apparent* existence. The concept of Genii (or Powers of Nature) and its Forces are personified and incorporated into the Sacred Science of initiation with the different beings displayed within the Sanctuary. It was a result of the belief in the providence and oversight by the Gods as taught in the initiation. The administration of the Universe entrusted to the subordinate Genii from who *416* good and evil are dispensed in the world was a consequence of this belief. The Mysteries of Mithras taught that Ahura Mazda (Ormuzd) and Angra Mainyu (Ahriman) shared the world egg. Each established twenty-four Genii to dispense the good and evil in the world. These were subordinate to twelve Superior Gods of who six were on the side of Light and Good and the other six were on the side of Darkness and Evil.

This principle of the Genii as organizers of the Universe was closely connected to the Ancient Mysteries, and the idea was used for sacrifices and initiations among Greeks and Barbarians. Plutarch said the Gods, through the Genii intermediaries, draw near to mortals in initiation ceremonies that the Gods have ordered them to assist by dispensing punishments and blessings. This accounts for how the Deity is kept neutral while His minister or the Principle and Power of Evil was the author of vice, sin, and suffering. The Genii, or angels, are different in their character as is humanity with some being good and some evil. Some are Celestial Gods, Archangels, or Angels and some are Infernal Gods, Demons, or fallen Angels.

The chief of the Evil Genii was Typhon, Angra Mainyu (Ahriman), Satan, or Shaitan as the Evil Principle who established disorder in nature and brings trouble, illness, and punishment to men for his crimes. Plutarch said that these truths Isis desired to teach and show in her Sanctuaries and Mystery ceremonies established with the memory of her sorrow and wanderings. In addition, Isis encouraged piety and consolation for other's misfortune. He said, the principle of Providence and administration of the Universe through intermediary Powers to maintain man's connection with the Divinity was established in the Mysteries of the Egyptians, Phrygians, Thracians, Magi, and Zoroastrians is evident by their initiations with mournful and funereal ceremonies. This was an essential part of the lessons given the Initiates in teaching them their own soul's relationship with Universal Nature. The lessons were meant to establish man's sense of dignity with himself and with his place in the Universe.

Thus, the whole system of the Universe was displayed to the eyes of the *417* Initiate in the symbolic cave of the Universe, adorned with its attributes. This world is organized with its double force being active and passive, light and dark. It is overseen by a living and intelligent Force, governed by the Genii, or Angels, who preside over its different areas. Their nature can be good or evil in proportion as they have more or less portions of dark matter in their make-up.

This is the world the soul is forced to descend into from the ethereal and luminous fire above. It enters the dark matter where the hostile Principle and his Genii are battling to keep the body as its prison and its passions in submission until it learns to return to its origin and native country. This life is the soul's exile from that place.

According to the philosophers, one thing remains to show the path to return through the constellations, planetary spheres, and back to its original home. It is the celestial fire, the soul of the world, a pure, simple, and unmixed universal principle above the Heavens in a region infinitely pure and luminous itself above the world. When a soul descends, it acts against its nature. It is urged by a desire of the intelligence in its love for matter that forces it to descend and learn of the conflict of good and evil below. The Soul is formed of a simple substance when it is unconnected with matter. When united with the body, it gravitates but struggles to return its portion to the Divine Fire whose home is in Heaven.

The Mysteries sought to teach man of his divine origin and show the path of its return. The great science the Mysteries acquired was the knowledge of man's self and his noble origin, his great destiny, and his superiority over the other animals of Earth that cannot acquire this knowledge though he will resemble them while he does not reflect upon his existence and the depths of his nature.

Only by acting, suffering, virtue, piety, and good deeds can the soul free itself from the body. Then it can ascend along the path of the Milky Way, the gate of Capricorn, and the seven spheres to return to the place where it had descended. Thus, the theory of the spheres, the signs and intelligences, and the whole system of astronomy was connected with the soul and its destiny. The Mysteries taught these great principles of physics, metaphysics, the soul's origin, its condition here below, its destination, and its future fate.

The Greeks set the establishment of the Mysteries of Eleusis in the year 1423 BC during the reign of Erechtheus of Athens. It was rumored that Ceres herself started them. According to Diodorus Siculus of Sicily, that Monarch who brought them from his native Egypt established it. Another tradition held that Orpheus introduced them into Greece as a copy of the Mysteries of Isis at the same time with establishing the ceremonies of Dionysus as a copy from the Mysteries of Osiris.

Outside of Athens, these Mysteries of Isis changed to worship Demeter (Ceres), and they became well established across the land. The Boeotians worshipped the Great or Cabeiric Ceres in the recesses of a sacred grove where only Initiates could enter. These ceremonies and the sacred traditions of their Mysteries were connected with those of the Cabeiri in Samothrace.

The Mysteries were celebrated everywhere the same revealing their common Egyptian roots and features including Argos, Phocis, Arcadia, Achaea, Messenia, Corinth, and many other parts of Greece. Pausanius informs us that the Greeks regarded the Mysteries of Eleusis superior to all the others Mysteries, as the Gods are superior to mere Heroes.

The Mysteries of Bona Dea, the Good Goddess, were celebrated at Rome from the earliest times of that city. Cicero and Plutarch tell us that men were not permitted to know her true name. These Mysteries were to be practiced by women alone, but was violated by Publius Clodius. These celebrations were held at the Kalends of May (first day of the new moon) and the ceremony greatly resembled the Mysteries of Bacchus, according to Plutarch.

The Mysteries of Venus and Adonis were principally local to Syria and Phœnicia from where they then entered Greece and Sicily. Venus (as Astarte) was the Great Female Deity of the Phœnicians and Melqart (as Adonis or Greek Hercules) was their Chief God. Adonis was the lover of Venus and was slain by a wound to his thigh from a wild boar in its hunt. The blood from his wound *419* produced the flower anemone. Venus received his corpse and was able to obtain from Jupiter six months of each year with him while the other six months he would spend with Proserpine in the Underworld. This was an allegory of the Sun's location in its two hemispheres throughout the year. In the Mysteries, a ceremony marked his death and mourning. After his six months, the mourning concluded, and his resurrection and ascent to Heaven was announced.

Ezekiel speaks of the festivals of Adonis or Tammuz, an Assyrian Deity, whom the women mourned seated at the doors of their dwellings every year. These Mysteries were celebrated in the Spring on the Vernal Equinox to mark his restoration to life. When the celebration began the Sun (ADON, Lord, or Master) was in the Zodiac of Taurus, the home of Venus.

Plutarch says that Adonis and Bacchus could be regarded as the same Deity. This was based upon the similarity in many details of the Mysteries of these two Gods.

The Mysteries of Bacchus were also known as the Festivals of Sabazios, Orpheus, and Dionysus. They are among the oldest festivals of the Greeks. They were attributed to the Greek Bacchus or Orpheus, but the similarities in the ceremonies, observances, mythology, and symbols with Osiris from Egypt prove their origin. The name Bacchus, word *orgies*, and sacred words used in his Mysteries are of foreign origin to Greece. Bacchus was originally an Asian Deity. He was worshipped in the East and his parties (orgies) were celebrated there long before the Greeks. He was originally worshipped in India, Arabia, and Bactria.

Bacchus was honored in Greece with simple public festivals and complicated Mysteries of varying degrees of ceremony. This was due to its migration to different regions and different times and its subsequent adoption of the rites that were passed along. The people who celebrated the most *420* complicated forms of the Mysteries were ignorant of the meaning of most words used, and symbols revered. In the Feasts of Sabazios the words EVOI and SABOI were used which are not Greek. A golden serpent was thrown at the Initiate. This allusion pointed to the fable that Jupiter (gold) had in the form of a serpent had sired with Proserpina as he sired Bacchus. There was a saying repeated to the Initiates, that a bull brings the serpent, and the serpent in turn brings the bull, who was Bacchus. The meaning of which was that the bull (Taurus of the Vernal Equinox and the Sun its Sign was Bacchus, Dionysus, Sabazios, Osiris, etc.) and the Serpent together. Both were represented by constellations in the Heavens and were situated so as one rose, the other set.

The serpent was a familiar symbol in the Mysteries of Bacchus. The Initiates held them in their hands, as Orphiucus (constellation) does in the Heavens. The purifier of candidates (Orpheo-telestes) did the same and yelled out EVOI, SABOI, HYES ATTE, ATTE, HYES!

The Initiates in these Mysteries preserved the ritual and ceremonies that agreed with the early simplicity. The rules set by Pythagoras were followed there. They buried no Initiate in woolen garments as they thought wool was unclean like the Egyptians did. They did not perform blood sacrifices choosing to live on fruits, vegetables, or inanimate things. They imitated the life practiced by the meditative Asian Sects to live in tranquility, free from trouble and crime in the cradle of peace. The promised to put their initiates in communion with the Gods by purifying the soul of all troubling passions that dim the divine light that is available to every soul ready to receive its purity. One of the degrees of initiation allowed the initiates to attain a state of divine inspiration. The Mysteries of the Lamb practiced at Pepuza in Phrygia professed, inspired, and
421 prophesied that the soul by means of the initiations and purified of all stains could see the Gods in this life as well as after death.

The sacred gates of the Temple were opened once in each year for the ceremonies of initiation to be performed, and no stranger was ever allowed to enter it. Night threw her veil over the Mysteries so that they were revealed to no one unlawfully. Inside the trials of Bacchus were replayed. He, like Osiris, died and descended to the underworld to rise to life again. Raw flesh was distributed to the Initiates for each to eat in memory of his death at the hands of the Titans.

These Mysteries were celebrated at the Vernal Equinox and the symbol of Earth's rebirth. It was meant to symbolize the active and reproductive power of Bacchus. The Initiates wore garlands and crowns of myrtle and laurel.

During the Mysteries three days and nights, the initiate candidates were kept in darkness and terror. After the ceremony representing the death of Bacchus (Osiris), he was called Αφανισμος or twice born. This was done by confining him in a small space so that he could meditate in solitude and darkness on the work he was engaged upon. His mind was prepared to receive the sublime and mysterious truths of primitive revelation and philosophy. This period was his symbolic death as well as his deliverance from it by regeneration. While in his cell, he could hear the reenactment of the Typhon's pursuit after the body of Osiris and the search by Isis (or Rhea) for his mangled body. The initiated together cried out the names of the Deity as derived from Sanskrit. It was then announced that the body had been found and the candidate was freed with shouts of joy.

He then passed through a depiction of Hell and Elysium. It was written, "Then they were entertained with songs and dances, taught the sublime principles of sacred knowledge, and witness wonderful and holy visions. Perfected and initiated, they are now FREE. Crowned with triumph they walk the blessed areas, converse with other pure and holy men, and celebrate these sacred Mysteries at their pleasure." They were taught the Mysteries objects and its nature, and ways to identify each other whereby they were called *Epopts*. They were fully instructed in the Deity's nature and attributes, the afterlife, the unity 422 and attributes of the Grand Architect of the Universe, and the truth behind the fables of Paganism. The great Truth was that, "Zeus is the primitive Source of all things. There is ONE God, ONE power, and ONE principle over everything." After receiving full explanations to the many symbols, they were dismissed with the saying Κογξ and Ομπαξ (corrupted from Sanskrit), *Kanska Aom Pakscha* that means, *object of our wishes, God, Silence*, or better phrased, *Worship the Deity in Silence*.

One of symbolic emblems was the rod of Bacchus. It was reported that once he threw it on the ground where it changed into a serpent. Another report indicates he struck the Orontes and Hydaspes (now Jhelum) Rivers with it to cause the waters to recede allowing him to pass over dry. By striking a rock with it, water issued forth. The Bacchae (Maenads) crowned their heads with vine leaves, carried serpents in vases and baskets, and finding (Ευςησις) the body of Osiris threw a live one at the aspirant's body.

The Mysteries of Attis in Phrygia and Cybele resembled that of Adonis, Bacchus, Osiris, and Isis. Their Asian origin is not in doubt, and the Phrygians were quite possibly one of the foundations of early civilization like Egypt. The Phrygians mingled allegory and fables with religious worship more than any other group. Their traditions surrounding Cybele and Attis were quite various despite its origin there. According to Julius Firmicus, they represented nature by allegory and held its facts under the veil of embellished history.

Their feasts were coincided with the equinoxes. They began with lamentation, mourning, groaning, and pitiful cries in remembrance of the death of Attis. They ended with joy and excitement at his restoration to life.

The numerous legends of Attis and Cybele will not be recounted as it is provided by the writers Julius Firmicus, Diodorus Siculus, Arnobius of Sicca, Lactantius, Servius, Saint Augustine, and Pausanias. We shall summarize by saying that Cybele was a Phrygian Princess who invented musical instruments and dances. She was enamored with Attis in his youth. Somehow, he mutilated himself or was mutilated by her out of jealousy; and he died from this wound. After he was restored to life, like Adonis. The Phœnician tale of their Sun-God 423 is similar in plot, though expressed with other terms, forms, and names.

In Syria, the figure of Cybele was called Rhea. The name Rhea is found among the creation story of the Phœnicians as written by Sanchuniathon. Lucian of Samosata said after Attis' mutilation he established her worship, built her a temple, established the Mysteries of Rhea, and taught its celebration to the Phrygians, Lydians, and people of Samothrace. Like Cybele, Rhea was depicted on a chariot being drawn by lions, holding a drum, and crowned with flowers. According to Varro, Cybele represented mother earth. She took of the characteristics of Minerva, Venus, the Moon, Diana, Nemesis, and the Furies. She was clad in precious stones while her High Priest wore a robe of purple and a tiara of gold.

Like the Roman Bona Dea, the Grand Feast of the Syrian Goddess and the Mysteries of Attis were celebrated at the Vernal Equinox. The Mysteries of Attis taught the Initiates of the reward of a future life. It described how Attis fled from the jealous Cybele, how he hid in a cave in the mountains, and of his self-mutilation. His priests famously continued to imitate his self-mutilation through time. The festival of Attis lasted three days whereby the first was for mourning and tears and continued to wild rejoicing. Macrobius said the Sun was worshipped with the name Attis. The ceremonies were purely allegorical with some easily explained and others more mysterious and hidden, according to the Emperor Julian. This is how symbols outlast their intentions and explanations. As in Masonry, man's ignorance and rashness to understand create new meanings.

Pausanias informs us in another legend that Attis died after being wounded by a wild boar in the genitals, like Adonis. The pine tree was sacred because he died under it. This symbol was found on many monuments near a bull and ram, which represented the Sun and Moon.

424   The Persians worshipped the Sun through Mithras and generated many of the wise symbols for worship. The Persians regarded the Sun as the home of Fire. Fire was considered to give life to the earth and exist throughout the Universe as its soul. These rites passed from Persia into Armenia, Cappadocia, and Cilicia before the Romans learned of it. However, the Mysteries of Mithras were the biggest in Rome. The Mysteries of Mithras began to gain traction under Emperor Trajan. Hadrian then prohibited them due to the graphic scenes of its ceremonies and the human victims who were burned to death its fortune-telling with the victims pulsing entrails. They gained great splendor under Commodus who personally had sacrificed a victim to Mithras. They continued their practice under Constantine and later. The Priests of Mithras were found throughout the Roman Empire and as far away as Britain.

Caves were made sacred for Mithras. Many astronomical symbols were collected within them. Initiates faced many cruel tests while in the ceremonies.

The Persians did not build traditional temples. They chose to worship upon the tops of the hills and in enclosures of unfinished stones. They discouraged images and made the Sun and Fire symbols of the Deity. The Jews borrowed these thoughts from them in the story of Abraham and God as Fire and as Moses with the Burning Bush at Horeb and Fire on Sinai.

With the Persians, Mithras as the Sun was the invisible Deity, Parent of the Universe, and the Mediator. In Zoroaster's initiation cave, the Sun, Planets, and Zodiac were represented overhead by gems and gold. The Sun emerged from the back of Taurus. Three great pillars labeled Eternity, Fertility, and Authority supported the roof. All was symbolic of the Universe.

Zoroaster, like Moses, was said to have conversed directly with the Deity and received a system of pure worship. It was to be shared only with the virtuous, devote, and students of Philosophy. His fame spread throughout the nations and pupils were recorded from everywhere. Pythagoras was even a scholar of his.

After an introductory period, the candidate entered the cavern for initiation. He was received on the point of a sword pressed to his naked left 425 breast that caused a small wound. He was crowned with olive branches, anointed with a perfume, purified with fire and water, and passed through seven stages of initiation symbolized by a seven-stepped ladder. He had many fearful trials of which darkness was a principal part. He saw the wicked in Hades portrayed and finally emerged from darkness into light. He was received in Elysium among the initiated where the Priest (Archimagus) presided, robed in blue. He assumed the obligations of secrecy and was entrusted with the Sacred Words primarily including the Ineffable Name of God.

Afterward, all the parts of his initiation were explained to him. He was taught that these ceremonies brought him closer to the Deity, and he should adore Fire as the gift of that Deity and His residence. He was taught the sacred characters known only to Initiates. He was instructed about the creation of the world. He had the true philosophical meaning of mythology explained to him. Primarily this included the legend of Ahura Mazda (Ormuzd) and Angra Mainyu (Ahriman), and the symbolism in the six created Amesha Spenta (Amshaspand). In Middle Persian these were known as: *Bahman*, the Lord of Light; *Ardwahisht*, the Genius of Fire; *Shahrevar*, the Lord of Splendor and Metals; *Spandar-Maz*, the Source of Fruitfulness; *Khordad*, the Genius of Water and Time; and *Amordad*, the protector of the Vegetable World and the prime cause of growth. Finally, he was taught the true nature of the Supreme Being, who was the Creator of Ahura Mazda (Ormuzd) and Angra Mainyu (Ahriman). This Absolute First Cause was called ZERUANE AKERENE and was part of the Zurvanism branch of Zoroastrianism.

There were several Degrees in Mithraic initiation. Tertullian details the first's name as the Soldier of Mithras. The ceremony presented the candidate a crown for his head, which was supported by a sword. It was placed near his head, and he was to refuses it saying, "Mithras is my crown." After this, he was a soldier of Mithras, and he had the right to call Initiates fellow-soldiers and companions-in-arms. From this we have the title *Companions* from the Royal Arch Degree of the American Rite.

Porphyry continues to explain that he then passed to the Degree of the Lion. The lion was the constellation Leo, home of the Sun, and symbol of Mithras on his monuments. Rome called these ceremonies Leontic or Heliac (*Coracia* or *Hiero-Coracia*) and was dedicated to the Raven. This bird was sacred
426 to the Sun and placed just below the Lion in the Heavens, along with the Hydra. It also appeared on Mithraic monuments.

He continued to pass to higher Degrees. There the Initiates were called *Perses* as children of the Sun. Above them were *Fathers*, who were the Patriarch of the group. The chief of the patriarchs was the Father of Fathers, or *Pater Patratus*. Initiates also had the titles of *Eagles* and *Hawks*, and both were birds sacred to the Sun within Egypt. There the eagle was sacred to the God Mendes while the hawk was an emblem of the Sun and Royalty.

The island of Samothrace was anciently a place for the Mysteries. Many people traveled there to be initiated. It is believed that the Pelasgians (original inhabitants) settled the island and had a dialect different from other Greeks though the ages. The Gods of these Mysteries were called CABEIRI, which may originate from the Semitic word *Cabar* (great). Varro called the Gods of Samothrace, *Potent Gods*. In Arabic, Venus is called *Cabar*. Varro said the Great Deities of those Mysteries were Heaven and Earth. These were the symbols of the Active and Passive Powers, or Principles, of universal generation. The Gemini Twins, Castor and Pollux, were worshipped on Samothrace. The remarks written by Apollonius, citing Mnaseas of Patrae, gave the names of Ceres, Proserpine, Pluto, and Mercury as the four Cabeiri of Samothrace. The Cabeiri were also known as Axieros, Axiocersa, Axiocersus, and Casmillus. Mercury was the messenger of the Gods. The young altar attendants and the children employed by the Temple were called Mercuries, or Casmilli. Similarly, the Etruscan in Tuscany and the Pelasgians who worshipped them there called them the Great Gods.

Tarquin the Etruscan King was an Initiate of the Mysteries of Samothrace. Etruria had its Cabeiri too as the worship of the Cabeiri spread from that island into Etruria, Phrygia, and Asia Minor. As Sanchuniathon mentions the Cabeiri and the word has Semitic origin, the worship must have originated in Phœnicia and spread to Samothrace.

The Twins, sometime referred to as Dioscuri, with Venus were patron Gods of Navigation and were invoked in the Mysteries of Samothrace. The constellation Auriga, or Phaeton, was honored there with grand ceremonies as
427 well. As told in the Argonaut expedition, Orpheus as an Initiate of these Mysteries, counseled his companions to anchor in Samothrace when a storm was rising. When they did so, the storm ceased and they all were initiated into the Mysteries there. After initiation, they continued their voyage with the assurance of good fortune as they were under the protection of the Dioscuri as patrons of sailors and navigation.

These Initiates were promised much more however. The Priests (Hierophants) of Samothrace consecrated man to the Deity. The Initiate was to lead a virtuous life and in return, he would be rewarded after death as right justice from the Gods. This pledge made the Mysteries revered by all men that inspired respect for its teachings and a desire for initiation. The Mysteries caused the island to be labeled and held *Sacred* by all nations. The Romans left its liberty and laws for the island though it ruled the whole area. It was a refuge and sanctuary for the unfortunate. On the island, men could be absolved of their crimes, even homicide, as long as it was not committed in a temple.

On Samothrace, young children were initiated. They were invested with the sacred robe, purple belt, crown of olive, and seated upon a throne just like other Initiates. The ceremonies told the death story of the youngest of the Cabeiri. The God was slain by his brothers. The brothers then fled into Etruria (around Tuscany, Italy) with an ark that held the God's genitals. In Etruria, the Phallus and ark were sacred objects. Herodotus said the Samothracian Initiates were taught in the Mysteries the origin and reason for revering the Phallus. Clement of Alexandria said the Cabeiri taught the Tuscans to revere it. It was considered sacred at the Syrian Heliopolis where the Mysteries resembled those of Attis and Cybele. The Pelasgians associated it with Mercury. It appears on the monuments of Mithras. Universally, it was a symbol of the life-giving power of the Sun at the Vernal Equinox.

In the Indian Mysteries, as the candidate made his three circuits, he would pause at the South each time and repeat, "I copy the Sun and follow his good and charitable example." Blue Masonry uses the Circuits, but it no longer has the explanation. It explained that the candidate represented the Sun in the Mysteries. First he descended Southward to the Evil Principle, Angra Mainyu *428* (Ahriman), Shiva, or Typhon as represented by darkness, winter, and death. Afterward, he would rise again and start to ascend Northward to light, summer, and life.

The death of Sita (wife of Vishnu) was lamented, as was the death of Kāma by Shiva where his ashes were thrown to the waves in a chest, like Osiris or Bacchus. Ghosts and noise terrified the candidate during these stories.

Then, the candidate personified Vishnu, his avatars (incarnations on Earth), and his labors. The first two taught the legend of the Deluge, but in the first, Vishnu is said to have taken three steps across the Universe creating the earth, air, and heavens. The candidate took these three steps at right angles to represent this. From this ritual, Masonry has extracted the three steps ending at right angles.

Nine avatars were completed, and the candidate had been taught that faith was superior to sacrifice, charity, or restraint. He was warned to avoid five crimes and obligated himself against committing them. He was shown an image of Paradise, with the Members of the Order magnificently displayed within it and the symbol of the Deity as a fire blazing on the Altar.

He was given a new name, dressed in a white robe and crown, and provided the signs, tokens, and lectures of the Mystery. His forehead was marked with a cross, and an inverted level (Tau Cross) was marked on his breast. He received the sacred cord and talismans and was told the sacred Word (Sublime Name) A. U. M., known only to the Initiates.

The candidate was taught the multitude of symbols and emblems, the secret science hidden under them, and the different virtues of the mythological figures. Through all this, he learned the meaning of those symbols that were unintelligible before initiation.

The third Degree meant a life of seclusion when the Initiate's dependents were able to provide for themselves. He lived in the wild, prayed, purified himself, and lived on vegetables only. He was said to be born again.

The fourth Degree was to abandon the material world through self-contemplation and self-torture. Perfection was attained in this manner so it could unify with the Deity.

429 In the second Degree, the Initiate was taught the Unity of the Godhead, the patriarchs, the Deluge, the evil in the heart, the need for a mediator, the instability of life, the final destruction of all created things, and the restoration of the world in a more perfect form. They were taught about the Soul's Immortality, its Eternity, the transmigration of the Soul, and future reward and punishment. They stressed that mere ceremonies and sacrifices could not atone for sins. Instead, man needed repentance, reformation, and voluntary punishment.

The Mysteries that developed among the Chinese and Japanese originated from India. They were founded on the same principles and had similar rites. The word given to the new Initiate was O-MI-TO-FO, in which we recognize the original name A.U.M. with Fo (Buddha) appended.

The equilateral triangle and the mystical **Y** were both symbols that alluded to the Triune God and the ineffable name of the Deity. The ring supported by two serpents was a symbol of the world being protected by the Creator's power and wisdom. In Masonry, two parallel lines (from the serpents) support the circle in our Lodge and show the Asian origin of this symbol.

Within Japanese Mysteries, the probationary period for their highest Degree was twenty years.

The Druidic Mysteries resembled the Asian Mysteries in its main features.

Their ceremonies began with a song to the sun. The candidates were ranked as *threes*, *fives*, or *sevens* as they were qualified and led nine times around the Sanctuary, between East and West. The candidate had many trials, and one was from the legend of Osiris. He was placed in a boat and cast out on the sea. He alone had to reach the opposite shore by using his skill and intelligence. The death of Hu was portrayed while he was in total darkness such that he could only hear the sorrow. He had many obstacles in which to prove his courage. He risked his life against armed enemies and had to represent many animals. When he finally attained the permanent light, he was taught by the Arch-Druid the Mysteries. The morality the Order taught tasked him to act bravely in war. He *430* was taught of the immortality of the soul and its future state. He was solemnly instructed to worship the Deity and instill rigid morality by avoiding sloth, contention, and folly.

He attained only exoteric knowledge by the first two Degrees. Only a few attained the esoteric knowledge of the third Degree. These were typically the powerful elites among the population. They spent nine months studying the arts and sciences from the Druids, in solitude, as part of their purification. This period represented death and burial within these Mysteries.

The dangerous voyage upon the actual sea while in a small boat on the evening of April 29th was the last trial of initiation. If he refused the trial, he was disgracefully dismissed. If he succeeded in his voyage, he was called thrice-born. He was eligible to receive all the dignities of State and thorough instruction in the philosophical and religious doctrines of the Druids.

The Greeks also styled the *Epoptes* (Εποπτης) initiates as thrice-born (Τριγονος). In India, perfection was in the Yogi who had been reincarnated many times.

Among the Norse the general features of initiation was like the other Mysteries. A long probation, fasting, shame, circular processions, and trials helped prepare the candidate to understand the symbolism of the ceremonies. These would include the procession of the heavenly bodies, the descent into the underworld, the killing of the God *Baldr* by the Evil Principle, *Loki*. Other similarities included Baldr's body being placed on a boat and sent upon the waters as a funeral pyre. The Norse Mysteries were the Eastern Legend with different names and slight variations.

The Egyptian Anubis reappeared as the guard dog at the gates of death. The candidate was enclosed in a symbolic tomb and when released went in search of the body of Baldr. When he finds the body, Baldr is restored to life and seated upon a throne. He was obligated upon a sword (as in the French *Rit Moderne*) and *sealed* his obligation by drinking *out of a human skull.*

Afterwards, all the primitive truths were taught to him that had survived through time. He was told of the origin of the Gods, the creation of the world, the deluge, and the resurrection represented by Baldr.

He was marked with the sign of a cross. A ring was given to him as a *431* symbol of Divine Protection and Perfection. From these rituals, we derive our custom of giving a ring in the 14th Degree.

He was taught that the Cube and the point within a Circle are emblems of Odin. He was also taught of the nature of the Supreme God, "the author of everything that exists, the Eternal, the Ancient, the Living and Awe inspiring Being, the Searcher for concealed things, the Being that never changes;" distinct and separate from Odin the Conqueror. The Triune God of the Hindus was altered represent ODIN AS the Almighty FATHER, FREA (*Rhea* or *Phre*) the mother (universal *matter*), and *Thor* his son (the Mediator). Here we recognize *Osiris, Isis,* and *Horus.* On the head of Thor, the twelve stars in a circle allude to his eastern origin.

He was taught of the destruction of this world, and the creation of a new one where the brave and virtuous would enjoy happiness and delight forever. He could achieve this eternal good fortune through the practice morality and virtue.

The Initiates were prepared for the lessons in all Mysteries by trial, abstinence, and chastity. For days, he would fast and drink liquids meant to diminish his passions and keep him chaste.

Purification by water was required as a symbol of the soul's purity, needed to escape from its bondage to matter. Sacred baths, baptisms, ceremonial immersions, sprinklings, and other ceremonies were used. In Athens, they bathed in the sacred Ilissos River. Before entering the Temple of Eleusis, they had to wash their hands in a vase of ceremonial water at the entrance. Clean hands and a pure heart were required of the candidates. Cleanliness was truly next to Godliness! Apuleius bathed in the sea seven times to symbolize the Seven Spheres through which the Soul must ascend. The Hindus continue to bath in the sacred river Ganges to purify their souls for its journey to heaven.

Clement of Alexandria cites a passage of the Greek Menander, who speaks of purification by being sprinkled three times with salt and water. Sulphur, resin, and the laurel also served to purify. In general, purification could be accomplished by the use of air, earth, water, or fire. Lucian said the Initiates at Heliopolis in Syria sacrificed a sacred lamb (symbol of Aries) when it was the 432 Zodiac sign associated with the Vernal Equinox. They ate the lamb (Passover) and would touch its head and feet to their own, and knelt upon its fleece. They would bath in warm water, drink the water, and sleep upon the ground.

There were differences between the lesser and greater Mysteries. First, one had to be admitted in the lesser before he could receive the greater. The lesser Mysteries were really a preparation for the greater. The lesser were of the Vestibule (antechamber) of the Temple while the greater of Eleusis, were in the Sanctuary. In the lesser Mysteries, initiates were prepared to receive the holy truths taught in the greater. The Initiates of the lesser were called *Mystes,* or Initiates. Those of the greater were called, *Epoptes,* or Seers. An ancient poet said Mystes were an imperfect shadow of the Epoptes, as sleep is to Death. After admission to the lesser, the Initiate was taught lessons of morality and parts of the symbolism of the sacred science as seeing the truth through a veil. The most sublime and secret part of the sacred science in full explanation was reserved for the Epopt who saw the naked Truth.

In the very beginning, the priests required the candidate to take a fear inspiring oath to never to divulge the secrets before the first secret or principle was shared. Then, he made his vows, prayers, and sacrifices to the Gods. The skins of the sacrificial victims to Jupiter were spread around the ground, and the candidate walked over them. He was taught some mysterious questions and answers by which he could make himself known to other initiates. He was placed on a throne, dressed with the purple belt (cincture), and crowned with wreaths of flowers, palm, or olive.

We are not certain of the time between the lesser and greater Mysteries of Eleusis., but most said it was five years. It was a unique occasion when Demetrius was made Mystes and Epopt in one ceremony. When admitted to the Degree of Perfection, the Initiate was taught of nature's entirety, the soul comprised the whole of man, its exile was on Earth, Heaven was its native country, and birth is the soul's death and death is a rebirth. When he was allowed entrance to the sanctuary he did not receive the whole instruction at once, but it continued over several years. There were many parts to advance through, all covered and hidden by thick veils from his eyes. Proclus said, there were Statues and Paintings in the inmost sanctuary displaying the forms used by the Gods. Finally, when the last veil was removed the sacred image of the Goddess was seen in all her splendor. Brilliant, divine light surrounded Her and filled the whole sanctuary, dazzled the eyes, and penetrated the soul of the Initiate. Symbolically, this is how the final revelation of the nature of Deity, the soul, and the relationship of each to matter was shared.

Vivid scenes were portrayed meant to alternate the Initiate's emotions between fear and joy, light and darkness. They used lightning and thunder, ghosts and specters, and magical illusions to astonish their eyes and ears. The Poet Claudian described the abduction of Proserpine and alluded to events in her Mysteries. He wrote, "The temple is shaken. Fiercely the lightning streaks and the Deity announces his presence. Earth trembles. A terrible noise is heard in among these terrors. The Temple of the Son of King Cecrops resounds with continuous roars. Eleusis lifts her sacred torches up. The serpents of Triptolemus hiss, and a fearful Hecate appears in the distance."

The celebration of the Greek Mysteries continued for nine days.

On the first, the Initiates gathered. This was the day of the full moon in the month Boedromion. This was counted when the moon was full at the end of Aries, close to the Pleiades and her place of exaltation in Taurus.

The second day they held a procession to the sea to bath and purify.

The third was full of offerings, atoning sacrifices, and religious rites of fasting, mourning, continence, etc. A fish was sacrificed with offerings of grain and other living animals.

On the fourth, they carried the mystic wreath of flowers in their procession to represent what Proserpine dropped when abducted by Pluto, and the Crown of Ariadne (wife of Dionysus) in the Heavens. It was carried on a wagon drawn by oxen. Women followed bearing mystic chests wrapped in purple, containing grains of sesame, biscuits, salt, pomegranates, the mysterious serpent, and the mystic phallus.

433

The fifth day held the procession of torches to remember the search for Proserpine by Ceres. The Initiates marched in threes with each holding a torch. The procession was lead by the Dadoukos.

The sixth day was for, as consecrated to Iacchus, an aspect of the Light-God (Dionysus) who was the son of Ceres (Demeter) reared in the sanctuaries. He held the torch of the Sun-God. The chorus in Aristophanes *Frogs* terms him the star that lighted the darkness of initiation. He was brought forth from the sanctuary with his head crowned with myrtle. He was carried from the gate of the Kerameikos cemetery on the Sacred Way to Eleusis with joyous and sacred dancing and singing with the mystic cries of *Iacchus*.

On the seventh, there were gymnastic exercises and bouts where victors were crowned and rewarded.

On the eighth was the feast of Aesculapius.

On the ninth day, the famous libation kykeon was drunk to commemorate the souls of the departed. According to Athenaeus, the Priests filled two vases and put one in the East and the other in the West. These faced the gates of day and night where they were overturned while chanting mysterious prayers. This is how they called upon the two great principles of nature, Light and Darkness.

During the days of the festival, no arrests or lawsuits could be made. No one was allowed to display great wealth or office in their dress, as the rites were far more sacred and should not be outshone. Everything was done for the Mysteries and religion.

These were the Mysteries and Old Thoughts. It has come to us in scattered fragments through history. To this day, the human mind contemplates the mysteries of nature. It finds the answers to these questions and concepts well formulated by the ancients. This can be seen in their wise symbols even more than in their written philosophies. The written word tries in vain to express the great ideas seen in the great circle of Birth, Life, Death, and Rebirth, which was the greatest mystery. Remember, as you study these symbols that they had a better sense of the depth of these wonders than we do. To them life was a greater mystery than the stars, and held even the beetle as sacred. Their faith was condensed into symbols and expanded into allegories to be understood through contemplation, as they could not be completely explained by words. There are thoughts and ideas that no language of man has words to express.

CHAPTER 25: KNIGHT OF THE BRAZEN SERPENT

THIS Degree is both philosophical and moral. It teaches the necessity of reformation and repentance as a means of obtaining mercy and forgiveness, but it is also devoted to an explanation of the symbols of Masonry. It pays close attention to those symbols that are connected to the ancient and universal legend representing a murder (or death) and the restoration to life, of which Khir-Om Abi (Hiram Abiff) is but one variation. Other variations of this legend include Osiris, Isis and Horus, Attis and Cybele, Adonis and Venus, the Cabiri, Dionysus, and many other representatives of the active and passive Powers of Nature. This legend taught the Initiates of the Mysteries that the influence of Evil and Darkness is only temporary, but Light and Good are eternal. 435

Maimonides said, "Seth's son Enos and several others committed grievous errors in pursuit of their ambition. They reasoned since they were God's ministers, it was His will that they should receive the same admiration and respect from the masses as the Court of a great King. Impressed by their own image of themselves, they built temples to the Stars, sacrificed to them, and worshipped them in the vain expectation this pleased the Creator of all things. In the beginning, they worshipped both the Stars and the Omnipotent Lord God. However, that great and venerable Name was forgotten as time went on, and their religion became nothing more than the idolatrous worship of the constellations." 436

The first learning in the world was done primarily with symbols. The wisdom of the Chaldæans, Phœnicians, Egyptians, Jews, Zoroaster, Sanchoniathon, Pherecydes, Syrus, Pythagoras, Socrates, Plato, and all of the ancients who we have knowledge of today was symbolic. Serranus said of Plato's Symposium, "it was the method of the Ancient Philosophers to represent truth with certain symbols and hidden images."

Strabo said, "All that can be said concerning the Gods is described by the old parables and fables. It was customary for them to communicate their thoughts and beliefs concerning Nature in enigma and allegory, and accordingly, it was not easily explained."

As explained in the 24th Degree, the ancient Philosophers believed the soul of man originated in Heaven, and Macrobius confirms this was a settled opinion among all of them. They believed the only true wisdom was that the soul originated in Heaven, and while united with the body, it always looked toward its source and strived to return to the place whence it came. It had dwelled among the fixed stars until finally being seduced by the desire of a physical body, and it descended to be imprisoned in matter. Once imprisoned, it only had the recollection of and attraction to its birthplace, and to return there, it must work and suffer in the body.

The Mysteries taught the great doctrine of the divine nature of the soul, its desire for immortality, the nobility of its origin, and the grandeur of its destiny. Although they struggled to express its *nature* by comparing it to Fire and 437 Light, they erred in its original source and mistook the mode and path it pursued while ascending to and descending from the stars and spheres. These allegories were the accessories of the Great Truth, designed to make the idea more impressive and accessible to the human mind.

We will follow the soul's descent in order to understand this old concept. The souls began and ended their journey in the sphere or Heaven of the fixed stars, that Holy Region or Elysium Fields that were their native home. All souls were permitted to remain in Heaven as long as they avoided any contact with matter or contamination from the body, but those souls who longingly looked toward the body and what we call *life* were victims of their own weaknesses. They are attracted by degrees to the inferior regions of the Universe. To a soul, this is the real *death,* and they conceived this secret terrestrial desire from the weight of thought. The journey towards a body required the soul to undergo three degradations (deaths) until it had passed through the several spheres and elements. The perfectly celestial soul slowly imprisons itself within the enclosure of the body by subtle and successive alterations in proportion to the distance it has moved away from its simple and perfect home. It first surrounds itself with a body made of the elements of the stars. Next, it descends through the several spheres and planets, gaining more and more dense matter. Thus, by degrees, it slowly descends into an earthly body with its number of degradations (or deaths) being equal to the number of spheres through which it traversed.

Macrobius said the Galaxy crossed the Zodiac at the two opposite tropical points in the sun's course, Cancer and Capricorn. These two points are called the Gates of the Sun. Before his time, these two tropics corresponded to those constellations, but in his day (~400 A.D,), they corresponded to Gemini and Sagittarius, due to the precession of the equinoxes. The *signs* of the Zodiac remained unchanged, and the Milky Way crossed at the *signs* Cancer and Capricorn, but they did not coincide with those *constellations.*

438 Souls descended to earth and re-ascended to Heaven through these *gates.* Macrobius said in his dream of Scipio, Cancer was the Gate of Man where souls descended to Earth, and Capricorn was the Gate of the Gods where souls re-ascended to become Gods at their seats of immortality. According to Pythagoras, the Milky Way diverted the souls' route into Pluto's region where

they were unable to begin their descent toward the terrestrial bodies until they left the Galaxy. Until they reached the sign Cancer, they had not left the Galaxy and were still considered Gods. Once they reached Leo, they began their apprenticeship for their future condition, and when they came to Aquarius (the sign opposite Leo) they were the farthest removed from human life.

Descending from the celestial limits where the Zodiac and Galaxy unite, the soul loses its Divine spherical shape as a point is lengthened into a line to form a cone. Then the indivisible soul (monad) suffers division, disturbance, and conflict as it divides itself into a pair (duad). It experiences the disorder inherent in matter as it unites itself with and becomes intoxicated from the flow of carnal matter. This event is symbolized by the cup of Bacchus or the cup of forgetfulness located between Cancer and Leo. Plato described it as the fields of oblivion, and souls gathered there to drink from the river Ameles, which caused them to forget everything. This account is also found in Virgil. Macrobius said, "If souls carried into their bodies all the divine knowledge they had acquired during their journey through the Heavens, people would not differ in their opinions about the Deity. So some souls forget more, and some of them forget less."

We must learn to look all the way through these images and allegories to the ideas struggling for expression and the great thoughts they enshroud, because even today we do not have a *better* way of representing the soul's origin and its manifestation into this body.

The highest and purest form of matter nourishes and constitutes divine existences. The poets term it *nectar* or the beverage of the Gods. The lower, more irregular, and carnal form of matter intoxicates the souls. The ancients symbolized it with the River Lethe, the dark stream of oblivion. Today, we shy away from any attempt to explain the soul's forgetfulness of its heritage or reconcile the lack of any memory of its former condition and essential immortality.

The soul is dragged down along the zodiac and through the Milky Way by the heaviness produced by this inebriating flow. During its descent through the lower spheres and planets, it adds a new coating of material from each luminous body, contributing to the different faculties it will need while it inhabits the body.

The soul acquires the power of reasoning and intelligence, or the logical and contemplative faculty, from Saturn. It receives the power of action from Jupiter. Mars gives it valor, self-reliance, and passion. The Sun contributes the senses and imagination, which produce sensation, perception, and thought. Venus inspires it with desires. Mercury provides the faculty of expression and enunciation for what it thinks and feels. Finally, the Moon bestows the force of generation and growth. The Moon is the last and lowest of the divine bodies, but it is first and highest to the terrestrial bodies. Although the lunar body assumed by the soul is the sediment of celestial matter, it is also the first

325

substance of animal matter. The Moon is the intersection between the celestial and terrestrial worlds.

The celestial spirits always aspire to rise, but as the soul descends towards its mortal body, it is deemed to die. Macrobius said do not be worried about the *death* of this soul we call immortal because it is neither annulled nor destroyed by this death, but rather it is impaired while on earth. It does not forfeit its right to immortality, because, after it is freed from the body and purified of the stains of vice contracted during its mortal existence, it is restored with all its privileges to the luminous residence of its immortality.

As the soul re-ascends, it returns to each sphere the vices and passions of the earthly faculties that it originally received from them. The Moon is returned the increase or decrease of the body. Mercury receives fraud, the architect of evils. Venus gets the seductive love of pleasure. The Sun is returned the passion for greatness and empire. Mars receives recklessness and overconfidence. Jupiter gets greed, and Saturn gets falsehood and deceit. Once the soul is at last relieved of all earthly vices and corruption, it enters into the eighth sphere, or highest Heaven, naked and pure.

This explanation is consistent with the doctrine of Plato, which says the soul cannot reenter Heaven until the revolutions of the Universe have restored it to its original condition and purified it from the effects of its contact with the four elements.

The preexistence of souls is a belief of great antiquity. Rabbi Manasseh ben Israel said this was always the belief of the Hebrews. Lactanius said the immortality of the soul was taught in the Mysteries, because most philosophers concluded that for the soul to exist *after* the body, it had to exist *before* it. Therefore, it was independent of the body. The same doctrine was adopted by most of the learned Greek Fathers and many of the Romans, and it would prevail today if people spent any time thinking about whether the soul's immortality included a prior existence.

Some philosophers believed the soul was imprisoned in the body as punishment for the sins it committed in a prior life. They concluded this by the soul's unawareness of any such prior life or sins committed there. Others believed that God commanded the soul to inhabit the body. The Kabbalists united these two opinions with four worlds in order of perfection, *Atziluth*, *Briah*, *Yetzirah*, and *Assiah* meaning the *emanation, creation, formation*, and *material* worlds. Each world was closer to perfection than the one that followed in both their own nature and the nature of the beings that inhabited them. All souls are pure and immortal spirits when they originate in the world Atziluth, the Supreme Heaven and House of God. Those who descend from it by God's order, and not by their own fault, are given a divine fire that preserves them from the contamination of matter and restores them to Heaven as soon as their mission is ended. Those whose descent is their fault are dragged down by their own weight from world to world, unconsciously losing their love of Divine things and self-contemplation until they reach the world Assiah. This concept is pure Platonism engaged in the images and words unique to the Kabbalists. Porphyry said the doctrine of the Essenes "believed that souls descended from the most subtle ether, attracted to bodies by the seductions of matter." Technically, it was the doctrine of Origen who studied the theory of the Heavens, the spheres, and the influences of the signs and constellations as taught by the Chaldæans.

The Gnostics believed souls ascended and descended through eight Heavens. During the ascent through each Heaven, there were certain Powers who opposed their return and often drove them back to earth if they were not sufficiently purified. Closest to the luminous residence of souls was the last of these Powers, a serpent or dragon.

In the ancient doctrine, certain angels (Genii) had the duty of conducting souls to the bodies prepared to receive them and retrieving them when their mortal existence was complete. Plutarch said this was the responsibility of Proserpine and Mercury. According to Plato, a familiar guardian angel (Genius) accompanies a person at their birth, follows and watches over them during their life, and at death conducts them to the tribunal of the Great Judge. These angels are the mode of communication between man and the Gods, and the soul is always in their presence. This doctrine was taught in the oracles of Zoroaster, and these angels were the Intelligences that resided in the planets.

Anciently, the secret science and mysterious emblems of initiation were connected to the Heavens, Spheres, and Constellations. This connection must be studied to understand the allegories and explore the meanings, ideas, and symbols that the ancient sages struggled to articulate but could not sufficiently and adequately explain, because words can only grasp what our senses have the capacity to define.

It is difficult for us to thoroughly appreciate the reverence the ancients had for the Heavenly bodies and the observations that gave rise to their ideas. We cannot put ourselves in their places and view the stars from their context, because our common knowledge regards the Stars, Planets, and Universes as *442* mere inanimate machines and collections of orbs that are no more amazing than a clock or a planetarium. Like the Ancients, *we are* astonished at the Power and Wisdom of the MAKER and his creations (a kind of Infinite *Ingenuity*), but the ancients also wondered *at* the *Work* endowing *it* with Life, Force, mysterious Powers, and mighty Influences.

The Nile River flows north through Ethiopia and into Egypt. Its floods have created the alluvial land of Upper and Lower Egypt, and they continue to shape and fertilize it with their sediment. These annual floods were originally devastating calamities until levees, drains, and artificial lakes were constructed for irrigation. Then the floods became blessings, and they were awaited with joyful anticipation rather than fear and terror. Once the Sacred River withdrew into its banks, the farmers sowed their seeds upon the rich new soil which the beneficent sun assured would produce an abundant harvest.

Likewise, Babylon was located on the Euphrates River. It flows from the Northwest to the Southeast, and like all rivers in the arid Orient, it blesses the countryside through which it flows. However, its rapid and uncertain floods also brought fear, terror, and disaster.

Without astronomical instruments, the ancients looked at the Heavens with the eyes of children. They had no idea that the earth was actually a globe and not just a vast plain of unknown extent with speculative boundaries. The differences in its surface were judged to be the irregularities of a plane, and they did not know if anything lived underneath its surface or what supported it. Every twenty-four hours, the sun arose from beyond the Eastern rim of the world, and it traveled over the earth and across the sky. It was always positioned south of the point overhead, sometimes closer, and sometimes further away. In 443 the evening it sank below the world's Western rim and darkness followed.

Every twenty-four hours, the Moon appeared in the Heavens. It was primarily visible at night but sometimes visible during the day. It also traveled across the sky, sometimes as a thin crescent or gradually increasing to a full globe, resplendent with silver light. It was also positioned south of the point overhead, sometimes closer and sometimes farther away but always within the same limits as the Sun.

Surrounded by the absolute darkness of night when everything has disappeared, man seems alone in an existence of nothingness under the black curtains that confine him. His memory recalls the glories and splendors of light, but everything is as dead to him as he is to Nature. How distressing and overwhelming was the thought, fear, and dread that the darkness *may be* eternal and that the light of day may never return while the solid gloom closes against him like a wall! What can restore him to life, energy, activity, fellowship, and communion with the great world which God has built around him? LIGHT restores him. Primitive man regarded light as the source of their real existence, and without it life would be but one constant gloomy despair. Everyone felt this need for light and its creative energy, and nothing was more alarming to them than its absence. LIGHT became their first Deity, and its single ray flashing into the dark tumultuous bosom of chaos caused man and all of the Universe to emerge from it. This was the first dogma of Orpheus, Moses, and the Theologians. Light became Ormuzd who was adored by the Persians, and Darkness became Ahriman who was the origin of all evils. Light was the life of the Universe, the friend of man, and the substance of the Gods and the Soul.

To the ancients, the sky was a great, solid, concaved arch or hemisphere of unknown material at an unknown distance above the flat, level earth where the Sun, Moon, Planets, and Stars journeyed in their chosen courses.

444 The Sun was the great globe of fire with unknown dimensions, at an unknown distance. The Moon was a mass of softer light, and the stars and planets were luminescent bodies armed with unknown but supernatural powers.

The ancients soon observed that at regular intervals, the days and nights were equal in length, and two of these intervals measured the same space of time as had elapsed between the successive floods, and also between the returns of springtime and harvest. They also recognized that the changes of the moon occurred regularly. The same number of days always elapsed between the first appearance of her silver crescent in the Western evening sky, her full globe rising in the Eastern evening sky at the same hour, and the next appearance of her silver crescent in the Western evening sky.

The ancients also observed that the Sun crossed the sky on a different line each day. The days were longest and the nights were shortest when the line of the Sun's path was furthest North. Likewise, the days were shortest and the nights were longest when that line was furthest South. The Sun's progress North and South was perfectly regular and divided into four equal seasons. The days and nights were equal at the Vernal and Autumnal Equinoxes, and the days were longest at the Summer Solstice and shortest at the Winter Solstice.

The ancients discovered that the Vernal Equinox (on or about the 21st of March) brought with it soft winds and the return of warmth caused by the Sun's Northward movement from the middle of its course. The Bull (Taurus) and the Ram (Aries) were valuable animals to the farmers and symbols. This is when these animals recovered their strong, generative power and vigor. The birds mated and built their nests, the seeds germinated, the grass grew, the trees put forth leaves, the vegetation of the new year sprang forth, and the impulse of amatory action overcame that part of the animal creation. At the Summer Solstice, the Sun reached the northern limit of its course and brought great heat, burning winds, weakness, and exhaustion. The vegetation withered, the Lion sought comfort far from his desert home, and man longed for the cool breezes of Spring and Autumn and the cool water of the Nile or Euphrates.

The Autumnal Equinox brought the harvests, falling leaves, and the cold evenings foretelling the coming wintry frosts. The Principle and Powers of Darkness began to prevail over those of Light, driving the Sun further into the ₄₄₅ South until the nights were longer than the days. The Winter Solstice was sprinkled with frost, the trees were leafless, and the Sun reached the most Southern path in its course. It hesitated to consider whether to continue south and leave the world to darkness and despair or to retrace its steps north again, bringing back springtime, green leaves, flowers, and all the delights of love.

Time naturally became divided into days, moons or months, and then years. These divisions and the corresponding movements of the Heavenly bodies became associated with and connected to all man's physical enjoyments and hardships. The primitive people of the Orient were keenly interested in the regularity of the phenomena performed by the two great luminaries of Heaven. Their crops, homes, and prosperity were at the mercy of the elements, changing seasons, and their predictive regularity.

The attentive observer soon noticed that some of the stars were even more regular than the Sun and Moon. Their risings and settings foretold with absolute certainty the periods and recurrence of the different phenomena and seasons on which the physical well-being of all man depended. They began to distinguish the individual stars, or groups of stars, and gave them names and designations that were both natural and imagined. It was observed that in the course of a year, the seasonal cycles coincided with the courses of the Sun, the rising and setting of certain Stars, and their position relative to the Sun and the Northern star. The conclusion was that the celestial and terrestrial objects were *in fact* connected, and they accordingly named particular Stars or groups of Stars according to the terrestrial events that seemed connected to them. Those that did not fit this naming convention were given arbitrary and fanciful names.

446   The Ethiopians of Thebes or Saba named the Stars that signaled the flooding of the Nile the Stars of Inundation, or *poured out water* (AQUARIUS).

The Stars of the Summer Solstice were named for the Crab (CANCER). The Sun could be found in this constellation once it had reached the Northern Tropic and began to *retreat* southward in a retrograde motion.

The Stars of the Autumnal Equinox were named the Stars of the Balance (LIBRA). Here the Sun had reached the middle point between the Northern and Southern extremes of its course, and the days and nights were equal.

The Sun could be found in the Stars of the Lion (LEO) during the heat of summer when the Lion's thirst drove it from the Desert to drink from the Nile.

During the harvest, the Sun could be found in the Stars named the Gleaning Virgin (VIRGO), who held a Sheaf of Wheat.

During February, the Sun could be found in the Stars of the Lamb (ARIES) when the Ewes delivered their young.

The stars that indicated it was time to plough in March were called the Stars of the Ox (TAURUS).

The stars that watched the hot, burning winds come from the desert like venomous and poisonous reptiles were called the Stars of the Scorpion (SCORPIO).

The annual flooding of the Nile was always accompanied by a beautiful Star that appeared in the direction of the source of that river, and it seemed to warn the farmers of the coming floods. The Ethiopians named it the Dog Star (SIRIUS) because they compared its arrival to a barking dog warning of danger.

The study of Astronomy was expanded, and the Stars were grouped by tracing imaginary figures over the Heavens. The most important stars were those that lay along the path the Sun traveled as it climbed Northward or descended Southward. This path extended an equal distance on each side of the Equinox (when days and nights were of equal length), forming a belt that curved like a Serpent and was divided into twelve Signs termed the Zodiac.

The Vernal Equinox of 584 B.C. saw the Sun entering the sign and constellation Taurus (the Bull), after having passed through the Signs Aquarius, Pisces, and Aries since beginning its northern ascent.

After TAURUS, the Sun passed through Gemini and Cancer, before *447* reaching LEO, where it ended its journey northward. The Sun proceeded through Leo, Virgo, and Libra and entered SCORPIO at the Autumnal Equinox. Then it continued south through Scorpio, Sagittarius, Capricorn, and finally AQUARIUS, where its journey south ended.

The path of the Sun through these signs was named the *Ecliptic*, and where it passed through the two equinoxes was named the *Equator*.

The ancients knew nothing about the immutable laws of nature. When the Sun journeyed southward, they always feared it might not stop, leaving the earth to be ruled forever by darkness, storm, and cold.

They rejoiced when the Sun began to return north after the Winter Solstice, struggling against the hostile forces of Aquarius and Pisces to be amicably received by the Lamb, Aries. They rejoiced even more when it entered Taurus at the Vernal Equinox and assured the days would again be longer than the nights. This event announced that the planting season had come.

They complained after the Autumnal Equinox, when the venomous Scorpio, the vindictive Archer (Sagittarius), and the ill-omened Sea-Goat (Capricorn) dragged the Sun down to the Winter Solstice.

The ancients portrayed the Winter Solstice as the slaying of the Sun. It passed into darkness for three days, after which it arose and began its journey northward again. The Sun redeemed the earth from the gloom and darkness of winter, which eventually became emblematical of sin, evil, and suffering, just as spring, summer, and autumn became emblems of happiness and immortality.

They personified the Sun under the name of OSIRIS and worshipped him by adapting the Sun's descent through the Winter Signs into a fable of his death, his journey into the underworld, and finally his resurrection.

The Moon was personified as Isis, the wife of Osiris. TYPHON, the Spirit or Principle of Evil who fought against and destroyed Osiris, became both winter and the desert or the ocean into which the Sun set each night.

The Sun's journey through the twelve signs became the legend of the *448* twelve labors of Hercules and the incarnations of Vishnu and Buddha. It also became the legend of Khūrūm's murder (Hiram, the Sun's representative) by the three Fellowcrafts (the three Winter signs: Capricorn, Aquarius, and Pisces) who assaulted him at the three gates of Heaven and killed him at the Winter Solstice. The search by the nine Fellowcrafts (the nine other signs) symbolized his discovery, burial, and resurrection.

The celestial Taurus was the sacred Creative Bull of the Hindus, who opened the new year by using his horn to break the egg from which the world was born. The bull APIS was worshipped by the Egyptians, and Aaron reproduced it as a golden calf in the desert. The palaces at Koyunjik and

Nimroud were adorned with the sacred and beneficent signs of Taurus and Leo, the human-headed winged lions and bulls, as was the Cherubim set by Solomon in his Temple and the twelve brazen (or bronze) oxen.

The Celestial Eagle was often substituted for Scorpio (because of Scorpio's negative influences), and the four great periods of the year became marked by the Bull, Lion, Man (Aquarius), and the Eagle. They were also upon the respective standards of Ephraim, Judah, Reuben, and Dan, and they still appear on the shield of American Royal Arch Masonry.

The Ram or Lamb (Aries) became an object of adoration because he opened the equinox and delivered the world from the wintry reign of darkness and evil.

A multitude of circumstantial details soon surrounded the simple idea of the annual death and resurrection of the Sun. Some details were derived from other astronomical phenomena, while many others were merely poetical ornaments or outright inventions.

In addition to the Sun and Moon, the ancients saw Venus as a beautiful shining Star with a soft, silvery light. They noticed that it always closely followed the Sun when it set and preceded it when it rose. Mars was an angry, red colored star that attracted their attention with its free movements among the fixed hosts of Heaven. Lastly, Jupiter was a kingly star that had an unusual brilliancy and regularly rose and set. Mercury and Saturn would not be noticed until astronomy began to be studied as a science.

449

The astronomical priests arranged the zodiac and constellations into a circle. The winter quadrant was adverse, opposed, and contrary to summer. The enlightened, intelligent, creative, and beneficent king OSIRIS (or ORMUZD) ruled over the angels of summer. The demons or Devs from the underworld of darkness and sorrow ruled over the fallen angels or evil spirits of winter. In Egypt, Scorpio was the first ruler of the winter signs, then the Polar Bear or Ass. The Ass was called Typhon (meaning *deluge*) due to the heavy rains while that constellation reigned. Later, the Persians personified the serpent as Ahriman, the Evil Principle in the religion of Zoroaster.

Every year, the Sun arrives on the Equinoctial point of the equator later than the previous year. Astronomy gives us the explanation of this effect, but the annual amount of precession is a little over 0 degrees, 0 minutes, and 50 seconds. This precession amounts to 30° or roughly one zodiacal sign every 2155.6 years, with a complete Revolution of the Equinoxes occurring every 25,856 years. As the sun now enters Pisces at the Vernal Equinox, it entered Aries in 300 B.C. and Taurus in 2100 B.C. The division of the Ecliptic now *called* Taurus lies in the Constellation Aries, while the *sign* Gemini is in the *Constellation* Taurus. Four thousand six hundred and ten years before Christ, the sun entered Gemini at the Vernal Equinox.

At 2100 B.C., 300 B.C., and today, the entrances of the sun at the Equinoxes and Solstices into the signs, were and are as follows:

2100 B.C.

Vern. Equinox, sun entered	**Taurus**...	from Aries.
Summer Solstice	Leo	from Cancer.
Autumnal Equinox	Scorpio	from Libra.
Winter Solstice	Aquarius	from Capricornus.

300 B.C.

Vern. Eq.	**Aries**	from Pisces.
Summer Sols.	Cancer	from Gemini.
Autumn Eq.	Libra	from Virgo.
Winter Sols.	Capricorn	from Sagittarius.

2007

Vern. Eq.	**Pisces**	from Aquarius.
Sum. Sols.	Gemini	from Taurus.
Aut. Eq.	Virgo	from Leo.
Winter Sols.	Sagittarius	from Scorpio.

450

The worship of the sun and stars began by confusing *signs* with *causes*, but what do we really know of *cause* and *effect* except that one regularly or habitually *follows* another?

Because Sirius's rising *preceded* the rising of the Nile, it was deemed to *cause* it, and in like manners, other stars were believed to *cause* extreme heat, bitter cold, and violent storms.

Anciently, a religious reverence for the zodiacal Bull (TAURUS) appears to have been universal throughout Eurasia and stretched from the Caucasus to the South Indian Peninsula, into Europe, and across East Africa.

This ancient practice probably originated when the path of the vernal equinox passed across the stars in the head of the sign Taurus (among which was Aldebarán). This period corresponds to the time when the arts and writing historically emerged for the first time.

451

The Arabian word AL-DE-BARÁN means the *foremost* or *leading* star, and its name implies that it *did* precede (or *lead*) all others. That year opened with the sun and moon in Taurus. There are a multitude of ancient Assyrian and Egyptian sculptures of a bull with moon-like or crescent horns and a sun disk between them. These sculptures are direct allusions to the important festival of the first new moon of the year. That year, the annual celebration of the festival of the first new moon opened with the Sun and Moon in Taurus.

The Psalmist sang, "At the time appointed, blow the trumpet for *the New Moon* on our solemn day of feast. This is a statute for Israel and a law of the God of Jacob. He ordained this to Joseph as testimony when he came out of the land of Egypt."

The reverence paid to Taurus continued long after the precession of the Equinoxes caused the vernal equinox to pass through Aries. The Chinese still have a temple called "The Palace of the horned Bull", and this symbol is also worshipped in Japan and India. The Cimbrians (German tribe) carried a brazen bull as the image of their God when they overran Gaul and Spain. They represented the Creation with the image of a bull, breaking the shell of an egg with its horns, that signified Taurus opening the new year by bursting the symbolic shell of the annually recurring orb.

Theophilus said that Osiris of Egypt was supposed to be dead or absent fifty days of each year. Landseer thinks the Sabean priests in the lower latitudes of Egypt and Ethiopia were accustomed to seeing the first or chief stars of the Farmer [BOÖTES] sink beneath the Western horizon. They began their mourning or instructed others to mourn, and once his prolific virtues were transferred to the vernal sun, bacchanalian revelry began.

The Pleiades were the leading stars of the Sabean year for seven or eight centuries before the precession of the Vernal Equinox passed into Aries but after it had passed from Aldebarán and the Hyades. Thus, we see on monuments the combined symbols of the sun and moon appearing successively, first on the head, then the neck, and then the back of the Zodiacal Bull, and more recently on the forehead of the Ram.

The crescent and disk symbol (♉) is still used to denote Taurus. This symbol originated in the remote ages when this conjunction in Taurus remarkably distinguished both the beginning of the Sabean year and the cycle of the Chaldæan Saros. A bronze Chinese statue depicts the crescent placed on the *back* of the Bull by means of a cloud, and a curved groove provided for the occasional introduction of the sun's disk, when the beginning of a solar year coincided with the beginning of a lunar cycle. This bronze bull was made in a year when the vernal equinox passed across the middle or later degrees of the constellation Taurus, and the Pleiades were, in China as in Canaan, the leading stars of the year.

The combined crescent and disk always represents the aligned Sun and Moon. When it was placed on the head of the Zodiacal Bull, the cycle was termed SAROS by the Chaldæans, Metonic by the Greeks, and alluded to in Job with the phrase, "Mazzaroth in his season." This cycle only happened once every eighteen years.

This symbol appeared on the head of a Ram on Alexander's sarcophagus, because the Ram was the leading sign during his time. In the sculptured temples of the Upper Nile, the crescent and disk also appeared on the forehead of the Ram or the Ram-headed God, which the Grecian Mythologists called Jupiter Ammon or the Sun in Aries.

By analyzing the stars that composed or were near these respective constellations, we may discover a clue to the symbols of the Ancient Mysteries and of Masonry.

When the Sun is *in* a particular constellation, the edge of that constellation will only be visible just before sunrise and just after sunset, but the constellations *opposite* it *will be* visible. For example, when the Sun is in Taurus (Taurus *sets with* the Sun) Scorpio rises and is visible throughout the night. *453* However, if Taurus rises and sets with the Sun today, then in six months it will rise at sunset and set at sunrise, because the stars gain two hours a month on the Sun.

During the time of the Chaldæan shepherds and the Ethiopian and Egyptian farmers:

> "The milk-white Bull with golden horns,
> Led the newborn year."

This means that the Pleiades were in the neck of TAURUS, the Hyades in its face, and Aldebarán was the brilliant chief. Orion is the splendid constellation to the southwest, with Betelgeuse in his right shoulder, Bellatrix in his left shoulder, Rigel on the left foot, and in his belt are the three stars known as the Three Kings. According to the legend, Orion persecuted the Pleiades, and Jupiter saved them from his fury by placing them in the Heavens. Orion still pursues them, but in vain. The Pleiades, Arcturus, and the Bands of Orion are also mentioned in the Book of Job. They are usually called the Seven Stars although only six are visible, but it is believed there *were* seven before the fall of Troy.

Pleiades is the Greek word *to sail*, and they have been observed for signs and seasons in all ages. Virgil said the sailors gave names to "the Pleiades, Hyades, and the Northern Car: *Pleiadas, Hyadas, Claramque Lycaonis Arcton.*" He added that Palinurus studied Arcturus, Hyades, the Twin Triones, and Orion surrounded with gold.

Taurus was the prince and leader of the constellations for more than two thousand years. When his head set with the Sun near the end of May, Scorpio rose in the southeast.

The Pleiades were sometimes called *Vergiliæ* (Virgins of Spring) because the Sun entered this cluster of stars during Spring. Their Syrian name was *Succoth*, or *Succothbeneth*, derived from a Chaldæan word meaning to *speculate* or *observe*.

The *Hyades* are five stars (the Greeks counted seven) in the form of a V, 11° southeast of the Pleiades. Aldebarán leads the starry host when the Vernal *454* Equinox is in Taurus, and when he rises in the East, Aries is about 27° high.

When Aldebarán approaches the meridian, the Heavens present a magnificent appearance. Capella is slightly to the north, Orion is to the south, Procyon, Sirius, Castor, and Pollux are to the east about halfway to the horizon, and the Pleiades are just to the west. Regulus is rising upon the ecliptic, and Virgo is lingering below the horizon. Fomalhaut is halfway past the meridian in the Southwest, and to the Northwest are the brilliant constellations, Perseus, Cepheus, Cassiopeia, and Andromeda.

ORION is visible throughout the world, because the equinoctial line passes through its center. When Aldebarán rises in the east, the Three Kings of Orion follow him. As Taurus sets, Scorpio rises in the East, and his sting is said to kill Orion. Orion rises at noon on or near the 9th of March, and he is accompanied by great rains and storms that threaten the mariners.

The Great Star ARCTURUS is in the constellation Boötes which the ancient Greeks called *Lycaon*, from the word *lukos* meaning wolf. The Hebrews called it Caleb Anubach meaning the Barking Dog, and when Taurus began the year, it corresponded with Summer.

The two human figures GEMINI (Twins) come next. Their heads have the bright Stars CASTOR and POLLUX which were also called the Dioscuri and the Cabeiri of Samothrace, which were the patrons of navigation. South of Pollux are the brilliant Stars SIRIUS and PROCYON, the greater and lesser Dog, and still further South is Canopus in the Ship Argo.

Sirius is the largest and brightest Star in the Heavens. When the Vernal Equinox began in Taurus, it rose with the Sun. When the Sun entered Leo on the Summer Solstice (about June 21st), it would rise before the Sun and signal that the rising of the Nile would begin in about fifteen days. Canopus also rose before the Sun as a precursor to the rising of the Nile, and Procyon rose before Sirius.

There are no significant Stars in CANCER. In the Zodiacs of Esne, Dendera, and in most of the astrological architectural remains of Egypt, the sign of this constellation was the sacred beetle (*Scarabæus*) that symbolized immortality and the Gate of Man where souls descended from Heaven. In the crest of Cancer is a cluster of Stars called *Præsepe* (the Manger or the Beehive). On each side of it is a small Star, and the pair are called *Aselli* (little asses).

Leo has the splendid Stars REGULUS directly on the ecliptic and DENEBOLA in the Lion's tail. Southeast of Regulus is the Star COR HYDRÆ.

The first labor of Hercules was to slay the Nemæan lion. Leo was the first sign the Sun passed into after the Summer Solstice, and it symbolized his struggle to reascend.

The Nile overflowed in Leo. It was first in the Zodiac of Dendera, and it was also in all the Indian and Egyptian Zodiacs.

In the left hand of VIRGO (Isis or Ceres), just a little South of the ecliptic, is the beautiful Star SPICA Virginis. Of less magnitude, VINDEMIATRIX is in the right arm, and Northwest of Spica in Boötes (the farmer, Osiris), is the splendid star ARCTURUS.

Aben Ezra said the first 10° of Virgo represents a beautiful Virgin with flowing hair sitting in a chair and holding two ears of corn in her hand while suckling an infant. Virgo was Isis, and she carried Horus in her arms. This

455

image was exhibited in her temple with the inscription: "I AM ALL THAT IS, THAT WAS, AND THAT SHALL BE. The fruit which I have brought forth is the Sun."

Nine months after the Sun enters Virgo it reaches the Gemini. When Scorpio begins to rise, Orion sets. When Scorpio is at the meridian, Leo begins to set, Typhon reigns, Osiris is slain, and Isis (the Virgin) follows him to the tomb weeping.

The Virgin and Boötes both set with the Sun at the Autumnal Equinox, and they deliver the world into the wintry constellations where they introduced it to the angel of Evil, represented by Ophiucus the Serpent. At the start of the Winter Solstice, the Virgin rose *with* the Sun (Horus) in her bosom.

LIBRA has four Stars of the second and third magnitude, 456 Zubeneschamali, Zubenelgenubi, Zubenelakrab, and Zubenalgubi. Near the last of these is the brilliant but hostile Star ANTARES in SCORPIO.

ANTARES is a star of the 1st magnitude and remarkably red. It is one of the four great Stars, including FOMALHAUT near Pisces, ALDEBARAN in Taurus, and REGULUS in Leo. Early astronomers noticed them because they answered to the Solstitial and Equinoctial points. Scorpio was sometimes represented by a Snake or a Crocodile, but on the Mithraic Monuments and the Zodiac of Dendera it was a Scorpion. This sign was vilified because it signaled the reign of Typhon.

There are no Stars of importance in Sagittarius, Capricorn, or Aquarius.

The brilliant Star FOMALHAUT is near Pisces, which is considered the most ominous sign in the Zodiac. It was deemed indicative of *Violence* and *Death*. The Syrians and Egyptians both abstained from eating fish out of animosity towards this sign, and the Egyptians Hieroglyphically represented odious things or expressed hatred by painting a fish.

The bright Star CAPELLA is in Auriga, and it never seems to set due to its close proximity to the North Star.

There are Seven Stars circling the North Pole known as Ursa Major (the Great Bear or Big Dipper) which have been observed in all ages. The Priests of Bel, the Magi of Persia, the Shepherds of Chaldæa, the Phœnician navigators, and the astronomers of Egypt revered them. The two stars MERAK and DUBHE always point to the North Pole.

Eusebius said the Phœnicians and Egyptians were the first to ascribe divinity to the Sun, Moon, and Stars, regarding them as the sole causes of the production and destruction of all beings. They disperse to the world all of the known opinions about the generation and descent of the Gods. The Hebrews were the first to practice a belief in an invisible Creator while the rest of the world worshipped the luminous bodies as Gods blazing in the Heavens. They offered sacrifices to the stars, bowed down before them, and neither raised their 457 souls nor their worship beyond the visible heavens.

The Chaldæans, Canaanites, and Syrians where Abraham lived practiced the same religion. The Canaanites consecrated horses and chariots to the Sun.

The citizens of Emesa in Phœnicia recognized Him under the name of Elagabalus, and the Tyrians worshipped the Sun as the Great Deity Hercules. The Syrians fearfully worshipped the Stars of the Constellation Pisces and consecrated images of it in their temples. The Sun as Adonis was worshipped in Byblos and near Mount Libanus, and there was a magnificent Temple of the Sun at Palmyra that was pillaged by Aurelian's Roman soldiers, rebuilt, and rededicated. The Babylonians who settled in Samaria worshiped the Pleiades under the name of Succoth-Beneth. Saturn was worshipped among the Copts under the name of Remphan. The Syrians, Assyrians, Phœnicians, and Canaanites worshipped the planet Jupiter as Bel or Baal; Mars as Malec, Melech, or Moloch; Venus as Ashtaroth or Astarte; and Mercury as Nebo.

Sanchoniathon said the earliest Phœnicians adored the Sun and honored it under the name of BEEL-SAMIN, meaning the *King of Heaven*. They built columns to the elements air (wind) and fire and worshipped them. Sabeism was the worship of the Stars, and it flourished everywhere in Babylonia. Abulfaragius informed us that each of the twelve Arab Tribes recognized a particular Star as their Patron. The Tribe Hamyar was consecrated to the Sun; the Tribe Cennah to the Moon; the Tribe Misa to Aldebarán; the Tribe Tai to Canopus; the Tribe Kais to Sirius; the Tribes Lachamus and Idamus to Jupiter; the Tribe Asad to Mercury; and so on.

The Saracens worshipped Venus whom they called CABAR (The Great), and they swore by the Sun, Moon, and Stars. The Arabic author Shahristan said the Arabs and Indians before his time had temples dedicated to the seven Planets. Abulfaragius said the seven great primitive nations of Persia, Chaldæa, Greece, Egypt, Turkey, India, and China were all originally Sabeans who worshipped the Stars. They all prayed at Sunrise, Noon, and Sunset by turning toward the North Pole and bowing. They prayed to the Stars and the Intelligences who inhabited them, offered sacrifices to them, and worshipped the fixed stars and planets as Gods. Philo said the Chaldæans regarded the stars as the sovereign arbiters of the world's order, and they did not try to imagine any invisible or intellectual being. They regarded NATURE as the great divinity who exercised its powers through the action of the Sun, Moon, Planets, Fixed Stars, the succession of the seasons, and the combined action of Heaven and Earth. The great Sabean feast was celebrated when the Sun reached the Vernal Equinox. They also celebrated five other feasts when the five minor planets entered the signs where they had their exaltation.

Diodorus Siculus informed us that the Egyptians recognized the Sun and Moon (Osiris and Isis) as the primary and eternal Divinities, who they believed governed the world, provided everything its nourishment and growth, and were the active and passive principles of generation, and that the perfection of all effects produced by nature depended upon them.

Porphyry said the learned priest of Egypt, Chæremon, and many other learned men recognized the stars composing the zodiac as gods, including all the

458

stars that marked its divisions by rising or setting, the subdivisions of the signs into 10° units, the horoscope, and the stars called Potent Chiefs of Heaven that presided there. They began their sacred legends by explaining the Sun as the Great God, Architect, and Ruler of the World. These legends included the fable of Osiris and Isis; the appearance, disappearance, and ascension of the stars; the increase and decrease of light in the phases of the moon; and the path of the sun dividing time and the heavens into two parts (one assigned to light and the other to darkness).

Lucian said the sacred Egyptian bull Apis was the image of Taurus, and the horned Jupiter Ammon was the image of Aries. Arid Clemens of Alexandria said the four primary sacred Egyptian animals were the emblems of the four *459* signs, or cardinal points, which divided the year into four parts at the equinoxes and solstices. They also worshiped fire, water, and the Nile River, which they styled Father, Preserver of Egypt, and sacred emanation from the Great God Osiris. The other elements, Air, Heaven, Earth, Sun, Moon, Night, and Day, were also revered as Great Gods whose names were inscribed on the ancient columns. Eusebius said they lastly regarded the Universe as a great Deity, composed of the different parts of itself with each part representing a different god.

This same worship extended into every part of Europe and Eurasia. The ancient Persians worshiped the Sun as Mithras, but they included the Moon, Venus, Fire, Earth, Air, and Water. They made sacrifices to the Heavens and the Sun, and they burned incense to the seven Planets on seven ancient *pyrea*. The Zend-Avesta contains prayers to Mithras, the stars, the elements, trees, mountains, and every part of nature. Taurus is summoned to unite with the Moon, and the four "royal stars" of the Persians, Taschter (Aldebaran), Satevis (Antares), Haftorang (Fomalhaut), and Venant (Regulus), the great Star Rapitan, and the other constellations kept watch over the different portions of the earth.

The Magi worshiped fire above all other elements and powers of nature, as did many ancient nations. The Ganges and Indus Rivers were worshiped in India, but the Sun was the Great Divinity. The Chinese built Temples to Heaven, Earth, Mars, the spirits of the air, water, mountains, stars, and the sea-dragon.

The twelve palaces of the Labyrinth were built in honor of the Sun. Like the twelve superb columns of the Temple at Hieropolis, they were consecrated and covered with symbols of the twelve gods or spirits of the signs of the Zodiac. The shape of the pyramid and the obelisk both resembled a flame, *460* because these monuments were consecrated to the Sun and Fire. Timæus of Locria said, "the equilateral triangle is used in the design of the pyramid to create four equal faces and equal angles, which resembles fire, the most subtle and mobile of the elements." An inscription upon an obelisk translated by the Egyptian Hermapion and found in Ammianus Marcellinus read, "Apollo the Son of God, He who made the world, true Lord of Lords, who fills Egypt with His glory."

The religious monuments of the ancient world most commonly divide the Heavens into groups of seven, which are the number of planets, and by twelve, which are the number of signs. The twelve Great Gods of Egypt can be found everywhere, and the Greeks and Romans adopted them. Individual altars were built to their images in Athens, and they were painted on the porticos. The People of the North had their twelve *Azes*, or Senate of twelve great gods where Odin served as chief. The Japanese, like the Egyptians, divided them into twelve classes, seven ancient and five modern.

The most striking proof of the universal adoration of the stars and constellations was the arrangement of the Hebrew camps in the Desert and the allegory of the twelve Tribes of Israel described in the Hebrew legends to Jacob. The Hebrew camp was a quadrilateral divided into sixteen parts. The four center divisions were occupied by images of the four elements, and the four divisions at the four angles of the quadrilateral were occupied by the four *fixed* signs influenced by the four great Royal Stars, Regulus in Leo, Aldebarán in Taurus, Antares in Scorpio, and Fomalhaut in the mouth of Pisces. The Celestial Vulture or Eagle represented Scorpio in the Hebrew emblems. The other signs were arranged on the four faces of the square.

461 There is a unique coincidence between the characteristics Jacob assigned to his sons and those of the signs of the Zodiac or the planets that reside in those signs.

Reuben was compared to Aquarius because he was unstable and unable to excel. The water from Aquarius flows toward the South Pole, and it was the first of the four Royal Signs that ascend from the Winter Solstice.

Judah was compared to the Lion (Leo), whose constellation is the domicile of the Sun. The strong grip of the Lion of the Tribe of Judah raised Khūrūm from the grave after the grip of the apprentice (Aquarius at the Winter Solstice) and the fellowcraft (Cancer at the Vernal Equinox) failed.

Ephraim was compared to the Ox (Taurus). *Dan* was compared to the Cerastes or horned Serpent, which is synonymous to the vulture or pouncing eagle. This bird was often substituted for the venomous scorpion because of the terror it inspired as the symbol of Typhon and his evil influences. Hence, in the sacred pictures of the Jews, Christians, and in Royal Arch Masonry, the four famous figures are the Lion, the Ox, the Man, and the Eagle. These are the four creatures of the Apocalypse copied by Ezekiel who saw them revolving around blazing circles in his thoughts and dreams.

Gad was compared to the Ram. It is the residence of Mars, chief of the Celestial Soldiery, and Jacob characterized it as a warrior and chief of his army.

Issachar was compared to the stars of *Aselli*, or little asses, which are in Cancer.

Zebulon was compared to the Capricorn of old, represented by the tail of a fish and called the Son of Neptune by astronomers.

Benjamin was compared to Sagittarius hunting the Celestial Wolf. The Romans placed Diana the huntress in that constellation. *Naphtali* is compared to 462 Virgo, the residence of Mercury, whose eloquence and agility are attributes of the Courier of the Gods. *Simeon* and *Levi* are united and compared to the two fishes of the Constellation Pisces.

Plato's Republic followed the divisions of the Zodiac and the planets, as did Lycurgus at Sparta, and Cecrops in the Athenian Commonwealth. The Chinese legislator Chun divided China into twelve Tcheou and specially designated twelve mountains. The Etruscan Empire was divided into twelve Cantons. Romulus appointed twelve Lictors. There were twelve tribes of Ishmael and twelve disciples of Jesus. The New Jerusalem of the Apocalypse has twelve gates.

The Chinese book Souciet spoke about a palace of four buildings with gates looking towards the four corners of the world. The East gate was dedicated to the new moons of Spring, and the West gate to those of Autumn. The South gate was dedicated to the new moons of Summer; and the North gate to those of Winter. In this palace, the Emperor and his noblemen sacrificed a lamb that represented the Sun at the Vernal Equinox.

In the Greek theaters, the march of the Choruses represented the movements of the Heavens and the planets, and Aristoxenes said the Strophe and Anti-Strophe imitated the movements of the Stars. The number five was sacred to the Chinese as the number of planets other than the Sun and Moon. Astrology consecrated the numbers twelve, seven, thirty, and three hundred and sixty. *Seven*, the number of the planets, was as sacred as *twelve*, the number of signs, months, oriental cycles, and sections of the horizon. We will elaborate about the numbers, which the ancients gave mysterious powers in a subsequent Degree.

The Signs of the Zodiac and the Stars appeared on many of the ancient coins and medals. The planet Venus was on the public seal of the ancient Italian city Locrians. Aries and the crescent moon were on the medals of Antioch. The Ram was an important Deity in Syria because it divided the astrological year. Taurus was on the Cretan, Mamertin, and Athenian coins. Sagittarius was on the Persian coins. All twelve signs appeared upon the ancient Indian coins. Scorpio 463 was engraved upon the medals of the Kings of Comagena, and Capricorn was on those of Zeugma, Anazorba, and some other cities. Nearly all the signs of the Zodiac are found on the medals of Antoninus.

Astrology was practiced among all the ancient nations. In Egypt, the book of Astrology and the animals symbolizing the equinoxes and solstices were ceremoniously carried in the religious processions. The same science flourished throughout Chaldæa, Asia, and Africa. The Indian astrologers of the Oxydraces disclosed their scientific secrets of Heaven and the Stars to the conquering

Alexander. The Brahmins taught Apollonius the secrets of Astronomy and how to see into the future from the stars with the ceremonies and prayers used to appease the gods. In China, astrology taught the mode of governing the State and families, and in Arabia it was deemed the mother of the sciences. It flourished in Rome, and Constantine had his horoscope drawn by Valens. It was a science in the middle ages and to this day, it is still practiced. Catherine de Medici was fond of it, Louis XIV consulted his horoscope, and the learned Casini began his career as an astrologer.

The ancient Sabeans and Chaldæans both held feasts to honor each planet on the day when it entered its place of *exaltation*, or the particular place in the Heavens where its influence upon Nature was supposed to have the greatest energy. The Sun's place of exaltation was in Aries, because at this point it awakened all of Nature and warmed into life all of the vegetation. In Egypt, this most solemn feast was called the Feast of Fire and Light. The Jews celebrated it with the Passover, and the Persians celebrated Neurouz. The Romans preferred the term "place of *domicile*" to exaltation, and they celebrated their feasts when the planets entered the signs deemed their *house*.

464 The order of the planets, as then understood from the nearest to the farthest, was the Moon, Mercury, Venus, the Sun, Mars, Jupiter, and lastly Saturn.

The Ancient Calendars, like the feasts, were also determined by the risings and settings of the Fixed Stars, their relation to the Sun, and their first appearance as they emerged from behind its rays.

The Roman games of the Circus were celebrated in honor of the Sun, Moon, Planets, Zodiac, Elements, and the most apparent parts and potent agents of Nature. They were personified, represented, and imitated in the Hippodrome. Four different colored horses representing the four elements and seasons pulled the Sun's chariot. The seven courses corresponded with the number of planets, and they ran from East to West like the circuits around the Lodge. The Seven Stars (Ursa Major) that revolved around the pole were also represented, as were the stars of Capella which signaled the new year when the Sun reached the Pleiades in Taurus.

The four different intersections of the Zodiac at the Equinoctial and Solstitial points have throughout history been used by many countries to start the new year. Some countries chose the Vernal Equinox because the days become longer than the nights and symbolize light's victory over darkness. Sometimes the Summer Solstice was chosen because the longest day symbolized the Sun's reaching the pinnacle of its glory and perfection. The Egyptians chose it because it corresponded with the beginning of the Nile's flooding. Some countries preferred the Autumnal Equinox because the harvests were gathered, and the hopes for a new crop were entrusted to the bosom of the earth. Others preferred the Winter Solstice because, as the shortest day, it symbolized the beginning of Light's conquest that was destined to end in victory at the Vernal Equinox.

The Winter Solstice began the Roman year when figuratively speaking, the Sun *died* and was *born again*. Then the Circus games were celebrated to honor the invincible Sun-God. Macrobius said many people of Italy compared the four ages of man to the four Equinoctial and Solstitial points: likening the Sun to an infant born at the Winter Solstice, a young man at the Vernal Equinox, a grown man at the Summer Solstice, and an old man at the Autumnal Equinox. This idea was adopted from the Egyptians. 465

The image of each Sign that started the four seasons became the image of the Sun for that particular season. Hercules wore the Lion's skin. The horns of the Bull adorned the forehead of Bacchus, and the autumnal serpent wound its long folds around the Statue of Serapis, 2500 years before our time. Over time, the precession of the Equinoxes forced these constellations to be replaced by the preceding symbol, causing their attributes to change. Then the Ram provided the horns for the head of the Sun under the name Jupiter Ammon. The Sun was no longer exposed to the waters of Aquarius, nor was it enclosed in an urn like the God Canopus. Rather, the Sun was in the Stables of Augeas or the Celestial Goat, and He completed his triumph mounted on an ass in the constellation Cancer, which then occupied the Solstitial point of Summer.

The Sun also borrowed other attributes from the new constellations for its images.

The Bull was the first regenerator of Nature through its union with the Sun, and next was the Ram (called the Lamb by the Persians). Both signs took their turn as an emblem of the Sun overcoming the wintry darkness by repairing the barrenness, disorder, and destruction of Nature wrought by the Scorpion and Serpent of Autumn. Mithras was represented sitting on a Bull (the image of Osiris), while the Greek Bacchus armed his head with its horns and was pictured with its tail and feet.

The Constellations were important to the farmers, because their rising or setting in the morning or evening indicated the coming planting and harvesting times. The location of Capella (the she-goat Amalthea that nursed Jupiter) over the equinoctial point (Taurus) and the Pleiades that signaled the Seasons spawned a multitude of the most observed and celebrated poetic fables in antiquity. 466

The original Roman year began with the Vernal Equinox. July was called *Quintilis*, the 5th month, August was *Sextilis*, the 6th, *September* was the 7th month, etc. The Persians also began their year at the Vernal Equinox, and they celebrated their great feast of Neurouz when the Sun entered Aries and the Constellation Perseus rose. Perseus was the first spirit to bring to earth the heavenly fire consecrated in the temples, and the ceremonies reminded people of the rejuvenation of Nature and the triumph of Ormuzd, the Light-God, over Ahriman and his powers of Darkness.

The Hebrews also began their year at the Vernal Equinox in the month of Nisan. This marked both the commemoration of the Passover and the Exodus when the Israelites were led out of Egypt by Moses. When Bacchus' army had long marched in the burning deserts, the Lamb (or Ram) led them to beautiful meadows and the Springs that watered the Temple of Jupiter Ammon. Bacchus was the great Divinity to the Arabs and Ethiopians, and they considered a Country abounding in springs and rivulets to be the perfect paradise.

Orion and Taurus are on the same meridian. Both die from the sting of the celestial Scorpion who rises in autumn when they both set. The Stars of the Autumnal Equinox are those malevolent spirits who are always at war with the Principle of good, and they destroy the life producing powers communicated to the earth by the Sun and the Heavens.

The Vernal Equinox was as dear to the sailor as to the farmer, because those Stars allowed navigation of the stormy Seas. Dioscuri or Chief Cabiri of Samothrace were the guardian Divinities of the sea who sailed with Jason in search of the golden fleeced ram (Aries), whose morning ascent announced the Sun's entry into Taurus. Jason the Serpent-bearer rose in the evening, and he was considered Dioscuri's brother. Orion rose after Taurus and rejoiced in the forehead of the new year. He was also the son of Neptune, and as the most effective administrator of the oceans, he decreed either calm or stormy seas.

The Summer Solstice was as important to the Egyptians as the Vernal Equinox. It marked the beginning of the decrease in the length of daylight, the *maximum* height of the Sun's elevation, and the peculiar annual rising of the Nile. The Nile seemed to rise and fall as the days grew longer and shorter, being the lowest at the Winter Solstice, and highest at the Summer Solstice. This solstitial point was chosen to signify the new year because the Sun seemed to regulate the Nile's water level. This began the Sothiac (Sirius) Period when the Dog Star's morning ascent marked this important period for the Egyptian people. This type of year was called the Year of God, the Heliac (Solar) year, and the Canicular year, and it consisted of exactly 365 days. This meant at the end of four years, or 4 years times 365 days equaling 1,460 days, an additional day was needed for earth to make four complete revolutions of the Sun. To correct this, some Nations made every fourth year consist of 366 days as we do now, but the Egyptians decided against this practice. At the end of 120 years, or 30 times 4 years, the 120th year would need 30 more days to complete 120 revolutions of the Sun, and the start of the 121st year would precede the Summer Solstice by a month.

Therefore, if the beginning of the year lost 30 days every 120 years, the beginning of the year would correctly begin again at the Summer Solstitial point at the end of 1,460 years or 12 times 120 years. The Sun would have made 1,459 revolutions although 1,460 would have been counted. The Sun would not have made its 1,460 complete revolution until the end of 1,461 years because each revolution is actually 365¼ days.

The Egyptian *Sothiac* period began on the Summer Solstice when Sirius first occupied Leo and later Cancer. Porphyry said it was this Solstitial New Moon, accompanied by the rising of Set or the Dog Star Sirius, which signaled the beginning of the year, the generation of all things, and the natal hour of the world.

Sirius alone did not determine the flooding period of the Nile. Aquarius with his urn and the stream flowing from it were in opposition to the sign of the Summer Solstice occupied by the Sun, and he received the full Moon in his cup when he began the march of Night. The feet of Pegasus rose above and with him, soaked by the flowing waters that the Muses drink. The Lion and the Dog were worshipped because they were supposed to *cause* the floods. The waters doubled their depth while the Sun passed through Leo, and the sacred fountains poured their streams through the lions' heads. Hydra spread across three signs when rising between Sirius and Leo. Its head rose with Cancer, its tail rose with the feet of Virgo and the beginning of Libra, and the floods continued as the Sun passed along its whole body.

The successive turns at being victor and vanquished in the contest between light and darkness for the possession of the lunar disk resembled exactly what happened to the earth during the Sun's journeys from one Solstice to another. The lunar cycle presented the same periods of light and darkness as the year, and it was the object of the reasonable religious legends. Pliny said that above the Moon, everything is pure and filled with eternal light. The cone of shadow which the earth projects to produce the night ends at the Moon, and the journey of night and darkness ends there too. Here we enter the pure substance. *469*

The Egyptians believed when Osiris (the Sun) and Isis (the Moon) united in the spring, he gave her the creative principles of generation to disseminate into the air and the elements. The Persians believed Taurus impregnated the Moon in the spring. People have always had a mysterious and unexplainable belief in the Moon's great influence upon vegetation, the birth, and growth of animals. The astrologers, the Naturalists like Pliny, the Philosophers like Plutarch and Cicero, the Egyptian Theologians, and the Metaphysicians like Proclus all believed in this lunar influence.

Diodorus Siculus said, "The Egyptians acknowledged the Sun and Moon (Osiris and Isis) as the two great gods who govern the world and regulate its administration with the seasons. It is the nature of these two great Divinities to impress an active and overflowing force that affects the generation of beings. The Sun does it with heat and the spiritual principle that forms the breath of the winds, while the Moon does it with humidity and dryness. Nature is maintained, born, grown, and vegetates by the combined action of the Sun and Moon and their five shared qualities: spiritual, fiery, dry, humid, and airy."

The five primitive powers, or elementary qualities of air, spirit, fire, water, and earth, are attributed to the Sun and Moon in the Indian theology, and they are the same five elements recognized by the Chinese. The Phœnicians and the

Egyptians both regarded the Sun, Moon, and Stars as the sole causes of generation and destruction.

The Moon, like the Sun, continually changes its course across the Heavens, moving between the upper and lower limits of the Zodiac. The Moon's different places, phases, aspects, and its relation to the Sun and the constellations have been a fruitful source of mythological fables.

470   The Zodiac termed the location of the planets their *houses*. The House of the Sun was in Leo and that of the Moon in Cancer. The other planets had two signs; Mercury had Gemini and Virgo; Venus had Taurus and Libra; Mars had Aries and Scorpio; Jupiter had Pisces and Sagittarius; and Saturn had Aquarius and Capricorn. This distribution of the signs and their places of exaltation provided many of the mythological emblems and fables. Diana of Ephesus (the Moon) wore the image of a crab on a necklace because that sign was the Moon's house. Leo carried the Sun, personified as the Egyptian Apollo, upon a throne of Horns for a like reason. The Egyptians consecrated the sacred scarabæus to the Moon because its place of exaltation was in Taurus, and for the same reason, Mercury was said to have presented Isis with a helmet like a bull's head.

The twelve signs of the Zodiac were further divided into three 10° parts called Decans. These 36 Decans of the Zodiac were equally divided among the seven planets, with Mars receiving the extra Decan because it opened and closed the series of planets. We know this subdivision was not established until after Aries opened the Vernal equinox because Mars, having its house in Aries, was listed first in the sequence of planets as follows: Mars, the Sun, Venus, Mercury, the Moon, Saturn, Jupiter, Mars, etc. until each Decan is assigned a planet, and each sign has three planets. Next, each Decan was assigned a unique God or Spirit (totaling thirty-six in all). According to the Chaldæans, every ten days one of them descended to earth and then re-ascended to Heaven ten days later as the next one descended. This division is also found on the Indian and Persian spheres, and on the Barbaric sphere, which Aben Ezra described. The God or Spirit of each Decan assisted with the effects produced by the Sun, Moon, and other planets, but their doctrine was extremely important and kept secret. Firmicus said the ancients protected these doctrines even though the Deity inspired them, and they only taught them to distinct Initiates with a great reserve cautiously disguised by an obscure veil so they would not become known to the masses.

471   These Decans also had *paranatellon*s or stars that lay *outside* of the Zodiac which rise or set with specific 10° divisions of each sign. Anciently there were 48 celestial figures or constellations associated with the 36 Decans, twelve were in the Zodiac and 36 were outside of it. For example, when Capricorn set, Sirius and Procyon (Canis Major and Canis Minor) rose because they were the Paranatellons of Capricorn although at the opposite end of the heavens. The rising of Cancer coincided with the setting of Corona Borealis and the rising of Sirius and Procyon, its three paranatellons.

The risings and settings of the Stars are always distinguished by its position to the Sun in one of three ways: cosmical, achronical, and heliacal.

When a Star simultaneously rises or sets on the same degree of the Zodiac sign occupied by the Sun, it *cosmically* rises and sets with the Sun. Because this star cannot be seen during this time due to the light or twilight of the Sun, it is necessary to know *its* place in the Zodiac to observe stars that rise just before or set just after it.

A Star rises and sets *achronically* when it rises in the East as the Sun sets in the West or sets in the West as the Sun rises in the East. This rising and setting in *opposition* to the Sun happens to each Star once a year as the Sun moves from West to East one degree a day in relation to the Stars.

A Star is considered to *heliacally* rise in the morning when it appears about an hour and a half before the Sun. It is said to *heliacally* set in the evening when it sets about an hour and a half after the Sun, because the Sun (*Helios*) seems to touch the star with its luminous glow. A heliacal Star will appear or disappear for several months as it gradually emerges from or disappears into the Sun's rays. A Star has set heliacally when it no longer remains visible above the western horizon after sunset and then completely ceases to be seen setting in the West. It remains invisible until the Sun passes far enough to the East that it can no longer be eclipsed, and then it reappears in the East about an hour and a half before sunrise. This is their *heliacal* rising. During this interval, the cosmic rising and setting occur. ₄₇₂

The Stars were also believed to produce different effects according to when they rose or set, whether they did so cosmically, achronically, or heliacally and according to the different seasons of the year in which these phenomena occurred. These effects were carefully marked on the Calendars, and many things in the ancient allegories referred to them.

The division of the Stars into good and bad, or beneficent and malevolent was very important. The Persians classified Aries to Virgo as good or beneficent and Libra to Pisces as bad or malevolent. The good Angels and Spirits, and the bad Angels, Devs, Evil Spirits, Devils, Fallen Angels, and Titans were assigned respectively. The other 36 Constellations were equally divided. When added to those of the Zodiac, they totaled 24 on each side.

The heavens were often represented as an Egg. This symbolic Egg was born from the mouth of the invisible Egyptian God KNEPH and known in the Grecian Mysteries as the Orphic Egg. From an Egg came the Coresian God CHUMONG, the Egyptian OSIRIS, and PHANES (the God and Principle of Light). In Japanese tradition, the world emerged from it when it was broken by the Sacred Bull. The Greeks placed it at the feet of BACCHUS TAURI-CORNUS, and the Magian Egg of ORMUZD produced the Amshaspands and Devs. The Constellations symbolized the breaking of the Egg into two halves, equally divided between the Good and Evil Constellations and Angels. The beneficent signs and stars of Spring were Aries, Taurus, Auriga, and Capella, while those of

Autumn were Libra, Scorpio, the Serpent of Ophiucus, and the Dragon of the Hesperides, and they were symbols of the Evil Principles and malevolent causes of the ill effects of Autumn and Winter. This explains the mysteries of the journey of the human soul as it descends through the spheres to the earth by the Sign of the Serpent, and then returns to the Empire of light by the Sign of the Lamb or Bull.

473   The most creative action and energy of Heaven always manifested at the Vernal Equinox, and they originated the fables that represent the victory of Light over Darkness by the triumphs of Jupiter, Osiris, Ormuzd, and Apollo. The triumphant god first takes the form of the Bull, the Ram, or the Lamb. Next, Jupiter wrestles his thunderbolts from Typhon, who had seized them during the Winter, and finally the God of Light overwhelms his foe who is symbolized by a large Serpent. This victory causes winter to end, and the Sun blazes in the Heavens, accompanied by Orion while seated on the Bull. Nature rejoices at Ahriman's victory against Ormuzd, and Order and Harmony are reestablished where dire confusion had reigned.

The Universal Soul of the World was believed to exercise its creative energy primarily through the Sun as it moved along the signs of the Zodiac. The influence of the signs is modified when they unite with the paranatellons who assist in furnishing the symbolic attributes of the Great Luminary as it regulates Nature's greatest powers. The action of the Universal Soul is displayed in the movements of the Spheres, the location of the Sun, and in the periodical risings and settings of the Stars. These movements explained the metamorphosis and the attributes of that Soul who was personified as Jupiter, Bacchus, Vishnu, or Buddha, and explains the worship of those animals that represented the Celestial Signs who were supposed to receive emanations from the Universal Soul.

The ancient Theologians, Astrologers, Poets, and Philosophers personified the Stars as dynamic and intelligent beings, eternal bodies, and active causes animated by a living principle. They were directed by an intelligence that emanated from, and was a part of, the life of the universal intelligence of the
474 world. The famous divisions of the eternal and divine Intelligences by seven (number of planets) or by twelve (signs of the zodiac) are found throughout the hierarchical order of the Gods, Angels, and the Spirits who were the representatives of the Divine Force.

These Intelligences have absolute authority over all parts of Nature, the elements, animals, vegetation, mankind, and all the actions, virtues, vices, good, and evil that compose every person's life. The passions of man's soul and the maladies of his body depend upon the heavens and the spirits who preside at his birth, control his fortunes, and receive his soul when it is reunited with the pure life of the lofty Stars. Portions of the Universal Soul are dispersed throughout the world to influence movement upon everything. Through the mysterious forces of Nature, It seems to give life to the plants and trees, direct a comprehensive plan of organization and development, impart eternal motion to the running waters, impel the winds to change their direction or be silent, calm or arouse the ocean, unchain the storms, pour out the fires of volcanoes, and shake the mountains and continents with earthquakes.

These invisible Intelligences were divided between the two great armies of the Principles of Good and Evil, Light and Darkness, Ormuzd and Ahriman, Osiris and Typhon. The Evil Principle was the driving force of brute matter. It was personified as Ahriman and Typhon and their armies of Devs, Fallen Angels, and Malevolent Spirits who continually battled the Good Principle of Celestial Light and Splendor, Osiris, Ormuzd, Jupiter, or Dionysus with their bright hosts of Amshaspands, Izeds, Angels, and Archangels in a warfare that wages in the soul of every person from birth until death.

The 24th Degree discussed the legend of Osiris and Isis, and the 25th Degree now explains the astronomical phenomena that became the basis for these mythological facts. 475

At the Vernal Equinox, the Sun initiated generation and his warmth poured upon the sublunary world all the blessings of Heaven. The beneficent guardian of all vegetation supplies new activity to the dull earth to warm her heart after the long, cold, Wintry frosts until her bosom bursts forth with all the greenness and perfumes of spring. Her joy is heard in the leafy forests, grassy fields, and flowery meadows promising abundant crops, grains, and fruits.

Osiris was the God of Cultivation and Benefactor of Man who poured onto the earth his magnificent blessings from the gift of the Divinity. Osiris' antagonist in the Egyptian mythology was Typhon, just as Ormuzd's antagonist in the Persian theology was Ahriman.

Diodorus Siculus said the native inhabitants of Egypt and Ethiopia were the first to identify the two great Divinities of the Heavens, the Sun (Osiris) and the Moon (Isis), who were considered the source of all the generations of earth. This idea was taught by Eusebius and also by the Phœnicians. These two Divinities were entrusted with the administration of the world, and all sublunary bodies received their nourishment during the annual revolution and the different seasons that divided it.

Osiris and Isis gave civilization the discovery of agriculture, laws, arts of all kinds, religious worship, temples, the invention of letters, astronomy, the gymnastic arts, and music. Osiris tried to share these valuable discoveries with the countries that he passed through. He built cities, taught men to cultivate the earth, and his first presents to men were wheat and wine. Europe, Asia, Africa, and India partook in the blessings he communicated, and they claimed him as one of their great gods.

His brother Typhon killed and dismembered him. Isis collected all of his parts except his generative organs which had been thrown into the Nile to 476 fertilize Egypt every year. Isis buried his remaining parts, erected a tomb over them, and remained single while furnishing her blessings to her subjects. She cured the sick, made the blind see, healed the paralytic, and raised the dead. Her son Horus (Apollo) learned spirituality and the science of medicine from her.

The Egyptians believed the beneficence of the two luminaries produced man, animals, and all bodies that are born, grown, and die in the eternal circle of generation and destruction.

When Taurus opened the new year at the Vernal Equinox, Osiris united with the Moon and gave her the seeds of fruitfulness, which she poured upon the air to impregnate the generative principles that gave activity to universal vegetation. When Apis the bull had a Crescent Moon on his shoulder, it represented the living image of the Sun (Osiris) uniting with the Moon (Isis) at the Vernal Equinox and cooperating with her to provoke everything into generation. Their prolific influence was explicitly expressed with images that were not misunderstood, but today they would be deemed lewd and offensive.

Osiris gave everything that is good in Nature like order, harmony, and the pleasant temperatures of the seasons. Typhon gave stormy passions and irregular impulses that agitate the sensual and material part of man, the diseases and afflictions of the body, inclement weather, inconsistent seasons, and eclipses.

Osiris was the image of generative power expressed by his symbolic statues and the sign that he entered into at the Vernal Equinox. The Nile and all the water in Nature were regarded as His emanations to Nature, and without this most fundamental generative element, there could be no vegetation.

477   Diogenes Laertius, Plutarch, Lucian, Suidas, Macrobius, Martianus Capella, and many other ancient writers confirmed that Osiris and Isis were the Sun and the Moon. His power was symbolized by an Eye over a Scepter. The Greeks termed it the Eye of Jupiter and the Eye of the World, and our Lodges call it the All-Seeing Eye. The oracle of Claros styled him the King of the Stars and the King of the Eternal Fire who creates the year and the seasons, dispenses the rains and winds, and causes daybreak and night. Osiris was invoked as the God who was enshrouded within the Sun's rays. He was the invisible and eternal force that modified the sublunary world by using the Sun's resources.

Osiris was the same God as Bacchus, Dionysus, and Serapis. Serapis was the author of precision and harmony in the world. Bacchus and Ceres (identified by Herodotus as Isis) presided over the distribution of all our blessings, and from the two emanated everything good and beautiful in Nature. The Sun furnished the seed and principle of every good, and the Moon received and preserved it. In both the Persian and Egyptian theology, the Moon directly acts on the earth, but she is impregnated in the Persian faith by the Celestial Bull (Taurus) and in the Egyptian faith by Osiris (Sun). She unites with both of them at the Vernal Equinox in the sign Taurus, which is her place of her exaltation. Plutarch said the force of Osiris was exercised through the Moon, because she was the passive cause relative to the Sun and the active cause relative to the earth.

The earliest changes in the water level of the Nile began to appear at the Vernal Equinox when the new Moon occurred at the Sun's entrance into the constellation Taurus. The Nile was believed to receive its fertilizing power from the union of the equinoctial Sun and the new Moon meeting in Taurus. Osiris was often mistaken for the Nile and Isis for the earth. Osiris was deemed to act on the earth by his emanations to the Moon and the Nile, and thus the fable of his generative organs being thrown into that river. However, Typhon was the principle of drought and barrenness, and his mutilation of Osiris meant that drought would cause the Nile to shrink and then dry up in Autumn.

Outside of Egypt, Osiris was the symbol of the refreshing rains that *478* descended to fertilize the earth. Typhon was the burning winds of Autumn; the stormy rains that rotted the flowers, plants, and leaves; the short, cold days of Winter; and everything in Nature that produced corruption and destruction.

In summary, Typhon (the Persian Ahriman) was the principle of corruption, darkness, the lower world where earthquakes originated, tumultuous winds, burning heat, lightning, fiery meteors, plague, and pestilence. This revolt of the Evil Principle and Darkness against the Good Principle and Light has been presented in various forms of every theory about the origin of the universe. However, Osiris (through Isis) filled the material world with the happiness, purity, and order which maintained the harmony of Nature. Legend has it he died at the Autumnal Equinox when Taurus or the Pleiades rose in the evening, and he did not rise to life again until Spring.

Taurus and Scorpio were the most prominent signs in the mythological history of Osiris, because they marked the two equinoxes, 2,500 years before our Era. The other constellations near the equinoxes fixed the duration of the fertilizing action of the Sun, and it should be noted that Venus, the Goddess of Generation, also has her domicile in Taurus.

The Sun in Scorpio signaled Osiris had lost his life. Typhon's hands and feet were composed of serpents, and his place of exaltation was under Scorpio. He bound Osiris in a crate and flung him into the Nile in the 17° of Scorpio. When the Sun entered Scorpio, his light diminished, Night began her domination, the Nile shrank, the earth lost her vegetation, and the trees lost their leaves. The Mithraic Monuments depict this as the Scorpion biting the testicles of the Equinoctial Bull, which Mithras (the Sun of Spring and God of Generation) is seated upon. On the same monuments we see two trees, one covered with young leaves and a little bull and a torch burning at its base, and the other is loaded with fruit, and at its base is a Scorpion and an extinguished torch. *479*

Ormuzd or Osiris, the beneficent Principle that gives the world light, personified the Sun. Typhon or Ahriman personified his natural enemy Darkness. The Sages of Egypt explained the necessary and eternal rivalry of these principles ever pursuing the other, one dethroning the other in the Spring under the Bull, and the other in Autumn under the Scorpion. This legendary history detailed by Diodorus and Synesius also personified the Stars and constellations Orion, Capella, the Twins, the Wolf, Sirius, and Hercules, whose risings and settings noted the start of one or the other equinox.

Plutarch gave us the position of the Sun and Moon in the Heavens, at the moment when Osiris was murdered by Typhon. He said the Sun was in Scorpio at the Autumnal Equinox, and the Moon rose alone in Taurus. Six months earlier, she had been in union with Osiris who Taurus had risen with on the day of the Vernal Equinox. Taurus remained in the luminous hemisphere for six months always setting before the Sun until Autumn when the Sun arrived at Scorpio. Taurus was now in complete opposition to the Sun, and he rose when the Sun set to complete his course across the sky during the night as he presided over the long nights. Osiris' death was commemorated in sad processions by carrying a golden bull covered with a black drape that symbolized the darkness that the sign of Osiris had entered. While the Sun's absence prolonged the nights, Taurus and Osiris would remain under the control of Typhon, the Principle of Evil and Darkness.

Setting out from Taurus at the Autumnal Equinox, Isis (the Moon) began searching for Osiris through all the superior signs. Every month she became full in each successive sign, but without finding him. We will follow her allegorical wanderings.

Typhon who had conspired with the Queen of Ethiopia slew Osiris. The paranatellons of Scorpio were the Serpents and reptiles which supplied the attributes of the Evil Spirits. Typhon was depicted as a serpent in the Egyptian astronomical maps, and at the division of Scorpio is Cassiopeia, the Queen of Ethiopia, whose setting brings stormy winds.

Osiris descended into the infernal regions where he took the name and identity of Serapis, who was identical to Pluto. He became associated with Serpentarius and was identical to Æsculapius, whose form he took in his passage to the lower signs where he takes on the names of Pluto and Ades.

Isis wept for the death of Osiris, and nature mourned the impending loss of her Summer glories, the advent of the empire of night, the withdrawing of the waters, the cessation of the winds that brought the rains which rose the Nile, the shortening of the days, and the despoiling of the earth. Directly opposite the Sun, Taurus enters into the earth's cone of shadow, which totally eclipses the Moon.

The body of Osiris was enclosed in a crate or coffin and cast into the Nile. Near Chemmis, Pan and the Satyrs were the first to discover his death and announced it with their cries, which created sorrow and alarm. Taurus and the full Moon then entered into the cone of shadow. He was above the Celestial Nile River, Perseus the God of Chemmis, and Auriga, who was himself identical with Pan, leading a she-goat styled after his wife Aiga.

Isis went in search of the body, she first met some children who had seen it, and she gave them the gift of prophecy for their information. The second full Moon was in Gemini who presided over the oracles of Didymus and included Apollo, the God of Prophecy.

She learned that Osiris had mistaken her sister Nephte (Typhon's wife) 481
for Isis when she discovered a crown of sweet clover leaves where they had
united. This connection bore a child that Isis looked for with the aid of her
dogs, found, reared, and adopted with the name Anubis, her faithful guardian.
The third full Moon occurs in Cancer, which is the domicile of the Moon. The
paranatellons of Cancer are the crown of Ariadne or Proserpine (the leaves of
the sweet clover), Procyon and Canis Major, one star of which was called the Star
of Isis, while Sirius himself was honored in Egypt under the name of Anubis.

Isis went to Byblos and met the women of the King's Court near a
fountain. They convinced her to visit the King, and she became the nurse of his
son. The fourth full Moon was in Leo, which was the domicile of the Sun, or
Adonis the King of Byblos. The paranatellons of Leo are the flowing water of
Aquarius, Cepheus the King of Ethiopia, and Regulus known simply as The
King. Behind Cepheus rise his wife and Queen of Ethiopia (Cassiopeia), his
daughter Andromeda, and his son-in-law Perseus, all paranatellons of both Leo
and Virgo.

Isis suckled the child with the end of her finger at night. She burned all
the mortal parts of its body, and then in the shape of a swallow, she flew to the
great column of the palace that was made from the tamarisk tree that grew
around the coffin still containing the body of Osiris. The fifth full Moon
occurred in Virgo which Eratosthenes called the true image of Isis. It pictured
Isis suckling Horus who was born near the Winter Solstice. The paranatellons of
Virgo are the mast of the Celestial Ship, the swallow-tailed fish, and a portion of
Perseus, the son-in-law of the King of Ethiopia.

Isis recovered the sacred coffin and sailed from Byblos toward Boutos
with the eldest son of the King. Anubis met them with her son Horus, and they
hid the coffin in a forest. Typhon recognized it while hunting wild boar by
moonlight, and he cut the body into fourteen pieces to represent the number of
days between the full and new Moon. The sixth full Moon occurred in Libra
over the division separating Virgo and include the Celestial Ship, Perseus the son 482
of the King of Ethiopia, and Boötes who is said to have nursed Horus. The
paranatellons of Libra are the river of Orion that sets in the morning, Ursa Major
(the Great Bear or Big Dipper), and the Dragon of the North Pole which was
also the celebrated Python whose attributes were borrowed by Typhon. These
stars surround the full Moon of Libra, the last of the Superior Signs and the one
that precedes the new Moon of Spring, which will be reproduced in Taurus.

Isis collected the scattered fragments of Osiris' body, buried them, and
consecrated the phallus, which is carried in the ceremony of the *Pamylia* feasts
held on the Vernal Equinox that celebrated the congress of Osiris and the Moon.
Osiris returned from the darkness to aid Horus and Isis against the forces of
Typhon. Some say he reappeared in the form of a wolf, but others say it was in
the form of a horse. Fourteen days after the Moon is full in Libra, she arrives at
Taurus and unites with the Sun, whose fires she accumulates for fourteen days

while going from new to full Moon. Then she unites the harmony and order of all the months from the superior portion of the world where light always reigns, and she borrows from Osiris the power to destroy the evil and chaos that Typhon wrought upon nature during the winter. When Osiris returns from the lower hemisphere, he assumes the attributes of the Sun as it passes into Taurus. This is marked by the Wolf and the Centaur rising in the evening and the heliacal setting of Orion, which is in conjunction with the Sun of Spring, in his triumph over Typhon or darkness.

During the absence of Osiris but after she had hidden the coffin in the forest, Isis united with Typhon to the objection of Horus. When Isis returned to Osiris as he was about to attack Typhon, Horus deprived her of her ancient crown, but Mercury gave her a helmet shaped like the head of a bull in its place. Then Horus the mighty warrior, in the image of Orion, fought and defeated Typhon who was in the shape of the Serpent or Dragon of the Pole. Apollo destroys the same Python in Ovid, and Io becomes Isis when, fascinated by Jupiter, she is turned into a cow and placed in the sign of the Celestial Bull. The equinoctial year ends when the Sun and Moon are united with Orion, the Star of Horus, and placed in the Heavens under Taurus. The new Moon becomes young again and shows herself for the first time as a crescent in Gemini, the domicile of Mercury. Then in conjunction with the Sun, Orion provokes his rival the Scorpion, causing him to set whenever he himself reappears on the eastern horizon, with the Sun. The days lengthened and the evil and chaos are eradicated by degrees. Horus (*Aur*, Light) reigns triumphant, symbolizing the eternal renewal of the Sun's youth and creative vigor by his succession to the characteristics of Osiris, at the Vernal Equinox.

These were the progressions of the astronomical phenomena within the legend of Osiris and Isis. They suffice to explain the origin of the legend although the ornamentation from the poetical and figurative spirits of the Orient became excessive.

All of the ancient nations have legends with the Bull, Lamb, Lion, and Scorpion or Serpent, and all the religions have traces of the worship of the Sun. The equinoctial and solstitial feasts are still practiced everywhere. Our ceilings continue to glitter with the greater and lesser luminaries, and the number and arrangement of our lights have astronomical references. Our Lodges are full of the ancient symbols. In the old churches, chapels, Pagan temples, and pagodas, the altar is in the East and the ivy over the east windows represents Bacchus. Even the cross had astronomical origins.

Landseer was the author of the Sabean Researches who depicted another theory about the legend of Osiris in which he makes the constellation Boötes play a leading part. He reasoned that because none of the stars were visible at the same time as the Sun, at any given time the Sabean astronomers could only determine his actual place in the Zodiac through their observations of the heliacal and achronical risings and settings of the stars. There were many solar festivals among the Sabeans, and some were agricultural. The signs associated with those festivals were the risings and settings of the stars of BOÖTES, the Farmer, Bear-driver, or Hunter. The Priests considered his stars to be the established nocturnal indices or signs of the Sun's place in the ecliptic at different seasons of the year. The festivals were named *Aphanism* (disappearance) and *Zetesis* (the search of Osiris or Adonis, or *Boötes).* 484

The returns of certain stars related to the spring (or seed time) and harvest seasons seemed to the ancients to be eternal and unchangeable. Those periodical returns were considered celestial oracles by the initiated and more especially the masses, because they announced the important coming changes on which the prosperity and the very existence of man depended. The oldest of the Sabean constellations that frequently appeared on the Sabean celestial maps seemed to have been an astronomical *Priest*, a *King*, a *Queen*, a *Farmer*, and a *Warrior*. The *King* was *Cepheus* or *Chepheus* of Ethiopia. The *Farmer* was *Osiris, Bacchus, Sabazeus, Noah,* or *Boötes*. The stars of the Farmer were the signal to begin the agricultural labors on which annual production depended. These stars came to be considered and hailed in Egypt and Ethiopia as stars of terrestrial productivity, and prayers, offerings, and vows were regularly offered to them by the devout Sabeans.

Landseer said the stars in Boötes including those of the 5th magnitude totaled *twenty-six*. Their apparent successive achronical disappearance produced the legend of Typhon cutting Osiris into twenty-six pieces. There are actually more stars in the constellation, but they could not be observed without telescopes.

Plutarch said Osiris was cut into *fourteen* pieces. Diodorus said it was into *twenty-six* pieces, and Landseer's ideas varied from the common beliefs as follows:

Landseer thinks Typhon was the *ocean* which the ancients imagined or 485 believed surrounded the Earth, and all the stars successively appear to sink into it. [Perhaps the ancients considered TYPHON to be DARKNESS personified. The old legend says he was hunting by moonlight when he met with Osiris].

The ancient Saba were probably near the latitude 15° north. Axoum is nearly in 14°, and the Western Saba or Meroë is north of that. Fifty centuries ago, Aldebarán was the leading star of the year, and at the Vernal Equinox he had attained an elevation of about 14° at daybreak which would have been sufficient for him to have emerged from the Sun's rays and be visible. The ancients allowed *twelve* days for first magnitude stars to emerge from the solar rays, and there is even less twilight the further South we go.

At that time, Cynosura was not the North pole star, rather it was Alpha Draconis. This caused the stars to rise and set at different angles from their current risings and settings. Landseer constructed a globe with swiveling poles that were capable of any adjustment for the zodiac. He ascertained that in that remote period at latitude 15° north, the 26 stars in Boötes (or 27 including Arcturus) did not set anchronically in succession. Instead, they set simultaneously in pairs and triplets, totaling fourteen separate settings or disappearances that correspond with the fourteen pieces into which Osiris was cut according to Plutarch. Kappa, Iota, and Theta in the uplifted western hand were the last triplet to disappear. They actually skirted the horizon but were invisible at such a low latitude. The women of Phœnicia and Jerusalem wept for Thammuz (Osiris or Adonis) while the *Zetesis* (search) proceeded. Shortly thereafter, they reappeared below and to the eastward of α Draconis.

Aldebarán rose heliacally in the East and became visible just before daybreak on the very morning after the achronical departure of the last star of the Farmer.

Spica Virginis also rose at the same moment of the heliacal rising of Arcturus. One is near the middle of the Farmer, and the other near the middle of the Virgin. Arcturus may have been the part of Osiris' body that Isis did not recover.

486   At Dedan and Saba, it was thirty-six days from the *aphanism (disappearance)* of these stars to the heliacal rising of Aldebarán. It was forty days at Medina and a few more at Babylon and Byblos. During these days, the stars of the Farmer successively set out of sight during the *crepusculum* or short-lived morning twilight of those Southern skies, the special season of ancient astronomical observation.

The forty days of mourning for Osiris were measured by the departure of his Stars. The vernal season began when the last star had set out of sight, the Sun arose with Aldebarán, the Tauric leader of the Hosts of Heaven, and the East rejoiced and kept holiday.

With the exception of the Stars χ, ι and δ, Boötes did not begin to reappear in the Eastern quarter of the Heavens for about four months. The Stars of Taurus had declined Westward, and Virgo was rising heliacally. In that latitude, the Stars of Ursa Major [anciently termed the Ark of Osiris] set, and the last one, Benetnasch, returned to the Eastern horizon with the stars in the head of Leo right before the Summer Solstice. A month later, the Stars of the Farmer followed, and Ras, Mirach, and Arcturus almost simultaneously rise heliacally.

The Stars of Boötes rose in the East right after Vindemiatrix, as if under the gentle influence of its rays. In the East, Nature rejoiced at his sign. He had his annual career of prosperity, reveled in the East for three months, and attained meridian height with Virgo. When the Stars of the Water-Urn rose and Aquarius began to pour his annual deluge, he declined Westward following the Ark of Osiris. As he declined toward the Northwestern horizon and the Solar year grew old, his generative vigor gradually diminished, and the world mourned as his Stars descended beneath the Western Wave, signaling the death of Osiris.

The Ancient Astronomers saw all the great Symbols of Masonry in the Stars. Sirius is the Blazing Star (*l'Etoile Flamboyante*), and the Sun is symbolized by the point within a Circle. The Sun, Moon, and Mercury (or Anubis) are the three
487   Great Lights of the Lodge. The figures and numbers exhibited by the Stars were assigned unique and divine powers, and the veneration paid to numbers

originated there. The three Kings in Orion form a straight line with each equidistant from the other. The two extreme Stars are 3° apart, and each of the three are 1° 30' to the nearest. Because the number *three* is unique to apprentices, the straight line is the first principle of Geometry by having length but no breadth, the extension of a point, an emblem of Unity and Good as the divided or broken line is a symbol of Duality or Evil. Near these Stars are the *five* Hyades, the number appropriate for Fellowcrafts. Close to them are the *seven* Pleiades, the master's number. These three sacred numbers are consecrated in Masonry as they were in the Pythagorean philosophy. They always appear together in the Heavens when the Bull, the emblem of fertility and production, glitters among the Stars and Aldebarán leads the Hosts of Heaven (*Tsbauth*).

Algenib in Perseus, and Almaach and Algol in Andromeda, form a right-angled triangle, illustrate the 47th problem of Euclid, and display the Grand Master's square upon the skies. Denebola in Leo, Arcturus in Boötes, and Spica in Virgo form the equilateral triangle which is the universal emblem of Perfection, and it represents the Deity with His Trinity of Infinite Attributes, Wisdom, Power, and Harmony, and the other, generative, preserving, and destroying Powers. The Three Kings with Rigel in Orion form two triangles included in one, and Capella and Menkalina in Auriga, with Bellatrix and Betelgueux in Orion, form two isosceles triangles with β Tauri, which is equidistant from each pair. The first four make a parallelogram, the oblong square so often mentioned in our Degrees.

Julius Firmicus' description of the Mysteries said, "Except for the funerals and mournings which are annually celebrated to honor Osiris, there is also a physical reason. They label the seeds of fruit as Osiris, the Earth as Isis, and the natural heat as Typhon. The fruits are ripened by the natural heat, collected for the life of man, separated from their marriage to the earth, and are sown again when Winter approaches. This sowing of the seeds would have to be the death of Osiris, and when the fruits begin generate a new procreation again, this is the discovery of Osiris."

The decay of vegetation and the falling of the leaves were regarded as emblems of destruction and evidence of the Power that changes Life into Death 488 upon all nature. Life was again brought out of Death by the springing of leaves, buds, and flowers. The spring was a sign of the restoration to life, but these were all secondary and referred to the Sun as the first cause. It was *his* figurative death that was mourned, not theirs, and His death and return to life was connected to many of the stars.

We have alluded to the twelve signs of the Zodiac as they apply to the legend of the Master's Degree. Some other coincidences have sufficient interest to warrant mentioning.

Khir-Om was accosted at the East, West, and South Gates of the Temple. The Ancients called the two equinoxes the Gates of Heaven, and the

Syrians and Egyptians considered the Fish (the Constellation near Aquarius) to be indicative of violence and death.

Khir-Om lay in the grave for several days, and at the Winter Solstice the length of the days did not noticeably increase for five or six days. Then the Sun began to climb Northward as Osiris was said to arise from the dead. Similarly, Khir-Om was raised by the power of the Lion (Leo), who drew him toward the Summer Solstice.

The names of the three assassins may have been derived from three Stars that we have already named. We search in vain for the Hebrew or Arabic names *Jubelo, Jubela,* and *Jubelum.* There is no explanation available for them in those languages, nor are the names *Gibs, Gravelot,* and *Hobben,* and the like in the Ancient and Accepted Rite any more plausible to any of the ancient languages. By the precession of the Equinoxes when the Sun was in Libra at the Autumnal Equinox, he met in that sign where the reign of Typhon started. Three Stars formed a triangle, *Zuben-es Chamali* in the West, *Zuben-Hak-Rabi* in the East, and *Zuben-El-Gubi* in the South below the Tropic of Capricorn that was within the realm of Darkness. In Zuben-Hak-Rabi we can see Jubelum Akirop; in Zuben-El-Gubi we can see Jubelo Gibs; and time and misinterpretation may even have changed Es Chamali into Gravelot.

489 Isis was the Moon personified who sought her husband. In the Legend of the Master's Degree, nine Fellowcrafts, the Nine Knights Elu (the York Rite counts twelve), in white aprons were sent to search for Khir-Om. There are nine conspicuous Stars along the path the Moon travels which sailors use to determine their longitude at Sea: Arietis, Aldebarán, Pollux, Regulus, Spica Virginis, Antares, Altair, Fomalhaut, and Markab. These are the stars who probably accompanied Isis in her search.

In the York Rite, *twelve* Fellowcrafts were sent to search for the body of Khir-Om and the murderers. They correspond with the Pleiades and Hyades in Taurus, where the Sun was found when Light began to prevail over Darkness and the Mysteries were held. The Pleiades were the Stars of the ocean to the nighttime mariner and the Virgins of Spring heralding the season of blossoms.

Only six Pleiades are now visible. The original twelve may have included Aldebarán and five Stars connected to the Pleiades (the Three Kings in the belt of Orion, Bellatrix, and Betelgueux on his shoulders with the latter two the brightest of the flashing starry hosts).

Job asked, "Can you bind the sweet influences of the Pleiades or loosen the bands of Orion?" In the book of Amos, we find these Stars connected with the victory of Light over Darkness when the Seer said, "Seek Him that makes the Seven Stars (the Pleiades) and Orion, AND TURNETH THE SHADOW OF DEATH INTO MORNING."

An old Masonic legend says a dog led the Nine Elus to the cave where Abiram hid. Boötes was anciently called Caleb Anubach, the Barking Dog, and he was personified by Anubis who had the head of a dog. Arcturus' fiery red star is also connected to Job with the Pleiades and Orion. Arcturus rose after the Sun when Taurus opened the year, and for sixty days after the Winter Solstice seemed to be searching through the darkness for him, until, they rose at the same hour. Orion rose at noon on the Winter Solstice, and at night he also seemed to be in search of the Sun.

490

When the Sun enters the Autumnal Equinox, there are nine remarkable Stars that come to the meridian at nearly the same time, rising as Libra sets and seeming to chase that Constellation. They are Capella and Menkalina in the Charioteer, Aldebarán in Taurus, and Bellatrix, Betelgueux, the Three Kings, and Rigel in Orion. Aldebarán passes the meridian first, giving him the title of *Leader*. Nowhere in the heavens are there so many splendid Stars as there are near the meridian. Closely following them but further South was Sirius, the Dog-Star, who led the nine Elus to the murderer's cave.

The division of the signs into the ascending (Aquarius to Cancer) and descending (Leo to Capricorn) series refer to the upward and downward progress of the soul. The signs were also divided into six superior and six inferior signs. The six superior signs in 2455 B.C. were Taurus to Scorpio, and in 300 B.C. they were Aries to Libra. The six inferior signs in 2455 B.C. were Scorpio to Taurus, and in 300 B.C. they were Libra to Aries. These two Hemispheres were considered the Kingdoms of Good and Evil, Light and Darkness, Ormuzd and Ahriman to the Persians, and Osiris and Typhon to the Egyptians.

For the Persians, the first six Spirits that Ormuzd created presided over the first six signs, Aries, Taurus, Gemini, Cancer, Leo, and Virgo. The six evil Spirits created by Ahriman presided over the other six signs, Libra, Scorpio, Sagittarius, Capricorn, Aquarius, and Pisces. The soul entered the realm of Evil and Darkness when it passed into the Constellations that follow the Autumnal Equinox, and it reentered the realm of Good and Light when it returned to those that follow the Vernal Equinox. Even today, some still believe that the soul loses its happiness at the Autumnal Equinox but regains it at the Vernal Equinox.

Sallust the Philosopher said the Feasts of Rejoicing at the Vernal Equinox celebrated the return of the soul to the Gods, the recovered principle of Light's superiority over Darkness, or day over night, and it was the most favorable time for souls desiring to re-ascend to their Principle. The Feasts of Mourning were in memory of the rape of Proserpine at the Autumnal Equinox, when Darkness and Night become the victors and the souls descended from the Heavens into the infernal regions.

491

According to Firmicus, this is the reason that the ancient astrologers fixed the location of the river Styx to the 8th degree of Libra and the reason that Styx allegorically symbolized the earth.

The Emperor Julian gives the following more fully developed explanation. He stated the reason the exalted Mysteries of Ceres and Proserpine were celebrated at the Autumnal Equinox was that, at that time of the year, man

359

most feared that the destructive and dark power of the Evil Principle might harm their souls as it conquered nature. The ceremonies were a safety precaution thought to be necessary as the God of Light passed into the opposite or adverse region of the world. There was less to be feared at the Vernal Equinox because God was present in one portion of the world, and He *recalled souls and showed Himself to be their Savior.* Julian barely developed the theological idea of the attractive force that the Sun exercised over souls, drawing them to him and raising them to his luminous sphere. He attributed this effect to the feasts of Attis or the feasts of Rejoicing, which lasted three days before the mourning for that death began. He concluded that the Mysteries were celebrated at the Vernal Equinox because, as the sun drew closer to the equinoctial point of Spring, the length of the days increased, and that time just seemed appropriate for those ceremonies. There is a great similarity between the substance of Light and the nature of the Gods. Souls are attracted toward the solar light because light is analogous to the Divine Nature. As light increases at the Vernal Equinox and the days prevail in length over the nights, the Sun has an attractive force besides the visible energy of his rays that is helpful to souls trying to return to their First Principle. He said he did not pursue the explanation further because it belongs to a mysterious doctrine beyond the reach of the masses and known only to those who understand the method of action of Deity. Like the Chaldæan author whom he cited, he had treated the Mysteries of Light as the God with seven rays.

The Ancients believed the Souls shared in the destiny here below because they emanated from the Principle of Light, and therefore they could not be indifferent to nor unaffected by the victory and defeat of the Great Luminary.

This belief is confirmed by examining some of the Symbols used in the Mysteries. One of the most famous symbols was THE SERPENT, also the Symbol of this Degree. The Hebrew and Gnostic theory of the Universe designated this the serpent as the author of the fate of Souls. It was consecrated in the Mysteries of Bacchus and Eleusis. Pluto overcame the virtue of Proserpine by using the form of a serpent, and like the Egyptian God Serapis, he was always depicted seated on or entwined by a serpent. This image is found on the Mithraic Monuments, and the Egyptians gave it some attributes of Typhon. The sacred basilisk coiled with its head and neck raised was the royal insignia of the Pharaohs. The Egyptian Monuments depicted two of them entwined and suspended from the winged Globe. A tablet found in a Tomb at Thebes had an image of a God piercing a serpent's head with a spear. Another tablet from the Temple of Osiris at Philæ depicted a tree with a man on one side, a woman on the other, and in front of the woman was a basilisk with horns on its head and a disk between the horns. Medusa's head was encircled by winged snakes, and once she was beheaded, they left the Hierogram or Sacred Cypher of the Ophites (Gnostic Serpent worshippers). The Serpent can be found upon the monuments of all the Ancient Nations in connection with the Globe or circle.

The Serpent being grasped by Serpentarius (the Serpent bearer) is found on the Celestial Globe over Libra, the sign where souls descended or fell. The head of the reptile is under Corona Borealis, the Northern Crown, also called *Libera*, or *Proserpine* by Ovid. These two Constellations rise with Libra, who follows Virgo (or Isis) whose feet are resting upon the eastern horizon at Sunrise on the day of the equinox. The Serpent extending above and between Libra and Scorpio created the gate through which souls descended, when those two signs marked the Autumnal Equinox. This alluded to the Serpent, which was flung onto the Initiate's chest in the Mysteries of Bacchus Saba-Zeus. *493*

Hence came the cryptic expression, *the Serpent creates the Bull, and the Bull the Serpent.* This alludes to the two adverse constellations of the two equinoxes. One rose as the other set, but both were the points of the heavens through which souls passed, either ascending or descending. Souls fell by the Serpent of Autumn and were regenerated by the Bull, whose attributes Bacchus-Zagreus and Osiris adopted in *their* Mysteries when the Bull was slain and restored to life to represent the fall and rise of souls.

Eventually the regenerating Sun adopted the attributes of *Aries* or the Lamb, and in the Mysteries of Ammon, souls were regenerated by passing through that sign, after falling through the Serpent.

The Serpent-bearer was Ophicus (Æsculapius) the God of Healing. In the Mysteries of Eleusis, that Constellation was placed in the eighth Heaven, and the feast of Æsculapius was celebrated on the eighth day of those Mysteries. It was also termed Epidaurus, or the feast of the Serpent of Epidaurus. The Serpent was sacred to Æsculapius, and it was connected to the mythological adventures of Ceres.

The ceremony of libations to the Souls referred to the ascent and descent of Souls by pouring wine upon the ground while looking towards the two gates of Heaven.

Cere and the Serpent, and Jupiter Ammon and the Bull were all part of the Mysteries of Bacchus. The fables of the generation of the Bull by the Serpent and the Serpent by the Bull, of the Scorpion biting the testicles of the Bull, and of Jupiter impregnating Ceres by tossing the testicles of a Ram into her bosom are explained. At the Autumnal Equinox place Aries (or Jupiter Ammon) into the West occupied by the setting Sun, and place Virgo (Ceres) on the Eastern horizon with the Crown, or Proserpine, in her train. Place Taurus setting in the West, and Jupiter Ammon (or the Sun of Aries) in the East with the Serpent, and the Crown will rise after Virgo with the Serpent in the train. Place the Sun at the Vernal equinox and Libra with the Serpent under the Crown *494* in the West, and the Bull and the Pleiades will rise in the East.

In the Mysteries of the bull-horned Bacchus, the officers held serpents in their hands, raised them above their heads, and cried out "Eva!" This was the generic name of the serpent and the particular name of the constellation where the Persians placed Eve and the serpent. The Arabians called it *Hevan*, Ophiucus himself, *Hawa*, and the brilliant star in his head, *Ras-al-Hawa*. The use of this word *Eva* or *Evoë* made Clemens of Alexandria believe that the priests in the Mysteries invoked *Eve*, who brought evil into the world.

The mystic winnowing fan surrounded by serpents was used in the feasts of Bacchus. A basilisk wrapped around the handle of the mystic vase in the Isiac Mysteries. The Ophites kept a serpent in a mysterious ark and allowed it to glide amongst the sacred bread when they celebrated the Mysteries. The Romans kept serpents in the Temples of Bona Dea and Æsculapius. The pursuit of Latona by the serpent Python was presented in the Mysteries of Apollo, and the dragon Typhon pursued Isis in the Egyptian Mysteries.

According to Sanchoniathon, TAAUT was the interpreter of Heaven and attributed something so divine to the nature of the dragon and serpents that the Phœnicians and Egyptians followed suit. They have more vitality and spiritual force than any other creature. They have a fiery nature demonstrated by the quickness and force of their motions, and they assume many shapes and attitudes. When they have reached old age, they shed off that age, are young again, and they increase in size and strength.

The Egyptian Priests fed the sacred serpents at the temple in Thebes. Taaut discussed the mysteries regarding the serpent in his writings. Sanchoniathon said the serpent never died unless by a violent death. It was immortal and reentered into itself, which according to some ancient theosophists, particularly those of India, was an attribute of the Deity.

495

The Phœnicians called the serpent *Agathodemon* (the good spirit), and Kneph was the Serpent God of the Egyptians.

Sanchoniathon said the Egyptians depicted the serpent with the head of a hawk because of that bird's swift flight. Actually, the hawk headed serpent was the symbol of the Sun. The head Priest was the sacred interpreter who gave very mysterious explanations of that symbol. He said such a serpent was a very divine creature that lit all the first-born space with the rays of his opened eyes, and when he closed them, it was dark again.

A snake was the letter T or DJ in the hieroglyphic characters, and it occurs many times on the Rosetta stone. The horned serpent was also the hieroglyph for a God.

According to Eusebius, the Egyptians represented the world with a blue circle, sprinkled with flames, and surrounding a serpent with a hawk's head. Proclus said that they represented the four quarters of the world with a cross and the soul of the world (Kneph) by a serpent surrounding it in the form of a circle.

Anaxagoras wrote that Orpheus believed that the vessel and the water it produced were the primitive principles of things, and when combined they gave existence to a two-headed serpent. One was the head of a lion and the other of a bull. Between these two heads was the figure of the God Hercules (or Kronos) who created the egg of the world that produced Heaven and earth by dividing itself into two hemispheres. From that egg, the God Phanes originated in the shape of a serpent.

The Egyptian Goddess *Ken* was depicted as standing naked on a lion while holding two serpents in her hand, and she was the same as *Astarte* or *Ashtaroth* of the Assyrians. *Hera* held a serpent by the head in her right hand, and she was worshipped in the Great Temple at Babylon. There were also two large silver serpents worshipped near *Khea*.

A sculpture from Kouyunjik had two serpents attached to poles near a fire-altar. Two eunuchs tended its sacred fire, and a bearded figure leads a wild goat to the sacrifice.

The serpent of the Temple of Epidaurus was sacred to the God of Medicine (*Æsculapius*), but it was taken to Rome following a pestilence 462 years after the city was built.

The Phœnicians symbolized the God *Nomu* (*Kneph* or *Amun-Kneph*) with a serpent. The good spirit, *Horhat*, was symbolized in Egypt by two cobras supporting a Sun, and the serpent with the winged globe was placed over the doors and windows of the Temples as a guardian angel. Antipater of Sidon called *Amun* "the renowned Serpent", and the Cerastes (cobra) is often found embalmed in the Thebaid Provinces.

A serpent coiled around a tree trunk was engraved on ancient Tyrian and Indian coins. The Serpent Deity, *Python*, was considered prophetic, and the tripod at Delphi was a triple-headed serpent of gold. The portals of all the Egyptian Temples were decorated with the sacred Circle and the Serpent. It was also found upon the Temple of Naki-Rustan in Persia, on the triumphal arch in Beijing, China, over the gates of the great Temple of Chaundi Teeva, in Java, upon the walls of Athens, and in the Temple of Minerva at Tegea. The Mexican emblem was formed by two Serpents converging in a circle, each with a human head in its mouth. The Buddhist crosses in Ireland had serpents carved upon them, and wreaths of snakes are on the columns of the ancient Hindu Temple at Burwah-Sangor.

The Serpent was an Egyptian symbol of Divine Wisdom, and it symbolized Eternity when forming a circle with its tail in its mouth. It was a symbol of the Universe in the rituals of Zoroaster, and the ring between two Serpents was the Chinese symbol of the world, governed by the power and wisdom of the Creator. The Serpent coiled around an Egg was the Indian, Egyptian, and Druid symbol of the creation of the Universe. A Serpent with an egg in its mouth was a symbol of the Universe beholding all the generative power of the Sun.

The Serpent shedding its skin and seemingly renewing its youth made it an emblem of eternity and immortality. Syrian women used it as a charm against barrenness, like the devotees of Mithras and Saba-Zeus. Fohi, Cecrops, and Erechtheus were the half-man, half-serpent, Earth-born civilizers of the early world. The snake was the guardian of the Athenian Acropolis. NAKHUSTAN

496

497

was the brazen serpent of the wilderness that was adopted by the Hebrews as a token power of healing. Christ said, "Be wise as serpents and harmless as doves."

The Serpent was often used as a symbol of jealousy and hatred. It appeared in the emblems of Siva-Roudra, the power of desolation and death. It was the bane of Aëpytus, Idom, Archemorus, and Philoctetes. It gnawed the roots of the tree of life in the Eddas, and it bit the heel of unfortunate Eurydice. To the Hebrew writers, it was generally a type of evil, and it is especially so in the Indian and Persian Mythologies. The Cosmic Serpent (Vasouki) churned the Sea by rotating Mount Mandar within its coils. It spit a terrible poison trying to produce the Amrita, or water of immortality, to infect the Universe, but Vishnu rendered it harmless by swallowing it. Ahriman, in serpent form, invaded the realm of Ormuzd, and the Bull, as the emblem of life, is wounded by him and dies. It became a religious obligation for devout followers of Zoroaster to kill reptiles, impure animals, and especially serpents. The moral and astronomical importance of the Serpent were connected. It became a belief of the Zend-Avesta that Ahriman, the Principle of Evil, made the Great Serpent of Winter, who assaulted the creation of Ormuzd.

A serpent ring was a well-known symbol of time. To dramatically express how time feeds upon itself, the Egyptian priests fed bull fat to vipers in a subterranean chamber that represented the Sun's Winter home. The dragon of Winter pursued Ammon (the golden ram) to Mount Casius. Virgo was bitten on the heel by Serpens, and together with Scorpio, they rise behind her. Honey was the emblem of purity and salvation, and it was thought to be an antivenom to the serpent's bite. The bees of Aristæus are emblems of nature's bounty, but they were destroyed by the serpent and restored within the entrails of the Vernal Bull.

The Sun-God is finally victorious. Chrishna crushes the head of Calyia, Apollo destroys Python, and Hercules slays Lernæan whose poison festered in the foot of Philoctetes Mopsus, Chiron, or Sagittarius. The infant Hercules destroys the deadly snakes, and wars against hydras and dragons like St. George of England and Michael the Archangel.

The solar and lunar eclipses were believed to be caused by the assaults of a demon in dragon form. This was the original Leviathan or Crooked Serpent of antiquity, paralyzed by the power of Jehovah and suspended in the sky like a glittering trophy, yet always in pursuit of the Sun and Moon. When it finally overtakes them, it entwines them in its folds and prevents them from shining. The last Indian Avatara and the Eddas both expected a fire-breathing serpent to destroy the world. The serpent became a formidable obstacle to the career of the Sun-God, because it dominated the close of the year by guarding the approach to the golden fleece of Aries and the three apples or seasons of the Hesperides. The Great Destroyer of snakes (Hercules) is occasionally married to them (the northern dragon), fathering the three ancestors of Scythia, because at one time, the Sun seems to rise victorious over darkness, and at another time, it sinks into its embraces. The northern constellation Draco is the astronomical belt of the Universe as it winds through the wintry bear like a river or the serpent encircling the egg in the Egyptian hieroglyphs.

The Persian Ahriman was called "The old serpent", "the original liar", "the Prince of Darkness", and "the nomad". The Dragon was a familiar symbol of the waters and rivers, and the pastoral Asiatic Tribes symbolized their powerful neighbor nations, who adored the dragon or Fish, were themselves symbolized under the form of dragons. Ophioneus warred against Kronos in the old Greek Theology, but he was defeated and cast into the sea (his proper element). There, he was crowned the Sea God Oannes (Dragon or Leviathan) of the watery half of creation, who spewed a flood of water at the persecuted woman of the Apocalypse. He was the monster who threatened to devour Hesione and Andromeda and who, for a time, became the grave of Hercules and Jonah. He is obscurely named Rahab, and in Job, he was overcome and defeated *499* by Jehovah.

The Sun-God appears in the Spring as Mithras or Europa riding a Bull, but in the opposite half of the Zodiac, he rides the emblem of the waters, the winged horse of Nestor or Poseidon. The Serpent rises heliacally at the Autumnal Equinox, besetting the cold constellation Sagittarius with a poisonous influence, and it is explained as the reptile on the path that "bites the horse's heels so that his rider falls backward." The same serpent, the Oannes Aphrenos or Musaros of Syncellus, was the Midgard Serpent that Odin sank beneath the sea, but it grew to such a size that it encircled the whole earth.

These Asian symbols of the contest between the Sun-God and the Dragon of Darkness and Winter were imported into both the Zodiac and the circle of European legend. Both Thor and Odin fought dragons, Apollo fought Python, Achilles fought Scamander, and Bellerophon fought the Chimæra. In the apocryphal book of Esther, dragons foretold "a day of darkness and obscurity," and St. George of England, the problematic Cappadocian Prince, was originally a varying form of Mithras. Jehovah was said to have "cut Rahab and wounded the dragon." The dragon was the leader of the rebellious stars. His tail drew a third part of the Host of Heaven and cast them to the earth. According to Enoch, "he did not come at the right time." Jehovah "divided the sea and broke the heads of the Dragons in the waters." According to the Jewish and Persian belief, near the end of time, the Dragon would enjoy a short period of amnesty that would be a season of the people's greatest suffering. In the end, however, he would be bound and destroyed in the great battle with the Messiah or eaten by the faithful, as suggested by the Rabbinical figure. Like Ahriman or Vasouki, he might ultimately be absorbed by and united with the Principle of good.

Diodorus said that there were two large, silver serpents (each weighing thirty talents) near the image of Rhea in the Temple of Bel at Babylon. There was also an image of Juno holding the head of a serpent in her right hand. The

500 Greeks called Bel *Beliar,* and Hesychius interpreted that word to mean "dragon" or "great serpent". From the book, *Bel and the Dragon,* we learn that a great, live serpent was worshipped in Babylon.

The Assyrians, Emperors of Constantinople, Parthians, Scythians, Saxons, Chinese, and Danes all measured the serpent as a standard. The *Persici Dracones* standards were among the spoils taken by Aurelian from Zenobia. The Persians depicted Ormuzd and Ahriman as two serpents competing for the global egg. A human body with a lion's head and encircled by a serpent represented Mithras. In the Sadder, was the precept: "Killing serpents repeats the Zend-Avesta and awards great merit as if you had killed so many devils."

Serpents encircling or emerging from rings and globes are common on the Persian, Egyptian, Chinese, and Indian monuments. Vishnu was represented as sleeping on a coiled serpent, whose folds formed a canopy over him. Mahadeva was represented with a snake around his neck, one around his hair, and armlets of serpents on both arms. Bhairava sits on the coils of a serpent whose head rises above his own. Parvati has snakes about her neck and waist. Vishnu is the Preserving Spirit, Mahadeva is Siva, the Evil Principle, Bhairava is his son, and Parvati is his wife. The King of Evil Demons in the Hindu Mythology was called *Naga,* the King of Serpents, whose name is traced to the Hebrew *Nachash,* meaning serpent.

Cashmere had seven hundred carved images of serpents that were worshipped, and in Tibet, the great Chinese Dragon ornamented the Temples of the Grand Lama. In China, the dragon was the crest and symbol of royalty, sculpted in all the Temples, displayed on furniture, and embroidered on the clothing of the nobility. The Emperor wore it as a protective badge, and it was engraved on his scepter, crown, and all the vases of the imperial palace. The Chinese believed that there was a dragon of extraordinary strength and sovereign power in Heaven, in the air, on the waters, and in the mountains. The God Fohi had the form of a man with the tail of a snake that will be explained in a subsequent Degree.

The dragon and serpent are the 5th and 6th signs of the Chinese Zodiac. 501 The Hindus and Chinese believed that the sun or moon, when eclipsed, had been seized by a serpent (*Asootee* of the Hindus) or dragon shrouding the globe and the constellation Draco, and it also refers to "the War in Heaven when Michael and his Angels fought the dragon."

Sanchoniathon said Taaut authored the worship of serpents among the Phœnicians and added, "He consecrated the species of dragons and serpents, and the Phœnicians and Egyptians practiced his superstition. He was also the first to make an image of Cœlus," the image representing the Heavenly Hosts of Stars using visible symbols similar to the Egyptian Thoth. The Tyrian coins during Alexander's reign had serpents etched in many positions: coiled around trees, erect in front of altars, and crushed by the Syrian Hercules.

The seventh letter of the Egyptian alphabet is *Zeuta* meaning *Life*. It was sacred to Thoth and symbolized by a serpent standing on its tail. The serpent was dedicated to the God of healing, who leans on a knotted stick with a snake coiled around it. The Isiac tablet that described the Mysteries of Isis had references to serpents as her emblems in every part. The *Asp* was especially dedicated to her, and it is seen on the heads of her statues, the bonnets of her priests, and the crowns of the Kings of Egypt. Serapis was occasionally illustrated with a human head and serpent tail, and one engraving placed him with two minor Gods: one a serpent with a bull's head and the other a serpent with lion's head.

An ancient sacrificial vessel found in Denmark had several compartments with an engraving of a serpent attacking a kneeling boy, pursuing him, fleeing him, and conversing with him. This is similar to the Sun at the new year represented by a child sitting on a lotus and the relationship of the Vernal Sun with the Autumnal Serpent, pursued by, pursuing, and in conjunction with him. There were also other figures of the Zodiac on this vessel.

The base of the *tripod* of the Pythian Priestess was a triple-headed serpent of brass, whose three heads in a triangular form supported the conical column of its body, which was coiled in decreasing circles as they moved up the column and away from the heads. There was a similar column placed in the Hippodrome at 502 Constantinople by the city's founder. It is said that Mohammed broke one of the heads with his hands and the other by a blow from his iron mace.

The British God HU was called "The Dragon - Ruler of the World," and his chariot was drawn by serpents. His ministers were styled *adders*. A Druid in a poem of Taliessin said, "I am a Druid, I am an *Architect*, I am a Prophet, I am a *Serpent* (Gnadi)." The chariot of the Goddess Ceridwen was also drawn by serpents.

A passage in the eulogy of Uther Pendragon described the religious rites of the Druids' mystic and obscure allusion to the Autumnal Serpent pursuing the Sun along the circle of the Zodiac, to the celestial cup, and finally to the Golden horns of Virgil's milk white Bull. It read, "The Sanctuary is earnestly praying to *The Gliding King*, who forces *the Fair One* to retreat to the evil that covers the huge stones while the Dragon moves over the vessels of drink-offering while they are in *the Golden Horns*." A couple of lines later, the Priest implored the victorious *Beli*, the Sun-God of the Babylonians.

The serpent is often found associated with the Cross on the Ancient Monuments. The Serpent upon a Cross was an Egyptian Standard that occurred repeatedly upon the Grand Staircase in the Temple of Osiris at Philæ and on the pyramid of Giza, which pictured two kneeling figures erecting a Cross, on the top of which is a serpent. The *Crux Ansata* was a Cross with a coiled Serpent above it, and it is probably the most common emblem on the Egyptian Monuments, because almost every Deity or Priest carried it their hand. It was shaped like the iron tether pins used to stake a young animal in a pasture, and it became a symbol of Royalty to the Shepherd Kings.

A Teutonic or Maltese Cross formed by four curved lines within a circle is also common on the Monuments and represented the Equinoxes and the Solstices.

503 The Caduceus, carried by Hermes or Mercury, and also by Cybele, Minerva, Anubis, Hercules Ogmius the God of the Celts, and the personified Constellation Virgo, was a winged wand with two entwined serpents. Originally, it was a simple Cross symbolizing the equator and equinoctial planes as four elements proceeding from a common center. A Cross enclosed in a circle then surrounded by a crescent, became a symbol of the Supreme Deity. The form improved, and the arms of the Cross were changed into wings. The circle and crescent were formed by two snakes emerging from the wand with their heads making the horns of the crescent.

The triple Tau in the center of a circle and a triangle symbolizes the Sacred Name; the Sacred Triad of the Creating, Preserving, and Destroying Powers; and the three great lights of Masonry. If we add the single Tau Cross to the Masonic point within a Circle and the two parallel lines, we have the Ancient Egyptian Triple Tau.

A column shaped like a cross with a circle above it was used by the Egyptians as a flood gauge for the Nile. The Tau and Triple Tau are found in many Ancient Alphabets, and they may be connected within two circles, the double cube, or the perfect ashlar.

The *Crux Ansata* is found on the sculptures at Khorsabad, the ivories from Nimroud, and the cylinders of the later Assyrian period.

The single Tau represented the one God, and the Triple Tau represented the Trinity of his attributes WISDOM, STRENGTH, and BEAUTY or HARMONY, the three Masonic pillars.

The Latin Vulgate and the most ancient copies of the Septuagint translate Ezekiel 9:4 as: "The Lord said, 'Go through the middle of Jerusalem and mark a TAU upon the foreheads of those who mourn for the wrongdoings done there." This *Tau* forms the cross of this Degree, and it is the emblem of *life* and *salvation*. The Samaritan *Tau,* the Hebrew *Tau,* and the Ethiopic *Tavvi* are the obvious prototypes of the Greek τ.

504 In ancient times, the *Tau* was a symbol of innocence marked on those acquitted of crimes by a judge. Military commanders marked it on soldiers who returned from the field of battle unhurt as a sign of their safety under the Divine Protection. The Druids would carefully prune a tree into the sacred shape of a Tau Cross and then consecrate it with solemn ceremonies. On the tree, they deeply carved the word THAU which meant God. On the right arm of the Cross, they inscribed the word HESULS, on the left, BELEN or BELENUS, and on the middle of the trunk, THARAMIS. This represented the sacred *Triad*.

The Indians, Egyptians, and Arabians all paid respect to the sign of the Cross thousands of years before the coming of Christ. It was a sacred symbol everywhere. The Hindus and the Celtic Druids built many of their Temples in the form of a Cross, as the ruins clearly show. The ancient Druidical Temple at Classerniss on the Island of Lewis in Scotland was a Circle of 12 Stones. On the east, west, and south sides were three stones, in the center was the image of the Deity. In the north were two rows of nineteen stones, and one stone at the entrance. The Supernal Pagoda at Benares and the Druidical subterranean grotto at New Grange in Ireland were also in the form of a Cross.

The Statue of Osiris at Rome had the emblem of a Cross. Isis and Ceres also bore it, and the initiation caverns were constructed in that shape with a pyramid over the *Sacellum*.

Crosses were cut into the stones of the Temple of Serapis in Alexandria, and many Tau Crosses are visible in the sculptures of Alabastion and Esné in Egypt. The symbol of the Egyptian God Kneph on coins was a Cross within a Circle.

The Crux Ansata was an emblem of Osiris and Hermes. It was deemed a Sublime Hieroglyphic that possessed mysterious powers and virtues, a wonder-working amulet.

The Sacred Tau is in the hands of the mummy shaped figures between the forelegs of the Sphinxes in the great avenue leading from Luxor to Karnac. The Kabbalists expressed the number 10 with a Tau Cross, the perfect number 505 denoting Heaven, the Pythagorean Tetractys, or the unspeakable name of God. The Tau Cross is also on the stones in front of the door of the Temple of Amunoth III at Thebes, who reigned near the time when the Israelites took possession of Canaan.

Tertullian had been initiated, and he informed us the Tau was inscribed on the forehead of everyone admitted into the Mysteries of Mithras. The Tau symbolized Life, the Circle symbolized Eternity, and when combined they symbolized Eternal Life. When an Egyptian King was initiated, the Tau was impressed upon his lips as the emblem of life and key of the Mysteries. The Tau Cross was used in the Indian Mysteries under the name *Tiluk*, and this mark, when placed on a candidate, signified he was to be set apart for the Sacred Mysteries.

The names of thirteen Great Gods (including YAV and BEL) were discovered at Nimroud on the upright tablet of the King. The left hand character of each name was a cross made of two wedge-shaped characters.

The Cross appears on an Ancient Phœnician medal found in the ruins of Citium, on the very ancient Buddhist Obelisk near Ferns in Rosshire, on the Buddhist Round Towers in Ireland, and upon the splendid obelisk from the same era at Forres in Scotland. The facade of a temple at Kalabche in Nubia has three regal figures each holding a Crux Ansata.

The Subterranean Mithraic Temple at New Grange, Scotland, like the Pagodas of Benares and Mathura, were in the form of a Cross. Magnificent Buddhist Crosses were erected and are still standing at Clonmacnoise, Finglas, and Kilcullen in Ireland. Wherever the monuments of Buddhism are found in India, Ceylon, or Ireland, we also find the Cross, because Buddha or Boudh was believed to have been crucified.

The Mystic Cross identified the planets that were known to the Ancients, in conjunction with the solar or lunar symbols. Saturn was a cross over a crescent. Jupiter was a cross under a crescent. Mars was a cross leaned against a circle. Venus was a cross under a circle, and Mercury was a cross crowned by a circle and that under a crescent.

506   The Solstices at Cancer and Capricorn and the two Gates of Heaven are the two pillars of Hercules which the Sun never journeyed beyond. They appear in our Lodges as the two great columns, Jachin and Boaz, and as the two parallel lines of the circle with a point in the center (an emblem of the Sun between the two tropics of Cancer and Capricorn).

In our Lodges, the Blazing Star represents Sirius, Anubis, or Mercury, the Guardian and Guide of Souls. Our Ancient English brethren considered it an emblem of the Sun. The old Lectures said, "The Blazing Star in the center refers to that Grand Luminary, the Sun, which enlightens the Earth and dispenses blessings to mankind with its amiable influence." It was also said to be an emblem of Prudence. The word *Prudentia* originally meant *Foresight*, and accordingly, the Blazing Star is regarded as an emblem of Omniscience or the All-Seeing Eye, which was the Sun to the Ancients.

The Dagger of the Elu of Nine, used in the Mysteries of Mithras with its black blade and white hilt, was an emblem of the two principles of Light and Darkness.

We learn from Eratosthenes that the Constellation Virgo was Isis (Ceres) portrayed by a woman holding an ear of wheat. The different emblems that accompany her in the description given by Apuleius were a serpent on either side, a golden vase with a serpent wrapped around the handle, and the bear, ape, and Pegasus that represented the Constellations that seemed to march in her train on the day of the Vernal Equinox.

The cup consecrated in both the Mysteries of Isis and Eleusis was the Constellation Crater or the Cup. The sacred vessel of the Isiac ceremony had its counterpart in the Heavens. The Olympic robe worn by the Initiate was a magnificent mantle, covered with images of serpents and animals. Under this robe were twelve other sacred robes that alluded to the starry Heavens and the twelve signs. The seven immersions in water alluded to the seven spheres that the soul plunged through to arrive here and take its place in a body.

507   During the three centuries before the Christian era, the Celestial Virgin occupied the horoscope, Eastern point, and the gate of Heaven where the Sun and Moon ascended above the horizon at the two equinoxes. It also occupied

this point at midnight during the Winter Solstice, the moment when the year began. It was very closely connected to the location of the Sun and Moon at the principal times of the seasons. The greater and lesser Mysteries of Ceres were celebrated at the equinoxes. When souls descended past the Sun in Libra, the Virgin rose before him, stood at the gates of day, and opened them for him. Her brilliant Star Spica Virginis and Arcturus in Boötes (northwest of it) heralded his coming. He returned to the Vernal Equinox at the moment that souls were generated, and again it was the Celestial Virgin who led the march of the signs of night. In her stars came the beautiful full moon of that month. In succession, she introduced night and day as they began to diminish in length, and she led the souls to the gates of Hell in the 8th Degree of Libra, where they passed the River Styx. She was the famous Sibyl who initiated Eneas and opened the way to the infernal regions to him.

This characteristic caused the Constellation Virgo to be included in all the sacred fables regarding nature under different names and varied forms. It was often named Isis (or the Moon), and when the moon was full at the Vernal Equinox, she was in union with Virgo or beneath its feet. Mercury's (or Anubis) domicile and exaltation was in the sign Virgo, and in all the sacred fables, he was the inseparable companion of Isis, without whom she did nothing.

This correlation between the emblems and ceremonies of the initiations, the Heavenly bodies, and the order of the world was more defined in the Mysteries of Mithras practiced in Asia Minor, Cappadocia, Armenia, Persia, and Rome. This is supported by the descriptions of the Mithraic cave, where the two movements of the Heavens, the fixed Stars, the Planets, the Constellations, the eight mystic gates of the spheres, and the symbols of the elements were figured. A Mithraic monument in Rome figures the succession and triumphs of the *508* Serpent or Hydra under Leo, the Celestial Dog, Bull, Scorpion, the Seven Planets represented by seven altars, the Sun, Moon, and the emblems relating to Light and to Darkness.

The Mysteries of Attis were celebrated when the Sun entered Aries, and among the emblems, was a ram at the foot of a tree being cut down.

This is a large part of the truth of the Pantheon in its infinite diversity of unusual names and personifications, completely different from its original allegory where physical phenomena and the Heavenly Bodies were the fundamental types. The glorious images of Divinity that formed Jehovah's Army were the Divine Dynasty or real theocracy that governed the early world. The men of the golden age interacted with the skies and watched the radiant rulers bring Winter and Summer with a poetic truth said to live in immediate communication with Heaven, seeing God face to face. Then the Gods introduced their own worship to mankind. Oannes, Oe, or Aquarius rose from the Red Sea to teach science to the Babylonians. The bright Bull legislated for India and Crete, and the Lights of Heaven were personified as Liber and Ceres grew vineyards on the Bœotian hills and gave the golden sheaf to Eleusis. The children of men were essentially allied or married to those sons of God who sang the jubilee of creation. The encircling Heavens, with its countless Stars, appeared as animated intelligences to the imagination of the solitary Chaldæan wanderer. They could easily be compared to a gigantic ladder upon which Angel luminaries ascended and descended between the earth and Heaven with their risings and settings. The original revelation was eventually forgotten, and they began to worship the Creature instead of the Creator. They united astronomy, astrology, and religion into one view by connecting all earthly things to eternal links of harmony and sympathy with the heavenly bodies. After wandering in error at length, they stopped looking up to the Stars and at external nature as Gods and began to focus their attention to the narrower world of self. They became reacquainted with the True Ruler and Guide of the Universe and used the old fables and superstitions as symbols and allegories to hide and convey the great truths, which had faded out of most memories.

509

The Hebrew writings defined the term "Heavenly Hosts" to include the advisors and representatives of Jehovah, the celestial luminaries, and the stars. These animated intelligences were the messengers or angels who presided over human prosperity, dispersed misfortune, and implemented the Divine commands. Their position in Heaven was determined by their power and authority on earth. The Morning Stars and the Sons of God are identified in the book of Job. They sang the same praises to the Almighty, had joy, walked in brightness, and were liable for impurities and imperfections in the sight of God. The Elohim originally included the foreign superstitious forms, and the host of Heaven was revealed in poetry, first to the shepherds of the desert, then an encampment of warriors, then in chariots of fire, and finally as winged messengers ascending and descending the ladder of Heaven to communicate the will of God to mankind.

Bereshith Rabba said to Genesis, "The Eternal called Abraham and his descendants from the Heavens. The Israelites were servants to the stars, born under their influence, but they became liberated from this degrading servitude by virtue of the law given to them on Mount Sinai." The Arabs had a similar legend in which the Prophet Amos explicitly asserted that in the desert, the Israelites worshipped Moloch, a Star-God equivalent to Saturn, not Jehovah. However, the Gods El or Jehovah were not merely planetary or solar. Their symbolism was consistent with nature and the mind of man, like every Deity. The astrological character assigned to Jehovah had him seated on the pinnacle of the Universe, leading the Armies of Heaven, and unerringly commanding them by name and number. His stars were His sons, and His eyes were used to keep watch over man's deeds. The remaining stars and planets were His angels. In Pharisaic tradition and the lexicon of the New Testament, the Heavenly Host appears as an Angelic Army, divided into regiments and brigades, led by transcendent generals such as Mazzaroth, Legion, Kartor Gistra, etc., each commanding 365,000 collections of stars. Spoken of by several Jewish writers,

510

the Seven Spirits who stood before the throne were thought to be derived from the Persian Amshaspands, who ultimately were the seven planetary intelligences of the seven branched golden candlestick, originally modeled to Moses on God's mountain. The stars were believed to have fought in their orbits against Sisera, and the heavens were said to have control over earth. They governed it by signs and ordinances containing the astrological wisdom identified and cultivated by the Babylonians and Egyptians.

The Hebrews supposed each nation to have its own guardian angel and provincial star. Jehovah, as the Sun, was the first of the Celestial Powers characterized as overlooking and governing all things from the height of Heaven. As time passed, the Sun became one of the angels, or subordinate planetary spirits, of Babylonian or Persian mythology, the patron and protector of their nation, "the Prince who stands for the children of our people." The conflicts of earth corresponded to the warfare in the sky, and no one had visitation from the Almighty without first chastising their guardian angel.

The fallen Angels were also fallen Stars. Early Hebrew Mythology first alluded to the feud among the spiritual powers when Rahab and his confederates were defeated in a battle against the Gods. It identified the rebellious Spirits as part of the visible Heavens, punished as proof of God's power and justice. It said God, "Stirs the sea with His might. By His understanding, He killed Rahab. His breath clears the face of Heaven, and His hand pierced the crooked Serpent. The confederates of Rahab bow beneath Him."

Rahab was a sea-monster similar to the legendary dragon in most mythologies. He was the adversary of Heaven, the demon of eclipse, whose "belly of Hell" Hercules, like Jonah, spent three days inside before eventually escaping with only the loss of his hair or rays. Chesil, the rebellious giant riveted to the sky, which Orion represented in Job, was compared to Ninus or Nimrod, *511* the mythical mighty hunter who founded Nineveh (the City of Fish) and who slew lions and panthers before the Lord. Rahab's confederates were probably the "High ones on High", the Chesilim, or constellations in Isaiah, the Heavenly Host or Heavenly Powers, where folly and disobedience were found.

Pseudo-Enoch said, "I beheld seven stars, blazing like great mountains, and the angel said until the consummation of Heaven and Earth, this place will imprison the Stars and the Army of Heaven who overstepped God's command and arrived before their proper season. These Seven Stars had transgressed the commandment of the Most High God and were bound there until the sentence for their crimes was served."

The Jewish and early Christian writers viewed the worship of the sun and the elements with comparative indulgence. Justin Martyr and Clemens of Alexandria claimed that God had designated the stars to be legitimate objects of heathen worship, provided to the world to establish some tolerable concepts of natural religion. This seemed to be a compromise between Heathenism and Christianity, because certain emblems and ordinances of faith were common to both. The advent of Christ was announced in the East by a Star, and His nativity was celebrated on the shortest day of the Julian Calendar, the same day when the memorials of Mithras or Osiris were celebrated in Persia and Egypt. The Host of Heaven and the loyal servants of the Sun surrounded the manger of His birthplace like the spring-dawn of creation, and in the words of Ignatius, "a star shined from the Heavens with an unexplainable light to destroy the power of magic and the bonds of wickedness. God Himself had appeared in the form of man to renew eternal life."

An infinite variety of things contributed to the development of the perception of Deity. The ancients may have substituted the worship of the creature for the creator and the parts of the body for the soul, but the ultimate 512 perception was still one of unity. The idea of one creative, productive, unity governing God presided in the earliest exertion of thought, but the monotheism of the primitive ages makes every subsequent interpretation except our current one appear as a deviating step towards error. Throughout the old faiths, we find ideas of a supreme or presiding Deity. Amun or Osiris resided among the many gods of Egypt, Pan directed the chorus of the constellations with the music of his pipe, and Zeus led the solemn procession in the astronomical theology of the Pythagoreans. Maximus Tyrius said, "Amidst an infinite diversity of opinions on all other subjects, the world is united in the belief of only one almighty King and Father of all."

There is always a Sovereign Power like Zeus, Deus, Mahadeva, or Adideva responsible for the order of the Universe. The doctrine of Divine Unity was always present among the thousand gods of India. The ethereal Jove was worshipped by the Persians as supremely comprehensive and independent of planetary or elemental subdivisions as the "Vast One" or the "Great Soul" of the Vedas long before Xenophanes or Anaxagoras.

The simplicity of belief in the patriarchs included the use of symbols because they satisfied the mind by *tangibly* delineating a feeling that strives to become a precise and durable idea. Even the ideas beyond the senses require the aid of forms and symbols for their expression and communication, as all ideas of God do. These representative forms and symbols constitute the external characteristics of every religion and ultimately seek to express the *same* religious sentiment. However, they vainly struggle to communicate spiritual ideas from one person to another using language and expressions, which have a surface meaning. The result is that the same idea of Deity is expressed in infinitely various forms, branching into infinitely diverse creeds and sects.

All religious expression is symbolism because we can only describe what can be seen, and the true objects of religion are unseen. The earliest educational tools were symbols, but their interpretation and understanding always differed 513 relative to external circumstances, imagery, and mental capacity. You cannot convey to people your interpretation of a symbol by simply showing them the symbol. The philosophers tried to solve this problem by creating explanations about these symbols, but they were less effective, obvious, and impressive than the painted or sculptured forms. Narratives were then added to these explanations, but even their true purpose and meaning was gradually forgotten. When the explanations and narratives were abandoned, philosophy resorted to the refined symbolism of definitions and formulas that struggled with attempting to illustrate ideas that were impossible to express. Language can only supply a *sign* or *symbol* for the most abstract expression of Deity, because it is an unknown object, no more truthful and adequate than the terms Osiris and Vishnu, but less superficial and explicit. To say He is a *Spirit* only says that He is not matter. In despair, we can only define *what* spirit is by resorting to calling it a subset of matter (like the Ancients did) as Light, Fire, or Ether.

The symbol of Deity is only appropriate or durable in a relative or moral sense, because we cannot worship words that have only a physical meaning. To call Him a *Power*, *Force*, or an *Intelligence* merely deceives us into believing that the words we use have more meaning than the ancient visible symbols did. To call Him *Sovereign*, *Father*, *Grand Architect of the Universe*, *Extension*, *Time*, *Beginning*, *Middle, and End, whose face is turned on all sides, the Source of life and death* only presents people with symbols that vainly try to communicate 'the same vague ideas which people in all ages have ineffectively struggled to express. It is doubtful that all our metaphysical theories and logical subtleties have succeeded in communicating any more distinct, definite, true, or adequate idea of the Deity than the primitive ancients did. They endeavored to symbolize and express His attributes by Fire, Light, the Sun and Stars, the Lotus, and the Scarabæus, all examples of unexplainable phenomena.

Primitive man recognized the many visible manifestations of the Divine Presence without losing faith in this invisible, supreme Unity, because they were *514* all God. They recognized Him as the evening breeze of Eden, as the whirlwind of Sinai, as the Stone of Beth-El, and as the fire, thunder, or immovable rock adored in Ancient Arabia. They saw the image of the Deity in everything wonderful. They saw the Sun as Jehovah, like Osiris and Bel, the Stars as His children, and His eyes "which ran throughout the world and watched over the Sacred Soil of Palestine throughout the year."

The wit of man wove this Symbolism into a complicated web of fiction and allegory that reproduced all the powers of Heaven on earth, which his limited means of explanation will never unravel. Like all religions, Hebrew Theism evolved into symbolism and image worship including the Tabernacle, the Temple, the Ark, the use of emblematic vessels, vestments, cherubs, Sacred Pillars, Seraphim, and the symbolic representations of Jehovah.

Chrishna said in the Bagvat Ghita, "Among the Adityas, I am Vishnu, the radiant Sun among the Stars, the ocean among the waters, the Himalaya among the mountains, and Meru among the mountain tops." The Psalms and Isaiah are full of similar attempts to convey ideas of God to the mind by ascribing tangible characteristics to Him. He rides the clouds and sits on the wings of the wind.

Heaven is His pavilion, and lightning flashes from His mouth. God needs a physical image, because Man cannot worship an abstraction. If they do not shape, carve, or paint visible images of Him, they have invisible ones within their minds that are equally inadequate and unfaithful.

The diverse and inconsistent images of God in the Orient emerged from the desire to represent a more complete notion of the Divine Attributes of the Infinite than was possible with a single, individual symbol. We do the same thing mentally, when we attempt to create our own images or try to analyze the mass 515 of infinite attributes we assign to the Deity or His infinite Justice, Mercy and Love.

We can quote Maximus Tyrius who said, "If man had recourse to words or names in his desire to obtain *any* concept of the Universal Father, then the most valued and most beautiful things would all be inscribed with the name of Deity. Because of our great fondness and affection for the Beloved, we should not discourage this universal practice of symbolism that is necessary to motivate the people of the world to worship the Deity. Let the physical image perform its task by bringing the divine idea before the eye. This image may be enhanced by the art of Phidias, poetry of Homer, Egyptian Hieroglyphs, or Persian element, but do not bicker over the external differences *so long as the great essential is attained* THAT PEOPLE ARE MADE TO REMEMBER, TO UNDERSTAND, AND TO LOVE GOD."

Man used to regarded Light, Fire, the Sun, Stars, and Planets as symbols of Deity that were infinitely superior to man and gifted with mighty powers and vast influences at a level that we can no longer comprehend. Fire and Light are now as familiar to us as air and water, and the Heavenly Luminaries have become as lifeless as our own world. Perhaps the characteristics man gave to them were as adequate as the mere words that we use today to symbolize the ineffable mysteries and infinite attributes of God.

There are inherent risks in the use of symbolism that offset its advantages, just as there are similar risks in the use of language. The mind 516 usurps reason and leaves it helplessly entangled in a web of names representing things that are confused with ideas, means mistaken for the ends, and the instrument of interpretation mistaken for the object. Subsequently, the symbols mutate into independent truths and persons. This was a dangerous but necessary path to approach the Deity, which Plutarch said, "many mistook the sign for the thing signified and fell into a ridiculous superstition, while others tried to avoid one extreme but plunged into the equally hideous gulf of irreligion and disbelief."

All great Reformers have battled against the intellectual evil caused by a degraded idea of the Supreme Being. They established an existence or distinct personality for their version of God, separate and distinct from the previous versions. In His name, they established new symbols and images to adorn His Temple. However, human effort is only limited to substituting relatively correct impressions for deficient ones and replacing a flawed symbolism with a more pure one. Every person unconsciously worships an image of Deity created in their own mind, because symbolism and language both share the subjective character of the ideas they represent. The names given to God only elicit visible or intellectual symbols, whose modes or forms manifest incomplete but progressive reverential feelings of religious sentiment. Each term or symbol confirms a partial truth that is always subject to improvement or modification, and in time, each will be superseded by other more accurate and comprehensive terms and symbols.

Idolatry occurs when a higher spiritualism is achieved than what the symbolism communicates, but the symbol is worshipped for what is being signified or a material object is substituted for a mental object of worship. To some degree, every religion and perception of God is idolatrous, because it imperfectly substitutes an incomplete and partial idea for the Undiscoverable Being.

The belief in both a Deity and the soul's immortality is a natural part of 517 self-consciousness and not a specific dogma. It grants eternity to man's nature, reconciles its seeming anomalies and contradictions, makes him strong in weakness, perfectible in imperfection, gives a suitable object for his hopes and powers, and values dignity in his pursuits. This is consistent with the belief in an infinite, eternal Spirit, because we learn to appreciate its evidences in the Universe through the dignity of the mind.

The great aim of ancient wisdom was to fortify and impart this hope through poetry or philosophy, like it was in the Mysteries, or as it is in Masonry. Life arising from death was the great mystery that symbolism represented delightfully under a thousand innovative forms. Nature was scrutinized for proof of the grand truth that seemed to transcend all other gifts of imagination, and it was easily discovered. It was found in the olive, the lotus, the evergreen myrtle of the *Mysta*, the grave of Polydorus, the deadly but self-renewing serpent, the wonderful moth emerging from the coffin of the worm, the phenomena of germination, the settings and risings of the sun and stars, the darkening and growth of the moon, and in sleep, "the minor mystery of death".

The birth of Apollo from Latona and the dead hero Glaucus were allegories of the changing cycles of life and death in nature. These changes were fabrications to preserve her sacred virginity and purity and to protect the majestic calm produced by her bounty. The typical death of the Nature God, Osiris, Attis, Adonis, or Hiram was a profound, but comforting mystery. The heating charms of Orpheus were connected to his destruction, and his bones were buried within the sacred tomb of his immortal equivalent as valued pledges of fertility and victory.

The doctrines of the Greek Philosophers stated their ideas about the immortality of the soul in the form of symbolic suggestion. Egypt and Ethiopia learned this from India, but the origin of this doctrine was as remote and 518 untraceable as the origin of man. Its natural expression is found in the language of Chrishna in the Bagvat Ghita: "I was never non-existent, nor were you or the princes of the Earth, nor afterwards shall we ever cease to be. The soul has not merely existed in the past, present and future. Rather, it is preexistent, changeless, eternal, and cannot be destroyed when this mortal frame perishes."

The dogma of antiquity believed that the thronging forms of life were a series of purifications, through which the fragments or sparks (souls) of the Universal Intelligence migrated to re-ascend to the unity of its source. Inebriated in the bowl of Dionysus and dazzled in the mirror of existence, the souls forgot their native dignity and passed into the terrestrial bodies they coveted. The spirit's most common descent was suggested by the sinking of the Sun and Stars from the North (Summer Solstice) to the South (Winter Solstice). Within the portals of Dionysus' empire was the scene of delusion and change, where the soul became clothed in a material form and the world became adorned with the Universal Spirit. The body received the soul like a vase or an urn, and the world was a mighty bowl that received the descending Deity. An image as old as the Grottos of the Magi and the denunciations of Ezekiel depicted the world as a dimly lit cavern, where the soul forgot its celestial origins in proportion to its material fascinations.

Another image portrayed the Soul's embodiment as the condensation of the breath of the Deity, and the aerial element assumed the common form of water. The vapor fell into the water and was viewed as the birth of vapors that would re-ascend and adorn the Heavens. If our mortal existence is the death of the spirit, then our mortal death is the revival of it. As physical bodies are exalted from earth to water, water to air, and air to fire, so man may rise into the Hero, and the Hero into the God. The soul must pass through a series of trials and migrations through the course of Nature to recover its lost effects. Those trials are located in the Grand Sanctuary of Initiations (the world) and their primary agents are the elements. Dionysus, the Sovereign of Nature or the personified sensuous world, was the official Arbiter of the Mysteries and guide who introduced the soul into, and dismissed it from, the body. He was the Sun and liberator of the elements, and his spiritual power was similar to the imagery of the supposed path of the spirits in their descent and ascent through the gates of Cancer and Capricorn in the Zodiac.

He was the Creator of the World and the guardian, liberator, and Savior of the Soul. He was ushered into the world amidst lightning and thunder, where he became the Liberator celebrated in the Mysteries of Thebes, delivering earth from Winter's chains, conducting the nightly chorus of the Stars, and leading the annual celestial revolution. His symbolism was the imagery used to complete the Zodiac: he was the Vernal Bull, the Lion, the Ram, the Autumnal Goat, and the Serpent. In short, He was the varied Deity, the personified manifestations, the all in the many, the varied year, the life passing into many forms, inferior to none, yet changing with the seasons and undergoing their periodical decay.

He assists and negotiates for man, and He emphatically strives to perfect the individualized spirit by first reconciling it to the Unseen Universal Mind with "the trials or test of an immortal Nature" and then symbolically, through the Mysteries. He holds the cup of generation and the wisdom or initiation that causes the soul to despise its material bonds and long for its return. When leaving the Heavens, the soul first drank from the Cup of Forgetfulness, and upon returning, it drank from the Urn of Aquarius. The Sun at the Winter Solstice symbolized the exchange of worldly memories for the recovered recollections of the glorious sights and enjoyments of its preexistence. Water nourishes and purifies, and the celestial urn, from which it flowed, was believed to be a symbol of Deity and an emblem of Hope that brightened the dwellings of the souls.

The second birth of Dionysus was a spiritual regeneration, like the rising of Osiris and Attis from the dead, and the raising of Khūrūm. Psyche (the Soul), like Ariadne, had one earthly and one immortal lover. The immortal suitor was *520* Dionysus, the Eros-Phanes of the Orphici, who was gradually elevated from the symbol of Sensuality to the torchbearer for the Nuptials of the Gods through the progress of thought. The Divine Influence awakens the soul from its Stygian trance and returns it to Heaven from earth.

The ancient scientific theories described in the Mysteries about the origin of the soul, its descent, its journey here below, and its return were a study of the process for perfecting the soul, morals, and society. They believed the Earth was the Soul's place of exile and Heaven was its home and birthplace. The soul had lost its wings during its descent, and it would recover them when it untangled itself from matter and began its upward flight.

Both, the ancients and St. Paul viewed matter as the principle of all the passions that troubled reason, misled intelligence, and stained the purity of the soul. The Mysteries taught the Initiate how to minimize matter's effect on the soul and restore it to its natural dominion. Baptisms, fasting, donations, self-denial, and initiations were at first merely symbolic of the moral purity required of the Initiates, but they eventually came to be regarded as necessary causes of that purity.

Initiation was meant to have the same effect as philosophy. It sought to purify the soul of its passions, to strengthen the divine part of man, and to give man an anticipatory happiness about a future vision of the Divine Beings to be enjoyed by him one day. Proclus and the other Platonists taught, "The Mysteries and initiations withdrew the souls from this mortal and material life to reunite them to the gods, and they revealed to the adepts the splendors of the Deity." *521* The precious fruits of the last Degree of the Mystic Science were to see Nature in her springs or sources and to become familiar with the causes and the real existences.

Cicero said that the soul must exercise itself in the practice of virtues if it wants to quickly return to its place of origin. While imprisoned in the body, the soul can free itself through the contemplation of superior beings and, in a sense, be divorced from the body and the senses. Those who remain enslaved to their passions only increase the time before they will be able to re-ascend to Heaven, because their souls require more purification.

The Initiate was required to free himself from his passions and the obstacles of matter so that he might rise to the contemplation of the Deity or the intangible and unchanging light, where the causes of all created natures live and subsist. Porphyry said, "We must leave behind everything sensual so the soul may easily reunite and live happily with God." Hierocles said, "The great work of initiation is to remind the soul of what is truly good and beautiful, comfort it from the pains and ills it endures on earth, facilitate its return to the celestial splendors, and reestablish its first position in the Fortunate Isles. Then, when the hour of death arrives and the soul is freed from its mortal garment that is left behind as a legacy to earth, it will buoyantly rise to its home among the Stars, rediscover its ancient condition, and approach the Divine nature as closely as it is possible."

Plutarch compared Isis to knowledge and Typhon to the ignorance that obscured the light of the sacred doctrine. He said that the most precious gift of the gods was the knowledge of the Truth and the Nature of the gods, so far as our limited capacities allowed us to understand them. The Valentinians called initiation LIGHT. Psellus said an Initiate became an Epopt when they were admitted to see THE DIVINE LIGHTS. In the language of an Initiate in the Mysteries of Bacchus, Clemens of Alexandria exclaimed to an Initiate he termed blind like Tiresias that Christ would blaze upon his eyes with greater glory than the Sun, "Oh Mysteries most holy! Oh pure Light! When the torch of the Dadoukos burns, Heaven and the Deity are revealed to my eyes! I am initiated, and I become holy!" The true objective of initiation was to be sanctified and TO SEE just and faithful concepts of the Deity, Whose knowledge was THE LIGHT of the Mysteries. The Initiate at Samothrace was promised to become pure and just. Clemens said souls are *illuminated* by baptism and led to *the pure light*, which mingles with no darkness nor anything material. The Initiate who was called A SEER became an Epopt. "HAIL NEWBORN LIGHT!" the Initiates cried in the Mysteries of Bacchus.

The effect of complete initiation was to illuminate the soul with rays from the Divinity, and according to the Pythagoreans, become the eye that contemplates the field of Truth. The soul is superior to the body in its mystical abstractions, and it annuls those sensual actions during the time needed to reenter into itself, so it may have a clear view of the Divinity and the means of coming to resemble Him.

This strengthens the soul against the power of the senses and the passions, and frees it from a wretched slavery. Our ancient brethren strove to prepare themselves to return to the bosom of the Deity through the steady practice of all the active and contemplative virtues. Do not let your objective as a Mason fall below theirs. We use the same symbols they used, and we teach the same great cardinal doctrines of the existence of an intellectual God and the immortality of the soul of man, which they taught. If the details of their ancient doctrines about the soul seem on the verge of absurdity to you, then compare them to the current notions being offered and judge for yourself. If it seems that they occasionally regarded the symbol as the thing symbolized and worshipped the *sign* as if it were a Deity, then reflect upon your own ideas of Deity and ask if you worship those ideas and images formed and fashioned in your own mind, rather than the Deity Himself. If you are inclined to smirk at the importance they attached to purifications and fasts, then pause and inquire whether the same weaknesses of human nature still exist today, causing rites and ceremonies to be regarded as *actively* sufficient for the salvation of souls.

We conclude this lecture with the words of an old writer, which you *523* should always remember. "It is a pleasure to stand on the shore and see ships tossed upon the sea. It is a pleasure to stand in the window of a castle and watch the adventures of a battle. However, no pleasure is comparable to having a scenic view of TRUTH, capable of seeing the errors, wanderings, mists, and tempests in the valley below, but, *You must have pity with this prospect and not be boastful or proud.* Certainly it is Heaven upon Earth to have a person's mind move to charity, rest in Providence, AND TURN UPON THE POLES OF TRUTH."

CHAPTER 26: PRINCE OF MERCY OR SCOTTISH TRINITARIAN

WHILE you were in darkness, you heard the Voice of the Great Past 524 repeat its most ancient doctrines. All can accept a Christian Mason's view of Jesus as the realization of the Divine WORD, which was foretold by similar writings regarding Krishna by the Hindus, Sosiosch by the Zoroastrians, and Osiris by the ancient Egyptians. In all these versions, a protagonist dies to rise again and redeem mankind. Likewise, the Christian Mason can accept if others interpret these as the LOGOS of Plato being the WORD, THOUGHT, meaning, proportion, logic, or Emanation of LIGHT while *he* interprets these as the WORD of the beloved Disciple that was with God in the beginning, was God, and from Whom everything was made. All trust, believe, and adore it as the Perfect REASON of the Great, Silent, Supreme, and Uncreated Deity.

We value the importance of *all* Truth. We do not suggest, utter, or condone any words that can be deemed disrespectful to any faith by anyone. We do not tell Muslims that only the belief in one God is important while Mohammed as His prophet is unessential. We do not tell Jews they are heretics if they will not believe that the Messiah was born in Bethlehem nearly two thousand years ago. We do not tell Christians that Jesus of Nazareth was a mere mortal and His history is a revival of an older legend. To do any of this is beyond Masonry's jurisdiction, because Masonry belongs to all time and all religion as it finds its great truths everywhere.

There is a GOD to every Mason. This ONE is Supreme, Infinite in Goodness, Wisdom, Foresight, Justice, and Benevolence, and He is the Creator, Disposer, and Preserver of all things. Masonry leaves to Religion to inquire and explain how He creates, acts, and manifests Himself.

Masons believe the soul of a man is immortal. It does not try to resolve 525 the questions of its origin, its relationship with God, or what its existence will be like hereafter. You judge these things for yourself.

WISDOM or INTELLIGENCE, FORCE, STRENGTH, or HARMONY, and FITNESS or BEAUTY are the threefold attributes of God. Due to the subtleties in Philosophy, Masonry does not declare the Existence of the Personifications of this Trinity in our reality. Nor does it state whether the Christian Trinity is such a personification or a Reality of the greatest importance.

Masons believe that the Infinite Justice and Benevolence of God are assurance that Evil will be defeated one day, and that afterwards, the Good, True, and Beautiful will reign triumphant forever. It knows, feels, and teaches that Evil, Pain, and Sorrow exist as part of a grand and wise plan. These parts work together under God's eye to achieve the result of perfection. Masonry does not try to explain or decide if evil is correctly depicted by any particular creed such as Typhon the Great Serpent, Angra Mainyu and his Armies of Wicked Spirits, the Giants and Titans that war against Heaven, Dualist Principles of Good and Evil, Satan's temptation and the fall of Man, or Loki and his offspring. Similarly, Masonry does not proclaim or try to determine how Light, Truth, and Good will achieve triumph over Darkness, Error, and Evil. It does not pronounce if the Redeemer, as expected by many nations throughout history, has appeared in Roman Judea or is yet to come.

It reveres all of the great reformers from mankind. It views Moses, Confucius, Zoroaster, Jesus, and Mohammed as Great Teachers of Morality and Esteemed Reformers, if nothing else. It allows every brother of the Order to believe one of these is the most important or Divine as his Creed teaches.

Masonry promotes the belief of truth as taught by any creed. It only protests when a creed lowers the concept of Deity, degrades Him with human passions, denies the destiny of man, challenges the benevolence of the Supreme God, strikes at Faith, Hope, and Charity as the pillars of Masonry, promotes immorality, or disregards the duties outlined by the Order.

526   Masonry is a worship all men can perform. It does not explain or determine the great mysteries among man that are above our comprehension and intellect. Masonry trusts in God. It HOPES and BELIEVES unquestioningly, and it is humble. It forces no one to adopt its beliefs or be content with its hopes. It WAITS with patience to understand the mysteries in Nature and God.

The greatest mysteries are those around us. They are so small and common we take them for granted. Wise men have refined equations that explain and predict the motions of the celestial bodies. Spinning on their axes and orbiting in huge ellipses, everything is also moving inconceivably across the fabric of the Universe while we blissfully ride along and dream of all that was made for *us*. They learnedly speak of weak, strong, gravity, electromagnetic *forces*, and all the derivative forces we can measure, but they still hide a need for deeper meaning. There is another force in the Universe.

Take this meaning from two small, similar seeds. Give one to the Scientists, who will tell us how plants are fed with carbon dioxide, water, phosphate fertilizer, potassium, calcium, sulphur, iron, and magnesium. Let them decompose, analyze, and torture the seed in all ways known. The net result of all the steps is sugar, gluten, water, carbon, potassium, and so forth.

Take the second seed and bury it in the ground, water it, and let the Sun warm it. Soon, a slender shoot springs up and continues to grow with its own force, power, and *capacity*. Think of the miracle in its mere growth! Think of the force, power, and capacity this feeble shoot develops. It extracts from the earth, air, and waters the necessary elements, as catalogued by its DNA, by which it steadily grows towards the sky.

One seed may grow to be a fragile, feeble stalk like an ordinary weed. One may grow to be a woody, thorny, and sturdy bush. A third may grow to be a palm tree, or a tall, broad, and mighty pine unhurt by frost, ice, or snow that 527 surrounds it for months.

See how the brown earth, invisible air, and clear rain undergo a chemical reaction to extract various *colors*. Different shades of green, the vivid colors of the flowers, and the hues of fruits and vegetables. From what influence do we get these *colors*? What causes *them* to be a product of earth, water, and air? It is a great miracle to make something out of nothing.

Pick the flowers. Smell their perfect and delicious *perfumes* and odors. Where did these come from? What would it take for a chemist to reproduce *them* from nature?

Then we get the fruit. Compare the colorful apples and golden oranges. Peal them and open them! The texture and fabric are completely different! They have dissimilar *tastes* and distinct *odors*. Why do we have new tastes and new odors? They spring from the same earth, air, and water but return different tastes, looks, smells, and textures. Not only are they different between each other, but there are differences between the flower and the fruit of the same.

Moreover, look in each fruit we find new seeds! Each is gifted with the same wondrous power and *force* contained within it waiting to evolve. These forces survived for three thousand years in the grain of wheat found within an Egyptian mummy. These forces remain as mysterious to science and wisdom as the nature and laws of God. What can *we* truly know of nature? We can measure its mechanisms, but *we* do not know what force sets them in motion. If the glossy leaves, colorful flowers, and sweet fruit of plants are miracles to our comprehension, how can we expect to understand the powers and operation of the soul?

Are the phenomena of thought, will, and perception of the mind any more wondrous than the origins of the colors, perfumes, taste, and textures of the fruit and flower?

We hide our real ignorance in science and words. These words are without any fundamental meaning. What is gravitational force? It describes the 528 *tendency* for attraction of masses! What external "*force*" instructs that attraction to exist?

What force creates gravity? By what forces do we move the muscles that raise the arm against gravity when we think it should rise? Where are thought and *will* originated? Is it a spontaneous occurrence or is it a response to something? These are miracles and as inexplicable as creation or the existence of God.

Who can explain the passions, instincts, memories, and affections of a canary? What is the self-consciousness and dreams of a dog? What is the reasoning of the elephant? Who knows the wondrous instincts, passions, government, civil policy, and communications of the ant and the bee?

Who has deciphered and described how heat and light travel from the Sun through a vacuum. What triggered the big bang and why is that singularity so different from all the other laws of the universe? How does the brain register images received upon the discrete rods and cones of the retina and signal them through the ganglions to form a coherent thought we process as the wondrous thing called SIGHT? How do the wave concussions within the atmosphere strike the eardrum and transform into the equally wondrous phenomenon of HEARING which we learn to process and recognize as the crash of thunder, roar of the ocean, chirp of the cricket, music, song, or conversation?

Our senses are as mysterious to us as we are to ourselves. Philosophy has proven to be nothing but *words* about the *nature* of our senses, perceptions, realizations, thoughts, or ideas. Man is not capable of realizing his conscience as an identity separate from his body. While he may separate the heart from the brain, he cannot separate the soul from the mind. How can we identify our core being and separate it from our bodies? Do we understand that touch, sight, hearing, smell, and taste are sensations that travel across our nerves to our minds and that this forces us to react with or without conscious reasoning?

529 What do we know of Substance? Men can doubt if it even exists or is mere perception. Philosophers inform us that our senses only share the *attributes* of substance, size, mass, color, etc. Our senses do not inform us of the *thing* itself *being* large, solid, black, or white, for example. Likewise, we know the *attributes* of the Soul through its thoughts and perceptions, but we do not know the Soul itself, that which perceives and thinks.

We find wondrous mystery in the existence of heat and light though we do not know how. Its limits are narrow when compared to infinity. On every side of lights deepest reaches stretches infinite space and the blackness of unimaginable darkness and the unattainable temperature of absolute zero. The darkness of Midnight and the cold of the Arctic Islands are nothing in comparison. One photon decimates absolute darkness, yet darkness swallows our universe. Think of the mighty Power required to maintain the warmth and light within such infinity. Yet, GOD is everywhere.

What mysteries in water are affected by heat and cold! What mysteries lies hidden in the transformation between states in every snowflake, ice crystal, water, and vapor molecule as they settle, flow, and rise up again over the summits of the mountains!

Chemistry has unveiled many wonders before our eyes! Imagine if one law enacted by God, such as gravity, was repealed. The whole world with its granite, gold, silver, iron, coal, and our own bodies would instantaneously dissolve. So too would all the Suns, Stars, and Worlds throughout the Universe of God. Without them, light and heat would disappear unless the Deity Himself was the Eternal Light and the Immortal Fire, as the Ancient Persians thought.

There are great mysteries within the Universe of God! How *can* we expect to grasp and comprehend them with our limited mental vision? Think of the infinite SPACE without limit and infinite TIME without beginning or end. Then think of the WE, HERE, and NOW in the center of it all! An infinite number of suns, the nearest of which only *diminish* our size when viewed with a powerful telescope. Around those are multitudes of worlds. There are stars so remote that their light does not perceptibly reach us, but have their own journey through this infinity of time. The light that *does* reach us and we *seem* to see has been traveling for centuries. All the while, our world continued to spin on its axis and orbit our sun while this sun orbits about the Milky Way pulled back and forth. Meanwhile, in every drop of water we drink, the air around, the earth under, and the sea surrounding there are incredible numbers of creatures invisible to the naked eye. These are all organized, living, feeding, *perhaps* with consciousness of identity, memory, and instinct. 530

These are just some of the mysteries of God's Universe. Our lives in this world form just a spec in the center of infinite Time. We would gladly learn, "how God created this Universe and understand His Powers, Attributes, Emanations, Mode of Existence, and Action. We would gladly know the plan, profound as God Himself, according to which all events proceed. We would know the laws by which He controls His Universe. We would gladly *see* and *talk* to Him face to face. If we do not *believe*, it is because we do not *understand*.

He commands us to love our neighbor, but we dispute, wrangle, hate, and slay each other. We cannot agree about anything. We debate the Essence of His Nature and His Attributes. We debate if He became a man and was crucified, if the Holy Ghost is the *same* or *similar* to the Father, if a feeble old man is God's deputy, if some are His chosen people, if damnation is eternal, and if a particular doctrine is heresy or truth. We drench the world in the blood of massacred nations. We turn fertile lands into barren deserts under the auspices of holy war, persecution, and mission. For many centuries, the Earth has been a scene of human gore where one brother slays another over different opinions. Our blood has soaked the Earth, polluted her veins, and made her an abomination to her sisters in the Universe.

If all men were Masons and obeyed its gentle teachings, then our world 531 would be a paradise; intolerance and persecution make it otherwise. The Masonic Creed is BELIEVE in God's Infinite Benevolence, Wisdom, and Justice. HOPE for the final triumph of Good over Evil and Perfect Harmony for the Universe. Be as CHARITABLE as God towards the faithless, error, folly, and fault in man. We all can make a great brotherhood.

INSTRUCTION

Sen∴ W∴ Brother Junior Warden, are you a Prince of Mercy?

Jun∴ W∴ I have seen the Delta and the Holy NAMES upon it, and like you, I am an AMETH in the TRIPLE COVENANT, of which we bear the mark.

Qu∴ What is the first Word upon the Delta?

Ans∴ The Ineffable Name of Deity, the true mystery of which is known only to the Ameth.

Qu.:   What do the three sides of the Delta denote to us?

Ans.:   The three Great Attributes or Developments of the Essence of the Deity. WISDOM is the Reflective and Designing Power from which the Plan and Idea of the Universe was formed when there was nothing but God. FORCE is the Executing and Creating Power which acted instantaneously to the Idea formed by Wisdom and realized the Universe, Stars, Worlds, Light, Life, Man, Angels, and all living creatures. HARMONY is the Preserving Power, Order, and Beauty that maintains the Universe in its State, and it forms the law of Harmony, Motion, Proportion, and Progression. WISDOM *thought* the plan, STRENGTH *created* it, and HARMONY *upholds* and *preserves* it. The Masonic Trinity, three Powers from one Essence represent the three support columns of the Universe. They are the Physical, Intellectual, and Spiritual symbolized by every Masonic Lodge. To the Christian Mason, they represent the FATHER, WORD, and HOLY SPIRIT that are ONE.

Qu.:   What do the three Greek letters upon the Delta, I∴ H∴ Σ∴ [Iota, Eta, and Sigma] represent?

Ans.:   The three Names of the Supreme Deity from the Syrians, Phœnicians, and Hebrews . . . IHUH [יהוה]; *Self-Existence* . . . EL [אל]: *the Nature-God, or Soul of the Universe.* . . SHADDAI [שדי] *Supreme Power.* Also, three of the Six Chief Attributes of God according to Kabbalah. WISDOM [IEH], the *Intellect* (Νους) of the Egyptians, the *Word* (Λόγος) of the Platonists, and the *Wisdom* (Σοφία) of the Gnostics. MAGNIFICENCE [EL] is Symbolized by the Lion's Head. VICTORY and GLORY [*Tsabaoth*] are the two columns JACHIN and BOAZ that stand in the Porch of the Temple of Masonry. To the Christian Mason, they are the first three letters of the name of the Son of God who redeemed mankind.

Qu.:   What is the first of the THREE COVENANTS to which we bear the mark?

Ans.:   The one God made with Noah when He said, "I now establish my covenant with you, your descendants, and with every living creature on Earth: never again will all life be cut off by the waters of a flood; never again will there be a flood to destroy the earth. This is the sign of the covenant I am making between you and Me and with every living creature, a covenant for all generations to come: I have set my rainbow in the clouds, and it will be the sign of the covenant between the earth and Me. Whenever I bring clouds over the earth and the rainbow appears, I will remember my everlasting covenant between you and Me and all living creatures of every kind. Never again will the waters become a flood to destroy all life (Genesis 9:8-15)."

Qu.:   What is the second of the Three Covenants?

Ans.∴   The one God made with Abraham when He said, "I am God Almighty. I will make My covenant between you and Me, and you will be fruitful, the Father of Many Nations, and Kings shall come from you. I will establish My everlasting covenant between Me and you and your descendants after you for generations to come, to be your God and the God of your descendants after you. The whole land of Canaan, I will give as an everlasting possession (Genesis 17:1-8)."

Qu.∴   What is the third Covenant?

Ans.∴   The one God made with all men through His prophets when He said, "I will gather all nations and tongues, and they will come and see My Glory. The new Heavens and the new Earth will endure before me, and the former will not be remembered (Isaiah 66:18-22). The Sun will no more be your light by day, nor will the brightness of the Moon shine on you, for the Lord will be your everlasting light, and your God will be your glory (Isaiah 60:19). His Spirit and His Word will remain with man forever. The heavens will vanish like smoke, the earth will wear out like a garment and its inhabitants will die like flies. However, my salvation will last forever, my righteousness will never fail. (Isaiah 51:6) I will also make you a light for the Gentiles, that you may bring my salvation to the ends of the earth (Isaiah 49:6). The redeemed of the Lord will return. They will enter Zion with singing and everlasting joy will crown their heads. Gladness and joy will overtake them, and sorrow and mourning will flee away (Isaiah 51:11)." 533

Qu.∴   What is the symbol of the Triple Covenant?

Ans.∴   The Triple Triangle.

Qu.∴   What else is it a symbol of to us?

Ans.∴   The Trinity of Attributes of the Deity as well as the triple essence of Man being the Principle of Life, the Intellectual Power, and the Soul or Immortal Emanation from the Deity.

Qu.∴   What is the first great Truth of the Sacred Mysteries?

Ans.∴   No man has ever seen God. He is One, Eternal, All-Powerful, All-Wise, Infinitely Just, Merciful, Benevolent, Compassionate, Creator, Preserver of all things, Source of Light and Life, and as big as Time and Space. His Thought created the Universe, all living things, and the souls of man. He is the one THAT IS, the PERMANENT, while everything else is a perpetual genesis.

Qu.∴   What is the second great Truth of the Sacred Mysteries?

Ans.∴   The Soul of Man is Immortal. It is not the result of organization, a composite of modes of action in matter, a succession of phenomena and perceptions. It is EXISTENCE, one and identical, a living spirit, a spark of the Great Central Light that has entered and dwells within the body to be separated at death to return to God who gave it. It does not disperse or vanish at death like smoke. It cannot be annihilated, but continues to exist, be active, and retain intelligence, as it existed before it was enveloped in the body with God.

Qu∴   What is the third great Truth in Masonry?

Ans∴   The duty that leads to right conduct and deters from crime is older than nations and cities, and as old as the Divine Being Who sees and rules both Heaven and earth. The principle that impels us to right conduct, and warns us of guilt springs from the nature of all things. While his reign might not have had written laws against such violence, King Tarquin the Proud violated that Eternal Law. This law does not *originate* when *written* for it is as old as the Divine Intelligence itself. A virtuous result is not always made from a virtuous deed. These actions must have deeper roots and motives to give them the stamp of virtue.

Qu∴   What is the fourth great Truth in Masonry?

Ans∴   The moral truths and metaphysical truths are absolute. Even the Deity cannot have an effect without a cause, or experience without matter. He could not make it sinful and evil to respect our pledge, love truth, or moderate our passions. The principles of Morality are self-evident truths, just like the principles of Geometry. Moral laws are a necessary consequence to our nature. They were not created by God, but have existed eternally within God. Their continuance does not depend on His WILL. Truth and Justice are His ESSENCE. God is the principle of Morality and therefore they do not exist because of His will but because He is. It is not our duty to obey His law only because we are weak and God is omnipotent. We are not forcibly bound to obey the stronger. Good is the expression of His will. His will did not create the eternal, absolute, uncreated justice, which is *in* God. His will executes and decrees as *our* will decrees and executes the ideals of good within us. He has provided us the law of Truth and Justice but He has not arbitrarily instituted that law on us. Justice is inherent in His will because it is in His intelligence and wisdom. It is within His very nature and essence.

Qu∴   What is the fifth great Truth in Masonry?

Ans∴   There is an essential distinction between Good and Evil and what is just and unjust. Attached to this distinction is the obligation among the intelligent and free to conform to what is good and just. Man is intelligent and free. He is free because he is conscious of, and *made* his duty obedience to, truth and justice. It is necessary that he have the power to obey which means having the power *not* to obey as well. He can comprehend the difference between good and evil, justice

534

and injustice, and right and wrong. He therefore is obliged to adhere to that obligation, in the absence of any contract or law which may also urge him to resist the temptation to do evil or injustice. He must comply with this sacred law of eternal justice.

535

Man is not governed by Fate or Destiny, but he is free to choose between good and evil. Justice, Right, Good, and Beautiful are of the essence of the infinite Divinity. Therefore, these are laws to man. We are conscious of the freedom of action as our own identity and connected existence. We have the same evidence between one and the other. If we put *one* in doubt then we have no certainty of *either*, and everything is unreal. If we deny our free will and action as an impossible idea, we would deny the Omnipotence of God.

Qu∴ What is the sixth great Truth of Masonry?

Ans∴ Our *obligation* makes practicing moral truths necessary. Reason dictates that moral truths are an obligation on our will. Like the foundation of moral truth, moral obligation is *absolute*. Necessary truths are necessary and the obligation is obligatory. There are degrees of importance among different obligations, but an obligation is complete. We cannot be *nearly* obliged or *almost* obliged. We are *wholly* obliged or not at all. There is no place to escape and seek refuge from an obligation. The obligation is absolute, unchangeable, and universal. What is today is the same as tomorrow and what is obligatory on *me* is the same on *you*. The principle of all morality is to repress by force every wrong and unjust act and equal punishment for the act if committed despite law or contract. Man recognizes the distinction between right and wrong action, justice and injustice, or honesty and dishonesty. He naturally feels it is wrong for vice to be rewarded or unpunished, and virtue to be punished or unrewarded. He does not need to be taught these distinctions or have a civil law published to enforce this obligation. As the Deity is infinitely just and good, it must follow as law that punishment is not arbitrary vengeance and will be the inevitable result of Sin.

Qu∴ What is the seventh great Truth in Masonry?

536

Ans∴ The unchangeable law of God requires us to respect the absolute rights of others, be just, do good, be charitable, and obey the dictates of the generous and noble intentions of the soul. Charity is an obligatory law because our conscience requires us to relieve the suffering, distressed, and destitute. It means to *give* what another has no right to *take* or *demand*. We are to be the givers of God's bounties. The obligation is not as precise and inflexible as *justice* is. Charity has no rule or limit and goes beyond all obligations. Its beauty is in its liberty. "He that does not love does not know God, FOR GOD IS LOVE. If we love one another, God dwells in us and His love is perfected in us. God is love and he that lives in love, lives in God, and God in him." To be kind, affectionate, practice brotherly love, provide relief to the needy, be generous, liberal, and hospitable, not practice evil, rejoice with others in good fortune, sympathize with them in sorrow, live in peace, and repay injury with kindness are the sublime dictates of the Moral Law as taught by Masonry since the infancy of humanity.

Qu∴ What is the eighth great Truth in Masonry?

Ans∴ The laws of motion and harmony control and regulate the Universe of God. We only witness isolated incidents and cannot discern the connection with our limited capacity and vision. We are not aware of any mighty mechanisms that harmonize the apparent discord. Evil is a façade to the underlying good and perfect in nature. Pain, sorrow, persecution, hardship, affliction, destitution, sickness, and death are the means to develop noble virtues. As a reaction needs a catalyst these sorrows, sins, errors, wrongs, and outrages cause the virtues of patience in distress, prudence in difficulty, temperance in avoiding excess, courage in danger, truth amid hazard, love despite ingratitude, charity for the destitute, forgiveness of injuries, toleration of bias and erroneous opinions, justice in judgment taking account of motive and action, patriotism, heroism, honor, self-denial, and generosity. These virtues would have no existence and be unknown while other virtues would scarcely deserve the name if life would be one flat emotion above which none of the lofty elements of human nature could emerge. Man would be content in idleness instead of becoming the brave, strong soul against Evil and rude Difficulty.

Qu∴ What is the ninth great Truth in Masonry?

Ans∴ The JUSTICE, WISDOM, and MERCY of God are infinite, perfect, and not in conflict. They form the Great Perfect Trinity of Attributes like the doctrine of this Degree. Three are as one. There is an absolute principle of good and bad, where good actions deserve reward and bad ones deserve punishment. God is just and good. Yet, there are examples in this world where crime, cruelty, oppression, tyranny, and injustice are prosperous, happy, fortunate, and content. They rule, reign, and enjoy the blessings of God's charity while the virtuous and good are unfortunate, miserable, destitute, repressed, suffering, starving, oppressed, and victims to the villains that govern. Without existence beyond, this life would be one great theater of pain, wrong, and injustice whereby God would disregard His own law of reward and justice. Therefore, there must be another life where these injustices are resolved. All the powers of man's soul care for infinity, immortality, and the universal hope of another life. All creeds, poetry, and traditions establish that man is not an orphan but has a

537

Father nearby. The day must come when Light, Truth, Justice, and Goodness will be completely victorious over Darkness, Error, Wrong, and Evil. The faiths of all nations since the primitive ages agree that the Universe is in Harmony, and therefore Light and Good will ultimately prevail over Darkness and Evil. The myriad souls that have emanated from the Divinity, purified and ennobled by its effort, will return to perfect bliss with God. It will no longer be possible to offend against those laws. *538*

Qu∴ As Masons, what is the one great lesson taught to us in this Degree?

Ans∴ That in the absolute realm of Light, Truth, and Perfection which all good men on earth work to emulate with the certainty that death will convey their bodies to darkness and dust, there is another certain law which conducts their souls to a state of Happiness, Splendor, and Perfection with their Father and their God. Nature cannot reverse itself because everything evolves towards Eternity. Since the birth of Time, a force is steering all people toward that destination. Heaven is attracting that which is agreeable to its nature, enriching itself with the rewards of the Earth, collecting within its spaciousness whatever is pure, permanent, and sublime to adorn its Eternal City, and leaving nothing but our lifeless mass and matter.

Let every Mason obey the voice that calls him there. Let us pursue what is above and not be content with the world we live in so shortly, thus neglecting to prepare for the world we shall dwell in forever. Everything within and without us speaks of our approaching death and teaches us that it is not our final resting place. We should increase our preparations for the next world and implore help and strength from our Father who can put an end to the fatal wars that our desires have waged with our real destiny. When these worlds move in harmony and we no longer fear death's bridge between them then all things will be ours. Life will no longer have its vanity and death will not carry its terror.

Qu∴ What are the symbols of the purification necessary to make us perfect Masons?

Ans∴ Washing and cleansing with pure water as with a baptism or mikvah. Cleansing the body is a symbol of purifying the soul. Washing contributes to bodily health just as virtue provides a healthy soul. Sin and vice are maladies and illness. Anointing with oil (unction) sets us *539* apart and dedicates us to the service of the Beautiful, True, and Good. Robes of white are emblems of openness, purity, and truth.

Qu∴ What is the chief symbol of man's ultimate redemption and regeneration?

Ans∴   The fraternal supper consisting of bread, that nourishes and of wine, which refreshes and exhilarates. It is symbolic of the time to come when all mankind will be one harmonious brotherhood and teach the great lessons. Just as matter may change form yet never be annihilated, we can state that the noble soul will continue its existence beyond the grave. The bodies of those who died before us can claim their joint ownership with the particles that compose our mortal bodies. Our bodies are but new combinations of the ancients, patriarchs, kings, and commoners all decomposed into their elements and carried upon the winds over all the continents. They fall and then rise again as part of the habitations where new souls are brought to life. We are living bonds and a brotherhood among all living creatures, people, and races. From the bread we eat to the wine we drink there *may* enter into our bodies the same particles of matter that once formed the mortal bodies called Moses, Confucius, Plato, Socrates, Buddha, or Jesus. In a true sense, we eat and drink the bodies of the dead. We cannot say there is a single atom of our blood or body that some other soul might not claim with us. The supper also teaches us the infinite kindness of God who sends us seasons to sow and harvest, makes rains shower, shines the sun upon all, bestows us with His unsolicited and innumerable blessings, and asks for nothing in return. There are no angels about His creation who call the world to prayer or sacrifice. He bestows His benefits in silence, does not ask for thanks, and despite our ingratitude does not cease His kindness. Thus, the bread and wine teach us that our Mortal Body is no more WE than the house in which we live or the garments we wear. But the Soul is I, the ONE, identical, unchangeable, immortal emanation from the Deity, that returns to God to be happy forever in His good time. Our mortal bodies dissolve and return to the dust from which we came as the particles come and go in a perpetual genesis. To our Jewish Brethren, this supper is symbolic of Passover. To the Christian Mason, it is symbolic of the Last Supper of Christ and His Disciples at Passover. He broke bread and gave it to them saying, "Take and eat; this is my body." He then gave them the cup and He said, "Drink from it, all of you. This is my blood of the covenant, which is poured out to many for the forgiveness of sins. (Matthew 26:26-28)" He thus symbolized the perfect harmony and union between Himself and the faithful. His death upon the cross was for the salvation of man.

540

The history of Masonry is the history of Philosophy. Masons do not pretend to instruct the human race. Asia produced and preserved the Mysteries while Masonry has throughout Europe and America given regularity to its doctrines, spirit, and action. It has developed moral advantages that humanity may reap. Masonry is more consistent and simple in its procedures. It has attempted to simplify the diversity of allegories that survived from the ancient mythologies to become a science itself.

No one can deny that Jesus taught morality. "Love one another. Forgive those that spitefully use you and persecute you. Be pure of heart, meek, humble, and content. Do not be content on earth but save it for Heaven. Submit lawfully to authority. Become like little children, or you cannot be saved, for of such is the Kingdom of Heaven. Forgive those who repent. If you have sinned, you should not cast a stone at another sinner. Do unto others as you would have others do unto you." These were His simple and sublime teachings to the people and not difficult questions of theology.

The early Christians followed this advice. The first practitioners of that faith were not thinking of domination. They were called to action by the words and sayings of Jesus, the desire to spread the word, devoted, humble, modest, charitable, and teachers of the spirit of humanity to the churches under their direction. The first churches were simply random gatherings of all Christians in the same location. Even their persecutors had to admire their characteristic morality and religious enthusiasm. Everything was shared between them 541 including their property, joys, and sorrows. At night, they would meet for instruction and prayer. A meal ended these reunions and all social ranks were leveled in the presence of a paternal Divinity. Their object was to make people better. They had simple worship based on universal morality. They did away with the typical sacrifices found elsewhere upon the altars of the gods. It helped regulate domestic life and made woman equal and influential. It admitted slaves to their reunions and meals and raised them from oppression there. This is how Christianity reformed the world and obeyed the teachings of its founder.

This original message taught by Jesus was the same early religion communicated by God to the Patriarchs. This was not a new religion, but the reintroduction of the oldest of all. Its true and perfect morality was the same as every creed of antiquity, and it is the same as the morality of Masonry.

There was an initiation in the early days of Christianity that people were admitted into with special conditions. Complete knowledge of the doctrine was taught to initiates through three degrees of instruction. The first were the *Auditors*, second were *Catechumens*, and third were *the Faithful*. The Auditors were the novices who were prepared through ceremonies and instruction to receive the dogma of Christianity. A portion of this dogma was made known to the Catechumens after the purification of a baptism and initiation into the ideas of *divine genesis (theogenesis)*. Only *the Faithful* were initiated into the grand mysteries of that religion which included incarnation, nativity, passion, and the resurrection of Christ. These doctrines, the celebration of the Holy Sacraments, and the Eucharist were kept in secrecy. These Mysteries were in two parts. The first was the Mass of the Catechumens while the second was the Mass of the Faithful. They also celebrated the Mysteries of Mithras as *a mass* and kept the same ceremonies. This Mystery contained all of the sacraments of the Catholic Church including the Confirmation's breath of life. The Priest of Mithras promised the Initiates deliverance from sin by means of confession and baptism with a future life of happiness or misery. He celebrated the offering of bread as an image of the resurrection. The baptism of the newborn, anointing of the deathly sick (known as Extreme Unction), and the confession of sins originated with the Mithraic rite. A candidate was purified by baptism, his forehead was impressed with a mark, and he was offered bread and water while pronouncing certain mysterious words.

Early Christians were persecuted and they took refuge in the Etruscan catacombs that stretched for miles under the City of Rome. There they could perform the ceremonies of the Mysteries amid the maze-like passageways, deep caverns, hidden chambers, chapels, and tombs.

The Basilideans were a Gnostic sect of Christians founded by Basilides in Alexandria shortly after the death of Jesus. Their teaching originated from a disciple of St. Peter and they performed the Mysteries with the old Egyptian legend. They symbolized Osiris by the Sun, Isis by the Moon, and Typhon (Set) by Scorpio, and they wore crystal amulets bearing the emblems of a star and serpent to protect them from danger. The amulets were copies of talismans from Persia and Arabia and given to every initiate.

Irenaeus told us the Simonians were one of the earliest Gnostic sects that had a Priesthood of the Mysteries.

Tertullian told us the Valentinians were a major Gnostic movement that imitated and perverted the Mysteries of Eleusis. Irenaeus informed us in his writings of the Mysteries practiced by the Marcionians. Origen wrote about the Ophites and their Mysteries. There is considerable evidence that all Gnostic sects had Mysteries and initiation. They all claimed to possess a secret doctrine coming from Jesus Christ that interpreted the Gospels and Epistles differently and with deeper meaning. They did not communicate this secret doctrine to every one. Among the large numbers of Basilideans, maybe one in one thousand knew about it according to Irenaeus. The name of the highest class of their Initiates were called *Elect* or *Elus* ['Εχλεχτόι] and Strangers to the World [ξένοι ἐν χόσμαῳ]. There were lesser and greater Mysteries with at least three Degrees which included the *Material*, *Intellectual*, and *Spiritual*. Few Basilideans attained the highest Degree.

Baptism was one of their most important ceremonies. The Basilideans celebrated the 15th of Tybi (January 6th) as the anniversary of the day on which Christ was baptized in the River Jordan.

They performed the ceremony of laying on hands to purify. The mystic banquet was symbolic of their future admission to the Heavenly Wisdom [Πλήsωμα].

Their ceremonies were more similar to the Christians than the Greeks, but they combined them with Asian and Egyptian aspects. They taught the primitive truths, but accidentally included numerous errors and fictions.

The discipline of the secret was the concealment (*occultatio*) by denial of certain tenets and ceremonies. Here it was described as what it was not and only those who knew it understood the description according to Clement of Alexandria.

The early Christians feared persecution and held their meetings of the Faithful in private at night. They assembled and guarded against the imposters and spies who might lead to their arrest. They spoke figuratively and used symbols to prevent pretenders and eavesdroppers from understanding. Among them was a select Order who were further initiated into Mysteries, which they were solemnly bound not to disclose without explicit approval. They were *Brethren, the Faithful, Stewards of the Mysteries, Superintendents, Devotees of the Secret,* and ARCHITECTS.

According to the writings of St. Dionysius the Areopagite (the first Bishop of Athens) in the *Ecclesiastical Hierarchy*, the sacraments were divided into the three Degrees of *purification, initiation,* and *perfection*. It also mentions *the bringing to sight* as part of the ceremonies.

Clement, Bishop of Rome, described the early church's position in The Apostolic Constitutions when he states, "These regulations must on no account be communicated to all persons, because of the Mysteries contained in them." It speaks of the Deacon's duty to keep the doors closed and permit only the initiated to enter for the offering (oblation). The doorkeepers, *Ostiarii*, were to keep guard, notify the time of prayer and assembly, and by secret signal they 544 would alert those within of danger. The Mysteries were only open to the *Faithful* and no spectators were allowed for communion.

Tertullian (death ca. 220 AD) wrote in his *Apology*, "No one is admitted to the religious Mysteries without an oath of secrecy. We appeal to the Thracian and Eleusinian Mysteries. We are bound to be cautious because if we were faithless, we would provoke Heaven and incite the severest human displeasure. Strangers could betray us, as they only know what they hear from rumor and hearsay. All holy Mysteries implore the unfaithful to keep away."

Clement, Bishop of Alexandria (born ca. 150 AD), wrote in *Stromata* that he cannot explain the Mysteries because it would be like putting a sword in a child's hands. He frequently compares the Discipline of the Secret with the heathen Mysteries for the internal and obscure wisdom contained.

Whenever the early Christians were in the company of strangers, which they called *the Profane*, they never spoke of the sacraments but used symbols and secret words to convey their meaning.

Origen (born ca. 185 AD) answered Celsus's objection to the concealed doctrine of the Christians by writing, "So far as the essential and important doctrines and principles of Christianity are taught openly, it is foolish to object to other things that are secret. This is common in the Christian discipline because our philosophers taught things that were general and some that are particular and esoteric. It was the same among the disciples of Pythagoras."

When preparing to celebrate its Mysteries, the early congregation would pronounce, "Depart, you uninitiated! Let the Catechumens and others not admitted or initiated leave."

Archelaus, Bishop of Cascara (in Mesopotamia), conducted a debate with Manichaeus in 278 AD and said, "The Mysteries the church teaches to those who have passed through the introductory Degree are not explained to the Gentiles. They are not openly discussed when among the Catechumens, but are 545 conveyed in disguised terms and double-meanings that the Faithful [Πιστοί] recognize and those who are not knowledgeable about them are not disadvantaged in the disclosure of the first meaning."

Cyril, Bishop of Jerusalem (ca. 315 AD - 386 AD), wrote in a series of 23 lectures the *Catechesis*, "The Lord spoke in parables and allegories to the general public, but to the disciples he provided explanations about the public lectures. The glory is for those who are enlightened while obscurity and darkness are for the unbelievers and unlearned. Similarly, the church employs obscure terms within its lectures to hide its Mysteries from those who have not advanced beyond the class of Catechumens."

St. Basil the Great, Bishop of Caesarea (ca. 330AD - 379 AD) stated, "We have received from the Apostles the dogmas in writing and the mysteries through oral tradition. Several lessons were taught orally to prevent the masses who were familiar with the dogmas from losing a respect for them. . . . This is what the uninitiated are not permitted to contemplate. It would not be proper to write and share an account of them among the people."

St. Gregory Nazianzen, Bishop of Constantinople (329 AD – 379 AD) said, "You have heard as much of the Mysteries as we are allowed to speak openly of for everyone. The rest will be communicated to you in private and you must keep it to yourself. . . . Our Mysteries should not be made known to strangers."

St. Ambrose, Archbishop of Milan (ca. 337 – 397 AD) wrote in his work *De Mysteriis*, "All the Mystery should be kept concealed, guarded by faithful silence, otherwise it will be misunderstood by the ears of the uninitiated. . . . . It is not provided for all to contemplate the depths of our Mysteries . . . . They should not be viewed by those deemed unworthy to behold them. They should not be given to those who cannot keep them." In another of his works, "He who divulges the Mysteries to unworthy people sins against God. The danger is not in the violation of the promise not to tell, but in not explaining adequately the truth if hints of it are revealed to those who should not receive it. . . . . Beware of throwing pearls before swine! . . . . Every Mystery should conceal its 546 secrets by silence unless it is wrongly divulged to the uninitiated. Beware not to reveal the Mysteries accidentally!"

St. Augustine, Bishop of Hippo (354 AD – 430 AD), said in one of his discourses, "Without the Catechumens near, we have kept you to hear us. Besides that which belongs to all Christians together, we will instruct you in the sublime Mysteries, which none is qualified to hear except by the Master's favor . . . . To have taught them to the masses would have been to betray them." He continued with references to the Ark of the Covenant by stating it was a symbol of a Mystery, or secret of God, shadowed by the cherubim of glory and veiled in honor.

St. Chrysostom and St. Augustine wrote of initiation more than fifty times. St. Ambrose specifically wrote to those initiated into the Mysteries, not merely baptized or admitted into the church. The initiated had the Mysteries of religion unveiled to them. These secrets were kept from the Catechumens who were only permitted to hear the Scriptures and their ordinary discourses. The Mysteries were never discussed because they were reserved for the Faithful. When normal services and prayers ended, the Catechumens and spectators left.

Chrysostom, Archbishop of Constantinople (349 AD – ca. 407 AD) said, "I want to openly speak, but dare not because of the uninitiated. Therefore, I will use disguised terms to hide what are in the shadows. . . When the holy Mysteries are celebrated we close the doors to all uninitiated persons." He mentioned the glory of the initiated, "which here I skip in silence because it is forbidden to disclose such things to the uninitiated." Palladius, in his work on the Life of Chrysostom, was outraged by his description of a riotous crowd that forced its way into the *penetralia* and saw what was not intended for their eyes. Chrysostom mentioned the same incident in his epistle to Pope Innocent.

St. Cyril of Alexandria (ca. 378 AD – 444 AD) was made Pope in 412 AD and stated in his *7th Book against Julian*, "These Mysteries are so profound that they can be understood only by those who are enlightened. I will not speak of their admirable qualities because doing so might inform the uninitiated and break my promise not to share that holiness with the impure. I will not give pearls to those who cannot know their worth. . . . I would say more if I were not afraid of divulging information to the uninitiated. Men typically condemn or have contempt for what they should appreciate due to their lack of knowledge and misunderstanding." *547*

Theodoret (393 AD – ca. 457 AD) was made Bishop of Cyrrhus in Syria in 423 AD, and he wrote very extensively. In one of his three *Polymorphus* Dialogues, titled *The Immutable*, he introduces *Orthodoxus* who states, "Answer me in mystical and obscure terms because there may be some persons present who are not initiated into the Mysteries." In the preface to Ezekiel where he traced the discipline of the secret to the beginning of the Christian era he said, "These Mysteries are so majestic that we should keep them with the greatest caution."

Marcus Minucius Felix, an eminent lawyer of Rome, lived around 212 AD and wrote a defense of Christianity. He said, "Many of the Christians know each other by tokens and signs (*notis et insignibus*), and they form a friendship with each other almost before they become acquainted."

The Latin Word *tessera* originally described a square piece of wood or stone, used in making tessellated pavements. Afterwards, it meant a tablet on which anything might be written and it described a cube or a die. It was generally used to identify a square sign of metal or wood on which the watchword or password of an Army was written. Later, *tessera* came to mean the watchword itself. We know of the *tessera hospitalis*, which was a piece of wood split in two parts that formed a pledge of friendship. Each person kept one half and both swore fidelity to Jupiter. Breaking the tessera was how one dissolved the friendship. The early Christians used it as a Mark or the watchword of friendship, and it was generally a piece of bone in the shape of a fish. On it was inscribed the word Ἰχθῦς, a fish, and was an acronym for the Greek phrase, Ἰησοῦς Χριστὸς Θεοῦ Υἱὸς Σωτής; *Jesus Christ, the Son of God, the Savior.*

In *de Fide et Symbolis* St. Augustine said, "These few words represent the faith given to the *Novices* that were known among all the Faithful; by believing, you may submit to God; by submitting, you may live rightly; by living rightly, you may purify your heart; and, with a pure heart, you may understand what you believe."

Maximus Taurinus said, "The tessera is a symbol and sign by which to distinguish between the Faithful and the uninitiated."

There are *three* Degrees in Blue Masonry. There are two words of two syllables, and they embody the binary. There are three words of three syllables. The three Grand Masters of the Temple were the two Kings and Khir-Om (Hiram) the Artisan. The candidate gains admission with three knocks. Three gavels raise the Brethren to their feet. There are three principal officers of the Lodge, three lights at the Altar, and three gates of the Temple, and all are located in the East, West, and South. The three lights represent the Sun, Moon, and Mercury; Osiris, Isis, and Horus; Father, Mother, and Child; Wisdom, Strength, and Beauty; Chokmah, Binah, and Daath; or Chesed (Gedulah), Geburah, and Tiphareth. The candidate makes three circuits of the Lodge. There were three assassins of Hiram (Khir-Om), and he was murdered after three blows while trying to escape from the three gates of the Temple. Three times the exclamation at his gravesite was repeated. There are three divisions of the Temple, and it has three, five, and seven Steps. A Master works with Chalk, Charcoal, and Clay. There are three movable and three immovable jewels. The Triangle appears among other Symbols such as the two parallel lines tangent to the circle are connected at its top. The Columns Jachin and Boaz are connected at the top symbolizing the equilibrium, which helps explain the great Mysteries of Nature.

This repetition of the number three is not accidental and has profound meaning. It is repeated in all Ancient philosophies.

400

The Egyptian Gods formed Triads. Two members were combined to establish a third. From the City of Thebes the Triad was of Amun, Mut, and Chons. At Philae the Triad was Osiris, Isis, and Horus. In the City of Elephantine and around the Cataracts there were Chnum (Neph), Satis, and Anuket. In the City of Memphis there were Ptah, Sekhmet, and Neferem. In the City of Heliopolis was the Ennead of Atum, Shu, and Tefnut. Hermopolis had Thoth, Mu'ut, and Ra.

Osiris, Isis, and Horus were respectively the Father, Mother, and Son. Horus was the Light, the Soul of the World, and the First-Born.

Sometimes this Egyptian Triad was identified with SPIRIT, MATTER, and the Universe. SPIRIT was the *active* Principle or Generative Power. MATTER was the PASSIVE Principle or Productive Capacity. The Universe was generated by the other two Principles just as a son or daughter is made from the father and mother.

Egypt viewed the Triad of Amun-Ra, Osiris-Ra, and Horus-Ra (Ra-Herakhty) and they were respectively referred to as the Creator, the Giver of Life, and Ra-Herakhty, the Controller of Light. These symbolized the Summer, Autumn, and Spring Suns as the Egyptians recognized only three Seasons. Accordingly, they only built three gates for the Temples. The Deity appeared in these different forms because of the differing effects of the Sun during these three Seasons.

549

The Canaanite trinity mentioned by Damascius spoke of Ulomos (Eternity), Chusor (Artisan Kothar-and-Hasis), and an egg from which heaven and earth originated.

The Zurvan Triad consisted of Zurvan Akarana, Ahura Mazda (Ormuzd), and Angra Mainyu (Ahriman) whereby the Good and Evil Principle came from the Father of boundless time. The world produced its harmony from their equilibrium. Angra Mainyu would rule for the first period, and Ahura Mazda would rule to eternity.

The *Chaldæan Oracles* of Zoroaster spoke of the Monad and the Triad animating Fire, Light, Ether, and Worlds.

Orpheus celebrated the Ennead or three Triads. The first Triad was Chronos (time), Anake, and Chaos. The second was Phanes (manifestor), Uranus (sky), and Cronus. The third was of Metis (intellect), Ericapaeus (power), and Phanes (father). Damascius said the Orphic Trinity consisted of Metis, Phanes, and Ericapaeus and represented Will, Father, and Power. Phanes, Eros, and Mithras represented Light, Love, and Life. Acusilaus of Argos made it consist of Metis, Eros, and Ether representing Will, Love, and Ether. Pherecydes of Syros made it of Fire, Water, and Air (or Spirit) so that from fire and water we recognize the parallel to Osiris and Isis as the Sun and the Nile.

The first three of the Persian Amshaspands were Vohu-Man (BAHMAN), the Lord of wisdom and LIGHT; Asha-Vahishta (Ordibehesht), the Lord of FIRE;

and Khshathra-Vayria (Shahrivar), the Lord of SPLENDOR. These lead us back to Kabbalah.

Plutarch said, "There are three aspects of a better and more divine nature. First is the Intelligible or that which exists within the Intellect. Second is Matter (το Νοητος and Υλη). The Greek Kosmos that emanates from the first two together is the third. Plato refers to the first as the Intelligible, Idea, Exemplar, or Father. Matter is the Mother, Nurse, receptacle, or place of generation. The third, coming from the other two is the Offspring or Genesis."

The Pythagorean fragments state, "Before Heaven was made there existed Idea, Matter, and God the Demiurge as craftsman or creator of the former two. He made the world from matter completely created within itself to be perfected with a soul and intellect, and then he generated a divinity for it."

Plato told us of Thought as the Father and Primitive Matter as the Mother. Kosmos is the Son and is the product of the other two Principles. Kosmos was the Universe with a soul.

Later Platonists stated the Triad composed of Potency, Intellect, and Spirit. Philo of Byblos retells Sanchuniathon's described triad as the three sons of Genos (son of Aeon and Protogonus) being Fire, Light, and Flame. This is an Alexandrian idea, not Phœnician.

The Neoplatonic philosopher Amelius said the Demiurge (Creator) is three and its three Intellects are the three Kings: He who *exists*; He who *possesses*; and He who *beholds*. The first is that which *exists* in itself. The second *exists* to itself, but it *possesses* the idea of the first, which encompasses it. The third *exists* to itself, and it *possesses* the second that surrounds it, and can only *behold* the first surrounding both yet remains distant from the third. The three are the Creators, formed and fashioned intellectually with separate existences. The Third exists within the Second and the Second within the First. These equate to the Orphic triad of Phanes, Uranus, and Cronus.

The most ancient doctrine of the Brahmins is interpreted by some as Trinitarian. It speaks of one supreme, indivisible, unchangeable Purushottoma (PARABRAHMA). He appears in different forms as needed with the first as BRAHMA the *Creator*, then as VISHNU the *Preserver*, and as SHIVA the *Destroyer* and *Renovator*. The Supreme Essence revealed himself in the material Universe but was soon regarded as three separate deities collectively called the TRIMURTI. Later each God was separated from this single entity, and each was considered an independent supreme deity with other manifestations of it by different names. Hindus have a Universal saying for all religions, "The truth is One, but different Sages call it by Different Names."

The Persians under Zoroastrianism received the idea of these three principles from the Indians. These three were reduced to two principles. The first was of Life represented by the Sun and the second of Death represented by cold and darkness. These were intended to be a parallel of the moral world with the continual struggle between light and darkness, life and death, or good and evil principles as embodied by the legend of Ahura Mazda (ORMUZD) and Angra Mainyu (AHRIMAN). MITHRAS, an Ahura, was considered the protector of truth and justice and the source of cosmic light. BUDDHA is considered by Hindus to be an incarnation (Avatar) of Vishnu on Earth.

The Trimurti among the Hindus were taken by the Ethiopians (Abyssinians) as NEPHTHYS, Khenmu (PTAH), and Satis (NEITH). They represented respectively the CREATOR as a ram, MATTER as the globe or an egg, and THOUGHT or LIGHT that contained the seed of everything. This triple manifestation of one God (THOTH) with the three aspects *creative power*, *goodness*, and *wisdom* was common to the triad. Other Deities were rapidly created along the Nile river. Among these were OSIRIS representing the Sun, ISIS representing the Moon, and TYPHON representing Evil and Darkness or the offspring to 551 Osiris and Isis. The Triad of OSIRIS, ISIS, and HORUS replaced the latter triad and was the Chief triad of worship among the Egyptians in later dynasties.

The ancient Etruscans (a people of unknown origin within Italy whose language is unlike any other) acknowledged a divine power that was divided into different manifestations to interact with man and the world. They built Temples to these deities. Each town had one National Temple, dedicated to the three great attributes of God, STRENGTH, LIGHT (or sometimes RICHES), and WISDOM, or *Tinia* (father), Uni or *Thalna* (mother), and *Minerva* (daughter). The Triad was worshiped under one roof (as in Egypt) with the supreme divinity identified by different names in the different geographical regions. Each Etruscan city may have had several gods, gates, and temples but there were always three sacred gates and one Temple to the three Divinities. This was the same wherever the laws of Tages (or Thoth) were found. At Volterra, Italy the Porta all'Arco, or Etruscan Gate, has upon it the three heads of the National Divinities where one is at the top of the arch and one above each of the two pillars.

The Buddhists recognize a Trinity known as the Three Jewels of Buddhism, and it is comprised of BUDDHA, DHARMA, and SHANGHA that are the Mind's Enlightenment or *Intelligence*, Teachings or *Law*, and Community or *Harmony* respectively.

The Chinese Taoism represents the *Supreme Deity* as composed of SHANG-TI or Hong-Jun Lao-Zu as the great primal originator and teacher. The Three Pure Ones are then composed of YU-CH'ING, the One of *Origin*, SHANG-CH'ING, the One of *Divinities* and *Treasures*, and T'AI-CH'ING the One of TAO and *Virtues*. From the *Tao Te Ching* we understand the TAO as the Way of Love, Moderation, and Humility that was existent before all, from Chaos, in silence, void, alone, infinite, unchanging, everywhere, always moving, and the source of all. The Tao produced one, one produced two, two produced three, and three produced everything.

The Slavic myth of the Unity in Three Gods, a Trinity called TRIGLAV, was composed of Svarog (creator), Perun (firmament), and Svetovid (light and

earth). The Prussians had the Triad of PERKUNAS (creation, *light*, *thunder* and
sky), PATULAS (*hell*), and PATRIMPAS (*Earth* and spring). The Norse had the triad
of ODIN (father, wisdom, sun, and war), THOR (son and thunder), and FRIGG
(mother, sky, love, and fertility).

KABBALAH stated that the Infinite Deity was beyond the reach of the
Human Intellect and was without Name, Form, and Limitation (Ain Soph). He
was said to have revealed Himself through ten *emanations*, called SEPHIROTH,
allowing creation through "restriction". The first world of creation is ATZILUTH,
and it is the light that filled the void from the Deity. KETHER (*Crown*) is how we
understand the Divine Will or Potency. Next are the pair CHOKMAH and BINAH.
CHOKMAH is Wisdom and it is associated with the FATHER and active *Power*.
BINAH is Understanding, and it is associated with the MOTHER and passive
Capacity. DAATH is Knowledge and represents Unity. This seems to parallel the
"WORD" of Plato and the Gnostics. It is the *ineffable* word *within* the Deity. The
Father, Mother (Holy Spirit), and Offspring (Son) are common themes among *all*
religious Trinities.

Another Trinity within Kabbalah is commonly composed of the Sephirah
of CHESED (GEDULAH), GEBURAH, and TIPHARETH. Chesed translates to *Mercy*
and *Love*, and it is associated with FATHER (*Aba*). Geburah translates to *Severity*,
Strength, Power, or *Judgment* is associated with MOTHER (*Imma*). Completing this
group is TIPHARETH that translates to Adornment, Peace, *Beauty*, or *Balance* and is
associated with the SON. It is the force that integrates the other two and creates
harmony. The ZOHAR states, "Everything happens according to the Mystery of
Balance," or by the equilibrium of Opposites. Thus, the HARMONY of the
Universe flows from the equilibrium of POWER and WISDOM. Power and Justice
are a pillar and Wisdom and Mercy are a pillar of these emanations of God's
Nature. POWER and WISDOM when in Equilibrium produce BEAUTY or
HARMONY and it is the Word or utterance of the Thought of God.

Philo of Alexandria explains that the Supreme Primitive Light when
united with WISDOM [Σοφια], the mother of Creation, forms all things within
Himself. He then acts in the Universe through the WORD [Λογος . . Logos] that
dwells in God and from which all His powers and attributes reveal themselves.
This doctrine was borrowed from Plato.

Simon Magus and his disciples taught that the Supreme Being, or Center
of Light, produced the first three couples of united emanations that were
male/female pairs [Συζυγίας . . . Suzugias] and the origin of all things. REASON
and INVENTIVENESS, SPEECH and THOUGHT, and CALCULATION and
REFLECTION [Νους and Επίνοια, Φωνή and Εννοια, Λογισμὸς and Ενθύμησις . . . Nous
and Epinoia, Phōne and Ennoia, Logismos and Enthumēsis] of which WISDOM
was the first produced and the Mother of all that exists.

Valentinus Gnostics adopted and modified this doctrine. They taught
that the Pleroma (Πλήρωμα), or FULLNESS, of the Superior Intelligences had the
One at its head and was composed of eight primary Aeons [Αἰών] of alternating

sexes: Depth (PROFUNDITY) and Idea (SILENCE), Mind (SPIRIT) and TRUTH, WORD and LIFE, and MAN and CHURCH. Βυθὸς, Σιγὴ, Πνεῦυα, Ἀλήθεια, Λόγος, Ζωή, Ἄνθρωπος, and Ἐκκλησία which transliterate to Bythos, Sige (Ennoia), Nous, Aletheia, Logos, Zoe, Anthropos, and Ekklesia.

Bardesanite doctrines were long embraced by Syrian Christians. They taught that the Father of Life first produced 'Mother' as a Companion for Himself [Σύζυγος . . . Suzugos], and gave birth to CHRISTOS, the Son of the Living (see also Fragments of a Faith Forgotten, pg. 404). After the Son came the Sister and Companion, the Holy Spirit. They produced sons and daughters known as Mayo (water) and Yabsho (land), Nuro (fire) and Rucho (air) [see also A New General Biographical Dictionary, BAH-BEE, Rose, 1857], then Seven Mystic Couples of Spirits, the Heaven, Earth, and everything within, then seven spirits who ruled the planets, twelve Aeons who governed the Zodiac Constellations, and finally thirty-six Starry Intelligences or Deacons. The Holy Spirit [*Sophia Achamoth*] was the Holy Intelligence and the Soul of the physical world. She went from the Pleroma to that material world and was afflicted by the suffering of humanity until CHRISTOS her former spouse came to her with his Divine Light and Love and guided her way to purification and reunited herself with him as his Companion.

Basilides, a Christian Gnostic, taught that there were seven emanations from the Supreme Being, Abraxas: The Supreme, Mind, Word, Reflection, Wisdom, Power, and Righteousness [Πρωτογονος, Νους, Λογος, Φρονησις, Σοφια, Δυναμις, and Δικαιοσύνη transliterated as Protogonos, Nous, Logos, Phronesis, Sophia, Dunamis, and Dikaiosune]. From these more emanations continued in succession until all three hundred and sixty-five, inclusive of Abraxas, were realized. This composed the Plenitude of the Divine Emanations of which the Thought [or Intellect, Νους. . . Nous] descended upon the man Jesus at his baptism in the river Jordan. He was the servant [Διάκονος . . . Diakonos] of the human race. The Thought did not suffer with him upon the cross. The Basilideans taught that the Νους only had the appearance of humanity, and Simon of Cyrene was crucified while it ascended to Heaven.

Basilides held that Abraxas was the head of the emanations and was the most exalted [Ὁ ἀκατονόμαστος, ἄῤῥητος]. Abraxas evolved seven living, self-subsistent, ever-active material powers:

FIRST: INTELLECTUAL POWERS.

1	Nous	Νους	Mind
2	Logos	Λόγος	Reason
3	Phronesis	Φρόνησις	Moral Thought
4	Sophia	Σοφία	Wisdom

SECOND: ACTIVE OR OPERATIVE POWER.

5	Dunamis	Δυναμις	Might, accomplishing the purposes of Wisdom

THIRD: MORAL ATTRIBUTES.

6	Dikaiosune	Δικαιοσύνη	Holiness or Moral Perfection
7	Eirene	Εἰϛνη	Peace

These Seven Powers (Δυνάμεις. . Dunameis) and the Primal from which they evolved constitute the First Octave [Πρωτη Ογδοας . . . Prote Ogdoas] in this scheme, and it is the root of all Existence. Many gradations of existence proceeded to evolve from this spiritual life. Each lower one was the impression, or *prototype*, of the immediate adjacent higher one. He proposed 365 of these gradations expressed within the mystical word Abraxas [Αβραξας].

The Abraxas is interpreted by numerology with the Greek letters as. . . .
555 α, 1 . . β, 2 . . ρ, 100 . . α, 1 . . ξ, 60 . . α, 1 . . ϛ, 200 = 365. This was the entire Emanation-World as thought developed by the Supreme Being.

According to Basilides, there was a dualist aspect of the universe where Light, Life, Soul, and Good were opposed to Darkness, Death, Matter, and Evil.

Among Gnostics, God was represented as the immanent, incomprehensible and original source of all. Valentinus' incomprehensible ABYSS (βυθος . . bythos) was exalted as beyond and above all possibility of designation, the ἀκατονόμαστος of Basilides, and the ὢν of Philo. Direct and *immediate* interaction with finite things was inconceivable based on this immeasurable Essence of God. *Self-limitation* is the beginning of communication to life on the part of God. He had to allow others to exist, which resulted in a manifestation of His interaction with life. Still, He is a hidden Deity and all further self-developing manifestations proceed from this Divine Essence. This primal link in the chain of life first evolved the powers or attributes in the divine Essence. Until that first self-comprehension, they were hidden in the boundless Abyss of His Essence. Each of these attributes relay the divine Essence as one particular aspect. In this respect, the title of God may be applied to each. These Divine Powers evolved themselves and became the principles and seeds of all further developments of life. The life within them unfolds and individualizes itself in successive grades descending towards the material world. The spirits become weaker the further removed they are from the source.

The first emanation was called the first comprehension of God [πρώτη κτάληψις τούτου, *prote katalēpsis heautou*, or πϛῶτον καταληπτὸν τοῦ θεου transliterated as *proton Katalepton tou Theou*] which was a distinct substance and was represented by the Mind or Word, [νούς or λόγος . . . *Nous* or *Logos*].

In the Alexandrian Gnosis, the Platonic notion of matter [Hule . . ὕλη], predominates. This inanimate boundary limits the evolution of life in its advancing progression. The Perfect is ever evolving itself into the less Perfect. This ὕλη is represented under various dualistic images: darkness with light, Void
556 [κένωμα, κενὸν. . . . Kenoma, Kenon] with Fullness [Πλήρωμα . . . . Pleroma] of the

Divine Life, shadow with light, or simply as chaos. This dead matter possesses no inherent tendency to seek the Divine. The evolution of the Divine Life (the essences developing themselves out of the progressive emanation) becomes weaker the further it is from the first link in the series. Their connection with the first becomes less at each successive step until there arises an imperfect, defective product unable to retain its full connection with the chain of Divine Life, and it sinks from the World of Eons into the material chaos. According to the same notion somewhat differently expressed [according to the Ophites and to the Bardesanes], a drop from the fullness of the Divine life bubbles over into the bordering void. Here the dead matter receives animation by mixing with the living principle. At the same time, the divine essence of the living becomes corrupted by mingling with the chaotic mass. Existence multiplies itself, and there arises within it a subordinate and defective life. There is ground for a new world, and creation starts from beyond these emanations. Since this chaotic matter has acquired vitality, there arises a distinct and active power in opposition to the God-like. This slightly negative, blind, ungodly, nature-power resists the Divine influence. The products of the spirit of the ὕλη, (of the πνευμα υλικον . . Pneuma Hulikon) are Satan, malignant spirits, and wicked men who have no reasoning, moral principle, or rational will. Blind passions alone drive them. Platonism supposes there is a similar conflict within the soul between the influence of Divine reason [the νους . . . Nous] and the natural blind resistance to reason. [between the προνοια (pronoia) and the αναγη (anage)].

The Syrian Gnosis proposed an active kingdom of darkness and evil. Its encroachment on the kingdom of light brings a mixture of light and darkness or the Godly and the ungodly.

Some Platonists believed that with organized, inert matter of the material world there existed a blind, lawless power with an ungodly soul from the beginning. As God organized the chaos (ὕλη or the inorganic matter) into the material universe the same laws organized the mundane soul into a spiritual, rational being which animated the universe. The same laws also organized the ungodly into an irrational, passionate, and hungry force that developed into evil spirits and persuasion.

The Gnostics *all* agreed on the belief that the world emanated from God, and our creation evolved as a mixture of this emanation and pre-existing matter. The first emanation was from the Divine Essence and the noblest creation. God's formation and organizing power on this emanation generated a creator of *our lower world*. This creator, Demiurge [Δεμιουργος], was not the Supreme Father of *that higher world* of emanation, but a being of a similar nature with the Universe, which His will organized and governed. This world, our world, was inferior to that higher world and its Father.

Some of the Hellenistic Jews of Alexandria conjectured that the Supreme God created and governed the world by His angels. He was the Artificer and Governor of the World who directed and controlled these angels. This

557

Demiurge they compared to the animating spirit of Plato as described by Timaeus and the Platonists [δευτερος θεός . . Deuteros Theos or θεός γενητός . . Theos Genetos] who represented the IDEA of Divine Reason by what is *becoming* and what dies. It is different from that which *is*, being immortal and timeless. This angel was a representative of the *Supreme Good* and existed on an emanation, or lower stage. He is not independent, but acts according to the ideas provided to him by the Supreme God. This is similar to the Platonist's reasoning of how the worldly soul patterns the creation of all things after the ideas communicated by the Supreme Reason [Νούς . . . Nous, the η έστι ζόον . . . . ho esti zoon, the

558 παςάδειγμα . . . paradeigma of the Divine Reason objectified]. The concepts communicated are beyond this limited essence. Therefore, he would not understand their entire scope or the meaning of his work, as he is simply their enactor, the creator. As a tool under the operation of a higher being, he reveals higher truths than he can comprehend. It was believed that the Jews did not recognize this angel in all the supposed manifestations of God described in the Old Testament and that they believed God *revealed* Himself. The Jews did not know the Demiurge and his relation to the hidden Supreme God, *who never reveals Himself* to this world. They confused the source with the model and the idea with the symbol. They looked no higher than the Demiurge and took him as the Supreme God Himself. However, the spiritual men among them perceived, or *divined*, this idea veiled within Judaism. They extended their thought beyond the Demiurge to know the Supreme God. Therefore, they were His proper worshippers [θεραπευταί . . Therapeutai].

Sabeans, or Nazarene Gnostics, regarded the Demiurge as a being *hostile* to the Supreme God. They believed that despite the Demiurge's finite nature he and his angels wished to establish their independence. They would not tolerate a remote ruler within their realm. If a higher nature descended to their kingdom, they would try to imprison it there. In this belief system, the kingdom of these Angels equates to those of the Star-Spirits who try to rob man of his freedom, deceive him, and rule over his world. The seven Planet-Spirits and twelve Star-Spirits of the zodiac sprang from Fetahil and the Spirit of Darkness to play an important part in everything that is bad. The Demiurge is a limited and limiting being, proud, jealous, and vengeful. His character was defined within His Old Testament description, which they believed came from him. Whatever aspects of God that appeared as non-ideal were transferred to the concept of the Demiurge. The ύλη was rebelling against this will and rule which He, the creator,

559 might exercise over it and destroyed the work He had begun. This jealous being was imagined as nature. It was limited in power and ruled as a despot. The Demiurge tried to check the divine aspects that had descended without direct connection from the Supreme God of Holiness and Love into daily mundane life. Only a few spiritual men knew the perfect God of the Mysteries.

The Gospel of St. John is largely an argument against Gnosticism. Those different sects designated philosophical problems, debated solutions, and introduced rituals for these different problems. These problems included the creation of a material world by an immaterial Being, the fall of man, the incarnation, and the redemption and restoration of the spirit man. This was accomplished by a series of intelligences or operations, called *The Beginning* (ἡ αρχή, Arkhe), *the Word* (Λογος, Logos), *the Only-Begotten, Life, Light,* (Μονογενες, Ζωη, and Φως, Monogenes, Zoe, and Phos), and Spirit [Ghost] (Πνεύμα, Pneuma). In the opening of the Gospel, St. John declares in the Beginning was the WORD, Life, and Light, the Only Begotten was flesh as Jesus Christ, and diffused among men as the Holy Spirit [or Ghost].

Pleroma [Πλήρωμα], or Fullness, was a favorite term among the Gnostics as were Truth and Grace Gnostic Aeons. The Simonians, Docetes, and some other Gnostics held that an intermediary Aeon, Jesus Christ, was sent to earth but was never real and only appeared as human. St. John's gospel states that the Word became Flesh and lived among us. Through Jesus, man was brought back into unity with the Pleroma, Truth, and Grace.

According to the Gnostic Valentinus, who was a Christian from Alexandria, God was Bythos, the Abyss [Βυθός] who was unintelligible, unfathomable, and incomprehensible. No mind could comprehend the duration of His existence as He has always been. He is the Primitive Father or the Beginning [Προπάτωρ and Πρόαρχή . . Propator and Proarkhe]. He will always BE and does not age. His Perfections emanated and produced the intellectual world. After having passed infinite and unknown ages in rest and silence, He thought. This thought was the source of all His manifestations that became His creation. From within Him emanated the Aeons first of which included Idea [Εννοια . . Ennoia], Grace [Χάρη, Chari], or Silence [Σιγή, Sige]. The first manifestation of Divinity from this pair was Mind [Νους, Nous as the Only-Begotten [Μονογενες, Monogenēs] whose dualist companion was Truth [Αλήθεια . . Alitheia]. From them emanated the Word [Λογος. . Logos] and its counterpart Life [Ζωη . . Zoe]. From them emanated Man and Church [Ανδρας and Εκκλησία . . Anthropos and Ekklesia]. From these two, twelve more were generated, six of whom were Faith, Hope, Charity, Intelligence, Happiness, and Wisdom [*Kesten, Kina, Amphe, Ouananim, Thaedes,* and *Oubina*]. The harmony of the Aeons in their struggle to reunite with the Primitive God was disturbed. In order to redeem and restore them, the Intelligence [Νους] produced Christos and Wisdom (Sophia) or Holy Spirit as His companion who restored the Aeons to their state of harmony. These two formed the Aeon Jesus, born from a Virgin, with whom Christos united in the baptism. Jesus Christ and his companion Sophia Achamoth saved and redeemed our world.

The Gnostic Marcosians taught that the Supreme Deity produced the Word [Λογος, Logos] or Plenitude of Aeons. His first utterance was a syllable with four letters. Each letter became a separate being. His second word of four letters, third word of ten letters, and fourth of twelve letters generated: thirty in all. These were the Pleroma [Πλήρομα].

560

The Valentinians and other Gnostics identified three levels of existence. First was the divine in life due to their nature and similar to the Sophia [Σοφία], soul, and Pleroma of spiritual natures [φύσεις πνευματικαί, Phuseis Pneumatikai]. Second was the physical nature [φύσεις ψυχικαί, Phuseis Psuchikai] and the origination of life which was separated from the first by mixing with the Hule [ὕλη] and began a new level of existence with the image of higher mind and system but in a lesser form. Third was the ungodly material nature that resists all improvement and tends to destroy through blind lust and passion.

The nature of the spiritual [πνευματικον, pneumatikon] is in its relationship with God (the Ηομουσιον το θεο . . Homoousion to Theo), and it develops the

561 concept of Unity, the undivided, and the simple (Ουσια ηενική μονοειδής . . Ousia henike, monoeides).

The essence of the physical [ψυχικοί, psuchikoi] is multiple derivatives which are subordinate to the higher unity. This allows them to be guided by the higher unconsciously and perhaps consciously.

The essence of the material world [ὑλικοί, Hulikoi] with Satan as its chief is the opposite of unity. It is unharmonious and disunion itself. It has no sympathy, no focus, no warmth, no organization, and it is a force for destruction and chaos among everything. It has no positive power and is therefore unable to create, produce, or form because it is only able to destroy and scatter.

According to Valentinus' disciple Marcus, the idea of a WORD [Λογος του Ontov, logos tou ontos] showing the Divine Essence that was hidden in Creation was a continuous utterance of the Ineffable. Its creation story was detailed by the aspects of divine life [σπέρματα πνευματικα . . spermata pneumatika] that continued to unfold and individualize themselves through the Aeons. It was represented as several *names* of the Ineffable generated from their several *sounds*. It is an *echo* of the Pleroma that descends into the Hule [ὕλη] and creates a new, but lower, world.

One ceremony of ethereal baptism among the Gnostics was described. The assembly said, "In the NAME which is hidden from all the Divinities and Powers [the Demiurge], the name of *Truth* [Αλήθεια, Aletheia from the Bythos] which Jesus of Nazareth put into the light of Christ, the living Christ through the Holy Ghost for the redemption of the Angels, the Name by which all things attain Perfection…" The candidate then said, "I am *established* and redeemed. I am redeemed in my soul from this world and from all that belongs in it by the name of יהוה (Jehovah) who has redeemed the Soul of Jesus by the living Christ." The whole assembly then said, "Peace to all whom this name rests upon." (Neander, General History of Christian Religion and Church, p.477)

According to the Bacchic Mysteries, the Titans tore Dionysus in pieces as a boy. His body was destroyed except for his heart. This body was considered by the Manichaeans to represent the Soul that was swallowed by the powers of

562 darkness. Divine life was distorted into fragments by the influence of matter, and the pieces were the luminous essence remaining in the primitive man.

According to Mani, it was the Protos Anthropos [προτος ύνθρωπος]. To Valentians, it was the Praon Anthropos [πράων ύνθρωπος]. In Kabbalah, it was called the Adam-Kadmon. In the Zend-Avesta, it was the Kaiomorts. The powers of darkness swallowed these pieces, and the mundane soul mixed with base matter. The seed of divine life fell into matter and then needed to undergo a process of purification and development.

The Gnosis [Γνόσις] of Carpocrates consisted of the one Supreme Original being, the highest unity from which all existence emanated, and everything strives to return. The material spirits (archons) that rule over the Earth seek to stop this tendency towards unity. From their influence, laws, and arrangements all the checks, disturbances, and limits to this process exist. These spirits seek to retain mortal souls in their realm by encouraging the indulgence of the material and natural world to keep them from attaining Unity. From these spirits, the popular religions of all nations originated. The souls that remember their condition in the material world are freed to soar upward in contemplation of Unity. When attained, freedom allows nothing to disturb or limit the soul, and it can rise above the popular deities and religions. They provided as examples Pythagoras, Plato, Aristotle, and Christ. They made no distinction between Jesus and other wise and good men. They taught that any souls that attained the same freedom from the material world would be equivalent to any of those examples from before.

The Ophite Gnostic's system had a Supreme Being who was unknown to the majority of the Human race who was the Bythos [Βυθός] or Abyss and Source of Light. He was the source of Adam-Kadmon, the Primitive Man, created by the Demiurge and perfected by the Supreme God through communication with the Spirit [Πνεύμα . . Pneuma]. The first emanation was the Thought of this Supreme Deity [Εννοια . . Ennoia] and was the conception of the Universe in the Thought of God. Thought, also referred to as Silence (Σιγη . . Sige), produced 563 the Spirit [Πνευμα . . Pneuma] as the Mother of the Living and Wisdom of God. In this early, Primitive Existence Matter (Water, Darkness, Abyss, and Chaos) existed just as eternal as the Spiritual Principle. Bythos and Thought united with Wisdom to make her fertile with Divine Light whereby she produced the *Christos* and a Second wisdom, *Sophia-Achamoth*. The inferior wisdom fell into the chaos, became entangled, enfeebled, and forgot about the Superior Wisdom that birthed her. In her entanglement with Chaos, she produced the Demiurge Ialdabaoth, or the builder of Material Creation. Afterward, she reclaimed her position as the first emanation of creation. Ialdabaoth produced an angel in his image. The angel produced a second, and this continued six times after the Demiurge. There were then seven different *reflections* that lived in different areas. The names of these six were IAO, SABAOTH, ADONAI, ELOI, ORAL, and ASTAPHAI. Ialdabaoth desired to be the Supreme Being and made our world and man upon that world in his own image. His mother passed the Spiritual into man after him. Now, man is the focus of this contest between the Demiurge and his mother, light and darkness, good and evil. The image of Ialdabaoth as reflected in matter became the Satan. Eve and Ialdabaoth's sons had created children that were angels like themselves. Sophia withdrew spiritual light from man and the world became evil through its influence. With pleas from Wisdom, Spirit encouraged the Supreme Being to send Christos to redeem the world. Compelled by his Mother, Ialdabaoth caused Jesus to be born of a Virgin. In uniting with Wisdom, the Celestial Savior descended through the seven heavens disguised as each region's chief and entered, with his sister, the man Jesus at the baptism in Jordan. Ialdabaoth aware that Jesus was destroying his empire and abolishing his worship had the Jews crucify Him. Before the crucifixion, Christos and Wisdom ascended to heaven. From heaven, they restored Jesus to life and gave Him a spiritual body that allowed him to remain on earth for eighteen months. From

564 Wisdom he received perfect knowledge [Γνωσις . . Gnosis] and communicated it to a small number of His apostles. From there he arose to the region of Ialdabaoth where he takes the Souls of Light that have been purified by Christos. When Ialdabaoth has nothing from the Spiritual world to rule over anymore, the redemption will be complete. This time will mark the end of the world and the return of Light to the Plenitude.

The theologian Tatian adopted this theory of Emanation and of Aeons in his explanations. The theory advocates the existence of a sublime God who does not allow Himself to be known directly. Only through Intelligences emanating from Him does creation exist and become aware. The first emanation was His spirit [Πνευμα . . Pneuma] as God Himself, thinking, and conceiving the Universe. The second emanation was the Word [Λογος . . Logos] as a Creative Utterance beyond mere Thought or Concept. It was the manifestation of the Divine, but it was derived from Thought or Spirit as the First Begotten and creator of the tangible. This composed the Trinity of the Father, Spirit, and Word.

The Elcesaites adopted the Seven Spirits of the Gnostics in their theological blend and named them Heaven, Water, Holy Spirits, Angels of Prayer, Oil, Salt, and Earth.

The Gnostics generally adopted the same opinion of Jesus Christ as the Docetes. They thought the Superior World was too pure and antagonistic for physical matter to unite with it. Therefore, Christ as an Intelligence from that World appeared on the earth without material substance and only *appeared* as a body. As some have stated, he used the body merely as an envelope for his true self.

Noetus viewed the Son as the visible aspect of God, the Father. The Word was not merely an Intelligence but real flesh.

Paul of Samosata, the Patriarch of Antioch, taught that Jesus Christ was physically the Son of Joseph and Mary. However, the Word, Wisdom, or Intelligence of God [Νους . . Nous] united itself with him by adopting the physical body so that he might be both the Son and God Himself.

Arius, a theologian, asserted the idea labeled Arianism. It called the Savior the first created by God as the "only-begotten" due to the direct will of God. He existed before time and the ages. According to the Catholic belief, 565 Christ was of the same substance as God, but according to other beliefs, he was of the same nature as man. Arius adopted the theory that a similar nature existed in both, but that it was not identically the same. When God created the humans, He made a being as THE WORD, THE SON, THE WISDOM [Λογος, Γιος, Σοφια . . Logos, Gios, Sophia]. It was the son who gave existence to mankind. This WORD is the same idea as the Ormuzd of Zoroaster, Ain Soph of Kabbalah, Mind [Νους, Nous] of Platonism and Philonism, and the Wisdom or Demiurge [Σοφια or Δεμιουργος . . Sophia or Demiurge] of the Gnostics. Arius separated the Inferior from the Superior Wisdom. True to His nature, God would not communicate directly with any creature, but that from which the Son was made communicated to Him, and therefore it was called the Word and the Son.

Mani, the founder of Manichaeans, was born in the Parthian Empire and traveled among many lands evangelizing. He was distinguished among the Magi, learned from Scythianus the dualist principle at the time of the Apostles, understood Mandaeanism, knew Harmonius of the Bardesane Gnostics, and derived doctrines from Zoroastrianism, Christianity, Buddhism, and Kabbalah. He claimed to be the *Paraclete* [Παράκλητος], Comforter, Advocate, or the last prophet and Teacher of the Deity. He did not consider himself the Holy Spirit or Holy Ghost and began his writings in the *Fundamental Epistle* with words, "Manichaeus, an apostle of Jesus Christ, by the providence of God the Father. These are wholesome words from the perennial and living fountain." (Against the Fundamental Epistle of Manichaeus, Augustine, Ch.5) The dominant idea of his doctrine was Dualism supported by Pantheism. It was derived from various sources including Zoroaster, Jesus, and Buddhism from the Kushan Empire in India. The God of Light battles the power of Darkness, and mankind marks the middle ground between the two. Light represents the spiritual world and darkness represents the material world. The two Gods, one of Good and the other of Evil, are independent, eternal, and rulers of their particular worlds, and they constantly battle one another. All souls are from HIM, the light and all bodies are from darkness. The soul is pure but under the rule of the body. The evil God, "The Original Man", is purely matter. The good God, "The Father of Greatness" rules over the spiritual world. The soul transmigrates through many lives to find its place with God after freeing and separating itself from material domination. The Empires of Light and Darkness are eternal while matter is fleeting and was created by the battle between the two forces. In Him lay hidden 566 thousands of ineffable treasures. The Paradise of Light of the Father of Greatness is eternal, and it is inhabited by countless fortunate and glorious Aeons [Αιωνες]. From The Father, there were three creations. First, He created the Spirit or Mother of Life who in turn generated the Son. This Son creates five sons of his own as ether, air, light, water, and fire. The Prince of Darkness found the boundary between Light and Dark and desired to invade and own the Light. The Father of Light sent the Son [*Kaiomorts*, Adam-Kadmon, Πρῶτος Ανθρωπος . . Protos Anthropos, and Hivil-Zivah from the Zend-Avesta, Kabbalah, the Gnosis, and Sabeanism] to battle the forces of Darkness with the five Light Elements as shields. While losing the battle to Darkness, the Son casts off the five shields and distracts the forces of Darkness from their invasion, but they proceed to swallow the Light of the Shields. The Son, the First Man, remains unconscious in the abyss of Darkness and calls for help. His mother, the Spirit hears his plea and begs the Father to bring aid. The Father of Greatness performs his second creation of Gods. The Living Spirit calls and the response from the First Man is heard. Awakened from his unconsciousness the First Man is raised back to Light by the Mother of Life and the Living Spirit. The Living Spirit returns and defeats the powers of Darkness and makes the eight earths and ten heavens from their bodies and skin. With the Light recovered, the Celestial Soul makes the Sun and Moon. From other portions that were swallowed, he makes the stars in the eleventh sky, or our world's sky. The Father then generates the third creation of the redeeming gods. The contact between this third creation and the defeated archons of Darkness generates the plants and animals of the earth. Paradise is created and ruled over by the Son, the First Man. The path to Paradise is set and ruled by the gods of creation. In an attempt to retain Light and defeat redemption of light to the Kingdom of 567 Light, the Prince of Darkness made Adam and Eve in the image of the created gods. The light from the gods is captured with the human body and through the body's material and greedy nature entraps humanity's light on earth. Thus, man is constructed of light from the gods and darkness as matter. To prevent the light from escaping at once, the Demons forbade Adam to eat the fruit of "the knowledge of good and evil," by which he could have learned of the Empires of Light and Darkness. Adam obeyed this. An Angel of Light, Jesus Splendor, tried to persuade Adam to chastity to free himself from matter. However, the Demons mated with Eve to produce Cain and Abel. Later Adam and Eve produce Seth, and human bondage to Darkness propagates through sensual motives now as it did then.

To redeem the soul and its light, man must be virtuous. The Mind, the Nous, sends prophets, in *appearance* only, to man to teach the way to redemption. Light took the name of Jesus, as it did with the other prophets such as Zoroaster, Hermes, Plato, Buddha, and Mani. The Light did its work and turned man away from the adoration of the Evil Principle and Demons.

Christian theology would hold that Light was incorruptible by Darkness. Light could not have mixed with matter. Jesus would have suffered in appearance only. Death gave to all souls the symbol of their duty. The body of Jesus was crucified and disappeared from sight. In his place there was heard a cross of Light from which the celestial voice pronounced these words, "The cross of Light is called The Word, Mind, Jesus, Christ, Door, Way, Bread, Seed,

Resurrection, Sun, Father, Spirit, Life, Truth, Faith, and Grace. The Gate, Joy, The Bread, The Sun, The Resurrection, Jesus, The Father, The Spirit, Life, Truth, and Grace."

Priscillianists were Christians who derived part of their doctrines from the Manichaeans Gnostics. They believed in Dualism as the two principles of eternal Light and Darkness. Their doctrine was based upon several layers of interpretation from the Biblical passages to support their Dualism and their Christian beliefs. The Prince of Darkness is the lord of matter and the physical world. God is the ruler of light and the spiritual world. Angels and human souls were sent from God to combat Darkness but were entrapped in the material bodies and hence were severed from the Kingdom of Light. The twelve signs of the Zodiac act as agents of the Prince of Darkness to influence man for evil. The Twelve Patriarchs of Light attempted to intervene on man's behalf to show the path to redemption and Light. The human soul continued under the influence of evil and materialism so the Twelve Patriarchs sent the Savior to teach and show the path to Light by freeing our souls of the material and worldly. The soul will continue to reincarnate in various bodies until it is purified through redemption and is able to rise to God and Light once again. The Savior, as Jesus, was of the same substance as God and was a manifestation of the Divinity. He was not a second person, unborn and eternal, like the Divinity. He was simply the Divinity under another form. 568

It is useless to trace these Gnostic ideas further. We pause at the countless emanations of the Mandaean cosmology of God and Primitive Light. There are countless spirits and a series of triads composing Primitive Light, Mano, Ferho, Ish Amon, Jordan, Abatur, and Fetahil. Instead of pursuing this further, we return to the simple and sublime creed of Masonry.

These accounts of the ancient and Gnostic beliefs concerning the Deity combined with the details witnessed from the preceding Degrees afford you a true picture of the ancient speculations. Through all times, those who attempt to solve the mystery of creation, of a material universe created by an Immaterial Deity, have interjected between God and man. They have written and spoken of diverse emanations, attributes, agents, spirits, and demons from the infinite and boundless Supreme God.

The Asian belief held that the Supreme Being did not participate directly in the creation of man or material. The Book of Genesis begins by describing creation as *formation*, or *modeling*, of the world from pre-existing matter as chaos. The Phœnicians would see this creation as not by IHUH, but ALHIM, a Subordinate Manifestation or Deity. A second section of Genesis assigns creation to *the Substance* of the *Self*, IHUH-ALHIM. St. John assigns the creation to the WORD [Λογος] and argues that CHRIST is the WORD, LIGHT, and LIFE, among other emanations that were part of creation in other faiths.

The concept of absolute existence, immaterial, out of reach from our senses, root cause, without beginning or end, infinity of eternities, before Time and Space is beyond the grasp of understanding. Mankind can tire himself with these contemplations and be no wiser for knowledge of His nature, His essence, or His attributes than when he began. Due to the impossible nature of a true understanding of immaterial ideas, we are lost and adrift without anchorage or reference. Man can only know what he can physically see. Despite this, man 569 feels *the* Powers, Forces, and Causes that are *not* matter. We assign names to these feelings, but we remain truly ignorant about *what* they really are.

This does not mean that we cannot *believe* in what we cannot *comprehend* and *explain* it to ourselves. If we only believed what our senses and intellect could grasp, measure, and comprehend we would believe nothing. The senses are not sufficient witnesses to the loftiest truths.

The most difficult part is that human language is designed to express *things*, images, and material representations instead of ideas. When we use the word *"emanation"*, our mind involuntarily identifies something material to associate it with, an *out flowing* of something that is material. If we *reject* the material, only the unreal remains for the emanation. The word "thing" suggests material and sensible. If we take away materiality from "thing", we have *no* thing. It is only an intangible unreality to us. Our minds endeavor to grasp this because we feel we are smart enough. *Existence* and *Being* are other terms that carry the same ideas of the material world. When we hear *Power* or *Force* the mind imagines a tangible, physical, and material thing acting upon another. Eliminate that idea of the material from Power and Force and it becomes as unreal as our shadow that is merely the *absence* of light. To us the spiritual is that which is *not matter*.

Infinite space and infinite time are two fundamental ideas. We begin to conceive of it as our universe stretched to its ends, with the light that extends beyond since the dawn of time, and still is but a spec to infinity. The void extends endlessly beyond our comprehension. It is limitless because it *is* nothingness, and the void of nothingness *is* SPACE. The endless time before and after all events of our forever continue unabated. TIME is also endless because it too *is* void.

The ideas of endless space and time are *related* to ideas of matter and events that are limited and finite. We cannot understand an *infinity* of worlds or events. We can only describe an *indefinite* number of them. As we try to 570 comprehend the *infinity*, we remind ourselves that there must be *space* where there is *no* world and there must be *time* without event. If there is infinity before and after, how can we define our space or time within that which is boundless?

We do not comprehend how we are still *in the centre of space* if we have no reference for where we are, where we have gone, or where we will go within space. Nor, do we comprehend how the age of humanity, life, the Earth, the planets, our solar system, galaxies, the universe, or ourselves are still in the centre of eternity. No matter where or when we are, there is as much *space* and *time* before us as behind us. If this is so, then we might say that the world has not moved and we have not lived at all.

We do not fully comprehend how the infinite numbers of worlds is no larger or smaller than the infinite number of atoms. Nor do we see the infinite centuries as no larger than the infinite numbers of seconds as they are both infinite and only differentiated by our material, tangible perspective.

We do have the capacity to formulate ideas of the *immaterial*. We can use the word, but we only know it as the absence of the material, not for being immaterial itself. It is but the opposite of what we can understand. Its idea negates the material.

We do not know of an effect without a cause. If we trace the chain of cause-and-effect back through all time, as it cannot be *infinite*, we must come to *something* that is the first cause. Still this fact is beyond our comprehension. When we hear of the big-bang, our first instinct is to know what existed before and why it occurred. The mind refuses to grasp the idea of *self*-existence without a beginning.

The mind does not go so far in search of mysteries. We do not have the right to disbelieve the existence of the Great First Cause because our words are not adequate to share our ideas. Because we cannot comprehend something is not a reason to doubt its existence.

If we rub a needle on iron, the steel is given a *virtue*, a *power*, and a *quality*. We then balance it on a pivot and one point of the needle turns to the North by Magnetic power. This Power keeps the pole for years and centuries, and it will always point to the North Pole of the world despite land, water, day, night, rain, *571* or clear skies. This Power keeps man on course over an ocean without landmarks or visible stars. It keeps ships from danger, families from distress, nations secure, and peace over the world. Due to it, Napoleon reached the ports of France when returning from Egypt, and Nelson lived to fight and win at Trafalgar. Men call this Power *Magnetism*, and think they have it fully explained. Despite our claimed knowledge of it, we really have only given a new *name* to an unknown thing to *hide* our true ignorance. What is this wonderful Power, from materials, enacted by nature, which extends its benefits to man and our society? It is a real, actual, *active* Power that we can measure and test. How does it propagate? Though we can see it, we do not know its *essence* any more than we know the essence or the mode of action of the Creative Thought and Word of God.

Furthermore, what is the essence of *galvanism* and *electricity*? It evolves from the chemical reaction between a little acid on two metals. Its effects can circle the earth in less than a second and communicate the *Thoughts* of individuals and nations. It *is* a Power, like Thought and Will.

How does *gravitation* make everything on the earth attract to the center? How does it spread its influence throughout the universe? How does it capture and keep larger masses of rock in its orbit? It is a *power* of which we can still learn more.

What is the nature of *heat* that fuels our world and our economy? It is everywhere, within us, near us, and around us. It keeps matter in motion. Without heat, life and atoms would cease to move. Without that motion, time would slow and the universe would stop to us. Is its substance matter, spirit, or immaterial? Is it a Force or a State of Matter?

What is *light?* Is it a particle or a wave? It has *substance* and *matter* and travels to us from the sun and stars. Its rays are separable into distinct wavelengths in the visible and invisible realms. *When* it is a mass, what is its essence? What power does it hold that it can travel millions of miles and continues for thousands of years after it leaves the stars? What is the medium for these waves to propagate?

572   All power is a mystery. A solid iron globe can shatter simply by freezing a drop of water embedded within the iron. Put water within a confined cylinder and apply heat and the power from the thermal expansion will shatter the cylinder to pieces. A seedling in its infancy that is so fragile in the world can grow deep into the rocks of the earth with an energy not understood. What is the essence of these forces locked within the seed and molecules of water?

More troublesome is LIFE itself with its wondrous and mighty energy. It has powers that maintain our body temperature and regulate our unconscious actions keeping us from decay and death too soon. Without these powers, our bodies quickly return to dust. The miracle of Life has eluded the definitive explanation of its nature and essence despite all the philosophers and dissertations on it. Aren't these thoughts merely words meant to attempt to frame this miracle, but they constantly fall short of defining what, how, and why life is?

It is no wonder that the ancient Persians thought that Light and Life were the same emanations from the Supreme Deity. Their worship of the Sun is reasonable. God breathed the spirit into man, but not matter. He did this through an emanation from Himself and not from a creature *made* by Him or distinct from him. It was a *Power* of His. Light would have seemed the same to those soul searching ancients. It too was not a creature, nor like other material substances, but it was an emanation from the Deity, immortal and indestructible.

What is REALITY? Our dreams seem real while they last. To our minds, they are as believable, when asleep, as our regular actions are when we are awake. When dreaming, we continue to see, hear, feel, act, and experience as vividly as we do when awake. When a year of life is done, its memories can be crowded into the memory span of seconds, and these are as real then, looking back, as the dreams we remember from that same time.

Philosophers will argue that we have no knowledge of *substance* itself. We can only understand its *attributes*. For example, when we investigate a block of marble our perceptions provide information that it is there, solid, colored, heavy, and so forth, but we do not know the very *thing* itself. These attributes are adjectives of a substance, but these are meaningless without the substance. A *thing* or *existence* is not the hardness, weight, or color we describe by itself. The descriptors are not things that move about attaching themselves to one thing or another. They are common traits, but not an object itself. The attributes are not the subject, but we cannot describe the subject without them.

573

Therefore, we say that Thought, Will, and Perception are not the soul but simply *attributes* of it. We have no perception of the soul *itself*, but only of its *manifestations*. Nor do we perceive God directly, but rather we perceive His Wisdom, Power, Magnificence, Truth, and many other attributes.

Still, we know there is matter, a soul, and God in the Universe.

Let us discuss the attributes of the soul. I am conscious that I exist and am the same identical person that I was twenty years ago. I am conscious that my body is not me. If my arms and legs were amputated, this *person* that I call ME, would still remain, complete, entire, and identical as before. However, I cannot determine through the most intense and continued reflection what I am, where within this body I reside, nor whether I am a point or expanded substance. I have no power to examine or inspect it. I only exist, will, think, and perceive *that* which I know and nothing more. I think a noble and sublime Thought. What is that Thought? It is not Matter or Spirit. It is not a Thing, but it is a *Power* and *Force*. I mark characters on paper that *represent* that Thought, but there is no Power or Virtue in the *marks* I write. These forces reside only in the Thought they convey to others, not the marks themselves. I may die, but that Thought will live. It is a Power that causes men to act, excites an enthusiasm, inspires patriotism, governs conduct, controls destinies, and orders life and death. The spoken word is just a certain succession of sounds that communicate to others Immaterial, Intangible, and Eternal Thoughts when arranged properly. The mere existence of a Thought after its appearance to the soul proves it is immortal. There is nothing that can forcibly destroy that thought. Though spoken words may vanish into the air and written words can be burned, erased, or otherwise destroyed, the THOUGHT itself will live on forever.

The Thought is therefore an EXISTENCE, FORCE, and POWER. It is capable of controlling matter, action, and mind. God's existence as the immaterial soul of the Universe and whose THOUGHT is an Infinite Power of Creation, production, destruction, and preservation is as comprehensible as the existence of a Soul, its Thought separate from the soul, and the Power of the thought to control and influence the fate and Destiny of Humanity?

574

Still we do not know what the Thought will be or when it will come. It is not WE. We do not form it, shape it, and fashion it. It is not our tool or invention. It is spontaneous to the soul. The soul is an involuntary instrument of its revelation to the world. It comes to us as a stranger and seeks a home.

We can barely explain any better the power of the human WILL. Like Thought, it seems spontaneous and without cause. Circumstances may *provoke* it or serve for its *occasion* but these do not *produce* it. It generates from within the soul. Is it the manifestation of what is *within* the soul, or is it an outward emanation of the soul with its own Existence? We do not know. We do know that our Will acts, controls, directs, shapes, and legislates over other souls. Still, it is not material or visible, but its legacy passes to other souls.

God can only be a mystery to us because everything around us is a mystery. We know there must be a FIRST CAUSE. His attributes are unrealities. As color, volume, mass, and hardness are not separate entities from matter, so Goodness, Wisdom, Justice, Mercy, and Charity are not independent existences from God. We personify them as men might, but the *attributes* of the Deity are *adjectives* of the One Great Substance. We know that He must be Good, True, Wise, Just, Charitable, and Merciful. In all His attributes, He is Perfect and Infinite. We are conscious that these laws imposed on us are necessary because without them, the Universe would be confused and a God within confusion would be inconceivable. These are His *essence*. They are necessary just as His existence is.

He is the Living, Thinking, and Intelligent Soul of the Universe. He is the PERMANENT, the STATIONARY of Simon Magus[Εστως . . Estos], the ONE that IS always to Plato [Το Ον . . TO ON], and is different from change, or the *Genesis*, of *things*.

A Thought emanates *from* the Soul and becomes audible and visible in Words. Likewise, THE THOUGHT of GOD sprang up from within Him when conceived and uttered Itself in THE WORD. It manifested through the mode of communication and created the Material, Mental, and Spiritual Universe. Like Him, It *is* immortal because it never *began* to exist as it existed *before* creation, *in* Him.

This is the *real* idea of the Ancient Nations. GOD, as the Almighty Father and Source of All *conceived* the whole Universe with His THOUGHT and *willed* its creation. His WORD *uttered* the THOUGHT and became the Creator, or Demiurge, in whom is Life and Light. That Light is the Life of the Universe.

The Word did not *cease* as a single act of Creation. It set the great machine of the universe in motion. It enacted the laws of its motion, progress, birth, life, change, and death, but it did not go idle or cease to exist.

THE THOUGHT OF GOD LIVES AND IS IMMORTAL. Embodied by the WORD, it *creates* and *preserves*. It conducts and controls the Universe including all spheres, all worlds, all actions, humans, and every animate and inanimate creature. It speaks through the soul of every man who lives. The Stars, Earth, Trees, Winds, Nature, tempest, avalanche, Sea's roar, waterfall, thunder, babbling brook, song birds, love, human speech, and song are among the alphabet it uses to communicate itself to humanity and inform them of the will and law of God. From these truly *did*, "THE WORD BECOME FLESH AND DWELL AMONG MEN."

God, the unknown FATHER [Πατέρ Αγνωστος . . Pater Agnostos], is known to us only by His Attributes. The ABSOLUTE I AM, . . The THOUGHT of

God [Εννοια . Ennoia], the WORD [Λογος . . . . Logos] as manifestation and expression of the Thought. This is THE TRUE MASONIC TRINITY composed of the UNIVERSAL SOUL, the THOUGHT *in* that Soul, and the WORD as expression of the Thought. These are the THREE IN ONE of the Scottish Trinitarian dance.

Here Masonry pauses to leave its Initiates to implement and develop these great Truths as each may view their acceptability with reason, philosophy, truth, and their own religious faith. Each is instructed to go forth and learn with these words as a guide. Masonry will not arbitrate between religions or men's reason. It calmly accepts, each man's view of the intermediaries between Deity and Matter and how God's manifestations and attributes are personified to him, as whatever his reason, conviction, or persuasion allows. 576

While the Indian tells us that PARABRAHMA was composed of BRAHMA, VISHNU, and SHIVA who were the *Creator, Preserver,* and *Destroyer* as the first Triune God. . . .

The Egyptian triad of AMUN-RA, NEITH, and PTAH as *Creator, Matter,* and *Thought* or *Light.* The Persian Trinity of the Three Powers in ORMUZD as Source of *Light, Fire,* and *Water.* The Buddhist Trinity composed the Three Jewels of Buddhism with BUDDHA, DHARMA, and SHANGHA as *Intelligence, Law,* and *Union* or *Harmony.* The Chinese Taoists had *their* Trinity of *Shang-ti,* the Supreme Sovereign composed of YU-CH'ING, the One of Origin, SHANG-CH'ING, as the One of Divinities and Treasures, and T'AI-CH'ING as the One of *Tao* and Virtues. Who produced the Unit that made two, two made three, and three made all that is . . . .

In Slavic mythology, the Unity of Three Gods called *Triglav* was composed of *Svarog* (creator), *Perun* (firmament), and *Svetovid* (light and earth). The Prussians had the Triad of *Perkunas* (creation, *light, thunder* and sky), *Patulas* (*hell*), and *Patrimpas* (*earth* and spring). The Ancient Scandinavian had the triad of *Odin* (father, wisdom, sun, and war), *Thor* (son and thunder), and *Frigg* (mother, sky, love, and fertility). The old Etruscans had the three great attributes of God, *Strength, Light,* and *Wisdom* as TINIA (father), Uni or THALNA (mother), and MINERVA (daughter). . . .

While Plato tells us of the *Supreme Good,* the *Reason* or *Intellect,* and the *Soul* or *Spirit.* Philo tells of the *Archetype of Light, Wisdom* [Σοφια], and the *Word* [Λογος]. The Kabbalists tell of the Triads of the Sephiroth . . . .

While the disciples of Simon Magus, and the many sects of the Gnostics, confuse us with their *Aeons, Emanations, Powers, Wisdom Superior* and *Inferior, Ialdabaoth, Adam-Kadmon,* and even the three hundred and sixty-five thousand emanations of the Mandaeans (Maldaïtes) . . . .

The Christian believes the WORD dwelled in the Mortal Body of Jesus of Nazareth, suffered upon the Cross, and the HOLY GHOST was poured out upon the Apostles to now inspire every truly Christian Soul . . . .

All faiths assert their claim to exclusive possession of the Truth of God. Masonry simply teaches its long-standing doctrine and nothing more. God is 577

ONE. His WORD is His THOUGHT uttered that created the Universe as it preserves it by the Laws that are an expression of that Thought. God breathed the Soul into Man and it is as immortal as His Thoughts. Man is free to choose good or do evil. Therefore, he is responsible for his actions and is punishable for his sins. All evil, wrong, and suffering are temporary and an aspect of the one great Harmony. In His time, they will lead to the great and final harmonic in humanity of Truth, Love, Peace, and Happiness. It will ring forever and ever under the Arches of Heaven, among all the Stars and Worlds, and in all souls of men and Angels.

CHAPTER 27: KNIGHT COMMANDER OF THE TEMPLE

THIS is the first of the truly Chivalric Degrees of the Ancient and Accepted Scottish Rite. This Degree is a break to the continuity between previous Philosophical degrees and the following degrees. This degree reminds you to always remain active in the great warfare of life. The Initiate is a Moralist, Philosopher, and a Soldier who is succeeding those Knights of the Middle Ages that wielded the Sword as Soldiers of Honor, Loyalty, and Duty.

Times and circumstances change, but Virtue and Duty remain the same. The Evils to be fought against only take different shapes and different forms.

The same need for truth and loyalty exists today as it did during the Crusades.

The religious and military obligations to care for the sick and wounded and battle against the Infidel are no longer required. The same duties continue to exist and obligate us today, but they are in different forms.

The innocent virgin is no longer at the mercy of the brutal Baron or soldier, but purity and innocence still need guardians.

War is no longer the natural State of Society. The same high duty and obligation still rests upon all men, if necessary, but it is an empty obligation to assume that most men would not retreat before the enemy.

Truth is more rare today than in the days of chivalry. Lies have become commonplace and circulate with a degree of respectability because they have an actual value. Lying and Dishonesty have become the great vices of our time. People will use whatever principles are expedient and profitable to advance their own interests. In courts, churches, and the legislatures, people will argue against their own beliefs to prove to others what they themselves do not believe. Hypocrisy and deception are valuable to those who use them. The truth of an opinion or a principle no longer matters, but only the gain that may be realized from them has any value.

The Media is the great spreader of untruths. Slandering a political opponent, and misrepresenting or inventing what was said in order to defeat them is so commonplace that no one even notices or comments anymore.

There was a time when a Knight would rather die than break his word or lie. The Knight Commander of the Temple restores this spirit and devotes himself to the noble worship of Truth. Never state an opinion merely for expediency, profit, or fear of the world's displeasure. It is unjust to slander an enemy or twist the speech and acts of other men under any pretext. You must always speak the Truth, all of the Truth, no more or less, or choose not to speak at all.

The Knight Commander protects the pure and innocent everywhere. He must stand up against those who would use violence or treachery to injure the soul. He must alleviate the need and destitution that cause too many people to sell their honor and innocence for food or want.

Mankind has never had a better opportunity to display those majestic virtues and noble heroism that distinguished the three great military and religious Orders, before they were corrupted by prosperity and power.

When a dreadful epidemic ravages a city and there are not enough living to bury the dead, most people will flee in terror and return to live respectable and influential lives once the danger has passed. The traditional Knightly spirit of devotion, selflessness, and contempt of death still lives in the human heart. There are still a few people who will stand firmly and steadfastly at their posts while defying danger. They do not do it for money, honor, or to protect their own household, but they do it for humanity and the need to obey the dictates of duty. They nurse the sick while breathing the diseased air of the hospital. They explore the homes of need and misery. As gently as an Angel, they ease the pains of the dying and give hope to those healing and recovering. They perform the last rites for the dead and they seek no other reward than the approval of their own consciences.

These are the true Knights of our present age, like the captain who remains on the bridge of his shattered ship until the last boat is loaded with passengers and the crew is safe. Then, if necessary, he calmly goes down with his ship. The fireman climbs the blazing walls and plunges into the flames to save the lives of strangers and answers only to his conscience. These people stand at their assigned post and die if necessary, because they have sworn not to retreat before the enemy.

My Brother, by becoming a Knight Commander of the Temple, you have devoted yourself to the performance of duties and acts of heroism like these. Soldier of the Truth and Loyalty! Guardian of Purity and Innocence! Defier of Plague and Pestilence! Nurser of the Sick and Burier of the Dead! Knight, preferring Death to the abandonment of your Post of Duty! Welcome to the bosom of this Order!

CHAPTER 28: KNIGHT OF THE SUN OR PRINCE ADEPT

GOD is the author of everything that exists. He is Eternal, Supreme, 581 Living and Awe-inspiring, and nothing in the Universe hides from Him. We should not make idols or images of Him. We should worship Him as though we are in the deep solitude of a secluded forest, because He is invisible, yet He is the soul of the Universe. He does not live in any Temple!

Light and Darkness are the Eternal ways of the World. God is the foundation of everything that exists and the Father of all Beings. He is eternal, immovable, Self-Existent, and infinitely powerful. He sees the Past, Present, and Future. At once, He sees us in a procession with our most remote Descendents and Ancestors, even the builders of the Pyramids. He reads our thoughts before we know them ourselves. Every motion, event, and revolution in the Universe is an act of His will. He is the Infinite Mind and the Supreme Intelligence.

In the beginning, Man had the WORD as given from God. The Light of existence came from the living power within that WORD. No man may speak the WORD. By it, THE FATHER made Light and Darkness, and every living creature in the world.

The Chaldæans and the Phœnicians believed that Light was divine. They 582 built temples and towers, worshipped, and offered sacrifices upon a thousand altars. LIGHT is a creature of the unseen God who taught the true religion to the Ancient Patriarchs and is *no thing*. He inspires AWE. He is MYSTERIOUS. He is THE ABSOLUTE.

Man was created pure, and God gave him truth in the same way He gave him Light. Since that time, he has lost *truth* and found *error*. He has wandered far into the darkness, and he is now surrounded by Sin and Shame. The Soul that is impure, sinful, and defiled by mortal stains cannot unite with God. By long trials and extensive purification, the Soul will finally be saved from its tragedy, as Light overcomes and unseats the Darkness.

God is the First. He is indestructible, eternal, UNCREATED, and INDIVISIBLE. His essence is *Wisdom, Justice, Truth, Mercy, Harmony, Eternity, Infinity,* and *Love*. He is silent and acts through MIND, and through the MIND, the Soul knows God. All things were originally contained in God, and all things have evolved from him. From His Divine SILENCE and REST, after limitless time, the

WORD or Divine Power was revealed. Through the WORD, the Divine INTELLECT formed the numberless suns and systems of the Universe, *fire, light,* and the Souls and intellects of mankind.

In the beginning, the Universe was One SOUL. HE was THE ALL, alone in TIME and SPACE. Infinite. HE THOUGHT, *"I Create Worlds"*, and *the Universe* was created, ruled by the laws of *harmony* and *motion.* Birds, beasts, and every living thing except Man, light, air, electricity, and mathematics were all created at this thought.

HE THOUGHT, *"I Create Man, whose Soul shall be my Image, and he shall rule"*, and *man* was created with senses, intellect, and a reasoning mind!

583   Yet MAN was merely an *animal* until a spark from God's own Infinite Being became his Soul. Thus, MAN IS IMMORTAL! Thus, man has three natures. He sees, hears, and feels. He thinks, reasons, and loves. He acts in harmony with the Universe.

When the world was young, the original Truth faded from the Souls of men. He asks, *"What am I?"* *"Where did I come from?"* *"Where am I going?"* Looking inward, the Soul tries to learn if "I" is more than mere matter. It tries to learn if thought, reason, passions and affections are more than mere chemistry. Man seeks to learn if he is a physical Being surrounding a Spirit. If so, he seeks to know whether that spirit is independent, with its own immortality, or just a small part of a single Great First Principle. In this manner, men have wandered in a maze of error, imagined vain philosophies, and found themselves consumed by materialism in a vacuum of abstract ideals.

When the first trees were putting forth their first leaves, man had already lost the perfect knowledge of the One True God, the Infinite Mind. He drifted helplessly without direction or destination. The Soul struggled to know if the Universe was a chance combination of atoms or the work of Infinite Wisdom. It struggled to find out if God was disconnected from the Universe or if He could be personally experienced. It wanted to know if God controlled matter directly by will or subjected it to unchangeable, eternal laws. With his limited vision, man sought to know the source of Evil, Pain, and Sorrow. He wandered more deeply into darkness and was lost. Without God, he was left only with a great, dumb, soulless Universe, full of meaningless symbols.

In some of the previous Degrees, you have seen and heard much of the ancient worship of the Sun, Moon, and heavens. You have heard of the worship
584 of the Elements and the Powers of the Universal Nature. You are now familiar with how these things have been made into suffering or triumphant Heroes, and personal Gods or Goddesses, with human characteristics and emotions. You have learned of the legends that allegorically represent the revolutions and motions of the heavenly bodies.

We do not intend for you to see this form of worship as the most ancient and original form of worship, because it was not. The Great Luminary of Heaven was known to the most ancient nations by many names. They proclaimed the primitive truths known by the Fathers of the human race. Only later did men, in error, begin to worship the visible manifestations of the Supreme Power and Magnificence and the Supposed Attributes of the Universal Deity in the elements of nature and the glittering array of constellations in the night sky.

We now draw your attention to another development of this truth by adding some explanation to the names and characteristics of the imaginary Deities that represented the Chief Luminary of Heaven among the ancient nations.

ATHOM or ATHOM-RE was the chief and oldest Supreme God of Upper Egypt. He was worshipped at Thebes. This is the same deity worshiped by the Hindus as OM or AUM, whose name was unpronounceable, and like BREHM (also Hindu) was "The Being that was, is, and is to come; the Great God, the Great Omnipotent, Omniscient, and Omnipresent One, the Greatest in the Universe, the Lord." His symbol was a perfect sphere, demonstrating that He was first and last, in our midst, and without end, superior to all the other Gods of Nature and all of the lesser Deities that were worshipped as powers, elements, and heavenly bodies. He was symbolized by Light, the Principle of Life.

AMUN (AMUN-RE) was the Spirit of Nature. He was worshiped at Memphis in Lower Egypt, in Libya, and in Upper Egypt. In Libya, he was Jupiter. He represents the intelligent and organizing force as seen in the order of Nature. He is the same as KNEPH, from whose mouth was born the Orphic egg from which came the universe.

DIONYSIUS was this same God of Nature to the Greeks. In legend, Dionysius and Hercules were both Heroes of Thebes and both were born to mortal mothers. Both were the sons of Zeus and persecuted by Hera. With Hercules, the divine half is overshadowed by his heroism. However, Dionysius always retains his divine nature in legend. He is identical to Iacchus, the presiding genius of the Mysteries. He represents the Sun in the sign of Taurus. He is depicted with ox hooves, saving the Earth from the harsh Winter. He conducted the stars and the celestial revolution of the year, bringing change in the seasons and the cycle of decay. He was the Sun as invoked by the Eleans as Πυριγενης, who came into the world with lightning and thunder. He is the Might Hunter of the Zodiac. He is ZAGREUS the Golden to the followers of Orphism. The Mysteries taught the doctrine of Divine Unity, a Power that seems to be a mystery, but it is actually true. This was Dionysius, the God of Nature or of the Life of Nature. While in darkness, he is the light preparing for the return of life and vegetation. In the Aegean islands, he was Butes, Dardanus, and Himeros or Imbros. In Crete, he was Iasius or even Zeus, whose reverent and orgiastic worship would have been misunderstood and misinterpreted by the uninitiated if the veil of the mystery had been lifted.

Zagreus, the son of Persephone, was ancient and subterranean. He was the horned progeny of Zeus in the Constellation of the Serpent. Zeus entrusted

585

him with the thunderbolt and encircled him with a protecting dance of Curetes (attendants). With help from the envious Hera, the Titans broke through this protection and dismembered him. Pallas recovered his still-beating heart for Zeus, who commanded Apollo to bury the dismembered remains upon Parnassus.

Like Apollo, Dionysius was a leader of the Muses. In the yearly cycle, the death of one marks the celebration of the other. They were similar, but different, playing separate parts of the same story. The mystic and heroic characters, the God of Nature and of Art, seem to have come from a common source in remote history. Their difference is only in appearance and not in substance. From the time of the initiations of Hercules from Triptolemus and Pythagoras into the Orphic Mysteries, the ideas of the mystic and the hero began to combine. It was said that Dionysius or Poseidon preceded Apollo as an Oracle, and Dionysius was known as a respected Healer, Savior, and Author of Life and Immortality. The dispersed followers of Pythagoras, the "Sons of Apollo" easily adapted to the Orphic Service of Dionysius. There was always something Dionysian in the worship of Apollo.

Dionysius is the Sun and a liberator of the elements. His followers meditated upon the constellations of the Zodiac, which represented the descent and return of Spirits. His second birth, as an offspring of the Highest, represents spiritual regeneration within man. No severe self-denial was required of his followers. Their joyful songs merely celebrated a golden age of eternal spring, fountains of milk and honey, and flowing wine. He is the "Liberator". Like Osiris, he frees the soul and guides its journey after death to protect it from a slipping back into corrupt matter or an animal form. All souls are a part of the Universal Soul, whose completeness is represented by Dionysius. He leads the drifting spirit home and accompanies it in its purifying journey. He died and descended into Shadow, and his suffering was the great secret of the Mysteries, as death is the greatest mystery of our existence. He is the immortal suitor of the Soul (or Psyche), the divine influence which actually called the world into being. He awakens the soul from its trance and restores it from Earth to Heaven.

HERMES, Mercury to the Greeks, Thoth to the Egyptians, and Taaut to the Phœnicians has been discussed in previous material. He was the inventor of writing and rhetoric. He was the winged messenger of the Gods, bearing the Caduceus wrapped with serpents, and the ORATOR represents him in our Council.

The *Hindus* called the Sun SURYA. The *Persians* called it MITHRAS. The *Egyptians* called it OSIRIS. The *Assyrians* and the *Chaldæans* called it Bel. The *Scythians* and the *Etruscans* called it the ancient Pelasgi, ARKALEUS, or HERCULES. The *Phœnicians* called it ADONAI or ADON, and the *Scandinavians* called it ODIN.

Among the Hindus, the *Souras* were the sect who showed particular adoration for the Sun. Their painters show his chariot drawn by seven green horses. The Temple of Visweswara at Benares contains an ancient sculpture depicting him being drawn by a horse with twelve heads. The charioteer is ARUN (from אור or AUR the *Twilight*), or the Dawn. He has twelve titles that distinguish his powers in each of the twelve months of the year. These powers are collectively called Adityas. Surya was said to have often descended to Earth in human form. It was said that he left a race upon Earth equal in renown among the Hindus as the Heliades of the Greeks. He was often called the King of the Stars and Planets, which reminds us of Adon-Tsbauth (the Lord of the Starry Hosts to the Hebrews).

MITHRAS was the Sun-God of the Persians and was said to have been born in a cave at the Winter Solstice. His feasts were celebrated during that time when the Sun began to grow stronger during the year. This was the great Feast of the Magi. Constantine fixed this Feast to December 26th in the Roman calendar. The images and statues of Mithras were inscribed *Deo-Soli invicto Mithras* (to the invisible Sun-God Mithras), *Nomen invictum Sol Mithra.. Soli Omnipotenti Mithra*. Gold, incense, and myrrh were consecrated to him. A hymn to the Sun of Martianus Capella says, "You, whom the dwellers on the Nile adore as Serapis, and who Memphis worships as Osiris. In the sacred Persia, you are Mithras. In Phrygia, you are Atys, and Libya bows down to you as Ammon, and Phœnician Byblos as Adonis and thus the whole world adores you under different names."

OSIRIS was the son of Helios (Phra), the "divine offspring created with the dawn." At the same time, he was the embodiment of Kneph or Agathodæmon, the Good Spirit, with all possible physical and moral manifestations. He represented, in a familiar form, the beneficent aspect of all higher emanations. He expressed the idea of a being of pure good. Because of this, it became necessary to establish another power as his adversary, which they called Seth, Babys, or Typhon, to account for the negative influences of Nature. *588*

Osiris was believed to have created agriculture, and the religious truth of the Egyptians was therefore tied to agriculture. The soul of man was symbolized by the seed hidden within the darkness of the ground (representing his mortality). Osiris was also the ruler over the dead, like Hades, Serapis, and Rhadamanthus. Death was just another name for *renewal*, since its God renewed the life in Nature. Every corpse that was properly embalmed was called "Osiris", and in the grave, the soul might be united or at least brought into the presence of Divinity. When God became embodied for man's benefit, it was necessary that he submit to *all* the conditions of physical existence. In death as in life, Isis and Osiris were patterns and precursors of mankind. Their tombs stood within the temples of the Superior Gods, even though their remains were in Memphis of Abydus. Their divinity was uncompromised. They either shone as the stars in the heavens or presided over the spirits of those whom death had brought to them.

The idea of the dying God frequently appears in Eastern legend, and it has been explained in the previous material. This idea was a natural evolution from the literal interpretation of nature-worship. Nature goes through changes and cycles. To the earliest religious thinkers, Deity was understood through these changes as well as Nature's vitality. The unseen Mover of the Universe was identified through these changes. The Deity suggested by this drama of Nature was worshipped by imitation and sympathy. A period of mourning was observed at the Autumnal Equinox, and a celebration took place with the return of Spring. Phrygians, Paphlagonians, Bœotians, and even Athenians also observed these cycles. Syrian women wept for Thammuz (Adoni) who was wounded at Winter and symbolized by the boar. These rites, like those of Osiris and Atys were inspired by the death or hibernation of vegetation as the Sun seemed to lose its life-giving power in the Winter.

The legendary history surrounding Osiris (like the Syrian ADONI) is just a narrative form of the popular religion of Egypt. The Sun is the hero, and the agricultural calendar is its lesson. The annual inundation of the Nile brought fertility, and it seemed to be life itself when compared to the death of the surrounding desert. This flooding appeared to be tied to the cycle of the Sun, so Egypt became the female power dependent upon the influences of its God, like a heart in the burning chalice of the desert. Typhon, the brother of Osiris, represented darkness, drought, and sterility. He threw the body of Osiris into the Nile, and thus the "Savior" perished in the 28th year of his life or reign and on the 17th day of the month of Athor (13th of November). He rises from his Winter death with the early flowers of Spring, and the joyful festival of Osiris is celebrated. Osiris also died in the heat of early Summer, when from March to July, the Earth perished from intolerable heat. The vegetation became scorched, and the Nile receded. From this death, he rises again as the Solstice Sun brings the inundation, and Egypt celebrates the approach of the second harvest of the year.

In the same way, Jemsheed (the Persian sun-hero) was quickly cut off by Zohak, the tyrant of the West. He was cut by a fish-bone and immediately the brightness of Persia changed to gloom. Ganymede and Adonis, like Osiris, were cut down in their strength and beauty. The premature death of Linus of Greece was like that of the Persian Siamek, the Bithynian Hylas, and the Egyptian Maneros, Son of Menes or the Eternal. The eulogy of Maneros was sung at Egyptian banquets, and an entombed effigy was passed around to remind the guests of their brief mortal life. The beautiful Memnon also perished in his prime, and Enoch, whose death was lamented in Iconium, lived 365 years (the number of days in the year). This was but a short time when considered among the long lives of his patriarchal brethren.

The story of Osiris is reflected in those of Orpheus and Dionysius Zagreus, and perhaps in the legends of Absyrtus and Pelias of Æson, Thyestes, Melicertes, Itys, and Pelops. Io mourns Isis or Niobe. Rhea mourns her dismembered lord Hyperion and the death of her son Helios, who was drowned in the Eridanus. The immortal Apollo and Dionysius died under other names

589

590

430

like Orpheus, Lunis, and Hyacinthus. The tomb of Zeus could be seen in Crete. Hippolytus became associated with Apollo after he was torn to pieces like Osiris. He was kept in darkness in the secret grove of Egeria until he was restored to life by the Pæonian herbs of Diana. Zeus left Olympus to visit the Ethiopians. Apollo served Admetus. Theseus, Peirithous, Hercules, and other heroes descended into Hades for a time, and a dying Nature-God appeared within the Mysteries. The Attic woman fasted while sitting on the ground, during the Thesmophoria, and the Bœotians mourned the descent of Cora-Proserpine to the Shades.

However, the death of this God was not understood in the East to be inconsistent with his immortality. The temporary decline of these Sons of Light is just an episode in their continuous cycle. Just as the day and year are convenient divisions of infinite time, these deaths are merely breaks in the Phoenix-like process of perpetual regeneration. In this way Osiris lives forever in the succession of Memphian Apis. Every year saw the revival of Adonis. The amber tears shed by the Heliades for the premature death of their brother are actually full of hope, and in them, Zeus descends from Heaven to the bosom of the parched Earth.

BAL was the representative of the Sun in Syria, Assyria, and Chaldæa. His name is found upon the monuments of Nimroud, and it appears in the Hebrew writings. He was the great Nature-God of Babylonia, the Power of heat, life, and generation. His symbol was the Sun, and he is depicted to be sitting upon a bull. All the features and accessories of his great temple were emulated in the Hebrew tabernacle and temple (to a smaller scale), where only his golden statue would be missing. The word *Bal* or *Baal*, like the word *Adon*, means Lord and Master. He was the Supreme Deity of the Moabites, Amonites, Carthaginians, and Sabeans. The Gauls worshipped the Sun by the name of Belinus, and Bela is found among the Celtic Deities on their ancient monuments.

The Northern ancestors of the Greeks preferred to emphasize the masculine ideals they so esteemed in their religious symbolism through *Perseus*, HERCULES, and MITHRAS. In contrast, the Southern cultures preferred feminine ideals.

Almost every culture had a mythical being, whose strengths and weaknesses, virtues and defects, follow the Sun's cycle through the seasons. There was a Hercules-like figure among the Celts, Teutone, Scyths, Etruscans, and the Lydians, and all of these legends spring from the story of that Greek Hero. Herodotus believed that the name Hercules originated earlier in Egypt or in the East, and that it may have originally belonged to a much greater figure. The temple of Hercules at Tyre was reported to have been built 2300 years before the time of Herodotus. Hercules, a Greek name, is thought to be of Phœnician origin, referring to a "carriage" of Earth and the "Hyperion" of the sky. Hyperion was the patron of navigators. They created altars in his name throughout the Mediterranean and to the extremities of the West, where

431

"ARKALEUS" built the City of Gades, which had a perpetual fire burning in his service. Hyperion was a direct descendant of Perseus. He is the luminous child of darkness, conceived within a subterranean vault of brass. He is a representation of the Persian Mithras, with his emblematic lions rearing above the gates of Mycenæ. He brought the sword of Jemsheed to fight against the Gorgons of the West. In the Zend-Avesta, Mithras is similarly described as the "mighty hero, the rapid runner, whose piercing eye embraces all and whose arm bears the club for the destruction of the Darood."

Hercules Ingeniculus, bending on one knee, raised his club and trampled on the Serpent's head. Like Prometheus and Tantalus, he was one of the many aspects of the Sun's continuous cycle. The victories of Hercules are illustrations of the power of the Sun, which must be sustained. In the far and gloomy North, among the Hyperboreans, he removed his Lion's skin and went to sleep for a long time. He lost the horses of his chariot. Therefore this place was called the "place of the death and revival of Adonis," the meeting place so close to the heavens (like the Indian Meru) that the Sun seemed to rise and set on it. To the Greek imagination, it became the final abode of Winter and desolation, the pinnacle of the arch connecting the upper and lower worlds. This was the place for the banishment of Prometheus. The daughters of Israel weeping for Thammuz (mentioned by Ezekiel) looked to the North while waiting for his return from that region. While Cybele and the Sun-God had gone from the Hyperboreans, Phrygia suffered the horrors of famine. Delos and Delphi waited for the return of Apollo from the Hyperboreans, and Hercules brought the olive from there to Olympus. To all Masons, the North has always been the place of darkness, and there are no lights there within the Lodge.

Mithras, born of the rocks (Πετρογενης), announced the return of the Sun in Spring. Prometheus was imprisoned in his cavern to illustrate the continuing Winter. The Persian beacon on the summit of the mountain represented Mithras in his most worthy temple. The great fires at the funeral of Hercules represented the Sun dying in glory behind the Western hills. Although the temporary manifestation of the Sun suffers or dies, the ever-lasting, eternal power of the Sun liberates and saves. Every Titan rose after his fall, because the renewal of Nature is as certain as its decline, and its cycles are controlled by a greater power.

"God," says Maximus Tyrius, "did not spare His own Son (Hercules), or exempt Him from the calamities incidental to humanity." Hercules had his share of pain and trial. He proved his affinity with Heaven by victory in his Earthly trials. His life was a continuous struggle. He fainted before Typhon in the desert, and at the beginning of the Autumn season (cum longæ redit hora noctis), he descended into Hades under the guidance of Minerva. There he died, but he first applied for initiation to Eumolpus to foreshadow the state of religious preparation that should precede the momentous change. In Hades he rescued Theseus and removed the stone of Ascalaphus, reanimated the bloodless spirits, and dragged the monster Cerberus into the light of day. Cerberus was an emblem of time itself, known to be invincible (unavoidable). Hercules breaks the chains of death (Busiris represents the grave) and is triumphantly restored to Eternal Youth after his labors. He is rewarded with eternal rest in the heavenly mansions of Zeus.

ODIN is said to have had twelve names among the old Germans, and to have had 126 names in all. He was Apollo to the Scandinavians, as written in the Voluspa, and he was destined to slay the monstrous snake. Then the Sun will be extinguished, the Earth will be dissolved in the ocean, the stars will lose their brightness, and Nature will be destroyed so that it may be renewed again. From these waters, a new and abundant world will emerge. Harvests will grow and ripen where no seed was planted, and evil will disappear.

This web of myths and legends was sacred to the faithful ancients. Unlike the modern mind, they did not distinguish their borrowed beliefs from those of other cultures. They did not regard their beliefs as superior or view other legends as common and unclean. Imagination, reason, and religion revolved around the same symbol. Every symbol carries serious meaning, if we could just find it. They did not create lifeless stories, because they were not hindered by convention. Imagination and reason must guide our interpretation of these myths, and many modern controversies have arisen from great misunderstandings of ancient symbolism.

Earth was the center of the Universe to these ancient peoples, because there were no other worlds with living beings with whom to share the care and attention of the Deity. The world was a great plain of unknown (perhaps unknowable) limits. The Sun, Moon, and Stars journeyed above that plain to give them light. The worship of the Sun became the basis for all the religions of antiquity. Light and heat were mysteries, and they still are today. The Sun caused the day, and his absence was the night. Spring and Summer came with him in his journey Northward, and when he again turned South, Autumn and Winter ruled the Earth. His influence produced the leaves and flowers, ripened the harvests, and brought the life-giving rains and floods. The Sun became the *594* most interesting object of the material Universe. He was the inner fire of nature within physical bodies. He was the Author of Life, heat, and flame and the cause of all creation. Without him, there was no movement, no existence, and no form. He was immense, indivisible, undying, and omnipresent. All men needed his light and creative energy. Nothing was more fearful to them than his absence. His beneficent influence identified him as the Principle of Good, the BRAHMA of the Hindus, the MITHRAS of the Persians, the ATHOM, AMUN, PHTHA, and OSIRIS of the Egyptians, the BEL of the Chaldæans, the ADONAI of the Phœnicians, and the ADONIS and APOLLO of the Greeks. These figures represented the Sun and the regenerating Principle that perpetuates and rejuvenates the world.

The struggle between the Good and Evil Principles was also personified, as was the struggle between life and death, destruction and re-creation. The

allegories and fables poetically represented the cycle of the Sun descending toward the Southern Hemisphere. It was figuratively said to be conquered and put to death by darkness (Evil). Returning toward the Northern Hemisphere, he seemed to be victoriously arising from the tomb. This death and resurrection also represented the succession of day and night. It represented death, which is a necessity of life, and the new life that is born from death. The ancients saw the conflict between these two Principles everywhere. This contest was represented in allegories and legendary histories. Astronomical events were ingeniously woven into these stories, and with them the changes of the Seasons and the beginning and end of the seasonal rains and floods. This was the basis for the great struggles between Typhon and Osiris, Hercules and Juno, the Titans and Jupiter, Ormuzd and Ahriman, the rebellious Angels and the Deity, and the Evil Genii and the Good. These fables can be found in Asia, in northern Europe, and even among the Mexicans and Peruvians of the New World. The Scythians mourned the death of Acmon, and the Persians mourned the death of Zohak
595 who was conquered by Pheridoun. The Hindus mourned Soura-Parama, who was slain by Soupra-Muni. The Scandinavians mourned Balder, who was torn to pieces by the blind Hother.

The idea of infinite space and time existed among the first men, just as it exists in us. We cannot truly conceive how one thing can be added to another thing, or one event may follow another, forever. It seems that just beyond us there must be an *empty* void or nothingness *without* limit. In the same way, the idea of *time* without beginning or end forces upon us a *void* in which *nothing* has yet happened.

In that empty space, primitive man knew there was no light or warmth. They *felt* what we know scientifically. There must be a thick darkness there and an intensity of cold beyond our understanding. They believed the Sun, the Planets, and the Stars descended into that void when they set below the Western Horizon. To them, Darkness was an enemy, a dread, and a terror. It was the very embodiment of the evil principle. They believed that Evil was formed from the darkness. When the Sun turned Southward toward that void, they felt tremendous dread. At the Winter Solstice, the Sun returned Northward and they rejoiced and feasted. They celebrated the Summer Solstice when he appeared to stand in his greatest place of strength and pride. These days have been celebrated by all civilized nations ever since. Christians have made them feast days of the church and assign them to the two Saints John. Masonry has done the same.

Today, the vast Universe has become but a great *machine*. It does not contain a great SOUL, but is reduced to a *clockwork* of unimaginable proportions, infinitely less than infinite. With our models, we have measured the distances and dimensions of a portion of it. We have learned of gravity and determined the orbits of the moon and the planets. We know the distance to the Sun and its size. We have measured the orbits of comets and the distances of the fixed stars.

We know the stars to be Suns like our Sun, each with its own worlds, all governed by the same unerring, mechanical laws. With telescopes, we have classified the galaxy and the nebula into other stars and groups of stars. We have discovered new planets by measuring their influence upon those we can see. We have learned that the planets (Jupiter, Venus, the fiery Mars, Saturn, and the others) and even the bright and ever-changing Moon are merely dark, dull, opaque orbs, without a brilliant fire and heavenly light of their own. We have counted the mountains and caverns in the moon with powerful telescopes. We no longer imagine that the stars control our destinies, though we can calculate the eclipses of the sun and moon, backward and forward, for ten thousand years. We have vastly increased our knowledge of the powers of the Grand Architect of the Universe, but our view of the Universe is now entirely material and mechanical. We can no longer perfectly *imagine* how these great, primitive, simple-hearted children of Nature felt about the Heavens as they stood upon the slopes of the Himalayas, on the Chaldæan plains, in the Persian and Median deserts, and upon the banks of the great Nile. To them, the Universe was *alive* and full of forces and powers that were mysterious and beyond their comprehension. It was no machine, but a great living creature, at times sympathetic and at other times harmful. All was a mystery and a miracle. The pulsating stars spoke to their hearts in an almost audible language. Jupiter, with his kingly splendors, was the Emperor of the heavens. Venus looked lovingly upon the earth and blessed it. Mars, with his crimson fires, threatened war and misfortune. Saturn, cold and grave, instilled fear. The ever-changing Moon was a faithful companion of the Sun, a constant miracle and wanderer. The Sun was the visible emblem of the creative and generative power. The Earth was a great plain, over which the sun, the moon, and the planets revolved to give it light. Some of the stars were beneficent influences bringing with them the Spring with its fruits and flowers, foreshadowing the coming rains of the season. Some stars, together with the eclipses, were heralds of Evil and warned of storms and deadly winds. The regular cycles of the stars, the return of Arcturus, Orion, Sirius, the Pleiades, and Aldebaran, and the travels of the Sun were voluntary and not mechanical to the ancients. Astronomy became the most important science, and those who studied it became rulers. The vast edifices, the Pyramids, the tower or temple of Bel, and other buildings throughout the East were built for astronomical purposes. In child-like simplicity, the ancients worshipped and personified Light, the Sun, the Planets, and the Stars. They eagerly believed in the legendary histories invented for them in an age when the capacity for belief was infinite. Upon reflection, we find this capacity still exists and will endure forever.

If we tried to interpret these myths as literal history, history would be an incomprehensible chaos. All the Sages would seem deranged, as would Masonry and those who instituted it. However, when these allegories are explained, they cease to be absurd fables or literal local stories. They become lessons of wisdom for all of humanity. No one who seriously studies these legends can doubt that they all originated from a common source.

The myths, legends, and fables of antiquity have their foundation in the phenomena of the heavens. The Heathen Gods share their names with the Sun, Stars, Planets, Zodiacal Signs, Elements, Powers of Nature, and Universal Nature herself. However, it would be a great mistake to assume that these ancient peoples actually worshipped all the physical things that seemed to them to have influence upon human destiny.

In all cultures, from the remotest antiquity, we find a single higher Deity, seated above all the gods representing these luminaries, powers, and elements. He is the one silent, undefined, incomprehensible, and Supreme God, from Whom all the rest flow or emanate. All are created through Him. Above the Time-God Horus, the Moon-Goddess or Earth-Goddess Isis, and the Sun-God Osiris, the Egyptians placed Amun, the Nature-God. Above him ruled the Infinite, Incomprehensible Deity (ATHOM). To the Hindus, BREHM was the silent, self-contemplative, one original God and the Source of Brahma, Vishnu, and Siva. Before Zeus, were Kronos and Ouranos. Over the Alohayim was the great Nature-God AL. Beyond him was the Abstract Existence, IHUH--He that IS, WAS, and SHALL BE. Above all of the Persian Deities was the Unlimited Time, ZERUANE-AKHERENE, and over Odin and Thor was the Great Scandinavian Deity ALFADIR.

The worship of Universal Nature as a God was very close to the worship of a Universal Soul. It could not have been the instinctive creed of primitive men. Imagining that the seemingly independent parts of nature formed one, consistent whole required a degree of wisdom beyond the scope of an uncivilized mind.

In the beginning, man had the WORD; and that WORD was from God; and out of the living POWER communicated to man in and by that WORD came THE LIGHT of His Existence.

God made man in His own likeness. HE had prepared the earth to be his habitation. He created man and placed him in that part of Asia that we now call the cradle of the human race. The stream of human life flowed through India, China, Egypt, Persia, Arabia, and Phœnicia. HE communicated to them the knowledge of the nature of their Creator, and of the pure, primitive, undefiled religion. The unique magnificence and the real essence of the primitive man and his destiny is found in his likeness to God. HE stamped His own image upon man's soul. That image has existed within every individual and within mankind in general, though it has been altered, impaired, and defaced. It may still be found on the pages of primitive history, but every reflecting mind may discover it within itself.

The original revelation to mankind (the primitive WORD of Divine TRUTH) remains as scattered traces in the sacred traditions of all the primitive Nations. Taken separately, they appear to be broken remnants of a mighty

598

edifice that has been destroyed, like the old Temples and Palaces of Nimroud. With the increasing immorality of mankind, this primeval word of revelation was tainted with various errors and hidden by innumerable falsehoods, and it has been confused and disfigured beyond recognition. However, a profound inquiry will reveal in early religions a luminous Truth. 599

These old beliefs were still supported by a foundation of Truth. If we could separate the pure insights about nature and its symbols from the additions of fiction, these earliest traces of instinct and imagination would be found to agree with truth and a true knowledge of nature. They provide an image of a complete, free, pure, and comprehensive, philosophy of life.

The eternal struggle between the Divine will and the natural will in the souls of men began immediately after the creation. Cain slew his brother Abel and brought forth generations of people who defied the true God. The other Descendants of Adam intermarried with the daughters of Cain's Descendants, and as a result, both the righteous and the unrighteous may be found within all nations and cultures. The ancients expressed this in their distorted legends of the wars between the Gods, the Giants, and the Titans. A similar division occurred when the Descendants of Seth preserved the true primitive religion and science, transmitting them through ancient symbolism on monuments of stone. This narrative was preserved among many cultures in the legends of the columns of Enoch and Seth.

Then the world fell from its original happy and fortunate condition into idolatry and barbarism. However, all nations retained the memory of that old wisdom, and the poets (the historians in this early time) commemorated the succession of the ages of gold, silver, brass, and iron.

From this sacred tradition flowed many variations among each of the most ancient cultures. Many of these variations brought fertility and life to favored regions of the world. For others, human error scorched the seed of truth and wrought nothing but sterile earth.

After the internal and Divine WORD, originally communicated by God to man, had become obscured and man's connection with his Creator had been broken, the myths and legends fell into disorder and confusion. The simple and Divine Truth was overlaid with absurd fictions and buried under illusive symbols. In the end, the Divine Truth was perverted into a horrible phantom. 600

Through idolatry, the worship of the object gradually obscured the higher principle it was intended to represent. The early nations received a great deal from the primeval source of sacred tradition, but pride (inherent to human nature) led each to recast the original truth as a possession unique to their specific culture. This change exaggerated that culture's value and importance, making them the peculiar favorites of the Deity. In order to make the remaining fragments of truth their own, they wrapped them in their own symbols, concealed them in allegories, and invented fables to account for their own special possession of them. Instead of preserving the blessings of the original revelation in their primitive simplicity and purity, they overlaid them with poetic language and fable. Only by close examination can we discover the truth.

Through compounded error, the original Truth degraded, and the spirit of man turned from God to nature and false faiths. Religions became coarse and vulgar. They were impressive as a spectacle, but lack the pristine purity of Truth that was once guarded so closely. This was most pronounced among the Eastern nations, the Indians, the Chaldæans, the Arabians, the Persians, and the Egyptians, who all had a profound imagination and a deep reverence for nature. The Northern sky contains the largest and most brilliant constellations, and the ancients were more aware of the impressiveness of these bodies than we are today.

601   The Chinese were a patriarchal, simple, and secluded people. Idolatry had very little impact upon their culture. They invented writing within three or four generations after the flood, and they long preserved the memory of much more of the original Truth than other cultures remembered. They were among those who stood closest to the source of sacred tradition. Many passages in their old writings contain remarkable examples of the eternal truth, and of the WORD of primitive revelation.

Among the other early cultures, wild enthusiasm and idolatry overshadowed the simple worship of the Almighty God. The pure and original belief in the Eternal Uncreated Spirit was disfigured and cast aside. The great powers and elements of nature, the powers of production and procreation, heavenly bodies with the great Sun and the mysterious, ever-changing Moon were worshiped in physical form as divine, and they were regarded as animated, living substances with power over man's destiny. Then the genii, guardian spirits, and even the souls of our ancestors were worshipped as divine. The animals represented by the constellations, originally revered only as symbols, became gods. The heavens, earth, and the cycles of nature were personified. Fictional characters were invented to account for the origins of science and the arts as well as the remaining fragments of the original religious truths. The good and bad principles, represented as mythical figures, became objects of worship, but in every case, there remained a small glimmer of the original Truth.

The ongoing study of the records of Eastern cultures continues to suggest that these principles originally emanated from a single source. The eastern and southern slopes of the Paropismus, or Hindukusch, appear to have been inhabited by related Persian peoples with similar habits, languages, and religions. The earliest Indian and Persian Deities are essentially symbols of celestial light, and they are said to be locked in constant struggle with the powers of Winter, storm, and darkness. The religion of both cultures was originally a worship of outward nature, particularly the forms of fire and light. These cannot be mere coincidences. Deva (God) is derived from the root *div*, meaning "to
602 shine". Indra, like Ormuzd or Ahura-Mazda, is the bright sky. Sura or Surya (the Heavenly) is a name of the Sun, similar to the Zend word Huare, as are

Khur, Khorshid, and Corasch. Uschas and Mitra are Medic and Zend Deities and the Amschaspands or "immortal Holy Ones" of the Zend-Avesta are similar to the seven Rishis or Vedic Star-God, of the constellation of the Bear. Zoroastrianism, like Buddhism, was an innovation or revision of an older religion and both are very similar. The original Nature worship, which combined Universal Presence and endless action, developed somewhat differently among the Indian and Persian cultures.

The early shepherds of the Punjaub in the "country of the Seven Rivers" held the Veda as their inspired wisdom. Their form of worship contains what are perhaps the most ancient religious expressions found in any language. They represent the physical objects of their worship as living beings. Highest in this order of Deities stands Indra, the God of the "blue" or "glittering" firmament. He was called Devaspiti, Father of the Devas or Elemental Powers. He measured out the circle of the sky and fixed the foundations of the Earth. Varouna, "the All-encompasser," held dominion in the air and water, the night, and the expanse between Heaven and Earth. Agni lives within the fire of sacrifice, and he is found in the center of domestic life and in lightning. He is the great Mediator between God and Man. Uschas, or the Dawn, leads the Gods in their morning rise to take their daily meal from the abundance offered by Nature. Then came the various Sun-Gods, Adityas or Solar Attributes, Surya the Heavenly, Savitri the Progenitor, Pashan the Nourisher, Bagha the Felicitous, and Mitra the Friend.

The Eternal Being's act of creation was represented as marriage to his first emanation, the universal mother. She was supposed to have existed with him from the beginning of time as a potential. Metaphorically, she is "his sister and his spouse." She eventually became the Mother within the Indian Trinity, which represents three Attributes of the Deity: Creation, Preservation, and Change or Regeneration.

The most popular representations of Vishnu the Preserver portray the 603 Deity leaving the incomprehensible mystery of His nature and revealing Himself at particular times throughout history, which seemed to mark the beginning of new periods of prosperity and order. The Divinity in various forms is really the same when combating the power of Evil, whether in agricultural or social matters, in traditional victories over rival creeds, or in constant physical change. The prototype of Hercules and Mithras was Rama, the Epic hero armed with sword, club, and arrows. He wrestled with the Powers of Darkness, much like Jacob, the Hebrew Patriarch. As Chrishna-Govinda, the Divine Shepherd, he is the Messenger of Peace, with dominion over music and love. Although he is occasionally seen in human form, he never ceases to be the Supreme Being. In the Bhagavad Ghita he says, "The foolish are unacquainted with my Supreme Nature and despise me in this human form, but men of great minds, enlightened by the Divine principle within them, acknowledge me as incorruptible and before all things. They serve me with undivided hearts. I am not recognized by all, because I am concealed by the supernatural power that is in me. I know all things past, present, and future. I existed before Vaivaswata and Manu, and I am the Most High God, the Creator of the World, the Eternal Poorooscha (Man-World or Genius of the World). In my own nature, I am exempt from birth or death, and I am Lord of all created things. As long as virtue is enfeebled in the world and vice and injustice prevail, I become manifest, and I am revealed from age to age to save the just, destroy the guilty, and reassure the faltering steps of virtue. He who acknowledges me in this way does not enter another mortal frame after death. He enters into me, and many who have trusted in me have already entered into me. They are purified by the power of wisdom. I help those who walk in my path, even as they serve me."

Brahma, the creator, sacrificed himself by descending into material forms. He became part of his creation, and his mythological history was interwoven with that of the Universe. Thus, although spiritually allied to the Supreme and Lord of all creatures (Prajapati), he shared a part of the world's imperfection and corruption. Like the Greek God Uranus, he was mutilated and killed. He combined the two balanced aspects: formless form, immortal and mortal, being and non-being, and motion and rest. As Incarnate Intelligence, or THE WORD, he communicated to mankind what the Eternal had revealed to him. He is the Body and Soul of all Creation. The Divine Word is written in living letters, and the enlightened spirit must interpret it.

The fundamental principles of Hinduism include a belief in the existence of only One Being, the immortality of the soul, and the future state of reward and punishment. Its followers practice virtue as a necessity for obtaining happiness in this temporary life, and their happiness in their future lives depends upon it as well.

In addition to the idea of reincarnation, Hinduism proclaims the existence of one God, from Whom all things proceed, and to Whom all must return. They constantly apply these expressions to Him: The Universal and Eternal Essence, that which has ever been and will ever be; and that which gives life to and exists within all things. He is omnipresent. He causes the motions and cycles of the celestial bodies. Secondly, they divide the Good Principle into three aspects or powers: Creation, Preservation, and Renovation by change and death. Thirdly, it acknowledges the necessary existence of an Evil Principle to counteract the benevolent purposes of the first. The Devata (Subordinate Genii) are entrusted with control over the various aspects of nature and play a role in this.

They believe that one great and incomprehensible Being has alone existed for all Eternity. Everything we behold, including ourselves, is a part of Him. The soul, mind or intellect of gods, men, and all sentient creatures are separate portions of the Universal Soul. At some point, all will return to that source. However, the mind of finite beings is distracted by an unceasing series of illusions that they believe to be real. This distraction will continue until we are united to the great fountain of truth. Of these illusions, the first and most essential is the notion of individuality. When the soul becomes detached from its source, it becomes ignorant of its own nature, origin, and destiny. It believes 605 that it represents a separate existence that no longer holds a spark of the Divinity, one link of an immeasurable chain and an infinitely small but indispensable portion of one great whole.

Their love of imagery caused them to personify what they believed to be the attributes of God, perhaps in order to simplify the nebulous idea of an indescribable and invisible God. From this intention came Brahma, Vishnu, and Siva or Iswara. These aspects were represented as various physical forms, but no emblem or visible sign exists of Brihm or Brehm, the Omnipotent. They considered the great mystery of the Supreme Ruler of the Universe to be beyond human comprehension. Every thinking creature must be conscious of the existence of a God (the first cause). However, any attempt to explain it or frame it in human terms would be ridiculous or extremely disrespectful.

The following extracts from their books will serve to illustrate the real tenets of their creed:

"This Universe, every world in the whole circle of nature, is pervaded by one Supreme Ruler. There is one unshakeable Supreme Spirit swifter than the thought of man. That Supreme Spirit moves at pleasure, but in itself is immovable. It is distant, yet near. It pervades this whole system of worlds, but it is infinitely beyond it. The man who considers all beings as existing in the Supreme Spirit, and the Supreme Spirit as pervading all beings, will not view any creature with contempt. All spiritual beings are part of the Supreme Spirit. The pure, enlightened soul assumes a luminous for with no physical body, no perforation, no veins or tendons, unblemished, and untainted by sin. It is a ray from the Infinite Spirit, which knows the Past and the Future and pervades all. It existed with no cause but itself and created all things as they are in an ancient time. I am *like* the all-pervading Spirit that gives light to the visible Sun, though infinitely greater in *degree*. Let my soul return to the immortal Spirit of God, and let my body, which ends in ashes, return to dust! O Spirit, who pervades fire, lead us in a straight path to the riches of happiness."

"You, O God, possess all the treasures of knowledge! Remove each foul 606 stain from our souls!"

"From what root springs mortal man when he is felled by the hand of death? Who can make him spring again to birth? God is perfect wisdom and perfect happiness. He is the final refuge for the man who has liberally bestowed his wealth, been firm in virtue, and knows and adores that Great One. Let us adore the supremacy of that Divine Sun, the Godhead who illuminates all, who re-creates all, from whom all proceed, to whom all must return, whom we invoke to direct our understandings aright, in our progress toward his holy seat. The Sun and Light are to this visible world, what truth is to the intellectual and visible Universe. Our souls acquire certain knowledge by meditating on the light of

Truth, which emanates from the Being of Beings. That Being sees without eyes, hears without ears, and knows everything that can be known, but there is no one who knows him. The wise call him the Great, Supreme, Pervading Spirit. Perfect Truth and Perfect Happiness are without equal and immortal. Absolute unity cannot be described or understood. He is without cause and the first of all causes, all-ruling, and all-powerful. He is the Creator, Preserver, and Transformer of all things."

"My soul of mine mounts aloft in my waking hours as an ethereal spark, and even in my slumber, it has a like ascent. Soaring to a great distance as an emanation from the Light of Lights, it is united by devout meditation with the supremely blessed and supremely intelligent Spirit! May that soul of mine, which was itself the primeval gift placed within all creatures, be united by devout meditation with the supremely blest and supremely intelligent Spirit! That gift is a ray of perfect wisdom, which is the inextinguishable light fixed within created bodies. No good act is performed without it, and it is as an immortal essence comprised of the past, present, and future."

"The Being of Beings is the Only God, eternal and present everywhere, who comprises everything. There is no God but He. The Supreme Being is invisible, incomprehensible, immovable, and without figure or shape. No one has ever seen Him; time never comprised Him; His essence pervades everything; all was derived from Him."

"The duty of a good man, even in the moment of his destruction, consists not only in forgiving, but in a desire to benefit his destroyer, just as the sandal-tree sheds perfume on the axe which fells it."

The Vedanta and Nyaya philosophers recognized a Supreme Eternal Being and the immortality of the soul. Like the Greeks, however, they differ somewhat in their ideas on those subjects. They speak of the Supreme Being as an eternal essence that pervades space and gives all things life or existence. From that universal spirit, the Vedanti identify four aspects (all in union with the whole) that are never taken as individual identities. Creation is not an instantaneous event, but the manifestation of what eternally exists in the one Universal Being. The Nyaya philosophers believe that spirit and matter are eternal, but they do not claim that the world has always existed in its present form. Only the primary matter from which it sprang exists forever. The almighty Word of God, the Intelligent Cause, and the Supreme Being produced the combinations of matter that compose the material Universe. While the soul is an emanation from the Supreme Being, they believe it is distinct from that Being and an individual entity. Truth and Intelligence are the eternal attributes of God. In contrast, the soul is susceptible to knowledge and ignorance, and pleasure and pain. Even when the soul returns to the Eternal and attains supreme bliss, it does not cease. It is not *absorbed* into Supreme Being, but retains the abstract nature of visible existence.

"The dissolution of the world consists in the destruction of the visible forms and qualities of things. Their material essence remains, and new worlds are formed from it by the creative energy of God. The Universe is dissolved and renewed in endless succession."

The Jainas, a sect in Mysore, hold that the ancient religion of India and the whole world consisted in the belief in one God as a pure Spirit, indivisible, omniscient and all-powerful. God gave every thing its appointed order and course of action. He gave man a portion of reason to guide him in his conduct and free will, so he could be held accountable for his conduct. 608

Manu, the Hindu lawgiver, revered "that divine and incomparably greater light," as opposed to the physical Sun. In the words of the most venerable text in the Indian Scripture, it is that light "which illumines and delights all, from which all proceed, to which all must return, and which alone can irradiate our intellects." He begins:

"Be it heard!"

"This Universe existed only in the first divine idea yet unexpanded, as if involved in darkness, imperceptible, indefinable, undiscoverable by reason, and undiscovered by revelation, as if it were wholly immersed in sleep"

"Then the Sole, Self-existing Power, Himself undiscovered, but making this world discernible, with five elements and other principles of nature, appeared with undiminished glory, *expanding His idea*, or dispelling the gloom."

"He Whom the mind alone can perceive, whose essence eludes the eternal organs, who has no visible parts, who exists from Eternity, even He, the soul of all beings, Whom no being can comprehend, shone forth."

"Deciding to produce various beings from His own divine Substance, He first created the waters with a thought. *That which is* (precisely the Hebrew יהוה), the first cause, not the object of sense, existing everywhere in substance, not existing to our perception, without beginning or end" (the A∴ and Ω∴, or the I∴ A∴ Ω∴), "produced the divine male famed in all worlds under the appellation of Brahma."

Then reflecting upon the different things created by Brahma, he adds: "After creating the Universe, He (meaning Brahma, the Λογοσ, the WORD), whose powers are incomprehensible, was again absorbed in the Supreme Spirit by exchanging the time of energy for the time of rest."

The *Antareya A'ran'ya*, one of the Vedas, describes this primitive idea of the creation: "In the beginning, the Universe was but a Soul, and nothing else (active or inactive) existed. Then HE had this thought, *I will create worlds*; and thus HE created the different worlds, air, the light, mortal beings, and the waters." 609

"HE had this thought: *Behold the worlds; I will create guardians for the worlds*. So HE took of the water and fashioned a being clothed with the human form. He looked upon him and contemplated. The mouth opened like an egg, and a fiery speech came forth. The nostrils opened, and through them went the breath of respiration, and by this breath, the air was propagated. The eyes opened and from them came a luminous ray that produced the sun. The ears dilated and from them came hearing, and from hearing space." After the body of man with his senses was formed, "HE, the Universal Soul, then reflected: *How can this body exist without Me?* He considered the way in which He might penetrate it. He said to Himself: *If the World is articulated, breath exhales, and eyes sees without Me, if ears hears, skin feels, minds reflects, mouths swallow, and reproductive organs fulfill their function, then what am I?* And separating the suture of the cranium, He penetrated into man."

Behold the great and fundamental original truths! God is an infinite Eternal Soul or Spirit. Matter is not eternal or self-existent, but it is created by a thought of God. After matter and the worlds, God made man by a thought. Finally, after endowing him with the senses and a thinking mind, a portion or spark of God Himself penetrates man and becomes a living spirit within him.

The Vedas describes the creation of the world in this way:

"In the beginning there was a single God, existing unto Himself, Who, after having passed an eternity absorbed in the contemplation of His own being, desired to manifest His perfections outwardly, and He created the matter of the world. The four elements were produced, but still mingled in confusion, He breathed upon the waters, which swelled up into an immense ball in the shape of an egg and became the vault and orb of Heaven, which encircles the earth. Having made the earth and the bodies of animal beings, this God (the essence of movement) gave to them a portion of His own being to animate them. Thus, the soul of everything that breathes is a fraction of the universal soul. No one perishes, but each soul merely changes its mold and form by passing successively into different bodies. The form that most pleases the Divine Being is Man, because it comes closest to His own perfection. When a man absolutely disengages himself from his senses and absorbs himself in self-contemplation, he comes to discern the Divinity, and becomes part of Him."

The Ancient Persians were similar to the Hindus in many respects. They shared similar language, poetry, myths, and legends. Their conquests brought them in contact with China, and they defeated Egypt and Judea. Their ideas about God and religion more closely resembled those of the Hebrews than any other culture. Some ideas we now regard as essential to the original Hebrew creed were borrowed from them.

They believed in the King of Heaven, Father of Eternal Light and the pure World of LIGHT, created by the Eternal WORD. They conceived of the Seven Mighty Spirits who stand next to the Throne of Light and Omnipotence, and the glory of those Heavenly Hosts surrounds that Throne. They had similar ideas about the Origin of Evil and the Prince of Darkness, who was the leader of the rebellious spirits and all the enemies of good. They were repulsed by Egyptian idolatry, and they tried to destroy it under the leadership of Cambyses. When Xerxes invaded Greece, he destroyed the Temples and erected fire-chapels along his march. Their religion was eminently spiritual, and their earthly fire and sacrifice were symbols of another devotion to a higher power.

Originally, the ancient religions of India and Persia simply venerated nature and its pure elements and powers. Above all, they revered the sacred fire or Light, the breath of Heaven that animates and pervades the breath of mortal life. This pure and simple veneration of nature is perhaps the most ancient, and by far the most prevalent in the primitive and patriarchal world. Originally, there was no deification of nature, nor a denial of the sovereignty of God. For the earliest men, who were still in communication with Deity, the pure elements and essences of creation were natural and true symbols of Divine power. In the *611* Hebrew writings, the pure light or sacred fire is an image of the all-pervading and all-consuming power and omnipresence of the Divinity. His breath was the first source of life, and the faint whisper of the breeze announced to the prophet His immediate presence.

"All things are the descendents of one fire. The Father perfected all things and delivered them to the Second Mind, whom all nations of men call the First. Natural works co-exist with the intellectual light of the Father. The Soul adorns the great Heaven like the Father. The Soul is an immortal fire from the power of the Father, and as mistress of life, it fills up the recesses of the world. The fire beyond fire, the mind of mind concealed his power in matter with mind, not action. He sprang from mind and clothed fire with fire. Father-begotten Light! He alone received the essence of intellect from the Father's power. He alone is able to understand the mind of the Father and instill into all sources and principles the capacity of understanding in a continuing, ceaseless, revolving motion." This was the language of Zoroaster, and it expresses the old Persian ideas.

Zoroaster also spoke of the Sun and Stars: "The Father made the whole Universe of fire, water, earth, and the all-nourishing ether. He fixed a great multitude of motionless stars that willingly stand still forever, without the desire to wander, fire acting upon fire. He congregated the seven firmaments of the world and surrounded the earth with the convexity of the Heavens. There He set seven living existences: six planets arranged in regular orbits and the Sun, as the seventh, placed in the center, from which all lines, diverging in every direction, are equal. The swift sun himself, revolving around a principal center, is always striving to reach the central and all-pervading light, bearing with him the bright Moon."

Yet Zoroaster added, "Do not measure the journeys of the Sun or attempt to reduce them to rules, because he is carried by the eternal will of the Father and not for your sake. Do not endeavor to understand the impetuous course of the Moon, because she runs under the impulse of necessity. Neither *612* should you be concerned with the progression of the Stars, because they were not generated to serve any purpose of yours."

Ormuzd says to Zoroaster in the Boundehesch, "I hold the Star-Spangled Heaven in ethereal space and make this sphere, once buried in darkness, a flood of light. Through me, the Earth became a firm and lasting world, where the Lord of the world walks. I make the light of Sun, Moon, and Stars pierce the clouds. I make the corn seed, which perishing in the ground, sprouts anew. I created a plan, whose eye is light, and whose life is the breath of his nostrils. I placed within him life's inextinguishable power."

Ormuzd or Ahura-Mazda represented the primal light, separate from the heavenly bodies, but necessary for their existence and splendor. The Amschaspands, the "immortal Holy Ones", each presided over a special aspect of nature: Earth and Heaven, fire and water, the Sun and Moon, the rivers, trees, and mountains. Even the artificial divisions of days and years were revered in prayer as enacted by the Divine beings. Each ruled separately within his own sphere. Fire, the "most energetic of immortal powers", was considered the visible representation of the primal light, and it was called the "Son of Ormuzd". The Sun, worshipped by the name of MITHRAS, was the most noble and powerful example of divine power, who "steps forth as a Conqueror from the top of the terrible Alborj to rule over the world which he enlightens from the throne of Ormuzd." Mithras was a beneficent and friendly genius, who was known as the "Invincible" and the "Mediator" to the Greeks. He was invincible because he never ceased in his daily struggle with darkness. He is the mediator through which Heaven's greatest blessings are communicated to man. He is "the eye of Ormuzd", the radiant Nero, pursuing his triumphant course. He brings life to the deserts, and He is the most exalted of the Izeds or Yezatas, the "never-sleeping protector of the land." "When the dragon foe devastates my provinces," says Ormuzd, "and afflicts them with famine, he will be struck down by the strong arm of Mithras, together with the Devs of Mazanderan. With his lance and his immortal club, the Sleepless Chief hurls down the Devs into the dust, and as Mediator, he interposes to guard the City from evil."

613   According to some Parsee sects, Ahriman was considered older than Ormuzd, because darkness is older than light. He was unknown as a Malevolent Being in the early ages of the world. In the Boundehesch, the fall of man is attributed to a deviant worship of Ahriman, and it took a succession of prophets (ending with Zoroaster) to deliver man from this misguided path.

Mithras is not only light, but also intelligence. He is the luminary who was born in obscurity to dispel darkness and conquer death. This will be carried out by the "Word", the "ever-living emanation of the Deity by which the world exists," and of which the repetitive liturgies of the Magi are but a representation. Zoroaster cried, "What shall I do, O Ormuzd, in my battle with Daroodj-Ahriman, the father of the Evil Law, so I may make men pure and holy?" Ormuzd answered, "O Zoroaster, invoke the pure law of the Servants of Ormuzd, the Amschaspands who shed abundance throughout the seven Keshwars, the Heaven, Zeruana-Akarana, the birds travailing on the high, swift winds of the Earth. Invoke my Spirit. I am Ahura-Mazda, the purest, strongest, wisest, and best of beings. I have the most majestic body and through purity, I am Supreme. My Soul is the Excellent Word; all people invoke me as I have commanded you, Zoroaster."

Ahura-Mazda is the living WORD. He is called the "First-born of all things and the express image of the Eternal. He is the very light of very light and the Creator, who, by the power of the Word which he never ceases to pronounce, made the Heaven and the Earth in 365 days." According to the Yashna, the Word existed before all and was itself a Yazata, a personified object of prayer. It was revealed in Serosch, in Homa, and under Gushtasp, and it was again revealed by Zoroaster.

Mithras is the current representation and mediator of the Primal Unity that originated and will ultimately absorb all opposing forces: life and death, sunshine and shade. His annual sacrifice is the Passover of the Magi and is a symbolic atonement or pledge of moral and physical regeneration. In the beginning, he created the world, and with each successive year, he releases the new cycle of life to invigorate a fresh cycle of creation. At the end of time, he *614* will sacrifice the weary world like a hecatomb before God. He will release the Soul of Nature from her mortal chains and take her to a brighter and purer existence.

Iamblichus (*On the Egyptian Mysteries*, viii. 4) says, "The Egyptians are far from ascribing all things to physical causes. They distinguish life and intellect from physical being, both in man and in the Universe. First, they place intellect and reason as self-existent, and from these they derive the created world. The Parent of generated things was a Demiurge. They acknowledge a vital force both in and before the Heavens. They place Pure Intellect above and beyond the Universe, and another (that is, Mind revealed in the Material World), consisting of one continuous mind that pervades the Universe, which is apportioned to all its parts and spheres." The Egyptian idea was the same as all transcendental philosophies: a Deity of immanence and transcendence, a spirit passing into matter without becoming compromised.

The writings of Hermes are regarded as the most authentic expression of transcendental wisdom that human curiosity can ever discover. Thebes is said to have revered a being without beginning or end, called Amun or Amun-Kneph. It was the all-pervading Spirit, the Breath of Nature, or even some higher object of reverence, which must not be named. In theory, this Spirit would rank higher than the three orders of Gods mentioned by Herodotus. Those orders were arbitrary classifications of similar or equal beings arranged in successive emanations and ranked according to dignity. The Eight Great Gods, or primary class, were probably aspects of the one, whole, emanated God expressed in the objects and powers of the Universe.

In the ancient Hermetic books quoted by Iamblichus, the following passage appears about the Supreme Being:

"Before all things existed, and before all beginnings, there was one God, prior even to the first God and King. He remained unmoved in the singleness of his own Unity. Nothing comprehensible by intellect is woven within him, or anything else. He is the example of the God who *is* good, who is his own father, the self-begotten, with only one Parent. For he is greater and prior to everything and the fountain of all things, He is the foundation of all the first species conceived by the intellect, and from this ONE, the self-originated God caused himself to shine forth. He is a beginning and God of Gods, a Monad from the One, prior to substance and the beginning of substance. From him comes substantiality. These are the most ancient beginnings of all things, which Hermes places before the ethereal, empyrean, and celestial Gods."

In the old Chinese creed, CHANG-TI (the Supreme Lord or Being) is the principle of everything that exists and the Father of all living things. He is eternal, immovable, and independent. His power knows no bounds. He sees at once the Past, Present, and Future. His knowledge penetrates the innermost recesses of the human heart. He rules the Heaven and the earth, and every event is a consequence of His direction and will. He is pure, holy, and impartial. Wickedness offends His sight, and He looks with favor upon the virtuous actions of men. At once, both severe and just, He punishes vice in an exemplary manner, and no Prince or Ruler escapes his judgment. As He casts down the guilty, He honors the man who follows his own heart and rises from obscurity. Good, merciful, and full of pity, He forgives the wicked upon their repentance. Human tragedies and the irregularity of the seasons are merely the warnings that He gives to men with fatherly goodness to encourage them to reform and amend their ways.

The cultures in the far Eastern regions of Asia were more strongly influenced by reason than imagination. They did not fall into idolatry until some time after Confucius and within two centuries of the birth of Christ. This began when the religion of BUDDHA or Fo was brought from India. For centuries, they practiced a pure worship of God, and the foundation of their moral and social existence was laid upon reason and conformity to the Truth of the Deity. They had no false gods or images, and their third Emperor, *Hoam-ti*, erected a Temple (probably the first ever erected) to the Great Architect of the Universe. Although they offered sacrifices to many lower-order angels, they honored them infinitely less than XAM-TI or CHANG-TI, the Sovereign Lord of the World.

Confucius prohibited the making of images or representations of the Deity. He considered Him a Power or Principle, pervading all Nature, and the Chinese designated the Divinity with the name of THE DIVINE REASON.

The Japanese believe in a Supreme Invisible Being who is not to be represented by images or worshipped in Temples. They call him AMIDA or OMITH, and he is without beginning or end. He came to earth and remained here for a thousand years. He became the Redeemer of our fallen race, and he is

448

the judge of all men. Good men will live forever, while bad men are condemned to Hell.

Confucius said the visible sky (particularly the Sun and Moon) and the Earth symbolize the Chang-ti, because it is by these objects that we enjoy the gifts of the Chang-ti. "The Sun is the source of life and light. The Moon illuminates the world by night. By observing the course of these luminaries, mankind is enabled to distinguish the times and seasons. The Ancients connected the act with its object and established the practice of sacrificing to the Chang-ti at the Winter Solstice. The Sun, having passed through the twelve places considered by the Chang-ti to be its annual residence, began its career by distributing blessings throughout the Earth."

Confucius said the TEEN is the universal principle and creative source of all things and the Chang-ti is the universal principle of existence.

In contrast, the Arabians never practiced or believed in an elaborate system of Polytheism. Their historical traditions were very similar to those of the Hebrews and there are several areas of perfect correlation. Among their culture, there always existed a tradition of a purer faith and a simple Patriarchal worship of the Deity. Idolatry did not have much influence until shortly before the time of the Prophet Mohammad. He promoted a return of the primeval faith and restored the doctrine of one God.

As with many other cultures, only fragments remain of the primitive doctrines of the Hebrews. The Hebrew culture did not pursue a strong interest in metaphysical speculations into the Divine Nature until after the period of their captivity among the Persians. It is evident from the Psalms of David that there was some preserved knowledge of the Deity, which was unknown to most. Those chosen to receive this wisdom became its preservers for later generations.

For Greek and Egyptian scholars, the higher ideas and exact doctrines concerning Divinity (his Sovereign Nature and Infinite Might, the Eternal Wisdom and Providence that directs all things to their proper end, the Infinite Mind and Supreme Intelligence that created all things) raise far above external nature. Pythagoras, Anaxagoras, and Socrates preserved these loftier ideas and nobler doctrines. Plato and his successors further developed them in a beautiful and luminous manner. Many deeply spiritual and significant ideas are found within the popular religion of the Greeks, although they are momentary flashes of a vague and ancient revelation: a belief in a Supreme Being, Almighty Creator of the Universe, and Common Father of Mankind.

Much of the primitive Truth was taught to Pythagoras by Zoroaster, who received it from the Indians. His disciples rejected the use of Temples, Altars, and Statues, because they recognized the error in imagining that Deity had any connection to human nature. The tops of the highest mountains were the places chosen for sacrifices, and hymns and prayers were their principal form of worship. According to Herodotus, these were addressed to the Supreme God, who fills the wide circle of Heaven. They regarded light as the most pure and lively emblem of the Eternal God and the first emanation. Man required light as a visible or tangible symbol to exalt his mind to the degree of adoration, which is due to the Divine Being.

There was a surprising similarity between the Temples, Priests, doctrines, and worship of the Persian Magi and the British Druids. The Druids did not 618 worship idols in any human form. They believed that the invisible Divinity should be adored without being seen. They believed in the Unity of the Godhead, and their invocations were made to the One All-preserving Power. Because this power was not composed of matter, they asserted that it must be the Deity. The secret symbol they used to express his name was O. I. W. They believed that the earth had been destroyed once by a deluge, and that it would be destroyed a second time by fire. They believed in the immortality of the soul and a final day of judgment. They held ideas about the redemption of mankind through the death of a Mediator. However, around these fragments of Truth, they wove a web of idolatry. They worshiped two Subordinate Deities under the names of Hu and CERIDWEN, male and female (identical to Osiris and Isis) and maintained a belief in reincarnation.

The early inhabitants of Scandinavia believed in a God who was "the Author of everything that exists; the Eternal, the Ancient, the Living and Awful Being, the Searcher into concealed things, the Being that never changes." Idols of the Deity were originally forbidden, and He was to be worshiped in the lonely solitude of isolated forests, where He was said to dwell invisibly in perfect silence.

Like their Eastern ancestors, the Druids held odd numbers as sacred. Odd numbers could be reduced to Unity or Deity, while even numbers ended in nothing. The number 3 was particularly revered. The numbers 19 ($7+3+3^2$), 30 ($7×3+3×3$), and 21 ($7×3$) were frequently used in the construction of their temples.

They were the sole interpreters of religion. They presided over all sacrifices, because no private person could offer one without their permission. Druids held the power of excommunication and punishment by execution. Even war or peace could not be declared without their permission. They claimed to possess the knowledge of magic, and they practiced divination as a public service.

The Druids cultivated many of the liberal sciences, and they were 619 particularly proficient in Astronomy. They considered the day to be the offspring of the night, and therefore made their calculations by nights instead of days. They divided the heavens into constellations, and they practiced the strictest morality. They held the most sacred regard for that peculiarly Masonic virtue of Truth.

The Icelandic Prose Edda contains the following dialogue:

"Who is the first or eldest of the Gods?"

"In our language he is called ALFADIR (All-Father, or the Father of All); but in the old Asgard he had twelve names."

450

"Where is this God? What is his power and what has he done to display his glory?"

"He lives in all ages. He governs all realms, and sways all things both great and small. He has formed Heaven, earth, the air, and all things. He has made man and given him a soul that shall live and never perish, although the body will have disintegrated or burned to ashes. All that are righteous shall dwell with him in the place called *Gimli* or *Vingolf*, but the wicked shall go to *Hel* and then to *Niflhel* which is below it in the ninth world."

Almost every heathen nation with a spirituality known to us maintained a belief in one Supreme Overruling God whose name must not be spoken.

"When we ascend," says Müller, "to the most distant heights of Greek history, the idea of God as the Supreme Being stands before us as a simple fact. Next to this adoration of One God, the Father of Heaven, the Father of men, we find in Greece a Worship of Nature." The original Ζεὺς was the God of Gods, called by the Greeks the Son of Time, meaning that there was no God before Him, and He was Eternal. "Zeus," says the Orphic line, "is the Beginning, Zeus the Middle; out of Zeus all things have been made." The Peleides of Dodona said, "Zeus was. Zeus is. Zeus will be; O great Zeus!" Ζεὺς νῆ, Ζεὺς ἐστὶν, Ζεὺς ἐσσεται ὦ μεγάλη Ζευ: and he was Ζεὺς χύδιστος, μέγιστος, Zeus, Best and Greatest.

The Parsees retain the old religion taught by Zaradisht. The following 620 dialog comes from their catechism: "We believe in only one God, Who created the Heavens, the Earth, and the Angels. Our God has no face, form, color, shape, or fixed place. There is no other like Him, nor can our mind comprehend Him."

The Tetragrammaton (יהוה) was forbidden to be pronounced. To prevent the loss of its correct pronunciation among the Levites, the High Priest uttered it in the Temple once each year, on the 10th day of the Month Tisri (the great feast day of atonement). During this ceremony, the people were directed to make a great noise so that the Sacred Word might not be heard by any who had no right to know it. It was believed that anyone other than the High Priest who heard the word would be stricken dead.

Before the time of the Jews, the Great Egyptian Initiates held the word Isis to be incommunicable in a similar regard.

Origen says, "There are names which have a natural potency such as those which the Sages used among the Egyptians, the Magi in Persia, and the Brahmins in India. What is called Magic is not a vain and chimerical act, as the Stoics and Epicureans pretended. The names SABAOTH and ADONAI were not made for created beings, but they belong to a mysterious theology that goes back to the Creator. From Him comes the virtue of these names when they are arranged and pronounced according to the rules."

The Hindu word AUM represented the three Powers combined in their Deity: Brahma, Vishnu, and Siva (the Creating, Pre-serving, and Destroying Powers) A, the first; U or Ŏ-Ŏ, the second; and M, the third. This word could not be pronounced except by the letters. They believe that the pronunciation of these letters as one word would make the Earth tremble and the Angels of Heaven quake with fear.

The Ramayan says that the word AUM represents, "the Being of Beings, One Substance in three forms; without mode, without quality, without passion: Immense, Incomprehensible, Infinite, Indivisible, Immutable, Incorporeal, and Irresistible."

An old passage in the Purana says, "All the rites ordained in the Vedas, the sacrifices to the fire, and all other solemn purifications shall pass away, but that which shall never pass away is the word A∴Ŏ-Ŏ∴ M∴ for it is the symbol of the Lord of all things."

Herodotus says that the Ancient Pelasgi built no temples and worshipped no idols. They had a sacred name for Deity, which should not be pronounced.

The Clarian Oracle of unknown antiquity was asked which Deity was named IAΩ and answered in these remarkable words: "The Initiated are bound to conceal the mysterious secrets. Learn, then, that IAΩ is the Great God Supreme that rules over all."

The Jews consider the True Name of God to be irrecoverably lost. They regard its pronunciation as one of the Mysteries that will be revealed with the coming of their Messiah. They attribute its loss to the law against the application of the Masoretic points to so sacred a Name. This caused the knowledge of the proper vowel sounds to be forgotten. It is even said in the Gemara of Abodah Zara that God permitted a celebrated Hebrew Scholar to be burned by a Roman Emperor, because he had been heard to pronounce the Sacred Name with these sounds.

The Jews feared the Heathen would gain possession of the Name. In their copies of the Scriptures, they wrote the Name in Samaritan characters instead of the Hebrew or Chaldaic script. They believed the Name was capable of working miracles and held that Moses performed the miracles in Egypt with this name engraved on his rod. Any person who knows the true pronunciation of the Name would be able to do as much as he did.

Josephus says the correct pronunciation was unknown until God communicated it to Moses in the wilderness, and that it was lost through the wickedness of man.

Muslims have a tradition regarding a secret name of Deity possessing wonderful properties. Initiation into the Mysteries of the *Ism Abla* is the only way to acquire knowledge of it.

H∴O∴M∴ was the author of the new religion among the Persians, and His Name was Ineffable.

Only the Priests pronounced the name AMUN among the Egyptians.

The old Germans adored God with profound reverence without daring to name Him or worship Him in Temples.

The Druids expressed the name of Deity by the letters O∴I∴W∴

Among all the ancient nations, the doctrine of the immortality of the soul was not just a hypothesis or *Faith*. It was a lively *certainty*, like the feeling of one's own existence and identity. It was actually present, exerting its influence on all earthly affairs. It inspired mightier deeds and endeavors than any earthly interest could.

Even the doctrine of reincarnation, which was universal among the Ancient Hindus and Egyptians, rested on a basis of the old primitive religion. Because man had gone astray and wandered far from God, he must make many attempts (a long and painful pilgrimage), before rejoining the Source of all Perfection. They held a strong conviction that nothing defective, impure, or defiled with earthy stains could enter the pure region of perfect spirits or be eternally united to God. The soul had to pass through long trials and purification before it could attain that blissful end. The objective of all these systems of philosophy was the final deliverance of the soul from the old calamity, the dreaded fate of wandering through the dark regions of nature and the various forms of the brute creation, ever changing its terrestrial shape. The goal was union with God, which they held to be the lofty destiny of the wise and virtuous soul.

Pythagoras gave the same meaning to reincarnation that the Egyptians gave to it in their Mysteries. He never taught the doctrine in the literal sense, as it was understood by the people. No emphasis upon a literal interpretation can be found among what remains of his teachings or the written fragment from his disciple Lysias. He held that men always remain in essence just as they were originally created, and they degrade themselves by vice and improve themselves by virtue.

Hierocles, one of the most zealous and celebrated disciples of Pythagoras, specifically states that it is misguided to literally believe that the soul of man after death may enter the body of a beast or plant as a punishment for vice or stupidity. Such an interpretation shows an absolute ignorance of the eternal form of the soul, which never changes. The soul always remains within man. It becomes God or beast symbolically through its own virtue or vice.

Timæus of Locria, another disciple of Pythagoras, says that to warn men and prevent them from committing crimes, God inflicted strange humiliations and punishments. He says their souls would pass into new bodies. A coward would enter the body of a deer. A ravisher entered into the body of a wolf. A murderer entered into the body of some still more ferocious animal, and those with impure appetites would enter the body of a hog.

Lysias said that the soul, once purified of its crimes, leaves the body, returns to Heaven to enjoy eternal happiness, and is no longer subject to change or death. According to the Hindus, it becomes a part of the universal soul that animates everything.

623

The Hindus believe that Buddha descended to earth to raise all human beings up to the perfect state. He will ultimately succeed, and all will be merged in Unity.

Vishnu will judge the world on the last day. The world will be consumed by fire, the Sun and Moon will lose their light, the Stars will fall, and a New Heaven and Earth will be created.

The obscured and distorted legend of the fall of the Spirits is preserved in the Hindu Mythology. Their traditions acknowledge and revere the first ancestors of mankind, the Holy Patriarchs of the primitive world. They are the Seven Great RISHIS or Sages of antiquity. Their history is embellished in a cloud of myth.

The Egyptians believed that the soul was immortal, and that Osiris was to judge the world.

A Persian legend states:

"After Ahriman has ruled the world until the end of time, SOSIOSCH, the promised Redeemer, will come and annihilate the power of the DEVS (or Evil Spirits), awaken the dead, and sit in final judgment upon the spirits and man. After that, the comet *Gurzsher* will be thrown down, and a great conflagration will take place that will consume the whole world. The remains of the earth will then sink into *Duzakh*, and become for three periods a place of punishment for the wicked. Eventually, all will be pardoned (even *Ahriman* and the *Devs*) and admitted to the regions of bliss, and thus there will be a new Heaven and a new earth."

The doctrines of Lamaism have fragments of the primitive truth, which may be found obscured in legend. According to that faith, "There is to be a final judgment before ESLIK KHAN. The good will be admitted to Paradise, and the bad will be banished to hell, where there are eight burning hot regions and eight freezing cold."

Wherever the Mysteries were practiced, the primitive revelation of the existence of One Great Being, Infinite and pervading the Universe was taught. This Being was worshipped without superstition, and His marvelous nature and attributes were taught to the Initiates. The masses attributed His works to Secondary Gods, personified and isolated from Him.

These truths were hidden from the masses, and the Mysteries were carried into every country without disturbing the popular beliefs. Those who were capable of understanding would know the truth, the arts, and the sciences. The true doctrine would remain uncorrupted. People prone to superstition and idolatry would remain unaware, just as they do today. The numerous modern doctrines and sects that degrade the Creator by crediting Him with the passions of humanity prove that even now the old truths must be given only to a select few. Otherwise, they will be overlaid with fiction and error and irretrievably lost.

Masonry is a less than perfect image of the Ancient Mysteries. It lacks their complete brilliance, and it is only the ruin of their grandeur. It has undergone numerous changes and suffered the influence of social and political events and circumstances. Egyptian in origin, the Mysteries were adapted to the habits of the different nations where they were introduced. Originally, they were primarily moral and political rather than religious, but they soon fell under the custody of the priests and became essentially religious institutions. Originally, they taught the initiates (presumably the most intelligent among the populace) 625 the absurdity of the creeds of the masses. Eventually, the Mysteries were adapted to the religious systems of the countries into which they were transplanted. In Greece, they were the Mysteries of Ceres; in Rome, of *Bona Dea*, the Good Goddess; in Gaul, the School of Mars; and in Sicily, the Academy of the Sciences. The Hebrews followed the rites and ceremonies of a religion that placed all knowledge and all the powers of government in the hands of the Priests and Levites. The pagodas of India, the retreats of the Magi of Persia and Chaldæa, and the pyramids of Egypt were no longer the sources at which man drank in knowledge. Every civilized culture had its Mysteries. Ultimately, the Temples of Greece and the School of Pythagoras lost their reputation, and Freemasonry took their place.

Masonry is an interpretation of the great book of nature, the purest philosophy, an explanation of physical and astronomical phenomena, and the place where all the great original truths that form the basis of all religions are safely guarded. The modern Degrees convey an image of primeval times, the varied and great causes of the Universe, and the importance of the book containing the moral and ethical truths of all cultures, which lead to happiness and prosperity.

The Kabbalistic doctrine has long been the religion of the wise Sages. Like Freemasonry, it guides the individual toward spiritual perfection and a universal view of the creeds and cultures of the world. In the eyes of the Kabbalist, all men are his brothers. Their relative ignorance is just another reason to teach them. There were illustrious Kabbalists among the Egyptians and Greeks, whose doctrines the Orthodox Church has accepted. In the Medieval period, there were also many among the Arabs.

The Sages proudly wore the name of Kabbalists. Kabbalah embodied a noble philosophy, pure and full of symbolism. It taught the doctrine of the Unity of God, the art of knowing and explaining the essence and actions of the Supreme Being, the spiritual powers and natural forces, and the means of determining their influence through symbolism, the arrangement of the alphabet, the combinations of numbers, the inversion of letters in writing, and the 626 concealed meanings discovered through these methods. Kabbalah is the key to the occult sciences, and the Gnostics were an offshoot from the Kabbalists.

The science of numbers did not only represent arithmetical qualities, but it also included the grandeur and proportion of all things. By it, we arrive at the discovery of the Principle or First Cause of things (THE ABSOLUTE).

UNITY is a lofty term to which all philosophy directs its attention. The human mind is compelled to collect and organize its thoughts around Unity. It is the Source and the center of all systematic order. It is the principle of existence, the central point, unknown in its essence, and apparent in its effects upon everything. It is the sublime center and the first of all causes. It was the central idea to which the ideas of Pythagoras converged, but he refused the title of *Sage*, which means *"one who knows"*. He invented and preferred that of *Philosopher*, meaning *"one who is fond of or studies things secret and occult"*. The mysterious astronomy, which he taught, was *astrology*. His science of numbers was based upon Kabbalistic principles.

The real teachings of the Ancients and Pythagoras are often misunderstood, because they were never meant to attach special virtue or abstract ideas to mere numbers. The Sages of Antiquity agreed upon the existence of ONE FIRST CAUSE (material or spiritual) of the existence of the Universe. Therefore, UNITY became the symbol of the Supreme Deity. UNITY represents God without attributing to the *number* ONE any divine or supernatural virtue.

These Pythagorean ideas are partially expressed in the following:

LECTURE OF THE KABBALISTS

Q: Why did you seek to be received a Knight of the Kabbalah?
A: To know, by means of numbers, the admirable harmony that exists between nature and religion.
Q: How were you announced?
A: By twelve raps.
Q: What do they signify?
A: The twelve bases of our temporal and spiritual happiness.
Q: What is a Kabbalist?
A: A man who has learned, by tradition, the Sacerdotal Art and the Royal Art.
Q: What means the device, *Omnia in numeris sita sunt?*
A: That everything lies veiled in numbers.
Q: Explain that.
A: I will do so, as far as the number 12. Your intuition will discern the rest.
Q: What signifies the *unit* in the number 10?
A: God, creating and animating matter, expressed by 0, which, alone, is of no value.
Q: What does the unit (1) *mean*?
A: In the moral order, a Word incarnate in the bosom of a virgin-- or religion. . . . In the physical order, a spirit embodied in the virgin earth-- or nature.
Q: What do you mean by the number *two*?
A: In the moral order, *man* and *woman*. . . . In the physical order, the *active* and the *passive*.

627

Q: What do you mean by the number 3?
A: In the moral order, the three theological virtues. . . . In the physical, the three principles of bodies.
Q: What do you mean by the number 4?
A: The four cardinal virtues. . . . The four elementary qualities.
Q: What do you mean by the number 5?
A: The quintessence of religion. . . . The quintessence of matter.
Q: What do you mean by the number 6?
A: The theological cube . . . The physical cube.
Q: What do you mean by the number 7?
A: The seven sacraments . . . The seven planets.
Q: What do you mean by the number 8?
A: The small number of Elus . . . The small number of wise men.
Q: What do you mean by the number 9?
A: The exaltation of religion . . . The exaltation of matter.
Q: What do you mean by the number 10?
A: The ten commandments . . . The ten precepts of nature.
Q: What do you mean by the number 11?
A: The multiplication of religion . . . The multiplication of nature.
Q: What do you mean by the number 12?
A: The twelve Articles of Faith, the foundation of the Holy City, the twelve Apostles who preached throughout the whole world for our happiness and spiritual joy . . . The twelve operations of nature, the twelve signs of the Zodiac, the foundation of the *Primum Mobile*, extending it throughout the Universe for our temporal felicity.

628

The Rabbi (President of the Sanhedrin) then adds: From all that you have said, it results that the unit develops itself in 2, is completed in three internally, and so produces 4 externally; whence, through 6, 7, 8, 9, it arrives at 5, half of the spherical number 10, to ascend, passing through 11, to 12, and to raise itself, by the number 4 times 10, to the number 6 times 12, the final term and summit of our eternal happiness.

Q: What is the generative number?
A: In the Divinity, it is the unit; in created things, the number 2: Because the Divinity, 1, engenders 2, and in created things 2 engenders 1.
Q: What is the most majestic number?
A: 3, because it denotes the triple divine essence.
Q: What is the most mysterious number?
A: 4, because it contains all the mysteries of nature.
Q: What is the most occult number?
A: 5, because it is enclosed in the center of the series.
Q: What is the most salutary number?

A: 6, because it contains the source of our spiritual and corporeal happiness.

Q: What is the most fortunate number?

A: 7, because it leads us to the decade, the perfect number.

Q: Which is the number most to be desired?

A: 8, because he who possesses it, is of the number of the Elus and Sages.

Q: Which is the most sublime number?

A: 9, because by it religion and nature are exalted.

Q: Which is the most perfect number?

629 *A:* 10, because it includes unity, which created everything, and zero, the symbol of matter and chaos, from which everything emerged. In its figures it comprehends the created and uncreated, the beginning and the end, power and force, life and annihilation. By the study of this number, we find the relations to all things, the power of the Creator, the faculties of the creature, and the Alpha and Omega of divine knowledge.

Q: Which is the most multiplying number?

A: 11, because with the possession of two units, we arrive at the multiplication of things.

Q: Which is the most solid number?

A: 12, because it is the foundation of our spiritual and temporal happiness.

Q: Which is the favorite number of religion and nature?

A: 4 times 10, because it enables us, rejecting everything impure, eternally to enjoy the number 6 times 12, the end and summit of our happiness.

Q: What is the meaning of the square?

A: It is the symbol of the four elements contained in the triangle, or the emblem of the three chemical principles: these things united form absolute unity in the primal matter.

Q: What is the meaning of the center of the circumference?

A: It signifies the universal spirit, life-giving center of nature.

Q: What do you mean by the squaring the circle?

A: The investigation of squaring the circle indicates the knowledge of the four vulgar elements, which are themselves composed of elementary spirits or chief principles; as the circle, though round, is composed of lines, which escape the sight, and are seen only by the mind.

Q: What is the profoundest meaning of the figure 3?

A: The Father, the Son, and the Holy Spirit. From the action of these three results the triangle within the square; and from the seven angles, the decade or perfect number.

Q: Which is the most confused figure?

A: Zero, the emblem of chaos, formless mixture of the elements.

Q: What do the four devices of the Degree signify?

A: That we are to hear, see, be silent, and enjoy our happiness.

The *unit* is the symbol of identity, equality, existence, conservation, and general harmony, the Central Fire, the Point within the Circle. *Two*, or the *Duad*,   630 is the symbol of diversity, inequality, division, separation, and change.

The number 1 signifies the living man (a body standing upright), because man is the only living being that truly has this capability. Adding to it a head creates the letter P, the sign of Paternity and Creative Power. A further addition produces R, signifying man in motion, going, *Iens, Iturus*.

The Duad is the origin of opposites. According to the Pythagoreans, it is the imperfect condition that results when a being detaches himself from the Monad, or God. Spiritual beings that emanate from God are captured in the Duad and there receive only illusions.

The number ONE signifies harmony, order, or the Good Principle (the ONE and ONLY GOD, *Solus* in Latin (*Sol, Soleil*), and the number Two represents its opposite. Here begins the fatal knowledge of good and evil. The number Two expresses everything double, false, and opposed to the single and sole reality. In nature, everything occurs in pairs of opposites: night and day, light and darkness, cold and heat, wet and dry, health and sickness, error and truth, male and female, etc. Because of this, the Romans dedicated the second month in the year to Pluto, the God of Hell, and the second day of that month to the *manès* of the dead.

To the Chinese, the number *One* signified unity, harmony, order, the Good Principle, or God, while the number *two* represented disorder, duplicity, and false-hood. In the earliest ages, their entire philosophical system was based upon two primary figures or lines, one straight and unbroken, and the other broken or divided into two. By placing one under the other (doubling) and three under each other (tripling), they made the four symbols and eight *Koua*, which referred to the natural elements and the primary principles of all things. Plato calls unity and duality the original elements of nature and the first principles of all existence. The oldest sacred book of the Chinese says: "The Great First Principle has produced two equations and differences, or primary rules of existence; but the two primary rules or two oppositions, namely YIN and YANG, or rest and motion, have produced four signs or symbols, and the four symbols   631 have produced the eight KOUA or further combinations."

The Hermetic fables among every ancient culture show first, 1, the Creating Monad, then 3, then 3 times 3, 3 times 9, and 3 times 27. This triple progression has its foundation in the three ages of Nature: the Past, Present, and Future, and the three degrees of universal creation: Birth, Life, and Death... Beginning, Middle, and End.

The Monad (1) was male, because its action produces no change *within* itself. It represents the creative principle.

The Duad or Binary (2) was female, ever changing by addition, subtraction, or multiplication. It represents matter capable of form.

The union of the Monad and Duad produces the Triad (3), signifying the world formed by the creative principle from matter. Pythagoras represented the world by a right-angled triangle with the two shortest sides equal in length, because the physical form of the world is equal to the creative cause.

The Triad (3) is the first of the *unequal* numbers. This mysterious number plays a great part in the traditions of Asia and the philosophy of Plato. It is the image of the Supreme Being that includes in itself the properties of the first two numbers. The Philosophers held that it was the most excellent and favorite number and a mysterious symbol revered by all antiquity. It was sacred to the Mysteries. There are only three essential Degrees among Masons, who honor the Sacred Triad in the symbol of a triangle as an object of their respect and study.

In geometry, one or two lines by themselves cannot form any shape. However, three lines may combine to form a TRIANGLE, considered the first and perfect geometrical figure. This is why it still serves to represent The Eternal as infinitely perfect in His nature, the Universal Creator, the first Being, and consequently the first Perfection.

It should be noted that the name of God in Latin and French (Deus, Dieu) has as its first letter the Delta or Greek Triangle. For all of these reasons, the triangle is still sacred. Its three sides are emblems of the three Kingdoms, Nature, or God. In the center of the triangle is the Hebrew JOD (the first letter of יהוה). It represents the Animating Spirit of Fire, the generative principle. This is similarly represented by the letter G, the first letter of the name for Deity in the languages of the North, which means Generation.

The first side of the Triangle offered to the Apprentice for study is the mineral kingdom, which symbolized by Tub∴

The second side of the triangle is the vegetable kingdom, which is symbolized by Schib∴ (an ear of corn), and it is the subject of meditations for the Fellow Craft. The Generation of bodies begins within the vegetable kingdom, and this is why the letter G, in its radiance, is presented to the adept there.

The third side of the triangle is the animal kingdom. This completes the instruction of the Master and is represented by Mach∴ (Son of putrefaction).

The number 3 symbolizes the Earth and the terrestrial bodies. The upper half of 3, like 2, symbolizes the vegetable world with the lower half hidden from our sight.

The number 3 also referred to harmony, friendship, peace, agreement, and temperance. It was so highly esteemed among the Pythagoreans that they called it perfect harmony.

Three, four, ten, and twelve were sacred numbers among the Etrurians, Jews, Egyptians, and Hindus.

The name of Deity in many Nations consisted of three letters. Among the Greeks, it was *I∴A∴Ω∴*; among the Persians, H∴O∴M∴; among the

632

Hindus, AUM; among the Scandinavians, I∴O∴W∴. On the upright Tablet of the King discovered at Nimroud, five of the thirteen names of the Great Gods consist of three letters each: ANU, SAN, YAV, BAR, and BEL.

The Tetrad or Quaternary (4) is the most perfect number and the root of other numbers. It is the root of all things. The tetrad is the first mathematical power. The number 4 represents the generative power, from which all combinations have derived. The Initiates considered this number to represent Movement and the Infinite. It symbolizes everything that transcends physical existence. Pythagoras taught his disciples that the number 4 is a symbol of the Eternal and Creative Principle and the Ineffable Name of God. In Hebrew, this name is composed of four letters.

In the number 4, we find the first solid figure in the form of a pyramid. *633* It is the universal symbol of immortality. The Gnostics claimed that the whole structure of their science was illustrated by a square whose angles were Σιγή (*Silence*), Βυθος (*Profundity*), Νοος (*Intelligence*), and Αληθεια (*Truth*). In the tetrahedron, the Triangle (the number 3) forms the triangular base and unity forms its point or summit.

Lysias and Timæus of Locria said that not a single thing could be named, which did not depend on the quaternary as its root.

According to the Pythagoreans, there is a connection between the gods and numbers. This connection constitutes the kind of Divination called Arithmomancy. The soul is a number. It moves itself and contains in itself the number 4.

Matter is represented by the number 9, which is 3 × 3. Since the Immortal Spirit is represented by 4, the Sages often said that when Man went astray, he passed from *4* to *9* and became entangled in an impossible labyrinth. The only way to emerge from this abyss of evil and deceit was to retrace his steps and return from *9* to *4*.

Like the triangle, the number 4 represented a living being, the bearer of the Triangle. It is Man, bearing within himself a Divine principle.

Four was a divine number. It referred to the Deity, and many Ancient Nations gave God a name of four letters. To the Hebrews it was יהוה, to the Egyptians AMUN and PHTA, to the Persians SURA, to the Greeks ΘΕΟΣ and ΖΕΥΣ, to the Romans DEUS, to the Scandinavians ODIN, to the Phœnicians THOTH, and to the Assyrians AS-UR and NEBO. This list could go on forever. This was the Tetragrammaton of the Hebrews, and the Pythagoreans called it the Tetractys.

The number 5 was mysterious, because it was composed of both the Duad (2), the symbol of the False and Double and the Triad (3). It clearly expresses the state of imperfection we see in the world: order and disorder, happiness and misfortune, and life and death. To the Mysteries, the number 5 was a fearful image of the Bad Principle (Duad) bringing trouble into the next *634* order (Triad).

461

In another sense the number 5 was an emblem of marriage, because it is composed of 2, the first even number, and 3, the first odd number. Juno, the Goddess of Marriage, had for her symbol the number 5.

Furthermore, like the number 9, it reproduces itself through multiplication. When multiplied by itself, there is always a 5 on the right hand side of the result. This led to its use as a symbol of material changes.

The ancients represented the world by the number 5. Diodorus says that it represents earth, water, air, fire, and ether or spirit. Therein lies the similarity between the Greek *pente* (the number 5) and Pan (the Universe, the All).

The number 5 identified the universal quintessence. It is no coincidence that its modern form resembles the serpent. It symbolizes the vital essence or animating spirit that flows (*serpentat*) through all nature. This ingenious figure is the union of the two Greek accents ' ' ordinarily placed over vowels when they should be emphasized or de-emphasized. The upper half of the figure (') is the potent and superior Spirit of God breathed into man. The lower half of the figure (') is the mild, secondary, purely human spirit.

The Pythagoreans regarded the triple triangle (a figure of five lines uniting in five points) as an emblem of Health.

The Pentalpha of Pythagoras or Pentangle of Solomon has five lines and five angles. Among Masons, it is the outline or origin of the five-pointed Star and an emblem of Fellowship.

The number 6 was a striking emblem of nature in the Ancient Mysteries. It illustrated the six dimensions of all bodies; the six lines which make up their form, etc. It was the four cardinal directions (North, South, East, and West) with the two directions of height and depth (the zenith and nadir in Astronomy). The sages applied the number 6 to the physical man, while the number 7 symbolized his immortal spirit.

Six may also be represented by the double equilateral triangle or Star of David, which is the symbol of Deity.

Six is an emblem of health and the symbol of justice, because it is the first so-called perfect number, whose even divisors (3, 2, and 1) added together, make itself.

635   Ormuzd created six good spirits, and Ahriman created six evil ones. These typify the six Summer and six Winter months.

No number has ever been as universally revered as the Septenary (7). This was the number of planets. Formed from the numbers 3 and 4, the Pythagoreans regarded 7 as the union of the material elements with the principle of everything that is immaterial. In essence, the number 7 was the emblem of everything that is perfect.

When expressed as a union of 6 and unity, it demonstrates the invisible center or the soul of everything with physical form. The 6 spatial dimensions cannot constitute a form without a seventh interior point or origin. This is the center and reality to which the body gives a physical appearance.

The ancient sages regarded the number 7 as having perfection, though to a lesser or subordinate degree than the perfection of Unity, because like unity, no other number could produce it. The number 4 occupies an arithmetical middle ground between unity (1) and 7, the difference being 3 each way.

Among the Egyptians, the figure of the number 7 symbolized life. This is why the letter Z of the Greeks was the first letter of the verb Ζάω (I live) and Ζεὺς (Jupiter, the Father of Life).

The number 8 (the Octary) is composed of the sacred numbers 3 and 5. Eight is the sum of 7 and 1 (the ogdoad of the heavens), the seven planets and the sphere of the fixed stars, or eternal unity and the mysterious number 7.

The Gnostic ogdoad had eight stars, which represented the eight Cabiri of Samothrace, the eight Egyptian and Phœnician principles, the eight gods of Xenocrates, and the eight angles of the cubical stone.

The number eight symbolizes perfection and its figure (8 or ∞) indicates the perpetual and regular course of the Universe.

It is the first cube (2 × 2 × 2), sacred to arithmetical philosophy, and signifies friendship, prudence, counsel, and justice. It was a symbol of the primeval law, which regarded all men as equal. 636

The number 9 (the novary) or triple ternary (3 × 3) was of no less importance than the number 3. Each of the three elements that constitute our bodies is itself a trinity: the water containing earth and fire, the earth containing particles deposited by fire and water, fire tempered by water and fed by earthly molecules. No one of the three elements is entirely separate from the others. All material beings may therefore be represented by the figurative number of three times three, which has become the symbol of all formations of bodies. The number 9 represents matter. The Pythagoreans observed that the number 9 reproduces itself incessantly and completely in every multiplication. This provides the mind a very striking emblem of matter that is incessantly composed before our eyes, after having suffered a thousand decompositions.

The number nine was dedicated to the Spheres and the Muses. It is the sign of every circumference, because a circle of 360 degrees is equal to 9, (3 + 6 + 0 = 9). Nevertheless, the ancients regarded this number with a sort of terror. As a symbol of versatility and change, it warned of the frailty of human affairs. They avoided all numbers where nine appeared, particularly 81, which is not only the product of 9 multiplied by itself, but its digits (8 and 1) also add to 9.

The figure for the number six (6) represented the earth animated by divine spirit. The figure for 9 (an inverted 6) was the earth under the influence of an Evil Principle. Nevertheless, the Kabbalists used the figure 9 to symbolize the generative egg. Its figure (9) resembled that of an embryo, receiving the nourishing flow of its life spirit by a connection to its lower side.

The Ennead, signifying a group of 9 things or persons, is the first square of unequal numbers.

Most are aware of the unique property of the number 9 that, when multiplied by itself or any other number whatsoever, gives a result whose final sum is always 9 or always divisible by 9.

Nine, multiplied by each of the ordinary numbers, produces an arithmetical progression, for example:

```
1...2...3...4...5...6...7...8...9..10
9..18..27..36..45..54..63..72..81..90
```

The first line gives the regular series, from 1 to 10. The second contains the product of 9 and the number from the first series. Upon close examination, it will be seen that the second series reflects upon itself, as if a mirror lies between 45 and 54.

Furthermore, the numbers comprising each half of the second set may be summed to values that reduce to 9, and when aligned in columns, the matching pairs of each half again produce sums that reduce to 9:

```
   9...18..27..36..45 = 135  ..and 1 + 3 + 5 =  9
+ 90..81..72..63..54 = 360  ..and 3 + 6 + 0 =  9.
  99  99  99  99  99   495  ..and 4 + 9 + 5 = 18 = 9.
```

Furthermore:

$9^2 = 81..81^2 = 6561 = 18 = 9...9 \times 2 = 18..18^2 = 234 = 9.$
$9 \times 3 = 27..27^2 = 729 = 18 = 9. \ 9 \times 4 = 36..36^2 = 1296 = 18 = 9.$

And so with every multiple of 9 (45, 54, 63, 72, etc.)
Thus $9 \times 8 = 72...72^2 = 5184 = 18 = 9.$
And further:

```
     18              27               36                72
    ×18             ×27              ×36               ×72
    144 = 9         189 = 18 = 9     216 = 9           144 = 9
    180 = 9         540 = 9         1080 = 9          5040 = 9
    324 = 9         729 = 18 = 9    1296 = 18 = 9     5184 = 18 = 9

    108
   ×108
    864 = 18 = 9
  10800 = 9
  11664 = 18 = 9.
```

464

And so with the cubes and the 4ᵗʰ power, for example:

$$
\begin{aligned}
27 = 729 &= 18 = 9 \\
\times 729 & \\
\hline
6561 &= 18 = 9 \\
14580 &= 18 = 9 \\
510300 &= 9 \\
\hline
531441 &= 18 = 9
\end{aligned}
\qquad
\begin{aligned}
18 = 324 &= 9 \\
\times 324 & \\
\hline
1296 &= 18 = 9 \\
6480 &= 18 = 9 \\
97200 &= 18 = 9 \\
\hline
104976 &= 27 = 9
\end{aligned}
\qquad
\begin{aligned}
81 = 6561 &= 18 = 9 \\
\times 6561 & \\
\hline
6561 &= 18 = 9 \\
393660 &= 27 = 9 \\
3280500 &= 18 = 9 \\
39366000 &= 27 = 9 \\
43046721 &= 27 = 9
\end{aligned}
$$

The number 10 (the Denary) is the measure of everything and reduces multiplied numbers to unity. It contains all numerical and harmonic relations and all the properties of the numbers that precede it. It concludes the Abacus or Table of Pythagoras. To the Mysteries, the number 10 represented the collection of all the wonders of the Universe. They wrote it as θ. It is Unity in the middle of Zero. It is the center of a circle and the symbol of Deity. In this figure they say everything that should lead to contemplation. The center, the ray, and the circumference represented God, Man, and the Universe.

Among the Sages, this number was a sign of friendship, love, and peace. To Masons it is a sign of union and good faith, because it is expressed by the joining of two hands. It is the Master's grip with 10 fingers. It was represented by the Tetractys of Pythagoras.

The number 12, like the number 7, is celebrated in the worship of nature. The two most famous divisions of the heavens, the 7 planets and the 12 Signs of the Zodiac, are found upon the religious monuments of all the peoples of the Ancient World, even in the remote extremes of the East. Although Pythagoras does not speak of the number 12, it is nonetheless a sacred number. It is the image of the Zodiac, and accordingly it represents the Sun, which rules over it.

These are the ancient ideas with respect to the numbers that so often appear in Masonry. Correctly interpreted, as the old Sages understood them, they contain many deep and meaningful lessons.

Before we begin the final lesson of Masonic Philosophy, we will pause a few moments to recall the Christian explanations and interpretations of the Blue Degrees. There are seven significant symbols in the Blue Degrees as described below.

In the First Degree, there are three relevant symbols: the preparation of the candidate, the manner of his reception, and his being brought to light.

1st. Man, after the fall, was left naked and defenseless against the just anger of the Deity. Prone to evil, the human race staggered blindly onward into the thick darkness of unbelief, tightly bound by the strong cable-tow of the natural and sinful will. Moral corruption was followed by physical misery. War, Famine, and Pestilence invaded the earth, and in the face of misfortune and wretchedness, man toiled with naked and bleeding feet. The Redeemer came in this condition of blindness, destitution, misery, and bondage to save the world.

This is symbolized by the condition of the candidate when he is brought up for the first time to the door of the Lodge.

2nd. In spite of the death of the Redeemer, man can only be saved by faith, repentance, and reformation. To repent, he must feel the sharp sting of conscience and remorse like a sword piercing his bosom. His confidence is in his guide, whom he is told to follow and fear no danger. His trust is in God, which he is caused to profess. The point of the sword that is pressed against his naked left breast (over the heart) represents the faith, repentance, and reformation required to bring him to the light of a life in Christ.

3rd. Having repented and reformed, and bound himself to the service of God by a firm obligation, the light of Christian hope shines down into the darkness of the heart of the humble penitent. It blazes upon his path to Heaven. This is symbolized as the candidate is brought to light after having been obligated by the Worshipful Master (in this respect a symbol of the Redeemer). He brings the candidate to light with the help of the brethren, as Christ taught the Word with the aid of the Apostles.

In the Second Degree there are two relevant symbols: the obligation and the middle chamber lecture.

4th. The Christian assumes new duties toward God and his fellow men. Toward God he owes his love, gratitude, veneration, and an anxious desire to serve and glorify Him. Toward his fellow man, he owes kindness, sympathy, and justice. This assumption of the duty of good works is symbolized by the Fellowcraft's obligation. He was bound as an apprentice only to secrecy and set in the Northeast corner of the Lodge. Now he descends as a Fellowcraft into the body of the brethren and assumes the active duties of a good Mason.

5th. The Christian, reconciled to God, sees the world in a new light. This great Universe is no longer a mere machine, wound up and set going six thousand or sixty million years ago and left to run forever. It does not function by virtue of a law of mechanics created at the beginning without further care or consideration on the part of the Deity. It has now become to him a great emanation from God, the product of His thought, not a mere dead machine, but a thing of life, over which God watches continually. Every movement immediately produced by God's present action. The law of harmony is the essence of the Deity and is re-enacted every instant. This is represented by the less than perfect instruction provided in the Fellowcraft's Degree regarding the sciences, and particularly geometry. Geometry is connected with God in a Mason's mind, because the letter suspended in the East represents both. Astronomy, the knowledge of the laws of motion and harmony that govern the celestial bodies, is merely an extension of the science of geometry. Here in the Second Degree, for the first time, the candidate receives instruction in something other than morality.

There are also two relevant symbols in the Third Degree, making 7 all together:

466

6th.   After passing through the first part of the ceremony, the candidate imagines himself to be a Master and is surprised to be informed that he is not. It is uncertain whether he ever will be.   A difficult and dangerous path yet to be traveled will determine whether he will become a Master.   This represents the words of our Savior to Nicodemus.   In spite of his excellent moral conduct, he could not enter the Kingdom of Heaven unless he were born again, symbolically dying and re-entering the world reborn, like a spotless infant.

7th. The murder of Hiram, his burial, and his being raised again by the Master are symbols of the death, burial, and resurrection of the Redeemer.   It also alludes to the death and burial of sin of the natural man and his being raised again to a new life or born again, by the direct action of the Redeemer.   Morality (symbolized by the Entered Apprentice's grip) and Philosophy (symbolized by the grip of the Fellowcraft) failed to raise him.   The strong grip of the Lion of the Tribe of Judah cannot be broken.   Christ, of the royal line of that House, has clasped to Himself the entire human race.   He embraces them with His wide arms as closely and affectionately as brethren embrace each other upon the five points of fellowship.

Entered Apprentices and Fellowcrafts are taught to imitate the noble example of those Masons who worked at the building of King Solomon's Temple.   They are to plant firmly and deeply in their hearts the foundation stones of principle, truth, justice, temperance, fortitude, prudence, and charity. This is the foundation of a Christian character that will prevail against the storms of misfortune and all the powers and temptations of Hell.   This is the most proper homage that can be paid to the Grand Architect and Great Father of the Universe.   The heart becomes a living temple built to honor Him.   The unruly passions are made to submit to rule and measurement, and excesses are struck off with the gavel of self-restraint.   Every action and principle is corrected or adjusted by the square of wisdom, the level of humility, and the plumb of justice.

The two columns (Jachin and Boaz) represent a profound faith and implicit trust in God and the Redeemer.   This is the source of a Christian's *strength* and his desire to perform good works, by which faith moves salvation to act.

The three pillars that support the Lodge are symbols of a Christian's HOPE in a future state of happiness, his FAITH in the promises, divine character, and mission of the Redeemer, and his CHARITABLE JUDGMENT of other men.

The three murderers of Khir-Om (Hiram) symbolize Pontius Pilate, Caiaphas the High Priest, and Judas Iscariot.   The three blows represent his betrayal by Judas, the refusal of Roman protection by Pilate, and the condemnation by Caiaphas.   They also symbolize the blow on the ear, the scourging, and the crown of thorns.   The twelve Fellowcrafts sent in search of the body are the twelve disciples, who doubt whether to believe that the Redeemer would rise from the dead.

The Master's word, supposed to be lost, symbolizes the Christian faith and religion, supposed to have been crushed and destroyed when the Savior was
642 crucified. Judas Iscariot had betrayed Him, Peter deserted Him. The other disciples doubted whether He would arise from the dead, but he arose from His tomb and inspired the civilized world. In this way, that which was supposed to be *lost* was *found*. It also represents the Savior Himself. He is the WORD that was in the beginning, that was *with* God, and that *was* God; the Word of life, that was made flesh and dwelt among us and was supposed to be lost. He lay in the tomb, for three days, and His disciples "did not yet know the scripture that He must rise again from the dead," and doubted it when they heard it. When He appeared among them, they were amazed, frightened, and yet they still doubted.

The shrub of acacia placed at the head of the grave of Khir-Om is an emblem of resurrection and immortality.

These are the explanations for our Christian brethren. They are entitled, as are all other Masons, to respect and consideration.

CLOSING INSTRUCTION

Masonry is not infallible. It is not for us to dictate to any man what he should believe. Up to this point, in the instruction of the several Degrees, we have confined ourselves to the great thoughts and ideas expressed in the different ages of the world. You are left to decide for yourself as to the portion of truth or error of each. This course will not change as we now deal with the highest questions that have ever stimulated the human mind: the existence and the nature of a God, the existence and the nature of the human soul, and the relationship between the divine and human spirit in the material Universe. There are no questions more important to an intelligent being. None have a more direct and personal interest. The following instruction is merely the completion or rounding-off of what we have already said in several of the preceding Degrees. Recall the previous lessons upon the Old Thought and the Ancient Philosophies. Without this consideration, the instruction would seem incomplete or imperfect.

Masonry rewards a faithful and intelligent workman by conferring upon
643 him knowledge of the True Word. In this way, Masonry perpetuates a very great truth. The idea that a man forms about God is always the most important influence upon his speculative theory of the Universe. It guides his personal view with respect to the Church, State, Community, Family, and his own individual life. A people's belief in a Supreme God as a cruel Deity of blood and sacrifice or as a God of Love has a great impact upon their conduct in times of war or peace. An individual's speculative theory about the level of control God exercises versus his own free will and responsibility greatly influences the course of his life.

Every day we can see the vast influence of the popular ideas about God. All of the great historical civilizations have grown through that influence. The popular Religion begins as an abstract idea in the heads of philosophers. Eventually it appears in laws, punishments for crime, churches, ceremonies, sacraments, festivals, fasts, weddings, baptisms, funerals, hospitals, colleges, schools, and social charities. It affects a nation's relationships between husbands and wives, between parents and children, and the daily work and prayer of everyone.

As the world grows, it *out*grows its ancient ideas of God. These ideas were only temporary placeholder anyway. Any man who has a greater conception of God than the current popular ideas will very likely be called an Atheist by those who are in reality far less believers in a God than he is. When the Christians declared that the Heathen idols were not Gods, they labeled them Atheists and put them to death. Jesus of Nazareth was crucified as an unbelieving blasphemer.

A man can deny God in certain *terms*, but not in *reality*. He may say there is no God, no God that is self-originated, or no God that always WAS and HAD BEEN, no God who is the cause of existence, and no God who is the Mind and the Providence of the Universe. He may say that the order, beauty, and harmony of the world of matter and mind do not require any plan or purpose of Deity. Then he says, NATURE (the whole sum-total of existence) is powerful, active, *644* wise, and good. He says that *Nature* is self-originated or always was and had been. He says Nature is the cause of its own existence, the mind of the Universe, and the Providence of itself. He recognizes a plan and purpose to order, beauty, and harmony, but he considers it the plan and purpose of nature.

In these cases, the absolute denial of God is not real. The *qualities* of God are admitted to be real. The possessor of those qualities has been assigned to *Nature* instead of *God*. The real question is whether such Qualities exist. It is not by what particular name we designate these Qualities. One man may call these Qualities "Nature", another "Heaven", a third "Universe", a fourth "Matter", a fifth "Spirit", and a sixth "God", "Theos", "Zeus", "Alfadir", "Allah", etc. Every one of them acknowledges the existence of the Being, Power, or simply ENS (something that just exists). The name matters very little.

Real Atheism is the denial of the existence of *any* God. It denies all possible ideas of God. It denies that there is *any* Mind, Intelligence, or ENS that is the Cause and Providence of the Universe. It denies any Thing or any Existence, Soul, Spirit, or Being that *intentionally* or *intelligently* produces Order, Beauty, and Harmony. It must deny that there is any law, order, harmony, or regularity in existence. It is utterly impossible for any human creature to conceive (though he may *pretend* to do so) of any of these except by the action of Intelligence. He should at least recognize a wholly unknowable cause of these.

The *real* atheist must deny the existence of the Qualities of God. He must deny that there is any mind within the Universe, any self-conscious Providence, or any Providence at all. He must deny that there is any Being or Cause of Finite things that is self-consciously powerful, wise, just, loving, and

469

faithful to itself and its own nature. He must deny that there is any *plan* in the Universe. He must claim that matter has existed forever or created itself. 645 Otherwise, he admits the existence of God. It is beyond our grasp to imagine *how* matter began in a space where there was nothing but God. It is equally beyond our reach to imagine matter as eternal without beginning. It is absurd to deny that the specific forms of matter, the seed, the rock, the tree, the man, and the solar system all came by chance, without planning, purpose, or intelligence. It is reasonable to believe that that the meaning we have attached to these words is incomplete, imperfect, or in error. If there never was a plan, the word would be nonsense. The *word* plan, like *purpose* or *Providence*, means and was intended to mean to us exactly what the Universe demonstrates.

The denial of a Conscious Power, Providence, or Mind and Intelligence that arranges man in reference to the world and the world in reference to man fails to satisfy our *human* nature or explain the world around us. Why would we contemplate the birth of the Universe and man, drifting without direction or cause, without knowledge of his purpose, without Mind, Providence, or Power? Is the Universe a waste of Time? Do heroism, bravery, and self-denial amount to nothing? When you die, will your nobility and your charity do mankind no service? If there is no plan or order in all these things, then everything comes and goes by complete chance. Does this explanation ever truly satisfy the human 646 mind? Nonetheless, the theory of Atheism is still put forward. Some have said, "Death is the end. This is a world without a God. You are a body without a soul. There is a Here, but no Hereafter. There is an Earth, but no Heaven. Die and return to the dust. Man is nothing but bones, blood, bowels, and brain. Mind is matter. There is no soul in the brain. It is nothing but a collection of nerves. We can see all the way to a little star in the nebula of Orion's belt, so distant that its light takes thousands of years to reach earth. There is no Heaven this side of that. You see all the way through, and there is no trace of Heaven. Do you think there is any Heaven beyond it? If so, when would you reach it? There is no Providence. Nature is a fortunate interaction of atoms. Thought is a fortunate function of matter, a fortunate result of a fortunate result. It is a lucky roll of the Universal dice. Things *happen*, but they are not *arranged*. There is good luck, and there is bad luck, but there is no Providence. Die and return to the dust!" Does all this satisfy the human instinct of immortality? Does this satisfy our instinctive desire to rejoin our loved ones who have gone before us? Does this satisfy our instinctive desire for immortality? Does it fulfill our need to come closer to the Eternal Cause of all things?

Real men are not content to believe there is no mind within man, no conscience to enact eternal laws, and no heart to love those who need it most. We cannot accept that there is no will of the Universe to guide the nations to wisdom, justice, and love. History is not (thank God!) the fortunate series of coincidences. We cannot believe there is no plan and no purpose in Nature.

We cannot accept that all beauty, wisdom, affection, justice, and morality in the world are an accident that could end at any time.

All over the world, heroism is unrewarded or paid with misery. There is corruption in high places, and the virtuous suffer in poverty or even in chains. The gentle devotion of a woman is rewarded by brutal neglect or more brutal abuse and violence. Everywhere there is want and misery. Many are overworked and underpaid. What does the Atheist's creed say of this? "We are a body without a soul on an earth without a Heaven, in a world without a God." What a *647* chaos we would make of this world!

The mind of the Atheist finds matter everywhere and Cause or Providence nowhere. His moral sense accepts no Equitable Will, no Beauty of Moral Excellence, no Conscience enacting justice, no unchanging law of right, and no spiritual Order or Providence. He is left with only Fate and Chance. He loves only finite things and his loved ones who have passed away are like yesterday's rainbow. They lived for a moment and are gone. His soul flies directionless through a vast darkness without Reason, Conscience, or the Heart of all that is. It finds no God, just a Universe in disorder. It senses no Infinite, no Reason, no Conscience, no Heart, and no Soul of things. It has nothing to revere, to esteem, to love, to worship, or to trust. It knows only an Ugly Force, alien and foreign to us, that strikes down those we love and makes us mere worms on the hot sand of the world. No voice speaks from the Earth to comfort him. The Earth is a cruel mother that devours her young. He sees no kind smile of Providence in the stars of the night sky. In storms, there is nothing but violence, and Lightning stabs into the darkness seeking men to murder.

No real man can ever be content with that. The evidence of God is built into the fabric of Nature and so deeply woven into the texture of the human soul, that Atheism has never become a faith. It is just a theory. Religion is natural to man. He instinctively turns to God, reveres, and relies upon Him. He looks to the Mathematics of the Heavens, written in gorgeous diagrams of fire, and sees law, order, beauty, and harmony without end. In all Nature, animate and inanimate, he sees the evidences of a Design, a Will, an Intelligence, and a God who is beneficent, loving, wise, merciful, indulgent, and powerful.

Man is surrounded by a material Universe. He is conscious of the influences that his material environment exerts upon his destiny. He is confronted with the splendors of the starry heavens, the regular march of the seasons, and the beauty of sunrise and moonrise. All the evidence of intelligence *648* and design are forced upon him. Every imaginable question about the nature and cause of these phenomena demands to be solved. They refuse to go unanswered. Nonetheless, after endless ages, the questions continue to prey upon the human mind and demand answers, perhaps in vain.

When man ceased to look upon the separate parts and individual forces of the Universe as gods and came to see it as a whole, this question occurred to him. "Is this material Universe self-existent, or was it created? Is it eternal, or did it originate?"

Immediately followed these other questions:

"Is this material Universe merely a set of accidental combinations of atoms, or is it the result and work of intelligence, acting upon a plan?"

"If there *is* such an Intelligence, what is it and where is it? Is the material Universe *itself* an Intelligent being? Is it like man, with a body and a soul? Does Nature act upon itself, or is there a Cause beyond it that acts upon it?"

"If there is a *personal* God that is *separate from* the material Universe, who created all things, but is Himself uncreated, does He have a body? Is He matter or spirit? Is He the soul of the Universe or completely separate from it? If He is Spirit, then what exactly is spirit?"

"Was that Supreme Deity active or at rest before the creation? If He was at rest for a previous eternity, what made Him decide to create a world? Was it a mere whim that had no purpose?"

"Was matter existent with Him, or was it created by Him out of nothing? Did He *create* it or just *give shape* to a chaos that already existed?"

"Did the Deity *directly* create matter or was creation the work of inferior deities, emanations from Himself?"

"If He is good, just, and knows everything, then why does He allow sorrow and evil to exist? How do we reconcile His benevolence and wisdom with the vice and misfortunes of this world?"

649   Then in reflecting upon his own nature, man asks:

"What is within us that thinks? Is Thought the result of material interactions or is there within us a *soul* that thinks, separate from but within the body? If there is a soul, is it eternal and uncreated? If not, how was it created? Is it distinct from God or an emanation from Him? Is it *inherently* immortal, or only so because God has willed it? Will it return to God and be merged into Him, or will it always exist, separate from Him, with its present identity?"

"If God has foreseen and planned all that occurs, how does man have any real free will or the least control over his circumstances? How can anything be done *against* the will of Infinite Omnipotence? If all is done *according* to His will, how is there any wrong or evil? Why with Infinite Wisdom and Infinite Power does he not choose to prevent it?"

"What is the foundation of moral law? Did God enact it for His own mere pleasure? If so, can He not repeal it when he pleases? Who will assure us that He will not repeal it, and make right wrong and virtue a vice? Is the moral law a necessity of His nature? Who enacted it? Does that not require a power superior to Deity?"

After these come the great questions of the HEREAFTER, another Life, the soul's Destiny, and a thousand other questions regarding matter, spirit, the future, and God. This is the source of all the systems of philosophy, metaphysics, and theology since the world began.

We have already discussed the thought of the ancient philosophic mind upon these great questions. We have examined the doctrine of Emanation among the Gnostics and in the East. You have learned of the Kabbalists, the Essenes, and Philo the Jew. We have shown that the old mythology was derived from the daily and yearly cycles of the heavens. We have illustrated the means by which the ancients explained existence and evil. We have touched upon their metaphysical ideas about the nature of Deity. Much more remains to be done than we can do here. We stand upon the rhythmic shore of the great ocean of 650 Time. Before us stretches out the boundless waters of an infinite Past. As waves roll up to our feet along the sparkling slope of the sandy beach, they deposit only a few tiny remnants, a shell, a piece of torn algae, and a rounded pebble. That is all. We have nothing else of the vast treasures of ancient thought that lie buried in that thundering sea.

Let us once more, and for the last time, along the shore of that great ocean, gather a few more relics of the Past. Let us listen to its mighty voices as they come in fragmentary music and in broken and interrupted rhythm. They whisper to us from the great abyss of the Past.

Rites, creeds, and legends directly or symbolically illustrate how the Mysteries of Being are supposed to be explained in Deity. The complex mythical genealogies represent the mysterious nature of the Omnipotent Deity. They symbolize the first efforts of the mind to communicate with nature. They are the flowers strewn before the youthful steps of Psyche when she first set out in pursuit of the immortal object of her love. In all their varieties of truth and falsehood, they are machinery designed to work upon the same end. Every religion began as a philosophy. Each was an attempt to interpret the unknown by thought and mind. When Philosophy outgrew its original aim, religion became something separate. It clung to unalterable dogmas and ideas that philosophy had abandoned. It became arrogant and elaborate, and it claimed to possess what Philosophy had long pursued in vain. Through its initiations and Mysteries it classified all that its limited view could discover of the well-being of mankind, the means of purification and atonement, the remedies for disease, the cure for the disorders of the soul, and the means to obtain the favor of the gods.

Why should we attempt to confine the idea of the Supreme Mind within an arbitrary barrier? Why should we ignore other concepts of the Deity and deem them inadequate, when they may only be a bit more inadequate than our 651 own? "The name of God," says Hobbes, "is used not to make us *conceive* Him, for He is inconceivable, but that we may *honor* Him." "Believe in God and adore Him," said the Greek Poet, "but investigate Him not. The inquiry is fruitless. Seek not to discover who God is, for by the desire to know, you offend Him who chooses to remain unknown." "When we attempt," says Philo, "to investigate the essence of the Absolute Being, we fall into an abyss of perplexity; and the only benefit to be derived from such research is the certainty of its absurdity."

Man is ignorant of the composition of the dust on which he walks. Nonetheless, he continues to speculate upon the nature of God and to define dogmatically in creeds the one subject he is the least capable of understanding. He even hates and persecutes those who will not accept his views as true.

Although knowledge of the Divine Essence is impossible, the ideas that man has formed reveal a great deal about his intellectual development. The history of religion is the history of the human mind. The ideas that man has formed of Deity have a direct effect upon his moral and intellectual achievements.

According to Philo, the only way for man to truly understand the nature of God is to analyze God in the *negative* and systematically rule out what is inferior or finite. After exhausting all avenues of symbolism, we compare the Divine Greatness with human smallness. Eventually, we employ expressions that appear to be affirmative, such as "Infinite", "Almighty", "All-wise", "Omnipotent", "Eternal", etc. In reality, this is just removing the limits upon God that we know confine man. In the end, we remain content with a name, which is nothing more than custom and a confession of our ignorance.

The Hebrew יהוה and the Greek *To ON* express an abstract idea of existence. It does not specify an outward manifestation. Similar to this are vague definitions like, "God is a sphere whose center is everywhere and whose circumference is nowhere", "God is He who sees all, Himself unseen", and finally, that of Proclus and Hegel, "the *To μη ον,* which has no outward or positive existence." Most of the so-called ideas or definitions of the "Absolute" are only a collection of negative statements affirming and teaching nothing.

652 God was first recognized in the heavenly bodies and in the elements. When man's consciousness of his own intellect matured, he became convinced that his internal thoughts were of something more subtle than the world around him. This new idea was applied to the object of his worship, and he deified a mental principle instead of a physical one. He made God in his own image. No matter how hard we try, the highest efforts of human thought can conceive nothing higher than the supremacy of intellect. For this reason, his devotion turns to no more than an exalted idea of human nature. He deifies nature, and then he deifies himself.

The eternal ambition of man's religious ideas is to become united with God. Originally, this wish and its fulfillment were simultaneous through unquestioning belief. As the concept of Deity was exalted, the idea of His earthly presence was abandoned. The complexity of Deity's influence upon the actions of the Universe and the evil that rises from its misinterpretation threatened the belief in Deity altogether.

Even the stars, once "bright potentates of the sky," directing our destinies upon earth now shine dim and distant. We no longer see the Archangel Uriel in a sunbeam. The real change is the progressive improvement in man's abilities, not in the Divine Nature. The Stars are no more distant now than before, but there is a little sense of disappointment and humiliation with the first awakening of the soul. Reason looks upward toward the Deity with a dizzy sense of having fallen.

Left with this hopelessness, every advanced nation felt compelled to fill the chasm, real or imaginary, separating man from God. This has been the great task of poetry, philosophy, and religion. Man bridges the chasm to commune with God by humanizing God's attributes, actions, and manifestations. These become his "Powers", "Intelligences", "Angels", and "Emanations".

The Persians, Indians, Egyptians, and Etrurians identified numerous ranks and orders of mythical beings with control over various aspects of nature. Each of these served to bring man closer to the Deity. This continued to a lesser degree as the Deities and Heroes of Greece and Rome changed names to receive a place among the Saints and Martyrs. The rational, idealistic, and metaphysical systems of Zoroaster, Pythagoras, and Plato were merely a more refined form of these poetical illusions that satisfied the masses. Man still looked back with a longing for the lost golden age when his ancestors communed face to face with the Gods. He hoped that by satisfying Heaven, he might bring about a renewal of that golden age in the islands of the Far West, under the scepter of Kronos or in a new center of political power in Jerusalem. This eager hope even overcame his terrors of the grave. Divine power was as infinite as human expectation could imagine. The newly entombed Egyptian in the Catacombs was supposed to be on his way to the Fortunate Abodes under the guidance of Hermes, there to obtain a prefect reunion with his God.

Remembering the value we place upon the old ideas concerning the Deity, let us again put ourselves in communion with the Ancient poet and philosopher. Let us learn how they solved the great problems that have always tortured the human mind.

The division of the First and Supreme Cause into two parts (Active and Passive, Father God and Mother Earth) is one of the most ancient and widespread dogmas of natural philosophy or theology. Almost every ancient people gave this division a place in their worship, mysteries, and ceremonies.

Ocellus Lucanus, who probably lived shortly after Pythagoras, opened his School in Italy five or six hundred years before the common era, during the time of Solon, Thales, and the other Sages who had studied in the Schools of Egypt. He not only recognized the eternity of the Universe and its divine character as an un-produced and indestructible being, he distinguished the Active and Passive causes in what he calls the Grand Whole, a single Being (both male and female) that comprehends all existences. It is both cause and effect. It is a regular, perfect, and ordered system of all Natures. This idea addressed the line that separated unchanging existence from perpetual change. This line separated the celestial from the terrestrial bodies, separated causes from effects, and distinguished what *is* from what *BECOMES*. These divisions were natural to the human mind.

653

654

We shall not quote his words in full. He believed the heavenly bodies were the first and most noble. They moved on their own, ever revolving, without change of form or essence. In contrast, fire, water, earth, and air change continually in form, but not in place. In the Universe, there is cause and effect. The cause moves and acts and in effect, the recipient is made and moved. In his view, everything above the Moon was the domain of the gods. Everything below the Moon was the domain of Nature and discord. *This* world breaks down and destroys what has been made. *That* world creates the things that are being created. Because the world is un-produced and indestructible, and because it has no beginning or end, it follows that the principle that creates apart from itself and that which creates *within* itself have always co-existed.

Of these two parts, one is active, and the other is passive. One is divine and always unchanging. The other is mortal and always changing, composing every part of what we call the "world" or "universe".

These ideas align with the Egyptian philosophy, which held that man and the animals had always existed together in the world. The divisions of nature (active and passive, generative and destructive, and Heaven and earth) united to form all things. According to Ocellus, this will always continue to exist. He concludes, "The Universe, the generations and destructions within it, the mode in which it now exists, and the mode in which it will always exist, illustrate the eternal qualities of the two principles: one always moving, the other always moved; one always *governing*, the other always *governed*."

655 This is a summary of the doctrine of this philosopher. His work is one of the most ancient that has survived. His subject occupied the minds of all men. The poets sang of the beginnings of the universe and of gods. The philosophers wrote treatises on the birth of the world and the elements of its composition. The Hebrew story of creation is attributed to Moses. The Phœnicians story is credited to Sanchoniathon. The Greek story was composed by Hesiod, while Diodorus Siculus influenced the Egyptians, the Atlantes, and the Cretans. The theology of Orpheus was shared among many different writings: the books of the Persians (Boundehesh), those of the Hindus, the traditions of the Chinese and the people of Macassar. The chants of Universal Creation that Virgil puts in the mouth of Iopas at Carthage, and those of the old Silenus, the first book of the Metamorphoses of Ovid. All these sources testify to the antiquity and universality of these myths regarding the origin of the world and its causes.

Heaven and earth were placed ahead of all the other *active* causes of nature, especially the sun, moon, fixed stars, planets, and above all, the zodiac. The elements were considered to be among the most *passive*. Each cause within this progressive order of energy was assigned a gender according to their mode of operation.

The doctrines of Ocellus were generally accepted everywhere, so everyone understood the need to make this distinction. The Egyptians did so in their selection of animals as emblems of these qualities. They symbolized the double gender of the Universe. Their God KNEPH issued the Orphic egg from his mouth. The author of the Clementine Recognitions makes a hermaphroditic figure emerge from the mouth of Kneph. This unites the two principles of which Heaven and the earth are but the forms. There is a double power, active and passive, which the ancients saw in the Universe and represented it with an egg. Orpheus borrowed this symbol from the theologians of Egypt, where he studied. These mysterious forms veiled the science of nature. The egg issues from itself a *656* hermaphroditic being, whose division into two parts (or causes) represents the composition of Heaven and earth.

The Brahmins of India expressed the same idea with a statue that represented the Universe, uniting within itself both sexes and called a Lingam. The male aspect was an image of the sun, the center of the active principle. The female aspect was an image of the moon, the highest sphere where the passive region of nature begins. The Lingam is still venerated in Indian temples. It is the conjunction of the sexual organs of the two sexes and an emblem of the same idea. The Hindus have always shown the greatest veneration to this symbol of ever-reproductive nature. The Greeks utilized the same symbol in their Mysteries. It was exhibited in the sanctuaries of Eleusis. Tertullian accuses the Valentinians of venerating it, a custom he claims to have been introduced by Melampus from Egypt into Greece. We learn from Plutarch and Diodorus Siculus that the Egyptians consecrated the Phallus in the Mysteries of Osiris and Isis. Siculus goes further in saying this was not unique to the Egyptians, but common to every people. It was common among the Persians and Assyrians. Everywhere, it is symbolic of the generative and productive powers of all animated beings. In those early ages, the works of Nature and all her agents were as sacred as Nature herself.

The union of Nature with herself is a chaste marriage, of which the union of man and woman was a natural image. Their anatomy provides an expressive symbol of the double energy that manifests itself in Heaven and Earth and unites to create all beings. "The Heavens," says Plutarch, "seemed to men to fulfill the functions of father, and the Earth of mother. The father impregnated the earth with its fertilizing rains, and the earth, receiving them, became fruitful and brought forth." Heaven covers and embraces the earth everywhere, and It is her potent spouse. He unites himself with her to make her fruitful. Without Heaven, she would languish in everlasting sterility, buried in the shades of chaos and night. Their union is their marriage. The offspring of the world are their children. The skies are our Father, and Nature is the great Mother of us all.

This was the general opinion of all the Sages. Cicero said, "Nature was *657* divided into two parts, one active, and the other that submitted itself to this action to be received and modified. The former was deemed to be a Force, and the latter the material on which that Force exerted itself." Macrobius repeated the doctrine of Ocellus. Aristotle called the earth the fruitful mother, surrounded on all sides by the air. Above the earth was Heaven, the dwelling-place of the gods and the divine stars. Its substance was ether, a fire constantly moving in circles, unchanging, divine, and incorruptible. Below Heaven lay nature and the elements, which were corruptible and mortal.

Synesius said creation occurred in the portion of the Universe we inhabit, while the cause of creation resided in the portions above us. Proclus and Simplicius deemed Heaven to be the Active Cause and the Father. He considered the World or the Whole to be a single Animal, containing action and acting itself. The same World *acts*, and *acts upon itself*. He divided the World into "Heaven" and "Generation". He placed the causes of creation in Heaven, governed by the Genii and Gods. The Earth (Rhea) was the mother of creation and Heaven (Saturn) was the father. The womb or bosom received the fertilizing energy of the God that gave life to the ages. The great work of creation is primarily performed by the action of the Sun, and secondarily by the action of the Moon. The Sun is the primitive source of this energy. It is the father and chief of the male gods that form his court. It follows all the actions of the male and female principles in nature. Proclus attributes the origin of stability and identity to the male principle, while diversity and mobility originate in the female principle. Heaven is to the earth, as the male is to the female. The movement and revolution of the heavens furnished the male generative forces. Received by the earth, the female forces became fruitful and produced animals and plants of every kind.

Philo says that Moses recognized this doctrine of two causes, active and passive. However, he identified the active principle with Mind or Intelligence, external to matter.

658 The ancient astrologers divided the twelve signs of the Zodiac into six male and six female entities, assigning them to six male and six female Great Gods. Among the most ancient cultures, Heaven and Earth (Ouranos and Ghê) were the first and most ancient Divinities. We find them in the Phœnician history of Sanchoniathon and in the Grecian Genealogy of the Gods given by Hesiod. In all cases, they marry and produce additional Gods by this union. "In the beginning," says Apollodorus, "Ouranos or the Heavens was Lord of all the Universe. He took to wife Ghê or the earth, and had by her many children." They were the first Gods of the Cretans, the Armenians according to Berosus, and of Panchaîa (an island South of Arabia) according to Euhemerus. Orpheus made the "Great Whole" both male and female, because it could produce nothing unless it united within itself the creative force of both sexes. He called Heaven PANGENETOR, the Father of all things, the most ancient of Beings, the beginning and end of all, containing within Himself the incorruptible and undying force of Necessity.

The same idea developed in Northern Europe. The Scythians identified earth as the wife of Jupiter. The Germans adored her under the name of HERTA. The Celts worshipped the Heavens and the Earth, and without the one, the other

478

would be sterile. Their marriage produced all things. The Scandinavians called the Heavens BÖR. He gave the Earth as a wife to his son FURTUR. Olaus Rudbeck adds that their ancestors were persuaded that Heaven intermarried with the Earth. The union of his forces with hers produced the animals and plants. This marriage of Heaven and Earth produced the AZES (the Genii of the North). The Phrygians and Lydians recognized the ASII, who were born of the marriage of the Supreme God with the Earth. According to Firmicus, the Phrygians attributed to the Earth supremacy over the other elements, and considered her the Great Mother of all things.

Virgil sings of the impregnation of the joyous earth by the Ether. It descends upon the earth's bosom, fertilizing it with rains. Columella sings of the loves of Nature and her marriage with Heaven annually consummated in the spring. He describes the Spirit of Life, the soul that animates the world, fired with the passion of Love and uniting with Nature. The Spirit of life is part of Nature, and Nature fills its own bosom with new productions. Columella calls this union of the Universe with itself, and the mutual action of two sexes, "the great Secrets of Nature" and "the Mystery of the Union of Heaven with Earth illustrated by the Sacred Mysteries of Atys and Bacchus." 659

Varro tells us that the great Divinities adored at Samothrace were the Heavens and the Earth. They were the First Causes or Primal Gods. As male and female agents, one is the Soul and Principle of Movement, and the other is the body or the matter that receives it. These were the gods revered in the Mysteries of that Island as well as in the orgies of Phœnicia.

Everywhere, the sacred body of Nature was covered with the veil of allegory, which concealed it from the unworthy masses. It was seen only by the sage who found it to be worthy of study and investigation. She showed herself only to those who loved her in spirit and in truth. She abandoned the indifferent and careless to error and ignorance. Pausanias said that, "the Sages of Greece only wrote in a veiled manner, never naturally and directly." Sallust the Philosopher says that, "Nature should only be sung in a language that imitates the secrecy of her processes and operations. She is herself an enigma. We see only bodies in movement. The forces that move them are hidden from us." The inspired poets, the wisest philosophers, all the theologians, the chiefs of the initiations and Mysteries, even the gods uttering their oracles have borrowed the figurative language of allegory. According to Proclus, the Egyptians preferred to teach and speak of the great secrets of Nature only in myth and mystery. The Gymnosophists of India, the Druids of Gaul, and the Hierophants of Phœnicia gave to science the same enigmatic language.

The division of all things into active and passive causes leads man to contemplate the two Principles of Light and Darkness. Light comes from the ethereal substance that composes the active cause. Darkness comes from the earth or the gross matter of the passive cause. In Hesiod, the Earth created Typhon (Chief of the Powers or Genii of Darkness) from its union with

660 Tartarus. However, the Earth unites with the Ether or Ouranos when it creates the Gods of Olympus or the Stars, the children of Starry Ouranos.

Light was the first Divinity worshipped by men. It is the brilliant spectacle of Nature. It seems to be an emanation from the Creator of all things, and it reveals the Universe that darkness hides from our eyes by giving it existence. Darkness reduces all nature again to nothingness and almost entirely annihilates man.

Two substances or forces of opposite natures were imagined, and the world was subject to their influence. One contributes to its happiness and the other to its misfortune. Light brings the world enjoyment, and Darkness steals it away. Light is a friend, and Darkness is an enemy. One was completely good. The other was entirely evil. Thus the words "Light" and "Good" became synonymous, as well as the words "Darkness" and "Evil". Good and Evil could not flow from the same source any more than Light and Darkness. Men naturally imagined two opposing Causes or Principles. One provides the Universe with Light and Good, while the other brings only Darkness and Evil.

This distinction between the two Principles formed one of the foundations of all religions. It is a key component of the sacred fables, the creation myths, and the Mysteries of antiquity. Plutarch said, "We are not to suppose that the Principles of the Universe are inanimate bodies, as Democritus and Epicurus thought, nor that matter devoid of qualities is organized and arranged by a single Reason or Providence, Sovereign over all things as the Stoics held. It is not possible that a single good or evil Being is the cause of all, because God cannot be the cause of any evil. The harmony of the Universe is a combination of opposites, like the strings of a lyre, or that of a bow, which is alternately stretched and relaxed." Euripides adds, "The Good is never separated from the Evil. The two must mingle for all to go well." Plutarch informs that this opinion "is that of all antiquity. The Theologians and Legislators passed it to the Poets and Philosophers. Its author is unknown, but the opinion itself is established by the traditions of the entire human race. It is consecrated in the mysteries and sacrifices of both the Greeks and Barbarians, who recognized the *661* dogma of the opposing principles in nature, which by their opposition, produce the mixture of good and evil. We must recognize the two contrary causes or opposing powers, which lead one to the right and the other to the left and thus control our life. For if there can be no effect without a cause, and if Good cannot be the cause of Evil, it is absolutely necessary that there should be a cause for Evil, just as there is a cause for Good." This doctrine was well received among the wisest nations. This idea acknowledges two gods with different occupations in nature, one creating good and the other evil. They have been called "God" and "Demon". The Persians and Zoroaster named the Good god Ormuzd, the nature of Light. The Evil god Ahriman was the nature of Darkness. The Egyptians revered Osiris, but Typhon was his eternal enemy.

After returning from the Persian captivity, the Hebrews had a good Deity and the Devil, a bad and malicious Spirit, who always opposed God. He was the Chief of the Angels of Darkness, just as God was chief of the Angels of Light. In Hebrew, the word "Satan" simply means, "The Adversary".

According to Plutarch, The Chaldæans classified both good and evil stars. The Greeks similarly classified Jupiter and Pluto. They had the Giants and the Titans. A Serpent encircled Pluto (or Serapis), and the shape of the Serpent was assumed by Typhon, Ahriman, and the Satan of the Hebrews. Every culture had a similar concept.

The people of Pegu believe in the two Principles, the author of Good and the author of Evil. They attempted to satisfy the evil principle and found it useless to worship good principle since he was incapable of doing evil. The people of Java, the Moluccas, the Gold Coast, the Hottentots, Teneriffe and Madagascar, and the Tribes of America tried to avoid the anger of the Evil Spirit by appealing to his good will.

Among the Greeks, Egyptians, Chaldæans, Persians, and Assyrians, the doctrine of the two Principles formed a complete and conventionally arranged theological system, and it was the basis of the religion of the Magi and of Egypt. The author of an ancient work attributed to Origen said that Pythagoras learned 662 from Zarastha, a Magus at Babylon (perhaps Zoroaster), that there are two principles of all things: *father* and *mother*, Light and Darkness. Pythagoras believed that warmth, dryness, lightness, and swiftness resulted from light. Coldness, wetness, heaviness, and slowness resulted from Darkness. The world derived its existence from both principles, as from the male and female. According to Porphyry, Pythagoras conceived of two opposing powers. The first was good, which he called Unity, Light, Right, Equal, Stable, and Straight. The other was evil, which he called Binary, Darkness, Left, Unequal, Unstable, and Crooked. He received these ideas when he lived for twelve years in Babylon and studied with the Magi. Varro says that Pythagoras identified two Principles in all things: Finite and Infinite, Good and Evil, Life and Death, Day and Night, White and Black, Light and Darkness, Heat and Cold, Dry and Wet. The world combines all of these in equal proportions. Summer was the triumph of heat, and Winter was the triumph of cold. They were equal in strength during Spring and Autumn, one favorable to birth and health, the other to deterioration and sickness. He applied the same idea to the rising and setting of the sun. Like the Magi, he held that in the body, God (or Ormuzd) resembled light, and in the soul, he resembled truth.

Aristotle and Plato acknowledged a principle of Evil that resided in matter and in its eternal imperfection.

The Persians said that Ormuzd was born of the pure Light, and Ahriman was born of Darkness. They were always at war. Ormuzd produced six Gods: Beneficence, Truth, Good Order, Wisdom, Riches, and Virtuous Joy. The emanations of the Good Principle blessed mankind. Ahriman produced six

Devs in opposition to the six emanations from Ormuzd. Then Ormuzd made himself three times as great as before, ascended as far above the sun as the sun is above the earth, and adorned the heavens with stars. He made Sirius the sentinel or advance guard. Ormuzd and Ahriman each created twenty-four other Deities and placed them in an egg. Ahriman broke the egg, and Good and Evil became mixed within the world. According to Theopompus, the Magi held that each of the two Principles would be victorious against the other for two terms of three thousand years. Then, for three thousand more years, they will battle each other. They will each destroy the works of the other in retaliation, and finally, Ahriman will perish. Men wearing transparent bodies will enjoy unutterable happiness.

The twelve great Deities of the Persians, the six Amshaspands of Light and the six Devs of Darkness, are the twelve Zodiacal Signs or Months. The six supreme signs of Light begin in Spring with Aries and continue through the Summer. The six inferior signs of Darkness begin in Autumn with Libra and continue through the Winter. As opposed to Eternity, Limited Time is created and measured by the celestial revolutions, each divided into twelve parts, and these subdivided into a thousand parts, which the Persians called years. The yearly cycle of the Sun was divided into 12,000 parts, or each season into 3,000. Thus, each year, the Principle of Light and Good triumphed for 3,000 "years". The Principle of Evil and Darkness triumphed for 3,000 "years", and they mutually destroyed each other's labors for 6,000 "years". The Zodiac was equally divided between them. Ocellus Lucanus, the Disciple of Pythagoras, held that the principal cause of all earthly effects resided in the Zodiac. The good and bad flowed from the influences of the planets that moved through it.

The twenty-four good and twenty-four evil Deities enclosed in the Egg are the forty-eight constellations of the ancient heavens. They are equally divided between the realms of Light and Darkness. The celestial sphere enclosing the world and planets was the mystic and sacred egg of the Magi, the Indians, and the Egyptians. This egg issued from the mouth of the God Kneph. It is the Orphic Egg in the Mysteries of Greece. It issued from the God Chumong of the Coresians, from the Egyptian Osiris, and the God Phanes of the Modern Orphics. It is the egg that was crushed by the Sacred Bull of the Japanese from which the world emerged. The Greeks placed it at the feet of Bacchus, the bull-horned God. Aristophanes causes Love to spring from the egg to join with Night and bring order to Chaos.

The Balance, Scorpion, Serpent of Ophiucus, and Dragon of the Hesperides became malevolent Signs and Evil Genii. Nature was divided between two principles and their subordinates: Michael with his Archangels and Satan with his fallen angels. This is the meaning behind the wars of Jupiter and the Giants, in which the Gods of Olympus fought on the side of the Light-God against the dark progeny of earth and Chaos. Proclus added that this war symbolized the resistance of dark and chaotic matter to the active and beneficent

663

664

force that organizes it. Here again is the idea of an active, creative Heaven giving form to the inert, dark substance of matter.

Osiris conquers Typhon, and Ormuzd conquers Ahriman at the Vernal Equinox, when the creative action of Heaven is strongest. The principle of Light and Good overcomes that of Darkness and Evil, and the world rejoices. The world is spared from cold and wintry darkness by the beneficent Zodiacal Sign that the Sun triumphantly enters after its resurrection.

From the doctrine of the Active and Passive Principles grew the idea of a Universe animated by a Principle of Eternal Life and a Universal Soul. Every being received an emanation of the Universal Soul at its birth. At the death of that being, the emanation returned to its source, and the life of matter remained with nature and matter itself. Life is manifested in motion, so it naturally follows that the sources of life must come from the luminous and eternal bodies in the Heaven, whirling along in a rapid course that is swifter than all other movement. Fire and heat are so similar to life that cold (like the absence of movement) seemed to represent death. Therefore, the vital fire that blazes in the Sun and produces the heat that gives life to everything was regarded as the principle of organization and the source of life for all earthly beings.

The Universe is not merely a great machine, moved by powerful gears and forced into continual motion. It acts and reacts in every possible direction, 665 and it reproduces in succession all the varied forms of matter. It is not a cold and purely mechanical action. A mere machine could never produce life.

The Universe was thought of as an immense Being, always living and moving in an eternal activity inherent to itself and subordinate to nothing outside itself. That Being connects everything together and makes the world a complete and perfect whole. It brings order and harmony to rule over matter according to various designs and plans. All organized beings would have emanated from its Supreme Intelligence. It is the source of all other Intelligences, and nothing exists outside of it. It is the beginning and end of all things, including man.

Chæremon was wrong in his assertion that the Ancient Egyptians saw the Universe only as a machine, devoid of life and intelligence. They revered the Sun and the other luminaries, and holding such an opinion would exclude all religious worship. Wherever there is worship, there must be intelligent Deities to receive the homage of their adorers. No other people were as religious as the Egyptians.

The Egyptians identified an immense, unchanging, and Eternal Being that they called "God" or "the Universe". The earthly life and intelligence was a small and temporary part of it. It was as if the Ocean that supplied the waters to the springs, brooks, and rivers through evaporation and received the water again as it flowed in return from these tributaries. Like man and the animals, the machine of the Universe was animated by a Principle of Life. In fact, man was so only because the Universe was essentially so. For a few moments, it breathed an infinitely small portion of its own eternal life into inert matter. Without that 666 piece of eternal life, man and animal alike would die, and the Universe would be alone, living and circulating around the wrecks of their bodies. By its eternal movement, it organizes and animates new life. Everything is a part of its universal soul.

The ancient ideas held that no Principle BEING existed apart from this Great GOD, the Father of all the gods or the World. The Principle of all things and the Universal cause were called God. The Soul of the Universe was eternal, immense, supremely active, and penetrating all parts of the Universe, but it was subordinate to the UNIVERSE-GOD, which the ancients adored as Supreme Cause and God of Gods. The Soul of the Universe causes the regular and symmetrical movement of the celestial bodies and brings order to the elements. It mingles, organizes, gives life, and preserves everything.

In the Æneid, Anchises taught Æneas the Pythagorean doctrine of the Soul and Intelligence of the Universe from which the souls and intelligences of all living things emanate. He said that Heaven, Earth, the Sea, the Moon and the Stars are moved by a principle of internal life, which sustains their existence. A great intelligent soul penetrates every part of the vast body of the Universe. It interacts with and animates everything from the eternal fire that burns in Heaven. It is the source of life in all living things. In the Georgics, Virgil repeats the same doctrine. He said that at the death of every animal, the life that animated it returns to its Principle and to the source of life that circulates in the sphere of the Stars.

Servius makes God the active Cause organizing the elements into bodies. He is the life-giving breath or spirit that activates matter and creates all things. The elements make up the substance of our bodies, but God composes the souls, which give life to these bodies. From the soul come the instincts and life of animals. He says when they die, that life returns to and re-enters the Universal Soul, and their bodies return to Universal Matter.

667 Timæus of Locria and Plato his Commentator wrote of the Soul of the World and expanded upon the doctrine of Pythagoras. According to Cicero, Pythagoras held that God is the Universal Soul, present everywhere in nature, and from which our Souls emanated. According to Justin Martyr, Pythagoras said that, "*God is one.* He is not, as some think, *outside* the world, but within it and complete in its completeness. He sees all that *becomes*, forms all immortal beings, is the author of their powers and performances, the origin of all things, the Light of Heaven, the *Father*, the *Intelligence*, the *Soul* of all beings, and the Mover of all spheres."

According to Pythagoras, God is ONE, a single continuous substance extending throughout the Universe, without separation, difference, or inequality like the human soul. Pythagoras rejected the doctrine of the spiritualists who separated Divinity from the Universe, making the Universe no more than a material work isolated from the Abstract Cause. The Ancient Theology did not separate God from the Universe. Eusebius wrote that only a small number of wise men, like Moses, sought for God or the Cause of all outside of that ALL.

The real authors of the original creation stories, the Philosophers of Egypt and Phœnicia, placed the Supreme Cause *in* the Universe itself. In their view, the world and all its parts are *in* God.

The World or Universe was then compared to man. The Principle of Life that moves the Universe was compared to that which moves man. The Soul of the World was compared to the Soul of man. Therefore, Pythagoras called man a *microcosm*, or little world, possessing in miniature all the qualities found on a great scale in the Universe. By his reason and intelligence, man drew from the Divine Nature. By his abilities to heal, grow, and reproduce, he drew from elementary Nature. Thus, the Universe was a great intelligent Being, like man. The Universe has in itself what man has in him: movement, life, and intelligence. However, the Universe is eternal and man is not. Therefore, the Universe is the Supreme Cause of all.

Pythagoras held that this Universal Soul does not act everywhere equally or in the same manner. The highest part of the Universe was the guiding power 668 of the rest of the world. The seven concentric spheres form an eternal order, the fruit of the intelligence or the Universal Soul. It moves the celestial bodies of the great system of the heavens in a constant and regular harmony.

Manilius said, "I sing the invisible and potent Soul of Nature; that Divine Substance inherent everywhere in Heaven, Earth, and the Waters of the Ocean, which forms the bond that holds together and unites all the parts of the vast body of the Universe. It balances all Forces and harmoniously arranging the various members of the world and maintains the life and regular movement within it. The action of the living breath or single spirit that lives within everything circulates in all the channels of universal nature. It quickly flashes to all its points and gives animated bodies their proper form and organization. This eternal Law and Divine Force maintains the harmony of the world and makes use of the Celestial Signs to organize and guide the animated creatures that breathe upon the earth. It gives each of them the appropriate character and habits. By the action of this Force, Heaven rules the condition of the Earth and its cultivated fields, and it gives or takes away the vegetation and harvest. It makes the great ocean swell and recede again at the ebbing of the tide."

Thus, the heavens and the earth are truly alive. This is not just poetic language. They live with a life of their own that is eternal like their bodies. Each is gifted with a life and perhaps a soul like man's as its portion of the universal life and universal soul. The other bodies that they form only live through them, with their life. It is like the embryo in a mother's womb, maintained by the active power of her own life. Such is the universal life of the world, reproduced in all beings.

"The soul of the world," says Macrobius, "is nature itself." The soul of 669 man is man himself. The soul of the world "always acts through the celestial spheres which it moves, and which follow the irresistible impulse it impresses on them. The heavens, sun, signs, stars, and planets act only with the activity of the soul of the Universe. That soul provides all the variations and changes of sublunary nature, and the heavens and celestial bodies are but secondary causes. The zodiac is an immortal and divine existence organized by the universal soul, and it and produces or gathers into itself all the varied emanations of the different powers that make up the nature of the Divinity."

This doctrine was of the earliest antiquity, and it was held by the old Sabeans. It was taught by Timæus, Plato, Speusippus, Iamblichus, Macrobius, Marcus Aurelius, and Pythagoras. Once man assigned a soul to the Universe that contained within itself the life of all beings, they supposed that soul to be essentially intelligent. They assumed that the soul was the source of intelligence, and subsequently the Universe became intelligent as well. Each soul became the repository for its piece of the Universal intelligence. Without a soul, there could be no intelligence, because the soul of the world contained in itself the intelligence of the world. All the agents of nature received a portion of Its intelligence, and the Universe became filled with intelligences. Wherever the divine soul acted as a cause, there also was intelligence. The Heaven, stars, elements, and all parts of the Universe became the seats of the many divine intelligences. Every minutest portion of the great soul became a partial intelligence, and the more detached from gross matter it was, the more active and intelligent it became. The old worshippers of nature, the theologians, astrologers, poets, and the most distinguished philosophers supposed that the stars were animated, intelligent beings. They were eternal bodies and active causes of effects on earth. Each received life from Universal life and received their direction from the intelligence of the world.

The Universe itself was regarded as a supremely intelligent being. This was the doctrine of Timæus of Locria. The soul of man was a part of the intelligent soul of the Universe and therefore intelligent itself. Many other philosophers agreed. Cleanthes, a disciple of ZENO, regarded the Universe as God, the eternal and universal cause of all manifested things. He assigned a soul and intelligence to the universal nature, and this intelligent soul was divine. The intelligence of man shared in its divinity. Chrysippus, the most subtle of the Stoics, saw in universal reason the divine force or essence of the Divinity he assigned to the world. This divine force was moved by the universal soul that pervades its every part.

One of Cicero's characters from *De Natura Deorum* argues that the Universe must be intelligent and wise, because man, who is an infinitely small portion of it, is intelligent and wise. Cicero makes the same argument in his oration for Milo. The physicists came to the same conclusion as the philosophers. They theorized that movement originated in the soul, and the control of regular and ordered movements originated with the intelligence. Therefore, because movement and order exist in the Universe, it must contain both a soul and intelligence.

The argument was that the Heavens and the Stars are *animated*, because they possess a portion of the Universal Soul. They are *intelligent* beings, because that Universal Soul is supremely intelligent. They share *Divinity* with Universal Nature, because Divinity resides in the Universal Soul and Intelligence. By this process of logic, Cicero assigned Divinity to the Stars, and they became animated beings gifted with sensibility and intelligence. They were composed of the noblest and purest portions of the ethereal substance, unmixed with matter, and containing only light and heat. He concluded the Stars were gods of an intelligence that is active, eternal, and superior to that of other existences. This was exemplified by the lofty height in which they moved with perfect regularity and admirable harmony. The realm of Heaven was host to many Eternal Intelligences, celestial Genii or Angels, sharing the universal Divinity. They held dominion over earthly nature and man.

671

Today, *we* reduce the planetary motions to mechanical laws and explain them with a combination of two forces: centripetal and centrifugal. We can calculate the effects of these *forces*, but we cannot demonstrate their *origin*. The ancients believed they were moved by an intelligent force that had its origin in the first and universal Intelligence. Are we so certain that we are any nearer to the truth than they were? What *are* "centripetal and centrifugal forces"? What *is* a *force*? To us, the entire Deity acts upon and moves each planet in the same way that sap circulates in a little blade of grass or particles of blood flowing through the tiny capillaries of the human body. To the Ancients, the Deity of each Star was a portion of the Universal God, the Soul of Nature. Each Star and Planet was moved and directed by *its own* unique intelligence. This was the opinion of Achilles Tatius, Diodorus, Chrysippus, Aristotle, Plato, Heraclides of Pontus, Theophrastus, Simplicius, Macrobius, and Proclus. In each Star resided an immortal Soul and Intelligence, part of the Universal Soul and Intelligence of the Whole. This was the opinion of Orpheus, Plotinus, the Stoics, and in reality, many Christian philosophers as well. Origen held the same opinion. Augustin believed that an Angelic Power controlled every visible thing in the world. Cosma the Monk believed that every Star was under the guidance of an Angel. The author of the Octateuch, written in the time of Emperor Justin, says that the Stars are moved by the impulse communicated to them by Angels stationed above the earth. Christian antiquity did not render a clear opinion, but many of the Christian theologians believed the Stars were living entities. Saint Augustin and Saint Jerome assumed that Solomon assigned souls to the Stars. Saint Ambrose does not doubt they *have* souls, and Pamphilus says that many members of the Church believe they are intelligent beings. Many do not, but he acknowledges that neither opinion is heretical.

672

The ancient mind believed there was a Soul *inherent* in the Universe and in its individual parts. The next step was to *separate* that Soul from the Universe and give it an external and independent existence and personality. This personality is still contained within every particle of matter, but it is apart from Nature. It is the Cause and Creator. This is the middle ground between Pantheism (all is God, and God is *in* all and is all) and Atheism (all is nature, and there is no other God). Reduced to the simplest terms, they seem to be the same.

We seem to pride ourselves for our recognition of a *personal* God, as something more suitable to the human condition and devoid of the mysticism of Pantheism. However, Divinity remains a mystery, regardless of the symbolism found in organic and inorganic creation. Our personification of Deity is itself a symbol (perhaps more subject to distortion) that degenerates into a mere reflection of our own human problems. In the end, *any* positive idea that we can form in our own minds about Deity must be infinitely inadequate.

According to its scholars, the spirit of the Vedas (the sacred Indian Books of great antiquity) is pantheistic monotheism. That is, His is one God and in all things. The many divinities and prayers addressed to them ultimately refer to attributes of THE ONE. Personification of these attributes into several deities was an effort to make up for the inability of language to convey the intended meaning. The Mimansa was interpreting the true meaning of the Mantras when it proclaimed that, in the beginning, "Nothing was but Mind, the Creative Thought of Him which existed alone from the beginning, and breathed without breath." This idea is dogmatically asserted and further developed in the 673 Upanischadas. The Vedanta philosophy, took on the mystery of the "ONE IN MANY" as the fundamental article of faith. This included both Divine Unity and the identity of matter and spirit. The unity that it promotes is unity of mind. Mind is the Universal Element, the One God, the Great Soul, Mahaatma. He is the matter and the creator, and the world is a tapestry of which he is both the web and the weaver. He is the Macrocosmos, the universal organism called Pooroosha, of which Fire, Air, and Sun are only the chief members. His head is light. His eyes are the sun and moon. His breath is the wind, and his voice is the language of the Vedas. Everything proceeds from Brahm, like the web from the spider and the grass from the earth.

The limitation of language in expressing the nature and creation of matter and spirit is at fault for giving the Hindu philosophy any appearance of materialism. Deity Himself is formless, but He is present in every form. His glory is displayed in the Universe as the image of the sun in water. He is not specifically the sun itself, because all material appearance is subjective. Were it not merely a symbol, it would come from ignorance. His domain is a middle ground between reality and non-reality. These other gods are unreal, because nothing exists except Brahm, but to some degree, they are as real as the attributes of Him. Multiple essences of Deity compose One Essence. Every aspect of Nature (animate and inanimate), at every moment, is one with the Pantheistic Spirit.

The goal of using reason is to generalize or create a general rule from apparent confusion. We try to separate the accidental and temporary from the stable and universal. In contemplating Nature, we intuitively perceive a general plan among endless varieties of form and action. These solemn and reverential instincts may be hardened by intellect to become a fruitful philosophy.

Consciousness of self and our personal identity is a part of our existence. We cannot conceive of thought without self. This is not a result of reflection, logic, observation, experiment, or even experience. It is a gift from God. It is our instinct. We have a sense that the consciousness of a thinking soul is really 674 who we are. We have the same instinctive belief in a Power upon which we are dependent. We cannot define or imagine that Power any better than we can *define* the soul, but we *feel* It and *know* It exists. We cannot *adequately* form true and correct ideas about the Power of the Absolute Existence because of our own limited faculties. The ideas we can form, though incomplete and inadequate, are the result of direct inspiration and the exploration of philosophy.

The idea of the universal preceded the system to explain it. It was *felt* long before the grand idea of philosophy received deliberate investigation and development. Plato described the self-conscious mind as "a Divine gift, bestowed upon mankind by some Prometheus, or by those ancients who lived nearer to the gods than our degenerate selves." The mind supposed the existence of a general Cause or Antecedent from its first experiences, and shortly thereafter, the mind gave a name to that Cause and personified it. At the time, this idea was just an obscure theory, because *the Cause explained all things except itself.* It was a *true* but *incomprehensible* cause. Ages passed before this idea was fully appreciated. It became the object of faith instead of science, because man had to confine himself to things within his ability to comprehend. Initially, intellect and reason were overshadowed by imagination, and inadequate ideas resulted from turning symbols into realities. The idea took on a thousand arbitrary forms.

The idea of Divine unity in poetry and Nature became obscured by complex symbolism, and the transcendental ideas failed to develop beyond the original profound thoughts of the earliest symbolists. However, the idea of Unity survived. Xenophanes criticized Homer, because he overlooked or played 675 down the idea of Unity in his poetry. The first philosophy reasserted the unity which poetry had lost, but the world had again lost its definition in a bewildered materialism. They merely reduced the Whole or First Element to a refined state of matter, unchanging, but subject to mutations, decay, and regeneration. This evolving theological system compared it to water, air, or fire.

Poets and popular beliefs fragmented the Divine Activity into a race of personifications. The idea of evolution and cause was diminished and replaced, and eventually pantheistic ideas were restored to nature without division or limitation. They initially recognized a mechanical *force* or *life,* but this evolved into an all-pervading *soul* or inherent *thought.* Finally, it became a controlling, external *Intelligence.*

The Ionian revival of pantheism was materialistic. The Moving Force was with matter, and it was a subtle but visible ingredient. The principle of life was associated with the most obvious material machinery of nature, *air* or *fire*. Everything was said to be alive and full of gods. The wonders of the volcano, the magnet, and the ebb and flow of the tide were the breath or movement of the Great World-Animal. The ether of Anaximenes had no qualities beyond air. The "Infinite" of Anaximander was free from states of quality or quantity, but it was merely an ideal chaos more defined by what it was not. It was the unlimited storehouse or Pleroma from which everything evolved. A moving Force was recognized *in* matter but only thought of as a *part* of it. Space, Time, Figure, Number, and other abstract ideas were treated as *substances* with a physical connection to the object they described. All the conditions of material existence were supposed to have evolved from the Pythagorean Monad.

676   The Eleatic philosophers considered ideas to be the only entities possessing stability, certainty, and reality. They said, "All *real* existence is *mental* existence; non-existence. Being inconceivable is therefore impossible. Existence fills the whole range of thought and is inseparable from its exercise. Thought and its object are one."

Xenophanes wrote in ambiguous language. He used material imagery to illustrate an indefinite meaning. He looked to the visible heavens for inspiration in defining universal being and called it *"spherical"*, a physical concept. He said that God was neither moved nor unmoved, limited nor unlimited. He did not attempt to express clearly, what cannot be understood. He felt (according to Simplicius) that such speculation was above physics. Parmenides took a similar approach, comparing his metaphysical Deity to physical abstracts like a sphere, heat, a combination of many things, or a continuity.

The Atomic school divided the All into Matter and Force. It considered matter unchangeable, though infinitely variable in its forms. All variety in existence resulted from various combinations of atoms without any external cause or direction. There was no universal Reason. There was only Mechanical Eternal *Necessity*, like that of the Poets. Regardless of this apparent materialism, it is doubtful that reason was ever entirely abandoned. The earliest contemplation of the external world brings it into an imagined relationship with ourselves and assigns to it the experience and will that belong to our own souls.

Anaxagoras and Empedocles supposed the existence of elementary particles creating all material phenomena through their combinations. However, Anaxagoras considered the Moving Force to be Mind. He clearly saw the impossibility of demonstrating or defining this beyond simple faith, but he also chose to define the nature of this non-matter or mind in physical symbols and 677 terms, although he tried to draw a distinction. In his view, human reason or the regulating Principle in nature had to be essentially different from all other things in character and effect. It was neither Matter nor a Force combined with matter. It was independent, distinct, unique, pure, and unmixed. It was the source of all motion, separation, and thought. It was unhindered by any external influence. It was independent and held Supreme Empire over all things in all the worlds. It was penetrating and powerful. It mixed with other things, but nothing mixed with it. It wielded universal control and thought and included the *Necessity* written about by the Poets. It was the independent power of thought that we exercise within ourselves. It was the self-consciousness of the Universe, the Supreme External Mind that sees, knows, and directs all things.

Thus Pantheism and Materialism were both avoided. Matter was infinitely varied but bound by unity under the direction of the Prime Mover. That Power was moved by nothing and governed by nothing. If this organizing Principle was *inherent* in matter, then there could be no chaos. If it was *external* to matter, then according to the old Ionian doctrine, there must have been a "beginning" when the Arranging Intelligence started its work.

This grand idea of an all-governing, independent mind proves difficult, because matter would exercise its own independent and eternal self-existence in a state of chaos. Thus began a dualism of mind and matter. In the Mind or Intelligence, Anaxagoras included life, motion, and the moral principles of noble and good. He probably preferred "Intelligence" to "God", because it was less susceptible to misinterpretation and distinguished his ideas from others. His "Intelligence" had many of the same problems as the "Necessity" of the poets. It was the prelude to a great idea, which was impossible to explain at the time. The road by which it might be understood had not yet been paved. 678

The mind cannot go further than self-deification in metaphysics. It makes itself God in its own limited understanding and therefore limits God. Plato discovered realities within his own mind that he did not see in physical phenomena. In the same manner, the old philosophers ranked the mind's creations among the gods. Plato considered the Supreme Being to be Intelligence and left any further definition deliberately vague, drifting somewhere between Theism and Pantheism. Plato recognized the demoralizing nature of poetry, but he was wise to avoid replacing it with more positive language. He said that spiritual things are only understood through figures and the old and natural form of allegory was the most appropriate vehicle for theological ideas.

As the layers of symbolism were gradually stripped away in order to get to the root idea, the religious feeling originally connected to the symbol was stripped away with it. The advocates of Monotheism, Xenophanes and Heraclitus, only spoke out against the making of gods in human form. They did not attempt to strip nature of its divinity. They tried to redirect religious thought from an overzealous symbolism to a purer one. They continued the veneration for the Sun and Stars, the Fire or Ether. Socrates, like Xenophanes, paid homage to the rising Sun and the celestial bodies, which also retained a secondary and limited Divinity in the Schools of the Peripatetics and Stoics.

The theme of philosophy moved toward the unseen being or beings revealed only to the Intellect. The more ancient symbols were discredited and dismissed as nothing more than the ancestral stories of the ancients. The Theism 679 of Anaxagoras was more subversive toward Mythology and the whole religion of outward nature. It was considered a misdirected, outward appeal to the consciousness of the spiritual dignity within man.

For Aristotle, the world moves on eternally, always changing, and always the same. Like Time, the Eternal Now, it knows neither rest nor death. It is possible to fail to *identify* something clearly but succeed in defining it to some extent with the use of multiple *analogies*. Physical objects lose their *individual* identity because matter is continually destroyed and renewed in its present *form*. This regular eternal *movement* requires an Eternal Mover who is always *acting*, not an inert Eternity such as the Platonic *Eidos*. His *essence* is *to act*, otherwise he might *never* have acted. What would inspire Him to act after so much inactivity? The existence of the world would be an accident. He cannot partially act or be anything except determined to act. That would leave motion conditional and unpredictable, not eternal. He is either *entirely action*, pure and untiring, or he is completely immaterial. For this reason, Aristotle avoided the idea that God was inactive and self-contemplative, creating and acting out of some unknown reason or motive after an eternity of doing nothing. However, he erred in denying that there was any actual moment when His creative action *began*.

According to Aristotle, The First Cause is unmoved and moves all. His *action* was *first*, and the Universe has existed forever, persistently and continuously. The *unity* of the First Mover follows from His immateriality. If He were not unmoved, the series of motions and causes of motion would be infinite. Unmoved and unchangeable, He causes all movement and action. He is necessary. Through the necessity of His being, we can account for those necessary eternal relations that make a science of Being possible. Aristotle leaned toward a seemingly personal God, not a Being of parts and passions like the God of the Hebrews or the God of most men in our own day, but a Substantial Head of all the categories of being. This Individuality of Intelligence, like that of Anaxagoras, is derived from an elaborate and profound analysis of Nature. It is similar to the living, unambiguous Principle of the old poets. Before the physical manifestation of the universe from Night and Chaos, it was Ouranos or Zeus. However, the personality is quickly removed from this vision, and a conclusion is reached where the real and idea are blended. Moral action and thought acting upon the material world are discounted. The divine action in the world remains an impenetrable mystery, and the efforts to understand it result in contradiction. At this extreme, the series of causes resolve into the Final Cause. That which moves, itself *un*moved, can only be Thought or Form. God is formal, efficient, and the final cause. God is the One Form comprising all forms, the one good including all good. Moving the world as the object of love moves the individual. He is the internal, self-existing Final Cause. He has no end beyond Himself. He is not a moral agent. Otherwise, He would simply be a tool to produce something higher and greater than Himself. Only one action of mind or thought can be assigned to Him. That act must be what we call our highest pleasure. It distinguishes wakefulness and sensation from hope and

680

memory. His existence is unending enjoyment, which is powerful to us but only temporary. The divine quality of active and tranquil self-contemplation demonstrates the intelligence inherent to the divine mind. His thought is His existence. If He can enjoy what exists beyond Himself, then He can also be displeased and pained by it, and He would then be an imperfect being. To suppose He receives pleasure from something outside Himself makes His *previous* enjoyment and happiness imperfect, and it would be a sort of dependency. Man's Good is beyond himself, but not God's. The eternal act that produces the world's life is the eternal desire of good, and the object of the Absolute Thought is the Absolute Good. Nature is entirely movement. Thought is entirely rest. In contemplating absolute good, the Finality can only contemplate upon itself, and any distinction between the thought and the thinker disappears. Divine Thought *681* is "thinking of thought". God is that pure and perfect energy of thought. He is life itself, eternal and perfect. This is the sum of all that is meant by the term "God". However, after all this transcendentalism, the essence of thought is found in its ability to transfer from object to object. We cannot conceive of thought without something beyond itself to think about. No act of self-contemplation is complete without an external action, movement, or manifestation.

Plato attempted to show how the Divine Principle of Good could be seen in Nature. He considered Divine Soul to be a principle of movement. He made his Deity a free and intelligent Force, turning his ideas into reality. Aristotle tried to prove that all Nature tends toward a final good. To him, the Soul is the motionless center from which all motion radiates, and to which it all returns. God is also unmoved. The Deity of Plato creates, manages, and rejoices in the universal joy of His creatures. The Deity of Aristotle is the perfection of man's intellectual activity extended to the Universe. If the Deity is a continuous act of self-contemplation, the world is part of His thought. He contemplates it within Himself. He is separate from the world, but He mysteriously intermingles with it. He is universal and an individual. His organizing thought is necessary and makes the physical world both real and good.

Plato gave the unformed world an animal nature like the Ionians. He added an Intelligence to it, like Anaxagorean, that brought organization to the simple idea of Necessity. He added Good Will to the Intelligence, and Force and Strength became subordinate to Gentleness and Goodness. It seemed that further progress was impossible and that the Deity could not be more than The Wise and The Good.

Unfortunately, the contemplation of Good requires the contemplation of Evil. When God is held to be "The Good", it is not because Evil is unknown, but that it is absolutely excluded from His attributes. However, if Evil is separate and independent, how can God represent Unity and Supremacy? To answer this problem, one has to return to the ideas of antiquity. One must concede *682* ignorance and deny the ultimate reality of evil. Plato, Aristotle, and Speusippus taught that evil is only one of the many ideas that simply exist as part of our finite understanding and be dismissed through the progress of philosophy. We must revert to the original idea of "The Absolute", a single Being in whom all mysteries are explained. Evil is simply a rough spot on the ocean of Eternity, which does not really exist as an object of faith.

"The Absolute" must be closely tied to this non-existent notion. Matter and evil presented themselves too often and too clearly to be eliminated by the subtleties of Logic. It is vain to attempt to merge the world with God when our experience reflects conflict, imperfection, and instability instead of the perfection of its source. Philosophy was simply another name for uncertainty. The mind had deified Nature and its own ideas without any useful result. The reality it sought either externally or internally seemed to elude its grasp, and the intellect aimed for a truth that was attainable and applicable to its present condition.

The Deity of Plato is related to human sympathies. He is the Father of the World and its Creator. He is the author of good but not evil. He says, "Envy is far removed from celestial beings, and if willing and braced for the effort, man is permitted to aspire to a communion with the solemn troops and sweet societies of Heaven. God is the Idea or Essence of Goodness, the Good itself (τὸ αγαθόν) in goodness. He created the World and gave it the greatest perfection it could sustain. The world was as close an image of Himself as possible. This sublime symbol of all excellence is an object of veneration and love." The Sages of old had already suggested that God was the Author of Good. Like the Sun in Heaven and Æsculapius on earth, He is "Healer", "Savior", and "Redeemer". He is the destroyer of Evil, healing the problems inflicted by Herè, the irrational power of nature.

Plato resurrects the dogma of antiquity when he identifies LOVE as the highest and most beneficent of gods, who gives life to nature. Love is the physician healing the Universe, like medicine to our bodies. This concept was so important to Socrates that he sacrificed to Æsculapius as he was dying.

This symbolic idea and connection to the Universe was inspired by the earliest instincts and feelings. Through intellectual progress, it was refined until it also gained the approval of reason and understanding. Even the Scythians, Bithynians, and Scandinavians called God their "Father". All nations traced their ancestry more or less directly to Heaven. Olen the Hyperborean considered Love the First-born of Nature. No one could determine when God was first worthily and truly honored or identify when man first began to sense the silent eloquence of nature? To the mystical Theologers who preceded Greek philosophy, Love was the Great First Cause and Parent of the Universe. Proclus said, "Zeus changed Himself into the form of Love when entering upon the work of creation. He brought forth Aphrodite as the principle of Unity and Universal Harmony to display her light to all. He contains the principle of love within the depths of His mysterious being, where creative wisdom and blessed love are united."

683

"From the first
Of Days on these his love divine be fixed,
His admiration; till in time complete
What he admired and loved, his vital smile
Unfolded into being."

The philosophers of the East suggested that an Eternal Being, superior to all affection and change, existed in serene and independent bliss. This left the creation of the world a bit difficult to explain. If He required nothing external to Himself to complete His already-existing Perfection, why would He leave His unrevealed and perfect existence and become involved in chaotic nature? The solution to this problem is Love. The Great Being saw the beauty of His own idea, with Him from the beginning. Maia (Nature's loveliness) is the seed of 684 passion and the source of the physical world. Love became the universal parent Deity, separated into both Love and the thing loved.

Here again is the problem of a pre-existing eternity in which God dwelt alone. His uncompromised unity had no object to love. The very idea of love implies the existence of an object to love. If God's essence is love and He is unchangeable, could He have created a Universe to love that, by existing, gave His love existence? The only reasonable conclusion is that the Universe and God always co-existed.

How is the existence of evil is to be reconciled with the wisdom, goodness, and omnipotence of God? To what extent does man have free will? Is he controlled by an inherent need or destiny? Is it really a combination of both? In some respect, these are questions about the qualities and attributes of God. We must try to learn about His moral nature by studying the way in which He governs the Universe. This investigation delves into His intellectual nature. It directly concerns the moral responsibility and destiny of man. The importance of the answers to these questions inspires man to fathom the profound mysteries of Nature, our own Existence, and the actions of an incomprehensible God.

Does the Deity govern the Universe by fixed and unchangeable laws or more subtly by direct interference? Can we encourage Him to change His plan through prayer?

God alone is all-powerful, but the human soul has claimed to be a part of the Divine. Van Helmont said, "The purity of the spirit is shown through energy and the effect of will. God, by the agency of an infinite will, created the Universe. The same sort of power, to an inferior degree and limited by external influences, exists in all spiritual beings." The further back in time we look, the more often prayer takes the form of incantation. Even today, prayer retains the 685 form of incantation to some degree. The rites of public worship are not just considered an expression of reverence, but real spiritual acts with an expected result for the mind of the worshipper. It may be the attainment of some desired object, health, wealth, or some other supernatural gift for the body and soul. It might be to escape from danger or for vengeance upon enemies. Prayer was able to change the purposes of Heaven and make evil tremble under the abyss. It held a compulsory influence over the gods. It attracted the sympathy of spirit with spirit. Hindu and Persian poems were addressed to both the Deity Himself and to His many diverse manifestations. These manifestations were the necessary unified emanations from the living or creative Word, which supports the framework of the universe by continuous repetition.

The story of the Fall details the Hebrew method of explaining the great moral mystery, the origin of evil, and man's apparent disconnection from Heaven. All ancient creeds have a similar narrative. Man had been innocent and happy in the beginning, but he lost it to temptation and his own weakness. This story connects an increase of knowledge to an increase of misery and identifies death as a penalty of Divine Justice. Secondary to this are several questions. Why is the earth covered with thorns and weeds? What is the origin of clothing? What is the origin of sexual shame and passion? Why is childbirth painful? Why is the serpent to be feared and hated?

All the variations of this story account for the apparent imperfection in the work of a Perfect Being. In Eastern philosophy, the Soul lapsed and parted from its pre-eminence, since it was originally a part of the Universal Mind. The theory of its reunion with the Universal Mind accompanies the idea of its fall. Its individuality must cease in order to again become part of the Infinite. All things must eventually return to God. This process is carried out by spiritual meditation or self-denial and completed in the magical transformation of death.

The Angels of Evil fell just like man. In God's good time, they too would be restored, and the reign of evil would cease forever. All the Ancient Theologies are concerned with this process. This is how Sin and Evil were reconciled with the perfect and undeniable wisdom and beneficence of God.

With man's independence of thought come freedom and responsibility. Man has a moral part to play. The limitations of his nature are exposed by his freedom. He has a duty and the capacity to act in accordance with Good. Man is *conscious* of his own freedom to act. How can man have ever imagined himself to be otherwise? Experience teaches him this freedom is limited and controlled. When any external influence tries to restrain and limit this freedom, he instinctively rebels against it as an injustice. Our freedom is determined by external factors, but our happiness is dependent upon effects in the physical World and the moral character of its Ruler.

This leads to another problem. The God of Nature must be One, and His character cannot be anything other than good. Therefore, what is the origin of evil, which preceded or accompanied man's moral development? Human opinion has consistently flowed between two conflicting extremes. One is inconsistent with God's Omnipotence, and the other is inconsistent with His beneficence. If God is perfectly wise and good, evil must arise from some *independent* and *hostile* principle. However, if all things are subordinate to One, then Evil exists only if it was created by God. Is this a Beneficent Author? 687

The dualistic natures of both moral and physical realities ran counter to the doctrine of Divine Unity. Many of the Ancients rejected the idea of one Supreme Being, like Homer's Jove who distributed good and evil out of two urns. They preferred the doctrine of two distinct and eternal principles. Many saw the cause of evil to be the inherent imperfection of matter and the flesh, without explaining how God was not the cause of it. Others personified the suggested Evil Principle, whose origin involved all the difficulty of the original problem. However, if these limitations were overlooked, dualism satisfied the curiosity of the masses. The difficulties were ignored and supposed not to exist. It is the world supported by an elephant, supported by a tortoise.

The simpler and older idea treated the one and only God as the Author of all things. Jehovah said, "I form the light and create darkness. I cause prosperity and create evil. I, the Lord, do all these things." Maximus Tyrius said, "All mankind is agreed that there exists one only Universal King and Father, and that the many gods are His Children." There is nothing improbable in the simple idea that there is only one God. It combines Nature's Unity with the all-pervading Spiritual Essence, which is derived from the earliest instincts of the Human Mind. It is like a shadow of the original truth taught by God to the first men.

The Deity of the Old Testament is often represented as the direct author of Evil, sending evil and deceitful spirits to men. He hardened the heart of Pharaoh and punished a whole people for the acts of an individual sinner. The sacrifices of Abraham and Jephthah (proposed, even if not executed) suggest the dominance of severity over mercy in the Deity. It was not uncommon, in any age or culture, for men to acknowledge the existence of one God without assuming anything about His dignity or benevolence. The causes of both good 688 and evil are assigned to a mysterious center, which varied in character by the culture defining it. Therefore, Deity was often depicted with feelings of envy and jealousy. This is illustrated with the narratives about the healing skills of Æsculapius and the punishment Prometheus received for giving fire to man. The spirit of Nature, represented by Orpheus, Tantalus, and Phineus was killed, confined, or blinded for divulging the Divine Mysteries to mankind. The Divine Envy can still be seen today. For the God of Moses, it is jealousy of his unquestionable control. The prescribed penalties for worshipping other gods seem to spring from a jealous hold upon His greatness, rather than any immorality or degradation inherent to the nature of the worship itself. Herodotus philosophically justifies these punishments as a strict adherence to moral balance and as a punishment for pride, arrogance, and disrespect.

God provides for the universe through regular and universal laws. He takes care of material things without violating physical laws, and he acts according to the nature of the things He has made. In the material and unconscious world, He works *through* its materiality and unconsciousness, not against them. In the animal world, He acts *through* its brutality and semi-consciousness, not against them. He takes care of human things by acting in accordance with human nature. He works in the human world through man's consciousness and partial freedom, not against them.

God acts by general laws for general purposes. The Universal Law of Gravity is a good thing, because it keeps the world together. A plane may crash into the Earth, killing hundreds, because of gravity, but the same law preserves countless millions. It cannot be overturned for the sake of hundreds, nor can it be overturned to allow the plane to stay in the air.

689 It is difficult to conceive of a Perfect *Will* without confusing it with the mechanics of the world. Language offers no name for a combination of the Unchanging with the Moral. The old poets personified them separately as Ananke or Eimarmene and Zeus. How can an All-Powerful God, whose Essence demands justice and mercy, maintain these universal laws? It is impossible for His unchanging nature to become unjust, merciless, cruel, or fickle. He cannot repeal the great moral laws that make crime wrong and the practice of virtue right.

All we know about Free Will is what we experience ourselves. The idea of Supreme Will guided by Infallible Law (even if self-imposed) is always easy to strip of its essential quality of Freedom. Subdued by something inadequately labeled Necessity, it loses its moral and intellectual dignity.

When we elevate the idea of law above bias or tyranny, we discover that the self-imposed limitations of the Supreme Cause are actually the sources and safeguards of human freedom. This returns us to the question "Is there a law above God Himself?" Is it self-imposed? Can it be repealed? If not, what power prevents it?

Homer's Zeus is a paradox of conflicting ideas. He combines strength with weakness, wisdom with folly, universal fatherhood with specific children, and omnipotent control over events with submission to a superior destiny. The obscure word DESTINY was used to avoid the theological problems the human mind failed to decode. It is like a fly ensnaring itself further by trying to escape the spider's web.

The oldest idea of Deity was deliberately vague. The addition of specific attributes was a later innovation. The God of nature reflects the changing character of the seasons, which vary from dark to bright. He is either angry or 690 serene, lavishly abundant or barren. Although Nature seems erratic, she is capable of fulfilling the highest moral feelings in her mysteries. The dark side of Nature becomes Siva, Saturn, or Mexitli, a patron of debauchery and bloodstained altars. All the old poetic stories reflect this ambiguity where Nature is neither wholly immoral nor purely beneficent.

No civilization ever deliberately made their Deity malevolent. Any questions that resulted from assigning the origin of all things to God were dismissed in trust and hope. The Supreme Ruler was unquestionably revered, and His beneficence was never doubted because of startling conflicts or contradictions. Men were not dissatisfied with His rule, and although fear might have caused anxiety, it did not overcome hope. Only after abstract ideas began to assume the shape of reality did a distinction between Good and Evil become necessary.

To account for moral evil, the philosopher had to devise an explanation that still allowed for the piety of the inventor. Evil was blamed upon the perversity of woman or an agent distinct from God. Typhon or Ahriman is created, and the Gods are divided into two classes. The Ancient Divinity is dethroned, and a Devil or Demon enters the story. In the East, the source of corruption was inherent to the material flesh. The Hebrews assigned everything illegal and immoral to Satan. The Greeks occasionally promoted the older and truer view, and blamed man exclusively for his calamities. Good things were seen as voluntary *gifts* from Heaven. Homer's Zeus exclaimed, "It is grievous to hear these mortals accuse the Gods. They pretend that evils come from us, but they create them with their own wanton folly." Solon writes, "When destruction comes, it is the fault of man and not of God." Euripides decided that, in spite of knowing what is right, people neglect to do it.   *691*

Approaching the real truth, Pindar, Hesiod, Æschylus, Æsop, and Horace suggested that all virtue is a struggle. Life is not a thing of rest, but frenzied action. Suffering is another name for learning through experience, and Zeus is the father of instruction and the schoolmaster of life. He is the giver of all understanding. He put an end to the golden age, gave venom to the serpents, and made the wolves fierce predators. He shriveled the fruit on the vine, stopped the flow of wine, hid the secret of fire, and made life harsh and unpredictable. In all these things, his intention was always beneficent. The goal was not to destroy life but to improve it. The burden of making his living by sweat and tears was a blessing to man, not a curse. Nothing is as great or excellent as what is attained by effort. Safe and easy virtues are worthless to gods and mankind. The sting of nature awakens the sleeping fire within man and inspires useful action through meditation and thought.

Ancient religious reformers decried the worship of "idols" as the root of all evil. While we know with certainty that the worship of idols is not the source of all evil, its irrational arrogance has caused much of it. Idolatry is as common now as it ever has been. People are always engaged in worshipping the fanciful images of their own imaginations.

Human wisdom is always limited and incorrect. Even the right ideas fall somewhere between ignorance and knowledge. Progress is natural to mankind, and philosophy is the educational journey that never quite arrives at the perfect truth. Like Socrates, a Mason should assume the modest title of "a lover of wisdom". You must always long for a greater knowledge than you presently possess, something still beyond your reach that you desire to make known for all time.

Philosophy was associated with poetry and religion under the broader idea of Love. Before the birth of Philosophy, Love received little attention. This mightiest and most ancient of the gods who co-existed with the world had been 692 unconsciously felt, but not honored or celebrated. In order for Love to wield a proper influence over religion and philosophy, the God of Nature must cease to be a God of terror. God cannot represent mere Power or arbitrary Will, a pure and stern Intelligence, an inflictor of evil, or an unmerciful Judge. The philosophy of Plato explicitly promoted the idea of Love. To him, Love was the first inspiration of the physical arts and the heavenly art of wisdom, which supports the Universe. Love inspires noble and generous deeds, and nothing would be beautiful or great without it. Love is our best pilot, ally, supporter, and savior. Love is the beauty and ruler of all things human and divine. Love and divine harmony forever soothe the minds of men and gods.

Man is capable of a higher Love. Uniting the mind with the Universe inspires all that is noblest in him, and he rises beyond himself. This higher love is neither mortal nor immortal. It exists between the human and the Divine, filling up the mighty interval, and binding the Universe together. Love is the highest of the celestial messengers who carry the prayers of mankind to the gods and convey their gifts to the world. "Divine Love is forever poor, and far from being beautiful as mankind imagines, for he is squalid and withered. He flies low along the ground. He is homeless and barefoot. He sleeps without covering before the doors and in the unsheltered streets. He possesses his mother's nature, always a companion of want. Yet, sharing the nature of his father, he is always trying to obtain things that are good and beautiful. He is fearless, determined, and strong. He is always cautiously devising some new, creative plan. He is wholly a philosopher, a powerful enchanter, and a subtle sophist."

The ideal result of Platonic science is to achieve the idea of something that has no earthly comparison, the Supreme Prototype of all beauty, pure and 693 uncontaminated by physical nature. The one who has obtained this thought has discovered real virtue. He has nurtured the beauty of virtue within himself, avoided the shadows, and conversed with the truth. He has become the friend of God as far as any mortal human can be.

Socrates and Heraclitus believed in a Universal Reason pervading all things and all minds, revealing itself through ideas. Therefore, Socrates looked for truth in general opinion and considered the sharing of ideas (mind with mind) as a great path to wisdom and a powerful method of progress. He believed that true wisdom was attainable. The moral instincts of temperance, conscientiousness, and justice were given to man by the gods, and they would never lead him astray.

This metaphysical direction put philosophy on par with prophecy and vision. If truth was discovered in thought, then thoughts should be treated as truths. Philosophy became an idolatry of ideas. Ideas became phantoms emanating from the pre-existent divine thought. Thus, philosophy creates a mythology of its own by escaping the bondage of one tyrant only to be caught in the web of another. Theories and ideas created and defended the false gods or "idols" of philosophy. The word *idolon* means *image*, and a false *mental* image of God is as much an idol as a false *wooden* image of Him. Exploring the problem of universal being, the first philosophy attempted to supply a substantive solution to every question by making the most sweeping assumptions. Poetry had filled the vast void between the human and the divine by personifying its Deity. Likewise, philosophy bowed down before the mind of the philosopher as though it were a reflection of the divine image. The philosopher deified himself by worshipping his own ideas, and nature was imprisoned by common ideas that were defined and limited by common words.

The clash of differing opinions led philosophy to be reduced gradually to a disgraceful chaos of utter skepticism. Xenophanes and Heraclitus mournfully recognized the failings of philosophy in their own acceptance of a universal doubt. The efforts of Socrates to rally the frustrated champions of truth ended *694* with a similar concession.

The worship of abstractions continued the error that personified Evil or deified Fate. Mystical philosophy evolved into mystical religion. The great task of understanding the outer world and its principles was left unfinished, and there was no reconciliation of the supreme power of reason with the demands of human sympathies.

The ancients perceived a natural order in the purpose and regularity of creation. Human institutions were supposed to be derived from the laws represented in Heaven. However, this assumed a divine law, which was actually little more than a logical extension of human law, unintelligible and unmoral. It did not matter if chance or reason governed the Universe, because misunderstood reason is nothing more than chance. Epicurus said, "It is far better to accept the fables of tradition than to acknowledge the oppressive necessity of the physicists." Menander speaks of God, Chance, and Intelligence as being indistinguishable. Unrecognized law is classified as *Chance*. It is perceived but completely misunderstood. It becomes *Necessity*. The Stoics completely submitted to the arbitrary rule of Law, while the Epicureans enjoyed a less restrictive lifestyle, though bound by the equally oppressive Chance.

Ignorance sees no need for anything and abandons itself to a tyrannical power without bounds. This tyrannical god is a paradox, because it permits evil, though it is assumed to be unlimited, all-powerful, and perfectly good. Identifying the Supreme Cause as a custodian of perfect reason but not using reason to understand it leaves the individual bound by the asceticism of the Stoics. This ignorance is free will combined with the universal rule of Chance. It is Fatalism and Necessity coupled with Omniscience and a fixed and unalterable Law. Human minds have always revolved around these ideas. The *695*

Supernaturalists conceived of a Being acting through impulse and superhuman wisdom. This Being demanded strenuous and constant service according to his will, and they considered the best man to be the most attentive to that duty. This is an irreconcilable contradiction between free will and the unavoidable demands of service. In the words of one archbishop, "if the production of the things we ask for depends upon natural causes, then our desires may be just as well fulfilled without prayer. Therefore, prayer is in vain."

The final stage in the evolution of religious thought is a religion of action justified by a solid comprehension of its aims and conditions. Man only becomes morally free when both Chance and Necessity are displaced by Law. Law as applied to the Universe is absolute and unchanging. The ideals and standards of this Law can be discovered and acted upon by human intelligence. Freedom exists when an individual develops his independence according to his own laws without external influence or constraint. Moral choice would not exist unless it was bound by conditions determining its ideals. Duty requires that rules be both intelligible and certain. Uncertain rules are unintelligible and impose no responsibility. An unknown law need not be obeyed. The Roman Emperor who enacted his own laws by putting them at such a height that no one could read them was justly denounced.

Man controls his destiny only by selecting from the pre-ordained options suited to his situation. Absolute or divine morality is the final cause or purpose of those comprehensive laws that often seem harsh and rigid to the individual. Universal inflexibility is just and impartial, and speculation must take refuge in faith. The immediate and obvious application of the law is very small in proportion to its wider and unknown application. The unseasonable rain that ruins my hopes of an abundant crop makes different crops in another region 696 prosperous. The sudden snowstorm or unexpected change in the wind may threaten my life, but that is in small proportion to the great benefit spread across the continent. This is the way of good and misfortune in the world. They initially seem irreconcilable and random, but good holds its ground, and in the end, misfortune diminishes with complete explanation. In a world of many individuals, suffering from conflicting interests and clashing passions, the practice of chivalry and generosity does not endure. The comfort and convenience of one man is often given priority.

The educated mind begins to appreciate the moral superiority of a clear and defined system of law. The chaos of causes and effects is brought into perspective. Apparent good is cheerfully replaced by disinterested and universal good. Self-restraint does not imply self-sacrifice. The true meaning of what appeared to be the arbitrary Power of Necessity is found to be Strength and Force acting in the service of Intelligence. God made mankind, placed us in a world of perpetual change, and gave us the capacity and means for happiness. We eventually learn that it is absurd to complain that we are not perfect, while living in a world of change, conflict, and passion.

Although the mystery of the world remains, it is sufficiently solved to inspire confidence. We must admit that if every person would do the best they are able to do and what they know they should do, there would be no better world than this. Mankind, surrounded by necessity, is free. We are not bound by an isolated will. In complying with nature's laws, we are able to improve our own condition and destiny. This preserves a balance between the powers of nature and the force of individual will.

This is a summary of the many conflicting opinions of antiquity and Ancient Thought. They demonstrate how human intellect always struggles to pass beyond the narrow bounds of its limited power and vision. It travels endlessly around a circle, as if lost in the woods, encountering the same unavoidable and impenetrable barriers. Science has many instruments. Astronomy has the telescope, Physics has the microscope, and Chemistry has its equations and combinations. All of these have significantly expanded our ideas about the Deity. We have discovered the vast expanse of the Universe, macroscopically and microscopically. We have observed and classified its star systems and the invisible swarms of the minutest animal life. We have harnessed the power of electricity, an apparent link between Matter and Energy. Despite all of this discovery, the Deity still becomes more incomprehensible to us than ever. Despite all of our formulas and speculations, we continue to return to the Ancient Thought. 697

Among all of these conflicting ideas, where is the True Word of a Mason?

My Brother, it is not within the reach of the Human Intellect to answer most of the questions that have tortured men's minds. With only our limited understanding, we have explained in the preceding pages what we may and must *believe*.

The True Word of a Mason is found in the concealed and profound meaning of the Ineffable Name of Deity. God conferred it upon Moses, but its meaning was long lost by the very precautions taken to conceal it. The true pronunciation of that name was a genuine secret, but the profound secret of its meaning was far more serious. The meaning of the Name contains all the truth that can be known by us concerning the nature of God.

He is AL, AL SCHADAI, ALOHAYIM, and ADONAI. He is the Chief or Commander of the Heavenly Armies. He is the collection of all Forces (ALOHAYIM) of Nature. He is the Mighty, Victorious Bal and Osiris. He is the Soul of Nature. He is Nature itself, a God that was personified in Man, and a God with human passions. He is the God of all faiths by another name. In his communication with Moses, he is יהוה. He said to him, אהיה אשר אהיה (AHIH ASHR AHIH), I AM WHAT I AM. Let us explore the esoteric or inner meaning of this Ineffable Name.

היה (HIH) is the imperfect tense of the verb To BE. The imperfect tense of any verb implies a condition or action that has occurred in the past and will continue indefinitely. The imperfect tense of the verb To BE describes a condition or state that is inseparable from the object described. The present tense of that verb is יהיה (IHIH). The Hebrew אהי (AHI) adds the truncated personal pronoun א (I), and יהי (IHI) contains the third person (He). The verb has the following forms:

Past Tense	היה	HIH	he existed, he was
	היו	HIU	they existed, they were
Present Tense	יהי / יהיה	IHIH / IHI	he exists, he is
	אהי / יהוא	IHUA / AHI	I exists, I am
Infinitive	היו / היה	HIH / HIU	exist
Imperative	הוי / היה	HIH / HUI	(you) exist
Participle	היה	HUH	existing, existence

This verb "to be" is never used as a common connecting word in Hebrew as it is in Greek, Latin, and English. It always implies *existence* or *actuality*. The *present* tense also includes the *future* sense (*shall* , *may* be, or exist). The Chaldaic forms of the imperfect tense of the verb הוה and הוא (HUH and HUA) are the same as the Hebrew הוה and היה (HUH and HIH) and mean "*was*", "*existed*", and "*became*".

הוא and היא (HUA and HIA) are the masculine and feminine personal pronoun HE and SHE. For example, in Genesis 4:20 appears the phrase הוא היה (HUA HIH) meaning HE WAS, and in Leviticus 21:9 we find אביה היא את (ATH ABIH HIA) meaning HER Father. However, the feminine pronoun "her" is often written as הוא (HUA), and היא (HUA) occurs only eleven times in the Pentateuch. Occasionally, the feminine form of the word means "it", but *that* pronoun is usually in the masculine form.

When either י, ו, ה, or א (Yōd, Vav, He, or Aleph) terminates a word and has no vowel either immediately preceding or following it, it is often dropped as in גי (GI) for גיא (GIA) meaning a valley.

So הוא היא (HUA-HIA), He-She, could properly be written הו הי (HU-HI). The Talmudists, who occasionally and deliberately transposed letters might write it as יה וה (IH-UH), which is the Tetragrammaton or Ineffable Name.

In Genesis 1:27 is written "So the ALHIM created man in His image, *in the image* of ALHIM created He him, MALE and FEMALE created He them."

Sometimes the word is written triangularly:

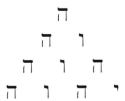

Among the Hebrews, this representation of the Ineffable Name was a symbol of Creation. The mysterious union *of God with His creatures* was in the letter ה, which they considered the Agent of Almighty Power. The letter enables the possessor of the Name to work miracles.

The personal pronoun הוא (HUA), meaning "he", is often used *by itself* to 699 express the Deity. In such cases, IHUH, IH, ALHIM, or some other name of God is *intended*, and it is not necessary to specifically write these names. In these cases, "He" means the Male, Generative, or Creative Principle or Power.

It was a common practice among the Talmudists to conceal secret meanings and sounds of words by transposing the letters.

The reversal of the letters in words was common to many cultures. For example, the Egyptian Goddess *Neitha* was reversed by the Greeks to form *Athenè* (Minerva). The Arabic name for the planet Venus is *Nahid*. Reversed, it gives *Dihan* (Diana) who was, like the Persian *Nihad*, a goddess of Nature. Strabo writes that the Armenian name of Venus was the phonetically related *A-nait-is*.

Tien (Chinese for Heaven) when reversed yields *Neit* or *Neith*, worshipped at *Sais* in Egypt. *Mitra* was the name of Venus among the ancient Persians. Herodotus, who tells us this, also identifies Venus among the Scythians as *Artim pasa*. *Artim* is *Mitra* reversed. By reversing it, the Greeks identified Artemis (Diana).

In Sanskrit, one of the meanings of *Rama* is *Kama*, the Deity of *Love*. Reversing Rama results in *Amar*, from which is derived the Latin verb for Love *Amare*, and the noun *Amor*. Similarly, the Sanskrit word *Dipaka* (often written as *Dipuc*) meaning love reverses to form the Latin *Cupid*.

The Arabic letters RHM (pronounced *RAHM*) signify *compassion* or *mercy*. Reversed they become *MHR*, the Persian word for *love* and the *Sun*. In Hebrew, the word *Lab* (the *heart*) is the reverse of the Chaldæan *Bal*, which has the same meaning.

The Persian word for *head* is *Sar*. Reversed, it becomes *Ras* in Arabic and Hebrew, *Raish* in Chaldæan, *Rash* in Samaritan, and *Ryas* in the Ethiopian language, which all mean *head, chief*, etc. In Arabic the word *Kid* is *rule*, regulation, or obligation. Reversed, it becomes the Greek *dikè* (justice). The Coptic *Chlom* (a crown) similarly becomes the Hebrew *Moloch* or *Malec* (a King).

In the Kou-onen (the oldest Chinese writing) the Hieroglyphic *Ge* (also *Hi* or *Khi*) was the Sun. So were the Persian *Gaw* and the Turkish *Giun*. The Moon was *Yue* (☽), *Uh* in Sanskrit, and *Ai* in Turkish. In Egypt and elsewhere, 700 the Sun was originally feminine, and the Moon was originally masculine. In Egypt, *Ioh* was the moon, and in the feasts of Bacchus the following cry was frequently heard: "*Euoï Sabvi! Euoï Bakhè! Io Bakhe! Io Bakhe!*"

Bunsen identifies the following personal pronouns for *he* and *she*:

	He	She
Christian Aramaic	Hû	Hî
Jewish Aramaic	Hû	Hî
Hebrew	Hû'	Hî'
Arabic	Huwa	Hiya

Thus the Ineffable Name simultaneously embodies every aspect of Great Philosophical Idea, that the Deity is Absolute Existence, the ENS, the TO ON. The Essence of the Deity is To Exist. He is the BEING that must have always existed. It is impossible that it should be otherwise. He is not Nature or the Soul of Nature but that which created Nature, separate from anything that has *become* or has been created. The Deity contains the Male and Female Principles in the highest and most profound sense. God originally encompassed all things within Himself. Matter was not co-existent with Him or independent of Him. He did not just bring shape and order to a pre-existing chaos. His Thought manifested itself outwardly into the Universe. It began to exist, and before that time, it only existed as an idea within Him. The Generative Power or Spirit and the Productive Matter (always deemed by the ancients to be the Female) originated in God. He Was and Is all that Was, that Is, and ever Shall be. All else lives, moves, and has being *in* Him.

This was the great Mystery of the Ineffable Name. This is the true arrangement of its letters, its true pronunciation, and its meaning. This idea was lost to all except the select few who received it. It was concealed from the masses, because the Deity and its metaphysical name were not personal or whimsical, and they believed in a tangible God within the reach of their understanding.

According to Diodorus, the name given by Moses to God was *IAΩ*. Theodorus adds that the Samaritans called God *IABE*. Philo Byblius refers to the form *IEYΩ*, and Clemens of Alexandria writes it as *IAOY*. Macrobius writes that it was an accepted truth among the "Heathen" that the three-letter *IAΩ* was the sacred name of the Supreme God. The Clarian oracle said, "*IAΩ* is the great God Supreme, that rules over all." The letter "I" signifies Unity, and A and Ω are the first and last letters of the Greek Alphabet.

This is the basis for the well-known expression, "I am the First and I am the Last. Besides Me, there is no other God. I am *A* and *Ω*, the First and the Last. I am *A* and *Ω*, the Beginning and the Ending. I am that which Is, Was, and Is to come, the Omnipotent." All of these statements illustrate the same great truth. God is all within all. He is the Cause and the Effect, the beginning, Impulse, or Generative Power. He is the Ending, Result, or that which is produced. He is in reality all that is, all that ever was, and all that ever will be.

701

Nothing besides Himself has existed eternally with Him. Nothing is independent of Him. Nothing else is self-existent or self-created.

The expression ALOHAYIM is a *plural* noun used in the account of the Creation in the opening of Genesis. In Genesis 2:4, it appears again, but with a singular verb: IHUH-ALHIM, which makes the meaning clear. The ALHIM is the combined unity of the manifested Creative Forces or Powers of Deity (His Emanations). IHUH-ALHIM is the ABSOLUTE Existence, or the Essence of these Powers and Forces from which they emanate.

This was the profound truth hidden from the masses in the ancient allegories by a double veil. These veils are found in the esoteric meaning of the generation and production in the Indian, Chaldæan, and Phœnician stories of Creation. These veils are the Active and Passive Powers, the Male and Female Principles, Heaven's Luminaries generating and the Earth producing. All of these obscure the doctrine that matter is not eternal and that God was the only original Existence, the ABSOLUTE, from Whom everything has proceeded, and to Whom all return. They conceal the idea that all moral law springs from His Wisdom and Essential Justice, as the Omnipotent Legislator. This WORD is correctly said to have been *lost*, because its *meaning* was lost, even among the Hebrews. However, the name still exists (its real meaning unknown) in the Hu *702* of the Druids and the FO-HI of the Chinese.

When we consider the Absolute Truth, Beauty, or Good, we cannot stop at an abstraction. We must frame their foundation in the context of a living, physical Being that is the beginning and end of each one.

Moral Truth, like every other universal and necessary truth, cannot remain a mere abstraction. Abstractions are unrealities. Within man, moral truth is just an idea. There must be a Being *somewhere* that not only *conceives of* moral truth, but also *embodies* it. It is not just a universal and necessary truth, as we understand it. It obligates our will. It is A LAW. *We* do not establish that law *ourselves*, because it is imposed upon us *in spite* of ourselves. It is a principle *without* us. There must be a *legislator*. He cannot be subject to that law, but He must possess the highest degree of all the characteristics of that moral truth. The moral law must have an Author, Who is composed of boundless justice and charity.

All *beautiful* and *true* things allude to a Unity, which is absolute BEAUTY and absolute TRUTH, and these *moral* principles unite in a single principle, which is THE GOOD. This leads to the idea of ABSOLUTE GOOD *within itself*, superior to all *particular* duties, but defined within those duties. This Absolute *Good* must be an attribute of the *one* Absolute BEING. Absolute Truth and Absolute Beauty cannot be different from that realized within Absolute Good, because the Absolute implies complete Unity. The True, Beautiful, and Good are one and the same essence. We believe the fundamental attributes that we perceive are within the Absolute and Infinite Perfection. Truth, beauty, and good appear separate from each other in the Finite and Relative World, but this is a distinction made by our minds. The human mind understands things only by division and classification. In the Being from Whom they emanate, they are 703 indivisibly united. This Being (at once three and one), Who sums up within Himself perfect *Beauty*, perfect *Truth*, and perfect *Good*, is GOD.

God must be the principle of Moral Truth and personal morality. Man is a moral being, endowed with both reason and liberty. He is capable of Virtue in the form of love and respect for others, *justice*, and *charity*.

Man cannot possess any real and essential attributes that the *Creator* does not possess. The *effect* only draws its reality and existence from its *cause*. The *cause* contains within itself everything essential to the *effect*, even if the effect is inferior and falls short of the perfection of its cause. It bears the marks of its dependence upon that cause, and its imperfection proves the perfection of its cause.

God cannot be explained by logical deduction or proven by so many equations or calculations. Trying to rigorously prove or derive the attributes of God yields nothing but abstractions. We must move beyond empty logic to arrive at a true and living God. The first idea we form of God is that of an *Infinite* Being, limited to our experience. It is the consciousness that we are a Being and a limited Being. It immediately takes us to the idea of a Being who is the principle of *our* being, Himself without limits. If our own existence forces us to conceive of a cause possessing that same existence to an infinite degree, each of the material attributes of our existence also requires its own infinite cause. God, then, is no longer the Infinite, Abstract, Indeterminate Being who our reason and heart cannot grasp. He is a real moral Being, like ourselves. The study of our own souls will lead us to a conception of God as sublime and having a connection with ourselves.

If man is free, God must be free. It would be strange if, while the creature has the marvelous power of free will, the Being that has made him 704 should be subject to a necessary development cause, even if that cause lies within Himself, an abstract, mechanical, or metaphysical power, inferior to the free will that we clearly experience. God is free *because* we are free, but He is not free *as* we are. He is at once *everything* that we are and *nothing* that we are. He possesses the same attributes that we do, extended to infinity. He possesses infinite liberty. He is united to an infinite and infallible intelligence. He is exempt from uncertainty and decision. At a glance, He perceives the Good, and His liberty accomplishes it spontaneously and effortlessly.

When we assign to God the liberty that is the basis of our existence, we transfer to His character our own justice and charity. In man, they are virtues. In God, they are attributes. For man, virtue is a difficult conquest of our liberty, but it is God's very nature. The idea of what is right is an indication of the dignity of our existence. If respect for rights is the very essence of justice, the Perfect Being must know and respect the rights of the lowest of His creatures. He provided them with those rights. Sovereign justice resides in God. It renders to everyone what is due him according to the truth of things. If man, a limited being, has the power to ignore his own needs to love and devote himself to another person's happiness, dignity, and perfection, then the Perfect Being must have this tenderness in an infinite degree. This is Charity, the Supreme Virtue of the human race. God has an infinite tenderness for His creatures, demonstrated by His giving us existence, which He could have withheld. Every day brings innumerable examples of His Divine Providence.

Plato understood God's love and expressed it in these great words: "Let us speak of the cause which led the Supreme Arranger of the Universe to produce and regulate that Universe. He is good and has no kind of ill will. Exempt from that, He willed that created things should be like Himself, to the greatest extent possible." Similarly, Christianity has said, "*God has so loved man that He has given them His only Son.*"

We are not suggesting that Christianity has *discovered* this noble sentiment. We must not lower human nature in order to raise Christianity. Antiquity knew, described, and practiced charity. The first feature of Charity, thankfully a 705 common trait among man, is goodness. At its loftiest, it is heroism. Charity is devotion to another, and it is ridiculous to pretend that there was ever an age of the world when the human soul was deprived of that part of its heritage, the power of devotion. However, there is no doubt that Christianity has spread and popularized this virtue. Before Christ, these words were never spoken: "LOVE ONE ANOTHER; FOR THAT IS THE WHOLE LAW." *Charity* requires *Justice*. He that truly loves his brother respects the rights of his brother, but he also does more. He forgets his own. Egoism *sells* or *takes*, but love delights in *giving*. In God, love is what it is in us, but to an infinite degree. God is inexhaustible in His charity, and He is inexhaustible in His essence. With Infinite Omnipotence and Infinite Charity, God unceasingly bestows upon humanity great favors born from the bosom of immense love. This teaches us that the more we give, the more we possess.

God is all just and all good. He does exactly and whatever He wills to do, and He can will nothing but what is good and just. The world is the work of God, and it is therefore perfectly made.

Yet there is disorder in the world that seems to undermine the justice and goodness of God.

A principle connected to the idea of good suggests that every moral agent deserves reward when they do well. Similarly, punishment results when they do ill. This principle is universal and necessary. It is absolute. If it does not apply in this world, then either it is false or the world is badly ordered.

However, good actions are not always followed by happiness. Evil actions do not always lead to misery. This is often more in appearance than fact. Virtue may be full of dignity, but it may also be full of sorrow and pain. The pains that follow vice are even greater. Virtue may often lead to health, strength, and long life, but the peaceful conscience that accompanies virtue creates internal happiness. Public opinion usually judges correctly with respect to a man's character. It rewards virtue with esteem and consideration, and vice with contempt and infamy. Justice does reign in the world. The surest road to happiness is still that of virtue, but there are exceptions. In this life, virtue is not always rewarded, and vice is not always punished.

706   The core of this problem is as follows: 1. The principle of reward for good action and punishment for bad action is absolute within us. 2. God is both just and all-powerful. 3. In this world, there are specific events or cases that contradict the necessary and universal law of reward and punishment. What is the result?

To reject that either of the first two principles is absolute is to destroy the foundations of the whole edifice of human faith.

To maintain them is to admit that the present life is to be completed or continued elsewhere. The moral person, whose actions are good or bad, and who awaits reward or punishment, is connected with a body. He lives with it, makes use of it, and depends upon it to an extent, but he is not *it*. The *body* is composed of parts. It is divisible even to infinity, but this body has a consciousness of *itself* that uses words like "I" and "ME". It feels free and responsible. It feels that it is a *single, simple* being. It senses that ME cannot be halved. When a limb is cut off and thrown away, no part of the ME goes with it. The identity, indivisibility, and absolute unity of the person are its *spirituality* and very essence. It is not merely a hypothesis that the soul differs in essence from the body. The soul is one with the consciousness of its own *thought* and *will*. Existence without consciousness is an abstract being, not a person. It is the *person* that has a unique identity. Its attributes develop it. They do not divide it. It is indivisible and may be immortal. If absolute justice requires this immortality, it does not require what is impossible. The spirituality of the soul is the required foundation of immortality. The law of reward and punishment is the direct metaphysical and moral proof of the existence of the soul. Add to this the tendency of all the powers of the soul to pursue the Infinite (the principle of final causes), and the proof of the immortality of the soul is complete.

God, therefore, in the Masonic creed, is INFINITE TRUTH, INFINITE BEAUTY, and INFINITE GOODNESS. He is the Holy of Holies. He is the Author
707   of the Moral Law. He is the PRINCIPLE of Liberty, Justice, and Charity. He is the Dispenser of Reward and Punishment. This is not an abstract God but an intelligent and free *person*, Who has made us in His image. From Him, we receive the law that presides over our destiny. We await His judgment. His love inspires us in *our* acts of charity. His justice governs the justice in *our* society and laws. We continually remind ourselves that He is infinite, because we would otherwise degrade His nature. If His infinite nature were not expressed by our own reason and soul, it would be as though He did not exist.

When we love Truth, Justice, and Nobility of the Soul, we love God as the foundation of these ideals. We should link them all into one great act of complete virtue. We should feel the presence of the vast forces of the Universe as the Forces of God. In our studies, when we attain a truth, we have glimpsed the thought of God. When we learn what is right, we learn the will of God, laid down as a rule of conduct for the Universe. When we feel genuine, unselfish love, we are experiencing a small feeling of the Infinite God. Only then will our reverence for the mighty cosmic force not be a blind Fate in an Atheistic or Pantheistic world. Only then are we feeling and knowing the Infinite God. Then we shall be mindful of the mind of God, conscious of God's conscience, and feeling His feelings. Our own existence will be in the infinite being of God.

The world is one harmonious whole, because God is One. God could make nothing but a complete and harmonious work. The harmony of the Universe responds to the unity of God. Any apparent lack of definition in the Universe is merely a defective sign of the infinite nature of God. To say that the Universe is God is to acknowledge only our physical existence and deny God. Whatever this belief may be called, it differs little from atheism. On the other hand, to suppose that the Universe is completely apart from God is an equally unsupportable if not impossible abstraction. To distinguish God from the Universe is not to separate Them. I distinguish myself from my qualities and actions, but that does not separate me from them. Likewise, God is not the Universe, although He is present everywhere in spirit and in truth.

For Plato (as with us), absolute truth is in God. It is God Himself under one of His phases. The original and unchanging principles of reality and intelligence are in God. In Him, all things receive both their existence and their understanding. By participating in the Divine reason, our own reason possesses something of the Absolute. Every judgment of reason surrounds a necessary truth, and every necessary truth requires the necessary Existence. 708

From every direction (metaphysics, esthetics, and morality above all), we arrive at the same Principle. It is the common center and the ultimate foundation of all truth, all beauty, and all good. The True, the Beautiful, and the Good are but multiple reflections of one Being. Thus, we reach the threshold of religion. Here we are in harmony with the great philosophies, which all proclaim a God. Here we meet the religions that have covered the earth, all of which rest upon the sacred foundation of natural religion. This religion reveals to us the natural light given to all men, without dependence upon any particular creed. When philosophy does not arrive at religion, it is below all forms of worship. Even the imperfect forms of worship give man a Father, a Witness, a Counselor, and a Judge. Through religion, philosophy connects itself with humanity. Everywhere in this world, humanity aspires to God, believes in God, and hopes in God. Philosophy contains in itself the common basis of all religious beliefs. It borrows their principles and returns them, surrounded by light, elevated above uncertainty, and secure against all attack.

The Nature of the Infinite Being requires that He must create, preserve, and give something of His own essence to the Finite. We cannot conceive of any finite thing existing without God. We cannot conceive of God existing without something. God is the necessary logical condition and cause of the world. Our world is the necessary logical condition of God and His effect. In His Infinite Perfection, He creates, preserves, and blesses what He creates. That is the conclusion of modern metaphysical science. The stream of philosophy runs down from Aristotle to Hegel and settles with this conclusion. Here again we encounter the ancient problem. If it is His nature to create, and if we cannot conceive of His existing *alone* without creating (or without *having* created), then His creation was co-existent with Himself. If He could exist an instant without 709 creating, He could do so for all eternity. Again, we arrive at the old doctrine of a God, the Soul of the Universe and co-existent with it. His creation had a *beginning*. However long ago that creation occurred, it had followed an eternity. The difference between *a* beginning and *no* beginning is infinite.

However, of some things we can be certain. We are conscious of ourselves, not merely as substances, but as Powers that exist, act, and suffer. We are conscious that we did not create and do not sustain ourselves alone, but we depend upon something beyond ourselves for existence and support.

Among the first ideas of consciousness, we inseparably find the idea of God. Carefully examined by the scrutinizing intellect, it is the idea of God as infinite, perfectly powerful, wise, just, loving, and holy. God is absolute being without limitation. God made us and everything. God sustains us and everything. God made our bodies in a series of acts extending over a vast succession of years. Man's body is the result of all created things. God made our spirit, our mind, and our conscience. God created our affections, soul, and will. He appointed to each of these its natural mode of action and its aim. Thus, self-consciousness leads us to consciousness of God and finally to consciousness of an infinite God. That is the highest evidence of our own existence, and it is the highest evidence of His.

If there is a God at all, He must be omnipresent in space. He must be as present beyond the last Stars as He is here. He is there with the smallest particle of dust in the sunbeam and with the littlest cell of life discovered through the microscope.

He must also be omnipresent in time. God was in every second that elapsed before the Stars began to burn. God is in the most distant nebulous spot in Orion's belt and in the millions of deceased organisms composing a cubic inch of limestone. He is in the smallest imaginable or even unimaginable portion of time. To Him, in every second is a vast and unimaginable volume of time. His Here is the All of Space. His Now is the All of Time.

Through all this Space, in all this Time, His Being extends without end. God, in all His infinity, is perfectly powerful, wise, just, loving, and holy. His 710 being is an infinite activity, creating and giving of Himself to the World. The World's being is actually a *becoming*. The World was created and continues to be created. It is so now and was so for incalculable and unimaginable millions of ages.

All of this is philosophy. It is the unavoidable conclusion of the human mind. It is not just the *opinion* of Coleridge and Kant, but also the application of their *science*. It is not what they *guessed*, but what they *knew*.

In order to describe the presence of God in matter, we say that the world is a revelation of Him. He is *in* His work. The countless actions of the Universe are only His mode of operation. All material things are connected to Him. Everything grows, moves, and lives in and through Him. If He withdraws from the space occupied by anything, it ceases to be. If He withdraws any quality of His nature from anything, it ceases to be. Everything depends upon Him. He dwells within all things, and yet he transcends all things.

The failure of fanciful religion to become philosophy does not prevent philosophy from arriving at the same ideas as the true religion. The aim of philosophy is the divine order of the Universe. It is the intellectual guide that religion needs. As philosophy explores the real nature of the finite, it constantly improves and corrects its understanding of the perfect law of the Gospel of Love and Liberty. Philosophy reveals a means of realizing the spiritualism of revealed religion. It establishes law by discovering its rational basis. It guides the spirit along a path to a better and happier life. While religion is fixed and unchanging, science cannot develop and grow. Once science and religion are understood to be progressing toward a specific (perhaps the same) objective, both flourish. Aristotle demonstrated how religion might be founded upon an intellectual foundation, but his basis was too narrow. Bacon gave philosophy a clear direction and method with an ever-expanding scope. We are intellectual beings surrounded by limitations. Within these limitations, we must identify the practical value of laws by following the inspiring and ennobling paths of both religion and philosophy. The title of Saint has often been applied to those who despise philosophy, but our faith will stumble. Our instincts will mislead us. Knowledge must be present to purify our faith and give direction to our instincts.

Science is the sum of all well developed theories from our collective 711 experience. It is not a complete, fixed system beyond the need for change. It guides us along an infinite path between ignorance and wisdom. As conceived by Plato, its highest goal is happiness, and it is driven by the highest kind of love. Science unites all that was truly valuable in both of the old ideas: the grand principles of cause and effect and the mystical theory of spiritual, contemplative communion. Galen said, "Listen to me as to the voice of the Eleusinian Hierophant, and believe that the study of nature is a mystery as important as theirs and is as well adapted to display the wisdom and power of the Great Creator. Their lessons and demonstrations were obscure, but ours are clear and unmistakable."

513

Because of science, no individual is any longer entitled to consider himself the central point around which the whole Universe of life and motion revolves. The Universe was not made to indulge the convenience and luxurious ease of one man. Science has shown us an infinite Universe of stars and suns and worlds at incalculable distances from each other. In their majestic and awesome presence, we (and our world) sink into insignificance. Through the microscope, science has revealed new worlds of organized creatures (with senses, nerves, appetites, and instincts) living in a single drop of water.

Science teaches us that we are merely a tiny part of a great whole that stretches out on every side, above and below us. This whole is infinite in its complexity. Infinite wisdom has arranged the infinite succession of beings through the cycles of birth, decay, and death. The greatest virtues are only made possible through these conflicts, losses, trials, and hardships.

Knowledge may lead to power, and truths may become practical rules and the definition of duty. Pure science benefits humanity and communicates openly. It is moral, intellectual, powerful, peaceful, and selfless. Science binds individual to individual and each of us to the Universe. It provides us with clear proof of the equality of all motives, needs, and obligations. Cooperation takes the place of rivalry and jealousy. Science effectively makes the spirit of religion a reality by healing our habitual greed and selfishness, which are rooted in ignorant assumptions about the limitations of Providence and lead one man to steal from another rather than quietly enjoy his own.

We will probably never reach the highest levels of understanding nor fully discover the complete nature of self or essence. We will always fall short of the most simple, yet ultimate and complete, law. We explain many things with broad theories, as did the ancient philosophers and astronomers. We cannot express the cause or explain the whole condition of existence. We may reproduce a portion of it in practice, but we cannot comprehend the whole without completely understanding the essence of each of its parts. Therefore, we cannot assert our theories with absolute certainty as the ancient did their religious creeds. We cannot allow the mind to forget that it displaced common ideas with reasoned science and return to a blind self-deception and superstition.

Skepticism is an essential component of progress and discovery. Man's intellectual life is a perpetual beginning, a preparation for a birth. Without doubting and questioning our judgment would be useless. Knowledge is always imperfect or at least incomplete. Discovery multiplies doubt, and doubt leads to new discovery. The value of science is not in its conclusions, but in its inherent imperfection and incompleteness, its unlimited capacity for progress. The true religious philosophy of an imperfect being is not a system of creed, but rather, as Socrates suggested, it is an infinite search or approximation. Finality is another name for confusion or defeat. Science satisfies our religious feelings without limiting us. It opens up the unfathomable mystery of the One Supreme into a comprehensible form. While it avoids an inquiry into His Essence, which is beyond our reach, it feeds our endless enthusiasm for the investigation of His Will. We have long observed that knowledge is profitable, but we are beginning to discover that it is also moral. Ultimately, we will find that it is religious.

God and truth are inseparable. To know God is to know truth. To the extent that an individual's thoughts and purpose conform to the rule of right, his happiness grows and the purpose of his existence is fulfilled. In this way, a new life arises within him. He is no longer isolated. He is a part of the eternal balance around him. His own imperfect will is guided by the influence of a higher will, gently pushing him down the path of true happiness.

Man's power to ascertain outward truth is limited. Even when an instinctive or revealed truth is deceptive or imperfect, the excitement of sudden discovery has always led man to believe it to be full, infallible, and divine. Human weakness always needs to return to the pure and perfect source, and these popular revelations take on an independent form, carrying with them the derivations and mistakes propagated in their name. The mists of error thicken under the shadows of rules and regulations. Eventually, the free light rises again upon the night of ages, redeeming the genuine treasure from the superstition that clung to it.

Even to the Barbarian, Nature reveals a mighty power and a wondrous wisdom that continually points to God. It is no wonder that men worshipped the varied forms and processes of matter. A settler in the harsh Northern climates trembled at his deity in its palace of ice and snow. The lightning, storm, and earthquake startled the primitive man, and he saw the divine in the extraordinary.

The great powers of Nature always direct men to think of their Author. The Alps are the great altar of Europe. The night sky has forever been the 714 dome of a great temple, inspiring mankind to reverence, trust, and love. The Scriptures for the human race are revealed in earth and Heaven. No hymn touches the heart like the peaceful swell of the sea or the ocean waves. Every year the old world celebrates Pentecost with the glorious blossom of Spring upon each shrub and tree. Autumn is a long All-Saints' day, and the harvest is All-Hallows to Mankind. Even before the human race spread across Asia, Chaldæa, and Egypt, men marked each annual crisis, the solstices, and the equinoxes. They celebrated religious festivals around these events. Now, as then, the material world is a sacred connection between man and God.

Nature is full of religious lessons to the thoughtful man. He reduces the physical matter of the Universe to its forces. He wipes away the phenomena of human history to reveal the immortal spirit. He studies the laws and actions of these forces and this spirit. He cannot fail to be filled with reverence, trust, and the boundless love of the Infinite God, the Author and Support of the Universe. Science has its own New Testament, and the beatitudes of Philosophy are profound. Knowledge of the grass and trees teaches us deeper lessons of love and trust than we can glean from the writings of Fénélon and Augustine. The great Bible of God is always open before mankind, and the eternal flowers of Heaven shed sweet influence upon the mortal blossoms of the earth. The mountain preached to Jesus, and He delivered the great sermon to the people on a mountain. His figures of speech were originally natural figures of fact.

If I am to die tomorrow, then I will only seek advice for today and seek things that last no longer. My ancestors would be nothing more than the ground from which wheat grows. The dead would rot in the earth and their memory would be of little value to me. "I care nothing for the future of mankind! I am one atom in the trunk of a tree. I pay no regard to the roots below or the branches above. I will sow only seeds that yield a harvest for me today. Passion may govern my actions today, and ambition may govern me tomorrow. I will know no other laws or morality." Heroism would be replaced by the savage ferocity of the wolf, the brute cunning of the fox, and the plunder of the vulture. The calm courage inspired by truth and love that looks death firmly in the face would cease to be. Affection, friendship, and charity would be nothing more than the wild notion of the zealot, inspiring ridicule and pity.

Knowing that we will live forever and that the Infinite God loves all of us, we look upon all the evils of the world and know that it is the last hour of darkness before dawn. We may also see a small burning taper, providing just enough light to wait out the return of Spring. Eternal morning follows the night. A rainbow follows the storm that brings life to land and sea. Life rises out of the grave. The soul cannot be contained forever by flesh. No dawn is hopeless, and disaster is only the threshold of delight.

Above the great wide chaos of human error shines the brilliant light of natural human religion. It reveals God as the Infinite Parent of all, perfectly powerful, wise, just, and loving. Every stretch of the Universe beautifully illustrates the Great Bible of God. Material nature is its Old Testament. It is billions of years old and thick with eternal truths under our feet. It glitters with everlasting glory over our heads. Human Nature is the New Testament from the Infinite God. Every day, it reveals a new page as Time turns over the leaves. Immortality stands waiting to repay every virtue not rewarded, every tear not wiped away, every sorrow undeserved, every prayer, and every pure intention and emotion of the heart. Throughout all Nature, Life, and Time, the infinite Loving-kindness of God the Father comes to protect and bless everything that ever existed and ever will exist.

Everything is a thought of the Infinite God. Nature is His prose, and man His Poetry. There is no Chance and no Fate. God's Great Providence permeates the whole Universe and feeds it with everlasting life. Throughout history, there has been evil that we cannot understand or explain. It is impossible to square that evil with God's perfect goodness by any theory our feeble intellect allows us to spin. There is suffering, error, and sin for all mankind. All of these were foreseen by the infinite wisdom of God. His infinite power and justice provided for them all, and they are consistent with His infinite love. To believe otherwise would be to believe that He made the world to amuse His idle hours with the agonies of mankind. Then we might despairingly join in the horrible cry of Heine: "Alas, God's Satire weighs heavily on me! The Great Author of the Universe, the Aristophanes of Heaven, is bent on demonstrating with crushing force to me, the little, earthly, German Aristophanes, how my wittiest sarcasms are only pitiful attempts at jesting in comparison with His, and how miserably I am beneath Him, in humor, in colossal mockery."

No! God is not amused with the results of human suffering. The world is not a Here without a Hereafter. It is not a body without a soul. It is not a chaos with no God. Neither is it a body tormented by a soul, a Here with a worse Hereafter, a world with a God that hates more than half the creatures He has made. There is no Savage, Revengeful, and Evil God. There is an Infinite God, seen everywhere as the Perfect Cause, everywhere as Perfect Providence, transcending all, yet existing in all things. God is perfect power, wisdom, justice, holiness, and love providing for the future welfare of all. God foresees and worries about every bubble that breaks on the great stream of human life and history.

The object of existence in this world is happiness found in and through virtue. Virtue is suffering in this world and happiness in another life. Take away suffering, and there is no more humanity or self-sacrifice. There is no more devotion, heroism, or sublime morality. We are subjected to suffering, because we are intelligent and we ought to be virtuous. If there were no physical evil, there would be no possible virtue. The world would be badly adapted to the destiny of man. The apparent disorders of the physical world and the evils that 717 result from them do not occur in spite of the power and goodness of God. God does not merely allow them. It is His will that there shall be pain in the physical world to provide man an opportunity for virtue and courage.

Anything that favors virtue, increases moral liberty, and serves the greater moral development of the human race is good. Suffering is not the worst condition of man on earth. The worst condition is the moral decline that a lack of physical evil would enable.

Physical evil (internal or external) is connected to our goal of fulfilling the moral law here on earth. Whatever the consequences, we hope that virtue will not fail to be rewarded in another life. Moral law is its own sanction and purpose. It owes nothing to that law of punishment and reward that accompanies it. Though punishment and reward should not be our only inspiration to virtuous action, this law offers a legitimate foundation of comfort and hope.

Morality is the recognition of our duty, whatever the consequences.

Religion is the balance between duty and goodness that must be made in another life through the justice and omnipotence of God.

Religion is as true as morality. Once we acknowledge morality, we must acknowledge its consequences.

The whole of moral existence is included in the harmony of these two words: DUTY and HOPE.

Masonry teaches that God is infinitely good. What motive, what reason, and what possibility can there be for Infinite Power and Infinite Wisdom to be anything but good? Our sorrows in the loss of those so dear to us demonstrate His Goodness. The Being that made us intelligent cannot Himself lack intelligence. He Who has made us to love and sorrow for what we love must love the creatures He has made. In our sorrows, we take refuge in the assurance that He loves us. We know that He does not cause our suffering out of indifference or anger. His chastisements are only the consequences of our acts according to Universal Law, and we may profit by them. He could not show so much love for His creatures by leaving us immoral, untried, and undisciplined. We have faith in the Infinite. We have faith in God's Infinite Love, and it is that faith that must save us.

Suffering and bereavement are not an indication of God's Anger. He is incapable of Anger. He is higher above any such feelings than the distant stars are above the earth. Bad men do not die because God hates them. They die because it is best for them, and it is better for them to be in the hands of the infinitely good God than anywhere else.

Darkness and gloom lie upon the paths men. They stumble at difficulties and trouble. They are trapped by temptation. They are anxious and fearful. Pain, affliction, and sorrow follow them at every step. All this is permanently written upon the tablets of the human heart. It cannot be erased, but Masonry sees and reads it in a new light. It does not expect these trials and sufferings to be removed from life. Masonry expects that the great truth will eventually be believed by all men: that they are the means by which the heart is purified and the soul is energized. This world is our school.

Masonry endorses no creed except the most simple and Sublime One, the universal religion taught by Nature and Reason. Its Lodges are not Jewish, Muslim, or Christian Temples. Masonry promotes the tenets of morality that are common to all religions. It honors and teaches the greatest lessons from every age and every country. It extracts the good and discards the evil. It embraces the truth and rejects the error from all creeds. It acknowledges that a great deal that is good and true lies in us all.

Above all the other great teachers of morality and virtue, it reveres the character of the Great Master, Who died upon the Cross according to the will of the Father. Everyone must admit that, if the world were filled with beings like Him, the great ills of society would be just a memory. All coercion, injury, selfishness, and revenge would cease. All wrongs and sufferings would vanish at once. These human years would be happy, and eternity would be filled with brightness and beauty. The sad music of Humanity, now filled grief and sadness, would be an anthem bursting form the heart of the world, set to the March of Time.

If every man truly imitated that Great, Wise, Good Teacher, clothed with all His faith and all His virtues, how the circle of Life's ills and trials would be narrowed! Our material passions would not overcome our hearts. Desire would no longer successfully tempt men to act wrongly. Curiosity would not make men rash. Ambition would not swerve them from their great allegiance. Injury and insult would be shamed by forgiveness. "Father," men would say, "forgive them; for they know not what they do." None would seek to profit from another's loss. Every man would feel the brotherhood of the entire human race. Perfect faith and trust in the Infinite Goodness of God would soothe every sorrow, pain, and misery. The world around us would be new. Every man would recognize and feel the presence and the beneficent care of a loving Father.

However a Mason may believe with respect to creeds, churches, miracles, and missions from Heaven, he must admit that the Life and character of Jesus, as depicted in the few texts that remain, are worthy of imitation. That Life is an undeniable Gospel. Its teachings cannot be overlooked or discarded. Everyone must admit that it would be happiness to follow Him and perfection to imitate Him. However, men may judge His followers and successors, no one may hold Him in sincere contempt, accuse Him of poor reasoning, nor judge His doctrines as immoral. Whether He was Divine or human, inspired or merely a reforming Essene, His teachings are far nobler, far purer, far less marred by imperfection, and far less earthly, than those of Socrates, Plato, Seneca, Mohammed, or any of the other great moral Reformers of the world.

If our goals were beyond selfish gratification (like His), if our thoughts, 720 words, and actions were used to benefit mankind (the true work we were placed here to do), if our nature was as gentle and tender as His, and if society, country, family, friendship, and home were as dear to us as they were to Him, we would find relief from more than half of the difficulties, diseases, and pain in our lives. Virtuous conduct rather than self-interest, self-improvement without regard to the opinion of others, and acting with a focused purpose from the heart instead of devious motives would free our meditations from many disturbing and irritating questions.

Masonry requires us to preserve the nobler and better affections of our natures. It does not expect us to reject the happiness, love, and honor we receive from others. It does not make us vilify ourselves, abandon self-respect or self-worth, nor overlook the righteousness of our virtue. Our imitation of Him would require nothing less. Both require us to renounce our vices, faults, passions, and self-flattering delusions. We are asked to forego all outward advantages, because they are only gained by sacrificing our inward integrity or by anxious and petty schemes. We are asked to keep a good conscience and let opinion come and go as it will. We are asked to foster self-respect and let go of self-indulgence. We are to renounce our selfishness and the anxiety about what others may think of us. We are to be happy and content with God's great mercies. Unrestrained devotion to ourselves is nothing but a stumbling block. It spreads questions, traps, and problems around us. It darkens the way of Providence and makes the world a far less happy place than it should be.

Masonry teaches as He taught. It promotes affection for our family, tenderness to our friends, gentleness and patience toward our inferiors, pity for the suffering, and forgiveness for our enemies. We are expected to carry a gentle and affectionate nature throughout our lives. We endure pain, toil, agony, and
721 even death with serene and holy beauty. Masonry clearly speaks against selfishness and pride. We must care for the world even though it cares nothing for us. We must not ignore society even though it is unjust. We must not live quietly alone with ourselves, communing only with the mighty dead through their books. No man has ever found peace or light that way. Our experiences of hate, scorn, and neglect of mankind may test us, but there is nothing to do for people except to love them, admire their virtues, pity and accept their faults, and forgive their injustices. Hating your enemies will not help you. Killing them would be worse. Nothing within the compass of the Universe will help you except pity, forgiveness, and love.

We could relieve many of our own difficulties by showing His gentleness, affection, love, and compassion for the errors of mankind. So much depression and trouble would end. How our hatred might soften! A single word, spoken in the sincerest truth, could untie many knots of mystery and misunderstanding. Our rough paths would become smooth, and our crooked paths would straighten. Dark places would be filled with light.

Like science, Morality has its basic truths, and they are justly called moral truths. Moral truths are as certain as mathematical truths. A promise has a requirement to keep it faithfully, just as a triangle has the rule that its angles sum to 180 degrees. You may violate that promise, but you cannot change its nature. You only mislead yourself. The effort of emotion and reason to justify your violation of that trust does not change the essence of what it means to make a promise. Therefore, moral truths are absolute. They do not reshape themselves to satisfy our whim. They are unchanging and always present whether we like it
722 or not. Truth relentlessly condemns the guilty will that thinks denying or pretending to deny truth makes it cease to exist.

Moral truths differ from other truths in that as soon as we perceive them, they become the rule of our conduct. If a promise is made to be kept, it *must* be kept. In addition to *believing* the truth, we must *practice* it.

Practicing these moral truths is an obligation. Moral truths that seem necessary to reason and intellect are obligatory to the will. The moral obligation, like the moral truth behind it, is absolute. Because necessary truths are not *more* or *less* necessary, this obligation is not more or less *binding*. There are degrees of importance among different obligations, but there are no nuances to *obligation itself.* You cannot be *partially* or *nearly* bound by an obligation. You are either *completely* obligated, or *not at all.* The obligation ceases to exist if there is any relief from it.

If an obligation is *absolute*, it is *unchanging* and *universal*. Otherwise, what is an obligation *today* that is not so *tomorrow?* If *my* moral obligation differs from *yours*, it would be relative and conditional. This fact of absolute, unchanging, universal moral obligation is certain. *The good* is the foundation of obligation. If not good, then obligation has *no* foundation, and that is impossible. If one action should be done and another should not be done, there must be an essential difference between the two; otherwise, the moral obligation is arbitrary.

To place *conditions* upon the Good is to annihilate it. Either Good is the basis of our actions or it is nothing. An honest man who keeps his promise, even to his disadvantage, does so because it is *his duty*. When asked why, he answers that it was his duty, because it was *right, just*, and *good*. Beyond that, there is no answer to be made and no question to be asked. No one allows a duty to be imposed upon them without a reason. We satisfy ourselves that duty is commanded by justice, because justice is its own principle. Primary truths justify themselves, and justice, the essential difference between good and evil, is the first truth of morality.

Justice is not a *consequence*, because no other principle is its foundation. 723 Moral truth *forces itself* on man. It does not *emanate from him*. Justice and truth are equally subjective and necessary. We must look to the very nature of the true and good to discover the reason for their necessity. Moral obligation is founded upon the necessary difference between good and evil. It is itself the foundation of liberty. If man has his duties to perform, he must have the ability to fulfill them. He must be able to resist desire, passion, and self-interest in order to obey the law. He must be free. Otherwise, human nature is nothing but a contradiction. The certainty of moral *obligation* requires the certainty of *free will*.

The *will* is free to act, but it may not always accomplish its aim. The power *to accomplish* must not be confused with the power *to will*. Our success may be *limited*, but our will is *sovereign*. We are aware of this sovereign power of will. We feel a force within ourselves that can determine itself in one way or another. When we make a decision of will, we are simultaneously aware of our *ability* to choose the opposite. I am conscious that I am the master of my decision. When *the action* has ended, the consciousness of *the power* that willed it has *not*. That consciousness and the power remain. Free will is the essential and ever-present attribute of the will itself.

When we decide that a free individual has acted in a good or bad way, we have also judged that if he has done well, he deserves compensation. If his actions are ill, he deserves punishment. The severity of that judgment follows our own personal zeal. At times, it will be simply a kind feeling toward a virtuous man or a moderate hostility toward a guilty one. It may be support or great anger. The judgment of reward and punishment is intimately connected to the judgment of good and evil. Whether or not an actual reward or punishment is dispensed, the outcome that is deserved or earned remains. Conceding the 724 idea that consequences are deserved eliminates all real rewards and punishments.

When a wicked man obtains honor, it is merely the appearance of a reward. It is only a material advantage. Reward is essentially moral, and its value is independent from its form. A simple crown of oak, which the early Romans used to reward heroism, was of more real value than all the wealth of the world. It was a sign of the gratitude and admiration of the people. Reward that is deserved is a debt, but without merit, it is a theft.

Good is good in itself. It must be accomplished regardless of the consequences. The results of Good must be beneficial. Happiness is an effect of Good, and Good is a fact without an attached moral idea. Happiness completes it and crowns it.

Virtue without happiness (like crime without misery) is a contradiction. If virtue requires sacrifice, then eternal justice requires sacrifice to be accepted and courageously endured. Virtue is rewarded by happiness in balance with the happiness that was sacrificed. Likewise, crime is punished by unhappiness in proportion to the guilty happiness it sought.

The law that attaches pleasure and sorrow to good and evil is generally accomplished even here below. Order rules over chaos in the world, because the world lasts. Is that order sometimes disturbed? Are happiness and sorrow not always dispensed according to crime and virtue? The absolute judgment of Good, obligation, earned reward, and deserved punishment persevere. We must believe that as He implanted in us the idea of order, He must eventually reestablish the holy harmony of virtue and happiness by His own means.

The Judgment of the Good is the first fact, and it rests upon itself. Its resemblance to the judgment of the true and beautiful demonstrates the secret relationship to morality, metaphysics, and aesthetics. The good is particularly united to the true. Good is distinguished from truth only in that it is truth put into practice. The good is our obligation. They are two inseparable but not identical ideas. Moral Obligation borrows its universal and absolute character from Good.

The obligatory good is the moral law. That it is the foundation of all morality. By it, we separate ourselves passions and self-interest. We admit these exist, but we do not surrender to them.

Reason dictates that moral law coincides with liberty of action. Liberty must co-exist with obligation. Man is free and subject to obligation. Man is a moral being, and that involves the idea of rights. To this we add the notion of reward and punishment, which requires a distinction between good and evil.

Feelings play a key role in morality. Our moral judgments are accompanied by feelings in response to them. From the secret sources of enthusiasm, mankind draws the mysterious virtue that makes heroes. Truth enlightens and illuminates. Feelings inspire us to act. Self-interest also plays its part, because the hope of happiness is the work of God and one of the motives of human action.

This is the sum of the moral constitution of man. His Supreme Object is the Good. His law is Virtue, which often imposes suffering. This makes man greater than all other created beings known to us. This law is harsh and opposes the instinctive desire for happiness. However, the Beneficent Author of man's being has placed in his soul beside the severe law of duty, the sweet, delightful force of feeling. Man attaches happiness to virtue, and where he sees an exception to this, he retains Hope for the end of the journey.

Thus, morality touches religion. It is a sublime necessity of Humanity to see God as the supremely wise Legislator. He is the ever-present Witness and the infallible judge of virtue. The human mind, ever climbing to God, would see morality as fragile except that God is the first principle of the moral law. When we aim to apply a *religious* character to moral law, we run the risk of diminishing 726 its *moral* character. We may credit so much of it to God, that we make His will an arbitrary decree. The will of God as a basis for morality must be just if it is to have any moral authority. Good comes from the will of God alone, but only because His will is the expression of His wisdom and justice. The Eternal Justice of God is the sole foundation of Justice as Humanity perceives and practices it. We attribute good, obligation, reward, and punishment to God, but they exist through their own justification and authority. Religion is the crown of Morality, not its base. The foundation of Morality is in itself.

The Moral Code of Masonry is still greater than that developed by philosophy. To the law of Nature and the law of God, it adds the obligation of a contract. Upon entering the Order, the Initiate obligates himself to every Mason in the world. Once enrolled among the children of Light, every Mason on earth becomes his brother. He owes them the duties, kindnesses, and sympathies of a brother. He may call them for assistance in need, protection from danger, sympathy in sorrow, care in sickness, and a decent burial after death. Every Mason in the world is bound to go to his relief when he is in danger, if there is a greater probability of saving his life than losing their own. No Mason can wrong him of the value of anything, knowingly, nor allow it to be done by another if he can prevent it. No Mason can speak evil of him, to his face or behind his back. Every Mason must keep his secrets when they are lawful, defend his character when attacked, and protect, counsel, and support his widow and orphans. What many thousands owe to him, he owes to each of them. He has solemnly bound himself to be ever ready to carry out these duties. If he fails to do this, he is dishonest, and he has failed his duty. A Mason must never obtain honor or office under false pretenses. He is never to receive kindness and then fail to return that kindness, when needed, without a just reason.

Masonry holds him to his solemn promise to lead a purer life, to bear a nobler generosity, to practice charity of action and opinion. He must be tolerant and loving toward the entire human ace. He must zealously work for the benefit 727 and progress of mankind.

This is the Philosophy and the Morality that are the TRUE WORD of a Master Mason.

The ancients believed Seven Secondary Causes governed the world. These were the universal forces known to the Hebrews by the plural name ELOHIM. These forces, both similar and opposite to each other, produce equilibrium through their contrast and regulate the movements of the spheres. The Hebrews called them the Seven great Archangels and gave them names, each of which is a combination of a word with AL. AL was the first Phœnician Nature-God, the Principle of Light. These Hebrew names conveyed that these forces are His manifestations or emanations. Other cultures saw in these Spirits the government of the Seven Planets known at the time and gave them the names of their great divinities.

Similarly, in Kabbalah, the last Seven Sephiroth constituted ATIK YOMIN (the Ancient of Days). These Seven Sephiroth correspond to the Seven planets, the Seven colors of the spectrum, and the Seven notes of the musical octave.

Seven is the sacred number in all the ancient pantheons and symbols, because it is composed of 3 and 4. It represents the magical power in its full force. It is the Spirit assisted by all the Elemental Powers. It is the Soul served by Nature and the Holy Empire spoken of in the Clavicules of Solomon. There it is symbolized by a warrior, crowned, bearing a triangle on his armor. He stands on a cube, which harnesses two Sphinxes (one white and the other black) pulling in opposite directions and looking back.

There are Seven vices and Seven virtues. The virtues were anciently represented by the Seven Celestial bodies called (at that time) planets. The *Sun* represented FAITH, the opposite of Pride. The *Moon* was HOPE, the enemy of Greed. *Venus* was CHARITY, which opposed Luxury. *Mars* was FORCE, which was stronger than Rage. *Mercury* symbolized PRUDENCE, in contrast to Sloth. *Saturn* was TEMPERANCE, the opposite of Gluttony, and *Jupiter* represented JUSTICE, which overcomes Envy.

The Kabbalistic book of the Apocalypse is said to be closed with Seven Seals. In it, we find the Seven genii of the Ancient Mythologies. The doctrine it conceals is the pure Kabbalah, which was lost to the Pharisees by the time of Jesus. The images that flow through this wondrous epic reveal many symbols to which the numbers 3, 4, 7, and 12 are the keys.

The Cherub placed at the gate of Eden and holding a blazing sword is a symbolic bull or Sphinx with the body of a bull and a human head. It is the Assyrian Sphinx involved in the combat and victory of Mithras. It represents the law of the Mystery, which keeps watch at the door of initiation to ward off the Unworthy. It also represents the grand Magical Mystery expressed by the number 7. This is the "unspeakable word" of the Sages of the school of Alexandria. It is what the Hebrew Kabbalists wrote as יהוה and also אראריתא, (ARARITA – an acronym for the Hebrew: One is His Beginning; One is His Individuality; His Permutation is One). This simultaneously expresses the Unity

728

of the first Principle, the threefold nature of the Secondary Principle, and the dualism that lies in the middle. It is the union of the number 3 with the number 4 in a word composed of four different letters, but formed of seven (one occurring 3 times [א], and one occurring twice [ה]).

The vowels in the Greek language are also *Seven* in number, and were used to designate the Seven planets.

Tsadok was the Supreme God in Phœnicia. His Seven Sons were probably the Seven Cabiri, and he was the Heptaktis (the God of Seven Rays).

From Philo, we learn that Kronos (the Greek Saturn) had six sons or Great Male Gods (Zeus, Poseidon, Apollo, Arēs, Hēphaistos, and Hermes) and Seven daughters (the Titanides). The Persians worshiped Ahura Masda or Ormuzd and the Six Amshaspands. Three of these were Lords of the Empires of Light, Fire, and Splendor. The Babylonians similarly worshipped Bal and the Gods, and the Chinese revered Shangti and the Six Chief Spirits. The Greeks also identified Seven female deities: Rhea, the wife of Kronos, Hērē, Athēnē, Artemis, Aphroditē, Hestia, and Dēmētēi. In the Orphic pantheon, Gaia produced the fourteen Titans (Seven male and Seven female. Among these, Kronos was the greatest of the males. Like the number *Seven*, the number nine (3 x 3 or the triple triangle) appears in the three Mœraê or Fates, the three Centimanēs, and the three Cyclopēs (the offspring of Ouranos and Gaia or of Heaven and Earth).

The metals, like the colors, were Seven in number. A metal and a color were assigned to each planet. Gold was assigned to the Sun and silver to the Moon. 729

The palace of Deioces in Ecbatana had Seven circular walls of different colors. The two innermost walls were covered respectively by silver and gold.

The Seven Spheres of Borsippa were represented by the Seven Stories (each of a different color) of the tower or unfinished pyramid of Bel at Babylon.

Pharaoh saw in his dream, which Joseph interpreted, *Seven* good ears of wheat and *Seven* withered ears, blasted by the East wind. The Seven thin ears devoured the Seven good ears, and Joseph interpreted these to foreshadow Seven years of plenty followed by Seven years of famine.

Ebn Hesham described a tomb in Yemen containing a woman with *Seven* collars of *pearls* around her neck, Seven bracelets and armlets on each hand, and Seven rings around each ankle. A tablet accompanied her with an inscription stating that, after attempting in vain to purchase grain from Joseph, she (Tajah, the daughter of Dzu Shefar) and her people died of famine.

A deep study of the mysteries of science demonstrates that purely mechanical physics and the notion of a strictly material nature to the causes and actions of Divinity explain nothing and should leave anyone unsatisfied!

The traces of a single doctrine (always the same and carefully concealed) are found through the veil of all the ancient religious and mystical allegories, in all the sacred writings, in the worn stones of ancient ruins and temples, on the sphinx of Assyria or Egypt, in the marvelous pictures in the sacred pages of the Vedas of India, in the strange symbolism of alchemy, and in the initiation ceremonies practiced by all the mystery schools. This hidden philosophy seems to have been the forerunner of all religions. It is the secret lever of all the intellectual forces, the key of all divine mysteries, and the absolute Queen of Society. For a time, it was exclusively reserved for the education of Priests and Kings.

730   This doctrine had reigned in Persia with the Magi. It provided India with the most marvelous traditions and luxurious poetry, grace, and terror in its symbols. It civilized Greece by the sounds of the lyre of Orpheus. It veiled the principles of all the sciences and the whole progression of the human spirit. It is found in the calculations of Pythagoras. Fable is filled with its miracles, but history was confused with fable. Empires were shaken by its oracles. Tyrants turned pale on their thrones. Once confused, this doctrine weighed on all minds by either curiosity or fear. It seemed to everyone that nothing was impossible with this science. It commanded the elements, knew the language of the planets, and controlled the movements of the stars. At its command, the moon fell, bleeding, from Heaven. The dead rose from their graves and spoke by the wind whistling through their skulls. It controlled Love and Hate. It conferred upon the human heart either Paradise or Hell. It manifested all forms, distributing beauty or deformity as it pleased. It made men into animals and animals into men. It even dispensed Life and Death. It could bestow upon its masters riches (through the transmutation of base metals), and immortality (by its quintessence and elixir, compounded of gold and light).

This had been magic from the time of Zoroaster and Manes, from Orpheus and Apollonius Thyaneus. When the influence of Christianity overshadowed the splendid dreams and great aspirations of the school of Alexandria, this philosophy retreated into shadow and became more hidden and more mysterious than ever.

Nonetheless, the root of magic is science, just as the root of Christianity is love. In the Symbolism of the Christian Gospels, we find the incarnate WORD adored in its infancy by three magi guided by a star (the three-fold and the sign of the microcosm). He received gold, frankincense, and myrrh, another mysterious group of three that allegorically contains the highest secrets of Kabbalah.

Christianity should not have hated magic, but human ignorance always fears the unknown. Science was forced to conceal itself to avoid the
731   impassioned aggression of a blind love. It concealed itself in new symbols. It concealed its efforts and disguised its hopes. It created the jargon of alchemy and deceived the masses who were greedy for gold. Alchemy was only a living language to the true disciples of Hermes.

The Degrees of Masonry were utilized, if not invented, to partially unveil this doctrine to its Initiates. The Alchemists did not directly insert their own language, but the oral instruction following the initiation would be clear to one who had the key, even if it seemed incomprehensible or absurd to others.

The Prophecy of Ezekiel and the Apocalypse of St. John are poorly explained, and few Christians have ever attempted to understand them. These two Kabbalistic works were intended to explain this philosophy to Priests and Kings. They are closed with Seven seals for all faithful believers and would be perfectly clear to the non-believer initiated in the occult sciences.

Many Christians believe that the scientific and magical Clavicules of Solomon are lost. Nevertheless, it is certain that in the domain of intelligence governed by the WORD, nothing that is written is lost. The things that men no longer understand cease to exist for them alone, and their world descends into enigma and mystery.

The mysterious founder of the Christian Church was revered in His cradle by the three Magi. These men were priestly ambassadors from the three parts of the known world and represented the three worlds of the occult philosophy.

In the school of Alexandria, Magic and Christianity almost take each other by the hand in the work of Ammonius Saccos and Plato. The Hermetic Philosophy is expressed almost completely in the writings attributed to Dionysius the Areopagite. Synesius treatise on dreams, expanded by Cardan, includes hymns that could serve a Philosophical Church of Emanuel Swedenborg, if such a church could have a liturgy.

The reign of Emperor Julian encouraged this philosophical debate and regretted nothing in the loss of the old world except its magnificent symbols and gracious images. He was an enlightened Initiate of the first order, who believed in the unity of God and the universal Dogma of the Trinity. He was not a Pagan, but a Gnostic who embraced the allegories of Greek polytheism. It was *732* his misfortune to be more influenced by Orpheus than Jesus Christ.

When Religion and Philosophy become separate schools or paths, human intellect advances more than its Faith, and while habit may sustain faith for some time, its vitality is gone.

Those who tried to replace science with faith, experience with abstraction, and reality with fantasy were misguided fools who led primitive Christianity astray. For many ages, they tried to extinguish Magism, but they only shrouded in darkness the ancient discoveries of the human mind. Now, we grope in the dark to find the key to the phenomena of nature again. All natural phenomena depend upon a single and immutable law. It is represented by the philosopher's stone and its symbolic form is a cube. This law is expressed in Kabbalah by the number 4, and furnished the Hebrews with all the mysteries of their divine Tetragrammaton.

Everything is contained in the four letters of the Tetragrammaton. It is the *Azoth* of the Alchemists, the *Thoth* of the Bohemians, and the *Taro* of the Kabbalists. It provides the Adept with the last word of the human Sciences and the Key of the Divine Power. He who understands how to access this key also understands the necessity of never revealing it. If Œdipus, rather than *slaying* the Sphinx, had *conquered* it and driven it into Thebes bound to his chariot, he would have been King without the need for incest, disaster, and exile. If Psyche had persuaded Love to reveal himself with affection, she would never have lost him. Love is one of the mythological images of the grand secret and the grand agent, because it equally expresses an action and a passion, emptiness and fullness, and an arrow and a wound. The Initiates should understand this, but Masonry never says too much to prevent the unworthy from obtaining this truth.

When Science was defeated in Alexandria by the fanaticism of the murderers of Hypatia, it concealed itself under Christian disguises in the works of Ammonius, Synosius, and Dionysius the Areopagite. It became necessary to explain miracles with superstition and to veil science in confusing language. 733 Symbolic writing was revived, and figures and puzzles were created to express the whole doctrine in a sign. A single word might reveal a deep well of meaning. What was the goal of the seekers of knowledge? They sought the secret of the great work, the Philosophal Stone, perpetual motion, the method of squaring the circle, or universal medicine. This language spared them from persecution by making them a joke. In truth, each of these themes expressed one of the forces of the grand magical secret. This continued until the time of the Roman de la Rose. It explained the mysterious and magical meaning of Dante's poem. He borrowed it from the High Kabbalah, the vast, concealed source of the universal philosophy.

It is no surprise that man knows little of the powers of human will. He knows nothing of its nature or mode of operation. His own will can move his arm or compel another to obey him. His thoughts, expressed in writing, can influence and lead other men, but this is an incomprehensible mystery to him. No less a mystery is the will of Deity, with the strength to create a Universe.

The powers of the will are still unknown. We continue to debate whether many unusual physical phenomena result from the power of the will alone or some other natural cause. However, it is clear that a concentrated effort of the will is necessary for success.

These phenomena must be real, unless we dismiss the value of the human witness. If they are real, there is no reason to doubt the use of powers that were originally termed magical. Nothing is better documented than the extraordinary abilities of the Brahmins. No religion is supported by stronger testimony, and no one has successfully explained what might be called their miracles.

How far in this physical world can the mind and soul act independent of the body? We still do not know. The mystery of the will acting without physical contact or the phenomena of dreams continues to confound our wisest scholars. Their explanations are just a Babel of words.

Man still knows very little about the forces of nature. He is surrounded, controlled, and governed by them while he vainly thinks he is free from them. He is subject to the universal nature and her many infinite forces until he becomes their master. He cannot ignore their existence nor simply be their neighbor. *734*

There is a great force in nature, by which means, a single man who knows how to direct it could revolutionize and change the face of the world.

This force was known to the ancients. It is a universal force, whose Supreme law is equilibrium or balance. If science could only learn how to control it, it would be possible to change the order of the Seasons, to replace night with day, to send a thought in an instant around the world, to heal or harm at a distance, to give our words universal success, and make them reverberate everywhere.

This force was partially revealed by the blind guesses of the followers of Mesmer. It is exactly what the Adepts of the Middle Ages called the elementary matter of the great work. The Gnostics believed that it made up the fiery body of the Holy Spirit, and it was revered in the secret rites of the Sabbath or the Temple under the symbolic figure of Baphomet or the hermaphroditic goat of Mendes.

There is a Life-Principle of the world, a universal force, supporting two natures: love and anger. This force surrounds and penetrates everything. It is a ray released from the glory of the Sun and held by the weight of the atmosphere. It is the body of the Holy Spirit, the universal Agent, and the Serpent devouring its own tail. The alchemists recognized this ether of electricity, magnetism, life, light, and heat. Modern physical science speaks of it incoherently, identifying nothing but its effects. Theology might inappropriately apply to it all of its supposed definitions of spirit. It is at rest. It cannot be observed directly by any human sense. When it is disturbed or in motion, we cannot explain its mode of action. We may call it a "fluid" and speak of its "currents", but this simply covers our ignorance with meaningless words.

Force attracts force. Life attracts life. Health attracts health. It is a law of nature.

If two children constantly live together, day and night, and one is weak *735* and the other strong, the strong will absorb the weak, and the weak will perish.

In schools, some students absorb the intellect of the others, and in every circle of people, some individual comes to possess the wills of the others.

One man is often carried away by the crowd in morals as well as physics. The human will has an almost absolute power in determining one's acts, and every external demonstration of a will has an influence on external things.

Tissot blamed most sicknesses upon disorders of the will or the twisted influences of the wills of others. We are influenced and controlled by the wills of those who have similar interest. Those who share our problems have an even stronger effect. To embrace the weaknesses of an individual is to control him.

We make him an instrument in the cycle of mistakes and evils. When two individuals (one strong and one weak) with similar faults interact, the weaker is lost in the stronger. One mind is imprisoned by the other, and often the weaker, failing to free himself, falls lower than before.

We each have a dominant defect that an enemy can use to bind us. In some, it is vanity. In others, it is laziness. In most, it is egotism. If a cunning and evil spirit takes control of this defect, you are lost. You are in the grip of insanity, controlled by a force outside yourself. You instinctively fear anything that could free you from this cage, and you will not hear the words that might cure your insanity.

Miracles are the natural effects of exceptional causes.

The immediate action of the human will over our bodies, without apparent physical cause, is a physical miracle.

The influence upon the human will that captivates our thoughts, changes our firmest resolutions, and halts our most violent passions is a moral miracle.

It is a common error to regard miracles as effects without causes, as contradictions of nature, or fantasies of the Divine imagination. Men do not consider that a single miracle of this kind would break universal harmony and return the Universe to Chaos.

Absurd miracles are impossible for God Himself. If God could be absurd for a single instant, neither He nor the Universe would exist an instant afterward. To expect an effect of the Divine Free Will whose cause is unacknowledged or does not exist, is "tempting" God. It pushes us into the void.

God acts through His works in Heaven by angels and His works on earth by men.

In the heaven of human ideas, humanity creates God. Men think that God has made them in His image, because they make Him in theirs.

The domain of mankind is physical, visible nature. If he does not rule the planets or the stars, he can at least calculate their movement, measure their distances, and equate his will with their influence. He can modify the air, act to an extent upon the seasons, cure and inflict disease, preserve life, and cause death.

The absolute in reason and will is the greatest power that any man can obtain. This power causes what the masses admire as miracles.

POWER is the wise use of the will, which makes Death itself serve its own purpose.

Omnipotence is the most absolute Liberty, and absolute Liberty cannot exist without perfect equilibrium. The columns (JACHIN and BOAZ) are the unlimited POWER (VICTORY) and GLORY (SPLENDOR OF PERFECTION) of the Deity. They are the seventh and eighth SEPHIROTH of Kabbalah, whose equilibrium result in the eternity or STABILITY of His plans and works and an undivided, unlimited KINGDOM (the ninth and tenth SEPHIROTH). The Temple

736

of Solomon, with its stately symmetry, erected without the sound of any tool of metal is to us a symbol for this. The Most Perfect of Prayers says, "For Thine is the KINGDOM, the POWER, and the GLORY, for all the ages! Amen!"

The ABSOLUTE is the very *necessity* of BEING. It is the unchanging law of Reason and Truth. It is THAT WHICH IS, but THAT WHICH IS is, in some way, before HE WHO IS. God Himself *exists for a reason*. He does not exist *accidentally*. It is impossible that He could have *not* existed. His Existence is *necessary*. He exists for a Supreme and inevitable REASON. That REASON is THE ABSOLUTE. We must believe in IT in order for our faith to have a solid foundation. It has been said that God is a Hypothesis, but Absolute Reason is not so. It is essential to Existence. 737

Saint Thomas said, "*A thing does not exist just because God wills it*, BUT GOD WILLS IT BECAUSE IT IS JUST." If he had further developed this thought, he would have discovered the true Philosopher's Stone, the magical elixir that turns the trials of the world into golden mercies. Just as God must BE, He must be just, loving, and merciful. He cannot be unjust, cruel, or merciless. He cannot repeal the law of right and wrong or of merit and accountability. Moral laws are as absolute as physical laws. There are impossible things. Just as you cannot make two and two equal five, it is impossible to make a thing exist and not exist at the same time. Therefore, it is impossible for the Deity to make crime good, and love and gratitude evils. Likewise, it was as impossible to make Man perfect with his bodily senses and desires, as it was to make him responsive to pleasure and not pain.

Moral laws are the *enactments* of the Divine WILL, only because they *follow* Absolute WISDOM and REASON. They are the *Revelations* of the Divine NATURE. This alone gives Deity the *right* to enact them. Only in this way can we obtain a certainty of Faith that the Universe is one Harmony.

Belief in the Reason of God (and in the God of Reason) makes Atheism impossible. The Idolaters have made the Atheists.

This correspondence reveals all the forces of Nature to the Sage. It is the key of the Grand Arcanum, the root of the Tree of Life, and the science of Good and Evil.

The Absolute is REASON. Reason exists by means of Itself. It IS BECAUSE IT IS, and not because we suppose it exists. IT IS where nothing *exists*. Nothing could possibly exist without IT. Reason is Necessity, Law, the Rule of all Liberty, and the direction of every Initiative. If God IS, HE IS by Reason. The idea of an Absolute Deity separate from Reason is the IDOL of Black Magic and the PHANTOM of the Demon.

The Supreme Intelligence must be *rational*. In philosophy, God may be 738 no more than a Hypothesis, but God is a Hypothesis reinforced by Human Reason. To personify the Absolute Reason is to discover the Divine Ideal.

NECESSITY, LIBERTY, and REASON! Behold the great and Supreme Triangle of the Kabbalists!

FATALITY, WILL, and POWER! This corresponds to the Divine Triangle in human nature.

FATALITY is the inevitable linking together of effects and causes in a given order.

WILL is the power directing the forces of the Intellect, reconciling the liberty of the individual with necessity.

You must explore this philosophical path yourself. "Seek," say the Holy Writings, "and you shall find." Yet discussion is not forbidden, and without a doubt, the subject will be fully explained in your hearing hereafter. Verify, disprove, and discuss. By these actions, the truth is attained.

The greatest use of Thought is to explore the great Mysteries of the Universe and seek to solve them. This is the principal distinction between Man and the animals. In all ages, the Intellect has tried to understand and explain the Nature of the Supreme Deity.

It was obvious to the *philosophers* of all ages that one Reason and one Will created and governed the Universe. It was the ancient *religions* that tried to create many gods. The *Nature* of the One Deity and the means by which the Universe began have always tortured the human intellect. The Kabbalists have dealt primarily with these questions.

In one sense, we can have no actual knowledge of the Absolute Itself. Our means of obtaining what many consider knowledge depends only upon our senses. If *seeing* and *feeling* are knowledge, we would have no Soul. Science would have no electricity and no magnetism. We see, feel, and taste a chemical substance to discover something about its *qualities*, but it is only when we use the substance in combination with another that we truly learn its *effects*. Only then, do we really know something about its *nature*. The combinations and experiments of Chemistry give us knowledge of the nature and powers of most animal and vegetable substances. However, the Soul is beyond the knowledge of our senses, and it can only be known by its effects. Magnetism and electricity, when at rest, are equally beyond our senses. When they are in action, we see, feel, hear, taste, and smell only their effects. We do not observe what they *are*, but only what they *do*. Similarly, we can know the attributes of Deity only through His manifestations. To ask anything more is to ask for something we have given no name. God is a Power, and we know nothing of any Power *itself*, but only its effects, results, and actions. We know what Reason teaches us.

In modern times, we have tried so hard to escape from all *material* ideas of Deity and so narrowed our ideas about GOD that we are left with no idea of Him at all. In identifying Him as a pure immaterial Spirit, we have made the word *Spirit* mean *nothing*. We can only say that He is a *Somewhat* with certain attributes like Power, Wisdom, and Intelligence. Comparing Him to LIGHT would now be considered unphilosophical, if not the equivalent of Atheism. We think we must pity the ancients for their inadequate ideas of Deity as the Light-Principle, the invisible essence or substance from which visible Light flows.

Yet our own holy writings continually speak of Him as Light. Therefore, it is hardly surprising that the Sabeans and Kabbalists did the same, especially since they did not regard Him as the *visible* Light we see, but rather the Primordial Ether-Ocean from which light flows.

Before the creation, did the Deity dwell alone in the Darkness, or in the Light? Did the Light co-exist with Him or was it created after an eternity of darkness? If it co-existed with Him, did it flow from Him, filling all space as He did? Did He and the Light fill the same place and every place?

MILTON says, expressing the Hebraic doctrine:

"Hail, Holy Light, offspring of Heaven first-born,
Or of the Eternal, co-eternal beam!
May I express thee unblamed, *since God is Light.*
And never but in unapproached Light
Dwelled from Eternity; dwelled then in Thee,
Bright effluence of bright Essence uncreate."

740

An introduction to Kabbalah says, "LIGHT, the most supreme of all things and most Lofty, Limitless, and styled INFINITE, can be obtained by no thought or speculation; and its VERY SELF is withdrawn and removed beyond all understanding. Before all things, it existed, produced, created, formed, and formed by Emanation. In it was neither Time, Head, nor Beginning, since it always existed, and remains forever, without beginning or end."

"Before the Emanations flowed forth and before creation, the Supreme Light was infinitely extended and filled the whole WHERE. With respect to Light, no vacuum could exist. No space was unoccupied, but the ALL was filled with that Light of the Infinite, thus extended without end. Nothing existed except that extended Light, which, with a certain single and simple equality, was everywhere."

In the Introduction to the Zohar, AIN SOPH is called *Light*, because it is impossible to express it by any other word.

To conceive of God as an actuality and not as a mere non-substance or name (non-*existence*), Kabbalists (like the Egyptians) imagined Him to be "a most hidden Light." This is AUR, not our material and visible Light, but the Substance from which Light flows. It is like *fire* in relation to heat and flame. To the Sabeans, the Sun was the only manifestation of this Light or Ether. They worshipped it, but not as the symbol of dominion and power. God was the *Phôs Noëton*, the Light perceived only by the Intellect. God was the Light-Principle (the Light-Ether), from which souls emanated and to which they returned.

To the Phœnicians, Light, Fire, and Flame were the sons of Kronos. They are the Trinity in the Chaldæan Oracles, the AOR of the Deity manifested in flame that sprang from the invisible *Fire*.

In the first three Persian Amshaspands, the Lords of LIGHT, FIRE, and SPLENDOR are the AOR, ZOHAR, and ZAYO (*Light, Splendor,* and *Brightness*) of Kabbalah. The first of these is called AOR MUPALA (*Wonderful* or *Hidden* Light).

741 It is unrevealed or invisible. It is KETHER, the first Emanation or *Sephirah*, the *Will* of Deity. The second is NESTAR (*Concealed*). It is CHOKMAH, the second *Sephirah*, or the Intellectual Strength of the Deity. The third is METANOTSATS (*Sparkling*). It is BINAH, the third *Sephirah*, or the intellectual *creative* capacity. In other words, they are THE VERY SUBSTANCE of light *in* the Deity. *Fire* is that light, limited and furnished with attributes to make it visible, but it remains unrevealed in its *splendor.*

Masonry is a search for Light that leads us directly back to Kabbalah. The Initiate will find the source of many doctrines in that ancient and seldom understood mixture of philosophy and myth. He may come to understand the Hermetic philosophers, the Alchemists, all the Protestant Thinkers of the late Middle Ages, and Emanuel Swedenborg.

The Hansavati Rich, a celebrated Sanskrit Stanza, says: "He is Hansa (the Sun), dwelling in light; Vasu, the atmosphere dwelling in the firmament; the invoker of the gods (Agni), dwelling on the altar (i.e., the altar fire); the guest (of the worshipper), dwelling in the house (the domestic fire); the dweller amongst men (as consciousness); the dweller in the most excellent orb (the Sun); the dweller in truth; the dweller in the sky (the air); born in the waters, in the rays of light, in the verity (of manifestation), in the Eastern mountains; the Truth (itself)."

"In the beginning," says a Sanskrit hymn, "arose the Source of golden light. *He was the only born Lord of all that is.* He established the earth and the sky. Who is the God to Whom we shall offer our sacrifice?"

"He who gives life; He who gives strength; Whose blessing all the bright gods desire; *Whose shadow is immortality; Whose shadow is death;* Who is the God?"

"He through Whom the sky is bright and the earth for us; He through Whom the Heaven was established, no, the highest Heaven; He who measured out the light in the air; Who is the God?"

"He to Whom the Heaven and earth, standing firm by His will, look up trembling inwardly; He over Whom the rising sun shines forth; Who is the God?"

742 "Wherever the mighty water clouds went, where they placed the seed and lit the fire, thence arose He Who is the only life of the bright gods; Who is the God?"

In Indian philosophy, the WORD of God is the universal and invisible Light. It emits its blaze in the Sun, Moon, Planets, and other Stars and may be seen in this way by our senses. Philo calls it the "Universal Light", which loses some of its purity and splendor as it descends from the intellectual to the physical world. It manifests itself outwardly from the Deity. Kabbalah says that only part of the Infinite Light flowed into the emptiness that was prepared within the Infinite Light and Wisdom to receive creation. The Sephiroth emanating from the Deity were the rays of His splendor.

The Chaldæan Oracles said, "The intellect of the Creator stirred to action, spoke out, and formed the universals of every possible form and fashion within itself by thought. They flowed forth from the One Source . . . Before fabricating the Universe, Deity (in the form of Dominion) suggested a reasoned and unchangeable universal, the impression of the form of which pervades the Universe. That Universe, once formed and fashioned, became visibly beautified in infinitely varying types and forms. The Source and fountain of all these forms is one. . . . Ideas and forms from the Creative source succeeded each other in relation to ever-progressing Time and intimately received THE PRIMAL ETHER or FIRE. All these Universals, Primal Types, and Ideas flowed forth from (and are part of) the first Source of the Creative Power, which is perfect in itself."

The Chaldæans called the Supreme Deity ARAOR (Father of Light). From Him flowed the light above the world that illuminates the heavenly regions. This Light or Fire was the Symbol of the Divine Essence extending itself into inferior spiritual natures. The Chaldæan oracles said, "The Father took from Himself and did not confine His proper fire within His intellectual potency . . . All things are begotten from one Fire."

The Sabeans believed that all inferior spiritual beings were emanations from the Supreme Deity. Proclus wrote, "The progression of the gods is one and continuous, proceeding downward from the comprehensible and dormant unities, and ending in the last partition of the Divine cause."

It is impossible to speak clearly of the Divinity. Attempting to express 743 His attributes by using abstractions, limits us to negatives. We lose sight of our ideas and wander through a wilderness of words. We add Superlative to Superlative and call Him *best*, *wisest*, and *greatest*, but this is just an exaggeration of human qualities. Reason teaches us that there is only one God, and that He is a Perfect and Beneficent Being. However, our minds are incapable of penetrating the Divine *Nature*, the *Substance* of the Deity, the manner of His Existence, or the mode of creation of His Universe. We cannot clearly define Omnipotence, Omniscience, Infinity, or Eternity. We have no more right to assign intelligence to Him than any other human quality extended indefinitely. We cannot attribute our senses or bodily organs to Him, as the Hebrew writings do.

We satisfy ourselves by concluding that the Deity is not like anything that constitutes our own existence (as we understand it). Thus, He becomes logically nothing (*Non-Ens*). The Ancients saw no difference between this idea and Atheism. They thought of Him as something real. It is a necessary part of Human Nature. A non-idea of the Deity cannot be shared or appreciated by the masses. To them, God will always be The Father who is in Heaven. He is a King on His Throne and a Being with human emotions. He sympathizes with misfortune and becomes angry at their wrongs. He forgives them when they repent, and He listens to their prayers. It is the Humanity, more than the

Divinity, of Christ that inspires most Christians to worship Him more than the Father.

Kabbalists use the expression: "the Light of the Substance of The Infinite." According to Saint John, Christ was, "the Light that lights every man that comes into the world." "That Light was the life of men." "The Light shone in the darkness, and the darkness did not comprehend it."

The ancient ideas about Light were no less correct than our own. They did not see any of the qualities of matter in Light. Science may define Light to be a flood of particles of *matter*, flowing from the Sun and Stars and moving through space to reach us. But according to these theories, what mechanism and force could propel these minute particles across such vast distances of space? What has happened to the countless multitudes of particles that have reached the earth since creation? Have they increased the earth's mass? If Light is matter, why does it only travel in straight lines?

The normal characteristics of matter have nothing to do with Light, Heat, Electricity, and Magnetism. The electric spark produces light and so does the flint cutting off particles of steel. Molten iron radiates light. Organisms breaking down decaying wood emit it. Heat is produced by friction and pressure, and to explain this, Science identifies *latent* heat that is supposed to exist without producing actual heat. What quality of matter enables lightning to blaze so quickly from the Heavens that it splits an oak tree?

We are profoundly ignorant of the nature of these mighty agents of Divine Power, and we conceal this ignorance with words that have no meaning. Could we say for certain that Light does not flow from the Deity? All the religions of all the Ages of the World believed it did.

All truly authoritative religions are derived from Kabbalah and eventually return to it. All of the great scientific and religious dreams of enlightened philosophers (Jacob Bœhme, Emanuel Swedenborg, Louis Claude de Saint-Martin, and others) are borrowed from Kabbalah. All Masonic organizations and bodies owe to it their Secrets and Symbols.

Kabbalah venerates the union of Universal Reason with the Divine Word. It establishes an eternal equilibrium of being by two apparently opposed forces. It alone reconciles Reason with Faith, Power with Liberty, and Science with Mystery. It holds the keys to the Past, Present, and Future.

The allegories of the Bible express the religious science of the Hebrews in a veiled and incomplete way. The doctrine of Moses and the Prophets is founded upon the same ideas as that of the ancient Egyptians, which also had its own outward meaning and its veils. The Hebrew books were written to carry forward the memory of traditions, and they were written in Symbols that could not be read by the unworthy. The Pentateuch and poems of the Prophets were the elementary books of doctrine, morals, or liturgy. The true secret and traditional philosophy was added later under less transparent veils. Thus, a second Bible was born that was unknown to, or at least misunderstood by, the

536

Christians. They dismissed it as a collection of monstrous absurdities. The wise man knows that it contains everything that the geniuses of philosophy and religion have ever imagined of the sublime. It is a treasure surrounded by thorns, and a diamond concealed in rough stone.

Upon entering the Sanctuary of Kabbalah, one has to admire a doctrine that is so logical, simple, and absolute. It is the necessary union of ideas and symbols. It reveres the most fundamental realities by primitive characters (the Trinity of Words, Letters, and Numbers). It is a philosophy that is as simple as the alphabet. It is as profound and infinite as the Word. Its theories are more complete and luminous than those of Pythagoras. It may be summarized by counting on fingers, an Infinite held in the palm of a child's hand. It contains ten ciphers, twenty-two letters, a triangle, a square, and a circle. These are the elementary principles of the written Word. The reflection of that spoken Word created the world!

This is the doctrine of Kabbalah, which you will no doubt study.

According to the Kabbalists, the Absolute Deity has no name. The terms applied to Him are אור פשוט (AUR PASHOT, the Most Simple or Pure Light) and אין סוף (AIN SOPH or INFINITE). This is before any Emanation when there was no space or empty place. All was infinite Light.

Before the Deity created anything (Ideal, limited and comprehensible, or any form), He was alone and without form. There could be no thought or comprehension of Him in any way. It is forbidden to form any Idea or Figure of Him by any letter, not even by the letter He (ה) or the letter Yōd (י), even though these letters are contained in the Holy Name.

After He created this Idea, this limited and existing-in-thought Nature, which is represented by the ten SEPHIROTH or Rays and the First Man (ADAM KADMON), He descended into it. Only by means of this Idea might He be called by the name TETRAGRAMMATON. Only by this name could the created things know of His likeness. 746

When the Infinite God willed to create what was to flow forth, He contracted Himself in the center of His light to concentrate that most intense sphere of light. This is the first contraction called צמצם (Tsemsum).

אדם קודמן (ADAM KADMON, the First Man) is the first Atziluthic (Archetypal) emanation from the Infinite Light. It enters the emptiness of Space and gives all the other degrees and systems their beginnings. It is the Adam that is prior to all. It is the first. In it are revealed ten spheres of emanation. From these sprang the form of man with his ten spheres, reaching from the highest point to the lowest. From this flow all the systems.

The Infinite Light in its most Secret Nature is too brilliant to be experienced, except through the medium of this Adam Kadmon. Its illuminating light emanates in streams and pours through windows that might symbolize the ears, eyes, nostrils, and mouth.

The light emanating from this Adam Kadmon is one, but it becomes denser as it descends from one window or grade to the next.

Atziluth comes from the word אצל (ATZIL, to emanate or flow forth). This is the world of Emanation. When the primal space was emptied, the surrounding Light of the Infinite and the Light entered into the void without touching each other. The Light of the Infinite flowed into the void through a narrow path to begin its Emanation. Through that path, the Infinite Light is united with the Light that was within the void, which is always inferior.

Atziluth is the first of the four worlds or systems of Kabbalah.

747 The ten Sephiroth of the world of Atziluth are the ten Nekudot (vowels and points) of the Hebrew alphabet.

אין סוף (AIN SOPH) is the Cause of Causes. It means *"endless"*, because there is no limit to Its greatness. Nothing can comprehend it. This occasionally applies to KETHER (the CROWN and the first emanation), because it is the Throne of the Infinite and hiding place of Ain Soph.

The *Emech Hammelech* says that before anything existed, He (from His mere will) decided to make worlds. At that time, there was no empty space for creation, because all space, fixed within the center of Himself for the purpose of creation, was filled with the light of His Substance.

He then measured off within His own Substance the width, breadth, and length of a spherical space to be made vacant for the creation of these worlds. He compressed and folded the Light contained there and lifted it higher so that a place was created, unoccupied by the Primal Light.

This space was not completely devoid of that Light. Traces of the Primal Light remained where It had been.

Before the Emanations flowed from It, before all things were created, the Supreme Light was infinitely extended to fill the whole *Where*. Nothing *existed* apart from that extended light. It was AIN SOPH AUR, the Infinite Light.

When the mind of the Extended Light decided of Its own will to cause the creation of worlds, It compressed and receded in every direction from a 748 central point to form a perfect spherical void in space. This was the space where the Emanations could exist. This is where all Created things could receive their Form.

This void of space is clothed by the remaining traces of that withdrawn light of the Infinite. It is the innermost layer of form, and the nearest to His substance. It is the AUR PENAI AL, the *Light of the Face of God*.

There is a middle space surrounding the great sphere *between* the Infinite Light and the substance contained *within* It. It is the GREAT SPLENDOR.

The splendid light that surrounds the void of space is said to be like a point in the center of a circle. This point in the center of the Great Light is the Ether of space.

It is somewhat heavier than the Light and not as Subtle, *although it is not perceptible by the Senses.* It is the Primal Ether and the *Soul of the World* extending everywhere.

The Light *shining forth* from the Deity is still *connected* to Him. "It is flashed forth from Him, and yet all continues to be perfect unity . . . The Sephiroth, sometimes called the *Persons* of the Deity, *are His rays*, by which He is enabled to perfectly manifest Himself.

The Introduction to the Zohar says:

The first compression was caused in order to raise the Primal Light and create an empty space. In the Deity's joy and exhilaration in anticipation of the creation of His Holy People, the remaining traces of that raised Light compressed into points. He flowed forth in His delight, and from this commotion, an abstract power of judgment was generated. These compressed points of Light within the sphere are the collection of Hebrew letters. *By these individual letters, He writes the finite expressions and limited forms of Himself upon the Book.*

Fire and water are not greatly moved by the wind, but the Infinite was moved within himself. With great, blinding flashes of lightning, He flashed and shone within the sphere, from the center to the outside and back again. This motion is exhilaration. Dividing this exhilaration within Himself, He generated the form of the letters. 749

This same exhilaration within Himself determined the *forms* of creation. It was as if the Deity said, "Let this Sphere be the appointed place and let all worlds be created!"

By radiating and shining, He made the points sparkle. He combined different individual points to form the *letters*. In the image of these letters, THE BLESSED set forth the laws of His Wisdom.

It is impossible to obtain an understanding of the creation of man except through the mystery of letters. In this world, The Infinite is nothing except the letters of the Alphabet and their combinations. All the worlds are Letters and Names, but the Author of all has no name.

This void of space is "clothed" by the remaining traces of that withdrawn light of the Infinite. It is the *innermost* layer of form and the *nearest* to His substance. It is the AUR PENAI AL, the *Light of the Face of God*, by which we may understand the Light of the Substance.

After this clothing came into existence, He contracted it to lift up the lower half. This is the *third* contraction. In this way, He made an empty space for the worlds that could not use the great Light of the clothing. The end of this world was as bright and excellent as its beginning. By drawing up the lower half and with it half of the letters, He made the *Male* and *Female*, two sides of a connected whole.

This new empty space is the AUIR KADMON (PRIMAL SPACE). It was the first of all Spaces. It is not a *clothing* like the AUR PENAI AL (the Face of God).

750   The traces of the Light of the Clothing remain, and this world has a name *that includes all things*, IHUH. Before the world of empty space was created, HE and His Name existed: AIN SOPH and His clothing.

The EMECH HAMMELECH said:

With the third contraction, the lower half of the clothing was devoid of the light, but the traces of that light remained, and *this* clothing is called SHEKINAH, God dwelling within. It is the dwelling place of the male יה (Yōd He) and female הו (Vav He) combinations of letters.

This empty space was square. It was the *Primal Space* or Sublime Trace in Kabbalah (the *Auira Kadmah* or *Rasimu Ailah*). It was the remaining traces of the Light of the Clothing mixed with traces of the Very Substance. It was the *Primal Ether* but not empty Space. The Light of the Sublime remained in the place it occupied, but it was spiritual and diffused.

There were two Lights in this Ether: the Light of the SUBSTANCE (which was taken away) and the Remaining Traces of the Clothing. There is a great difference between these two. The Traces of the Clothing are *like the point in the center of a circle* that is what remains of the Light of Substance. We cannot call this Light, because Light is what remains from the removal of Ain Soph. It is the Yōd (י), the point in the center of Light. Light (Ether and Space) is a point in the center of the Great Light.

It is somewhat heavier than the Light and not as Subtle, although it is not perceptible by the Senses. It is the Primal Ether and the Soul of the World extending everywhere. Light is visible but imperceptible. *This Ether is imperceptible and invisible.*

The Introduction to the Zohar continues in the speaking of the Letter Yōd:

751   Worlds could not be formed in this Primal Ether, because of its thinness and the excess of Light. This was also prevented while the vital Spirits of the Remaining Traces of the Ain Soph Aur and the Light of the Clothing remained.

Therefore, HE caused the letter Yōd (less brilliant than the Primal Ether) to descend to capture the light remaining in the Primal Ether and again recede.

It descended five times to remove the vital Spirits of the Traces of the Ain Soph Aur, the Traces of the Light, and the Clothing from the Sphere of Splendor. By this, ADAM KADMON was created, and with the return of Yōd, a Trace of the Sublime Brilliance remained. It is a Spherical Shape that the Zohar calls *Tehiru* (Splendor). This is the First Matter. It is as formless as a vapor or smoke, although it retains spherical nature.

While descending, the Yōd left behind his own light, though it was not as great as the Shekinah. This Splendor was composed of the light of Yōd, and Yōd left itself with only a trace of that light. Without this light, He could not re-ascend to the Shekinah and join with it. The Holy and Blessed caused the letter He (ה, the female) to be given to Yōd from her Light, and sent him forth to descend and share *that* light with the Sphere of Splendor.

When he again ascended, he left behind the productive light of the letter He. By this light, another Sphere was created *within* the Sphere of Splendor. This is KETHER AILAH (*The Supreme Crown*), *The Ancient of Ancients*, and even the *Cause of Causes*. This Crown is still far smaller than the Sphere of Splendor, where a vast empty space remains.

The BETH ELOHIM said:

752

Before the Infinite God (the Supreme and First Good) gave form and shape to any of his ideas, HE was alone. He had no companion and no form. He completely lacked Ideal or Figure. It is forbidden to make a representation of Him whatsoever: no image, no letter, no form, not even a point.

After He had given this Idea form, limited and comprehensible, he descended through that medium. This is the Ten Emanations, the Adam Kadmon (the Primal or Supreme Man). Since He descended, all created beings know him by the name IHUH and through his likeness.

Wretched is the man who mistakes God for his attributes. Worse still is the man who would make Him like the earthly Sons of Men who perish and are consumed!

No idea can be formed about Him except through the ways in which He manifests Himself, exerting His influence through some attribute. Extending this, there can be no attribute, thought, or ideal of Him. He is like the Sea filling some great reservoir with its bed in the earth. Only by measuring the bed it has carved, can we begin to calculate the dimensions of the Sea itself.

For example, let us suppose there is *one* Source for all the water of the Ocean. From this Source there springs a fountain large enough to fill the space occupied by the Sea. Such is the letter Yōd. The Source is the first thing, and the fountain that springs from it is the second thing. Next, a great reservoir or basin is carved out. Filled with the waters of the fountain, it becomes the Ocean (the third thing). The water of this great Ocean then flows into seven rivers or streams. Here are the Source, Fountain, Ocean, and Rivers, making ten in all.

The Cause of Causes created ten emanations, and the Source of the Fountain is called KETHER (the Crown). The Light circulates and flows from 753 Kether without *end*. Therefore, He called Kether *endless*, like Himself, and like Him, this emanation has no form. Nothing similar to it exists. Now clear thought of it may be obtained.

After forming the Crown, He created a smaller vessel, the letter Yōd, and filled it from that source. This is the "Fountain gushing with Wisdom". In this emanation, He called Himself WISE. The vessel He called CHOKMAH (*Wisdom*).

He then created a great reservoir, which He called the Ocean. This is BINAH (*Understanding*). In this emanation, He is Intelligent or the *Conceiver*. HE is indeed the Absolutely Wise and Intelligent, but Chokmah is not Absolute Wisdom alone. Without the Understanding fulfilled in Binah, wisdom would be dry and unintelligent.

This was followed by the emanation of seven subsequent precious vessels. The first of these was CHESED (Mercy), which is also called GEDULAH (*Magnificence* or *Kindness*). The second of these was called GEBURAH (*Severity*). Next came TIPHARETH (*Beauty*). The fourth was NETZACH (*Victory*). This was followed by HŌD (*Glory*). The next was called YESOD (*Foundation*), and the last of these seven emanations (and the tenth in all) was MALKUTH (*Kingdom* or *Dominion*). In each of these emanations, He takes upon Himself its associated character.

These emanations (Sephiroth) are held in Kabbalah to have originally contained each other. That is, Kether contained Chokmah, and Chokmah contained Binah, which contained the last seven, and so on.

Rabbi *Jizchak Lorja* commented that our entire existence is contained in Binah. It projects all things, species by species, down into the lower worlds of Emanation, Creation, Formation, and Action. All are derived and flow from what is above them, and by this, all thing become real.

754   The Introduction to the Zohar says:

It is said in many places in the Zohar that all things that emanate or are created have their root above. Therefore, each of the Ten Sephiroth has its root above, with the very Substance of HIM. AIN SOPH had full consciousness and understanding of the essence of all the emanations and physical forms that were contained within Himself, even before they existed. When He came to the Sephirah of the Physical Form (MALKUTH), He concluded that worlds should be created. The first nine Sephiroth did not require the creation of worlds for Him to assume their attributes. MALKUTH, which is Kingdom or Dominion, would not apply until He ruled over the other Existences. From the point of MALKUTH, He created all the worlds.

There are ten of these spheres. Originating from individual points, they expanded to a spherical shape. This is the mystery of the ten Sephiroth (spheres), and within these ten spheres are ten Spaces. The sphere of Splendor is in the center of the space within MALKUTH in the First hidden Adam.

The First Adam *in the ten spheres above the sphere of Splendor* is called the First *hidden* Adam. In each of these spaces, many thousand worlds are formed. The first Adam is *linked* with the Primal Ether and is associated with the world of Binah.

KETHER contains all the other emanations so that they are indistinguishable from it, just as the four elements composing the body of man 755 cannot be isolated. This Crown (Kether) is The Cause of Causes and the Ancient of the Ancients.

Kether is the combination of all Ten Sephiroth. When it was first emanated, it consisted of all Ten. The Light extending from the Emanative Principle flowed into *it*, and two great *Universals* were manifested: the Light and the Vessel that receives It. This is identical to the *idea* of Humanity as a Unity within Deity, from which springs the individual soul. *This Light is the Substance of Kether, and the* WILL *of God is the Soul of all things.*

The Light of Ain Soph is infinite in every direction without end. A division was necessary to prevent that Light from flowing into the lesser empty space. This division is composed of the boundary of the sphere of Splendor and the boundary of the sphere Kether. These boundaries were the *Vessels containing* and enclosing the light of the sphere. Kabbalah regards these vessels "as somewhat opaque and not as splendid as the light they enclose."

The Light of Ain Soph is the Life and *Soul* of these vessels. It is active within them like the Human Soul in the human body. Kether began to exist at the same moment as its Vessel, like the flame upon burning coal. All the Sephiroth existed in potential within it.

This potential is illustrated in the conception of human life. When a child is conceived, a Soul is immediately sent into the embryo to become the infant. At this early stage, the Soul is the potential of all the organs and systems of the body. The strength of the soul *becomes* the human body of the child to be born.

Then the wisdom of God commanded that these potential emanations within Kether begin to exist, so that worlds might exist. HE directed Yōd to descend again to enter and shine within Kether. Upon Yōd's re-ascension, all the other emanations existed independently but remained within the sphere of Kether.

When God willed to produce the other emanations apart from Kether, HE sent Yōd down again. One half of Yōd was to remain outside, and the other half was to enter the sphere of Kether. HE then sent the letter Vav into the Splendor to pour its light onto Yōd.

Yōd received light from Vav, and his beauty illuminated and provided great energy to Chokmah. This gave Chokmah the ability to leave Kether and to gather and retain within itself all of the other eight emanations originally contained within Kether.

The sphere of Kether opened, and Chokmah descended to remain below Kether.

Through the same process, Binah was illuminated and separated from Chokmah by a second Yōd. Likewise, Binah had within itself the Seven lower Emanations.

The vessel of Binah was excellent and sparkled with rays the color of sapphire. It was so near in color and brilliance to the vessel of Chokmah that there was hardly any difference between them. Therefore, it would not quietly remain below Chokmah. It rose and placed itself on his left side.

The light from above flowed into and collected within the vessel of Chokmah. So much Light entered Chokmah that it overflowed. The Light escaped and, sparkling outside of Chokmah, it flowed to the left, strengthening the vessel of Binah. Binah is *female*.

756

By means of this extra energy and by virtue of the second Yōd, Binah possessed enough virtue and strength to project beyond herself the Seven remaining vessels. All were emanated continuously (one after the other). All were connected and linked with each other like the links of a chain.

757   The first three emanations (Kether, Chokmah, and Binah) manifested one below the other, without interaction between male and female. However, when Binah rose to a position beside Chokmah, with Kether remaining above them, the conjunction of the Male and Female (*Father* and *Mother*) began.

      The Source of All created Adam Kadmon (consisting of all the worlds) so that He would contain something from above and something from below. NEPHESH (the psyche or *Soul*) was the lowest spiritual part from the world of ASSIAH (one letter *He* from the Tetragrammaton). The RUACH (the *Spirit*) was the next higher spiritual part from the world of YETZIRAH (the *Vav* from the Tetragrammaton). NESHAMAH is the highest spiritual part from the world BRIAH (the other letter *He* from the Tetragrammaton). Finally, NESHAMAH LENESHAMAH came from the world of ATZILUTH (the YŌD of the Tetragrammaton).

      The Sephiroth were changed from their spherical form into the form of a person. This symbolizes BALANCE, because this form is both *Male* and *Female*. Chokmah is on one side with Binah on the other and Kether over both of them. Likewise, Chesed is on one side, and Geburah is on the other with TIPHARETH under both of them.

      According to the *Omschim*, some believe that the ten Sephiroth succeeded one another in ten degrees (one above the other) in a direct line from the highest to the lowest. Others believe that they were emanated in three lines, parallel with each other. One line was on the right, one on the left, and one in the middle. Beginning with the highest and going down to the lowest, Chokmah, Chesed, and Netzach are in one straight line on the right. Binah, Geburah, and Hōd are in one straight line on the left, and Kether, TIPHARETH, Yesod, and MALKUTH are in the middle column. Still others believe that all ten exist in ten concentric circles.

      The table of Sephiroth contains one more emanation often identified as a Sephirah. It is called Daath (thought). It lies between Chokmah and Binah, and is the result of their conjunction.

758   Adam Kadmon is the Idea of the Universe assigned to a human form by Kabbalah. Kether is the cranium. Chokmah and Binah are the two sides of the brain. Chesed (Gedulah) and Geburah the two arms. TIPHARETH is the torso. Netzach and Hōd are the thighs. Yesod is the male reproductive organ and Malkuth is the female.

      Each letter of the Tetragrammaton is assigned to one of the Sephiroth. Yōd is assigned to Chokmah. The first letter He is Binah. Vav is TIPHARETH, and the last He is Malkuth.

The Books concerning the *Hidden Mysteries* say that God intended to form Impersonations in order to diminish the Light. Therefore, HE gave form to Macroprosopos, Adam Kadmon, or Arik Anpin (three Heads). The first is called the "incomprehensible Head". The second is the "Head of that which does not exist", and the third is the "Actual Head of Macroprosopos". They are Kether, Chokmah, and Binah. They exist in the Glow of the World of Emanation or in Macroprosopos. The Zohar calls them ATIKA KADISCHA (The Most Holy Ancient). The Seven inferior Sephiroth (the Royalties of the first Adam) are called "The Ancient of Days". These compose the internal part (the Soul) of Macroprosopos.

The human mind has never struggled harder to understand and explain the process of creation and Divine manifestation than it has in Kabbalah. *At the same time, it tried very hard to conceal its thoughts from all but the initiated.* For this reason, much of it may seem like jargon. Macroprosopos or Adam Kadmon is the idea of the whole Universe held by and contained within Deity, Himself contained without form in the Absolute. Kether (the Incomprehensible Head) is the *Will* of the Deity or the Deity as Will. Chokmah, (Head of that which does not exist) is the Creative Power of Thought. This Thought is *within* the Deity and not in action. Therefore, it does not exist. Binah (the Actual Head of Macroprosopos) is the creative intellectual capacity. Impregnated by Chokmah, it *produces* the Thought. This Thought or Thinking Process is Daath.

This is better understood by comparison. In a human being, pain is a feeling or sensation. It must be *produced*. To produce it, there must be both the *capacity* to *produce* it (nerves) and the *power* to *generate* it by means of that capacity. This Power and the Passive Capacity together produce Pain, and they are like Chokmah, Binah, and Daath. 759

The four Worlds or Universals: Atziluth (Emanation), Briah (Creation), Yetzirah (Formation), and ASSIAH (Fabrication) are another mystery of Kabbalah. The first three are wholly contained *within* the Deity. The first world is the potential for the Universe, as it exists within the Deity and His Emanations. It is definite, imagined, but completely without form and undeveloped. The second is the idea of the Universe. This is a unified idea within Deity, but still lacking actual form. The third world is the same Universe without existence, but with defined forms. It has become a multitude of species and individuals. The fourth world is the potential of the Universe to become the Actuality, to exist as it exists for us.

The *Porta Cælorum* says that the Infinite Emanator uses the Sephiroth as His working tools. He operates with them and through them. They are the cause of existence of everything created. However, in these same *Sephiroth, Persons* and *Lights* are not creatures, but *ideas*. They are the *Rays* of THE INFINITE. Though they have descended from the Supreme Source, they are not severed from It. Through them, It is the Single and Perfect Universal Cause of All, working each specific operation through one of the Sephiroth.

God produced all things by His Intellect, Will, and free Determination. He willed to produce them through His Sephiroth. He manifests Himself *most* perfectly by producing the causes (and the Causes of Causes) instead of merely the effects.

In the first act of Emanation, God produced all the remaining causes. He Himself is most simply One, and the First Supreme Infinite Unity flowed forth at the same time, All and One. It is One, because it flowed from the Most Simple Unity. It is All, because It left that perfect immeasurable Singleness yet was still Absolute and Perfect in existence.

Emanation is the resulting form of what has no form. It is the finite derived from the infinite. It is the numerous and complex variety that springs by Infinite Power *and* Act from the Perfect Single and Simple Potential. It is movement from what is eternally motionless. It is diminished from His Infinite Perfection. The First Cause of all Infinite things emanates the First Causes for all finite things.

THE NECESSARY ENTITY cannot be divided into many, but He is multiplied in these Causes, by their Nature, Substances, and Vessels. From this multiplication, the Single and Infinite Essence is defined within external bounds and takes upon Itself definite form through these Vessels.

Just as Humanity is a microcosm, so Adam Kadmon is a macrocosm containing all the resulting Causes of the First Cause. Physical Man is the completion of all creation, and the Divine Man was its beginning. The inferior Adam *receives* all things *from* all, and the superior Adam *supplies* all things *to* all. The lesser is the *reflected* light and the end of light's descent from the Simple and Infinite Act, and the greater is the *Direct* Light and the end of man's ascent from the lowest matter to the First Cause.

The Principle of the Number Three brings duality to unity.

It restores stability to unity when it has ceased to be unity by becoming binary. Three is the first odd number. It contains in itself the first even number (two) and the unit (one), which are the Father and Mother of all Numbers. It has within itself the beginning, middle, and end.

Adam Kadmon emanated from the Absolute Unity and is himself a unit, but he descends and flows downward into his own Nature. This makes Him a duality. He returns to the Unity within Himself and to The Highest. This makes Him the Ternary and Quaternary.

This is why the Essential Name is composed of four letters, three of them unique and one of them repeated. The first letter He is the wife of the Yōd, and the second letter He is the wife of the Vav.

The Sephiroth, profoundly hidden in the First Cause, are its closest emanations. For this reason, they produce and control all the rest.

These Sephiroth give His Infinite Goodness being. They are the mirrors of His Truth and the closest likeness to His Essence, the Ideas of His Wisdom, and the representations of His will. They receive His power, and they are his working tools. They are His Treasury of Goodness and the Judges of His Kingdom. They reveal His Law, as well as His Attributes and Names. They are the ten categories containing and generating all things. They are the Second Causes by which the First Cause affects, preserves, and governs all things. They are the rays of the Divinity that illuminate all Forms, Ideas, and Species. They give being to Souls. They are the Powers by which essence, life, and movement are given to all things. They are the Basis of all Time and Space. They hold and enclose the Universe. Everything is connected to the One Eminent Limitless Perfection through the first three emanations (Supernals). They are the Causes of all dependent Perfections. They illuminate the Intelligences not tied to matter, the intellectual Souls, and the Celestial and Elemental bodies.

According to the Lesser IDRA of the Zohar, the Most Holy Hidden Eldest is continually more separated from everything that exists. However, HE does not completely separate Himself, because all things exist with Him. HE is 762 All that is and the Most Holy Eldest of All. HE is the most Hidden.

When HE takes shape, HE produces nine Lights, shining from Him. The rays they emit spread out on every side of the elevated Lamp. They may appear to diverge, but upon reflection, it becomes clear that they originate from a single Lamp.

The Space of creation is defined by THE MOST HOLY ANCIENT, and it is illuminated by the Light of His Wisdom.

HE takes form with three Heads, but these are really one Head. These three are extended into Microprosopos, and everything in existence shines from them.

This Wisdom gave form to what had no form, and it flowed into that creation.

Flowing forth, this Wisdom is called the "Father of Fathers". The whole Universe of Things is contained and defined through it. It is the principle of all things. It holds the beginning and the end.

Siphra de Zeniutha describes the equilibrium of the Balance. Before Balance existed, he says, forces did not oppose each other.

He adds that the Scales of the Balance are both Male and Female. In the Spiritual world, Evil and Good are *in equilibrium*. This is the World of the Balance. The World is restored when Evil becomes Good and when everything that exists is Good. This idea arranges the Sephiroth like a Balance of two Scales and a fixed support. Chokmah is on the right, and Binah is on the left. Kether is the support and Balance above them in the middle. Likewise, Chesed is on the right, and Geburah is on the left with TIPHARETH below, balancing them. Netzach is on the right, and Hōd is on the left. Under these is Yesōd.

Kether, the Supreme Crown, the Ancient Most Holy, and the most Hidden of the Hidden is considered both Male and Female.

763 Chokmah (the Father) and Binah (the Mother) are equal. Wisdom and the Mother of Thought dwell together. When the Intellectual Power emanates, the productive *Source* of Thought is included in Him.

When the First Adam was made to be both Male and Female, equilibrium was created. Before this division, the Father and Mother did not act as opposing forces. The Father represents perfect Love or Mercy, and the Mother represents perfect Severity or Justice. Before there was balance, the Mother turned away from the Father. Severity hid from Mercy.

In the Greater *IDRA of the Zohar*, there is no Left (Female) in the Ancient and Hidden One. His totality is Right (Male). HE is the totality of all things, and HE is hidden on every side.

Macroprosopos (Adam Kadmon) is distinct from ourselves and is referred to in the third person: HE (HUA).

In considering the Tetragrammaton, the commentary adds that Yōd is male. The letter He is female, and Vav is both male and female.

Yōd (ʼ) contains three individual points, an upper, middle, and lower. The upper point is the Supreme Kether. The middle, represented by Vav is Chokmah, and the lower point is Binah.

The Lesser IDRA of the Zohar says that the Universe was formed as both Male and Female. Wisdom was pregnant with everything that exists. All things flowed from Wisdom in the form of male and female. Chokmah is the Father, and Binah is the Mother. These two are in equilibrium as male and female. For this reason, all things are given the form of male and female. *If this were not the case, nothing would exist.*

Chokmah is the Generator of all things. When He and Binah join, she shines within Him and conceives. Their offspring is Truth.

Yōd impregnates the letter He, and she has a son. The Principle called Father (the Male or Generative Principle) is within Yōd, which flows downward from the energy of the Absolute Holy One.

Yōd is the beginning and end of all things that exist. The stream of existence that flows from Yōd is the Universe of things. For this reason, Yōd is called the Father of all.

764 All things flow from Chokmah, and all things are contained within It and formless. It is the Unity of all things and the Sacred Name, IHUH.

To the Kabbalists, all individuals are grouped into species, all species into more general orders, and ultimately everything into a Universal. This Universal is removed from any idea of individuality. It is not just a group of individuals, but also a Single real Being, ideal and intellectual. It exists above *any* individual and *contains* them all. Everything has evolved from this Universal.

If you find this disturbing, consider that if *all* things were originally in the Deity, the Universe sprang from Him. Therefore, it was not *created* out of nothing. The *idea* of the Universe, before it was given form, must have been as real as the Deity Himself. Humanity existed in the Deity as a Unit, without individuality.

Everything that exists must have first been *possible*. The whole Universe with its many individualities existed in Unity as possibility. This possibility or potential to exist was considered by the Kabbalists real Being. This was the Idea or Plan of the Universe that had to emanate from the Infinite Deity.

Geburah (Severity) is the Sephirah opposite to and paired with Chesed. Their union produces TIPHARETH (Harmony and Beauty). Geburah is also called *"Judgment"*. Judgment conveys *limitation* or *restriction*, whereas Goodness or Mercy (Chesed) is often considered Infinite. This subtly implies that everything contains both the *Finite* and the *Infinite*. The severity of judgment and the laws of the Infinite Absolute that limit all things below are relaxed by the *grace* of the Infinite. Therefore, the Spiritual and Material Natures are *in equilibrium*. Good counterbalances Evil everywhere. Likewise, Light is in equilibrium with Darkness. This is the Universal Harmony of things. Traces of the Light of Ain 765 Soph remained in the vacant space allocated for creation. This is the Light of the Substance of the Infinite. For this reason, Man is thus both human and divine. The *apparent* conflicts within his Nature are actually equilibrium *if he wills it to be so*. This balance results in the Harmony of Life, Action, Virtue, and Perfection.

The Sephiroth were assigned not only to the world of Emanation (Atziluth), but also to each of the other worlds (Briah, Yetzirah, and Assiah). They simultaneously convey the attributes of the Unmanifested Deity, Himself in limitation, and His actual manifestations. They are the qualities of the Universal Nature. They are Spiritual, Mental, and Material.

According to Kabbalah, God and the Universe were One. All things exist within God, and the form of all things flowed from Him. If this is generally true, then where does individuality begin? Is it the Hidden Source and Spring alone (the Unit)? Is it the flowing fountain that fills the ocean? Is it the ocean itself or its waves? Is the drops or the mist of those waves? The Sea and the River are each One, but the drops of water within each are many. The tree is one, but its leaves are many. The leaves may fall with colder temperatures, but the tree continues to grow. New leaves grow in the Spring. Is mankind the Tree? Are individual men the leaves? How else can the force of will and sympathy be explained? One man's life is always dependant upon another. Does this not demonstrate the unity of humanity? The links that bind all created things together are the links of a single Unity. The whole Universe is One, evolving itself into the many.

It is wrong to suggest that Kabbalah assigns sexual characteristics to the Deity. There is no basis for that assumption anywhere in the Zohar or any commentary upon it. Kabbalah is based on the fundamental idea that Deity is Infinite, extending everywhere without limitation. It has no specific form whatsoever. In order to begin the process of creation, He first created a vacant 766 space within Himself by contracting on all sides. His Nature is best described as

Light filling all space, formless and limitless. This space still contains the remaining traces of His Light. Into this spherical space, He emits His Emanations. These emanations contain a part of His Light or Nature, and some of these are given symbolic sexual characteristics.

The Infinite first limits Himself by flowing forth as *Will* (the decision to act). This *Will* of the Deity (or the Deity *as* will) is *Kether* (the *Crown*). In it are *contained* all other Emanations. This is a philosophical necessity. The Infinite does not *first* will and *then* decide to act. To will and act are not only simultaneous, but in reality *the same*. He does not only decide to act after His Omniscience tells Him that an action is wise. His Wisdom and His Will also act simultaneously. His decision that it was wise to create, *was* creation. Therefore, His Will contains within itself all the Sephiroth. This Will, by the exercise of thought, conceived the Idea of the Universe and caused the Power in Him to act upon the Idea. The Infinite, flowing from Ain Soph as Will, then flows forth as the Generative Power to stir the thoughts of Intelligence and Understanding (Binah). The Thought Itself is *Daath*. The *Siphra de Zeniutha* illustrates this by stating that the Power and Ability, the Creative and Productive, the Active and Passive, and the Will and Capacity unite to form the Act of Thought. They are *always* in conjunction and essential in the Act. The Will, Wisdom, and Ability are really the Father and Mother of all things. It was necessary that The Infinite form an idea *within* Himself of what HE willed to create. Since Time has no meaning with Him, his *Will was Creation*. To *plan* was to *Will* and *Create*. The Idea of the Universe contained the potential for all things in creation. After this, all formation was merely evolution and development.

767

Netzach and Hōd (the Seventh and Eighth Sephiroth) are called Victory and Glory respectively. Netzach is the perfect *Success* that awaits His creatures from His plan of Equilibrium. This equilibrium is the reconciliation of Light and Darkness, Good and Evil, Free Will and Necessity, and God's absolute power and Man's freedom. Without this balance, the Universe would be a failure. It is the inherent Perfection of the Deity given form in His Idea of the Universe. It is present in every spiritual, mental, or material part of the Universe. The *Perfection* of this plan *produces* perfect *Success*. It is the victory of Wisdom over Chance. This *is* the Glory of the Great Infinite Designer, whose plan is both Successful and Victorious.

The union of these two Sephiroth results in Yesod (Foundation or Basis). In the symbolic human figure assigned to the ten Sephiroth, Yesod represents the reproductive organ. From Yesod flows MALKUTH (Kingdom, Dominion, or Rule). Yesod is the Foundation of Stability and Permanence that *results* from the perfection of the Universal Idea. Whereas Hōd is the *Glory* or Self-Satisfaction of the Deity resulting from the Victory of His Perfect Idea, Yesod is the real outcome of that Success. The Deity is infinitely Wise and Time has no relevance. For Him, it is always HERE and NOW. He did not need to see the operation and evolution of His plan in order to know that it would succeed.

Creation is stable and permanent, not temporary. Its *Perfection* is its *Success*. His *Glory* is its *Permanence* and *Stability*. These Attributes of Permanence and Stability belong to the Universe, *because* they belong to the Infinite Himself.   768

This Stability and Permanence causes creation to continue without completion. By this continuous cycle, new Life comes through Death. New forms come from the end to old forms. Fatality is a consequence of Stability and Permanence. The absolute dominion (MALKUTH) of The Infinite Deity over all that He produces eliminates any chance or accident. Nothing exists in Time or Space with any power that does not originate in Him. Everything must be perfectly submissive to His Will. The Perfection of the plan, its success, His *Glory*, and its *Stability* bring about His Absolute Authority and the complete absence of Chance or Accident. As the Infinite Wisdom or Absolute Reason rules in the Divine Nature, It rules in its Emanations and in the worlds of Spirit, Soul, and Matter.

There are four worlds in Kabbalah. The first is the Atziluth, the world of emanations or archetypes. This is the Divine Nature or Divinity itself, somewhat fixed and limited, but without form. The second world is Briah, the world of *Creation*. This is the world of the first *Entities* (Spirits and Angels). The third world is Yetzirah, the world of *Formation*. This is the world of the first forms, souls, or intellects. The fourth world is Assiah, the World of *Fabrication*. It is the world of Matter. The Deity is *present* in each of these worlds *through* the Ten Sephiroth. Each begins with Kether, the Crown, as the HEAD. Next, *within* that Head are the two Hemispheres of the Brain (Chokmah and Binah). The result of their union is Daath. In each world, these are the three universals, producing the lower Sephiroth. In perfect balance, follow Law and Equity, Justice and Mercy, the Divine Infinite Nature and the Human Finite Nature, Good and Evil, Light and Darkness, Mercy and Severity, and Male and Female.

The whole Universe with its many beings and events existed with The   769
Infinite before any act of creation. His Mercy enabled Him to create. Without it, the strict and stern law of justice would have forced Him to destroy the Universe immediately. Therefore, Mercy is the essential component of the Permanence and Stability of the plan of Creation. For this reason, Kabbalah identifies Mercy with *Light* and *Whiteness*. It symbolizes the Very Substance of Deity. Paul had very similar ideas with respect to Law and Mercy (Grace). He may have studied the principles of Kabbalah under Gamaliel the Rabbi.

The dominion and control of the Deity is interwoven with this Mercy. Mercy is an essential *part* of dominion or rule (MALKUTH). Mercy enables Malkuth to give birth to the continuous cycles of generation that make up the Universe. Thus in Kabbalah, MALKUTH is *female*. All creation is born from this womb.

Kabbalah is an expansion from the original religious and philosophical traditions. It rests upon a principle of Magism: "what is visible to us is a portion of the invisible." The Ancients observed that equilibrium between the apparent opposition of two forces is the universal law. Extending the physical to the metaphysical, they concluded that God (the first living and active cause) possessed attributes balanced in apparently opposed pairs: stability and movement, necessity and liberty, order dictated by reason and the self-rule of Supreme Will, Justice and Love, and Severity and Mercy.

According to Kabbalah, the foundation of all religions and sciences is the equilibrium of all the attributes and emanations of Deity. Male is on one side, and female is on the other. The Supreme Will (which *is* also Absolute Reason) lies above, balancing the forces of each. This is the first and unchangeable idea of things. The Sephiroth compose a triple triangle and a circle. It is the Threefold Principle explained by balance and multiplied by itself in the domain of the Ideal. Then the Idea is made a reality through formation.

Unity can only take form through the Binary. Unity itself and the idea of Unity are already two.

Human unity is completed by the right and left. The first man was both masculine and feminine.

The Divinity has two essential conditions that serve as the basis of Its existence: Necessity and Liberty.

The laws of the Supreme Reason regulate the liberty of God, because He must be both reasonable and wise.

Knowledge requires a binary nature. An idea that is known cannot be separated from the being that knows.

The binary principle is the foundation of Society and the law. It is also the number of *Gnosis*, which implies knowledge through intuition. It is Unity multiplying itself by itself to create. For this reason, in the Sacred Symbols, Eve springs from the chest of Adam.

Adam is the human Tetragrammaton, conveyed by the mysterious Yōd of Kabbalah. Yōd is the image of the Kabbalistic Phallus. Adding to Yōd the three-letter name of Eve forms the name of Jehova, the *Divine* Tetragrammaton. It is the transcendent Kabbalistic and magical word: יהוה.

Unity is completed by the fertility of the Three-Fold Principle. Together they form the Quaternary (Four), which is the key of all numbers, movements, and forms.

A Square rotating on its Center produces a Circle of equal diameter. The circular movement of four right angles is the "squaring of the circle".

The Binary gives form to Unity, the equilibrium between the Above and the Below forms (with them) the Ternary (three-fold principle).

To us Creation is Mechanics and Motion. To the Ancients it was Creation, like the universe springing from the Orphic egg. Modern science now knows that all animal reproduction begins with the egg. This idea of creation pays reverence to the creative power, which is the philosophical cross of the Gnostics and the Masons.

The Sephiroth may be arranged according to the Tree of Life as illustrated in the 770
following diagram.

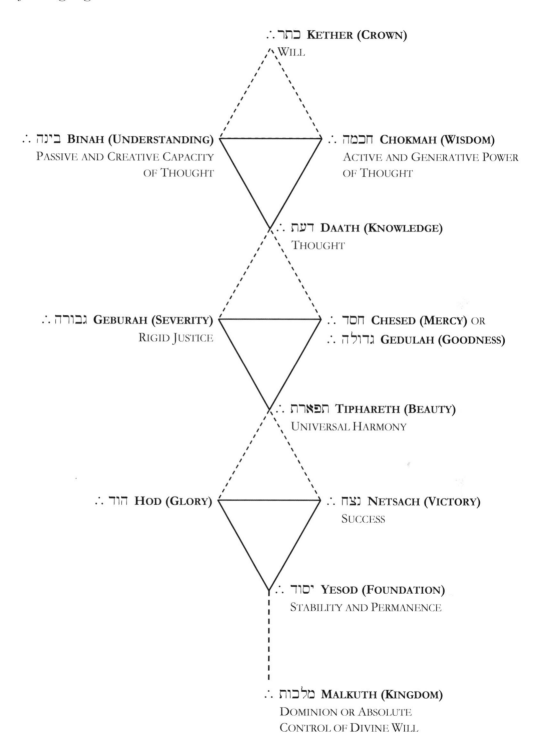

771
772 The Hebrew letter *Aleph* is the man. The letter *Beth* is the woman. *One* is the Principle. *Two* is the Word. A∴ is the Active, and B∴ is the Passive. Unity is Boaz, and the Binary is Jachin.

The two columns (Boaz and Jachin), through Kabbalah, explain all the mysteries of natural, political, and religious conflict.

Woman is man's creation, and universal creation is the female within the First Principle. When the Principle of Existence made Himself Creator, He produced by emanation an ideal Yōd. To make room for the radiating light of Yōd in the expanse of the uncreated Light, He had to hollow out a pit of shadow, according to his plan.

The Active Principle spreads out, while the Passive Principle collects and becomes fruitful.

Creation contains the Creator-Word. In order to create, the Creative Power and the Productive Capacity must unite. The Binary must again become Unity through conjunction. The WORD is the First-BEGOTTEN, not the first *created* Son of God.

Holy things are only revealed to the Holy, and the mysteries of Kabbalah will be holy for one who is worthy. The Scriptures say, "Seek and ye shall find. Knock and it shall be opened unto you." If you ever wish to find the Sanctuary, we have said enough to show you the way. If you do not, it is useless to say more, and it has been useless to say so much.

The Hermetic philosophers derived their doctrines from Kabbalah, particularly from the Treatise *Beth Elohim* or *Domus Dei* (known as the *Pneumatica Kabbalistica* of Rabbi Abraham Cohen Irira) and the Treatise *De Revolutionibus Animarum* of Rabbi Jitz-chak Lorja.

This philosophy was concealed by the Alchemists' Symbolism. It was hidden with the incomprehensible jargon of a flawed Chemistry. It appeared absurd, except to the Initiates. The key to this symbolism is within your reach, and the philosophy it contains is worth studying. The labors of the human mind always provide interesting instruction.

The dream of the Alchemists was to be rich and young and to live forever.

They sought a method of changing lead, mercury, and all the other metals into gold. They sought to discover a universal medicine to heal all ailments and
773 the elixir of life to halt death. This was how they hoped to accomplish these dreams.

Like all the Sacred Mysteries, the Secrets of the Alchemist's "Great Work" have a three-fold meaning: religious, philosophical, and natural.

The philosophical gold, in religion, is the Absolute and Supreme Reason. In philosophy, it is the Truth. In visible nature it is the Sun, and in mineral world it is the most perfect and pure gold.

The pursuit of the Great Work is called the Search for the Absolute, and the work itself is the work of the Sun.

It is impossible to obtain the material results (the transmutation of base metals into gold) without also obtaining (in the religious and philosophical domains) the universal medicine and the philosopher's stone. With these, the material work is simple. Otherwise, it vainly consumes the fortunes and lives of the seekers.

The universal medicine for the Soul is the Supreme Reason and Absolute Justice. For the mind, it is mathematical and practical Truth. For the body, it is the Quintessence. It is the fifth element, a combination of light and gold.

In the Superior World, the prima materia (primitive basis for all matter) is enthusiasm and action. In the intermediate world, it is intelligence and industry. In the lower world, it is labor. In Science, it is the Sulphur, Mercury, and Salt, which by alchemical process form the AZOTH (Universal Medicine) of the Sages.

Sulphur corresponds to the elemental Fire. Mercury corresponds to Air and Water. Salt is associated with the Earth.

The Great Work is the creation of man within himself. His effort in the Work determines his abilities and his future. The Great Work is the perfect freedom of his will, which assures him the universal empire of Azoth and complete power over the universal Magical agent.

This Magical agent, which the Ancient Hermetic philosophers disguised under the name of *"Prima Materia"* gives form to the Universal Substance. The Alchemists claimed that by means of this agent, they could transmute metals and create the universal medicine.

There are two Hermetic operations (one spiritual and one material) that *774* depend upon each other.

Hermetic Science is contained in the dogma of Hermes, which was legendarily cast into an emerald tablet. With respect to the Great Work, this tablet explains:

"Gently separate the earth from the fire, the subtle from the solid, with a great deal of industry."

"It ascends from earth to Heaven, and again descends to earth, receiving the force of things above and below."

"By doing this, you will possess the glory of the whole world. All truths will be revealed to you clearly."

"This is the potent force of all force. It will overcome the subtle and penetrate everything solid."

"This is how the world was created."

All the Masters of Alchemy use symbolic language when describing the Great Work. They were forced to do so to protect themselves from danger and to protect the philosophy from those who were unworthy. Their language was well understood by Adepts. It reveals the whole world of similarities governed by the single and sovereign doctrine of Hermes.

In their language, gold and silver are the King and Queen or the Sun and Moon. Sulphur is the flying Eagle. Mercury is a being that is both male and female, winged, bearded, crowned with flames, and mounted on a cube. Matter (Salt) is the winged Dragon. Molten metals are Lions of different colors, and the entire Work is symbolized by the Pelican and the Phoenix.

The Hermetic Art is a religion, a philosophy, and a natural science. It is the religion of the Ancient Magi and the Initiates of all ages. It is the philosophy that would be found in the school of Alexandria and in the theories of Pythagoras. It is the science of Paracelsus, Nicholas Flamel, and Raymond Lulle.

The Science becomes real only for those who believe and understand the philosophy and the religion. The process will only succeed for the Adept who has obtained absolute control of will. By doing so, he becomes the King of the elementary world. The great Cause behind the physical Universe is that force described in the Symbol of Hermes (the emerald tablet). It is the universal magical power. It is the spiritual, fiery, active power. It is the Od of the Hebrews and the Astral light to others.

775 It is the secret, living, and philosophical fire, the secret kept by the Hermetic philosophers. It is the Universal Seed that is symbolized by the figure of the Caduceus of Hermes.

This is the great Hermetic mystery. The Adepts call the bodies of nature "dead matter". "Living matter" is absorbed, energized, and operated by will.

The Great Work is far more than a chemical operation. It is a real creation of the human word initiated into the power of the Word of God.

The creation of gold in the Great Work results from transmutation and multiplication.

Raymond Lulle says that to make gold, one must have gold and mercury. To make silver, both silver and mercury are needed. He adds, "By mercury, I mean that mineral spirit so fine and pure that it improves the appearance of gold and silver." By this, he meant either electricity or Od, the astral light.

Salt and Sulphur are only used to prepare the mercury. Mercury is what we must absorb or join. It is the magnetic agent. Paracelsus, Lulle, and Flamel alone seem to have perfectly understood this mystery.

The Great Work of Hermes is essentially magical and the highest of all. It assumes the Absolute in Science and in Will. There is light in gold, gold in light, and light in all things.

Before obtaining the elixir of long life or the powder of projection, the disciples of Hermes had to seek the Philosopher's *Stone*.

The Ancients adored the *Sun* in the form of a black Stone, called Elagabalus or Heliogabalus. The faithful were promised a white Stone in Eternity.

Alchemists say that this *Stone* is the true *Salt* of the philosophers, which is one-third of the composition of Azoth, the great and true Hermetic Agent. They represent Salt in the form of a cubical Stone.

The Philosopher's Stone is the foundation of the Absolute philosophy, 776 the Supreme and unchangeable Reason. Before taking on the transmutation of metals, we must be firmly focused upon the Absolute principles of Wisdom. We must be guided by Reason, which is the test of Truth. A man who is the slave of his prejudices will never become the King of Nature and the Master of transmutations. Therefore, the Philosopher's Stone is necessary above all things. How is it found? Hermes tells us in his "Emerald Tablet" that we must separate the subtle from the solid with great care and focus. We must separate our certainties from our beliefs. We must clearly define the domains of science and faith. We must admit that we do not know the things we believe. We do not just believe anything we have come to know. Therefore, the essence of Faith is unknown and indefinite, and this is the opposite of Science. Therefore, Science is based upon reason and experience, while Faith springs from intuition and reason.

The Sun and Moon of the Alchemists perfect and stabilize the Philosopher's Stone. They correspond to the two columns of the Temple (Jachin and Boaz). The Sun is the symbol of Truth, because it is the source of Light. The rough Stone is the symbol of Stability. Thus to Medieval Alchemists, the Philosopher's Stone was the first means of making the philosophical gold, transforming life into Truth and Light. This is the first required operation of the Great Work leading to transformation. It allows the creators of the spiritual and living gold (who have found the true philosophical Salt, Sulphur, and Mercury) to discover material gold.

To find the Philosopher's Stone is to discover the Absolute, which has no flaws. It is the Steady result from the Volatile. It is the Law of the Imagination and the very necessity of Being. It is the unchanging Law of Reason and Truth. The Absolute is that which IS.

The Magnum Opus (the Great Work of the Sages), which Hermes called the "Work of the Sun", is the search for the Absolute in the Infinite, Indefinite, and Finite.

The Philosopher's Stone is the absolute foundation of true religious Faith, Philosophical Truth, and Metallic transmutation. This is the complete secret of Hermes.

This stone is one and many. It is broken apart by Analysis and 777 recombined by Synthesis. In Analysis, it is the powder of projection for the Alchemists. Before Analysis (and in Synthesis), it is a stone.

The Alchemist Masters say that the Philosopher's Stone must not be exposed to air. Nor should it be seen by the Uninitiated. It must be concealed and carefully preserved in the most secret place of the laboratory. Those who possess it must always guard the key to its hiding place.

The man who has the Great Mystery is a genuine King and more. He has no fear and no empty hopes or dreams. A single particle of this Stone will cure any sickness of the soul or body. As the Master says, "Let him hear, who has ears to hear!"

Salt, Sulphur, and Mercury are the passive tools of the Great Work. Everything depends upon the internal Magnet of Paracelsus. The entire work consists of *projection*, and projection is perfectly accomplished by the genuine understanding of a single word.

There is only one important step in the process: *Sublimation*. In material science, this is nothing more than the purification of a solid by heat, transforming it into the gaseous state.

Anyone who desires to understand the Great Word and obtain the Great Secret should carefully read the work of the Hermetic philosophers. By doing so, he will attain initiation, as many other have. To begin, he must have the key to their symbolism. This is the single doctrine of Hermes inscribed upon the Emerald Tablet. To succeed, he must follow his acquired knowledge and perform the work as explained in the Kabbalistic alphabet of the Tarot.

To make gold, we must first have gold. Nothing can be made out of nothing. We cannot actually *create* wealth. We increase and multiply it. Those who seek this path must take heed that no juggler's tricks or miracles are required to become an adept. The Hermetic science (like all *real* sciences) is mathematically provable. Its results, even its material effects, are as fixed as a correct equation.

778   The Hermetic Gold is not only a true philosophy, a light without Shadow, and a Truth without any particle of error. It is also material gold, real and pure. It is the most precious of any in the earth.

However, the living gold (Sulphur), the true fire of the philosophers, is found in the domain of Mercury. Fed by the air, it demonstrates its great power. It is like lightening, which begins with a dry and earthly outward breath. United with the moist vapor it takes on a fiery nature. It attracts the humidity inherent within it and changes its nature. Finally, it descends rapidly toward the earth, attracted to something of its own nature.

These mysterious words express what the philosophers mean by their Mercury, ignited by Sulphur, which becomes the Master and re-creator of the Salt. It is the AZOTH, the universal magnetic force, the grand magical agent, the Astral light, and the light of life. It is ignited by the force of thought, so similar to the Divine fire that they represent it as Sulphur.

Salt is Absolute Matter. To the Alchemists, anything composed of matter contains salt, and all salt (nitre) may be converted into pure gold by the interaction of Sulphur and Mercury. At times, this transmutation might occur in an instant or an hour without tiring the operator. At other times and under different *conditions*, it might require several days, months, or even years.

Two primary and essential laws exist in nature that balance each other to bring about the universal equilibrium of things. These are stillness and motion. In philosophy, they represent Truth and Fiction. In Absolute Thought, they are Necessity and Liberty, which are the very essence of Deity. The Hermetic philosophers gave the name *"fixed"* to everything that could be obtained by thought, everything that tended by its nature to rest. They called *"volatile"* everything that naturally obeyed the law of movement. The formation of the Philosopher's Stone is to volatilize the Fixed through Analysis and to fix the volatile by Synthesis. The agent of this synthesis is their salt, the combination of 779 Sulphur and Mercury, and the light of life, guided and made powerful by a Sovereign Will. Thus, they master all of Nature. Their stone is found wherever there is salt, which symbolically explains that no substance is outside the Great Work. Even the most despicable and apparently vile matter may be turned into gold. This is true in the sense that all matter contains the original salt principle symbolized by our own cubical stone.

Knowing how to extract the pure salt concealed within all matter is the Secret of the Stone. This Stone is composed of Salt. It is the Od, the universal astral light. It breaks down and rebuilds. It is one and many. It may be dissolved, like ordinary salt, and combined with other substances. It is the true *panacea* of the ancients. It cures the sicknesses of the soul and body. It is the medicine of all nature. By initiation, we may come to control the forces of the universal agent. We may have this stone at our disposal, always easy to extract. In its subtle state, it must not be exposed to air, which would deprive it of its virtue. It cannot be ingested or inhaled without danger. The Wise man protects it in its natural vessels. He extracts a piece from it through a single effort of his will and a single application of the Universal Agent to the vessels.

To illustrate this law of caution, they personify Mercury in Egypt as Hermanubis, a dog's head. Sulphur is represented by the Baphomet of the Temple, the goat's head that brought so much undeserved antagonism to the Mystery Schools of the Middle Ages.

Now, let us consider the words of the Alchemists themselves, and seek to learn their hidden meaning.

The RITUAL of the Degree of "Scottish Elder MASTER and Knight of Saint Andrew being the fourth Degree of Ramsay", as it is called in the Reformed or Rectified Rite of Dresden, uses these words:

"O how great and glorious is the *presence* of the Almighty God, which 780 gloriously *shines* through the Cherubim!"

"How venerable and astonishing are the *rays* of that glorious *Light* that sends forth its bright and brilliant beams from the Holy Ark of Alliance and Covenant!"

"With the deepest devotion, let us adore the great Source of Life, that Glorious Spirit who is the Most Merciful and Beneficent Ruler of the Universe and of all the creatures it contains!"

"The secret knowledge of the Grand Scottish Master is the combination and transmutation of different substances. In order that you may obtain a clear idea and a proper understanding, you are to know that all matter and all material substances are composed of combinations of three substances, extracted from the four elements. These three substances in combination are *Salt, Sulphur,* and

Sprit (Mercury). The first of these produces *Solidity*. The second produces *Softness*, and the third produces the *Spiritual*, gaseous particles. These three compound substances work together, and in this principle lies the true process for the transmutation of metals."

"These three substances allude to three golden basins. In the first of which was engraved the letter M∴. In the second, appeared the letter G∴, and in the third was nothing. M∴ is the first letter of the Hebrew word *Malakh*, which signifies *Salt*. G∴ signifies the Hebrew word *Geparaith*, which signifies *Sulphur*. There is no word in Hebrew to express the intangible *Spirit*, and there is no letter in the third basin."

"With these three principal substances you may bring about the transmutation of metals, which must be done by way of the five points or rules of the Scottish Mastership."

"The first Master's point shows us the Brazen Sea, where there must always be rainwater. Out of this rainwater, the Scottish Masters extract the first substance, which is Salt. This salt must afterward undergo a *seven-fold* manipulation and purification in order to be properly prepared. This seven-fold purification is symbolized by the Seven Steps of Solomon's Temple, which is provided by the first point or rule of the Scottish Masters."

781 "After preparing the first substance, you are to extract the second, which is Sulphur, out of the purest gold. To this, you must then add the purified or celestial Salt. They are to be mixed as the Art directs and then placed in a vessel in the form of a SHIP. It is to remain in this vessel, like the Ark of Noah, for one hundred and fifty days. Then bring it to the first damp, warm degree of fire in order to putrefy and produce the mineral fermentation. This is the second point or rule of the Scottish Masters."

If you consider, my Brother, that it was impossible for any one to imagine that common salt could be extracted from rainwater, or sulphur from pure gold, it will be obvious that some secret meaning was concealed in these words.

Kabbalah considers the spiritual part of man to be threefold: NEPHESH, RUACH, and NESHAMAH (*Psyche* or *Soul*, *Spirit*, and *Mind* or *Intellect*). There are Seven Holy Palaces, Seven Heavens, and Seven Thrones. Souls are purified by passing through Seven Spheres. The Hebrew word for *SHIP* is *Ani*, the same as the word for *I*, *Me*, or *Myself*.

The RITUAL continues:

"Multiplying the substance obtained from putrefaction is the third operation. This is done by adding the animate, volatile Spirit by means of the water of the Celestial Salt and Salt. This must be added daily and very carefully, adding neither too much nor too little. If you add too much, you will destroy that growing and multiplying substance. If you add too little, it will be self-consumed and destroyed. It will shrink away without enough substance to support its preservation. This third point or rule of the Scottish Masters gives us the symbol of the building of the Tower of Babel, used by our Scottish Masters. Because of its irregularity and the desire for due proportion and harmony, that work was stopped, and the workmen could proceed no further."

"Next comes the fourth operation, represented by the Cubical Stone, whose faces and angles are all equal. As soon as the work is brought to the point of multiplication, it is to be submitted to the third Degree of Fire, where it receives the necessary proportion of the strength and substance of the metallic particles of the Cubical Stone. This is the fourth point or rule of the Scottish Masters."

"Finally, we come to the fifth and last operation, represented by the Flaming Star. After the work has become a duly proportioned substance, it must 782 be subjected to the fourth and strongest Degree of fire. Here it must remain three times twenty-seven hours until it thoroughly glows. By this process, it becomes a bright and shining solution. With this new substance, the lighter metals could be changed by the use of one part to a thousand of the metal. This Flaming Star shows us the fifth and last point of the Scottish Masters."

"If you pass practically through the five points or rules of the Master, and by the use of one part to a thousand, transmute and purify metals, you may then in reality say that your age is a thousand years."

In the lecture of the Degree, the following hints to its true meaning are provided:

"The three divisions of the Temple, the Outer Court, Sanctuary, and Holy of Holies signify the three Principles of our Holy Order. They direct one to the knowledge of morality and teach those most practical virtues that should be practiced by mankind. Therefore, the Seven Steps, which lead up to the Outer Court of the Temple, are the emblem of the Seven-fold Light, which we need to possess before we can arrive at the height of knowledge and the ultimate limits of our order."

"In the Brazen Sea, we symbolically purify ourselves from all pollutions, faults, and intentional wrongful actions, as well those we commit through error of judgment and mistaken opinion. They all equally prevent us from arriving at the knowledge of True Wisdom. We must thoroughly cleanse and purify our hearts to their inmost recesses before we can correctly contemplate that *Flaming Star*, which is the emblem of the Divine and Glorious Shekinah (the presence of God). We must do all this before we dare approach the Throne of Supreme Wisdom."

In the Degree of The True Mason (*Le Vrai Maçon*), the self-proclaimed 23rd Degree of Masonry, or the 12th of the 5th class, the Tracing-board displays a luminous Triangle with a great Yōd in the center.

According to that Ritual, "The Triangle represents one God in three Persons, and the great Yōd is the initial letter of the last word."

"The Dark Circle represents the Chaos which God created in the beginning."

561

"The Cross within the Circle represents the Light by which He developed the Chaos."

783 "The Square represents the four Elements into which it was resolved."

"The Triangle, again, represents the three *Principles* (Salt, Sulphur, and Mercury), produced by the intermingling of the elements."

"God *creates*, Nature *produces*, and Art *multiplies*. God created Chaos, and Nature produced it. God, Nature, and Art have perfected it."

"The Altar of Perfumes represents the *Fire* that must be applied to Nature. The two *towers* are the two furnaces, moist and dry, in which it is to be worked. The bowl is the container of oak that will enclose the Philosopher's egg."

"The two figures surmounted by a Cross are the two vases (Nature and Art). Through these, the double marriage of the white woman with the red Servant is to be consummated. This marriage will spring a most Potent King."

"Chaos means universal matter, formless, but capable of all forms. Form is the Light enclosed in the seeds of all species, and its home is in the Universal Spirit."

"To work on universal matter, use the internal and external fire. This results in the four elements, the *Principia Principiorum* and *Inmediata*: Fire, Air, Water, and Earth. There are four qualities assigned to these elements: warm and cold, and dry and moist. Two of these apply to each element. Earth is dry and cold. Water is cold and moist. Air is moist and warm, and Fire is warm and dry. The dryness of Fire connects with the dryness Earth. As Hermes said, all the elements are moving in circles."

"From the mixture of the four Elements and their four qualities, spring the three Principles: Mercury, Sulphur, and Salt. These are the philosophical, not the material."

"The philosophical *Mercury* is a *Water* and SPIRIT, which dissolves and sublimates the Sun. The philosophical *Sulphur* is a *Fire* and SOUL, which softens and colors it. The philosophical *Salt* is an *Earth* and a BODY, which coagulates and fixes it. All of this occurs in the bosom of the *Air*."

"From these three Principles spring the four Grand Elements duplicated: *Mercury, Sulphur, Salt,* and *Glass*. Two of these are volatile: Water (Mercury) and Air (Sulphur), which is oil. All liquid substances by their nature avoid fire. They take from one (water) and burn the other (oil). The other two are dry and solid.

784 The Salt contains Fire, and *Glass* contains the pure *Earth*. Fire cannot do anything but melt or purify either of them, unless one makes use of a liquid alkali. Just as each element consists of two qualities, these great duplicated Elements take from two of the simple elements, or more accurately, they take from all four to a greater or lesser degree. Mercury receives more from Water. Oil or Sulphur obtains more from the Air. Salt has a greater share of Fire, and glass receives more from Earth. Earth is found, pure and clear, in the center of

all the elementary composites, and it is the last to disconnect itself from the others."

"The four Elements and three Principles reside in all the Compounds (Animal, Vegetable, and Mineral). In some, this is more evident than in others."

"Fire gives them Movement. Air provides Sensation. Water provides Nourishment, and the Earth satisfies the needs of Existence."

"The four duplicated Elements produce THE STONE if one is careful enough to supply them with the proper quantity of fire, and to combine them according to their natural weight. Ten parts of Air make one part of Water. Ten parts of Water make one part of Earth, and ten parts of Earth make one part of Fire. The whole combines the Active Symbol of one with the Passive Symbol of the other. The conversion of Elements is brought about by this means."

Here, the Ritual is clearly referring to the four Worlds of Kabbalah. The ten Sephiroth of the world of Briah proceed from MALKUTH, the last of the ten Emanations of the world of Atziluth. The ten Sephiroth of the world of YETZIRAH derive from MALKUTH in the world of Briah. The ten Sephiroth of the world of ASSIAH emanate from MALKUTH in the world of YETZIRAH. The Password of this Degree is "*Metralon*". This is a corruption of METATRON, the Cherub who, together with Sandalphon, is a Chief of the Angels. The Active and Passive Symbols are the Male and Female.

The Ritual continues:

"It is evident that in the Great Work, we must employ ten parts of philosophical Mercury to one part of Sun or Moon."

"This is obtained by *Solution* and *Coagulation*. These words mean that we must dissolve the body and solidify the spirit. These operations are worked by the moist and dry bath."

"Among colors, *black* is the Earth. *White* is the Water. *Blue* is the Air, and *red* is the Fire. This conceals very great secrets and mysteries."

"The tools used in pursuing 'The Great Work' consist of the Moist and Dry baths, the Vases of Nature and Art, the bowl of oak, clay (*lutum sapientiæ*), the Hermetic Seal, the beaker, the flame, and the iron rod."

"The work is accomplished in seventeen philosophical months according to the mixture of ingredients. It benefits the Initiate in two ways. It influences the soul by yielding *the knowledge of God, Nature, and ourselves.* It benefits the body by providing both health and wealth."

"The Initiate crosses Heaven and Earth. Heaven is the World that may be seen through the Intelligence, which is divided into Paradise and Hell. Earth is the World that we perceive through our Senses, also divided into Celestial and Elemental domains."

"There are Sciences specifically connected with each of these. *One is ordinary and common, but the other is mystical and secret.* The World of Heaven is studied through Hermetic Theology and Kabbalah. Celestial Astrology and the Elements are accessible through Chemistry. The use of fire to break down the

785

three kinds of Compound Substances into their basic components reveals the most hidden secrets of Nature. This last science is called the Hermetic Science, because it is what must be undertaken in the Great Work."

The Ritual of the Degree of Kabbalistic and Hermetic Rose ✝ uses these words:

"The true Philosophy that was known and practiced by Solomon is the foundation of Masonry."

"Our Ancient Masons have concealed from us the most important point of this Divine Art under symbols. This symbolism is nothing more than mystery and parable to all the Foolish, Wicked, and Ambitious."

"He who tirelessly works to discover this sacred place containing the clear and sublime Truth is supremely fortunate. He may be certain that he has found the True Light, Happiness, and Heavenly Good. He is one of the True Elect, because this *is the only real and most Sublime Science to which a mortal may aspire.* His life will be prolonged, and his soul will be freed from all vice and corruption, into which" (here the text adds, as if to mislead the unworthy), "*the human race is often led by hardship.*"

786   In this Degree, the symbolism of the Hall and the language of the ritual mutually explain each other. There are 12 columns in the hall. Each is white, marked with black and red. The hangings are black and crimson.

Over the throne is a great gold Eagle on a black background. In the center of the Canopy is the Blazing Star in gold with the letter Yōd in its center. To each side of the throne are the Sun in gold and the Moon in silver. The throne sits atop *three* Steps. *Ten* lights illuminate the hall and the anteroom (twenty in all), and a single light appears at the entrance. Black, white, and crimson appear in the clothing, and the Key and Balance are among the symbols of this degree.

In this Ritual the duty of the Second Grand Prior is, "to see if the Chapter is hermetically sealed, if the materials and elements are ready, if the Black is replaced by the White and the White with the Red."

"Be laborious," it says, "like the Star and procure the light of the Sages. Hide yourself from the Foolish and the Ambitious. Be like the Owl, which sees only by night and hides itself from treacherous curiosity."

"As the Sun enters each of his houses, he should be received there by the four elements. You must be careful to invite the elements to join you in your undertaking so that they may assist you. Without them, the House would be sad, giving him reason to feast upon the four elements."

"When he has visited his twelve houses, and you receive him and attended to him there, you will become one of his most favored. He will allow you to share in all his gifts. Matter will have no power over you. You will no longer dwell upon the earth. After certain periods of time, you will give back to the earth a body which is its own, and you will take in its place one that is entirely Spiritual. Matter is then deemed to be dead to the world."

"Therefore it must be restored. It must be reborn from its ashes. You will accomplish this through the fruit of the Tree of Life, symbolized by the sprig of acacia. The Sages say that whoever understands and completes this great work will know great things, but if you depart from the center of the Square and the Compasses, you will no longer be able to work with success."

"You will require another Jewel in certain undertakings. It is the 787 symbolism of Kabbalah. This holds the power to command the spirits of the elements. It is necessary for you to know how to use it. This you will learn through perseverance if you are a lover of the science of our predecessors, the Sages."

"A great Black Eagle, the King of Birds. He alone can scorch the Sun, physical in nature, formless, but deriving color from its form. The black anticipates the work. It changes color and assumes a natural form. From this emerges a brilliant Sun."

"The birth of the Sun is always announced by its Star, represented by the Blazing Star, which you will know by its fiery color. It is followed by the silver light of the Moon."

"A rough Ashlar is the shapeless stone which must be prepared in order to begin the philosophical work. It must be developed in order to change its form from triangular to cubic. This is accomplished by separating its Salt, Sulphur, and Mercury using the Square, Level, Plumb, Balance, and all the other *symbolic* implements of Masonry."

"We put these tools to philosophical use to construct a well-proportioned edifice from the rough stone, like a new candidate beginning his initiation into our Mysteries. When we build this structure, we must observe all rules and proportions. Otherwise, the Spirit of Life cannot lodge within it. You will build the great tower, and there will burn the fire of the Sages, the fire of Heaven. There the Sun and Moon will bathe in the Sea of the Sages. That is the basin of Purification, which holds the water of Celestial Grace. This water does not soil the hands, but it purifies the afflicted bodies."

"Let us work to instruct our Brother so that by his efforts, he may succeed in discovering the principle of life contained in the depth of matter. This principle is the universal solvent known as *Alkahest*."

"The most potent name of Deity is ADONAI. Its power puts the Universe in motion. The Knights who are fortunate enough to possess it have at their disposal all the power that inhabits it, the Elements, and an understanding 788 of all the virtues and sciences that man is capable of knowing. With its power, they would succeed in discovering the primary metal composing the Sun, which holds within itself the Principle of the seed. To this we may add six other metals, each containing the principles and primitive seed of the grand philosophical work."

"The six other metals are Saturn, Jupiter, Mars, Venus, Mercury, and Luna. The lesser science knows them as Lead, Tin, Iron, Copper, Mercury

(Quicksilver), and Silver. Gold is not included, because it is not (in essence) a metal. It is entirely Spirit and incorruptible. For this reason, it is the emblem of the Sun, which presides over the Light."

"The life-giving Spirit called Alkahest has within itself the creative virtue of producing the triangular Cubical Stone. It contains all the virtues that would make men happy in this world and in that to come. To determine the composition of Alkahest, we begin by working through the science of the union of the four Elements, which are drawn from the three Kingdoms of Nature: Mineral, Vegetable, and Animal. The rule, measure, weight, and balance of these each has its key. In one work we combine the work of animals, vegetables, and minerals, each in its appropriate season throughout the year."

"Something from each of the three Kingdoms of Nature is assigned to each Celestial House. In this way, everything is done according to sound philosophical rules. Everything must be thoroughly purified at the proper time and in the proper place. Only then may it be presented at the wedding table of the Spouse and the six virgins who hold the mystic shovel. This must not be done with an ordinary fire, but with an elementary fire. That fire burns primarily by *attraction* and by digestion in the philosophical bed, ignited by the four elements."

"At the banquet of the Spouses, the food is thoroughly purified and served in Salt, Sulphur, Spirit, and Oil. A sufficient quantity is compounded to form the Alkahest by means of the Balance of Solomon. This is served to the Spouses while they lie on their marriage bed. There they produce their embryo for the human race, the immense treasures that will last as long as the world endures."

789 "Few are capable of engaging in this great work. Only the true Freemasons may correctly aspire to it. Very few are worthy enough to attain it. Most of them do not know of the Clavicules and their contents. They have no knowledge of the Pentalpha of Solomon, which teaches us how to pursue the great work."

"The weight raised by Solomon with his balance was 1, 2, 3, 4, 5. This contains 25, 2 multiplied by 2, 3 multiplied by 3, 4 multiplied by 4, 5 multiplied by 5, and 9. These numbers thus involve the squares of 5 and 2, the cube of 2, the square of the square of 2, and the square of 3."

This alludes to the 47th problem of Euclid, a symbol of the Blue Lodge. It seems entirely out of place there, lacking significant meaning. The base of the right-angled triangle is 3, the perpendicular is 4, and the hypotenuse is 5. Using the rule that the sum of the squares of the two shorter sides equals the square of the longest, we have $3\times3=9$, $4\times4=16$, and $9+16=25$ (the square of 5). The triangle contains in its sides the numbers 1, 2, and 3. The Perpendicular is Male. The Base is Female, and the Hypotenuse is the product of the two.

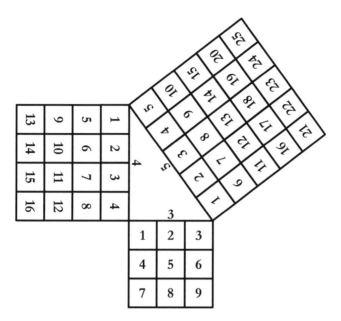

In the Hermetic language, to fix the volatile is to materialize the spirit. To volatilize the fixed is to spiritualize matter.

To separate the subtle from the gross (the first operation) is to internally 790 free our soul from all prejudice and vice. This is accomplished by the use of the philosophical SALT (WISDOM), MERCURY (personal ability and labor), and SULPHUR (the vital energy of will). In this way, we may change even the foul things of the earth into spiritual gold.

This is how we are meant to understand the parables of the Hermetic philosophers and the prophets of Alchemy. In their writings, as in the Great Work, we must skillfully separate the subtle from the gross, the mystic from the positive, and the allegory from the theory. To truly read them with understanding, you must first interpret them allegorically in their entirety. Only then may you descend from allegory to reality by way of the correspondences or similarities identified in this single statement:

"What is above is like what is below, and what is below is like what is above."

The "*Minerva Mundi*", legendarily attributed to Hermes Trismigestus, veils a philosophy under the most poetic and profound language. This is the doctrine of the self-creation of beings. It asserts that creation results from the balance of two forces. Alchemists identify these as the Fixed and the Volatile. In the Absolute, they are Necessity and Liberty.

The Masters in Alchemy say that it takes little time and expense to accomplish the works of Science. Only a single vessel is necessary, which they call the Great and Single furnace. It is within the reach of every man on earth, even though many do not know it. This alludes to philosophical and moral Alchemy. A strong and determined will can quickly become completely independent. Every one of us possesses this chemical tool, the Great and Single furnace. By it, we may separate the subtle from the gross and the fixed from the volatile. The Sages symbolize this tool, as complete and accurate as any science or mathematics, by a Pentagram or Star with five points. It is the absolute sign of human intelligence.

Alchemy represents the completion or perfection of the Great Work by a triangle surmounted by a cross. The last letter of the Sacred alphabet, Tau (ת), has the same meaning.

791

The "elementary fire that comes primarily from attraction" is probably Electricity or Magnetism, which is perhaps the secret of life or the vital force.

Paracelsus, the great Reformer in medicine, discovered magnetism long before Mesmer. He followed this great discovery to its end and into the magic of the Ancients. They understood the grand magical agent better than we do. They did not consider the Astral Light (Azoth), the universal magnetism of the Sages, to be an animal or substance, emanating only from certain special beings.

According to Hermetic Masons, the four Elements, the four symbolic animals, and the three Principles (with Azoth [the universal solvent]) correspond in the following way:

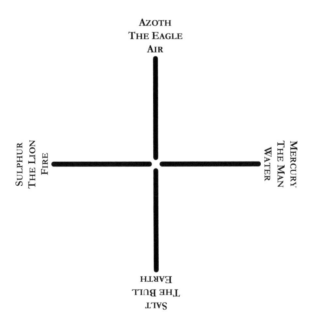

Air and Earth represent the *Male* Principle. Fire and Water belong to the *Female* Principle. These four forms symbolize four philosophical ideas: Spirit and Matter, and Motion and Rest.

Alchemy reduces these four things to three: the Absolute (Reason), the Fixed (Necessity), and the Volatile (Liberty).

All the great Mysteries of God and the Universe are hidden in the number Three, and it is natural that it should appear everywhere in Masonry and Hermetic Philosophy, under its mask of Alchemy. It even appears where Masons do not suspect it, teaching the doctrine of the equilibrium of Opposites and the resulting Harmony.

The double triangle of Solomon is explained by Saint John in a remarkable manner. He says there are three witnesses in Heaven: the Father, the Word, and the Holy Spirit. He also says there are three witnesses on earth: breath, water, and blood. Here he agrees with the Masters of Hermetic Philosophy. They call their Sulphur by the name of Ether. Their Mercury is the philosophical water, and they call their Salt the blood of the dragon or menstrual blood of the earth. The blood (Salt) corresponds to the Father. The Azothic water (Mercury) is the Word (Logos), and the breath (Sulphur) represents the Holy Spirit. Only the true children of Science understand the truths within the High Symbolism.

Alchemy has its Symbolic Triad of Salt, Sulphur, and Mercury, which symbolically divide man into Body, Soul, and Spirit. The Dove, Raven, and Phœnix are striking Symbols of Good and Evil, Light and Darkness, and the Beauty resulting from the equilibrium of the two.

To understand the true secrets of Alchemy, you must study the works of the Masters with patience and persistence. Every word is often a puzzle, and if you try to read quickly, it will all seem absurd. Even when they seem to teach that the Great Work is the moral purification of the Soul, they conceal their meaning. They are deceiving all but the Initiates.

Kabbalah refers to Yōd (י) as the *workman* of the Deity. The *Porta Cælorum* calls it single and primal, first among the letters. It is like a *point*, which is the first construction of Geometry. Stretched downward, it produces a *line* to form the letter Vau (ו). A line extended produces a *superficies*. Stretching the line of Vau (ו) forms Daleth (ד). Movement tends from right to left, and all communication is from above to below. The *name* of the letter Yōd is spelled Y-O-D (יוד). Vau (ו) has a numerical value of 6, and Daleth (ד) has a value of 4. They sum to 10, the numerical value of Yōd, their principle.

The *Siphra de Zeniutha* says that Yōd is the Symbol of Wisdom and the Father.

According to the *Lesser IDRA of the Zohar*, the Nature of the Father is contained in Yōd. It flows downward from the Holy power. Therefore, Yōd is the most secret of all the letters. He is the beginning and end of all things. The Supernal (Highest) Wisdom is Yōd, and all things are included in Yōd. He is the Father of Fathers and the Generator of the Universal. It is written: "*You have made all things in Wisdom.*" The All is Wisdom. The All is contained by Wisdom, and the Holy Name is the summary of all things.

The *Siphra de Zeniutha* adds that the Yōd (Father) approaches the letter He (Mother), and the result of their union brings Supernal Wisdom to Binah.

792

793

569

The name of Y-O-D (יוד) includes the Father, Mother, and Microprosopos or Seir Anpin, their offspring.

Wisdom (Chokmah) is the Principle of all things. It is the Father of Fathers. It is the beginning and end of all things. Microprosopos springs from the Father (Chokmah) and Mother (Binah). It includes the next six Sephiroth: Chesed, Geburah, Tiphareth, Netzach, Hōd, and Yesod. It is represented by the figure of a man. Microprosopos first occupied the place that was later filled by the world of Briah (Creation). After Creation, it was raised to the Atziluthic sphere, where It received Wisdom, Understanding, and Thought (Daath) from the Supernal Wisdom and Understanding.

The Vau in the Tetragrammaton represents these six members of Microprosopos. Vau was formed in the manner of Macroprosopos, but without Kether (Will), which remained in the first Universal. Vau received a portion of the Divine Intellectual Power and Capacity. The first Universal does not refer to itself in the first person ("I") but the third person ("HE"). The second Universal (Macroprosopos) speaks in the first person, calling itself "I".

The Greater IDRA of the Zohar, says:

The Eldest of the Eldest (the Absolute Deity) is in Microprosopos. All things are one. All was, all is, and all will be. There is no change. There has never been change, and there never will be.

He made Himself into a form that contained all forms, including the whole variety of Creation. This form is in the likeness of His own form (similar but not identical). The human form contains all that is above and below. The Most Holy took form, and the form of Microprosopos was determined. All things are equally one within each of the two Universals. However, in Microprosopos, His attributes are divided. Judgment is on our side and also opposite to us.

These Secrets are only revealed to those who cultivate this Holy Field.

The Most Holy Ancient is not called ATHAH (Thou), but HUN (He). However, in Microprosopos where everything began, He is called ATHAH and AB (Father). The beginning was in Him, and He is called Thou. He is the Father of Fathers. He sprang from non-existence. He is beyond mortal thought.

Wisdom is the Principle of the Universe and the source of thirty-two paths. They are twenty-two letters and the ten words. Wisdom is the Father of Fathers, and in this Wisdom are the Beginning and the End. There is wisdom in each Universal, one above and one below.

Rabbi Chajun Vital's commentary on the *Siphra de Zeniutha* says: At the beginning of emanation, Microprosopos flowed from the Father. It joined with the Mother under the mysteries of the letter He (ה). The result was Daleth (ד) and Vau (ו). Vau is the Microprosopos. Vau has a numerical value of six, and Microprosopos is composed of the six emanations that follow Chokmah and Binah. The Father is the Father of Fathers, because He is the source of these Fathers (Mercy, Severity, and Beauty). Microprosopos was like the letter Vau in the letter He, because He had no will. He then received the Divine Light from above through three separate vessels.

The vessels of the Sephiroth below Binah were broken, and evil was created from the fragments. Following the Supernal form, the fracture was repaired by the Balance of MALKUTH (Kingdom). This balance is illustrated in the symmetry of the human form. The conjunction of Microprosopos and Malkuth is called man.

The first world was superficial. It could not continue or survive, because 795 it had no human form. It lacked the system of Balance. The Sephiroth were lined up like points, one below the other. The first Adam, Microprosopos (not to be confused with Macroprosopos - the first *Hidden* Adam), was the beginning. In Microprosopos, the ten Emanations moved from potential alone into action.

Microprosopos is the second garment or separation between existence and the Elder Most Holy, who bears the name Tetragrammaton. The elder Universal is called Elohim, because He is Absolute Sympathy or Mercy in Microprosopos and acts as Severity in Macroprosopos. Although this Severity shines as Mercy compared to the lights of MALKUTH and the three lower worlds.

All of the formations of Macroprosopos come from the First Adam. To create the second garment, the First Adam caused a single spark to emit from the sphere of Severity, from whose five letters may be derived the name Elohim. This is a spark of air following the right side and a spark of fire on the left. Therefore, the white (Air and Mercy) and red (Fire and Judgment) do not intermix.

Microprosopos is the Tree of the Knowledge of Good and Evil. His Severities are the Evil.

MALKUTH (Kingdom) is given the name "Word of The Lord". It gives form to Heaven. Every formation is created by means of veiling. In this case, hiding is manifesting. As the excess light is veiled, it is reduced in intensity. Only through this reduction can it be received by those below. This veiling invests Briah in the World of Creation, continues into TIPHARETH in the World of Formation, and finally proceeds into MALKUTH in the world of Fabrication.

Before equilibrium brought balance, there was no direct opposition of principles. Microprosopos and his wife never joined. When the First Adam was made to be both Male and Female, equilibrium was created. Before this division, the Father and Mother did not act as opposing forces. The Father represents perfect Love or Mercy, and the Mother represents perfect Severity or Justice. The seven supernals that emanated from her (Binah) were all perfect severities. They had no direct connection to the Most Holy Ancient. They were all *dead*, 796 destroyed, and shattered. Then the balance of the Hidden Wisdom established equilibrium. Male and Female were formed, and with them Severity and Love. Only then was their connection from above restored.

The Father is Love and Mercy. With a pure and subtle Light or Goodness, He impregnates the Mother, who is Severity of Judgment. Their offspring is the mind of Microprosopos.

The introduction to the *Zohar* says the Deity decided to create Good and Evil in the world, according to what is said in Isaiah: *"who forms the Light and creates Darkness."* At first, the Evil was hidden. It could only receive form through the sin of the First Adam. Therefore, He determined that the first emanations, from Mercy downward, should be destroyed and shattered by the excessive flow of His Light. His intention was to create the worlds of Evil, but the first three emanations would remain. Among the fragments, there would be no Will, no Intellectual Power, and no Divine Capacity of Thought. The last seven emanations were forced to live *independently*, without companionship. This was the cause of their death and destruction.

There was no Love between them, but only a two-fold Fear. For example, Wisdom feared that it might re-ascend to its Source in Kether or descend into Binah. There was no union except between Chokmah and Binah, and this was imperfect. This is what is meant by saying that the world was created by Judgment or fear. This continued until everything was restored by Compassion. From Compassion came Love and Union. Six emanations were united into one person. Love is the attribute of Compassion or Mercy.

Binah produced the Seven Kings (Lower Sephiroth) all at once. The Seventh is Malkuth (Kingdom). It is the foundation or cornerstone of the palaces of the three lower worlds.

The six emanations above were shattered, but Kingdom was crushed into a formless mass. Otherwise, the evil demons created from the fragments of the others might receive bodies (life and growth) from it.

797 From the fragments of these vessels came all Evils, judgments, impurities, the Serpent, and Adam Belial (Baal). Their internal light re-ascended to Binah and then flowed down again into the worlds of Briah and YETZIRAH, where that light formed the clothing of the Seven Emanations. The Sparks of the great Influence of the shattered vases descended into the four spiritual elements: Fire, Air, Water, and Earth. From there it flowed into the lifeless, vegetable, living, and speaking kingdoms and became Souls.

Selecting the desirable from the undesirable lights (good from evil), the Deity first restored the universality of the Seven Kings of the Archetypal World (Atziluth). After this, He restored the three lower Worlds.

In each of these worlds, both good and evil remained. However, evil was limited by the Judgment and Severity that remained to prevent the broken vessels from ascending. Evil could not develop itself. It could not act. These Severities also remained, because a binary (pair) is necessary for creation. This need for Severity is the mystery of the pleasure and warmth of the creative appetite. It leads to the Love between husband and wife.

The introduction to the Zohar adds that if the Deity had not created worlds and then destroyed them, evil could not have existed in the world. All things would have been good. There would have been no reward for righteousness and no punishment for wrong. Good is only known by its relationship to evil. There would have been no fruitfulness or multiplication in the world. Without sexual desire, no man would seek to reproduce. In time, that desire will be called Laban (לבן, *white*), because it will have no impurity. It will return to the realm of Israel, and they will pray to the Lord to give them sexual desire in order to conceive children.

God intended His creatures to recognize His existence. For this reason, He created evils to afflict them when they sin, and He created Light and Blessing to reward the just. Therefore, man must have free will. He must be able to decide between Good and Evil in the World.

These Seven Kings died, because the equilibrium did not exist. Adam Kadmon was not yet male and female. The lower Sephiroth had no contact with life. They had no root or connection to Adam Kadmon or Wisdom. These were pure and simple mercies and severe judgments. Father was not attracted to Mother. Macroprosopos had no tie to Microprosopos. Malkuth (the Kingdom) was empty and devoid of thought. It had nothing. It received nothing. It was nothing. Judgment needed to receive Love from the Male. They must balance each other to produce creation (above and below). Left to Judgment alone, creation cannot carry on.

Balance must exist. There must be a root and connection from above. Judgment must be tempered so that all may live and not again die. As the Seven Emanations descend, all things achieve equilibrium. The measure of that Balance is the root from above.

In some interpretations of Kabbalah, the world of YETZIRAH (Formation) is composed of Kether (י), Chokmah and Binah (הי), and Chesed, Geburah, and Tiphareth (והי). Therefore, Vau (ו) is Tiphareth (Beauty and Harmony). *Man* represents Chokmah. Binah is the *Eagle*. Chesed is the *Lion*, and Geburah is the *Ox*. Kabbalists form a mysterious circle of connections or correspondences. Some suggest the following according to the Zohar: Michael, the Lion, and Water are in the South with the letter Yōd (י) of the Tetragrammaton. Gabriel, the Ox, and Fire are in the North with the first letter He (ה). Uriel, the Eagle, and Air are in the East with the letter Vau (ו). Raphael, the Man, and Earth are in the West with the second letter He (ה). The four letters also represent the four worlds in descending order.

Rabbi Schimeon Ben Jochai says that the four animals of the Mysterious Chariot, whose wheels are Netzach and Hōd, are Chesed (Lion), Geburah (Ox), Tiphareth (Eagle), and Malkuth (Man).

The *Æsch Mezareph* says that the Seven lower Sephiroth represent Seven Metals. Chesed and Geburah are Silver and Gold. TIPHARETH is Iron. Netzach and Hōd are Tin and Copper. Yesod is Lead, and MALKUTH is the metallic

Woman (Morn of the Sages). It is the field where the Seeds of the Secret Minerals are sewn. It is the Water of Gold, but these words conceal mysteries that cannot be spoken.

The word AMAS (אמש) is composed of the initials of the three Hebrew words that signify Air, Water, and Fire. Kabbalists assign these to Mercy and Justice, with Compassion balancing them.

The *Apparatus* calls Malkuth the *Haikal* (Temple or Palace), because it is the Palace that conceals and contains TIPHARETH. Haikal denotes the place where all things are contained.

To understand this more clearly, remember that Kether (the Crown) is treated as a person, composed of the ten Emanations. For this reason, it is also called Arik Anpin or Macroprosopos.

Chokmah is a person called *Abba* or *Father*.

Binah is a person called *Imma* or *Mother*.

Tiphareth (including all the Emanations from Chesed to Yesod) is a person called Seir Anpin or Microprosopos. The six emanations surrounding Tiphareth are represented by the interlaced triangle or the Seal of Solomon.

Malkuth is a person called the wife of Microprosopos. Vau represents the Beauty and Harmony that consists of Seir Anpin with its six members.

The wife (Malkuth) is *behind* the husband (Seir Anpin). She has no other knowledge of him. Every object that may be known is understood by either its cause or its effect. Near perfect knowledge is only obtained when the intellect knows the thing itself, in itself, and through itself. If it only reaches the object through similarity, an idea, or the object's effects, it achieves an imperfect knowledge. Malkuth (Kingdom) only knows her husband in this lesser way until she unites with him and obtains near perfect knowledge of him. Then the Deity (limited and manifested in Seir Anpin) and the Universe are one.

800 Vau is TIPHARETH. The Unity of the six members, including itself. TIPHARETH (Beauty) is the column that supports the world. It is symbolized by the column of the junior Warden in the Blue Lodge. The world was first created by Judgment, and it could not continue. Mercy conjoined with Judgment, and the Divine Mercies sustain the Universe.

The *Lesser IDRA of the Zohar* says that God formed all things as male and female. Without this division, the continuation of existence was impossible. The All-Embracing Wisdom shines from the Most Holy Ancient. Wisdom is the Father, and Understanding is the Mother. They are in equilibrium as Male and Female. They join and shine within each other. Their offspring is Truth. Wisdom and Understanding are the Perfection of all things when they are coupled and when the Son (the summary of all things) is in them.

These things are entrusted only to the Holy Superiors, who have entered and discovered the ways of the Most Holy God to avoid error. These things are hidden, and the lofty Holiness shines in them like brilliant light from the splendor of a lamp.

These things are revealed only to those who have entered and remain. Any man who enters and leaves would be better off if he had never been born.

All things are comprehended in the letters Vau and He. All are one system. These are the letters: הנובת (Tabunah, Intelligence).

CHAPTER 29: GRAND SCOTTISH KNIGHT OF ST. ANDREW

A MIRACULOUS tradition consecrates the Ancient Cross of St. Andrew, like the one related to the *labarum* of Constantine. This tradition began during the ninth century when Hungus reigned over the Picts in Scotland. The night before a battle he had a vision in which Saint Andrew, the Apostle, promised him victory. St. Andrew assured him of this victory by saying there would appear in the sky over the Pictish army a cross similar to the one he had suffered upon. Hungus awoke the next morning and saw the promised cross in the sky, as did the soldiers in both armies. After the victory, they gave thanks to the Apostle and made their offerings with humble devotion. Hungus and the Picts then vowed to wear a cross of St. Andrew in time of war as their badge of recognition.

John Leslie, Bishop of Ross, said the cross appeared to both Achaius, King of the Scots, and Hungus, King of the Picts, while they were on their knees praying the night before the battle when they fought together against Athelstan, King of England.

Every cross of Knighthood is a symbol of the nine qualities of a Knight of St. Andrew of Scotland, because every order of chivalry required the same virtues and excellencies of its devotees.

Humility, Patience, and Self-denial are the three essential qualities of a Knight of St. Andrew of Scotland. The Cross is an eloquent and unmistakable symbol of these three virtues. The Cross is sanctified by the blood of the holy ones who have died upon it.

Jesus of Nazareth bore it from the streets of Jerusalem up to Calvary, and upon it He cried, "Not My will, O Father! But Your will be done". He suffered upon it, because He taught and associated with the poor and lowly and found His disciples among the fishermen of Galilee and the despised tax collectors. His life was one of Humility, Patience, and Self-denial.

The Hospitallers and Templars took upon themselves vows of obedience, poverty, and chastity. The Lamb became the trademark and Seal for the Order of the Poor Fellow Soldiery of the Temple of Solomon. It conveyed the same lessons of humility and self-denial as the original trademark of two Knights riding a single horse. The Grand Commander warned every candidate not to be influenced to join the Order with the vain hope of enjoying earthly pomp and splendor. He told them they would have to endure many severe hardships that would challenge their tendencies, and they would be compelled to relinquish their own will and submit entirely to that of their superiors.

Henry VIII's daughter, Queen Elizabeth, dismantled the religious buildings of the Hospitallers, because they would not take an oath to maintain her supremacy. The Hospitaller facilities were charity houses, hospitals, and orphanages which relieved the State of many orphans and outcast children, ministered to their needs, and fed them breakfast and dinner each day. They also included Inns for traveling men who heard the sound of the dinner bell invite them in for fellowship and rest. The Hospitaller Knights were no less distinguished by bravery in battle than by the tenderness and zeal of their comfort to the sick and dying.

The Knights of St. Andrew vowed to defend all orphans, maidens, and widows of good families. They also vowed, to the best of their ability, to bring to justice murderers, robbers, or masterful thieves wherever they oppressed the people.

The vows of Rouge-Croix were, "If fortune finds you in distant lands or foreign countries, and you meet any gentleman of name and arms who has lost goods in worship and Knighthood in the King's service or in any other place of worship, and he has fallen into poverty, you shall aid, support, and relieve him, if you can. He may ask you for goods to provide for his sustenance, and you shall give him that part of such goods as God has provided to you, and as you can afford."

CHARITY and GENEROSITY have always been *very* essential qualities of a true and gentle Knight. CLEMENCY is the generous mark of a noble nature to spare the conquered. Valor is best tempered when it can turn relentless courage into consoling pity, and it shines brightest when it is clad in steel. The compassionate warrior will be rewarded with honorable victories during war and peace. The most famed men in the world have had both courage and compassion. A conquered enemy with his dignity still intact will become a stronger ally than those in a long train of captives from a Roman triumph.

VIRTUE, TRUTH, and HONOR are the three MOST essential qualities of a Knight of St. Andrew. The Knights were instructed in their charge, "you shall love God above all things and be steadfast in your Faith. You shall be true to your King, your word, and your promise. You shall not knowingly sit in any place where injustice is dispensed to anyone for any reason."

Virtue is a sanctuary so sacred that not even Princes or the law dare strike the virtuous person. Only Virtue and Wisdom perfect and defend mankind. Virtue is the decoration of the King of Heaven. It is the armor that protects us when we are unarmed, and it cannot be lost if we are true to ourselves. It is the embrace of Heaven, and without it, we are unprotected outlaws. There is no wisdom without virtue, but rather a clever way of guaranteeing our own undoing.

Peace is inevitable
Where Wisdom's voice has found a listening heart.
Amid the howl of more than winter storms,
The tranquil hears the voice of spring hours,
Already on the wing.

Sir Lancelot believed there was no chivalry equal to Virtue, a word which includes prudence. It primarily means manliness, and it includes what in old English was called *souffrance*, that patient endurance like the emerald, ever green and flowering.

It also includes *droicture* or uprightness, a virtue whose influence is so *804* strong and so powerful that all earthly things almost become unchangeable. Even our swords are formed to remind us of the Cross so that we may all live to show how much man can bear without dying. This world is a place of sorrow, tears, great evils, and constant calamity, and to attain real honor, we must maintain diligent familiarity with every Knightly virtue as though they are highly valued friends who are significantly more than ordinary acquaintances.

Do not look upon those who injure us with impatience or anger. It is inconsistent with our philosophy (and particularly with the Divine Wisdom) to express any concern about the evils that dishonorable people, rich or poor, can inflict upon the brave. When we combine the favor of God, the love of the Brethren, a generous temper, and a noble composure we have everything that the strength of malice cannot break. The consciousness of our honor and the spirit of our high chivalry must despise material and bodily evils if we are to be consistent with our commitment and retain the dignity of our nature as Masons. They should have no more influence upon us than a slap, dupe, superficial wound, or a dream.

The ancient days provide excellent examples of VIRTUE, TRUTH, and HONOR. You should nobly aspire to imitate the Ancient Knights, the first Hospitallers, the Templars, Bayard, Sydney, and Saint Louis. Pliny wrote to his friend Maximus and said, Revere the ancient glory when man was dignified in the sacred cities. Honor antiquity and great deeds. Do not detract from the dignity and liberty of anyone. We should defend the memory of the heroic Knights of former ages against those pretending to be the great, mighty, learned, and wise of the world who would conspire to denounce them. If they condemn or scorn your tribute of fidelity, then you are required to modestly and unashamedly bear it, because a day will come when it will be said they have lived poor and pitiful *805* lives, and the world will quickly forget them.

Reverent people may still be found in this very different age of commerce and trade, the vast riches of a few and the poverty of many, thriving towns and public housing swarming with the poor, churches with rented pews, theaters, opera houses, customs houses, banks, skyscrapers, malls and commercial palaces, factories and unions, Commodity and Stock Exchanges, newspapers, magazines, blogs, elections, Congresses, Legislatures, the alarming struggle for wealth and the constant battle for place and power, the worship of celebrity and greed, and the craving for and purchase of public office. Within this chaos, there are still some people who have heroic and knightly souls which preserve their dignity and composure amidst these conflicting passions, ambition, and the corruption that clamors around them.

Government always tends to become a conspiracy against liberty. Voters routinely elect people with very little dignity or chivalry. In this present age, people become distinguished for substandard accomplishments, for having name and celebrity, for being flatterers and lackeys, or for the gift of flattery. In a knightly age, these traits would have made them despised for lacking all true gentility and courage. The masses seem more likely to vote for these kinds of people despite their disgust and disregard for the truth, their pursuit of easy fortune, their hate of the oppressed, their willing readiness to worship the prosperous, their love of accusation, their hatred of apologies, and their eagerness and enjoyment to condemn those who do not worship them.

No country can ever be completely void of people with the traditional and heroic class and breed, whose word no person will dare to doubt, whose virtue shines brightly in all calamities and stands strongly amid all temptations, and whose honor radiates and glitters as purely and perfectly as the diamond. These people are not slaves to the material preoccupations and pleasures of life. They are not consumed by commerce, government regulation, the deception of the law, the objects of political envy, or the heartless, hollow vanities of an eternal indulgence. Every generation bequeaths their examples and images of people to be admired and imitated. Some of these people were among the Romans, under the most corrupt Emperors. They were in England while the Long Parliament ruled, in France during its festival of irreligion and murder, and in colonial and early America during the establishment of a new country.

When the management of a country's affairs and the customs of its people spawns a rejection of the belief in the virtue and honor of the Legislative, Executive, and Judicial branches of government; when there is a widespread spirit of suspicion and scorn of all who hold or seek office or have amassed wealth; when lies no longer dishonor a person, and oaths provide no assurance of the truth of their word, and one person hardly trusts another, states their real feelings, or is true to any party or cause when someone approaches them with a bribe; when everyone expects the media to report what they say with additions, perversions, and misrepresentations; when people privately profit from public misfortunes, when the media panders to the immoral and the amoral, and the pulpit is used for political sermons with long prayers to God eloquently delivered to admiring audiences and written out for publication like poems and political speeches; when the honesty and integrity of judges is doubted, and the honesty of legislators is a standing joke; then people may come to question whether the old days were not better than the new; the Monastery better than the Opera House, the little chapel better than the drinking saloon, the Convents better than the office buildings and factories devoid of antiquity, beauty, and holiness. These are the true Acherusian Temples where the nonstop rumbling of machinery can be heard and the bell rings to call its wretches to work and not to prayer, where they keep up a never ending tribute to the Devil, before furnaces which are never cooled.

Whatever withdraws us from the power of our senses, makes the Past distant, or the Future diminish the Present, advances our dignity as thinking beings. The modern hotel resorts with their flaunting pretenses, cheap finery, extravagant and superficial decoration, chronicles of dances, inelegant feasts, and bulletins of women's names and dresses are poor substitutes for the Monastery *807* and Church, which our ancestors would have built in the deep sequestered valleys between the rugged mountains and somber pine forests. A learned person of meditative temper and poetic feeling would gladly exchange the luxury hotel amid the roar and clamor of the city, or the pretentious country town tavern, for an old humble Monastery by the wayside, where they could peacefully rest without having to fear pride, arrogance, or dishonesty or pay for pomp, glitter, and gaudy ornamentation. There they could make their prayers in a church which resounds with divine harmony, and no pews would be available for wealth to isolate itself. They could behold the happy poor, informed and strengthened by the thoughts of Heaven. They could converse with learned and holy gentlemen, and before departure, they could exalt and calm their spirits with the melody of an evening song.

Freemasonry has added so many members that its obligations are less regarded than the simple promises people make to one another in the streets and markets. It clamors for public notice, courts notoriety with fanciful journals, and carries its controversies into the Courts. In some Orients, elections are conducted with all the heat and maneuvering of political struggles as office-seekers and management compete for place and position. The empty pomp of peaceful citizens in semi-military dress challenges that comparison to the noble Knights encased in steel and mail. Those Knights had a stern disdain for danger and death. They made themselves immortal when they won Jerusalem, fought at Acre and Ascalon, and were the fortress of Christendom against the Turkish legions that swarmed under the green banner of the Prophet Mohammed.

To be as respectable as those Knights and not merely a tinseled Knight of straw, you must diligently and devotedly practice the virtues you have professed in this Degree. Do not vow to be tolerant and then immediately denounce another for their political opinions? Do not vow to be zealous and constant in the service of the Order and then perform no work or contribute no *808* service to the Craft. The symbolism of the Square and Compasses is meaningless if your sensual desires and fundamental passions are not governed by them. If instead they domineer over your moral sense and reason, the animal over the divine, the earthly over the spiritual, then both points of the compasses *remain* below the Square. What a hideous mockery to call one a "Brother," whom he slanders to the masses, lends money to in usury, defrauds in trade, or plunders at law by deception?

You will be worthy to call yourself a Knight by possessing VIRTUE, TRUTH, HONOR, and by never bring false to your vows. Then Sir John Chandos, St. Louis, Falkland, Tancred, and Baldassar Castiglione might, if living, recognize you as worthy of their friendship.

A noble Spaniard said, "Chivalry is a religious Order that has Knights in the fraternity of Saints in Heaven." From this point forward, lay aside all uncharitable and remorseful feeling and exemplify disciplined passion and zeal. Learn to hate the vices and not the vicious. Be content with the discharge of the duties which your Masonic and Knightly professions require. Be governed by the noble principles of honor, chivalry, and reverence, and above all, always remember that jealousy is not our life, nor argument our end, nor conflict our health, nor revenge our happiness. Loving kindness is all these, greater than Hope, greater than Faith, able to move mountains, and the only thing which God requires of us to fulfill all of our duties.

We are compelled to confess in this Technological Age that people worship gods crafted from their own hands. The internal combustion engine, the television, and the silicon chip were the supreme gods of the twentieth century, and their idolaters are still everywhere. Throughout the civilized world, those who wield their tremendous power safely declare themselves gods.

We reluctantly confess that each scientific discovery makes the world a 809 smaller place with its gains. The satirist said of that self-absorbed century:

> - the clown's back turns away from the glory of the stars,
> We are gods by our own reckoning and may as well close our temples
> And carry on amidst the gasoline burning thunder of our cars:
> For we dispense self-thanking, self-admiring approvals
> At every step with, "Run faster, wonderful, wonderful age!"
> Little heeding if our souls are decorated as nobly as our jewelry,
> Or if angels will commend us for the goal of pilgrimage.

Deceived by their increased but still very imperfect knowledge and limited mastery of the brute forces of nature, people imagine they have discovered the secrets of Divine Wisdom, and in their own thoughts do not hesitate to replace the Divine with human prudence. Destruction was foretold by the Prophets against Tyre, Sidon, Babylon, Damascus, and Jerusalem as a consequence for the sins of their people. However today, if fire, earthquakes, or tornados destroy a city, those who venture to believe or say it was divine retribution or God's judgment are laughed at as fanatics, sneered at for indulging in hypocrisy, or berated for self-righteous vengeance.

Wandering in error, Science struggles to move God's Providence far enough away from us and the material Universe that it substitutes Forces of Nature and Forces of Matter for His supervision, care, and constant overseeing.

It cannot see that the Forces of Nature are the varied actions of God. This substitution is antagonistic to all Religion and Faith, which from the beginning have been the *Light* that illuminated human souls and constituted the consciousness of their own dignity, divine origin, and immortality.

The *Truth* that is the basis of all religions, even the spiritual creed of Masonry, is in danger. For all religions owe the life that they have had and their very being to the foundation on which they were reared, the undeniable and truthful proposition that the Providence of God rules directly in all the affairs and changes of material things. Science has its hands upon the pillars of the *810* Temple and is trying to rock it to its foundation. Yet as destructive as its efforts have been, they have only removed the worm eaten work of superstition from the ancient structure, and broken down some incoherent additions of owl-inhabited turrets of ignorance, and some massive props that supported nothing. The structure itself will only be overthrown when, "Human reason leaps into the throne of God and waves a torch over the ruins of the Universe."

Science only deals with phenomena. It is but charlatanism when trying to explain the powers, causes, or essence that produces these things that it gives names to. It no more knows what Light or Sound *is* than the Aryan cattle ranchers when they counted the Dawn, Fire, Flame, Light, and Heat as gods. Atheistic Science is not even half-science because it ascribes the Universe's powers and forces to a system of natural laws, an inherent energy of Nature, or unknown causes existing and operating independently of a Divine and Supernatural power.

The theories of science would be greatly fortified if it were capable of protecting life and property with the *certainty* of which it boasts. It would even secure human interests against the destructive agencies it develops in its endeavors to serve mankind. Fire, deemed the fourth element by the old philosophers, is His most useful and abject servant. How can man not be certain that at any moment his terrible subject may break forth and rise up into his master, tyrant, or destroyer? This is because fire is a power of nature which, in the ultimate trial of forces, is always superior to man. In a different sense from that as the servant of man, it is also the servant of Him Who makes His ministers a flame of fire, and Who is over nature, just as nature is over man.

There are powers of nature which man does not even attempt to control. Naples does nothing against Vesuvius. California only trembles with the trembling earth before the coming earthquake. The sixty thousand people who were buried alive in Lisbon by an earthquake had no knowledge of the causes and no possible control over the power that destroyed them. Science told us the exact time, size, and location of the 9.0 magnitude earthquake that swept a tsunami across the Indian Ocean on that fateful December 26, 2004, but it could not save the 250,000 people who drowned in its wake.

There are also powers of nature which man does attempt to control. *811* Mankind has made fire its servant in the kitchen and the factory, as the humble slave of the furnace, and as the spark of a match. However, in an instant, it can snap its brittle chain, break free from its prison, and leap forward with a destructive fury as if it sprang from the bosom of Hell. It consumes all of the prairies, forests, houses, and creatures in its path, while the firefighters stand helpless and in awe of the servant that is now the master.

Science becomes overly confident upon the strength of some minor success in the war of man with nature. It is inclined to substitute itself for Providence, which by the very force of the term is the only absolute science. Near the beginning of the twentieth century, medical science made incredible advances in the course of a few years. The great plagues which ravaged communities, cities, and countries throughout the world had been identified, diagnosed, and vaccinated. Parents no longer have to live in fear of their children dying from diseases such as Polio, Small Pox, Measles, Mumps, Tuberculosis, Rubella, Scarlet Fever, or Pneumonia, because science prevented them with vaccinations. From Fleming and Florey to Salk and Sabin, the healing arts had indeed taken long strides. The Medical Field might be excused had it said, "Man is mortal and disease will be often fatal, but there will be no more wholesale slaughter by infectious disease, no more general carnage, no more carnivals of terror, or high festivals of death."

This conceited boast hardly dies upon the lips when we are reminded of all the mysterious and monstrous specters that continually creep forth in spite of science, each more fearful than the last. Cholera, Malaria, SARS, Ebolavirus, Anthrax, West Nile Virus, Cancer, and AIDS all continue to defy science as they ravage mankind. Like the tiger's ability to sense blood in the jungle air, these invisible Destroyers, these fearful agents of Almighty Power, this tremendous Consequence of some Sufficient Cause, can sense the tainted atmosphere of countries during their devastating marches.

812   They have left no corner of the world, class, or profession untouched. They quietly leap and destructively descend upon the cities and countryside in every nation, upon the rich and the poor, the good and the bad, the faithful and the faithless alike.

Is *this* the judgment of Almighty God? A bold person would say it is, but they are even bolder to say it is not. How often have the words been fulfilled from the prophet to the daughter of the Chaldæan, the lady of kingdoms? "Your wisdom and your knowledge have perverted you, and you have said in your heart there are no others besides me. Should evil come upon you, you will not know where it came from. Mischief will fall upon you, and you will not be able to avoid it, and desolation shall come upon you suddenly."

It is easy to see the devastation wrought as judgment for the sins of each corner of the world. The United States is punished for the moral hypocrisy of its leaders and its vile celebrity culture. Russia and Southeast Asia are punished for the brutal political and religious persecution by their Communist governments. Africa is punished for its continued embrace of empty religions and the unrestrained greed of their leaders. South America is punished for the greed of its leadership and their unrepentant oppression of the poor. The Middle East and Eurasia are punished for their persecution of women, intolerance, and their silent acceptance of the slave-trade. And lastly, Europe is punished for its growing rejection of religion and its perpetuation of feudal empires under the new name of socialism that continues to oppress the poor to the benefit of the rich.

We should be slow to make conclusions from our petty human logic about the punishments dispensed by the ethics of the Almighty. Whatever the cruelty of greed, religious persecution, the slave-trade, or the oppression of the poor, we should still regard its supposed consequences to be wiser, and like Jesus we should probably say, "Do you suppose that these Galileans were the worst sinners of all the Galileans because they had suffered such things? Or those 813 eighteen whom the tower of Siloam fell upon and killed, do you think they were the worst sinners above all the men that dwelled in Jerusalem?"

Retribution prohibits retaliation, even in words. A city shattered, burned, destroyed, desolated, a land wasted, humiliated, made a desert and a wilderness, or wearing the thorny crown of humiliation and subjugation is invested with the sacred privilege and immunities of the dead. The celebration of revenge is disgraceful, and its fall and ruin should be ashamed in the presence of the infinite Divine chastisement. Freemasonry teaches us that "forgiveness is wiser than revenge, and it is better to love than to hate." Let those who see the hand of God in these great calamities be silent and fear His judgment.

People are great or small in stature as it pleases God, but their nature is great or small as it pleases themselves. Some people are not born with great souls, and others born with little souls. A person cannot add to their stature with knowledge, but they can enlarge their soul with it. The action of the will can make the soul into a moral giant or a moral dwarf.

The two natures of man are the great and the average, the spiritual and the material, and the honorable and the dishonorable. By his own volition, man must identify himself with one or the other. Freemasonry is a continual effort to exalt the honorable nature over the dishonorable, the spiritual over the material, and the divine over the physical. The purpose of the chivalric Degrees is to confirm and assist the magnificent lessons of morality and philosophy. Compassion, mercy, clemency, and a forgiving temperament are cardinal virtues to the character of a perfect Knight. The material and evil principle in our nature says, "Do not give, reserve your charity for impoverished friends, or at least unobjectionable strangers. Do not bestow it on successful enemies, or friends only in virtue of our misfortunes." But the more divine principle, spoken by the glorious Galilean says, "Do good to those who hate you, for if you love only those who love you, what reward do you have? The tax collectors, wicked oppressors, armed Romans, and renegade Jews, whom you count as your enemies, are also sinners."

CHAPTER 30: KNIGHT KADOSH

NOTE: Although recent discoveries in the Vatican archives have absolved the Knights Templars of the accusations previously leveled against them by King Philip IV of France and Pope Clement V, this chapter provides a good historical summary of the conflict that existed between the Vatican and Freemasonry.

WE frequently profit more from our enemies than from our friends. *"We support ourselves only on things which resist our pressure,"* and we owe our success to opposition. Mankind is the machine of Providence. Republics use the trinity of demagogues, fanatics, and scoundrels as the tools and instruments to affect the necessary changes they do not dare, but which they portray themselves as commissioned to prevent.

The best friends and worst enemies of Masonry in America may have been the Anti-Masons of 1826. They were composed of traitors, perjurers, and political opportunists who purified Masonry through persecution. In the end they proved to be its benefactors because persecution stimulates action and perseverance. Our current popularity is also due, in part, to the efforts of modern Anti-Masons.

In the mid eighteenth century, it become known that לדש were the Templars operating behind a veil. This Degree became forbidden, Masons ceased to confer it, and instead it became a brief and formal ceremony under another name. From the tomb where he rots, Clement the V cursed at the successors of his victims with the 1865 Allocution of Pio Nono against the Freemasons. The Allocution of Pio Nono is quoted and referenced many times in this chapter. Although the excommunications and condemnations against the Freemasons were a declaration of war, they were greatly needed to arouse us from our content and comfortable apathy and motivate us into action.

The Papacy revealed its secret hostility against the Templars in the passages quoted herein, taken from this Allocution. It is easy to separate the false from the true and the conjectures from the simple facts.

NOTE: The Papacy's passages are identified in "quotes" and the rebuttal or clarifying commentary is identified by [brackets].

"In the beginning, we were a power that ruled without conflict, without agreement, and consequently without control. This proved fatal to the early Apostolic Royalties. The (Roman) Republics had perished due to the conflict of liberties and franchises, and the absence of any sanctioned duty enforced by a governing bureaucracy. The Republics soon became rival tyrannies. The Christian Papacy was needed to establish a stabilizing institution and prevent the chaos of these collapsing governments. It would be an institution devoted to self-denial through solemn vows and protected by strict regulations. The members of this body would be recruited by initiation. Being the sole depository of the great religious and social secrets, it would accordingly be able to appoint Kings and Pontiffs free from the corruptions of Power. These secrets of the kingdom of Jesus Christ would also govern all its grandeurs."

"This concept presided over the foundation of the great religious orders, so often at war with the secular ecclesiastical or civil authorities. Its realization was also the dream of the dissident sects of the enlightened Gnostics who pretended their faith was really the primitive traditions of Saint John's Christianity. However, this rich and corrupt Order was really founded upon the mysterious doctrines of Kabbalah, and it increasingly became a menace to Church and Society. It seemed inclined to revolt against the legitimate authority of this established Hierarchy, threatening the civilized world with an immense revolution."

"The Templars, whose real history is largely unknown, were terrible conspirators. In 1118 nine Knights Crusaders in the East, including Geoffroi de Saint-Omer and Hugues de Payens, were consecrated by taking an oath to the Eastern Patriarch (at Constantinople) whose jurisdiction had been secretly and openly hostile to Rome for the 255 years since the time of Photius in 863 A.D. The declared purpose of the Templars was to protect the Christians who came to visit the Holy Places. Their secret purpose was to rebuild King Solomon's Temple based upon the model prophesied by Ezekiel."

816

"Formally predicted by the Jewish Mystics of the earlier ages, this rebuilding had become the secret goal of the Patriarchs of the Orient (at Constantinople). King Solomon's Temple, rebuilt and consecrated to Catholic worship would effectively become the Metropolis of the World. The East (Constantinople) would prevail over the West (Rome), and the Eastern Patriarchs would possess all of the Papal power."

"The Templars (*Poor Fellow Soldiery of the Holy House of the Temple*) were created using the example of the Warrior-Masons of Zerubbabel in the Bible. They worked while holding their sword in one hand and the trowel in the other. This is how the Sword and Trowel became the insignia of the Templars. Subsequently, they concealed themselves under the premise of *Brethren Masons*. [This name, *Frères Maçons* (in French), was adopted as the secret reference to the Builders of the Second Temple, but its English translation was corrupted into *Freemasons*. In England, *Pythagoras de Crotona* was altered into *Peter Gower of Groton*, and *Khairûm* or *Khûr-ûm* was mistranslated into *Hiram,* an artisan in brass and other metals who became the Chief Builder of the *Haikal Kadosh,* the Holy House of the Temple, the Ἱερος Δομος. Yet, the words *Bonai* and *Banaim* appear in the Masonic Degrees, meaning Builder and Builders.]

"The triangular plates of the four trowels of the Templars are arranged to form a cross. This forms the Kabbalistic pentacle (talisman) also known as the Cross of the East. The Knight of the East, and the Knight of the East and West have in their titles secret allusions to the Templars whom they were originally to succeed."

"In founding the Templars, the secret agenda of Hugues de Payens was broader in scope than serving the ambition of the Patriarchs at Constantinople. During that period in the East, a Sect of Johannite Christians claimed to be the only true Initiates of the real mysteries of the Savior's religion. They pretended to know the real history of YESUS the ANOINTED. In part, they had adopted the Jewish traditions and tales of the Talmud. They claimed that the facts written in the Gospels are only allegories. The key to their claim was given by Saint John, who said the world would be filled with the books that could be written about *817* the words and deeds of Jesus Christ. They believed these words would only be a ridiculous exaggeration that would be varied and have prolonged into infinity if he did not speak in allegory or legend."

The Papal Allocution continues: "The Johannites attributed Saint John, the founder of their Secret Church, and the Grand Pontiffs of the Sect assumed the title of *Christos, Anointed,* or *Consecrated.* They claimed to have directly succeeded from Saint John through an uninterrupted succession of pontifical powers. During the period when the Order of the Temple was founded, THEOCLET made claim to these imaginary birthrights. He knew HUGUES DE PAYENS and initiated him into the Mysteries of his pretended church. THEOCLET seduced DE PAYENS with the promise of Sovereign Priesthood, Supreme royalty, and being his designated successor."

"Thus, the Order of Knights of the Temple was at its very origin devoted to the opposition of the authority of Rome and the crowns of its Kings. The Apostolic authority of Kabbalistic Gnosticism was vested in its chiefs. Saint John is the Father of the Gnostics, and their translation of his assertion against the heretics and pagans of his Sect who denied that Christ was the Word is a complete misrepresentation, or at least a misunderstanding, of the whole Spirit of that Gospel."

"The tendencies and tenets of the Order were steeped in profound mystery. It openly professed the most perfect orthodoxy, but the Chiefs concealed the true aim of the Order, and their subordinates followed them without question."

"To acquire wealth, power, and establish the Johannite (or Gnostic) and Kabbalistic dogma by force, if necessary, were the goals and means presented to the initiated Brethren. They told the Initiates that the Papacy and its monarchies could be bought and sold, and would eventually destroy each other. Then the World would come to them for its Kings and Pontiffs, and this would become the heritage of the Temple. They claimed they would become the equilibrium of the Universe and the Masters of the World."

"Like many other Secret Orders and Associations, the Templars had two doctrines. The first was *Johannism* which was private and reserved for the Masters. The second was *Roman Catholicism* and was public. This public doctrine deceived the adversaries they strived to replace. Hence, Freemasonry is vulgarly imagined to have begun with the Dionysian Architects or the German Stoneworkers. It adopted Saint John the Evangelist as one of its patrons, and associated with him Saint John the Baptist to avoid arousing the suspicions of Rome. Covertly, they proclaimed themselves the child of Kabbalah and Essenism."

[The Johannism of the leadership was essentially Kabbalah of the earlier Gnostics. It degenerated into the heretical forms of Gnosticism to such an extent that even the ideas of Mani and his followers were nearly identical. Many adopted his doctrines of the two Principles represented by the handle of the dagger and the tesselated pavement ("*the Indented Tessel*" or floor of the Lodge). It was represented by great hanging tassels, although it really means a *tesserated floor* (from the Latin tessera) of white and black lozenges, surrounded by a *denticulated* or *indented* border or edging. In the higher Degrees, when the two colors black and white are displayed side by side for contrast, it alludes to the two Principles of Zoroaster and Mani. To others, the doctrine became a mystic worship of all Gods, descended from that of the Brahmans. It even devolved into an idolatry of Nature and a hatred of every other revealed dogma.

[This was all directly and inevitably caused by the misinterpretation of the established Church taking literally the figurative, allegorical, and mythical language of a collection of Oriental (Eastern) books from different eras in history. The same thing happened to the Hebrew books of the Old Testament during their translation by King James of England and John Knox of the Scottish Reformation.]

"In order to succeed and win partisans, the Templars sympathized with the conquered creeds and encouraged their hope for new worships. The Templars promised liberty of conscience and a new religion that would be the combination of all the persecuted creeds."

[Because of their own Christian convictions, it was not remotely possible that the Templars worshipped a monstrous idol called Baphomet or recognized Mohammed as an inspired prophet. Their ancient symbolism was designed to conceal what was dangerous to speak. This symbolism was misunderstood by those who were not adepts, and to their enemies it seemed to represent a belief or worship in all Gods. The golden calf made by Aaron for the Israelites (an oxen under a layer of bronze) and the Cherubim on the Propitiatory (mercy seat), were both details lost in the translations. What the Chiefs of the Order really believed and taught is indicated by the hints and symbols contained in the high Degrees of Freemasonry, which only the adepts understand.

[The Blue Degrees represent the outer court or portico of the Temple. In these degrees, parts of the symbols are displayed to the Initiate, but their explanations, while virtuous, are simplistic and incomplete. The Initiate is not intended to fully comprehend them, but it is intended that he will grasp their oversimplified meanings. Their complete explanation is reserved for well-read Masons. The whole body of the Royal and Spiritual Art of the High Degrees is hidden so carefully that for centuries we have been unable to solve many of the enigmas they contain. It is acceptable for the majority of Masons to believe that everything is contained in the Blue Degrees. Whoever attempts to convince them otherwise will labor in vain without any true reward and in the process violate his obligations as an Adept. Masonry is the veritable Sphinx, buried to its neck in the sands of the ages, the visible tip of the iceberg above the waters.]

"The seeds of ruin were sown for the Order of the Temple at its very beginnings. Hypocrisy is a mortal disease. The Templars conceived a great work, which they were incapable of performing, because they lacked humility and personal self-denial. It was further complicated because Rome was invincible, and the later Chiefs of the Order did not comprehend its mission. Furthermore, the Templars were generally uneducated and only capable of wielding the sword. They had no qualifications for governing and were required to restrict all differing Opinions." [The symbols of the wise are the idols of the masses and tend to be at least as meaningless as the hieroglyphics of Egypt to the nomadic Arabs. There must exist a common ground for the interpretation of the symbols to the mass of Initiates that is also meaningful to the Adepts.]

"Hugues de Payens did not have a keen and far-sighted intellect, nor that dignity of purpose which subsequently distinguished the military founder of another army who became formidable to kings. The Templars were unsuccessful Jesuits because they were unintelligent."

"Their goal was to become wealthy and buy the world. They succeeded, and riches became the reefs upon which they were wrecked. By 1312 in Europe alone, they possessed more than nine thousand feudal estates. They became *820* insolent, and arrogantly demonstrated their utter contempt for the religious and social institutions they intended to overthrow. Their flagrant ambition became fatal, and their objectives were discovered and thwarted. Pope Clement V and King Philip le Bel (the Fair) conspired in Europe to arrest, disarm, and imprison the Templars. The *Coup d' Etat* was more superbly executed than any before or since. The whole world was awestruck and eagerly awaited the strange confessions from a process that would echo through so many ages. [Rome has always been more tolerant of vice and crime than heresy. Rome traditionally approached philosophical truth as the most dangerous of heresies, and it has been rigidly intolerant of free thought. They began to fear the Templars and soothed their fear with an incredible cruelty.]

"It was impossible to reveal the Templar conspiracy against the Monarchies and the Papacy to the people. It was irresponsible to expose them to the doctrines of the Chiefs of the Order. The Templars were gravely accused of spitting upon Christ, denying God at their meetings, of gross obscenities, conversations with female devils, and the worship of a monstrous idol. [To reveal these secrets would have been to initiate the masses into the secrets of the Masters and lift the veil of Isis. To avoid this, the Templars were charged with magic and heresy, and false witnesses were summoned.]

"The end of the drama is well known. Jacques de Molay and his followers perished in the flames at the stake. In the gloom of prison before his execution, he organized and instituted what came to be known as the Occult, Hermetic, or Scottish Masonry. Grand Master de Molay created four Metropolitan Lodges: one at Naples for the East, one at Edinburgh for the West, one at Stockholm for the North, and one at Paris for the South." [The initials of his name, J∴B∴M∴ are found in the same order in the first three Degrees, and are one of the many internal and effective proofs this was the origin of modern Freemasonry. The legend of Osiris was adapted to symbolize the destruction of the Order. The resurrection of the Master KHŪRŪM ABAI after being slain in the Temple, symbolized the martyrdom of fidelity to Obligation, Truth, and Conscience. Finally, it foretold the restoration to life of the buried association.]

"The Pope and King Philip perished soon after the death of de Molay in a strange and sudden manner. Squin de Florian, the chief denouncer of the Order, was assassinated. Although the broken pieces of the Templar sword were crafted into daggers, their trowels could now only build tombs."

[The Order's wealth and estates were confiscated, and it seemed to cease almost immediately. However, it survived under other names, governed by unknown Chiefs. It carefully revealed itself only to those Initiates who had proven themselves worthy to be entrusted with such a dangerous Secret. The York Rite Order that styles itself after the Templars has assumed a name they do not represent.]

"The Successors of the Ancient Masters of Rose-Croix, quickly abandoned the pure and hierarchical Sciences their Ancestors used during initiation and instead became a Mystic Sect. They intermingled their dogma with that of the Templars, and they began to believe they were the sole depository of the secrets of the Gospel of St. John. The stories in their allegorical series of rites completed the initiation by reinforcing this belief.

"The Initiates in the eighteenth century believed their time had come to establish a new Hierarchy, others sought to overturn all authority, but they strived to throw down all the summits of the Social Order under the level of Equality."

The Symbol of the Rose has its mystical meanings based in the Kabbalistic Commentaries of the Canticles.

The Rose was represented to the Initiates as the living and blooming symbol for the revelation of the harmonies of being. It is the emblem of beauty, life, love, and pleasure. From the Book of the Jewish Abraham, Flamel made it the hieroglyphical sign for the accomplishment of the great Work. This is the key to the Roman de la Rose. The Conquest of the Rose was the problem proclaimed to Science by Initiation, while Religion was laboring to establish the exclusive, definitive, and universal triumph of the Cross.

The paradox proposed by the High Initiation was how to unite the Rose and the Cross. The mystical philosophy of the Universal Synthesis should 822 explain all of the phenomena of Being. Considered solely a physiological fact, religion is the revelation and satisfaction of a necessity for the soul. Its existence is a scientific fact and to deny it would be to deny humanity.

The Rose-Croix Masters respected the dominant, hierarchical, and revealed religion. They could no more be the enemies of the Papacy than of any legitimate Monarchy. If they had conspired against the Popes and Kings, it would have been because they personally considered them traitors to their duty and supreme advocates of anarchy.

A spiritual or temporal despot is nothing more than a crowned anarchist.

One of the magnificent symbols that express the esoteric and unexplainable part of Science is a Rose of Light with a human form in its center extending its arms out to form a cross.

Numerous commentaries and studies have been written about DANTE's *Divine Comedy*, but no one has pointed out its unique character. The great work of Ghibellin is a declaration of war against the Papacy with bold revelations of the Mysteries. Dante's Epic is Johannite and Gnostic. Like the Apocalypse, it is a bold application of the figures and numbers of Kabbalah to the Christian dogmas and a subtle rejection of everything absolute in these dogmas. His journey through the supernatural worlds is similar to the initiation into the Mysteries of Eleusis and Thebes. He finally escapes from the gulf of Hell *after symbolizing his acceptance of the direct opposite of the Catholic dogma by reversing the positions of his head and feet.* He then ascends to the light by using the Devil as a monstrous ladder. Faust ascended to Heaven by stepping on the head of the vanquished Mephistopheles. This demonstrated that Hell is impassable only to those who do not know how to turn away from it. We free ourselves from its bondage with courage.

Dante's Hell was a negative Purgatory, and his Heaven was composed of a series of Kabbalistic circles divided by a cross, like the Pantacle of Ezekiel. In the center of this cross blooms a rose, and we view the symbol of the Masters of the Rose-Croix for the first time publicly illustrated and almost categorically explained. It is interesting to discover that the Roman de la Rose and the Divine 823 Comedy are two opposite forms of the same work. They are both an initiation into the independence of the spirit, a satire of all modern institutions, and the allegorical formula of the great Secrets of the Society of the Rose-Croix. Most notable is that Guillaume de Lorris died in 1260, a full five years before Dante Alighieri was born. Guillaume had not completed his *Roman de la Rose* by the time of his death, and it was only completed a half century later by Chopinel.

The important manifestations of Mysticism coincide with the fall of the Templars. In Dante's old age, Jean de Meung (Chopinel) was the contemporary, and during the best years of his life he flourished at the Court of Philippe le Bel. The Roman de la Rose is the Epic of old France. It is a profound book penned in levity about a revelation learned from Apuleius about the Mysteries of Mysticism. The Rose of Flamel, the Rose of Jean de Meung, and the Rose of Dante all grew from the same stem.

Swedenborg's system was nothing more than Kabbalah without the principle of the Hierarchy. It is like the Temple without the keystone or a foundation.

Cagliostro was the Agent of the Templars when he wrote to the Freemasons of London declaring the time had come to begin rebuilding the Temple of the Eternal. He had introduced into Masonry a new *Egyptian* Rite and endeavored to revive the mysterious worship of Isis. The three letters on his seal (L∴P∴D∴) were the initials of the words *"Lilia pedibus destrue" (tread under foot the Lilies* [of France]). A Masonic medal of the sixteenth or seventeenth century had upon it a sword cutting off the stalk of a lily with the words *"talem dabit ultio messem"* (what a harvest revenge will give).

A Lodge chartered under the guidance of Rousseau (the fanatic of Geneva) became the center of the revolutionary movement in France. A Prince with royal blood went there to swear the destruction of the successors of Philippe le Bel on the tomb of Jacques de Molay. The record of the Order of Templars attests that the Regent, the Duc d'Orleans, was Grand Master of that formidable Secret Society. His successors were the Duc de Maine, the Prince of Bourbon-Condé, and the Duc de Cossé-Brissac.

The Templars compromised the King by saving him from the rage of the People, only to provoke that rage and bring on the catastrophe that had been prepared for centuries. It was the scaffold demanded by the vengeance of the
824 Templars. The secret forces of the French Revolution had sworn to overthrow the Throne and the Papacy upon the Tomb of Jacques de Molay. Half the work was completed when Louis XVI was executed, and the Army of the Temple then redirected all its efforts against the Pope.

Jacques de Molay and his companions were martyrs, but their avengers dishonored their memory. Royalty was reborn on the scaffolding of Louis XVI, and the Church triumphed. Overwhelmed in their victory, the captivity of Pius VI proved fatal to the Ancient Knights of the Temple. When he died as a prisoner from fatigue and sorrow in Valance, they perished too.

MORALS AND DOGMA FOR THE 21ST CENTURY

CONSISTORY

CHAPTER 31: GRAND INSPECTOR INQUISITOR COMMANDER (INSPECTOR INQUISITOR)

THE chief duties of a judge are to patiently hear, deliberately weigh, and 825
dispassionately and impartially decide. After the lessons you have received, I
need not enlarge further on them. You will be eloquently reminded of them by
the furniture on the Altar and the decorations of the Tribunal.

The Holy Bible will remind you of your obligation. As you judge, so will
you be judged by God, who does not have to try to determine the motives,
intentions, and purposes of people by their acts and words.

The Square, Compasses, Plumb, and Level are well known to Masons. 826
As a Judge, they should instill uprightness, impartiality, careful consideration of
facts and circumstances, accuracy in judgment, and uniformity in decision. You
are to bring up square work and square work only. You are to lean neither to
one side nor the other but be firm and steadfast in your convictions of right and
justice. You are to be true and weigh the facts and the law alone, forgetting
personal friendship or personal dislike. When reformation is no longer possible,
you are to strike relentlessly with the sword of justice.

The principal symbol of this Degree is the Tetractys of Pythagoras
suspended in the East where ordinarily the sacred word or letter glitters and it
represents the Deity. Its nine external points form the triangle, the chief symbol
in Masonry. You are familiar with many of its meanings.

To Masons, its three sides represent the three principal attributes of the
Deity that create, support, uphold, and guide the Universe in its eternal
movement. The three supports of the Masonic Temple are Wisdom, the Infinite
Divine Intelligence; Strength or Power, the Infinite Divine Will; and Beauty, the
Infinite Divine Harmony, the Eternal Law. Harmony ensures that the infinite
suns rush onward in their endless revolutions without clash or conflict in the
Infinity of space.

The triangle reminds Masonic Judges of the Pyramids, as everlasting as
the hills, and to stand as firm and unshaken as them when our belief is based on
solid truth.

The triangle includes numerous geometrical figures, all having a deep
significance to Masons. The triple triangle is particularly sacred, having long
been a symbol of the Deity. Extending their external lines creates a Hexagon

827 with six smaller triangles whose bases cut each other in the central point of the Tetractys. The Tetractys is a symbol of the generative power of the Universe, the Sun, Brahma, Osiris, Apollo, Bel, and the Deity. We can form twelve smaller triangles, three times three of which compose the Tetractys itself.

The Hexagon itself appears to us as a cube, not visible at first glance, but a fitting emblem of that faith in things invisible most essential to salvation. It is the first perfect solid and it reminds you of the cubical stone that sweat blood and of the stone deposited by Enoch. It teaches justice, accuracy, and consistency.

The infinite divisibility of the triangle teaches the infinity of the Universe, time, space, and God. The lines that diverge from the common centre increasing their distance from each other as they are infinitely extended. They may be infinite in number as God's attributes are infinite. They emanate from one centre, as the Universe emanated from God.

You have other duties to perform in addition to those of a judge. You should examine and carefully scrutinize the work in the subordinate Bodies of Masonry. You should ensure there are not excessive numbers of initiates in the higher Degrees. Improper persons should be excluded from membership and, in their life and conversations, Masons should testify to the value of our doctrines and institutions. You should also examine your own heart and conduct and keep careful watch over yourself. If you harbor malice, jealousy, intolerance, or bigotry, it is time for you to put your own house in order or call yourself a Mason in vain.

Everywhere in the universe, there is a law that seems to belong to the nature of things. This fact is universal. In different areas, we call this law by different names: the law of Matter, Mind, Morals, and the like. By this, we mean

828 a certain law that belongs to the material, mental, or moral forces in which they typically act. We know the ideal laws of matter from the fact that they are always obeyed. This obedience is the only evidence we have of the ideal rule. In respect to the material world, the ideal and the actual are the same.

We learn the laws of matter by observation and experience. Before experience of the fact, no man could tell that a body falling toward the earth would descend sixteen feet the first second, twice that the next, four times the third, and sixteen times the fourth. No law in our experience anticipated this rule of action. The same is true with all the laws of matter. The ideal law is known because it is a fact. The law is imperative. It must be obeyed without hesitation. There is no deviation or disobedience in the chemical laws of crystallization, proportion, or in any other law of Nature. Only the primal will of God works in the material world.

There are no exceptions to the law of Attraction, which binds atom to atom and gives unity to the world of things. There may seem to be exceptions to this law but all these are special cases of the one great law of attraction acting in various modes.

The various effects of this law at first surprises, but in the end the unity of the law astonishes the mind. Looked at in reference to the earth, an earthquake is no more than a chink that opens on a garden path in a dry summer day. A sponge is porous, having small spaces between the solid parts. The solar system is more porous, having more space between the several bodies. The Universe is even more so with even larger spaces between the systems. The same attraction holds together the atom, sponge, solar system, and the Universe. Every particle of matter in the Universe is related to each and every other particle and attraction is their common bond.

In the spiritual world, there is also a law for the spiritual forces of man. 829 The law of Justice is as universal as the law of Attraction, though we are unable to reconcile it with Nature. The lark has the same right to live, sing, and dart with pleasure through the sky, as the hawk has to spread its strong wings in the summer sunshine. Yet the hawk devours the harmless lark, as the lark devours the worm. As far as we know, there is no compensation anywhere for this apparent injustice. Among the bees, one rules, and the others obey. Some work and others are idle. Among the small ants, the soldiers feed on the proceeds of the workmen's labor. The lion lies in wait for and devours the antelope that has as good a right to life as it does. Among people, some govern and others serve. Money commands and labor obeys. Yet, for all this, no one questions the justice of God.

These varied phenomena are consistent with one great law of justice and the only difficulty is that we do not, and cannot, understand that law. It is very easy for a dreaming and visionary theorist to say that it is unjust for the lion to devour the deer, but we know of no other way that they could survive. Our scale of justice is not God's scale. His justice does not require us to free mankind from all labor.

Beneath the lives, wishes, wills, and plans of the six billion human beings on this earth resides the same eternal force they shape into their own special form. The same paternal Providence presides over them, keeping eternal watch over the great and small while producing a variety of effects from Unity of Force.

Justice is the foundation or fundamental law of the moral Universe, and 830 the rule of conduct for man. All human affairs are subject to it as the paramount law. What is *right* agrees with it and remains, while what is *wrong* conflicts with it and fails. Unfortunately, we always enact *our* notions of what is right and just into the *law* of justice and demand that God shall adopt our law as His. We are self-centered and try to amend our own little notions into the Universal Laws of God. Instead, we should try to learn by observation and reflection what His law *is*, then determine whether ours is consistent with *His* infinite justice and whether or not it corresponds with *our* limited notion of justice.

It might be difficult to prove how it is right or just for man to domesticate the horse or cow to his service and give in return only their daily food. Why is it just that we should kill and eat the harmless deer that only eats the greenery and drinks the water that God made common to all? It is difficult to prove it is just for one man's intellect or wealth to make another man's strong arms his servants for a daily wage.

To determine this universal law of justice is one thing, but measuring something with our own little ruler and calling *that* God's law of justice is another. The general laws enacted by God continually produce what our limited notions see as wrong. Before, men have been able to explain injustice only by assuming another existence in which all inequalities and injustices in this life will be remedied. It is very unjust that a child is made miserable by deformity or disease because of the vices of the parents, yet that is part of the universal law. The ancients said that the child was *punished* for the sins of its parents. *We* say that the deformity or disease is the *consequence* of the parent's vices, but as far as justice is concerned, that is merely the change of a word.

831   It is very easy to develop a broad, general principle embodying our own idea of what is absolute justice and to insist that everything conform to it. We may say, "All human affairs must be subject to that principle as the paramount law. What agrees with it is right and remains. What is wrong conflicts and fails. Personal feelings of love, friendship, or patriotism must be subordinate to this eternal right." Unfortunately, this Universe created by God will not conform to any such absolute principle or arbitrary theory, no matter in what grand words and glittering phrases it may be embodied.

Idealistic rules in morals are always injurious. People fall short of compliance with them and they turn real virtues into imaginary offences against false laws. Justice between man and man and between man and the animals below him is right and proper to be carried out with respect to the general and the individual interest. It is not a theoretical principle by which the very relations that God has created and imposed on us are to be experimented with and approved or condemned.

God has made the great system of the Universe and enacted general laws for its government. Those laws surround everything that lives with a mighty network of necessity. He chose to create the tiger with such organs that he cannot graze on grass, but must eat other flesh or starve. He has also made man carnivorous and some of the smallest birds are as carnivorous as the tiger. Every step we take and every breath we draw involves the destruction of numerous living things. Each, no matter how minute, is as much a living creature as ourselves. Among mankind, He has made necessary a division of labor both intellectual and moral. He has made necessary the various relationships of society and dependence, of obedience and control.

What God made necessary cannot be unjust, because if it is, then He is himself unjust. Legalization of injustice and wrong, justified by the *false* plea of necessity, is an evil that must be avoided. From the relationships of life, grow

832   duties, as natural as the leaves grow on trees. If we have the right to kill the lamb so we can eat and live, we have no right to torture it because that is not

necessary. We have the right to live, if we can, by the legitimate exercise of our intellect and to hire the labor of others to farm our lands, dig in our mines, and work in our factories, but we have no right to overwork or underpay them.

We can learn the law of justice and right from experience and observation, but God has given us an ability, our conscience, which is able to perceive this law directly and immediately. Mankind has in its nature a rule of conduct higher than what it has ever been able to live up to. It is an ideal of nature that shames its actual history, because mankind has always been prone to make any necessity society's own necessity. This notion must not be pushed too far. If we substitute this illusion for actuality, then we have within us an ideal rule of right and wrong that God Himself offends every day. We detest the tiger and the wolf for the brutality and love of blood, which are their nature. We revolt against the law by which the crooked limbs and diseased body of the child are the results of the parent's vices. We even think a God Omnipotent and Omniscient should not permit pain, poverty, or servitude. Our ideal of justice is loftier than the actualities of God. He has given us a moral sense for wise and beneficent purposes. We accept an ideal so exalted as significant proof of the goodness of human nature. We should attain as much of it as we can to be consistent with the relationships that He has created and the circumstances that surround us and hold us captive.

We develop our conscience and all its related powers when we apply it to our existing relationships and circumstances. We discover those duties that are obligatory and then learn justice, the law of right, and the divine rule of conduct for human life. If we attempt to define "the law of action that belongs to the infinitely perfect nature of God," and set up an ideal rule beyond our reach, then we will come to judge and condemn His work. *833*

A part of human nature is a sense of justice. People find a deep, permanent, and instinctive delight in justice. Inwardly, they revere this law of justice with a deep and abiding love. Justice is the object of the conscience, like light is the object of the eye, and truth is the object of the mind.

Justice keeps relationships between people honorable. It holds the balance between nations and between a person and their family, nation, or race so that their rights and their *ultimate* interests do not clash. The interests of anyone should not prove antagonistic to those of anyone else. We must believe this if we are to believe that God is just. We must do justice to all and demand it of all. It is a universal human debt and claim. However, the *temporary* interests and rights of man often interfere and clash. The self-interests of the individual often conflict with the permanent interests and welfare of society or what may seem to be the rights of another.

It is unreasonable to say that "one man, however little, cannot be sacrificed for another, however great." This is not only a fallacy, but a very dangerous one. Often one or more men must be sacrificed in the interest of many. The selfish coward seeks refuge in the comfortable fallacy that if they cannot be sacrificed for the common good, then their country has no right to demand of them *self-sacrifice*. The selfish coward also proclaims that anyone who gives their life or luxuries to ensure the safety or prosperity of their country is a fool. According to that doctrine, Curtius was a fool, Leonidas an idiot, and to die for one's country is an absurdity. The common soldier cannot be asked to sacrifice himself for the commander on whose fate hangs the freedom of his country and the welfare of millions yet unborn.

834   Necessity rules in the affairs of man and the interest and life of one man must often be sacrificed to the interest and welfare of his country. Someone must lead the lonesome hope and the physician must expose himself to contagious disease for the sake of others. The sailor on the open ocean must step calmly into the hungry waters if the lives of the passengers can only be saved by his sacrifice. The helmsman must stand firm at the wheel and let the flames take his own life to ensure the safety of those passengers on the doomed vessel.

People are always looking for what is just. The machinery of a State is an attempt by the people to organize a practical justice that may be attained in the real world. The small but widespread civil system that is composed of the law and the courts is mainly an effort to reduce to practice the theory of right. Constitutions are made to establish justice. The decisions of courts are documented to help judge more wisely the next time. The nation tries to gather together the most just men in the State so that they may incorporate into the law their aggregate sense of what is right. The people desire the law to be justice administered without passion. Even in the wildest ages, there has been a raw popular justice mixed with passion and administered in hate. Justice takes rude forms with rude people. It becomes less mixed with hate and passion in more civilized communities. Every progressive State occasionally revises its statutes and constitution to try to come closer to the most practical justice and right. Sometimes, when following theorists and dreamers in their adoration for the ideal they create injustice and then they have to retrace their steps.

In literature, people always look for practical justice and hope that virtue will have its reward and vice its appropriate punishment. They are always on the side of justice and the majority of humanity has an ideal justice that is better than
835 the world around them. The law is always imperfect and does not attain even the most *practicable* degree of perfection. No man is as just as his own idea of possible and practicable justice. His passions and his necessities always cause him to sink below his own ideal. The ideal justice that men look up to and attempt to reach will not be realized in this world. We must approach it as we would the ideal democracy that, "now floats before the eyes of earnest and religious men, fairer than the Republic of Plato, More's Utopia, or the Golden Age of fabled memory," taking care that we do not neglect to seize and hold fast its possible reality. To aim at the best, but be content with the best possible, is the only true wisdom. To insist on the absolute right, and eliminate the important and all-controlling element of necessity is the folly of a mere dreamer.

In a world inhabited by people with bodies, wants, and passions, the time will never come when there will not be need, oppression, servitude, and fear of man or God. As long as there are inferior intellects, indulgence, foolishness, improvidence, pestilence, war, and famine people will continue to need, serve, suffer, and fear.

The plough of justice is always drawn through the field of the world uprooting the savage plants. We always see a continual and progressive triumph of the right. The injustice of England lost America, the fairest jewel of her crown. The injustice of Napoleon cost him more than the snows of Russia and exiled him to a barren rock where his life served as a warning to mankind to be just.

We intuitively understand that justice is better than we can depict it. What justice is in a given case depends so much on circumstances that definitions of it are deceitful. Often it would be unjust to society to do what would be considered just to the individual. General pronouncements of a person's right to this or that are always fallacious. Often, it would be unjust to the individual to do what the theorist generally would say was right and his due.

We should always do unto others what, under the same circumstances, 836 we wish they would do unto us. There are many cases where one person must take care of themselves in preference to another. They may have to struggle for the possession of a plank that will save one but not two, or when attacked they can save their own life only by killing their attacker. A person must prefer the safety of their country to the lives of her enemies and sometimes of their innocent citizens. The retreating general may cut away a bridge behind him to delay pursuit or save the main body of his army though he surrenders a detachment, a battalion, or even a corps of his own force to certain destruction.

These are not departures from justice. Like other instances where the injury or death of an individual is beneficial to the safety of all, they may infringe upon some dreamer's idealistic rule of justice. Injustice, public or private, is inevitably followed by its consequences. The selfish, greedy, inhuman, and fraudulently unjust employer is detested by the people while the generous and humane employer has the good opinion of all. Those who stand up for truth and justice are honored. The world builds monuments to its patriots. Four great statesmen, now sculpted in stone, look down upon the citizens in South Dakota. How we admire the marble likenesses of Jay and Marshall, which look so calmly toward the living Bench of the Supreme Court of the United States. Washington built a great monument in the heart of America for the entire world with his constant effort to be practically just and not chase impractical dreams.

Only the greatest good for the greatest number, can legitimately interfere with the dominion of absolute and ideal justice. Government should not foster the strong at the expense of the weak, or protect the businessperson by taxing 837 the laborer. The powerful should not seek a monopoly of development and enjoyment. Politicians should not look for short-term solutions instead of the right and proper action. Justice should never be forgotten when taking a position or morality neglected in the interest of finance. We should not have national housekeeping as a substitute for national organization based on rights.

We may disagree about the abstract right of many things. Every question has many sides and few men look at all of them. We easily recognize cruelty, unfairness, inhumanity, partiality, and brutality by their ugly and familiar lines. We do not need to sit as a Court of Errors and Appeals to know, hate, and despise *them*.

There are certainly great evils in civilization today and many questions of humanity that have long been ignored. Poverty, crime, and vice in our cities tell us the rich, powerful, and intellectual do not perform their duty for the poor, feeble, and ignorant. Every wretched person who lives on minimum wage testifies to the injustice and inhumanity of mankind. The cruelties everywhere are a disgrace to their perpetrators and unwarranted by the lawful relation of control and dependence which it has pleased God to create.

A sentence is written by God against everything unjust and it is embedded in the nature of man and the nature of the Universe, because it is in the nature of the Infinite God. Trusting your senses and their truth is justice to yourself. An obedient life is justice toward mankind. No wrong is ever successful. The gain of injustice is a loss and its pleasure is suffering. Evil often seems to prosper, but its success will eventually bring defeat and shame. The day of reckoning will always come to a nation or an individual. The knave deceives himself. The miser may starve another's body, but he will also starve his own soul. When he dies his soul will creep out of his great estate of injustice, poor, naked, and miserable. Whoever escapes a duty loses a gain. Outward judgment often fails, but inward justice never does. A person who tries to love evil and do evil is eating stones and not bread. The swift feet of justice are following with wooden tread and her iron hands are round his neck. No person can escape this or themselves. Justice is the angel of God that flies from East to West. Where she spreads her broad wings, she brings the counsel of God and feeds mankind with angel's bread.

We cannot completely understand the moral Universe. The arc is a long one and our eyes reach but a little way. We cannot calculate the curve and complete the figure with the experience of sight. We can understand it by conscience and we know that it bends toward justice. Justice will not fail, though wickedness appears strong and has on its side the armies and thrones of power. Justice will not fail or perish from the world of man, nor will what is wrong and contrary to God's law of justice continually endure. The Power, Wisdom, and Justice of God are on the side of every just thought and it cannot fail, any more than God Himself can perish.

In human affairs, the justice of God must work through human means. Man is the instrument of God's principles. Our morality is the instrument of His justice that is incomprehensible to us and often seems unjust to us. It can silence

838

the oppressor's brutal laugh. Justice is the rule of conduct written in the nature of mankind. In our daily life we can help to prepare the way for the commonwealth of justice that is slowly, but, surely approaching. The justice we dispense will bless us here and hereafter, and at our death, we will leave it to the treasury mankind. Every Mason who enforces justice will help deepen the channel of human morality in which God's justice flows. The wrecks of evil that now block or obstruct the stream will soon be swept out and carried away by the resistless tide of Omnipotent Right. In this, as in all else, let us always endeavor to perform the duties of a good Mason and a good man.

CHAPTER 32: SUBLIME PRINCE OF THE ROYAL SECRET (MASTER OF THE ROYAL SECRET)

THE Occult Science of the Ancient Magi was concealed within the 839 Ancient Mysteries. It was disguised by the Gnostics, hinted at under the haze surrounding the pretended crimes of the Templars, and it is enshrouded in seemingly impenetrable enigmas that seem impenetrable in the Rites of the Highest Masonry.

Magism was the Science of Abraham, Orpheus, Confucius, and Zoroaster. The beliefs of this Science were engraved on the stone tablets of Enoch and Trismegistus. Moses purified and *re-veiled* them when he made the Holy Kabbalah the exclusive heritage of the people of Israel, and the Secret of its 840 priests. The Mysteries of Thebes and Eleusis preserved some of its symbols, but the key to the mysteries was lost among an ever-growing superstition. In its turn, Jerusalem had lost the Holy Word. Jesus came to destroy the veil of the old Temple by giving the Church a new body of legends and symbols that still conceals them from the masses but reveals the same truths to the Elect.

The memory of this scientific and religious Absolute was transmitted to the Elect of all the Ancient Initiations. This same memory was preserved in the celebrated Order of the Templars and became, for all the secret associations, the reason for their unique rites, signs, mutual devotedness, and power.

The Gnostics made the Gnosis forbidden to the Christians, and the official Sanctuary was closed for the high initiation. The Hierarchy of Knowledge was compromised by the violence of ignorance, and the disorders of the Sanctuary were mirrored in the State. Willingly or unwillingly, the Ruler is sustained by the Priest, because the Powers of the Earth must receive their consecration and force from the Sanctuary of the Divine instruction to remain viable.

The Hermetic Science of the early Christian ages, which was studied by the Arabs and Templars, is accurately defined as Kabbalah in active realization. Its three analogous Degrees are religious, philosophical, and physical realization.

Its religious manifestation is the foundation of the true Empire and the true Priesthood that rule in the realm of human intellect. Its philosophical manifestation is the establishment of the "HOLY DOCTRINE", and it is what PLUTARCH speaks of mysteriously in "de Iside et Osiride". Its physical manifestation is the discovery and application of the creative law that populates the great Universe.

841

If you measure a corner of the Creation and extend that knowledge of space by progression, the entire Infinite reveals still new universes. The summation of our knowledge always lies within the points of an ideal and ever-growing compass. Imagine that from any point of the Infinite above, a hand holds another Compass or Square. The lines of that Celestial triangle will meet that of the Compass of Science from below to form the Star of Solomon.

Scientifically probable hypotheses are the last gleams of fading knowledge. Faith begins where Reason ends, and beyond human Reason lies Divine Reason. Our feebleness is the great Absurdity that confuses us. For the Master Mason, the Compass of Faith is *above* the Square of Reason. *Both* rest upon the Holy Scriptures, and they combine to form the Blazing Star of Truth.

All eyes do not see alike. The visible creation is not one form or one color. Our mind is a book printed inside and out, and the two printings are more or less confused.

The primary tradition of the single revelation has been preserved under the name of "Kabbalah" by the Priesthood of Israel. The Kabbalistic doctrine is contained in the Sepher Yetzirah, the Zohar, and the Talmud. According to that doctrine, the Absolute is the Word that is the utterance and expression of being and life.

Magic is what it is. It is like mathematics, because it is the exact and absolute science of Nature and its laws.

Magic is the science of the Ancient Magi. The Christian religion reveres those Magi who came from the East guided by a Star, to adore the Savior of the world in His cradle.

842

Tradition also gave those Magi the title of "*Kings*". Initiation into Magism was considered a genuine royalty. The adepts called the grand art of the Magi, "*The Royal Art*", the *Holy Realm,* or *Sanctum Regnum.*

The Star that guided them is the same Blazing Star represented in all initiations. It was the sign of the Quintessence to the Alchemists, the Grand Arcanum to the Magists, and the Sacred Pentagram to the Kabbalists. The study of this Pentagram led the Magi to the knowledge of the New Name that was about to become supreme. It caused all creatures capable of adoration to bend down upon their knee.

Magic unites in a single science the most certain aspects of Philosophy with the Religion of the Infallible and Eternal. It perfectly reconciles the pairs of terms that seem so opposed to each other: faith and reason, science and creed, authority and liberty.

It supplies the human mind with an instrument of philosophical and religious certainty. It is as exact as mathematics, and it is responsible for mathematics' infallibility.

There is an Absolute in matters of Intelligence and Faith. Supreme Reason has not left human understanding to wander at risk, because there is an incontestable truth and an infallible method of knowing this truth. Those who accept it will give their mind the power to make themselves masters of all inferior things and spirits. It will make them the Arbiters and Kings of the World.

Science gives the intellectual world a life of regulated movements and progressive phases. With Truth, nothing concealed is lost and no discovery is entirely new. God is pleased to give Science (the reflection of His Glory) the Seal of His Eternity.

We must look to the religious symbolism of the Ancients and not the Philosophers for the footprints of Science to rediscover that Knowledge. The Priests of Egypt understood the laws of movement and life. They knew how to modify action with reaction, and they foresaw the results of these effects.

In the Magian traditions, the Columns of Seth, Enoch, Solomon, and 843 Hercules have symbolized the universal law of Equilibrium. This Science of Equilibrium led the Initiates to a universal gravitation around the centers of Life, Heat, and Light.

Thales and Pythagoras learned in the Sanctuaries of Egypt that the Earth revolved around the Sun. They did not attempt to make this widely known, because it would have required them to reveal one of the great Secrets of the Temple, the principle of Creation, and the cause of life. Skeptics ridiculed this Truth, and for many years, attempts were made to disprove it.

While the philosophers were busy reasoning, without replying or acknowledging their error, the Priests made the hieroglyphics that contained the Secrets of the Truth that created the dogmas and poetry.

When a Truth comes into the world, the Magi rush to adore the Infant who creates the Future. It is with Intelligence and the practice of obedience that one obtains Initiation. If Rulers have a Divine Right to govern, the true Initiate will cheerfully obey.

The orthodox traditions were brought from Chaldæa by Abraham. They were widely practiced in Egypt during the time of Joseph, as was the knowledge of the True God. Moses brought this Orthodoxy out of Egypt. The Secret Traditions of Kabbalah contain a Theology that has a consistency and harmony the world is still unable to comprehend. The Zohar is the Key to the Holy Books, and it reveals the depths, lights, and obscurities of the Ancient Mythologies and Sciences originally concealed in the Sanctuaries. To use it, the

Secret of this Key must be understood, but the Zohar is virtually incomprehensible and almost illegible for even the most penetrating intellects not initiated into this Secret.

844   The Secret of the Occult Sciences is of Nature itself. The Omnipotence of God is the Secret of the generation of the Angels and Worlds.

The Serpent in Genesis said, *"You shall be like the Elohim, knowing good and evil,"* and the Tree of Knowledge became the Tree of Death.

The Martyrs of Knowledge have toiled and died at the foot of this tree for six thousand years so that it may once again become the Tree of Life.

The Absolute, which is searched for unsuccessfully by the senseless, but can be found by the Wise, is the TRUTH, REALITY, and REASON of the universal equilibrium!

Equilibrium is the Harmony that results from the comparison of opposites.

Until now, Man has been trying to stand on one foot.

Civilizations have risen and fallen by the anarchical insanity of Despotism or the Despotic anarchy of Revolution.

The problem revolutionaries have and will always have to resolve is how to organize the Anarchy. The rock of Sisyphus will always fall back upon them. Out of necessity to exist even a single instant, they will always have to improvise a violent and blind despotism to survive. Man escapes from the harmony of Reason only to fall under the dictatorship of Folly.

Nations have been led astray by superstitious enthusiasms and calculations of materialist instinct, but God leads the world to believe in Reason and reasonable Beliefs.

We have seen prophets without philosophy and philosophers without religion. The zealous believers and apathetic skeptics resemble each other, and both are equally far from eternal salvation.

The great men and Seers have been ineffective in dealing with universal doubt and the conflicts of Reason and Faith. They have sought the ideal at the risk and peril of their reason and life.

Hoping to be crowned themselves, they are the first to do what Pythagoras prohibited of his admirable Symbols. They will destroy crowns and tread them under foot.

845   Light is the equilibrium of Shadow and Lucidity.

Movement is the equilibrium of Inertia and Activity.

Authority is the equilibrium of Liberty and Power.

Wisdom is the equilibrium of Thought and Intellect.

Virtue is the equilibrium of Affections, and Beauty is the harmonious proportion of Forms.

Beautiful lives are accurate ones, and the beauty of Nature is grace and splendor.

Everything just is beautiful and everything beautiful should be just.

• • • • • •

There is no void Emptiness in the Universe. For hundreds of centuries, Science has imagined that there was empty Space from the edge of our atmosphere to that of the Sun, Planets, and farthest Stars. Comparing finite knowledge to the Infinite, the Philosophers have proven they know almost nothing. In all that "empty" space are the Infinite Forces of God, acting in an infinite variety of directions. The Light that is the Visible Manifestation of God is in all of it. Darkness has no home in the Universe. Lighting one side of a sphere projects a cone of darkness on the other. The earth and every other planet or sphere that does not emit light carries the cone of its shadow as it rotates in its orbit. Error is the Shadow of the Truth that God uses to illuminate the Soul.

In all that "Empty Space" of the universe lay the Mysterious Electricity, Heat and Omnipresent Ether. The Invisible becomes Visible by the will of God. Two invisible gases are combined and compressed to become the water that fills the seas, flows in the rivers and rivulets, and drops upon the earth as rain or snow. God's manifestation fills everything we mistakenly call Empty Space and the Void.

Throughout the Universe, everything we call Life and Movement results 846 from a continuous conflict of Forces. When that activity ends, Death results.

Kabbalah says that if the Justice of God, which is Severity, was supreme, creation of imperfect beings like man would have been impossible. Because Sin is inherent in Humanity, after measuring the Sin, the Infinite Justice would have annihilated Humanity at the instant of its creation. Nothing imperfect would have been possible. However, if the Mercy of God was unrestricted, Sin would go unpunished, and the Universe would fall into a chaos of corruption.

If God repealed a single law of chemical attraction, the equally balanced forces would be released and instantaneously expand matter into intangible and invisible gases.

The great currents and rivers of air constantly flow, rush and roll from the equator to the frozen polar regions and back again to the hot equatorial regions. Typhoons, tornadoes, and cyclones result from conflicts between the rushing currents of equatorial heat and polar cold. These calamities and the benign trade winds result from the same great law. God is omnipotent. Effects without causes are impossible, but the effects will sometimes be evil. The fire would not warm, if it could not also burn human flesh. The most virulent poisons make the strongest remedies, when given in due proportion. Evil is the shadow of Good and inseparable from it.

Divine Wisdom balances the Omnipotence of the Divine Will and the result is Beauty or Harmony. The arch does not rest on a single column, but it is

847 supported by one on either side. So it is with Divine Justice, Mercy, Human Reason, and Faith.

The Categories of Aristotle and the Sentences of Peter Lombard argued instead of reasoned, ignored the Kabbalistic dogma, and wandered off into darkness. The Scholastic Theology was less a philosophy than a philosophical machine, and it substituted the human verb for the monotonous cry of machinery. The free application of rational necessities was the fatal precision of mechanism. With a single blow, ST. THOMAS AQUINAS crushed with a single blow the tower of words by proclaiming the eternal Empire of Reason. *"A thing is not just because GOD wills it; but GOD wills it because it is just."* The immediate consequence of this proposition became: *"A thing is not true because ARISTOTLE has said it; but ARISTOTLE could not reasonably say it unless it was true. Then first seek the TRUTH and JUSTICE, and the Science of ARISTOTLE will be given to you."*

The greatest Poets dream that Hell will be closed by the triumph of Heaven. The problem of Evil will receive its final solution, and Good will be triumphant and reign for Eternity. Persian dogma taught that AHRIMAN and his subordinate ministers of Evil would be reconciled with God by a Redeemer and Mediator and that all Evil would end. The philosopher forgets the laws of equilibrium and seeks to adorn the Light in a splendor without shadow and movement. However, as long as there is a visible light, there must be a shadow proportional to this Light. Whatever it illuminates will cast a cone of shadow. Resting will never bring happiness if it is not balanced by a similar and opposite movement of work. This is the unchanging law of Nature and the Eternal Will of JUSTICE, which is GOD.

This is why Evil and Sorrow in Humanity and the perils of this world are
848 indispensable. Harmony only results from the comparison of opposites. What is above exists only by reason of what is below. The depth determines the height. If the valleys are filled, the mountains disappear. If the shadows are dimmed, Light is ineffective. Light is only made visible by the contrast between brightness and darkness. Universal obscurity is produced by an immense dazzling. The color spectrum in Light only exists in the presence of a shadow.

The two great columns of the Temple that symbolizes the Universe are Necessity and Liberty. Although these forces seem antagonistic to human reason, God is capable of comprehending the balance between them. God's Power and Wisdom created the Universe to provide man a place to use his free will and free action as tools. A man anticipating the action of another may use that action as an instrument to implement his own purposes.

The Infinite Wisdom of God foresees what we will do and uses that as an instrument for the exertion of His Infinite Power. The result is Harmony, the third column that upholds the Lodge. The same Harmony results from the balance of Necessity and Liberty. The will of God is not for an instant defeated or thwarted, and he does not tempt or prohibit men from doing Evil. The result is Stability, Cohesion, Permanence, and the undivided Dominion and Autocracy of God. Victory, Glory, Stability, and Dominion are the last four Sephiroth of Kabbalah.

God said to Moses, I AM that which Is, Was and Shall forever Be.

The doctrine of all the ancient Wise Men was that the unmanifested God *849* has no Name, and it is expressly declared in Kabbalah. Jahweh is the Name of the Deity manifested in the act of Creation. He contains within Himself the whole Universe invested with form and materially developed in idea and actually. God has always existed and always THOUGHT and the Universe has always existed like Himself. The duration of the Universe is but a halfway point along the infinite line of eternity. God was not inert and uncreative during the eternity that stretches behind that point. The Archetype of the Universe has always existed in the Divine Mind. The Word was in the BEGINNING with God, and WAS God, and the Ineffable NAME was manifested as Being or Existence. The Philosophers said Existence or Being is a limitation, but the Deity is not limited or defined.

Reversing the letters of the Ineffable Name and dividing it, it becomes gender neutral like the word *Yod-He* or *JAH*. It reveals much of the obscure language of Kabbalah and represents The Highest, which are symbolized by the Columns Jachin and Boaz. We are told that, "God created Man in his image. From Male, He created Female." The writer, symbolizing the Divine with the Human, tells us that the woman, at first contained in man, was taken from his side. Minerva was born a woman in armor from the mind of Jove. Isis was the sister of Osiris before she was his wife. Within BRAHM, was developed MAYA, the Mother of all that is. The WORD is the First and Only begotten of the Father. The awe with which the Highest Mysteries were regarded has imposed silence upon the Nature of the Holy Spirit. The Word is Light, and the Life of Humanity.

Adepts understand the meaning of these Symbols.

For your last lesson, let us return to the Degrees of Blue Masonry and *850* receive an explanation of one of their Symbols.

You see upon the altar of those Degrees the SQUARE and the COMPASSES and remember how they lay upon the altar in each Degree.

The SQUARE is an instrument only used for plane surfaces, and it is appropriate for Geometry, or the measurement of the Earth. The COMPASSES are an instrument used for spheres and spherical surfaces, and they are adapted for spherical trigonometry.

The SQUARE is a natural and appropriate Symbol of this Earth and the things that belong to it. The COMPASSES are an equally natural and appropriate Symbol of the Heavens, all celestial things, and celestial natures.

At the beginning of this chapter is an old Hermetic Symbol. It has a Triangle upon a Square contained in a circle. Above this, a human body with two arms and two heads (one male and one female) is standing upon a dragon. Beside the male head is the Sun, and next to the female head is the crescent within the circle of the full moon. The hand on the *male* side holds the *Compasses*, and on the *female* side, a *Square*.

The Heavens and the Earth were personified as Deities by the Ancient Hindus, Zends, Bactrians, and Persians, and the Rig Veda Sanhita contains hymns addressed to them as gods. They were deified among the Phœnicians and among the Greeks as OURANOS and GEA.

The fertile Earth produces everything that ministers to the needs, comfort, and luxuries of man. From her bountiful and inexhaustible bosom come the fruits, grains, and flowers. She feeds the animals that serve man as 851 laborers and food. She is green with plentiful grass and the trees spring from her soil with their abundance of green leaves. In the earth are found useful and valuable minerals, seas that swarm with life, and rivers that furnish food and irrigation. The EARTH was always represented as a *female*, as the MOTHER.

The light and heat of the Sun and the rains of Spring make the Earth bountiful. They restore life and warmth to the chill brought by Winter and free the streams form their frozen silence. The Heavens and the Sun are the procreative and generative agents and have always been regarded as *male*.

The Hermaphroditic figure is symbolic of the double nature anciently assigned to the Deity as Generator and Producer. The Sun was male, and the Moon was female. The Compasses are the Hermetic Symbol of the Creative Deity, and the Square is symbolic of the productive Earth or Universe.

The spiritual and immortal part of man comes from the Heavens, and the Earth provides the material and mortal parts. The Hebrew Genesis says that JEHOVAH formed man from the dust of the Earth, and He breathed the breath of life into man's nostrils. The Souls given by God descend through the seven planetary spheres to be joined with their human bodies, and through those seven spheres, they must re-ascend to return to their origin.

The COMPASSES symbolize the *Heavens* and represent the spiritual, intellectual, and moral part of this double nature of Humanity. The SQUARE symbolizes the *Earth* and represents the material, sensual, and baser nature of Humanity.

852   Ancient Indian Philosophers said, "Truth and Intelligence are the Eternal attributes of God and not of the individual Soul. God and the individual Soul are distinct." This expression of Truth from the Nyaya Philosophers has been handed down through the ages in the lessons of Freemasonry. We are taught, "Truth is a Divine Attribute and the foundation of every virtue."

They said, "IN the body, the Soul is in a state of imprisonment and under the influence of evil passions. When the Soul acquires the knowledge of the elements and principles of Nature through intense study, it achieves THE ETERNAL."

The Hindu Philosophers believed the vitality that animates the body also perishes with it. They thought the Soul was a divine emanation of the Spirit of

God, but not a *part* of that Spirit. They compared it to the heat and light from the Sun or a *ray* of light, which does not lessen or divide its own being.

However created, the Soul does not know the means of its creation or understand its own individuality. It does not understand how the being created from the body and soul can feel pain, see, or hear. God has set bounds on the scope of our human and finite reason that cannot be exceeded. If we are capable of understanding the means of creating the Universe of things, He has concealed it from us by an impenetrable veil. The words we use to describe the act of creation do nothing to improve our comprehension of it.

Masonry teaches us that we are not entirely mortal. The Soul or Spirit is our intellectual and reasoning component, not subject to decay and dissolution, but surviving the death of the body. It is capable of improvement, advancement, and increasing its knowledge of divine things, making it ever wiser, better, and *853* more worthy of immortality. Working to benefit and improve others is the noblest ambition and the highest glory that we can attain in this imperfect life.

The Divine and Human are mixed in everyone. Everyone possesses Reason, Moral sense, and passions that prompt evil and sensual appetites. Paul wrote to the Christians at Rome, "If you live for flesh, you shall die, but if you seek spiritual redemption, you shall live. Those who are led by the Spirit of God are the sons of God. The flesh fights against the spirit, and the spirit against the flesh. They are contrary to each other." He wrote to the Romans, "I do not do what I want to do, but what I hate to do. It is not me that does it, but the sin within me. I want to do good, but I do not know how. I do not do the good that I want to do, but the evil that I do not want to do. I find then *a law* that when I want to do good, evil is present. I delight in the law of God inside, but my body fights against my mind. In my mind, I serve the law of God, but I sin with the flesh."

Fighting the battle of life heroically and well is the great purpose of every worthy person's existence. Overcoming adversity, advancing past all obstacles, snatching victory from the jaws of defeat, and becoming a leader of men through courage, perseverance, study, and hard work are some of the ways to fight the battle of life. Sadly, succeeding boldly in business, taking great chances, shrewd *854* dealing, unscrupulousness, market manipulation, and achieving status through disreputable means are thought by many to be success.

The greatest battle, which brings the truest honor and the most success, is the battle between our intellect, reason, moral sense, sensual appetites, and passions. These are the only glories of heroism to be won.

Everyone fights this battle. Those who win elsewhere often suffer crushing defeat in this encounter.

You have heard more than one definition of Freemasonry, but you have not yet heard the truest and most significant one. It is taught to the Entered Apprentice, Fellowcraft, and Master in every Degree. It is a definition of what Freemasonry, its purposes, and its very essence and spirit. For every one of us, it has the force and sanctity of divine law and imposes upon us a solemn obligation.

It is symbolized in the first three Degrees by the COMPASSES *and the* SQUARE, which you have taken so many obligations upon. As a Knight, you were taught it with the Swords symbolizing HONOR and DUTY. It was also taught to you by the BALANCE, the symbol of all Equilibrium, and the CROSS, the symbol of devotedness and self-sacrifice. Everything taught by these symbols is contained within the Compasses and the Square.

For the Entered Apprentice, the points of the Compasses are beneath the Square. For the Fellowcraft, one is above and one beneath. For the Master, both are dominant and have control and dominion over the symbol of the earthly and the material.

FREEMASONRY *is the subjugation of the Human by the Divine. It is the Conquest of the Appetites and Passions by Moral Sense and Reason. It is a continual effort, struggle,* 855 *and warfare of the Spiritual against the Material and Sensual.* That Victory and well-earned rest is the true HOLY EMPIRE.

The Mason must firmly believe that he has within himself a soul that will not die when the body is dissolved. That soul will continue to exist, advance toward perfection, and see more and more clearly as it draws nearer to God. The Ancient and Accepted Rite teaches this, and it encourages the Mason to persevere by believing that his free will is entirely consistent with God's Omnipotence.

Every Degree of the Ancient and Accepted Scottish Rite, from the first to the thirty-second, teaches the noblest purpose of life and that the highest duty of a man is to constantly and diligently strive to gain a mastery of everything. In him, Harmony and Beauty will be the result of a just equilibrium.

In the Lodge of Perfection, you have received a practical morality. You have been taught to be true regardless of the temptation to be false, to be honest in your dealings with others, to be charitable, to judge fairly and impartially, to be tolerant, and to wrong no man. Your spiritual nature is charged to overcome your appetites and passions despite all temptations and hardships.

856 The philosophical Degrees taught the value of knowledge, the excellence of truth, the superiority of intellectual labor, and the dignity and value of your soul. This assisted you in rising above the level of your animal appetites and passions, the pursuits of greed, and the struggles of ambition. The purist pleasure and noblest rewards are to be found in the acquisition of knowledge, expansion of the intellect, and the sacred writings of God upon the Book of Nature.

The Chivalric Degrees taught the superiority of generosity, forgiveness, compassion, disregard of danger, and the great obligations of Duty and Honor. They taught you to overcome the fear of death and to devote yourself to the great cause of civil and religious Liberty. You are to be a Soldier for all that is just, right, and true. No fear of danger or death, ambition, or greed can tempt a true Scottish Knight to dishonor himself and make his soul a slave to his appetites and passions.

A true and genuine Brotherhood cannot be based upon on any theory of human nature, theological or sectarian creeds, or the establishment of a system of association simply for mutual relief or support for those in distress.

There can be no genuine Brotherhood without mutual regard, good opinion and esteem, mutual charity, and mutual allowance for faults and failings. Only those who learn to always think better of each other, to look for and expect the good that is in each, and to allow for and overlook shortcomings can be Brethren to each other. Those who gloat over someone's failings and think everyone is naturally corrupt and immoral cannot be friends, much less Brethren. 857

No one can have a right to think poorly of others unless he also thinks poorly of himself. If he judges the character of another person from a single act and takes that as evidence of the whole nature of the man, he should consent to be judged by the same rule. Such judgments are impossible when he reminds himself that in every person there is an immortal Soul trying to do what is right and just. There is a portion of the Great Source of Light that struggles upward in spite of the obstacles from the passions. The Light is never wholly extinguished or annihilated. It is not victory that deserves honor but the struggle because no person can always be successful. The Mason will look for the good in everyone, even amidst the evil. He believes everyone is better than they seem to be, and that God cares for them. He will feel that even the erring sinner is his brother, entitled to his sympathy, and bound to him by the indissoluble ties of fellowship.

If there is nothing divine in man, he is just a more intelligent animal, with the same faults and vices and hardly (if any) moral excellence. Even animals show some degree of generosity, fidelity, and charity.

Bardesan said in his Book of the Laws of Countries that, "in the things relating to their bodies, people maintain their animal like nature. In the things which belong to their minds, they do what they wish." Bishop Meliton in his Oration to Antoninus Caesar said, "Let the ever-living God always be present in 858 your mind. Your mind is His likeness, because it is also invisible and without form. He exists forever as you will when you have shrugged off your body and stand before Him forever, living, and endowed with knowledge."

In Genesis, the words used to express the origin of things are of uncertain meaning, but with equal justification may be translated to the word "generated", "produced", "made", or "created". We do not need to argue whether the Soul or the Spirit is a ray that has emanated from the Supreme Intelligence, or whether the Infinite Power has called everyone into existence from nothing. In man, the Divine (the equilateral triangle) is united within the Human (the square) to symbolize this union.

Plato said we see the Soul deformed by the innumerable things that have harmed, mutilated, and defaced It, but we do not understand Its original nature as it left its Divine Source. The Mason who has the ROYAL SECRET can argue that the Soul's love of wisdom, its aspiration and tendency to seek the divine and immortal, and its struggles with the obstructions of the senses and passions will someday reveal its true form as it is freed from its deformities. By degrees, it will ascend the mystic ladder of the Spheres to its home and place of origin.

859 If you perceive the radiant and divine beauty of Philosophy, if you are a true Adept, you understand that the ROYAL SECRET, of which you are Prince, is that which the Zohar terms *The Mystery of the BALANCE*. It is the Secret of UNIVERSAL EQUILIBRIUM.

The Equilibrium between Infinite Divine WISDOM and Infinite Divine POWER provides the Stability of the Universe, the unchanging Divine Law, and the Principles of Truth, Justice, and Right. It is superior to all other law.

The Equilibrium between Infinite Divine JUSTICE and Infinite Divine MERCY provides Infinite Divine EQUITY. The Moral Harmony or Beauty of the Universe allows man to endure the presence of a Perfect Deity. It is better to love than to hate, and Forgiveness is wiser than Revenge or Punishment.

The Equilibrium between NECESSITY and LIBERTY (between Divine Omnipotence and Free Will) causes vices, ungenerous thoughts, and words to be crimes and wrongs justly punished by the law of cause and consequence. Nothing in the Universe can happen or be done against the will of God. Without the co-existence of Liberty and Necessity, there could be no religion, no law of right and wrong, and no human justice.

The Equilibrium between Good and Evil and between Light and Darkness assures us that everything is the work of Infinite Wisdom and Infinite Love. There is no rebellious demon or Principle of Darkness coexistent and in eternal conflict with God, or the Principle of Light and Good. By obtaining the knowledge of this equilibrium, we can see that the existence of Evil, Sin, Suffering, and Sorrow is consistent with Infinite Goodness as well as with the Infinite Wisdom of the Almighty.

Sympathy and Antipathy, Attraction and Repulsion are opposites in both the souls of man and in the Universe. Harmony results from the action and 860 opposition of each of them. They are not antagonists of each other. The force that repels a Planet from the Sun is no more an *evil* force than the force that attracts the Planet towards the sun. Each is created and exerted by God, and the result is the harmonious movement of the Planets in their elliptical orbits.

The Equilibrium between Authority and Individual Action establishes Government by balancing personal Liberty with Obedience to Law, and Fraternity with Subordination to the Wisest and the Best. There is an Equilibrium between the Will of the Present, expressed by the Vote of the People, and the Will of the Past, expressed in constitutions, laws, and customs that are sanctified by time. This Equilibrium is represented by the arch resting on the two columns Jachin and Boaz, which stand at the portals of the Temple. Masonry has placed the celestial Globe on one (a symbol of the spiritual part of our nature) and the terrestrial Globe on the other (a symbol of the material part of our nature).

Finally, Masonry labors to instill in its Initiates and demands of its Adepts and Princes the Equilibrium within ourselves between the Spiritual (Divine) and the Material (Human). The balance between the Intellect, Reason, and Moral Sense on one side and the Appetites and Passions on the other result in the Harmony and Beauty of a well regulated life.

The possibility of Equilibrium proves that our Appetites and Senses are Forces given to us by God for purposes of good and not by the malignancy of a Devil. They are the means by which we are strengthened and encouraged to perform great and good deeds. They are to be wisely used, but not abused. They must be kept within due bounds by our Reason and Moral Sense. You can make them useful instruments and servants, but do not permit them to become the managers and masters, using our reason and intellect for base purposes.

Above all, we are to revere ourselves as immortal souls with respect and charity for others. Those others share with us the Divine Nature, lit by a ray of Divine Intelligence, struggling towards the light. Everyone is capable of progressing towards perfection, and they deserve to be loved and pitied, but never hated or despised. Aid and encourage them, but do not abandon or leave them to wander in the darkness alone. *861*

From the mutual action and re-action of each of these pairs of opposites results the Triangle, which is the expressive symbol of the Deity to all the Ancient Sages. At the angles of one, stand symbolically the three columns that support the Lodge: Wisdom, Power, and Harmony or Beauty. One of the symbols found on the Tracing-Board of the Entered Apprentice's Degree teaches the last lesson of Freemasonry. It is the right-angled Triangle. It represents man as a union of the spiritual and material. The base is measured by the number 3, and it is the number of the Triangle, which represents God. The perpendicular is measured by the number 4, and it is the number of the Square, which represents the Earth. The hypotenuse is measured by 5, and it represents the nature produced by the union of the Divine and Human. The squares of the base and perpendicular, 9 and 16, when added together produce 25, whose square root is 5, which is the measure of the hypotenuse.

In each Triangle of Perfection, one is three and three are one. Accordingly, man is one although of a double nature. He realizes his purpose only when the two natures that are within him are in equilibrium. His life is a success only when it is in harmony and beautiful, like the great Harmonies of God and the Universe.

This, my Brother is the TRUE WORD of a Master Mason. This is the true ROYAL SECRET that makes possible, and shall at length make real, the HOLY EMPIRE of true Masonic Brotherhood.

GLORIA DEI EST CELARE VERBUM. (THE GLORY OF GOD IS TO CONCEAL THE WORD.) AMEN.

Stone Guild Publishing ™

Look for these and other great titles at:
http://www.stoneguildpublishing.com

Made in the USA
Middletown, DE
20 February 2016